ABAP® RESTful Programming Model

SAP PRESS is a joint initiative of SAP and Rheinwerk Publishing. The know-how offered by SAP specialists combined with the expertise of Rheinwerk Publishing offers the reader expert books in the field. SAP PRESS features first-hand information and expert advice, and provides useful skills for professional decision-making.

SAP PRESS offers a variety of books on technical and business-related topics for the SAP user. For further information, please visit our website: *www.sap-press.com*.

Kiran Bandari
Complete ABAP (2nd edition)
2020, 1,032 pages, hardcover and e-book
www.sap-press.com/4947

Puneet Asthana, David Haslam
ABAP 7.5 Certification Guide: Development Associate Exam (4th edition)
2018, 636 pages, paperback and e-book
www.sap-press.com/4605

Colle, Dentzer, Hrastnik
Core Data Services for ABAP
2019, 490 pages, hardcover and e-book
www.sap-press.com/4822

Winfried Schwarzmann
Test-Driven Development with ABAP Objects
2019, 594 pages, hardcover and e-book
www.sap-press.com/4882

Stefan Haas, Bince Mathew

ABAP® RESTful Programming Model

ABAP® Development for SAP S/4HANA®

Editor Will Jobst
Acquisitions Editor Hareem Shafi
Copyeditor Yvette Chin
Cover Design Graham Geary
Photo Credit Shutterstock.com/1107492197/© Suratchana Pakavaleetorn
Layout Design Vera Brauner
Production Kelly O'Callaghan
Typesetting III-satz, Husby (Germany)
Printed and bound in the United States of America, on paper from sustainable sources

ISBN 978-1-4932-1903-2

1st edition 2020

Library of Congress Cataloging-in-Publication Data
Names: Haas, Stefan (Information technology consultant), author. | Mathew, Bince, author.
Title: ABAP RESTful programming model : ABAP development for SAP S/4HANA / Stefan Haas, Bince Mathew.
Description: 1st edition. | Bonn ; Boston : Rheinwerk Publishing, 2019. | Includes index.
Identifiers: LCCN 2019039169 (print) | LCCN 2019039170 (ebook) | ISBN 9781493219032 (hardcover) | ISBN 9781493219049 (ebook)
Subjects: LCSH: ABAP/4 (Computer program language)
Classification: LCC QA76.73.A12 H335 2019 (print) | LCC QA76.73.A12 (ebook) | DDC 005.13/3--dc23
LC record available at https://lccn.loc.gov/2019039169
LC ebook record available at https://lccn.loc.gov/2019039170

Contents at a Glance

Dear Reader,

In this day and age, you need to do your research. Whether it's a new coffee shop or a different route to work, you'll know quickly if it's an improvement (the iced coffee is much better here and this commute has a great view over the bay), or if it's an unfortunate downgrade (the bagels are *just* okay and in poor weather the commute is twice as long).

Sometimes the choice is easy, and comes with a glowing recommendation from your peers!

That's what this author team has for you, a step-by-step guide to the ABAP RESTful programming paradigm. Breathe easy knowing that these industry experts have done the research, all with the intention of making your ABAP experience as frictionless as possible.

What did you think about *ABAP RESTful Programming Model: ABAP Development for SAP S/4HANA*? Your comments and suggestions are the most useful tools to help us make our books the best they can be. Please feel free to contact me and share any praise or criticism you may have.

Thank you for purchasing a book from SAP PRESS!

Will Jobst
Editor, SAP PRESS

willj@rheinwerk-publishing.com
www.sap-press.com
Rheinwerk Publishing · Boston, MA

Contents

Preface

SAP S/4HANA is SAP's latest suite of enterprise resource planning (ERP) software covering all core business processes of enterprises. Although SAP S/4HANA is to a large extent compatible to its predecessor SAP ERP 6.0 and is still based on the three-tier architecture consisting of a database, application server, and client layer, a huge technological shift has happened on how applications are developed for the SAP S/4HANA platform compared to previous SAP ERP versions. SAP S/4HANA is completely built on top of SAP HANA, SAP's in-memory database platform, and naturally one declared goal of the application architecture is to fully leverage the capabilities of SAP HANA to enable faster data processing and new types of analytical applications. Consequently, operations on data are supposed to be pushed down to the SAP HANA database as much as possible. Additional business logic is executed in ABAP on the SAP NetWeaver AS for ABAP. The SAP S/4HANA user interface (UI) is built using the new SAP Fiori design language, which puts the user in the center of the application development process and tailors apps to specific user needs. Specifically, SAP Fiori applications are developed using the SAPUI5 Software Development Kit (SDK), which is a responsive JavaScript framework that includes a rich set of UI controls. SAP Fiori apps run in the SAP Fiori launchpad in the browser, and it's no longer necessary (or even possible in the SAP S/4HANA cloud edition) for a business user to access the classic SAP GUI backend. The connection between the ABAP backend and the SAP Fiori apps running in the browser is established using the SAP Gateway and the OData protocol.

With the release of the ABAP RESTful programming model there is now a coherent programming model available for the development of SAP Fiori applications for S/4HANA. The ABAP RESTful programming model links together existing technologies in a consistent and transparent way. Additionally, the model significantly increases developer experience by providing an end-to-end Eclipse-based development flow. Moreover, the ABAP RESTful programming model is not only targeted at S/4HANA on-premise applications, which is the main focus of the book, but also for developing ABAP applications on the SAP Cloud Platform to extend the S/4HANA Cloud Edition.

Purpose of This Book

The new SAP S/4HANA application paradigm and all its associated technologies might be overwhelming in the beginning, especially when you're used to the monolithic development paradigms of previous SAP ERP versions. Our goal with this book is therefore to connect all of these different technologies that make up the new SAP S/4HANA programming model and give you a coherent end-to-end view of how to develop your own custom applications on the SAP S/4HANA platform. Throughout the book, we'll develop several fully functioning SAP S/4HANA SAP Fiori applications step by step, and you'll learn all the associated technologies and practices required, ranging from defining data models using ABAP core data services (CDS) over exposing them as an OData service to creating SAP Fiori UIs using SAPUI5 and UI annotations.

Target Audience

This book is primarily targeted at developers and consultants who want to learn how to develop applications for SAP S/4HANA. However, it might also be of interest for all kinds of people interested in SAP S/4HANA application development and its associated technologies and tools, for instance, technical-oriented business users and managers, project leaders, quality managers, or development managers.

Ideally, readers should be familiar with ABAP, JavaScript, and SQL as the book doesn't cover the basics of these programming languages. A basic understanding of SAP Fiori, SAP Web IDE, SAPUI5, CDS, Eclipse, SAP Gateway, OData, and the SAP Fiori launchpad is also beneficial, as we won't introduce those technologies in full depth. However, you'll receive all you need to understand and begin developing SAP S/4HANA applications.

Structure of This Book

Part I: SAP S/4HANA and SAP Fiori

- We'll start the book with **Chapter 1: SAP S/4HANA Architecture**, which will give you an introduction to SAP S/4HANA and its architecture in general and how it differs from previous SAP ERP three-tier architectures. Additionally, we'll outline the main differences between the SAP S/4HANA and SAP S/4HANA Cloud from a technical perspective.
- **Chapter 2: SAP Fiori and the Design-Led Development Process** introduces several UI-related topics beginning with the five core principles of the SAP Fiori design language: role-based, delightful, coherent, simple, and adaptive. After that, we'll look at the three phases of the design-led development process—discover, design,

develop—and how the process is key to a great user experience. Subsequently, the different SAP Fiori application types and their characteristics are explained. In general, we can distinguish between SAP Fiori elements applications, which are template based, and freestyle applications. Finally, the SAP Build tool is demonstrated as an easy-to-use cloud-based tool supporting all phases of the design-led development process.

- In **Chapter 3: ABAP RESTful Programming Model**, we take a closer look at SAP S/4HANA's application programming model and its associated technologies. We begin with core data services (CDS) as the key technology for exploiting SAP HANA's in-memory capabilities by enabling code-pushdown for all types of SAP S/4HANA applications from analytical to transactional. Then we look at the OData and SAP Gateway technologies, which enable access to ERP data from different clients and thereby enable the use of new UI technologies in conjunction with ERP data. The main purpose of the chapter, however, is to introduce the ABAP RESTful programming model in detail, beginning with an overview of its development flow and runtime components. Subsequently, we look at the different artifacts required to develop an ABAP RESTful application: queries, behavior definitions, behavior implementations, service definitions, and service bindings.

Part II: Developing Applications for SAP S/4HANA

- In **Chapter 4: Developing an SAP Fiori Elements List Report and Object Page**, we'll develop our first SAP Fiori elements application, based on the ABAP RESTful programming model, from the data model up to the UI. We'll create CDS views, add business object structure to them, implement business object behavior, and finally create a UI consisting of a list report and an object page. We'll also add unit tests for our backend and frontend business logic.
- **Chapter 5: Developing an Overview Page** will introduce the overview page (OVP) SAP Fiori elements application type in detail. We'll create an analytical overview page for our business scenario step by step and show you the end-to-end development processes ranging from CDS view creation to business service definition and the definition of the required UI annotations.
- In **Chapter 6: Developing an Analytical List Page**, you'll get to know another analytical SAP Fiori elements application type, the analytical list page (ALP). As in the previous chapters, we'll also develop an end-to-end application using this application type and show all the necessary steps for getting an ALP application up and running.

- If the SAP Fiori elements app types don't suit your needs, you must develop a freestyle application, which gives you full flexibility in terms of designing and implementing the UI of your application. In **Chapter 7: Developing a Freestyle Application**, we'll show you how to develop a freestyle application step by step using the SAP Web IDE full-stack. We'll show you all the necessary steps required to set up a freestyle application project, connect to an OData service, set up in-app navigation, and develop the UI using smart controls.
- In **Chapter 8: Deploying Applications to the SAP Fiori Launchpad**, we'll show you how to make the previously developed apps available to users in the SAP Fiori launchpad according to their business roles and how to connect all apps using cross-app navigation.

Part III: Operating Applications

- As the frontend part of SAP S/4HANA applications is based on JavaScript and no longer on proprietary ABAP-based technologies such as Web Dynpro, the UI source code can't be managed with the classic ABAP Change and Transport System (CTS) anymore. Usually SAPUI5 code is managed with the Git Source Code Management (SCM) system, which is also well integrated into SAP Web IDE full-stack. **Chapter 9: Version Control in SAP Web IDE Using Git** will therefore introduce you to the most important Git commands required when developing SAPUI5 applications in SAP Web IDE.
- Having a comprehensive automated test suite created using test-driven development (TDD) is a key enabler for good code quality, earlier detection of regression bugs, shorter release cycles, and, consequently, earlier customer feedback. Therefore, **Chapter 10: Automated Testing** will introduce you to the SAP S/4HANA testing pyramid. We'll start from the bottom up to show you how to write unit tests, integration tests, and end-to-end (E2E) tests for your SAP S/4HANA applications.
- Another key practice for shortening release cycles and reducing risk is continuous integration (CI). We'll teach you how to set up a CI pipeline for your frontend SAPUI5 code in **Chapter 11: Continuous Integration**. Additionally, we'll look at how you can establish kind of a CI pipeline in the backend as well using the ABAP Test Cockpit (ATC) and the ABAP Unit Runner.
- In Chapter 9, you learn how to use Git to manage your frontend SAPUI5 JavaScript source code. Nowadays, you can also manage your backend ABAP code with Git by using abapGit, a Git client for ABAP. Therefore, **Chapter 12: ABAP on Git** will give

you an introduction on how to use abapGit and its corresponding Eclipse plugin to manage ABAP source code. After reading this chapter you should also be able to import the source code attached to this book into your S/4HANA sandbox system.

Because SAP S/4HANA Cloud customers no longer have access to the SAP NetWeaver backend of SAP S/4HANA, SAP is providing another platform for doing side-by-side application development: the SAP Cloud Platform. In **Appendix A: Developing Applications on the SAP Cloud Platform**, we'll give you a quick tour of the SAP Cloud Platform programming model by developing a list report application similar to the application we developed in Chapter 4 on the SAP S/4HANA core platform.

Acknowledgments

We would like to thank our SAP PRESS editors Will Jobst and Hareem Shafi for the trust they have placed in us and for providing us with an opportunity to write this book. A special thanks also to you, the reader, for picking up this book. We hope it's helpful and gives you a kick start to developing applications for SAP S/4HANA.

Stefan Haas

I would like to thank my wife, Carolin, and my parents for their continuous support and understanding throughout the writing process of this book. A big thanks goes to my coauthor Bince Mathew for sharing this opportunity and experience with me. Thanks also to my friend Yingding who always has an open ear for technical discussions.

Bince Mathew

I would like to dedicate this book to my late father who was always very supportive and proud of me being an author. I would like to express my sincere gratitude to my mother, my wife and my brother who motivated me throughout the whole journey of writing this book. A special thanks to my wife Suzana who supported and encouraged me to keep up with the schedule of the book, she also took the time to read through the chapters and gave her feedback. A big thank you to my coauthor Stefan Haas: it was a pleasure working with you. Special thanks to Will Jobst for his help and guidance while writing this book and to Hareem Shafi for providing us with an opportunity to write this book.

PART I

SAP S/4HANA and SAP Fiori

Chapter 1
SAP S/4HANA Architecture

This chapter explores the technical building blocks of SAP S/4HANA and describes how they interact with each other. You'll learn about the main technical differences between SAP S/4HANA and the SAP Business Suite, as well as explore the differences between SAP S/4HANA and SAP S/4HANA Cloud.

Let's start with a high-level look at the core architecture of the system and its technical building blocks. We'll go more into detail in the next section where we'll cover SAP S/4HANA's Virtual Data Model (VDM) and its underlying ABAP technology, core data services (CDS). The VDM is also the foundation of transactional and analytical applications in SAP S/4HANA, and we'll look at the architectures of those app types in subsequent sections. Moreover, we'll explore SAP S/4HANA and SAP S/4HANA Cloud and their differences. We'll close the chapter with a short introduction to the SAP Cloud Platform as the main platform for developing side-by-side extensions for SAP S/4HANA.

1.1 Core Architecture

SAP S/4HANA is SAP's latest generation of enterprise resource planning (ERP) software and was initially launched in March 2015. Like its predecessor ERP solution, SAP ERP 6.0 Enhancement Pack (EHP) 8, which also serves as the basis for SAP S/4HANA, it offers an integrated suite of applications covering the key business functions of an organization, including Financial Accounting (FI), Controlling (CO) and Asset Accounting (AA) over Sales & Distribution (SD), Materials Management (MM), Product Planning (PP), Quality Management (QM), Plant Maintenance (PM), and human resources (HR).

Nevertheless, the technological shift between classic SAP ERP and SAP S/4HANA is immense because SAP S/4HANA is fully built on SAP's in-memory computing platform, SAP HANA, and offers a completely new consumer-grade user experience (UX) with SAP Fiori. SAP is, in general, trying to eliminate redundancies and simplify the system, which has grown over the past decades and has diverged in many places into overly complex transactions using different data structures and different architectures. In many cases, complex transactions have already been replaced by several new role-based SAP Fiori applications to reduce complexity for end users and improve the UX in general, which will continue in the future. Additionally, the exclusive use of SAP HANA has made it possible for certain application modules to simplify their data models and reduce their data footprints as SAP HANA significantly speeds up reporting and renders previously needed aggregate tables obsolete. However, in many cases, these simplifications are based on functional strategies that already exist in previous ERP versions, simplifying the transition to SAP S/4HANA. SAP publishes a list of simplifications periodically for SAP S/4HANA. Currently, SAP is offering three migration scenarios to SAP S/4HANA: a *system conversion*, where an already-existing SAP ERP system is converted to an SAP S/4HANA system; a *new implementation*, which is the "greenfield" approach; or a *landscape transformation*, where selective applications are moved to an SAP S/4HANA installation to consolidate the existing landscape.

1.1.1 Overview

Although SAP S/4HANA is a separate product in its own right, one of its clear goals is to stay compatible with previous SAP ERP releases to ease migration. Therefore, almost all its application, customizing, and system data are stored in the same database tables as in previous SAP ERP versions. From an architectural perspective, SAP S/4HANA is still based on the well-established three-tier client-server architecture, as shown in Figure 1.1, with SAP HANA being the sole Relational Database Management System (RDMS) underlying the system. The three main layers of the system, from the bottom up, are the database layer consisting of SAP HANA, the SAP NetWeaver Application Server for ABAP (SAP NetWeaver AS for ABAP), and the SAP Fiori frontend server (SAP Gateway). The SAP Fiori frontend server receives incoming HTTP client requests for SAP Fiori applications running in the SAP Fiori launchpad and the browser as well as for business data via the Open Data Protocol (OData), which uses HTTP as the data transfer protocol. The classic SAP GUI client has been replaced by the browser as the single client application and user interface (UI) runtime of the system, at least for SAP S/4HANA Cloud users. In SAP S/4HANA, on the other hand, you can still access classic backend transactions, but then you would miss out on the new SAP Fiori user experience. The SAP NetWeaver AS for ABAP contains several components for processing client application requests depending on the application type.

Enterprise Search (ESH) powers the search functionality in the SAP Fiori launchpad (also known as SAP Fiori search) and enables direct system-wide search access to applications and business data stored in SAP HANA. The Analytical Engine, which is included in SAP Business Warehouse (SAP BW), evaluates and executes analytical queries at runtime. For building SAP Fiori applications end-to-end (E2E), the ABAP RESTful programming model has been the framework of choice since SAP S/4HANA release 1909. Requests from the SAP Gateway layer are routed through the Service Adaptation Description (SADL) layer, and depending whether the request is read-only or requires write access, the request is either passed to the query runtime or the business object runtime, respectively.

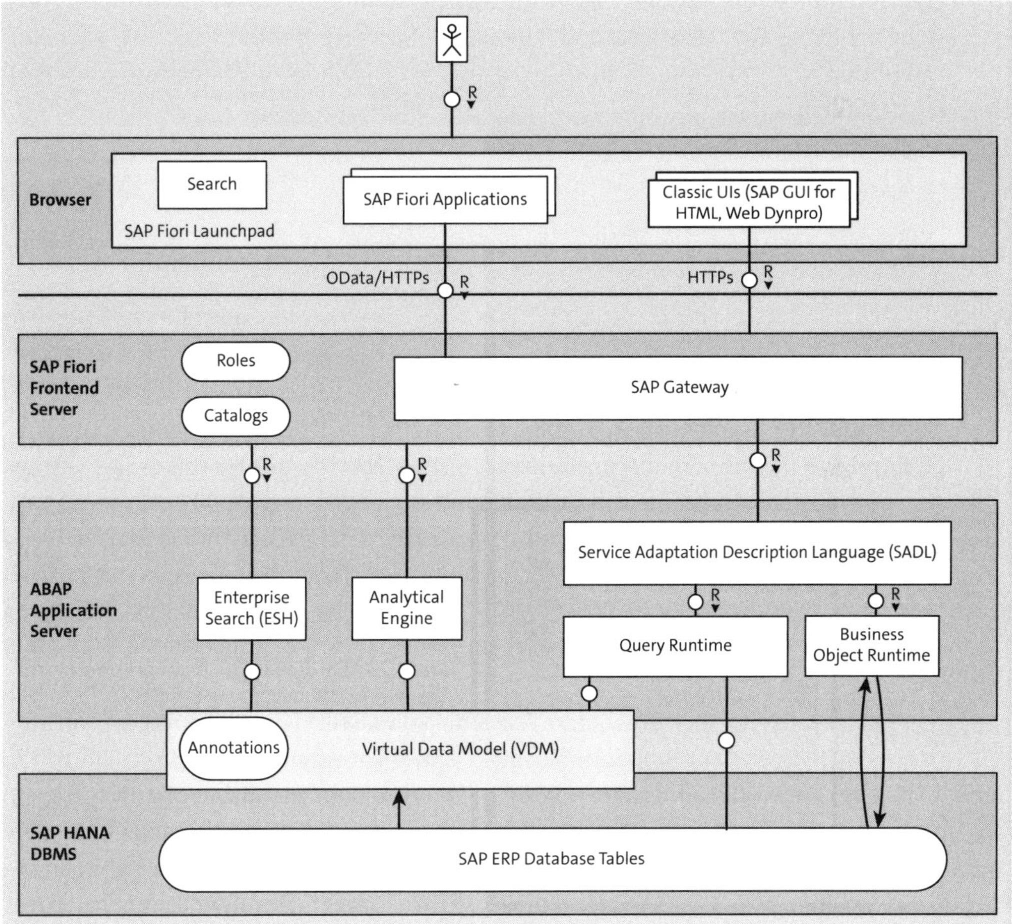

Figure 1.1 SAP S/4HANA's Three-Tier Core Architecture

1.1.2 Open Data Protocol (OData)

With the introduction of SAP Gateway and its OData channel, SAP has opened the ERP system up to external systems, clients, devices, and machines. All business entities of the system can be made network accessible by URIs. The OData protocol provides a standardized protocol for consuming business entities and their relationships via the RESTful paradigm based on HTTP. While making use of the same HTTP verbs `GET`, `PUT`, `POST`, and `DELETE` as a normal RESTful service, OData extends the standard paradigm with a set of best practices for building and consuming RESTful application programming interfaces (APIs). For instance, OData adds standard URL parameters for restricting the requested result set to particular properties (`$select`), to a certain number of entities (`$top`), or to entities fulfilling a certain condition (`$filter`). One could say that OData extends the RESTful paradigm toward SQL-like data consumption via HTTP, which, in turn, eases direct pushdown of queries to the SAP HANA database.

Note

To learn more about the Open Data Protocol (OData), take a look at the official website at *https://www.odata.org/*.

1.1.3 SAP HANA

Naturally, one of the most important goals for the SAP S/4HANA architecture is to fully exploit the in-memory capabilities of SAP HANA. To promote this usage, SAP has introduced a VDM layer on top of the existing business data tables that allows semantic consolidation of the more and more fragmented data model over the years without losing compatibility to previous ERP versions. ABAP core data services (CDS) is the core technology enabling the VDM; CDS is fully integrated in the ABAP stack but executed in SAP HANA. Using the CDS data definition language (DDL), you can define layered and semantically rich data views by selecting data from the old ERP tables. Technically, CDS views will generate SAP HANA database views on activation, pushing down calculations and semantic business entity composition and provision to the database. Putting a harmonized semantically rich virtual view layer on top of the old database tables abstracts away complex table structures and relationships that have developed over time and provides a harmonized and business-oriented view of the data. Business-oriented, SAP HANA-enabled provision of data significantly improves application performance because business data calculation and provisioning is, in the best case, completely pushed down to the SAP HANA database. This paradigm is called the Code-to-Data paradigm, in contrast to the classic Data-to-Code paradigm where large data sets are transferred to the application server and then processed in ABAP to provide the actually required business data. The latter paradigm, however, will never reach the full performance SAP HANA can reach.

As the SAP Basis technology, the VDM and CDS are the backbone of all SAP S/4HANA application types, including transactional applications, analytical applications, external interfaces, and Enterprise Search (ESH). The VDM is primarily a reusable and stable data foundation used for internal development at SAP but partners and customers can also use and develop on top of explicitly released views. The VDM increases development speed and efficiency by providing standardized and easy business entity consumption.

Note

For an overview of CDS views explicitly released by SAP, check out the View Browser app contained in the SAP_BR_ANALYTICS_SPECIALIST role.

1.1.4 SAP NetWeaver Application Server for ABAP

Although a clear focus has been set on SAP HANA exploitation, and the trend is toward a two-tier architecture, the middle tier of the SAP S/4HANA architecture still consists of the SAP NetWeaver Application Server for ABAP (SAP NetWeaver AS for ABAP), as in previous SAP ERP releases. SAP NetWeaver AS for ABAP contains several engines for transactional and analytical data processing, for instance, the Analytical Engine, which is also part of SAP Business Warehouse (SAP BW), the Business Object Processing Framework (BOPF), the business object and query runtimes of the ABAP RESTful programming model, and the Service Adaptation Definition Language (SADL). In the past, the implementation of business logic in SAP ERP was heterogeneous and fragmented, using many different ABAP frameworks or none at all, which led to unstandardized applications that were difficult to maintain and required a lot of application-specific domain expertise. When SAP S/4HANA was initially launched, no standardized coherent programming model for SAP Fiori applications was available, only a set of best practices, for instance, on how to develop an ABAP-based OData service for the OData Channel (ODC) of the SAP Gateway.

To standardize the implementation of business logic in SAP S/4HANA, SAP launched the ABAP programming model for SAP Fiori with SAP S/4HANA 1610 FPS01. Since then, SAP recommended to use this programming model for the E2E development of SAP Fiori applications. In the programming model, the underlying transactional Business Object Processing Framework (BOPF) node structure is derived from annotated CDS entities, and the business logic is implemented inside the BOPF in ABAP. The BOPF framework was initially developed for SAP Business By Design, which was then also reused and integrated into the SAP Fiori programming model to handle the ABAP-based business logic parts of applications. CDS views and BOPF business logic can be exposed in a model-based manner either via an SAP Gateway service builder project (Transaction SEGW) by simply referencing the CDS entities to be exposed (*reference data source* scenario) or via an annotation in the root view of the CDS data model (`@OData.publish: true`).

However, the ABAP programming model for SAP Fiori is still an heterogenous collection of new and existing technologies and tools. Even SAP GUI access is required for certain actions, for instance, to create an OData service using the Transaction SEGW or to activate an OData service using the Transaction /IWFND/MAINT_SERVICE. To overcome these shortcomings and to provide a cloud-ready programming model, in August 2018, SAP released the ABAP RESTful programming model for the ABAP environment (ABAP Platform 1808). The ABAP environment has since then been part of the SAP Cloud Platform, as a Platform-as-a-service (PaaS) offering that provides an E2E development experience for SAP HANA-optimized OData services such as SAP Fiori applications. Since SAP S/4HANA 1909, the ABAP RESTful programming model has also been available in on-premise installations of SAP S/4HANA and supersedes the ABAP programming model for SAP Fiori. As in the previous ABAP programming model for SAP Fiori, the semantically rich data model of applications is formed by CDS views. For transactional processing, business objects are derived from CDS entities; which operations a business object supports (e.g., create, read, update, and delete (CRUD) operations and custom actions) is defined via what's called a *behavior definition*. A behavior definition is a new ABAP repository object defined using a Behavior Definition Language (BDL). The data model and its behavior are then exposed as a *business service*, which is essentially a RESTful OData service. A business service consists of a service definition and a service binding. A *service definition* is an ABAP repository object that defines which parts of the data model are to be exposed as a business service. A *service binding* is an ABAP repository object used to bind a service definition to a specific client-server communication protocol, for instance, OData version 2. Unlike the ABAP programming model for SAP Fiori, the new ABAP RESTful programming model has been directly integrated into the ABAP language with new transportable development objects: behavior definition, service definition, and service binding. This integration provides a consistent Eclipse-based E2E development experience and enables you to use the programming model in the cloud without any additional required frameworks and tools, only the ABAP language core. Figure 1.2 shows the evolution of application development on the ABAP platform in general and in particular with SAP S/4HANA.

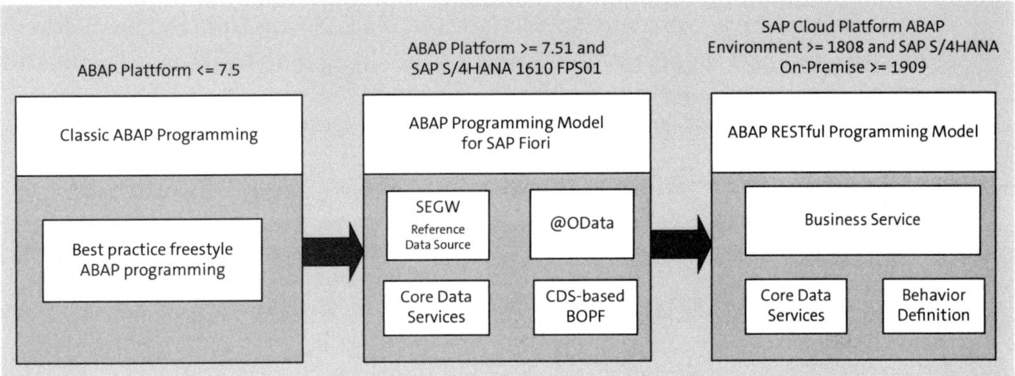

Figure 1.2 Evolution of the ABAP Programming Model in SAP S/4HANA

1.1.5 SAP Fiori Frontend Server Based on SAP NetWeaver Gateway

The SAP Fiori frontend server is based on the SAP Gateway component of SAP NetWeaver and manages the stateless communication between the user's browser, as the client application of the system, and the backend. The server hosts SAP Fiori applications that are downloaded for client-side rendering in the user's browser as well as the OData services or APIs used for fetching or changing the business data displayed in the applications. In native SAP Fiori applications, a clear separation exists between the UI and data, which fosters the reusability of backend components, whether business logic in ABAP or CDS views. The SAP Gateway component implements the OData protocol via its OData channel and takes care of all protocol-specific tasks, for instance, parsing and validating requests, rendering the response format in either JSON or XML, performing inbound and outbound conversions, and much more. The frontend and backend server communicate with each other via a trusted remote function call (RFC) connection.

SAP Gateway supports hub deployment as well as embedded deployment. In a hub deployment scenario, which used to be the recommended setup for SAP S/4HANA until SAP S/4HANA 1809, SAP Gateway components are deployed in a standalone frontend system and are decoupled from the SAP S/4HANA backend system. This setup, among other things, increases security since the external attack surface doesn't include the backend system. On the other hand, in an embedded deployment scenario, which has been the recommended deployment option since SAP S/4HANA 1809, both SAP Gateway and backend components reside in the same system, which reduces the Total Cost of Ownership (TCO) as only one system is required. However, this scenario increases the external attack surface, and upgrade cycles for both frontend and backend server are coupled. However, the SAP Fiori frontend has a dependency to the SAP S/4HANA backend, and vice versa (e.g., SAP Fiori for SAP S/4HANA 1809 requires a backend with SAP S/4HANA 1809). Therefore, we now recommend deploying the SAP Fiori frontend and the SAP S/4HANA backend in the same system to keep them in sync.

1.1.6 SAPUI5

The user interface (UI) layer consists of native SAP Fiori applications developed in SAPUI5, which is a JavaScript framework that enables the development of responsive HTML5 applications according to the SAP Fiori design language. Apps developed with SAPUI5 run in the browser and, by their nature responsive, adjust their layout depending on the screen size or resolution of the client device on which the browser runs. In addition to native SAP Fiori applications, older SAP UI technologies that support HTML-like Web Dynpro or SAP GUI for HTML are also supported in SAP S/4HANA and will get the same theming as native SAP Fiori apps when running in the SAP Fiori launchpad. For older UI technologies, the UI isn't rendered on the client side, and no decoupling of UI and business data APIs occurs. Instead, the UI is rendered on the server side, and because these applications were solely developed for the desktop, the classic UIs aren't responsive.

1.1.7 SAP Fiori Launchpad

End users can access SAP S/4HANA via browsers, and the single entry point to the system is the SAP Fiori launchpad. The home page of the SAP Fiori launchpad displays a grid of tiles, which provide access to apps assigned to the current user. SAP Fiori apps are organized in catalogs, which are created in the SAP Fiori launchpad designer and later assigned to Transaction PFCG roles. These roles are then in turn assigned to business users and comprise all applications the user needs to carry out his daily business tasks. The SAP Fiori launchpad also provides an integrated search functionality in the header area based on ESH, also known as SAP Fiori search, with which the user can search over all existing and ESH-enabled business entities in the system.

1.2 Backend

In the following subsections, we'll look at the backend components and technologies of SAP S/4HANA in detail. First and foremost, we'll look at the VDM of SAP S/4HANA, which is enabled by the CDS technology and fosters the Code-to-Data paradigm and code pushdown to the SAP HANA database. The VDM is the foundation for all application types in SAP S/4HANA and is enhanced with the BOPF (earlier than SAP S/4HANA 1909) or behavior definitions (since SAP S/4HANA 1909) for transactional applications and the Analytical Engine for analytical applications. In the following subsections, we'll provide a basic understanding of the different SAP S/4HANA application types and which technologies and components of the architecture are involved in developing different applications for SAP S/4HANA.

1.2.1 Virtual Data Model

On top of the classic SAP ERP tables, the VDM is a core architectural change with SAP S/4HANA compared to previous SAP ERP releases, as shown in Figure 1.3.

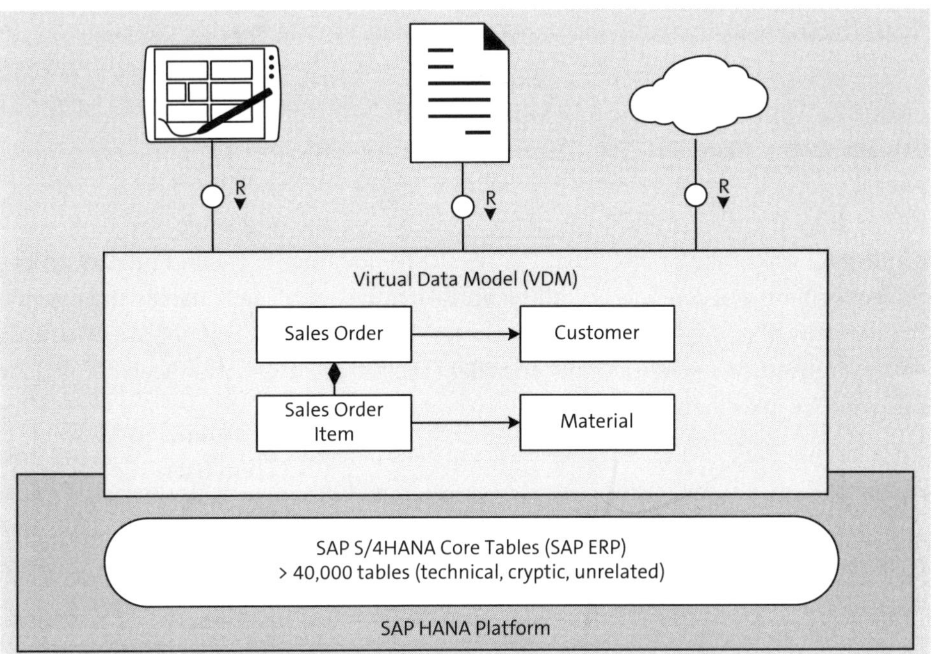

Figure 1.3 VDM on Top of Old SAP ERP Core Tables as the Cornerstone of All SAP S/4HANA Application Types

The VDM abstracts complex and heterogeneously grown table structures by putting a simplified and business-oriented layer of CDS views on top of the old database tables. The VDM provides understandable, semantically rich, and simplified access to business data in the form of consumable business entities without consumers having to understand the complex table structures and foreign key relationships that have grown for decades in the database tables.

ABAP Core Data Services

The technological core enabler of the VDM is the CDS technology, which consists of a DDL, a query language, and a Data Control Language (DCL). CDS artifacts are new development objects in the ABAP stack that use the standard transport lifecycle management system of ABAP, although these development objects are executed in SAP HANA.

The *data definition language (DDL)* can be considered an enhancement of SQL and allows the definition of semantically rich database views selected from either database tables or other CDS views. The CDS DDL has been available since ABAP 7.4 Service Pack (SP) 2. Relationships between views are expressed via a concept called *associations*. The DDL can also contain annotations to add domain-specific metadata.

Listing 1.1 shows an oversimplified example of a CDS DDL. The view selects data from table `EKKO`, which is a classic SAP ERP table containing purchasing documents and belongs to the Materials Management-Purchasing (MM-PUR) application component. As you can see, the syntax resembles SQL. The code includes a *projection* part, where we've included a few fields of the underlying table, and a *selection* part (`WHERE` condition), where we've restricted the results to documents created in 2018. In the projection part, you can hide cryptic technical database table field names and provide semantically meaningful names using aliases, which is also done in the SAP S/4HANA VDM; for instance, in our example, the alias `PurchasingDocument` has been defined for the database field `ebeln`.

Associations are used to express relationships between different CDS views and resemble joins but are easier to read because they don't directly program the joins. When selecting data from dependent views using path expressions, these joins will be materialized; otherwise, associations can be treated as metadata, and no joins are executed between the associated views. In the last line of the projection, we're propagating the association from purchase documents to purchase document items to other potential consuming views (`_PurchasingDocumentItemDDL`). A consuming view could then collect data from documents as well as items and form a new business entity; for instance, the expression `_PurchasingDocumentItemDDL.PurchasPurchasingDocumentItem` would select the purchasing document item field of the `Z_PurchasingDocumentItemDDL` view via the `Z_PurchasingDocumentDDL` view, which would result in the transformation of the association in an actual join on purchase documents and items.

```
@AbapCatalog.sqlViewName: 'ZPURCHDOCDDL'
@EndUserText.label: 'Purchasing Document'
define view Z_PurchasingDocumentDDL
  // (1) DB source table
  as select from ekko
  // (2) Association to items view
  association [0..*] to Z_PurchasingDocumentItemDDL
    as _PurchasingDocumentItemDDL
    on $projection.PurchasingDocument = _
PurchasingDocumentItemDDL.PurchasingDocument
{
  key ebeln as PurchasingDocument,
      ekorg as PurchasingOrganization,
      aedat as CreationDate,
      @Semantics.user.createdBy: true
      ernam as CreatedByUser,
      // (3) Exposure of association for
      //     consuming views
      _PurchasingDocumentItemDDL
}
// (4) Restrict documents to 2018
where
  aedat between '20180101' and '20181231'
```

Listing 1.1 Simple Example of a DDL File on Top of the Purchasing Document Table EKKO

CDS views can be consumed via Open SQL or other CDS views; therefore, Open SQL or CDS itself form the *query languages* of CDS, as shown in Listing 1.2.

```
SELECT * FROM z_purchasingdocumentddl INTO TABLE @DATA(lt_purch_
docs) UP TO 10 ROWS.
```

Listing 1.2 Open SQL Selected in ABAP to Select Data from the Purchasing Document CDS View

Data access via CDS views can be restricted by using the *data control language (DCL)* of CDS. In a DCL file, authorizations are declared via standard ABAP authorization objects. At runtime, the user's Transaction PFCG authorization objects and their values will be collected and pushed down to the database as filter conditions. This extremely important feature promotes the Code-to-Data paradigm. In the past, to check authorizations on individual database records or instance levels, the data had to be transferred to the application server. Then, the individual records were checked based on values found in the user's assigned authorization objects.

Listing 1.3 shows how this authorization process might have worked in the past. The data is selected from the database using Open SQL and stored in the internal table `lt_purch_docs`. In a loop, each entry is checked to determine whether the user has authorization to display the entry; if not, the entry is deleted from the table before being passed to the UI for display. However, as a result, we lose the Data-to-Code performance benefit gained with the CDS DDL because only the data selection part is pushed down to SAP HANA, whereas the required authorization check part is still executed in ABAP and requires the transfer of potentially large data sets from the database to the application server via the network.

```
LOOP AT lt_purch_docs ASSIGNING <fs_purch_doc>.
  AUTHORITY-CHECK OBJECT 'M_BEST_EKO'
    ID 'EKORG' FIELD <fs_purch_doc>-purchasingorganization
    ID 'ACTIVT' FIELD '03'.
  IF sy-subrc <> 0.
    DELETE lt_purch_docs INDEX sy-tabix.
  ENDIF.
ENDLOOP.
```

Listing 1.3 Classic AUTHORITY-CHECKs in ABAP after Reading Data from the Database Using Open SQL and Stored in an Internal Table (lt_purch_docs)

Fortunately, beginning with ABAP 7.40 SP 10, CDS DCL files can be used to push down these instance-level authorization checks to the database. Listing 1.4 shows a simple DCL file for the `Z_PurchasingDocumentDDL` view. Like the preceding ABAP code snippet, this code makes use of the standard ABAP authorization object M_BEST_EKO to restrict access to purchasing documents by purchasing organization, as shown in Figure 1.4. The purchasing organizations for which a user is authorized to see purchasing documents are derived from the Transaction PFCG roles. The user is assigned to Transaction PFCG roles, which, in turn, contain authorization objects that have certain authorization field values specifically required to carry out the user's specific business task according to the *least privilege* principle. In the following DCL, we'll make sure that users can only see purchasing document records with a PurchasingOrganization that is also contained in the EKORG field of the M_BEST_EKO authorization object instance assigned to the user via a Transaction PFCG role, for example, purchasing organizations 0001 and 0002. Additionally, we can check for display authority using the acvt field.

```
@EndUserText.label: 'Purchasing Document DCL'
@MappingRole: true
define role Z_PurchasingDocumentDCL {
    grant  select
        on Z_PurchasingDocumentDDL
    where
        ( PurchasingOrganization ) =
        aspect pfcg_auth (  M_BEST_EKO, EKORG, actvt = '03' );
}
```

Listing 1.4 Simple DCL File Using the Standard ABAP Authorization Object M_BEST_EKO to Filter the Purchasing Documents by Purchasing Organization

Display authorization object

Object	M_BEST_EKO
Text	Purchasing Organization in Purchase Order
Class	MM_E Materials Management: Purchasing
Author	SAP

Authorization fields

Authorization Field	Short Description...
ACTVT	Activity
EKORG	Purchasing Organization

Figure 1.4 Authorization Object for Purchasing Organizations in Purchase Orders

At runtime, the executed SQL SELECT statement will look like the following text:

```
SELECT * FROM Z_PURCHASINGDOCUMENTDDL WHERE PurchasingOrganization =
'0001' and PurchasingOrganization = '0002'
```

Notice how the DCL authorization checks are transparently pushed down to the database using an SQL WHERE clause.

Virtual Data Model Architecture

To foster reuse while still providing optimally tailored CDS views for different usage scenarios and applications, SAP has organized standard SAP S/4HANA CDS views in a layered architecture. The basis of the VDM architecture form the old SAP ERP core tables of the different application components ranging from FI to Logistics to HR. Figure 1.5 shows the different layers of the VDM architecture. From the bottom up, the architecture consists of the interface layer, formed by basic and composite views, and the consumption views layer, which sits on top of the interface view layer.

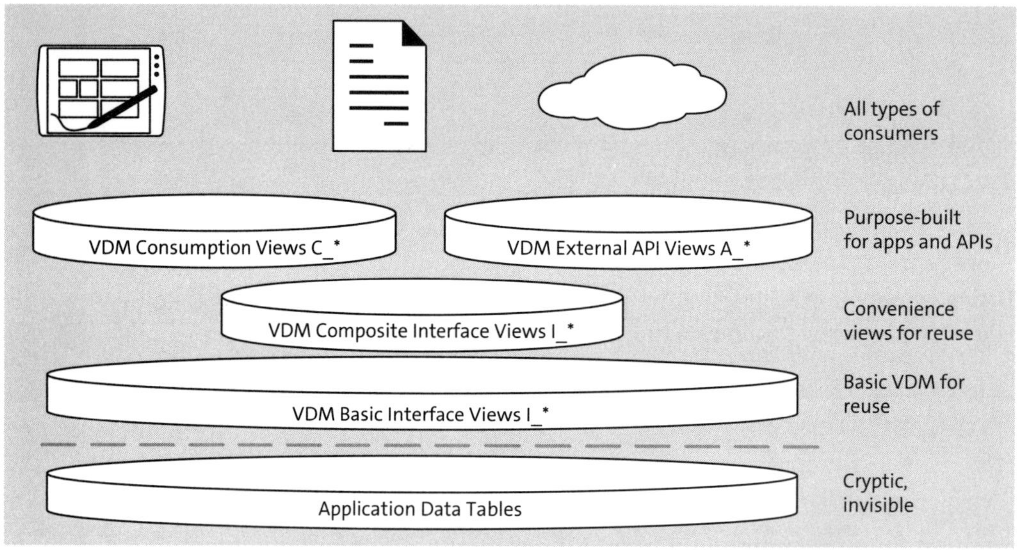

Figure 1.5 Different Layers of the VDM Architecture

The lowest layer of CDS views on top of the database tables is called the *interface view* layer, which serves as the reusable, application-agnostic base layer of the VDM. The interface view layer can be further subdivided into *basic* and *composite views*. By convention, names of CDS views of the interface view layer, basic as well as composite, start with `I_`, for instance, `I_Material`. Distinguishing between basic and composite views is done using the `@VDM.viewType: #BASIC/#COMPOSITE` header annotation.

The basic view layer of CDS views is the foundation layer of the VDM itself. All upper-layer CDS views of the VDM, both composite and consumption, are supposed to construct application-specific business entities and access data using those basic CDS views. However, direct database table access of upper-layer CDS views is a bad practice and is forbidden. Many other rules apply to the development of basic CDS views, but the main aspects and characteristics you should note are as follows:

- Basic views usually select data from one database table to allow fine-grained reuse.
- If the mandatory attributes of an entity are distributed over multiple tables, the basic view might already join those together.
- Basic views may only have associations with other basic views.
- Basic views aren't supposed to contain any complex calculations, aggregations, parameters, or `WHERE` conditions—only a projection of the underlying database table fields.
- Basic views provide semantic field names to hide the technical abbreviated database table field names.
- Basic views are agnostic to their potential consumers.
- Basic views are free of redundancies, which means that a piece of data can only be selected using one particular core view (e.g., there is exactly one view for the work center or cost center entity).

Due to their simplicity, basic CDS views are optimal candidates for fine-grained reuse and composition of new, more application-specific views and entities. CDS views already provide redundancy-free core business entities carrying semantic names and semantically labeled properties, but they are still usually based on a one-to-one relationship between the basic view and the SAP ERP table.

To compose new reusable business entities or bring together all business data required for a certain existing business entity in one view, the *composite view* layer is provided, which sits on top of the basic view layer. The further we move up the different layers, the more application specific and business oriented the views get. The main characteristics of composite views are as follows:

- Composite views are based on one or more basic CDS views and may also select data from other composite views.
- Composite views may have associations to other composite and basic views.
- Composite views may contain calculations, aggregations, parameters, or `WHERE` conditions.
- By nature, composite views introduce data redundancy; for instance, we might need a reusable view for an analytical use case and for a transactional app that might return the same data.

Like basic views, composite views are intended for reuse. Unlike basic views, however, composite views might already implement application type-specific scenarios, such as particular calculations, aggregations, annotations, or join scenarios, to provide business entities and data to application-specific consumption views sitting on top of them.

The uppermost layer of the VDM architecture, the *consumption view* layer, is intended for application-specific use cases. Unlike the interface view layers, consumption views aren't intended for reuse; instead, they address application-specific requirements. By convention, their names start with `C_`, for instance, `C_MaterialDailyDemand`. Consumption layer views are additionally annotated with the `@VDM.viewType: #CONSUMPTION` header annotation. External API views, which are used because they are application specific and nonreusable, are also assigned to the consumption view layer and are the basis for published OData APIs, for instance, via the SAP API Business Hub. Their names start with `A_`, for instance, `A_ProductionOrder`. The main characteristics of consumption layer views are as follows:

- Consumption layer views address application-specific requirements.
- Consumption views aren't intended for reuse as they are developed for a specific purpose, for instance, a certain SAP Fiori application or analytical query.
- Consumption views are supposed to access data using interface layer views.
- Consumption views may have associations to interface views as well as other consumption views.

Consumption views might contain application-specific complex calculations, aggregations, join conditions, or UI annotations, which is what renders their reuse impossible across application borders.

Figure 1.6 shows a complete E2E example of an application's VDM based on the sales order entity, which is part of the SD application component.

The lowest level contains the different SAP ERP tables from which data is brought together using several CDS view layers. The basic view layer (`I_SalesOrder`, `I_SalesOrderItem`, `I_Material`, `I_MaterialText`) directly performs projections on database tables, whereas the composite view layer provides reusable application-specific views for transactional (`I_SalesOrderTP`) and analytical applications (`I_SalesOrderItemCube`). Finally, the consumption view layer consists of application-specific views for transactional (`C_SalesOrderTP`), analytical (`C_SalesOrderItemQuery`), and external API applications (`A_SalesOrderItem`).

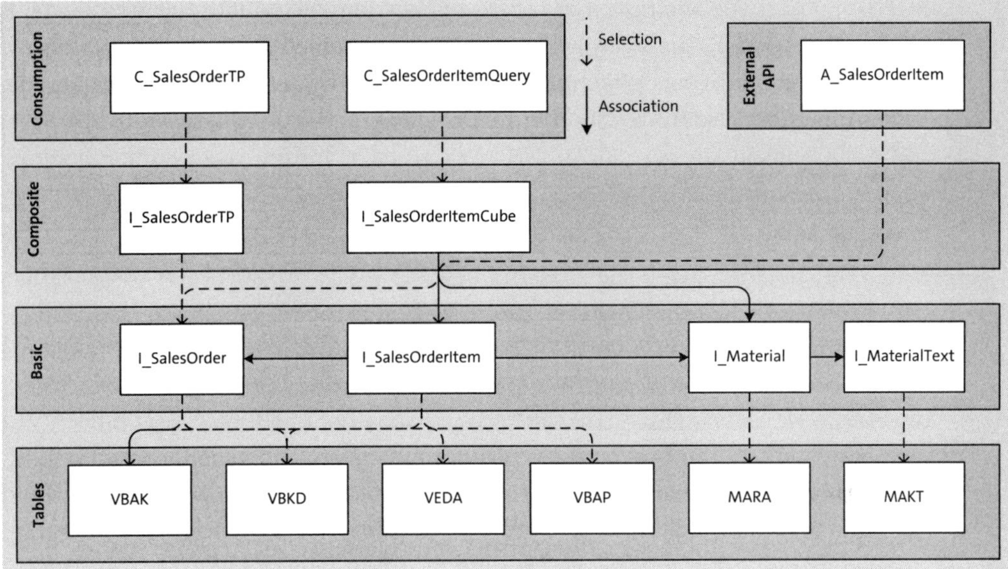

Figure 1.6 Example of the VDM Architecture for the Sales Order Business Entity

1.2.2 ABAP Programming Model for SAP Fiori

As mentioned in Section 1.1.4, the ABAP programming model for SAP Fiori is the recommended programming model for transactional applications up to and including SAP S/4HANA 1809 (initial release in September 2018). Thus, the focus of this book is the new ABAP RESTful programming model available since SAP S/4HANA 1909 (initial release in September 2019). Nevertheless, we'll provide a brief introduction to the ABAP programming model for SAP Fiori in this section, as you'll definitely stumble over many applications in your SAP S/4HANA system that are using this programming model.

Note

To learn more about the ABAP programming model for SAP Fiori, take a look at our other SAP PRESS book: *ABAP Programming Model for SAP Fiori: ABAP Development for SAP S/4HANA* at *http://www.sap-press.com/4766.*

An integral part of the ABAP programming model for SAP Fiori is the BOPF, which derives its *node* structure from annotated CDS view associations. Note that, whereas

BOPF only adds the business logic of the application, the underlying data model is always derived from the VDM by making use of specific hierarchy annotations for modeling the BOPF node structure on the CDS level. Generating the corresponding BOPF node structure from CDS business entities is supported from SAP S/4HANA 1610 SPS 03 onward.

The general idea of the ABAP programming model for SAP Fiori in SAP S/4HANA, as shown in Figure 1.7, is to provide direct high-performance access to CDS views for read-only scenarios using the SADL framework, which transparently passes OData requests via SAP Gateway down to the VDM layer using its query runtime. Modifying access is provided via the BOPF runtime to invoke business logic. If the modifying access doesn't invoke any business logic at all, a further optimization would be to directly access the database tables, which prevents the buildup of local buffers and caches.

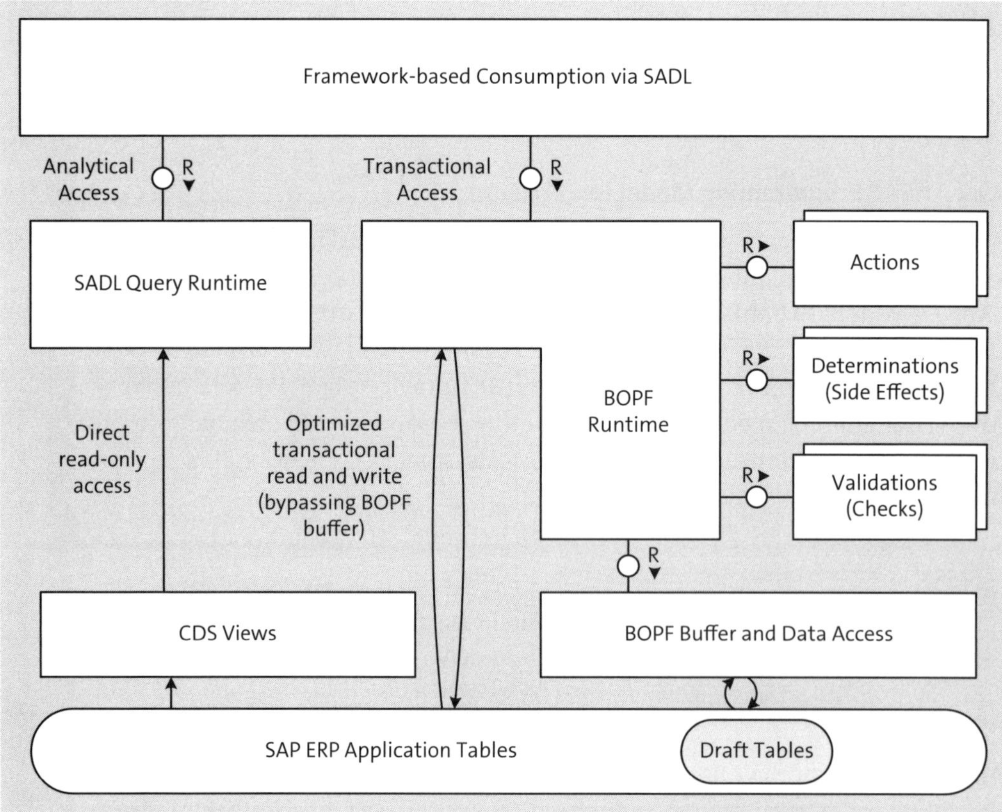

Figure 1.7 Architecture of the ABAP Programming Model for SAP Fiori

The SAP Fiori user experience requires a decoupling of the frontend and backend as well as a backend implementation optimized for stateless request handling. So far, BOPF has been aimed at stateful business applications, but a lot of effort has been put into optimizing BOPF for stateless data processing. Classic SAP Dynpro or Web Dynpro applications rely on an ABAP session along with application buffers that serve client requests until the user has finished his work and stored all the data changes. SAP Fiori applications, on the other hand, fetch data using RESTful OData services, which are stateless like the HTTP that is used as the data transfer protocol. Statelessness is also a core property of the RESTful paradigm and has some advantages over stateful applications:

- Statelessness enables horizontal scaling of APIs as any request can be processed by any server without any session-related dependencies.
- Stateless APIs are less complex as all information required to serve the request is contained in the current request, so no server-side state synchronization logic is needed.
- Reliability is also improved because, if one server crashes, another server can take over immediately as no previously stored state is required for serving requests.
- To improve network efficiency, the responses to requests can be cached on the client side.

You can also implement a stateful application scenario using stateless communication and BOPF, but instead of storing data in an in-memory ABAP session context, data must be stored on the database using draft tables, which are shadow tables of the original database tables. Users can work on the draft data for several interaction steps and roundtrips, and when finished editing the entity, the draft data can be activated and written to the actual database tables.

When a user is changing business data and jumps between the input fields on the screen, the changes are sent to the backend immediately via an OData request that updates the draft table(s) instead of the original database tables. Each draft update sent to the backend like this is called a *roundtrip*.

This information of a draft entity that is present for a certain business entity can also be used for locking the entity for other users (exclusive lock). In the past, locks were bound to an ABAP session; now, you can use *durable locks* to enable stateless locking of an entity beyond several ABAP sessions and requests.

Business Logic Implementation

Business logic implementation in BOPF comes in the form of actions, determinations, or validations:

- **Actions**
  Actions implement operations, for instance, changing the status of an invoice from **Outstanding** to **Paid**.
- **Validations**
  Validations don't change any data but check whether the data is consistent, for instance, whether price and quantity are defined for an invoice.
- **Determinations**
  Determinations execute side effects and are triggered on actions, for instance, if the quantity of items in an invoice changes, the overall price has to be updated as well.

Transactional Application Scenarios

In general, the ABAP programming model for SAP Fiori, available since SAP S/4HANA 1610 SPS 03, supports four different transactional application scenarios based on BOPF and CDS:

- New application with draft enablement
- New application without draft enablement
- Draft enablement of existing application
- Read-only application with quick actions (BOPF is only used for actions but not for CRUD operations)

1.2.3 ABAP RESTful Programming Model

As mentioned earlier, the main focus of this book is the new ABAP RESTful programming model, which supersedes the previously described ABAP programming model for SAP Fiori with SAP S/4HANA 1909. Moreover, SAP has promised migration support to the ABAP RESTful programming model for customers that have already invested in the ABAP programming model for SAP Fiori. Whenever possible, from now on, you should use the ABAP RESTful programming model for developing new applications as the ABAP RESTful programming model is planned to be the long-term solution for developing ABAP based RESTful OData services, in the cloud as well as in on-premise installations. We'll cover the ABAP RESTful programming model in detail in Chapters 3 and 4. However, we'd like to provide a high-level overview of the ABAP RESTful programming model in the following section.

Many core ideas in the ABAP RESTful programming model greatly resemble the ABAP programming model for SAP Fiori. However, one big difference is that the new programming model has been integrated into the core ABAP language, which also makes the model available on SAP Cloud Platform, by providing a core ABAP runtime without any additional tools and frameworks like SAP GUI or Transaction SEGW. In addition, this integration also enables a completely Eclipse-based E2E development experience without having to access SAP GUI transactions. A big difference to classic ABAP development in the cloud environment is also the use of ABAP on Git (abapGit) as the Source Code Management (SCM) tool, replacing the Change and Transport System (CTS) normally used for tracking changes in ABAP code and moving ABAP development objects between ABAP environments. However, in on-premise installations, you can still use the CTS when developing applications using the ABAP RESTful programming model.

Overview

Figure 1.8 shows the different building blocks of the ABAP RESTful programming model. As in the previous programming model, a data model based on CDS views serves as the foundation. If only read access to the database is required, the query component takes over the data retrieval for an OData service. The transactional counterpart of a query is a business object with additional ABAP-based behavior definition and implementation. The service definition defines which CDS entities of the data model should be exposed as OData entities. The service binding then binds the exposed entities to a client communication protocol, as of now OData version 2.0. The business service can then be offered as an SAP Fiori UI, by adding an SAP Fiori elements UI or other UI clients to the service, or as a web API, for any consumer capable of consuming an OData REST API, for instance, freestyle OpenUI5 applications.

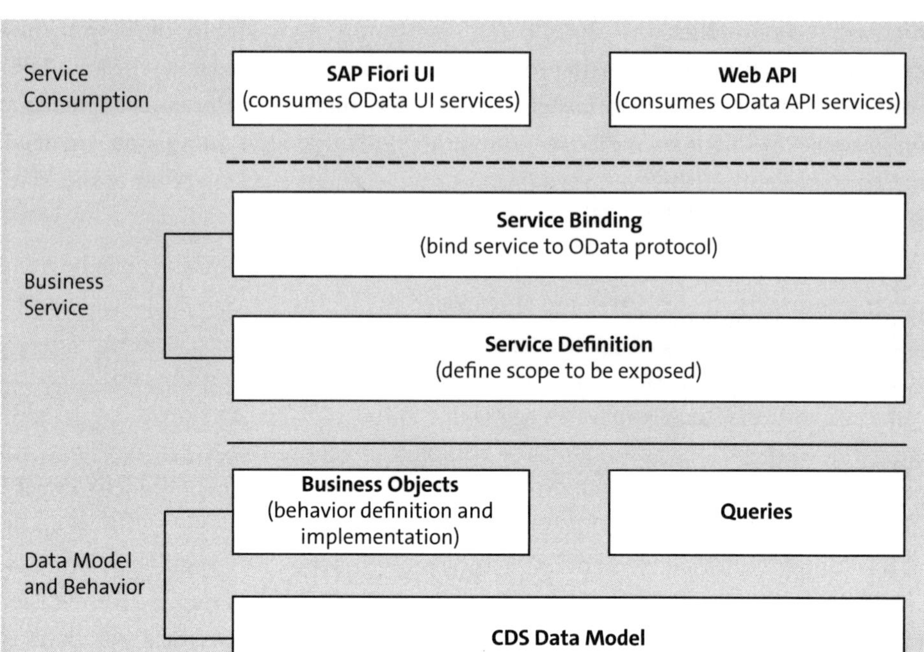

Figure 1.8 Architecture of the ABAP RESTful Programming Model

Business Objects

A business object is used for transactional processing and defines behaviors for the nodes of a CDS data model (e.g., CRUD operations or custom actions). To transform a CDS data model into a transactional business object node tree, the relationships between the nodes must be explicitly modeled. In the previous programming model, this modeling was performed using annotations, but in the ABAP RESTful programming model, modeling the structure of a business object has been integrated into the ABAP CDS language. The specific behavior for nodes in the business object hierarchy is defined using a new transportable ABAP development object called a behavior definition. The actual behavior implementation for a certain node is then established in a corresponding ABAP class.

Queries

The query runtime takes over the data retrieval from the database for a read-only OData service. In contrast to the business object behavior, no additional artifact is required to define the capabilities of the query runtime. In general, the query runtime can transform standard OData query options like filtering (`$filter`); paging (`$top`, `$skip`); and sorting (`$orderby`) into an SQL statement. This transformation occurs in a way that is transparent to the developer, which means that the developer won't have to deal with the construction of the SQL statement. Other capabilities like search, value helps, and text provisioning must be annotated in the CDS data model by the developer. The runtime of a query is usually managed by the query framework (SADL), which is also known from the previous ABAP programming model for SAP Fiori. SADL enables a model-based exposure of CDS entities and their relationships as OData entities, which SAP Fiori apps then consume in a stateless manner via the OData protocol over HTTP. Transparent to the application developer, SADL simply links together the different layers of the programming model without having to manually code access between the different layers.

As mentioned earlier, the ABAP RESTful programming model will be covered in detail in Chapter 3.

1.2.4 Analytics

An integral part of the SAP S/4HANA UX is its seamless integration of analytical content into standard process steps or applications. Business users in SAP S/4HANA will be supported with in-process contextual information to aid decision-making, such as which items to process next. For users who need a more generic view of the data, such as executives or data analysts, SAP still provides generic key-user tools to flexibly analyze business data, for instance, SAP Lumira, or SAP Analysis for Microsoft Excel. Embedded analytics scenarios for business users are, to a large extent, enabled by SAP HANA because it blurs the borders between classic online transaction processing (OLTP) and online analytical processing (OLAP) systems.

With SAP HANA, storing data column-based and in-memory, the speed of aggregating data has increased substantially and allows real-time analytical reporting and transactional processing in the same system. Another enabler of in-app analytics is SAP Fiori with its rich set of analytical controls and templates aimed at analytical use cases, for instance, the overview page (OVP) or the analytical list page (ALP).

As for other application types, the foundation of all analytical content in SAP S/4HANA is the VDM based on CDS views. Analytical CDS content can be consumed either via the OData protocol and the SADL engine or the Info Access Service (InA), Business Intelligence Consumer Services (BICS), and OData protocols and the Analytical Engine, as shown in Figure 1.9.

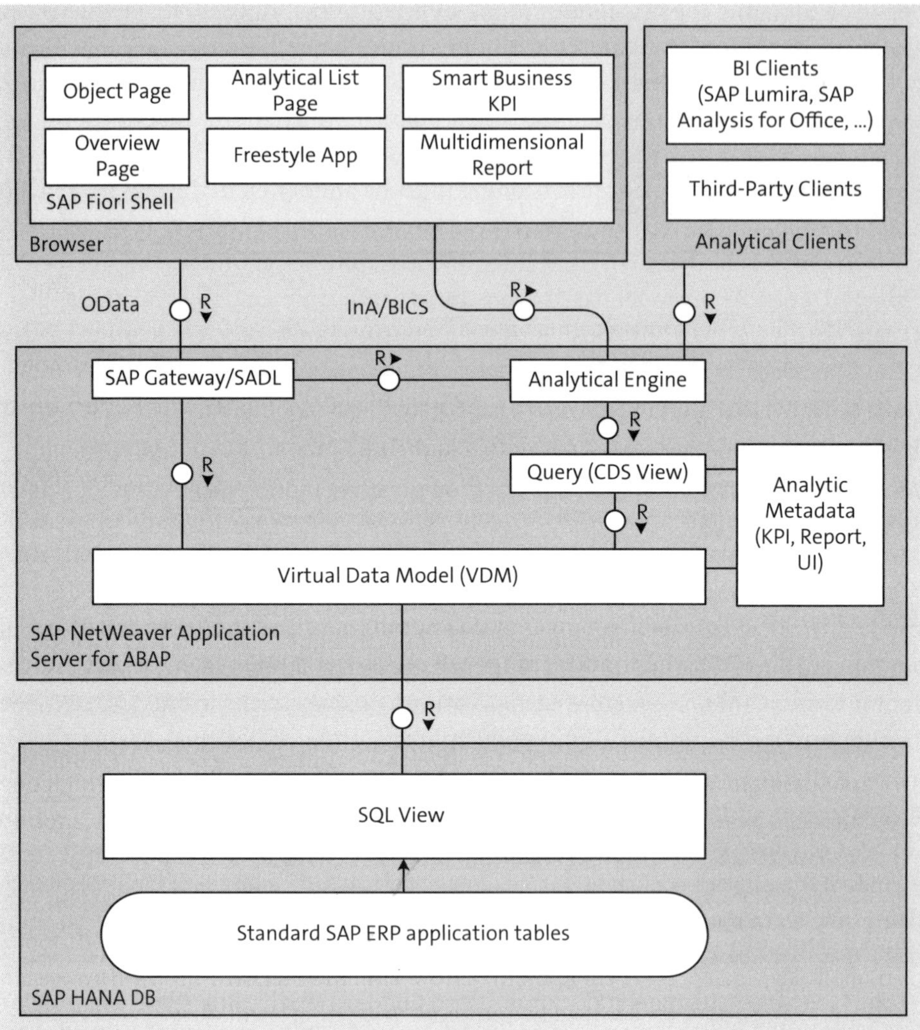

Figure 1.9 Analytical Parts of the SAP S/4HANA Architecture

Both engines use analytical CDS annotations, for instance, to determine which fields to aggregate the data. The `@DefaultAggregation: #SUM` annotation will mark a CDS view field as a measure on which data will be aggregated as a sum. All other fields in the view will be dimensions by default and form the context of the aggregation, for instance, the number of maintenance requests (measure) by machine type (dimension). For simple analytical use cases, the SADL engine can be used, but for more complex scenarios, such as hierarchy handling or exception aggregations, the Analytical Engine must be used.

The Analytical Engine is part of SAP BW in the ABAP server and will, like the SADL engine, use SQL SELECT statements on the CDS views to retrieve data. No application-specific ABAP code is executed at runtime, and the selection of data and the authorization checks are completely pushed down to the SAP HANA database.

1.3 User Experience

Another main objective of SAP S/4HANA is to offer an improved UX and to manage the transition from the UX found in traditional business software to a consumer-grade experience. The main pillar of this transition is the newly developed SAP Fiori design paradigm.

1.3.1 SAP Fiori

The UX of SAP S/4HANA is fully based on the SAP Fiori design language, which aims to provide lightweight role-based apps tailored to the users' specific tasks. Therefore, the UI of SAP S/4HANA is mostly based on web apps developed with the SAPUI5 framework, as SAPUI5 is one of the supported technologies for implementing the SAP Fiori user experience. SAPUI5 is a JavaScript framework that includes built-in support for architectural concepts such as the Model View Controller (MVC) pattern, two-way data binding, and routing. Apps developed with SAPUI5 run in the browsers of smartphones, tablets, and desktop PCs and will adapt according to the devices' capabilities. A subset of SAPUI5 has also been made open source under the Apache 2.0 license called OpenUI5 (*https://openui5.org/*).

1.3.2 SAP Fiori Launchpad

SAP Fiori apps within SAP S/4HANA are hosted by the SAP Fiori launchpad, which provides different services for the apps, for instance, inter-app navigation, personalization, and application configuration. This single entry point to SAP S/4HANA for end users on any device provides role-based access to all apps relevant for a user to carry out his specific business tasks.

1.4 SAP S/4HANA Editions

The SAP S/4HANA product offering currently consists of two different editions: SAP S/4HANA, which is the on-premise edition, and SAP S/4HANA Cloud. In the following section, we'll explore the different architectures, deployment options, and release strategies of both SAP S/4HANA editions.

1.4.1 On-Premise Architecture

The scope of SAP S/4HANA, in terms of functionality, localization, and content, can be considered equivalent to previous SAP Business Suite releases. Additionally, SAP S/4HANA provides you great flexibility over your system usage. You'll still have full access to well-known administration tools (e.g., Transaction PFCG for role and authorization management), and as with previous SAP ERP versions, you can tailor predelivered SAP content and applications to specific customer needs. Moreover, when choosing SAP S/4HANA, you can fully leverage the underlying SAP NetWeaver platform and SAP HANA database to develop custom SAP Fiori apps along with predelivered SAP Fiori apps. Development includes full access to the ABAP stack through ABAP in Eclipse, also known as ABAP development tools. One major change when compared to previous SAP ERP versions is that you no longer have the choice of selecting a supported database vendor. SAP S/4HANA depends on, and is exclusively built for, the SAP HANA database.

You can install SAP S/4HANA in your own data centers and have complete control over the software and your data. You'll be responsible for the whole lifecycle management of the system, including upgrades and applying corrections via SAP Notes. Using this deployment option, you'll have maximum flexibility when tailoring and customizing applications to your needs as well as for custom development on the SAP NetWeaver platform, rather than paying a license fee for the right to use the software, which usually involves high up-front investment.

1.4.2 Cloud Architecture

Compared to SAP S/4HANA, SAP S/4HANA Cloud is somewhat more restricted and standardized. SAP delivers ready-to-use content and specialized key-user tools to allow customizations and adjustments, but access to the SAP NetWeaver backend is no longer provided. This change prevents incompatible changes and modifications and ensures seamless quarterly upgrades of the system. All access to the system is browser based via the SAP Fiori launchpad, which is a shell that hosts all SAP Fiori apps, key-user applications for customizing the system, and end-user applications. The SAP Fiori launchpad is the single entry point to the SAP S/4HANA Cloud system. If end-user applications support customization, they can, to a certain extent, be customized and extended using key-user tools. This capability is called in-app extensibility because the extensions are created in the same system as the enhanced application. If, in addition to the SAP-delivered applications, custom applications are required, they must be developed and deployed in a side-by-side extensibility scenario using SAP Cloud Platform. Access to the SAP NetWeaver AS for ABAP via ABAP development tools in Eclipse isn't supported anymore.

In the cloud, two options for subscribing to SAP S/4HANA Cloud are available: public cloud or private cloud. Figure 1.10 shows a high-level overview of the different SAP S/4HANA editions, including on-premise.

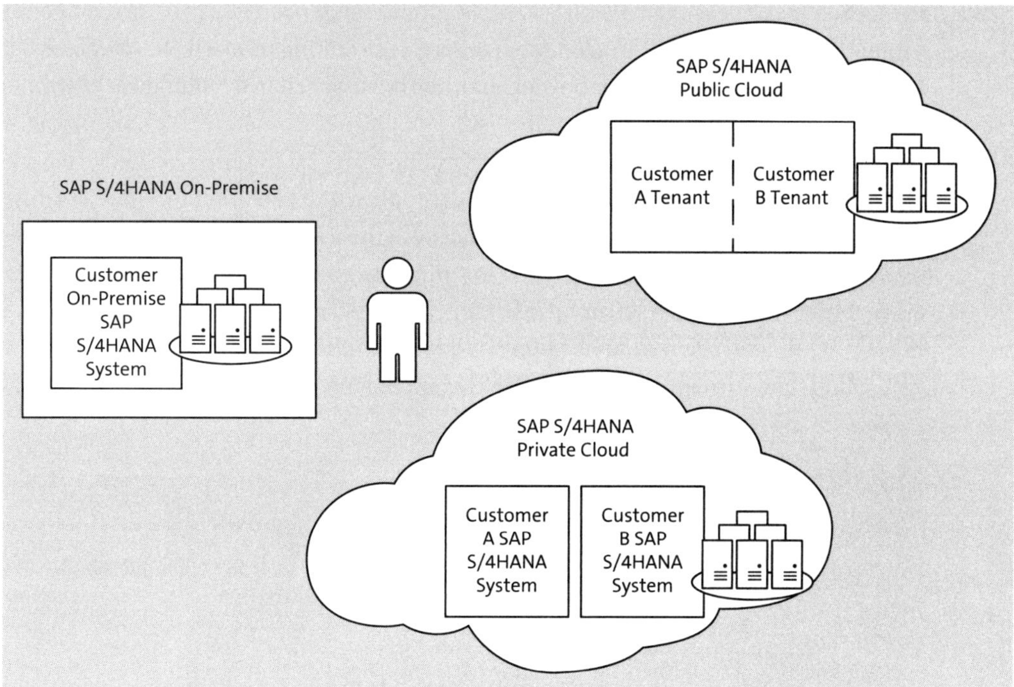

Figure 1.10 High-Level Overview of the Different SAP S/4HANA Deployment Options

Public Cloud

In a public cloud scenario, SAP S/4HANA Cloud is provided as Software-as-a-service (SaaS) by SAP and runs in a multitenant public cloud environment in SAP data centers.

From a cloud service provider view, using the available computing and infrastructure resources as efficiently as possible is important to reducing the TCO for providing the service.

This efficiency is best achieved by making subscribers share as many resources as possible while keeping them isolated from other subscribers in their own "tenants." From a subscriber perspective, being isolated from other subscribers of the cloud service is necessary for keeping data private. You'll subscribe to the service and continuously pay a subscription fee for using the service. Your key users and end users can access the system via the browser. SAP undertakes the lifecycle management of the system including system upgrades, patches, and hotfixes.

Private Cloud

In this deployment scenario, SAP S/4HANA Cloud is deployed in a private cloud environment managed by SAP in SAP data centers. Subscribing to a private cloud service implies a higher degree of isolation from other subscribers; instead of each customer having its own tenant within a shared system, each customer gets its own system. How far the responsibilities of subscriber and provider go in terms of lifecycle management of the system depends on individual contractual agreements. These arrangements can range from "hosting" scenarios, where the subscriber takes over the whole responsibility of the lifecycle management of the system, and the provider only provides the system and infrastructure, to fully managed scenarios, where the provider carries out all upgrade and maintenance activities. At the moment, the private managed cloud scenario can be realized with the SAP HANA Enterprise Cloud.

1.4.3 Release Strategies

Both SAP S/4HANA and SAP S/4HANA Cloud are supplied with quarterly updates. However, only SAP S/4HANA Cloud provides continuous access to the latest innovations provided by SAP as this edition is continuously supplied with quarterly *innovation releases*.

For SAP S/4HANA, on the other hand, SAP is providing one key release per year, which, for the next three quarters, is supplied with Feature Packs (FPs) that deliver nondisruptive innovations as well as software corrections and legal changes. After the third FP, the SAP S/4HANA release goes into maintenance-only mode, and eventually, a new SAP S/4HANA version is released.

In maintenance mode, Support Packages (SPs) bundle software corrections and may include legal changes for SAP S/4HANA releases on a quarterly basis. An SP might also contain refinements to existing functionalities, for instance, enhancements contracted in SAP customer connection programs, but no completely new functionality or innovations are released in SPs.

Technically, FPs and SPs are shipped as feature package stacks (FPS) and support package stacks (SPS), which are bundled sets of features or support packages that must be applied in the given combination.

Figure 1.11 summarizes the different release strategies for SAP S/4HANA and SAP S/4HANA Cloud.

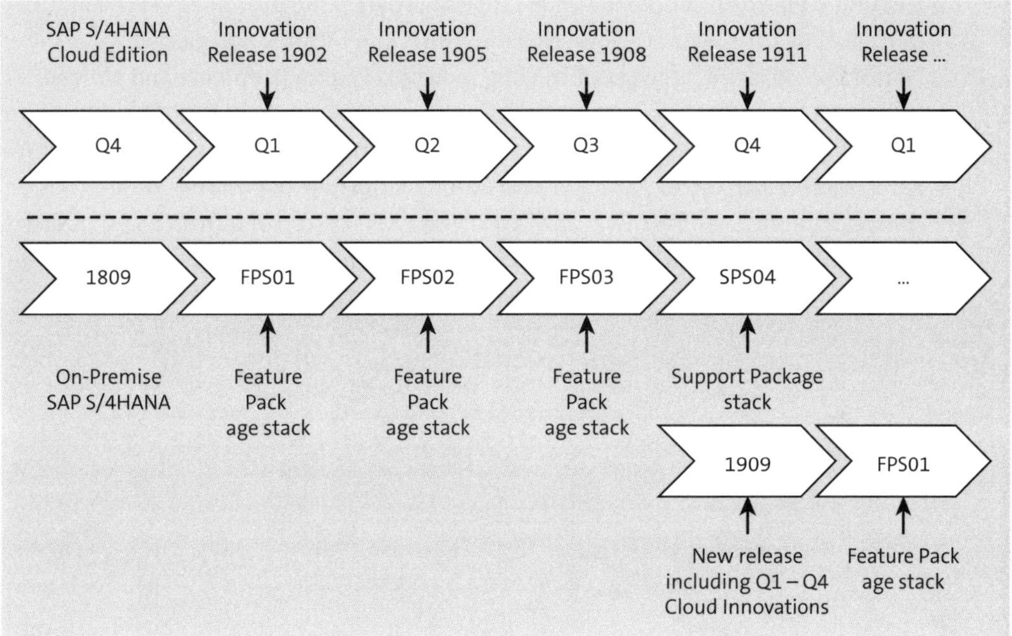

Figure 1.11 Different Release Strategies of SAP S/4HANA and SAP S/4HANA Cloud

1.5 SAP Cloud Platform

The SAP Cloud Platform plays an important role in extending SAP S/4HANA and SAP S/4HANA Cloud with state-of-the-art cloud services and applications, as shown in Figure 1.12. SAP Cloud Platform is SAP's Platform-as-a-service (PaaS) offering for developing cloud-native applications in Neo (SAP's own environment) or Cloud Foundry (an open-source cloud platform SAP is also contributing to). Additionally, SAP Cloud Platform hosts many of the innovative SAP Leonardo services and applications in areas such as machine learning and the Internet of Things (IoT). As a customer subscribing to the SAP S/4HANA Cloud service, you won't have access to the SAP NetWeaver AS for ABAP stack anymore using Eclipse. Instead, you'll develop custom applications on SAP Cloud Platform in a side-by-side extensibility scenario. SAP S/4HANA customers, on the other hand, still have the choice between developing their custom applications in SAP NetWeaver or switching to SAP Cloud Platform, which might facilitate a migration to SAP S/4HANA Cloud at a later point because custom code is already ported to a cloud-native platform environment and moved out of the core SAP ERP. SAP Cloud Platform supports a wide range of programming languages via containerized runtimes, for instance, Java, Node.js, ABAP, and HTML5. Additionally, SAP Cloud Platform provides a large set of backing services ranging from data and storage services (SAP HANA, Redis on SAP Cloud Platform, PostgreSQL) to SAP Cloud Platform DevOps (SAP Web IDE) over to business and integration services (SAP Tax Service, RabbitMQ on SAP Cloud Platform, SAP Cloud Platform Integration). To ease the consumption of the SAP S/4HANA VDM and OData APIs on top of it from SAP Cloud Platform, SAP has released the SAP Cloud SDK for Java and JavaScript/TypeScript.

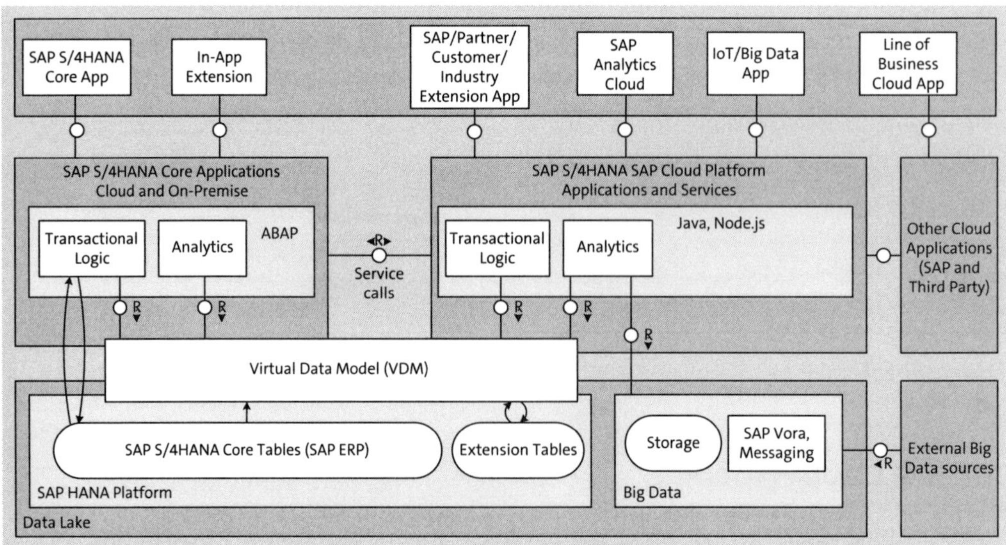

Figure 1.12 Overall Architecture of the SAP S/4HANA Application Suite Including SAP Cloud Platform for Developing Side-by-Side Extensions

1.6 Summary

SAP S/4HANA is based on a completely different architecture optimized for SAP HANA. Nevertheless, a major goal of the SAP S/4HANA architecture is to stay as compatible as possible with previous SAP ERP releases to ease migration and to leverage existing, well-established, and proven business processes developed by SAP, partners, and customers in recent decades. A cornerstone of SAP S/4HANA is the VDM based on CDS, which enables code pushdown to SAP HANA to a large extent according to the Code-to-Data paradigm. The VDM is the foundation of all application types in SAP S/4HANA, from transactional and analytical over to external interfaces and ESH. Explicitly released parts of the VDM can also be used by partners and customers as the foundation for developing custom applications. With SAP S/4HANA 1909 (released in September 2019), the ABAP RESTful programming model is now the recommended programming model for developing transactional SAP Fiori applications in SAP S/4HANA and supersedes the ABAP programming model for SAP Fiori. The renewed UX based on SAP Fiori is another big leap forward and will be discussed in detail in the next chapter.

Chapter 2
SAP Fiori and the Design-Led Development Process

In this chapter, we'll familiarize you with the design-led development process for creating SAP Fiori applications and describe the different developer tools for this process.

In this chapter, we'll introduce you to SAP Fiori, which is the new user experience (UX) for SAP S/4HANA. In addition, we'll cover the design-led development process, which helps with developing SAP Fiori applications; the different app types available for developers to choose from when starting with app development; and the different prototyping tools that support developers with the design process (e.g., SAP Build and Axure). We'll use the SAP Build tool to make a prototype design by following the design-led development process.

2.1 What Is SAP Fiori?

With SAP Fiori, SAP provides a consistent and elegant UX for creating stunning design with an emphasis on ease of use. The user interface (UI) is also simple to use and works seamlessly across multiple devices and screen sizes. The SAP Fiori user experience has five core characteristics: role-based, adaptive, simple, coherent, and delightful. SAP Fiori focuses on providing role-based applications to its users, which means the apps offer specific services relevant for a user's role.

SAP Fiori apps are also designed to simplify tasks by breaking down complex apps into multiple simple apps focusing only on a specific task. For example, the standard SAP transaction for creating a sales order or a purchase order has multiple options and tabs. This overwhelming array of options in the transaction might not be useful for all users and can be confusing and complicated. SAP Fiori apps take such big and complex transactions and split them into multiple simple apps to help users perform the required task with just a few clicks. A user who isn't familiar with the SAP GUI can still complete his task because there is little to no learning curve to using SAP Fiori apps. Users can focus on what they want to do rather than figuring out how to use the UI to complete their task.

At this point, SAP Fiori has gone through two iterations. Let's discuss those next.

2.1.1 SAP Fiori 1.0

Introduced in 2013, SAP Fiori was as a paid solution where customers had to buy a license for each user. On June 2014, during SAP's SAPPHIRE NOW event, the SAP Fiori user experience, as shown in Figure 2.1, and SAP Screen Personas were announced as free and included with the SAP software, which greatly increased the adoption rate of SAP Fiori among customers.

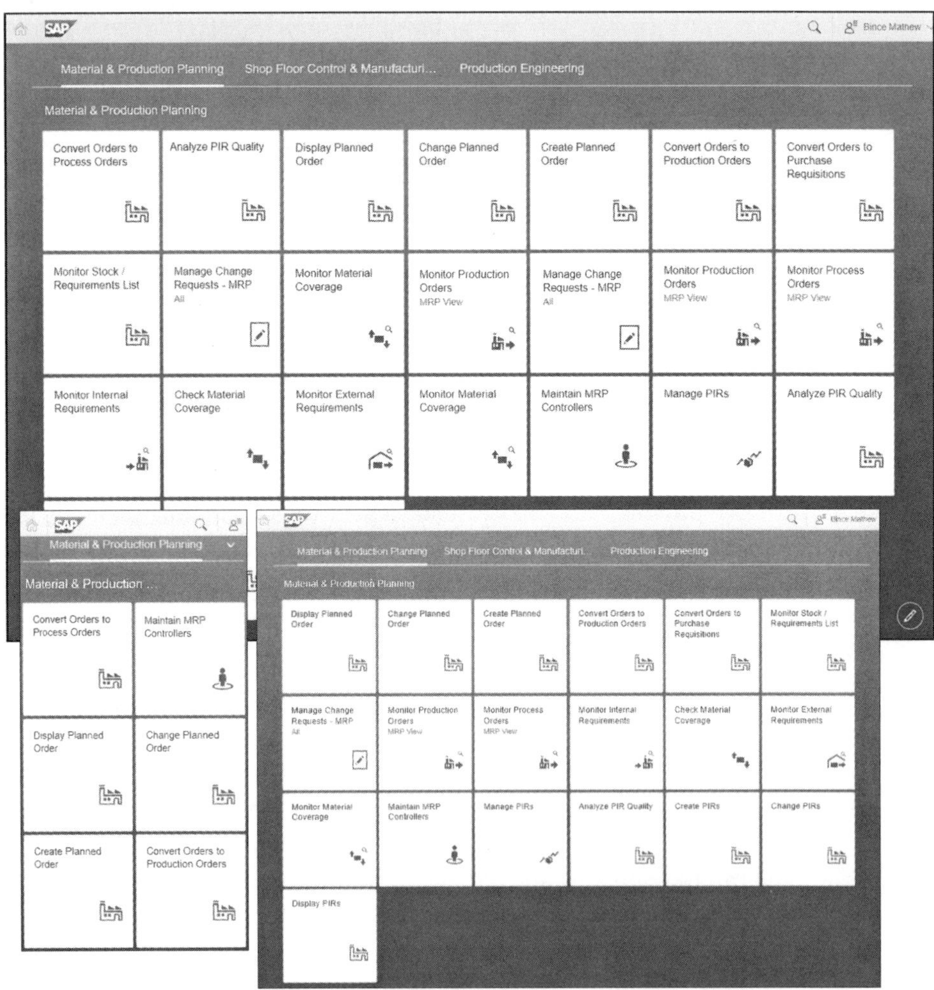

Figure 2.1 SAP Fiori 1.0 User Experience

SAP Fiori started with 25 apps that were developed by analyzing the most frequently used transactions in SAP. Later, more apps were added in the form of Wave I, Wave II, and so on, resulting in more than 500 apps. Over the years, SAP Fiori has evolved from just being a collection of apps to providing a totally new UX for SAP customers that comprise of solutions such as SAP Business Suite for SAP HANA (SAP S/4HANA), SAP SuccessFactors Employee Central, SAP Ariba Mobile, SAP Cloud for Customer, and more.

The SAP Fiori 1.0 design is valid with SAPUI5 versions 1.26 through 1.38.

2.1.2 SAP Fiori 2.0

On October 2016, SAP Fiori 2.0, shown in Figure 2.2, was launched, representing the latest evolution of the new UX for SAP S/4HANA and the SAP Business Suite.

Figure 2.2 SAP Fiori 2.0 User Experience

Based on the SAPUI5 version 1.40 and higher, this new version of the SAP Fiori user experience focuses on helping users concentrate on their specific tasks and to keep track of activities in other areas at the same time.

SAP Fiori 2.0 offers the following key features:

- A simple UX along with apps that can complete tasks quickly, thereby increasing user productivity
- Quick and direct accessibility to relevant information and applications
- Notifications on a timely manner for items that need attention
- Help for users when deciding what needs to be done next
- Options for quick and informed actions
- Focus on improving user satisfaction

2.1.3 SAP Fiori 3.0

SAP Fiori 3.0 is the new design that will be released to the public in multiple phases. In the first phase of SAP Fiori 3.0 launch, SAP is shipping the new SAP Fiori theme Quartz Light (successor to the Belize theme of SAP Fiori 2.0) along with SAPUI5 1.65 in SAP Cloud Platform. This release also includes a new shell bar that will replace the SAP Fiori 2.0 viewport design. The new shell bar has some new elements, and some old shell bar components have been rearranged. For example, the avatar icon that shows the user's details has been moved from the left to the right side of the new shell bar, which resides along with the search and notification icons, as shown in Figure 2.3.

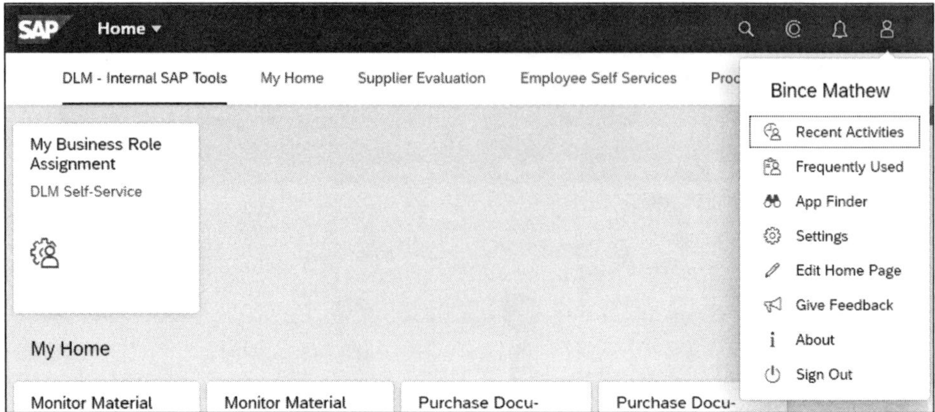

Figure 2.3 SAP Fiori 3.0 User Details Page

> **Note**
>
> If you want to know more about what is new with SAPUI5 1.65 version, see the SAPUI5 website: *http://s-prs.co/498800*.

The SAP Fiori 3.0 focuses on three priorities in UX design. Let's briefly discuss each next.

Consistency

Like previous versions of SAP Fiori, SAP Fiori 3.0 also focuses on providing a consistent user experience. This consistency helps in reduced costs in training the end users, which in turn results in fewer errors, higher productivity, and more. The less time your users spend searching for buttons or icons, the better the user experience will be, and users will be more motivated to use and app when the UI not only looks better but also behaves as expected. In turn, users will get even better at using the application.

To ensure the experience is fluid and consistent, SAP is taking an approach similar to how Microsoft releases new Windows 10 operating systems through future updates. The update to SAP Fiori 3.0 won't be a single release replacing SAP Fiori 2.0 completely, but instead, the transition will occur in several phases, such as first updating the theme to enhance the look and feel, then updating common functions, controls, floorplans, and so on. In the first phase, SAP has already released the new Quartz Light theme, which updated the existing shell bar of the SAP Fiori 2.0's Belize theme. This update has been available since April 2019 as part of SAPUI5 1.65 for SAP Cloud Platform. By the time you're reading this book, SAP might have already moved into the next phase of its update for SAP Fiori 3.0.

Intelligence

SAP Fiori 3.0 also takes advantage of machine learning/machine intelligence. In other words, SAP can leverage machine learning to analyze huge volumes of business data for your users and present this information to your users in a meaningful and timely manner. One concept utilizing machine learning is called a *situation*, which collects information from different areas of the ERP and updates/notifies users about a business situation that might need the user's attention. SAP Fiori can also make recommendations, such as what action can/should be taken to address that situation. The system also learns from the user's action on that situation, and in time, machine intelligence can collect and present relevant information for the user by learning from a user's past behavior on similar situations. This capability, in turn, helps users become more productive in their tasks as they become more confident in the system's ability to handle and alert users to situations occurring in the system.

An example use case could be material exceptions such as excess stock or the need to cancel a purchase order because the corresponding sales order was canceled in the system. In these cases, the situation handling feature powered by machine intelligence can be configured to alert the material requirements planning (MRP) controller directly in the SAP Fiori launchpad through notifications whenever such exceptions happen. By being notified on such situations in the SAP Fiori launchpad, your users will no longer need to go into every detail to find exceptions, which was time consuming, and such features in turn are increases the user's productivity.

Integration

Another plus for integration is conversational UX. Users can express what they want to do in a natural way to a digital assistant, either by speaking or typing. The system performs the hunting and gathering for so that users can work across products in one continuous conversation—all in a single screen. You can check out the preview of the new shell bar at *http://s-prs.co/498801*.

SAP Fiori 3.0 also provides users with a new search experience, including improved search previews, results page, and result visualizations—all, of course, fully integrated into the digital assistant.

Integration is a key factor customers expect in this modern age where everything is interconnected. This expectation is especially true for customers of SAP software: You might have multiple SAP products (or no SAP products) that you expect to be accessible through a single home page or a central entry point which gives you access to all the products in the landscape. This approach makes sense for end users so they don't need to be concerned about the different products (for example, SAP S/4HANA, SAP Concur, SAP Fieldglass, SAP SuccessFactors, or any other SAP product for that matter) to get the work done. Rather than opening each and every product individually through their own respective UIs, users want a single point of entry to all these functions. Needing to open every individual product to get the work done could affect efficiency greatly. So, SAP has come up with a solution as part of SAP Fiori 3.0 known as the SAP Fiori launchpad. This main entry point takes care of the integration between different products that customers might be using, thereby reducing the complexity in navigating between these products.

As an added feature to complement integration in the SAP Fiori launchpad, the conversational UI will also be introduced. Previously called SAP CoPilot, this digital assistant can interact with your users in a more natural way via text chats or spoken commands. For example, if you ask SAP CoPilot "Show me Sales Order XXXXX," the digital assistant will find the information related to your query and bring the results right to your launchpad. This feature can now work across various SAP products and is thus much more powerful than before. You can access the digital assistant from the icon in the center of the SAP Fiori 3.0 shell bar, as shown in Figure 2.4.

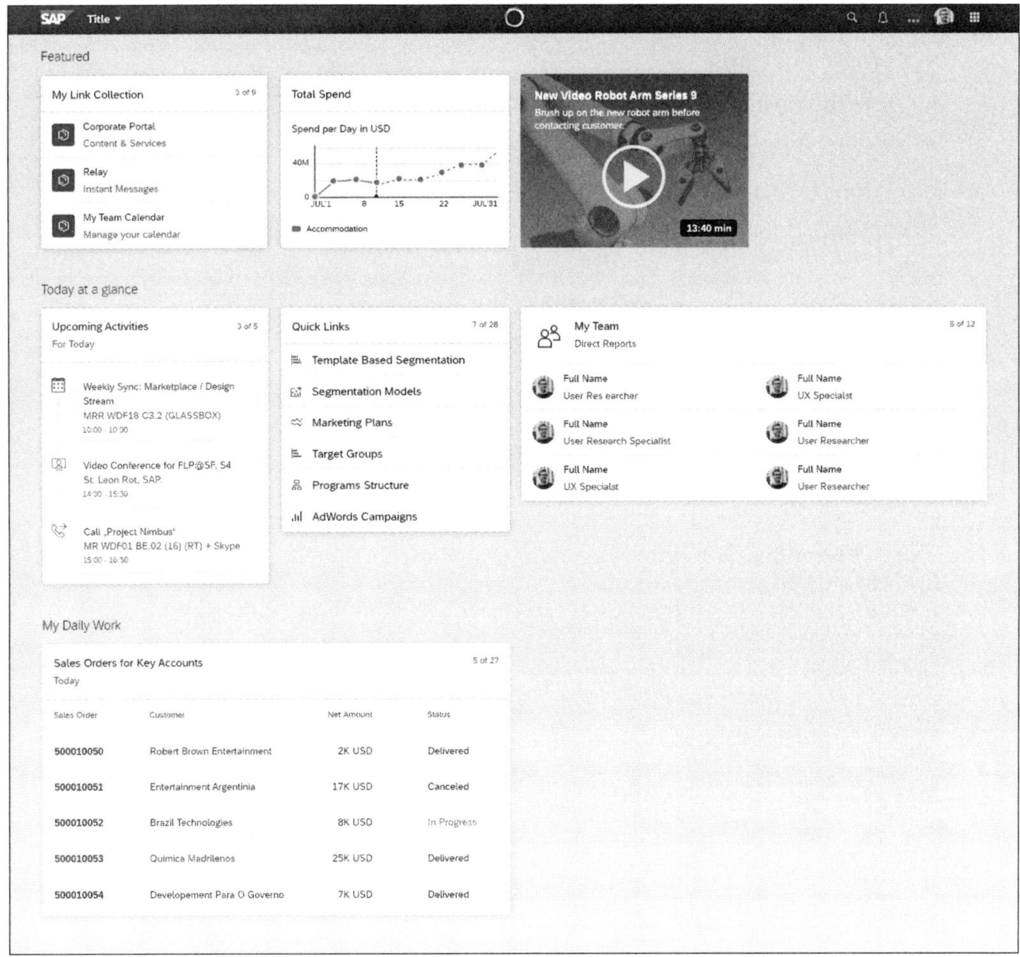

Figure 2.4 The SAP Fiori Launchpad Concept

As shown in Figure 2.4, multiple cards exist on the home page, called *integration cards*, as shown in Figure 2.5. These cards provide more information on home pages. The SAP Fiori launchpad also allows you to create custom pages with these cards integrated into the pages. These cards can also show previews of the data coming from a specific apps and are more robust than dynamic tiles. With the latest SAPUI5 1.65, you'll get six predefined cards:

- Table cards
- List cards
- Object cards
- Component cards
- Timeline cards
- Analytical cards
- Actions (not a predefined card, but a generic card containing actions as the content)

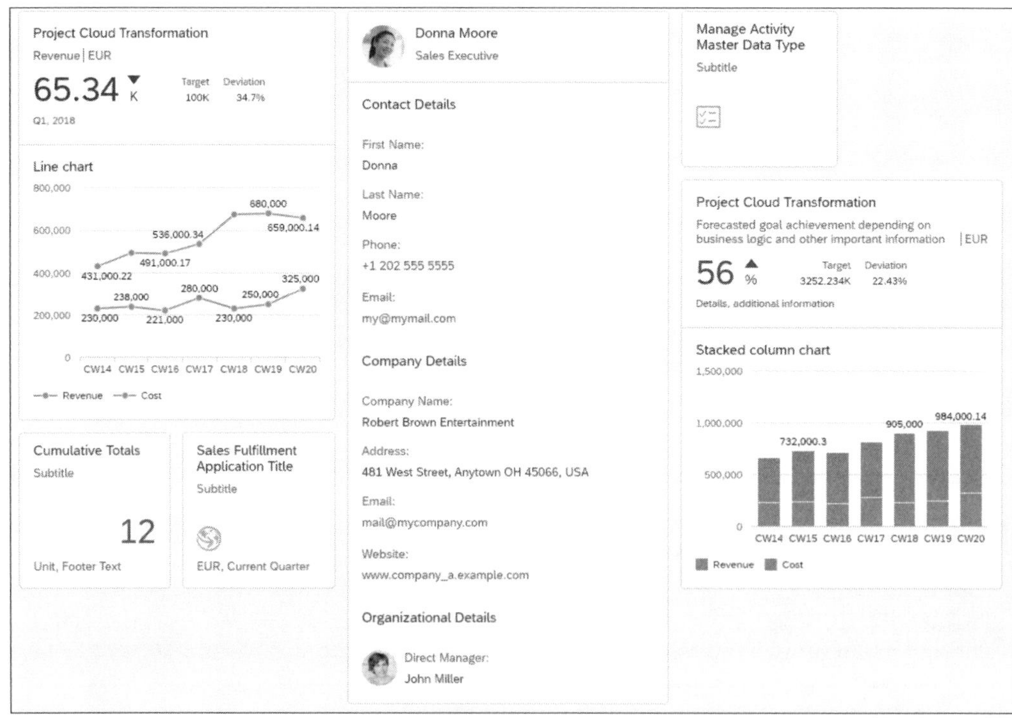

Figure 2.5 Integration Cards for SAP Fiori 3.0

By the time you're reading this book, even more cards may have been released for SAP Fiori 3.0. You can find more details about these cards at *http://s-prs.co/498802*. Integration cards support multiple visualization options, and each card can be configured using the `manifest.json` (as shown in Listing 2.1). The header and content area of each card can be configured as well.

```
{
  "sap.app": {
    "type": "card",
    ...
  },
  "sap.ui5": {
    ...
  },
  "sap.card": {
    "type": "List",
    "header": { ... },
    "content": { ... }
  }
}
```

Listing 2.1 Example manifest.json to Configure Cards

As shown in Figure 2.6, the new SAP Fiori launchpad approach integrates with different SAP and standard SAP products (both cloud and on-premise). This approach of using the SAP Fiori launchpad as a central hub to interact with every product linked to your business will make the SAP Fiori launchpad the main point of entry for accessing an SAP business system.

The following list summarizes the already released and upcoming features of SAP Fiori 3.0, which deeply integrates conversational UI and machine intelligence:

- New Quartz theme has been released to update the look and feel of the current UX.
- Personalized SAP Fiori launchpad helps users access all the different products that they need to complete their tasks.
- Integration of SAP CoPilot as a digital assistant with conversational UI.
- Situation handling to provide users with relevant information and insights and to propose appropriate actions.
- Dynamic content that supports apps powered by machine intelligence, analytics, etc.

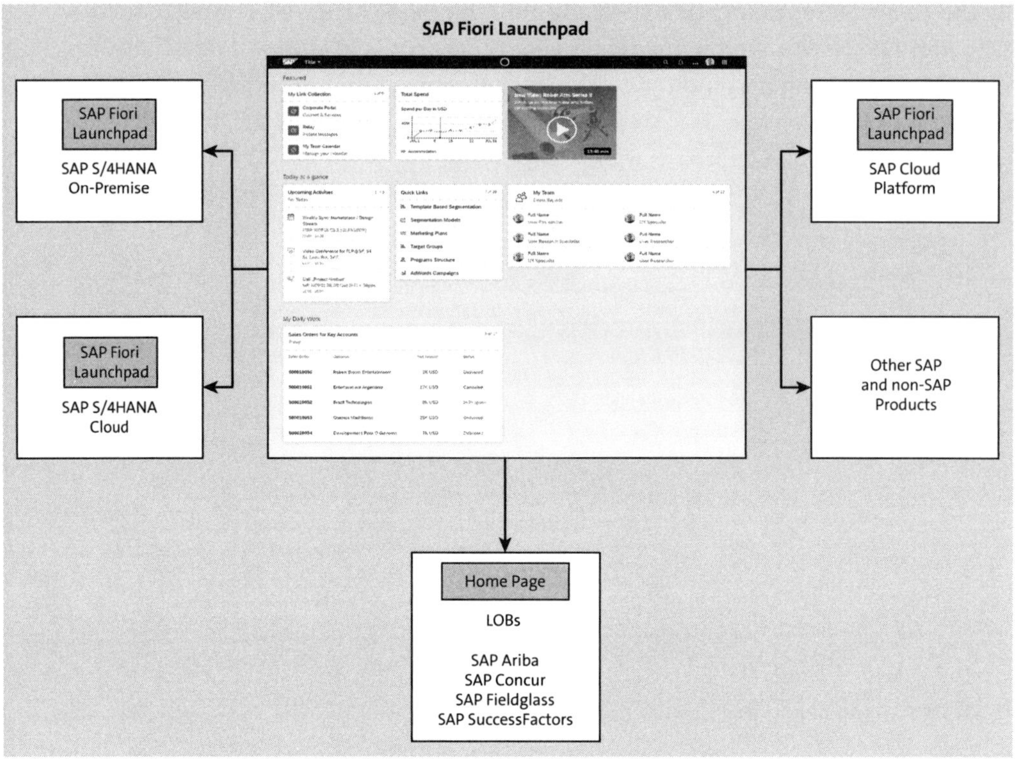

SAP Fiori Launchpad
SAP Fiori Launchpad
SAP S/4HANA On-Premise
SAP Fiori Launchpad
SAP S/4HANA Cloud
SAP Fiori Launchpad
SAP Cloud Platform
Other SAP and non-SAP Products
Home Page
LOBs
SAP Ariba
SAP Concur
SAP Fieldglass
SAP SuccessFactors

Figure 2.6 SAP Fiori Launchpad Integration with Different Products

2.1.4 Design Principles

As mentioned earlier, the basic design concepts for the SAP Fiori user experience are based on five core principles, as shown in Figure 2.7.

Role-Based
Delightful
Coherent
Simple
Adaptive

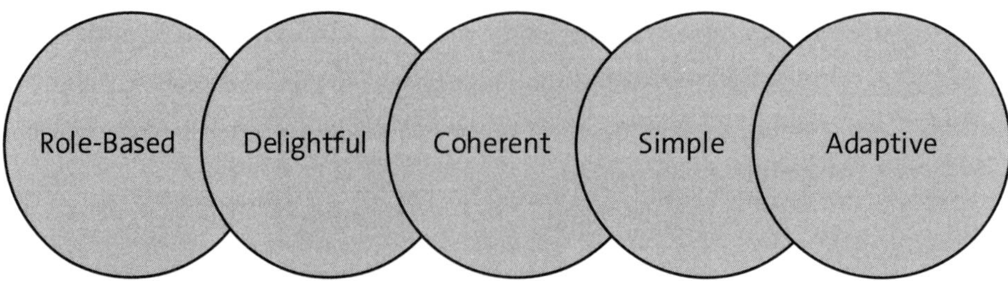

Figure 2.7 Core Design Principles of SAP Fiori

These principles are described as follows:

- **Role-based**
  Initially, SAP Fiori apps were made for specific type of users based on their roles, such as manager, employee, salesperson, and so on. The new SAP Fiori user experience provides information in a timely manner based on the way users work. In the new UX, SAP has now expanded those roles with more focus on your business, your needs, and how you work to be more in line with the multifaceted roles of today's workforce. Depending on the nature of a user's work, the user might have to perform different tasks within multiple business domains.
- **Delightful**
  In addition to creating a smarter UX for you to work in, SAP Fiori also adds value to the working environment by letting you focus on your work. A UX should neither be busy with information that isn't relevant to the role of the app's user nor should the UX be confusing for users using the app.
- **Coherent**
  A good design should be consistent with the UX throughout the app. Users shouldn't feel disconnected when navigating from one app to the other; instead, all the screens within the apps should feel as part of a coherent whole. Too much deviation in the design pattern between screens won't provide a pleasing user experience.

  Irrespective of which SAP Fiori app you use—for example, Approving Leave Requests, Creating Purchase Requisitions, Creating Sales Orders—SAP Fiori follows a consistent design and integration pattern that lets you enjoy a consistent experience.
- **Simple**
  If an app has too many buttons or features or too much information, users will find the app too complicated to use. Your app should focus primarily on the task based on the role of the user for which the app was designed. The goal is to let the user complete his task efficiently with the fewest clicks.

  SAP Fiori lets you complete a task quickly and intuitively by giving you only the essential functions to carry out your tasks with a simple UI. You can even personalize the UX to focus on your relevant tasks and activities.
- **Adaptive**
  An adaptive design should not only be able to resize its UX according to the device type but also be able to rearrange or slightly adjust the UX to cope with a smaller

or larger screen size. A modern UI should be designed by developers specifying what information and where it should be displayed within the app based on the available screen area.

All SAP Fiori apps follow this design guideline. So, in addition to an elegant, simple, and efficient UX, SAP Fiori also enables you to work on the go by seamlessly adapting the UX based on which device you're using. The SAP Fiori user experience adapts according to your task by providing relevant information that allows for meaningful insights.

2.1.5 Responsiveness and Adaptiveness

In today's world, we need everything on the go and instantly. SAP Fiori gives users the ability to switch seamlessly between desktops and mobile devices instantly. For this reason, developers must ensure that their apps deliver that same UX, which is why a responsive and adaptive design is important.

Responsive Design

One of the main highlights of the SAP Fiori user experience, when compared to its legacy GUI, is that it works across all devices irrespective of screen size to ensure a consistent UX on all devices. SAPUI5 offers a wide range of controls that can automatically adjust its size for different form factors and interaction styles, such as touch, tap, keyboard strokes, mouse clicks, and so on. SAPUI5 controls are also flexible enough that developers can manually adjust these properties, such as the size of the controls, to adjust the type of interaction based on the device, if necessary. The main advantage of using these controls for a responsive design is that you don't need any additional coding for these controls to adjust the size accordingly.

Adaptive Design

In certain scenarios, offering just a responsive approach might not be the suitable solution. For example, when using an SAP Fiori app on a desktop, you might prefer to see the maximum number of columns in a table so that you can edit or add data to some of the columns. In a tablet, on the other hand, you might not want to see all those columns at once and would rather see only the columns where you've already entered some data (you'll likely want to see even fewer columns on a smartphone). So, having different designs by adapting the complexity of apps that display a lot of data based on the device the app is being viewed on makes sense. This adaptive design approach requires developers decide logically which fields or information in the app make more sense based on the screen size or device. Although this approach requires some additional effort from the developer, a smooth UX will exist across all devices.

2.1.6 SAP Fiori Launchpad

The SAP Fiori launchpad, shown in Figure 2.8, is a single point of entry for all SAP Fiori apps, collecting different types of app tiles ranging from static tiles to tiles showing dynamic content, such as status indicators, number of pending approvals, open orders, and so on. These tiles are role based and represent a business application that can be launched by the user. In this book, we'll be focusing on the SAP Fiori launchpad for SAP Fiori 2.0.

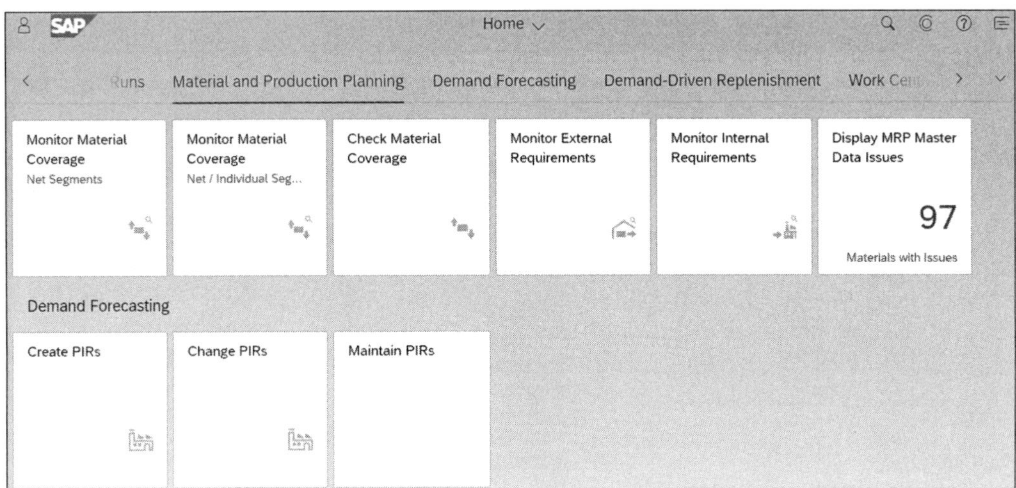

Figure 2.8 SAP Fiori 2.0 Launchpad

Viewport Design

The viewport, shown in Figure 2.9, is a design approach for SAP Fiori launchpad where certain portions of the launchpad's screen are visible only when the user clicks on the toggle buttons in the shell bar on the top-right and top-left corners. This design approach helps the launchpad provide users with additional user-specific information and notifications only when needed.

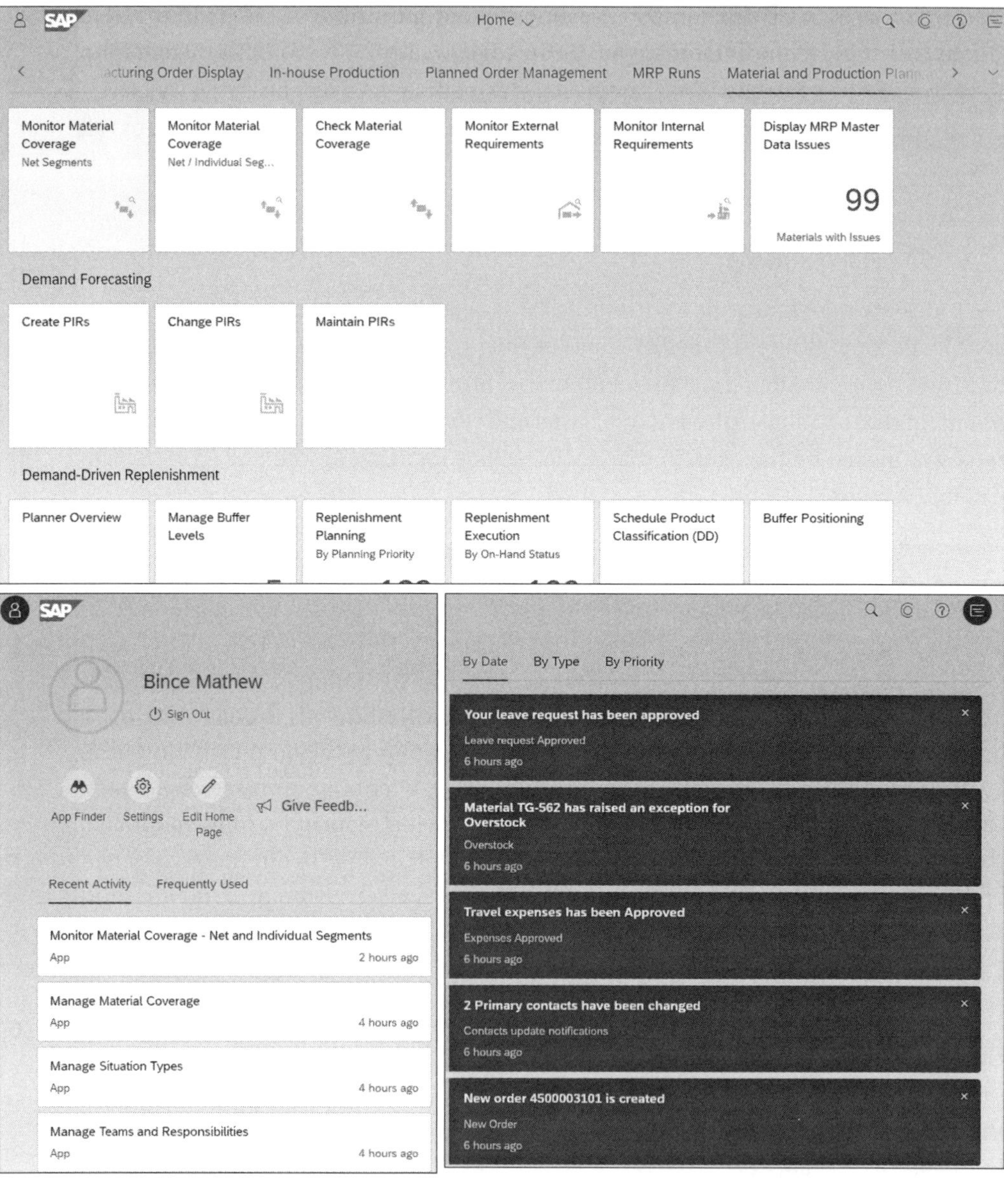

Figure 2.9 SAP Fiori 2.0 Viewport Design Approach

The transition animation to toggle these display areas itself is unique and smooth, which gives the user a sense of continuity within the launchpad, as shown in Figure

2.10. When a user clicks on either of the top toggle buttons on the shell bar, the whole screen smoothly slides to the left or the right to show the additional information area.

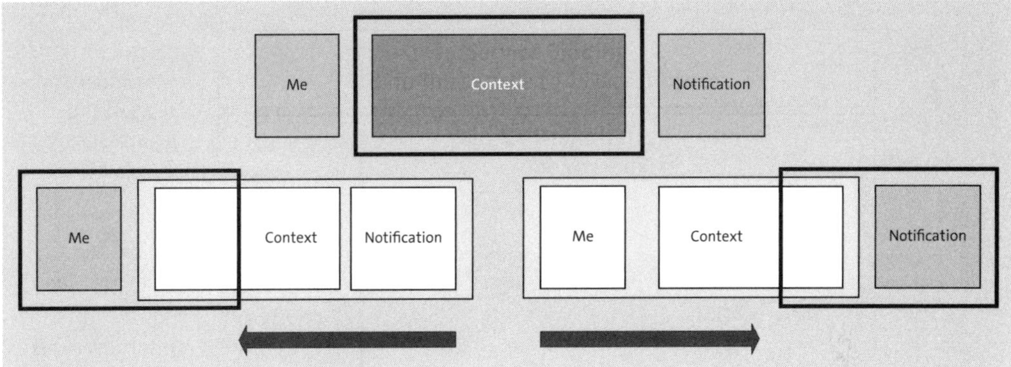

Figure 2.10 Animation Flow of a Viewport Design

Home Page

A home page is the starting page of the SAP Fiori launchpad and holds all the apps. The home page can also be personalized according to user preferences, including adding, removing, or grouping tiles. Because the launchpad is role-based, only the apps allowed for the roles assigned to the user will be available.

Me Area

The Me Area is one area of the SAP Fiori launchpad screen that is hidden by default as part of the viewport design approach. The Me Area, shown in Figure 2.11, is toward the left side of the launchpad and can be accessed by clicking on the toggle button on the top-left corner of the screen. This view is always accessible irrespective of whether you're in the home page or in any other apps in the launchpad.

The Me Area consists of the **Sign Out**, **App Finder**, **Settings**, and **Edit Home Page** buttons, as well as the **Recent Activity** tab, which shows the most recent actions by the user, such as which apps were recently opened, and a **Frequently Used** tab, which shows a list of apps most frequently used by the user.

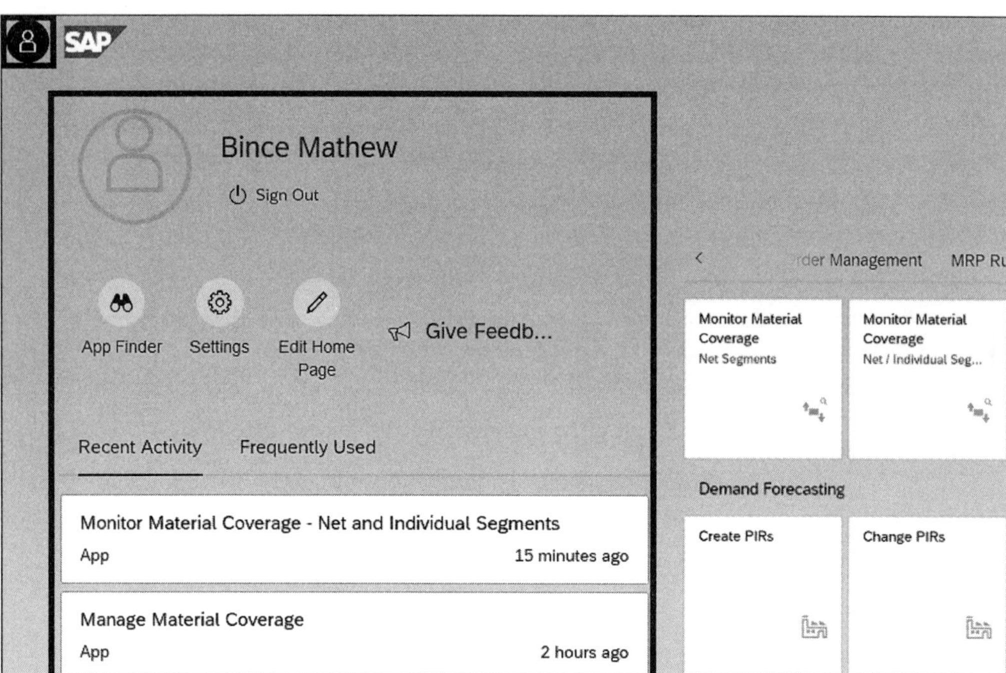

Figure 2.11 Me Area in the SAP Fiori Launchpad Home Page

In addition to the regular buttons, the Me Area also has an **About** button and an optional **App Settings** button, which can be made visible by the developer if the app needs to have some app-specific settings, such as selecting the area of responsibility for material requirements planning (MRP) controllers.

Notification Area

On the right side of the SAP Fiori launchpad, following the same viewport design principle, the Notification Area, shown in Figure 2.12, can be accessed by clicking the toggle button on the top-right side of the shell bar. This area is dedicated to system-specific notifications, such as workflows, chat notifications, and so on. These notifications can also be prioritized and grouped. This Notification Area provides users with more information on a specific notification and suggests actions a user can take within the Notification Area, such as approving workflows, approving leave requests, or similar actions. This level of flexibility helps users stay focused on the current tasks and yet perform such actions in parallel without navigating from the current app on which they are working.

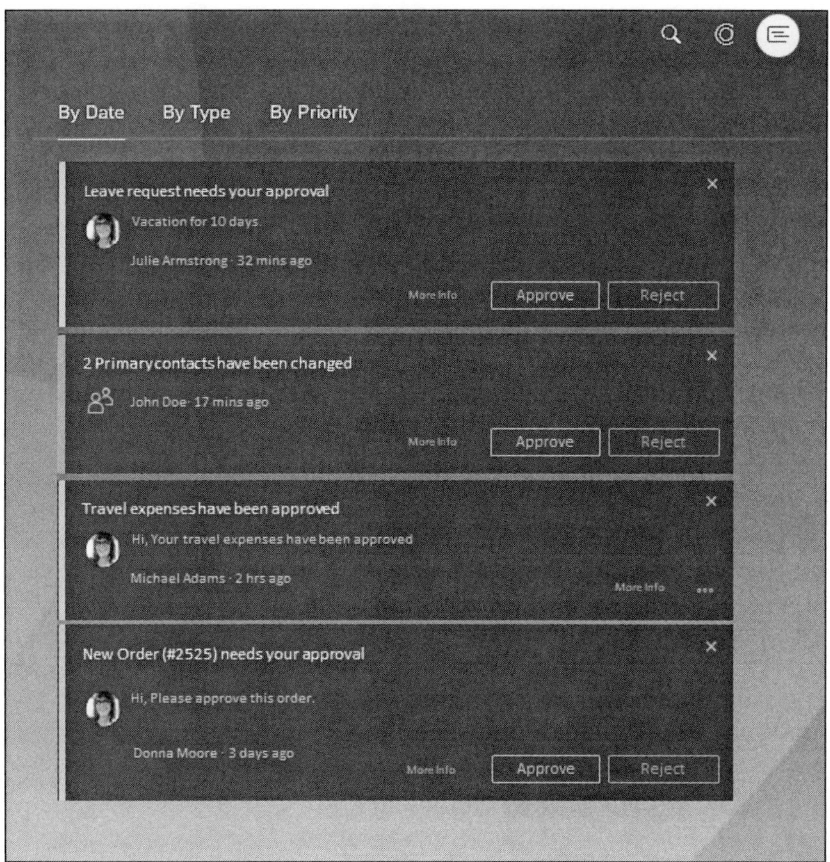

Figure 2.12 Notification Area of the SAP Fiori Launchpad

SAP CoPilot

SAP CoPilot is one of the latest and most powerful features added to SAP Fiori 2.0. SAP CoPilot was released with SAP S/4HANA Cloud 1705 (currently, this feature is not available for on-premise version) and is SAP's first step into integrating a virtual assistant to the enterprise sector. SAP CoPilot is always aware of your business context to give you relevant information on the apps within the SAP Fiori launchpad, to help you take actions, and so on. You can type in the chat window of the SAP CoPilot asking it, for example, to show you information about a certain purchase order or sales order, and the SAP CoPilot will list the results, as shown in Figure 2.13. You can even click on the results so that the purchase order or sales order will be opened in the relevant app.

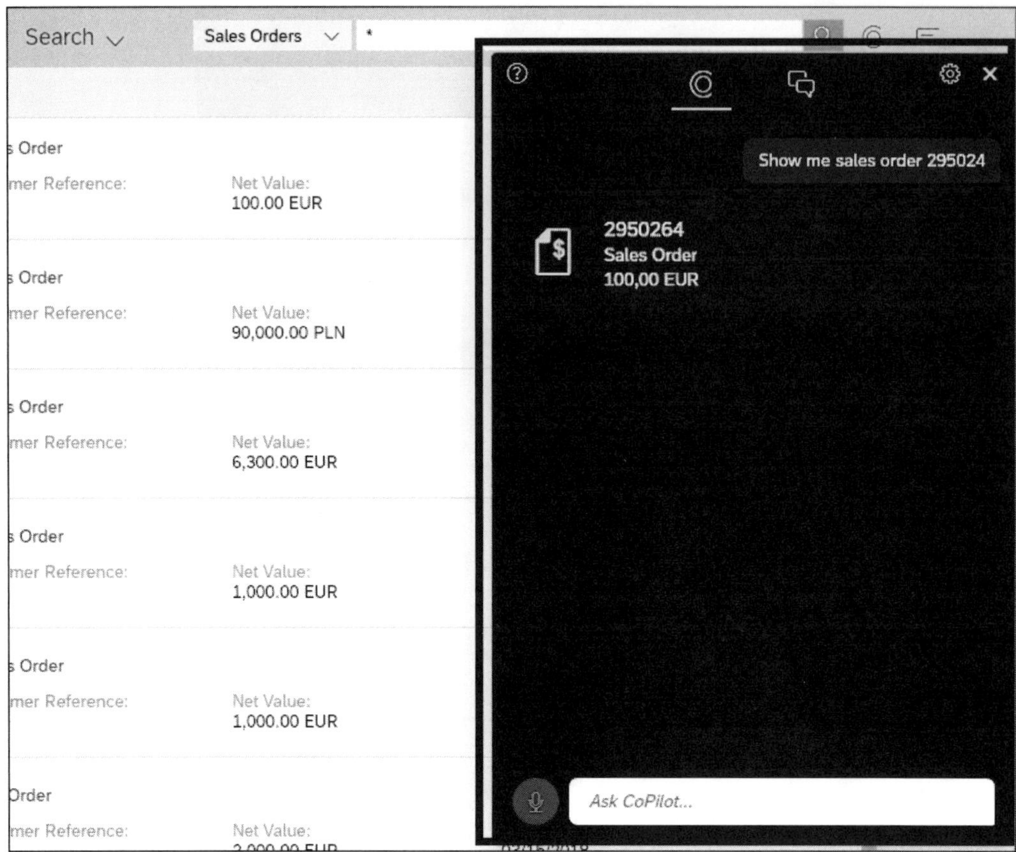

Figure 2.13 SAP CoPilot in SAP Fiori Launchpad

The main features of SAP CoPilot, as shown in Figure 2.14, are as follows:

- **Notes**
  Users can make use of SAP CoPilot to take notes while using the apps. SAP CoPilot will automatically link your notes to that specific app so that, whenever you return to that app, you can access all of the notes specific to that app by clicking on the **Linked to Current Screen** tab.
- **Screenshots**
  The **Screenshot** feature isn't just an image capture option; in fact, SAP CoPilot is intelligent enough to retain the navigation properties and filter parameters for that app so that, when the user clicks on the screenshot, the user is navigated to that app.

- **Recognizing business objects**
  SAP CoPilot has the ability to recognize the business context of the current application and allow you to add your own notes and screenshots.
- **In-context chat**
  This neat feature allows you to chat with other users in the SAP Fiori launchpad, enabling you to share notes, screenshots, and business objects with them. In addition, when users click on the screenshot, they can navigate directly to the app with all the filters and parameters you used at the time you took the screenshot, enabling fellow users to see exactly what you wanted to show them within the app.
- **Quick actions**
  Users can create business objects through many embedded Quick Create UIs. These fields are automatically filled in from the context by SAP CoPilot.

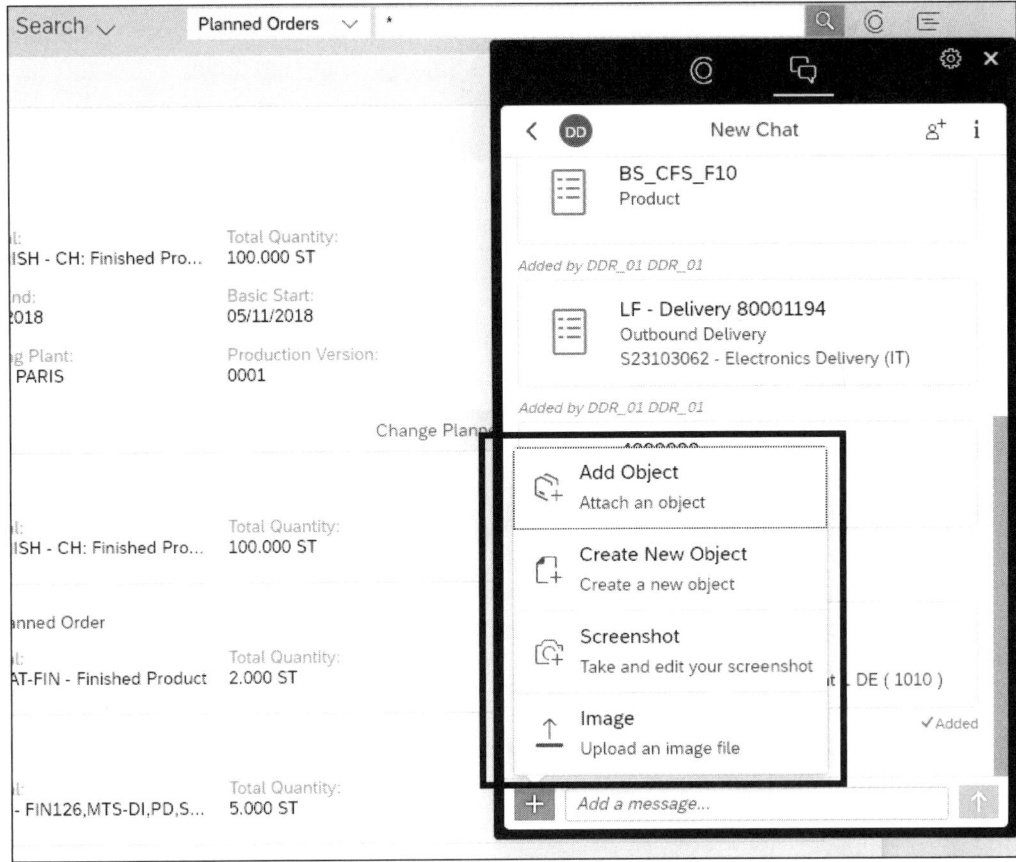

Figure 2.14 Different Features Offered in SAP CoPilot's Chat Option

SAP Fiori Launchpad Components

The SAP Fiori launchpad is comprised of multiple components, which are mainly divided into five categories:

- **Tile**
  A tile is like an application icon on your desktop—when you click on an app tile within the SAP Fiori launchpad, the relevant app will open within the launchpad.
- **App finder**
  The app finder is an easy way to search within the list of apps assigned to your role. You can use the app finder to quickly search for apps and add the app tiles to your launchpad. This capability replaces the old tile catalog option in the SAP Fiori 1.0 launchpad.
- **Enterprise Search (ESH)**
  ESH can search within all the available apps. For example, if you search for a specific sales order, ESH will list all the apps linked to that sales order.
- **Shell bar**
  A shell bar is like the main toolbar of the SAP Fiori launchpad and holds the Me Area, Notification Area, ESH, and SAP CoPilot. The shell bar also features the navigation button, the home button, and a dedicated area for displaying custom icons for branding.
- **Services**
  SAP Fiori launchpad has several services that can be leveraged by app developers, such as getting the local currency or date format of the current user, handling cross-app and in-app navigation, contacting support, and so on.

2.2 Design-Led Development Process

To create a great UX that caters to the needs of all your users across all lines of business and devices, you'll need a development strategy, which is where SAP's design-led development process comes in.

The process involves adopting proven design thinking methods that span the entire development process while also being simple, easy to implement, and scalable. Constant communication and understanding are required between the designers and developers. This approach ensures that your needs are met at both the visual and functional levels of the apps. SAP Fiori app development follows three main phases:

discover, design, and develop. The design-led development process, as shown in Figure 2.15, focuses on the first two phases.

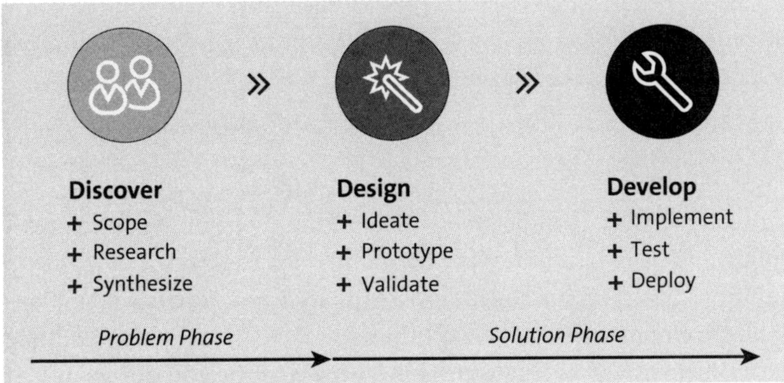

Figure 2.15 The Design-Led Development Process

Developing an app isn't just about coding because you must keep the end user in mind during development. Providing strong features within your app is great, but not at the cost of usability. So, developers must know about the user who will use the app. In the first phase of development, you should focus on the user and try to understand how user work, what exactly users expect from the app, and so on. Only after getting these fundamental things right should you move to the design phase to create the prototypes required for the development. After development is completed, you can then thoroughly complete the implementation and testing to make the app ready for deployment.

2.2.1 Discover

Sometimes, having a requirement list for an app to be developed doesn't give you the whole picture. You might need to visit your users and get to know their process in person. Therefore, having design thinking workshops with the end user is always a great way to understand business needs. By the time you're done with the discover phase, you should be aware of all the business roles and should have descriptions for the roles of each user that will use the app. These descriptions of roles are known as *personas*. A persona should be created for all the different types of users who will use the app and should describe the roles, tasks, and activities of those users. This information will prove vital during the design phase of your app because, by then, you'll have a clear picture of the requirements.

2.2.2 Design

When you're in the design phase, you can brainstorm with your team and come up with a storyboard using the personas as a reference for the users. Then, you can come up with multiple prototypes and cross-check the prototype designs with your users to come up with a final version of the design.

2.2.3 Develop

With a design mutually agreed upon between you and the users, now you can start building the app. During development, you might still need to tweak and come up with multiple iterations based on the continuous feedback from the customer at different stages of the development. You can split the app's development into multiple milestones to get users involved and gather their feedback at the end of each major milestone to further optimize the app. We also recommend involving users during this phase to make them aware of any unforeseen technical constraints that have come up during the development phase.

As the app is completed and being tested, more tweaking and optimizations may be required before having a finished product. After this phase, you're finally ready to deploy the app. You could also implement a concept called *design gates*, which comprise a team of UX experts to review the product during different stages of development to ensure that the app is consistent with the SAP Fiori design guidelines. This team can help the development team stay in line with the design guidelines and further optimize the UX.

2.3 Different SAP Fiori App Types

When developing SAP Fiori apps, multiple flavors of apps can be used, but apps are mainly divided into two categories: freestyle apps and SAP Fiori elements-based apps.

2.3.1 Freestyle

As the name suggests, with a freestyle app, you can start developing the app from scratch, and you're free to use any design style you want. However, the trade-off with going freestyle is that the increased probability that you are deviating from standard SAP design guidelines, and therefore, you might want to enforce a more strict UX review method, such as a design gate. Design gate reviews will ensure that you stay within SAP Fiori guidelines so that the app will still seem part of the consistent UX experience that SAP Fiori apps offer. But when your users demand a custom app, sometimes, going with a freestyle apps makes more sense than using the template-based options that we'll talk about in the next section.

2.3.2 SAP Fiori Elements

Before getting into SAP Fiori elements, let's consider some fundamental areas when designing and building an SAP Fiori app:

- Dynamic page layout (formerly known as full screen layout)
- Flexible column layout (formerly known as split screen layout)

Different layout types are called *floorplans*, shown in Figure 2.16, so a dynamic page layout will have one floorplan as a full screen app, and a flexible column layout will have two or three floorplans.

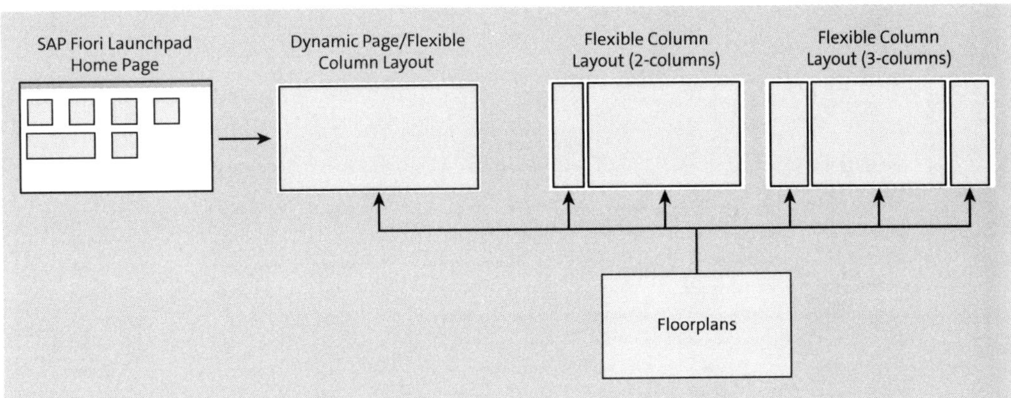

Figure 2.16 Overview of Layouts and Floorplans

SAP Fiori elements were formerly known as smart templates. Compared to freestyle apps, SAP Fiori elements provide app templates that cover most common app types. Developers can use SAP Fiori elements to make use of these layouts, floorplans, and an OData source to generate an app to display the data.

SAP Fiori elements also ensure that an app has a consistent design and follows the SAP Fiori design guidelines.

The following subsections describe the most commonly used SAP Fiori elements floorplans.

Technically, you can further subdivide the list report page (LRP) and object page apps into two. You can navigate from a list report page to its detail screen, which is an object page (object pages were formerly known as factsheets). Therefore, if your app only needs a list report page, all you need to do is disable the navigation to the object page. If an object page is all you need, then you can directly navigate to the object page. For example, when you click on a hyperlink for a process order number, for example, listed in the search results from an ESH, then you'll navigate to an object page directly, which will show the process order in detail.

List Report

First, let's consider a list report, shown in Figure 2.17, and discuss some use cases where choosing a list report makes sense. A list report gives users the option of working with large volumes of data, such as goods receipts, material lists for creating purchase orders, and so on. This type of floorplan is used in a scenario where, from a list of items, users can navigate to a details page.

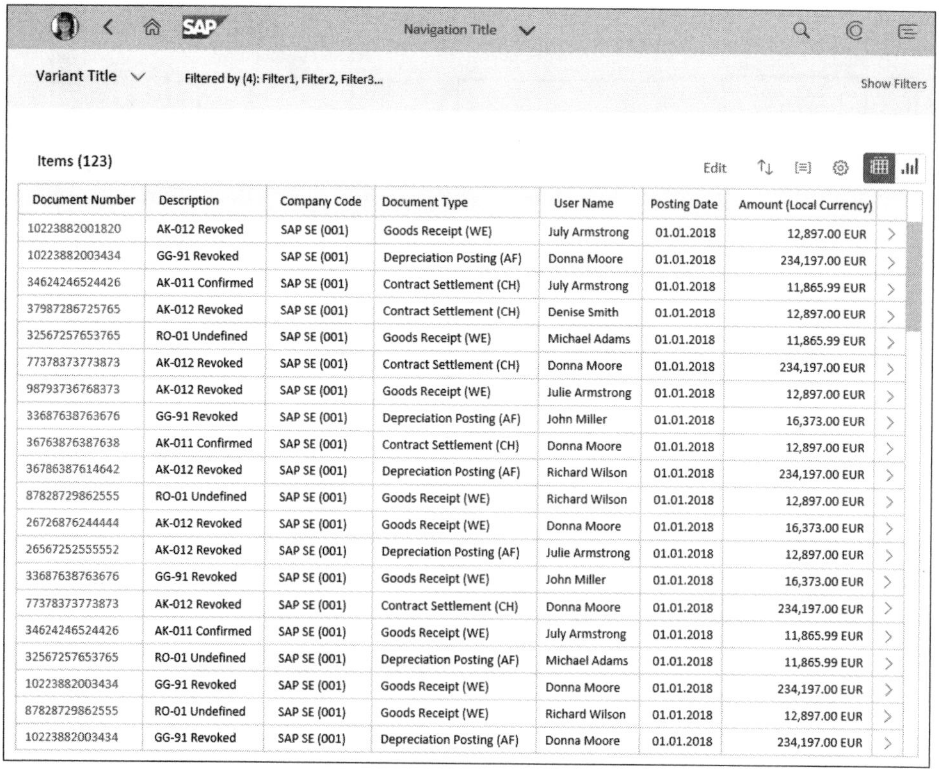

Navigation Title

Variant Title

Filtered by (4): Filter1, Filter2, Filter3...

Show Filters

Items (123)

Edit

Document Number	Description	Company Code	Document Type	User Name	Posting Date	Amount (Local Currency)
10223882001820	AK-012 Revoked	SAP SE (001)	Goods Receipt (WE)	July Armstrong	01.01.2018	12,897.00 EUR
10223882003434	GG-91 Revoked	SAP SE (001)	Depreciation Posting (AF)	Donna Moore	01.01.2018	234,197.00 EUR
34624246524426	AK-011 Confirmed	SAP SE (001)	Contract Settlement (CH)	July Armstrong	01.01.2018	11,865.99 EUR
37987286725765	AK-012 Revoked	SAP SE (001)	Contract Settlement (CH)	Denise Smith	01.01.2018	12,897.00 EUR
32567257653765	RO-01 Undefined	SAP SE (001)	Goods Receipt (WE)	Michael Adams	01.01.2018	11,865.99 EUR
77378373773873	AK-012 Revoked	SAP SE (001)	Contract Settlement (CH)	Donna Moore	01.01.2018	234,197.00 EUR
98793736768373	AK-012 Revoked	SAP SE (001)	Goods Receipt (WE)	Julie Armstrong	01.01.2018	12,897.00 EUR
33687638763676	GG-91 Revoked	SAP SE (001)	Depreciation Posting (AF)	John Miller	01.01.2018	16,373.00 EUR
36763876387638	AK-011 Confirmed	SAP SE (001)	Contract Settlement (CH)	Donna Moore	01.01.2018	12,897.00 EUR
36786387614642	AK-012 Revoked	SAP SE (001)	Depreciation Posting (AF)	Richard Wilson	01.01.2018	234,197.00 EUR
87828729862555	RO-01 Undefined	SAP SE (001)	Goods Receipt (WE)	Richard Wilson	01.01.2018	12,897.00 EUR
26726876244444	AK-012 Revoked	SAP SE (001)	Goods Receipt (WE)	Donna Moore	01.01.2018	16,373.00 EUR
26567252555552	AK-012 Revoked	SAP SE (001)	Depreciation Posting (AF)	Julie Armstrong	01.01.2018	12,897.00 EUR
33687638763676	GG-91 Revoked	SAP SE (001)	Goods Receipt (WE)	John Miller	01.01.2018	16,373.00 EUR
77378373773873	AK-012 Revoked	SAP SE (001)	Contract Settlement (CH)	Donna Moore	01.01.2018	234,197.00 EUR
34624246524426	AK-011 Confirmed	SAP SE (001)	Goods Receipt (WE)	July Armstrong	01.01.2018	11,865.99 EUR
32567257653765	RO-01 Undefined	SAP SE (001)	Depreciation Posting (AF)	Michael Adams	01.01.2018	11,865.99 EUR
10223882003434	GG-91 Revoked	SAP SE (001)	Goods Receipt (WE)	Donna Moore	01.01.2018	234,197.00 EUR
87828729862555	RO-01 Undefined	SAP SE (001)	Goods Receipt (WE)	Richard Wilson	01.01.2018	12,897.00 EUR
10223882003434	GG-91 Revoked	SAP SE (001)	Depreciation Posting (AF)	Donna Moore	01.01.2018	234,197.00 EUR

Figure 2.17 List Report Floorplan

If you use an SAP Fiori elements floorplan for a list report scenario, the basic layout will be automatically generated from the UI annotations coming from the CDS view in the underlying OData. We'll look at using UI annotation in detail for generating different types of SAP Fiori element floorplans in later chapters.

A list report has the following structure, as shown in Figure 2.18:

- **Shell bar**
  A shell bar is the area on the top of the launchpad. This shell bar is always visible irrespective of which page or tile you navigate to within the launchpad. The shell bar holds the **Me Area**, **Home**, **Navigation**, **Enterprise Search**, **Copilot** (if enabled in the launchpad), and the **Notifications** toggle buttons.
- **Header title**
  This area displays the title, filter information (if the header is collapsed), and toolbar.
- **Header content**
  This area displays the filter bar and the generic search field.
- **Content area**
  This area displays the icon tab bar, table/chart (per tab), and multiple tabs within the table/chart.
- **Footer toolbar**
  This area displays action buttons. (Alternatively, you can use UI annotation to bring action buttons on top of the table as Business Object Processing Framework [BOPF] actions instead of the footer, so buttons on the footer bar are optional.)

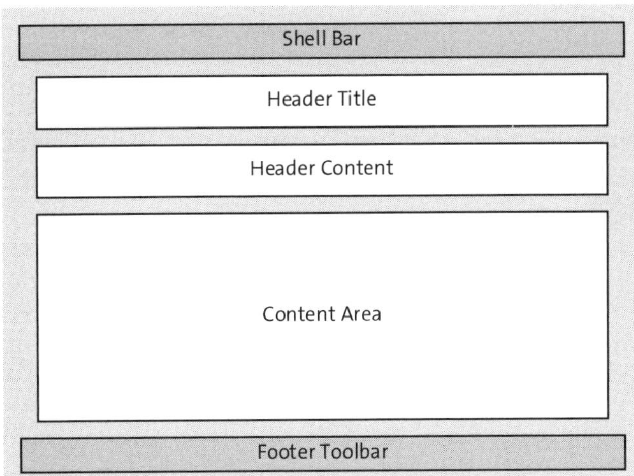

Figure 2.18 Structure of a List Report

While using a list report floorplan, consider the following scenarios to make sure this floorplan is the right one for your application:

- The user needs to go through a lot a record or items and then needs to search, sort, filter, and group them to complete the task.
- The user needs multiple views for the same content based on certain factors such as items that are **Open**, **In Process**, or **Completed**. This flexibility is possible because SAP Fiori elements enable having multiple tabs on the same screen. Switching between different tables shows the same contents but based on different filtering, sorting, or grouping parameters. In addition, SAP Fiori elements now support multiple tabs with tables bound to different entity sets; these tables in the different tabs can show different data. For example, the first tab might show a list of production orders, while the second table shows a list of process orders.
- Users need to work on multiple types of items.
- Further details aren't required to be shown on the same page, which means, if needed, further details can be shown in the object page (details page).
- The user needs to use this app for reporting purposes, using different visualization options to represent the underlying data in the form of tables or charts.

In these two scenarios, the list report floorplan might not be a good fit for your application:

- The user must go through a list of work items and view information based on priority.
- The user must see a single item in detail and edit that information.

Object Page

The object page floorplan, shown in Figure 2.19, is best for when a user needs to see all the details of a specific item. In addition, the user might want to edit or create the object. This floorplan has a flexible header, anchor-based navigation, and flexible layout.

In these two scenarios, an object page is the most suitable option:

- The details about an item need to be shown, and the user might need to edit or create an item.
- An overview of an object is required along with interacting with its different parts.

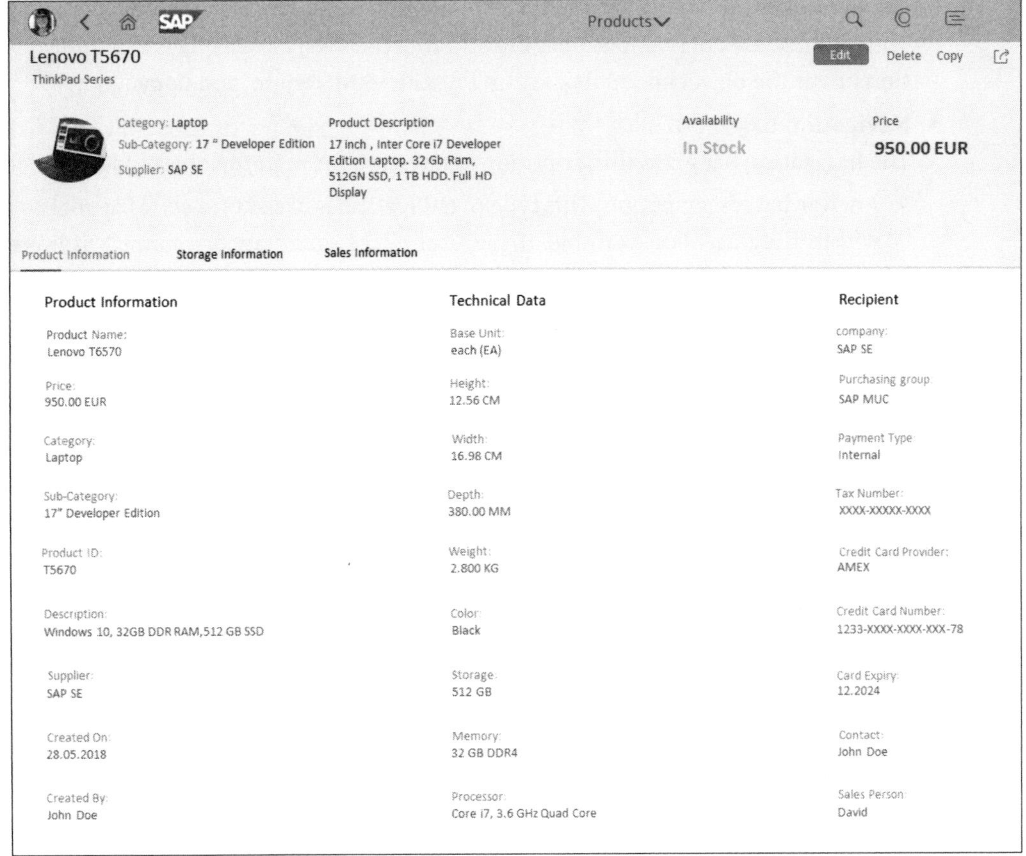

Figure 2.19 Object Page Floorplan

In these scenarios, an object page floorplan might not be the best choice:

- Several items need to be displayed on a single screen.
- The user must filter through multiple items or must find items without knowing the exact details.
- Guided steps are required for something like new object creation.

The object page presents users with display, create, and edit modes for the items they are working on. The object page structure is shown in Figure 2.20 and described in the following list:

- **Header area**
  The topmost area of the object page (excluding the shell bar) displays key information about the object and global action buttons: **Edit**, **Delete**, and **Copy**.
- **Navigation bar**
  The navigation bar gives three options to navigate through the object page.
  - Anchor-based navigation: This type of navigation is based on a series of anchors within the page. For example, if the user clicks on an anchor named **Storage Information** (as shown earlier in Figure 2.19), the page will scroll down until the item's area is reached.
  - Tab-based navigation: Instead of scrolling down to the required area, this control behaves like an icon tab bar. So, the information on the object pages will be stored in multiple tabs that users can switch to and from.
  - No navigation: No navigation is provided.
- **Content area**
  The content area is split into sections and subsections:
  - Sections: Act as containers for subsections and can't contain any content other than subsections. Sections can be reached via anchor-based navigation.
  - Subsections: Hold the actual contents, including multiple controls, global actions, and so on. Subsections are separated by gray lines.

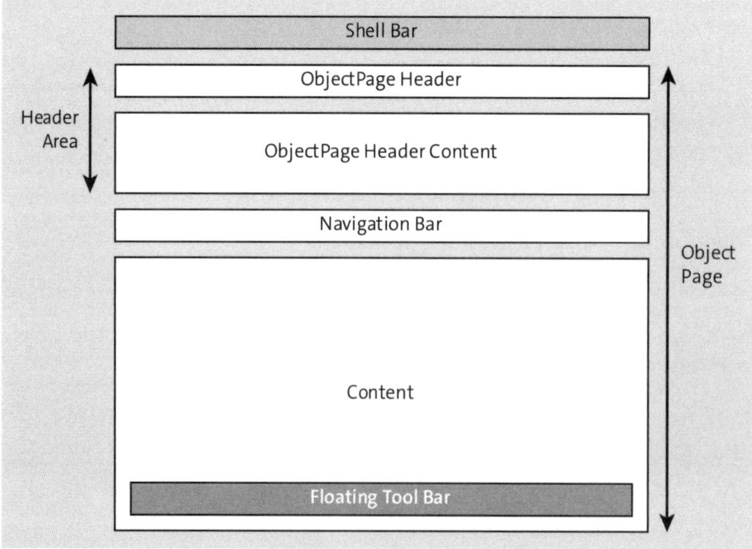

Figure 2.20 Structure of an Object Page

Overview Page

Overview pages (OVP), shown in Figure 2.21, are data-driven app types used when users need to access all the information on a single page based on role. OVPs can consist of charts, micro actions, data filters, and so on.

These different topics or pieces of information are displayed as different cards. An OVP will contain a group of these cards so that users can get all the information from multiple data sources and visualizations. Each card will give an overview of data from the underlying app, so that the user can get useful insights without navigating into the app.

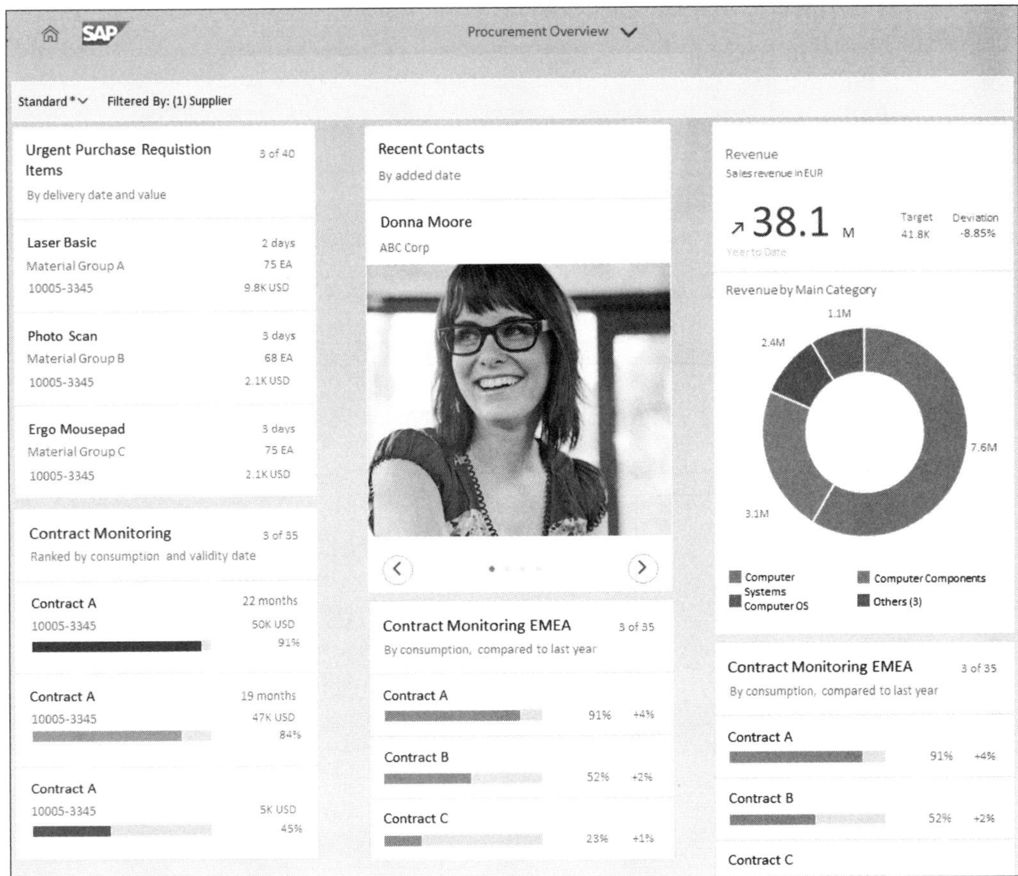

Figure 2.21 OVP Floorplan

The OVP structure shown in Figure 2.22 has two main elements:

- **Dynamic page header**
  This header displays four variants of dynamic pages, but all four variants have two common characteristics: no footer bar and no global actions in the header title area. These different versions of the page header will help cater to specific requirements for the OVP's main content. The four variants of dynamic pages are as follows:
  - Variant 1: Contains variant management and a smart filter bar.
  - Variant 2: Contains only a header title, which will be hidden automatically because the header content is empty.
  - Variant 3: No content in header title and header content area, which means the dynamic page header is completely hidden, and the cards will be displayed after the shell bar.
  - Variant 4: Contains a text in the header title and a smart filter bar in the header content area.

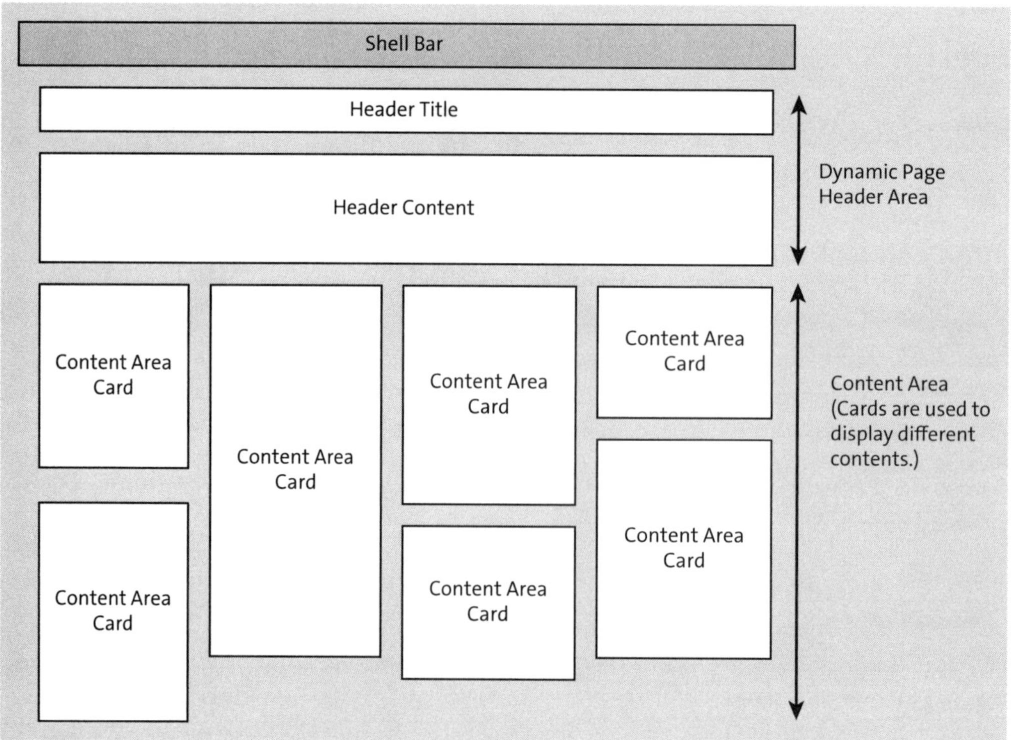

Figure 2.22 Structure of an OVP

- **Content area**
  The content area is filled with cards that act as containers for app content. These cards provide an entry-level view of the information from the underlying app it represents. Cards can represent data via visualization methods such as charts, lists, tables, and so on. However, cards don't have editable fields.

An OVP might be more suitable for some floorplans than others, such as in these use cases:

- An entry-level view of domain-specific content is required.
- Users need information from multiple apps so that they can make task-related decisions.
- Users need to see the information in different formats, such as charts, tables, and so on.

In the following scenarios, an OVP might not be the best floorplan to choose:

- The user needs to see only header level details of the items.
- The user needs to see information about one item in detail.
- The information to be displayed about the app doesn't need more than two cards (an object page is a better fit in this case).

Analytical List Page

Analytical list page (ALP) apps, shown in Figure 2.23, are used to analyze data from different perspectives, drill down through data, and take actions by viewing transactional data. All these different interactions with the data can be performed on the same page.

Tasks that involve going through a lot of transaction data might require viewing related information in the form of visualizations that will reduce the steps required to gain useful insights. In addition, visualization methods, such as charts, are visual pleasing and helpful in identifying relevant information quickly rather than going through each bit of data one by one.

Users with these types of tasks would also benefit from having both access to full transparent business data and the ability to act on that data. They would also need access to analytical views without the need to open a separate app or a view such as key performance indicators (KPIs). KPIs are small visual areas with charts or tables that can be drilled down into along with filters enriched with visualizations and measures. This capability also enables users to quickly identity some key values/points in the data such as spikes, sudden deviations, or any abnormal values that stand out within the data and might need immediate attention or action.

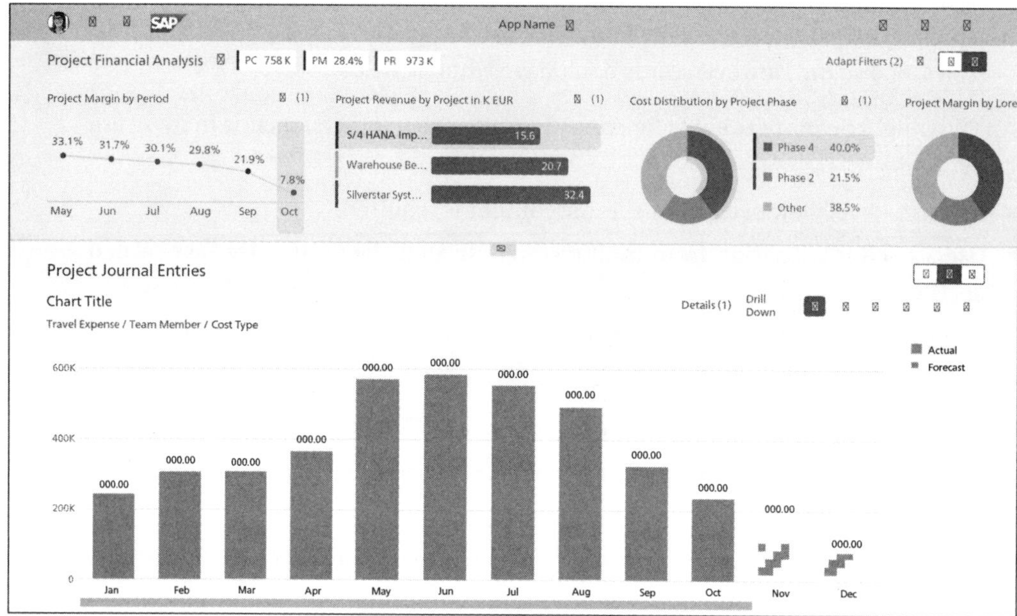

Figure 2.23 Analytical List Page

The analytical list page structure shown in Figure 2.24 has three main elements:

- **Page title**
  Contains page variants, KPIs, KPI cards, global actions, and so on.
- **Page header**
  Contains filter bars and visual filter bars.
- **Page content**
  Contains a chart only view, table only view, or a hybrid view that contains both tables and charts.

Analytical list pages can be used in the following scenarios:

- The user needs to pinpoint key information behind a certain situation or to identify the root cause behind a sudden spike or abnormality in certain areas.
- The user needs to analyze data from a different perspective, drill down into data, or view transactional data all on one page.
- The user needs interactive charts and tables.

- The user needs KPIs to keep track of key areas.
- The user needs to find a relevant date by analyzing a large number of items via drilldown, filters, searching, grouping, sorting, and so on, which would be comparatively difficult with other app types.

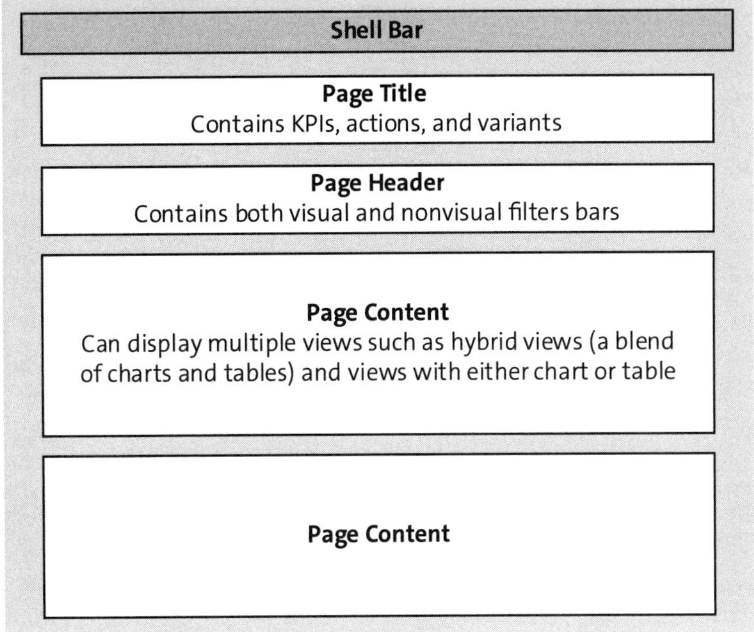

Figure 2.24 Analytical List Report Structure

You should avoid using analytical list pages in the following scenarios:

- The detailed view of the items isn't required on the same page.
- All the required information must be represented by just a table or chart.
- The user needs to see details about a single item.
- The user needs to see a set of relevant work items that must be sorted based on which needs to be processed first.

Worklist Page

The worklist page, shown in Figure 2.25, is used when a collection of items must be displayed so that the user can process those items. Each record needs a detailed review from the user to take actions on the records. A worklist page doesn't have a filter bar because only action items relevant to the user are shown. However, the data can still be sorted via the help of tabs, which lets the user see work items based on status.

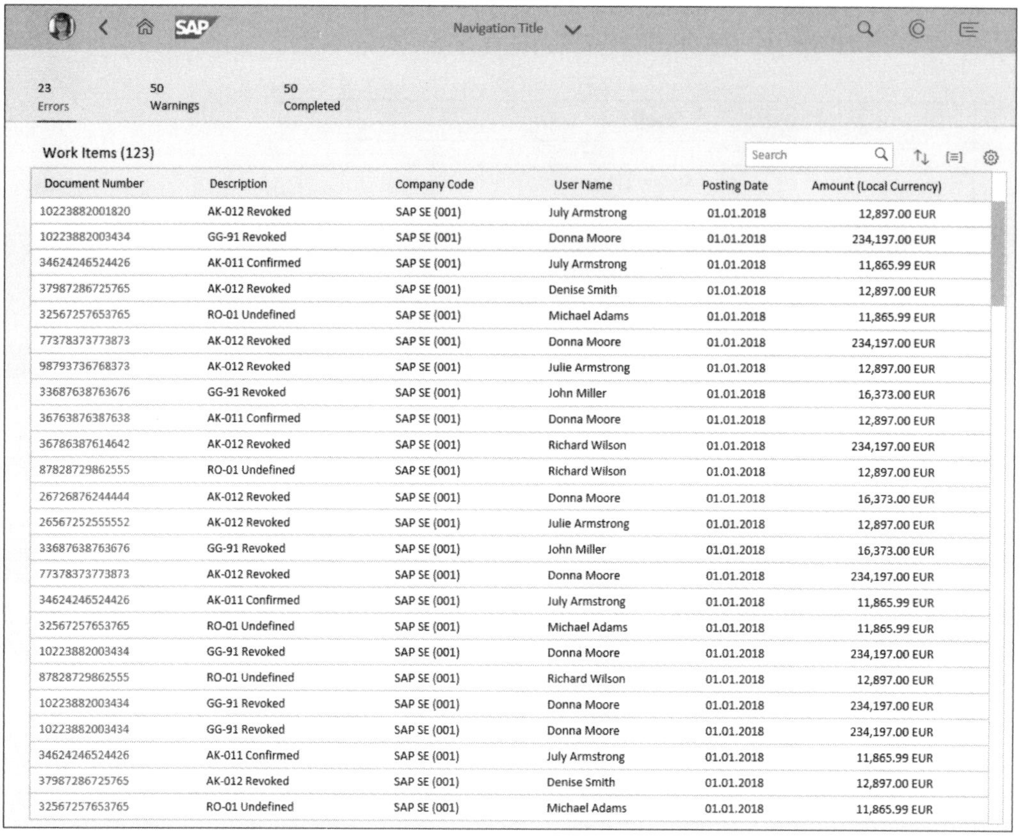

Navigation Title

23 Errors | 50 Warnings | 50 Completed

Work Items (123)

Search

Document Number	Description	Company Code	User Name	Posting Date	Amount (Local Currency)
10223882001820	AK-012 Revoked	SAP SE (001)	July Armstrong	01.01.2018	12,897.00 EUR
10223882003434	GG-91 Revoked	SAP SE (001)	Donna Moore	01.01.2018	234,197.00 EUR
34624246524426	AK-011 Confirmed	SAP SE (001)	July Armstrong	01.01.2018	11,865.99 EUR
37987286725765	AK-012 Revoked	SAP SE (001)	Denise Smith	01.01.2018	12,897.00 EUR
32567257653765	RO-01 Undefined	SAP SE (001)	Michael Adams	01.01.2018	11,865.99 EUR
77378373773873	AK-012 Revoked	SAP SE (001)	Donna Moore	01.01.2018	234,197.00 EUR
98793736768373	AK-012 Revoked	SAP SE (001)	Julie Armstrong	01.01.2018	12,897.00 EUR
33687638763676	GG-91 Revoked	SAP SE (001)	John Miller	01.01.2018	16,373.00 EUR
36763876387638	AK-011 Confirmed	SAP SE (001)	Donna Moore	01.01.2018	12,897.00 EUR
36786387614642	AK-012 Revoked	SAP SE (001)	Richard Wilson	01.01.2018	234,197.00 EUR
87828729862555	RO-01 Undefined	SAP SE (001)	Richard Wilson	01.01.2018	12,897.00 EUR
26726876244444	AK-012 Revoked	SAP SE (001)	Donna Moore	01.01.2018	16,373.00 EUR
26567252555552	AK-012 Revoked	SAP SE (001)	Julie Armstrong	01.01.2018	12,897.00 EUR
33687638763676	GG-91 Revoked	SAP SE (001)	John Miller	01.01.2018	16,373.00 EUR
77378373773873	AK-012 Revoked	SAP SE (001)	Donna Moore	01.01.2018	234,197.00 EUR
34624246524426	AK-011 Confirmed	SAP SE (001)	July Armstrong	01.01.2018	11,865.99 EUR
32567257653765	RO-01 Undefined	SAP SE (001)	Michael Adams	01.01.2018	11,865.99 EUR
10223882003434	GG-91 Revoked	SAP SE (001)	Donna Moore	01.01.2018	234,197.00 EUR
87828729862555	RO-01 Undefined	SAP SE (001)	Richard Wilson	01.01.2018	12,897.00 EUR
10223882003434	GG-91 Revoked	SAP SE (001)	Donna Moore	01.01.2018	234,197.00 EUR
10223882003434	GG-91 Revoked	SAP SE (001)	Donna Moore	01.01.2018	234,197.00 EUR
34624246524426	AK-011 Confirmed	SAP SE (001)	July Armstrong	01.01.2018	11,865.99 EUR
37987286725765	AK-012 Revoked	SAP SE (001)	Denise Smith	01.01.2018	12,897.00 EUR
32567257653765	RO-01 Undefined	SAP SE (001)	Michael Adams	01.01.2018	11,865.99 EUR

Figure 2.25 Worklist Page

The worklist structure, shown in Figure 2.26 has three elements:

- **Header title**
  Contains the title of the page and a header toolbar (consists of global actions).
- **Tab bar**
  This optional area can be used to display an icon tab bar. You can display a table or a chart in each tab.
- **Page content**
  If the tab bar is not used, then you can use an independent table or multiple tables

to display work items based on different priorities such as **Pending**, **In Process**, **Completed**, etc.

- **Footer toolbar**
  Contains a footer toolbar (consists of message buttons and action buttons).

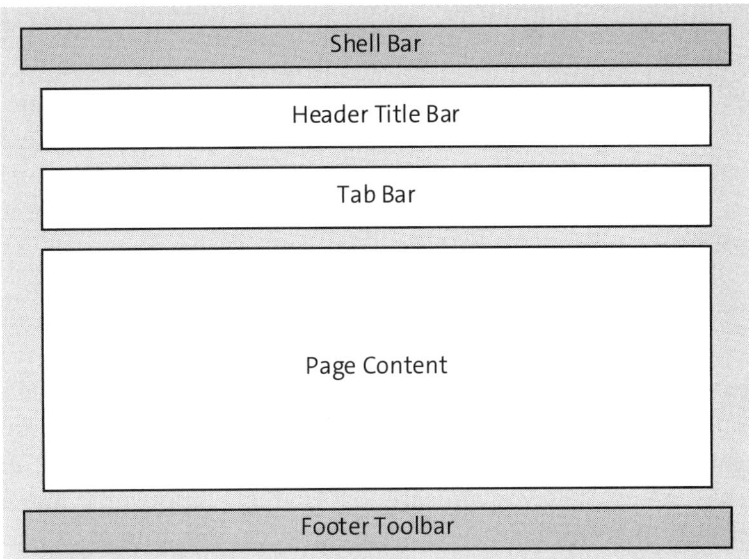

Figure 2.26 Structure of a Worklist Page

The worklist page is the right fit only for a few specific scenarios:

- The user needs to go through multiple work items and decide which one to process first based on importance or relevance.
- The user needs direct access to a work item for taking the required action.
- The same content needs to be displayed (with the help of tab bars) in multiple tabs based on status, for example, work items that are **Open**, **In Process**, **Completed**, and so on.

Worklist pages may not be the right fit for all scenarios, such as the following:

- The items in the list aren't work items.
- The user needs to work with a large list of items represented by tables or charts.
- The user needs to work with a large list of items by filtering, sorting, or searching through the results.

2.4 Prototyping Tools

For prototyping, developers can build on multiple methods, including designs drawn on paper (low-fidelity designs), Microsoft Excel sheet-based layouts, or interactive prototypes generated using wireframing tools (high-fidelity designs). To help developers reduce the initial effort to create a high-quality prototype, SAP has provided a set of prototyping tools.

Prototyping tools are a great way of coming up with mock-up designs of your apps. The most commonly used prototyping tools are Axure and SAP Build. These tools not only provide a static mock-up design but also features the option of making those designs somewhat interactive so that your prototype can mimic page navigation, button clicks, mock data, and so on.

2.4.1 Axure

Axure is a third-party wireframing/prototyping tool that SAP supports (download a 30-day trial version of Axure from *www.axure.com/download*). SAP provides a downloadable add-on stencils kit that can be imported into Axure to enable support for SAP Fiori prototyping and to help you visualize SAP Fiori app ideas within Axure (*http://s-prs.co/498803*). This downloadable package also contains a set of SAPUI5 icon fonts.

Another solution is to use design stencils available for Microsoft PowerPoint (*http://s-prs.co/498804*). However, this option is limited, and mock-ups will lack the interactivity and other rich features that a dedicated prototyping tool such as Axure or SAP Build can provide.

2.4.2 SAP Build

Compared to Axure, SAP Build is a dedicated prototyping tool for SAP Fiori apps. In addition, unlike Axure, SAP Build offers a set of prebuilt mock-ups, including mock data for multiple app scenarios. You can start with a prebuilt templates that most closely matches your app and then adapt the mock-up accordingly, or you can start a new template from scratch. You can use the SAP Build tool free of charge by going to *www.build.me*.

A gallery of prebuilt SAP Fiori app prototypes, shown in Figure 2.27, strictly based on the SAP design guidelines, will help you understand how a typical SAP Fiori app is designed, and you can even adapt these mock-ups to fit your design if you don't want to start designing a mock-up from scratch.

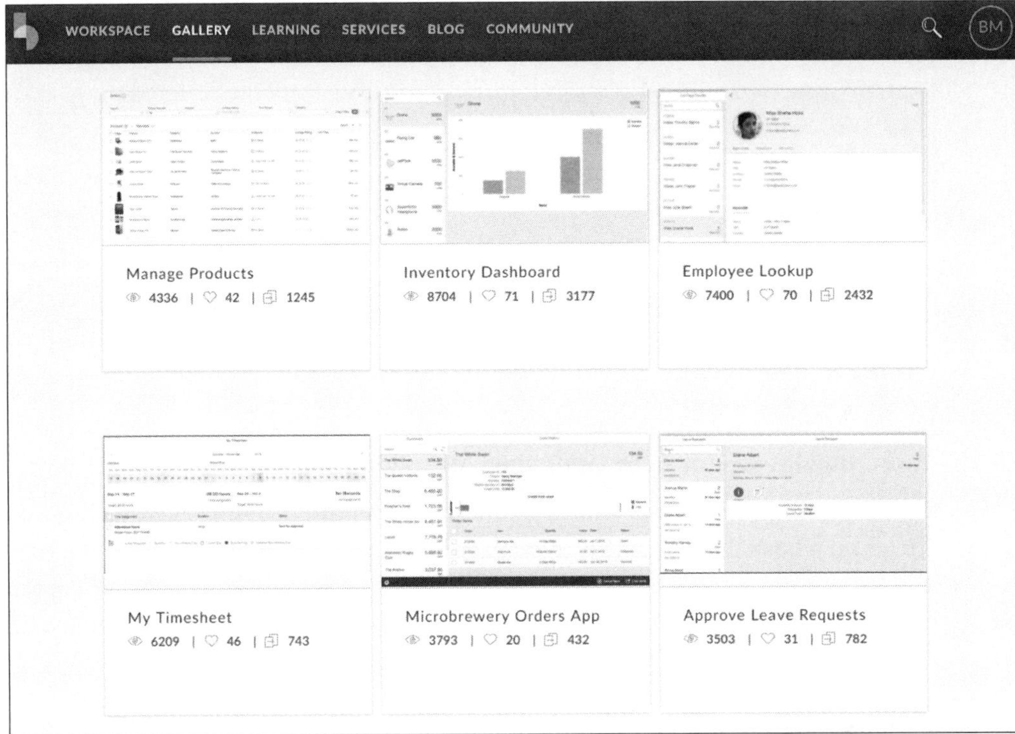

Figure 2.27 Prototype Gallery for SAP Build Tool

In addition to building a mock-up, you can add team members to your new SAP Build project so they can collaborate with you on the project.

After you're done with the mock-ups, you might want to share this mock-up with a customer or with other team members for their feedback. SAP Build allows you to generate a sharable URL instantly, so you can send your team members a working interactive prototype, instead of screenshots of the mock-ups or a ZIP file, enabling team members to get an idea of how the final app will look.

As mentioned earlier in this chapter, SAP Fiori user experience is all about design-led development or "humanizing our apps." SAP Build tools have an interactive learning cards section, which spans across the discover, design, and develop design phases of the SAP Fiori design guidelines. Clicking on one of the nodes, shown in Figure 2.28, within each of these design principles brings up a learning card explaining each phase.

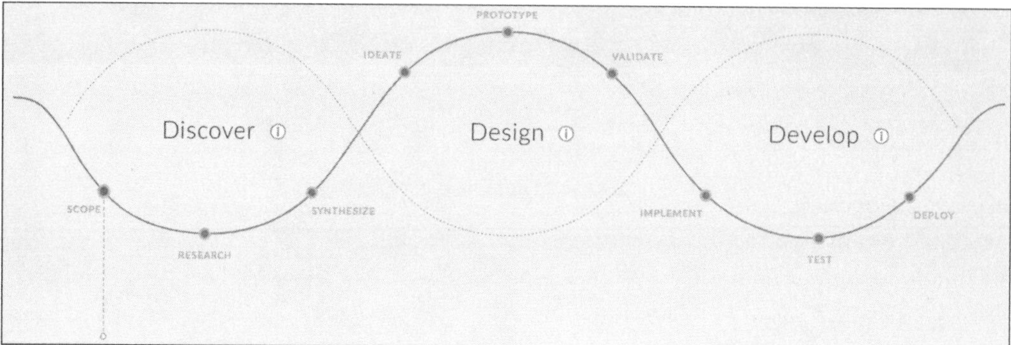

Figure 2.28 Design-Led Development Learning Cards in the SAP Build Tool

2.4.3 Building a Prototype Using the SAP Build Tool

Our aim in this section is to build a simple app for managing purchasing documents for a user whose primary role is to manage department expenditures. In our example, the user needs to keep track of all the purchase documents made by his department, needs to view detailed information of the purchasing documents, and needs the option to approve or reject purchasing documents if necessary.

Let's follow the design-led development process as you would in an actual project. We'll make this prototype with the SAP Build tool and build the actual app in the upcoming chapters. The following subsections describe the different phases of the design-led development process.

Discover Phase

In this phase, you'll identify the following: the app's scope, for whom the app is required, the challenges, and the possible bottlenecks. In addition, you'll talk to end users to create a persona for the app based on their needs. To simplify these tasks, we can further subdivide the discover phase into the several more manageable parts.

Scope

During this phase, communicating with your users and understanding what the project is about are essential. You'll need to document things so that you'll have a clear picture of what needs to be done so you can explain these tasks to your team. SAP

Build provides multiple templates to help you with the tasks defined in the different phases of design-led development.

> **Note**
> The following link provides a sample template you can use to document the project scope: *http://s-prs.co/498805*.

A project scope document will help you communicate with your team about what needs to be delivered. You'll also see the overall goal of the project, key deliverables, stakeholders, timeline, milestones, and so on. Table 2.1 contains the project scope details for our sample application for managing purchasing documents.

Project Scope Details: Manage Purchasing Documents	
Overall goal	To keep track of the expenses within the company, managers need an app with a UI that would help them identify high-value purchases, to monitor and approve or reject purchases accordingly. We'll build an app to manage purchasing documents.
Project scope	To deliver a solution that manages purchases within the organization; that can flag orders that are above the threshold limit; and that can show the status of the orders, including a detailed view of purchasing documents with items and options to approve or reject orders.
Project stakeholders	■ Sponsor: James Paul, Andre Green ■ Stakeholders: Evelin Smith, Julia Thomas
Project organization	■ Lead: Sebastian Joseph ■ Contributors: Richard Williams, Sam Andreas
Project deliverables	■ Personas, point of view (POV) statements ■ Storyboard ■ Prototype ■ Working software
Milestones	■ First draft review with Andre: 3/27/2019 ■ Executive review (Paul, Andre, Evelin): 4/1/2019 ■ Final draft: 4/5/2019 ■ Prototype: 5/5/2019 ■ Final product: 7/2/2019

Table 2.1 Project Scope Details

Research

This phase is all about gathering as much information as you can about your users to help you make meaningful decisions during project development. The best way to gather this information is by asking your users a set of questions like an interview. SAP Build also has a reference template to help you come up with a set of questions to gather that information.

> **Note**
>
> The following link provides an interview script template from SAP Build: *http://s-prs.co/498806.*

Synthesize

After the information gathering is done, now you'll sit down with your team along with the people who did the interview. Now, you can discuss the essential points from the information you've collected so far by writing all the essential points on a board. In this way, you can discuss among other team members to decide what information is relevant and further tweak the information, highlighting the potential problems/pain points of your app and discussing how to tackle those issues.

With an idea of who exactly your end user is based on the information at hand, you'll build personas for the potential users of the app. For creating personas, two options are available within the SAP Build tool: either use a template (available at *http://s-prs.co/498807*) or use the wizard/online form in the SAP Build tool.

To build a persona, as shown in Figure 2.29, you should list some key information about the user, such as an introduction about the user obtained from the interview phase, with whom the client mainly works, main goals for the user, what the user wants, job responsibilities, pain points mentioned by the user, and so on.

After you've created a persona, you can use the persona to make simple point of view (POV) documents for each requirement of the user (template available at *http://s-prs.co/498808*). This step will help you focus separately on each primary need instead of trying to tackle all the requirements at once. This document will help you and your team focus on specific problems and resolve the problems one by one. A typical POV should be minimal and focused on one requirement.

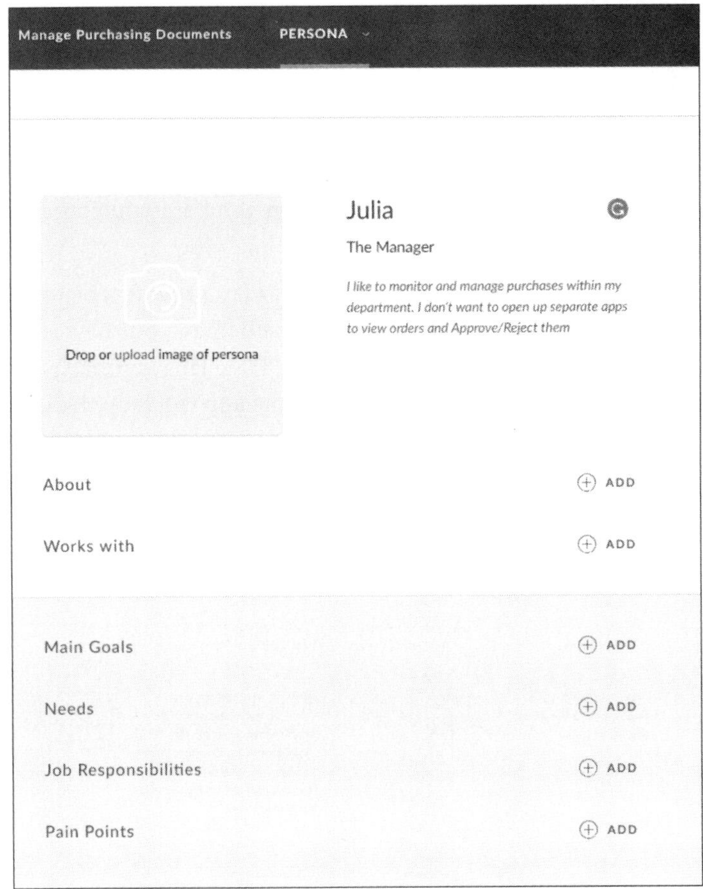

Figure 2.29 Persona Creation Wizard Using SAP Build

Design Phase

Now that you have an idea about the app, possible problems, and all the required information about users of the app, you'll need to come up with solution, build a prototype, test the prototype, share the prototype with end users, collect feedback, and tweak the designs based on feedback before coming up with a final prototype.

Ideate

In this phase, you'll try to understand how your users will use the existing system to complete their tasks and determine at which point they run into issues/problems with their current system and what alternatives they can take to overcome the problems.

You'll probably want to clearly record all the steps performed by users and re-create these steps on your end. Creating some flow diagrams will help you visualize these steps more accurately. Try to build separate use cases for the goals from the POVs (use the template at *http://s-prs.co/498809*).

With use cases in hand, now is the time for some brainstorming with your team. Think about how you'll resolve a specific issue. This session will help you come up with possible solutions and design concepts for the app.

After the brainstorming session, you can develop a storyboard to provide a pictorial representation of how the user will perform his task with the help of your new solution (download a storyboard template at *http://s-prs.co/498810*). This approach will basically give the team a high-level understanding of how the app will help the user in overcoming their current problems.

Shown in Figure 2.30 is a sample storyboard from SAP Build to give you an idea of how to visualize your prototype in a way that helps your customer complete his task. You can create storyboards based on the free available list of scenes at *http://s-prs.co/498811*.

Figure 2.30 Example Storyboard

Prototype

Now is the time to make the prototype. Sketch your design at least once on paper to get a feel for the app; these sketches are called low-fidelity designs. Now, let's decide which type of layout to make for our example, the Manager Purchasing Documents app. We need a list of all the purchasing documents on the same screen. A worklist page won't fit this requirement because the purpose of a worklist app is to list only the action items for a user. According to the personas, POVs, and use cases, the user needs more than a simple list of actionable items. He'll need to filter out, drill down on, and act on certain items as needed. Therefore, the obvious choice is a combination of a list report page for the purchasing documents and an object page to show items in detail.

> **Note**
>
> To help you make sketches for your prototype, you can download a template with various wireframe layouts for desktops, tablets, and a mobile devices at: *http://s-prs.co/498812*.

For this example, the sketch for the list report page is shown in Figure 2.31, which shows the first screen of the prototype. Notice the list of purchasing documents in the table, filter options, and action buttons for approve/reject. Furthermore, the table allows users to select multiple rows to perform mass approvals/rejections on the items.

Now that the first page sketch is done, let's focus on the object page for the second screen. As shown in Figure 2.32, this page lists all the items related to that purchasing document, so the user can see the cost breakdown of the item. This additional information will further help the user decide whether the purchase should be approved or not. The same approve/reject option is also provided here on the object page so that users don't need to go back to the first screen to approve/reject an item.

Now, we have the rough sketch of our prototype. But these sketches aren't professional looking enough to share with users to collect their feedback and these sketches aren't interactive either. If you can give your customer an interactive prototype design, their feedback will also help you further tweak the UX because users will get a feel for the final product you're trying to deliver.

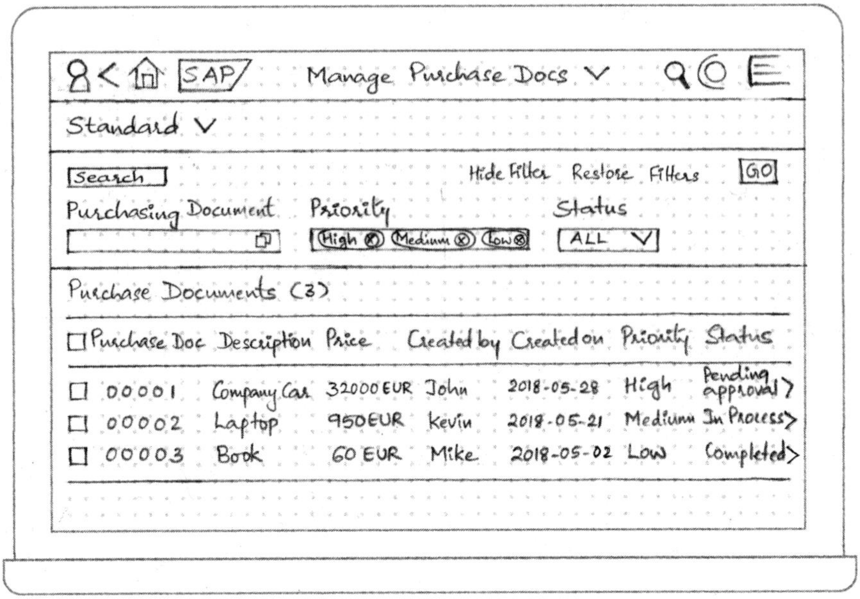

Figure 2.31 List Report Page Sketch on Paper

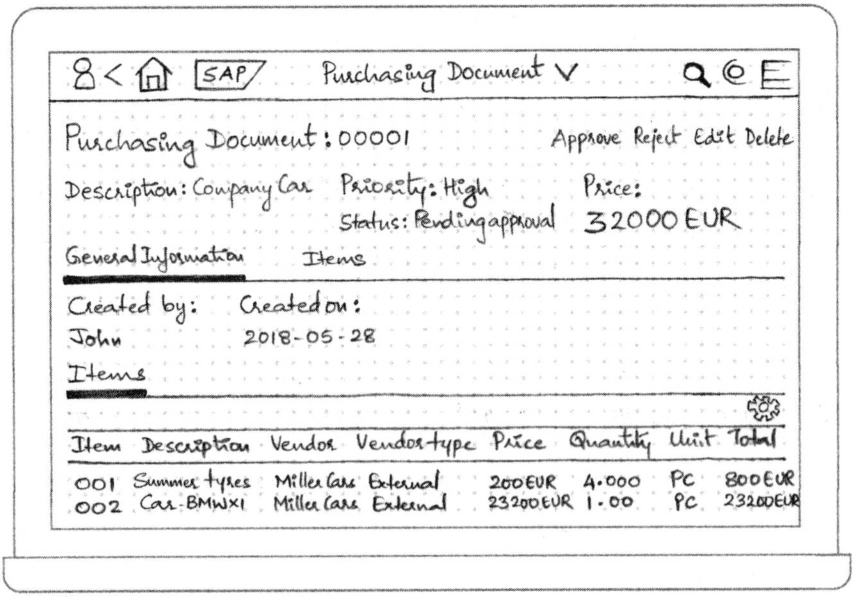

Figure 2.32 Object Page Sketch on Paper

To make a design closer to the final product and make it interactive, SAP Build has a set of templates to help you start. You can also start a new project from scratch, but because our designs are based on a list report page and an object page, we'll start with a template.

In the SAP Build tool, click on **New Project • Create New Project.** At this point, you'll also have the option of uploading the existing persona document you created from the template, or you can click the **Create a Persona** button to use the wizard. Then, you can click the **Start with Template** option, as shown in Figure 2.33.

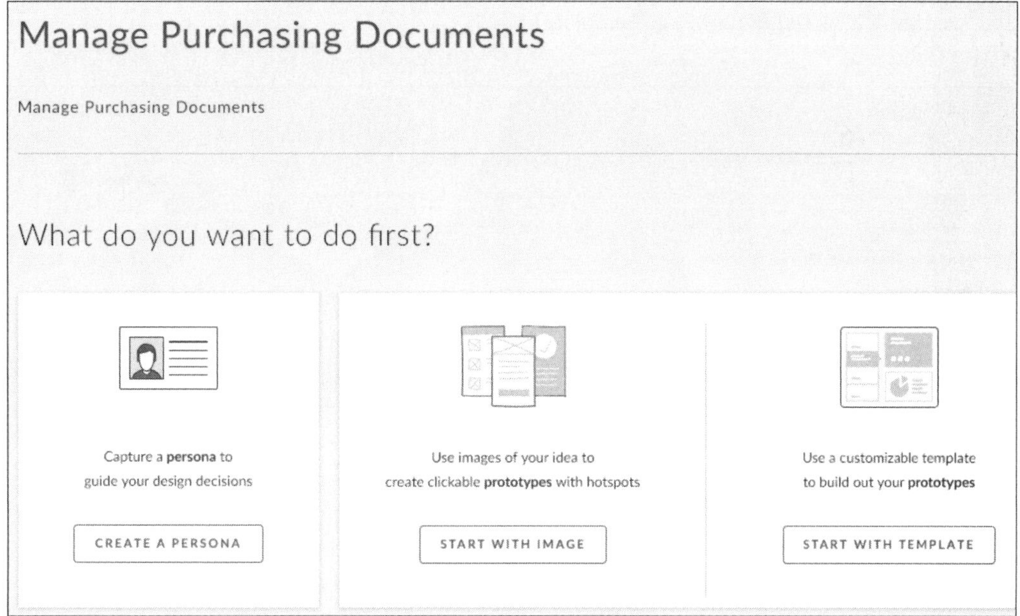

Figure 2.33 SAP Build Create Project from Template

From the list of templates, select **List Report**. Click on the **Edit Page** option to see a basic design of the list report, as shown in Figure 2.34. You can now modify the list report by adding the required filters, action buttons, and sample data for the table.

After all the UI elements are added to the template, the design should look like our sketch but closer to a real app, as shown in Figure 2.35. You can also create the required mock data for the table via the data editor feature of SAP Build. The layout editor also has useful features such as the option to view the mock-up on different device layouts (e.g., desktop, tablet, and phone) as well as the option to switch themes.

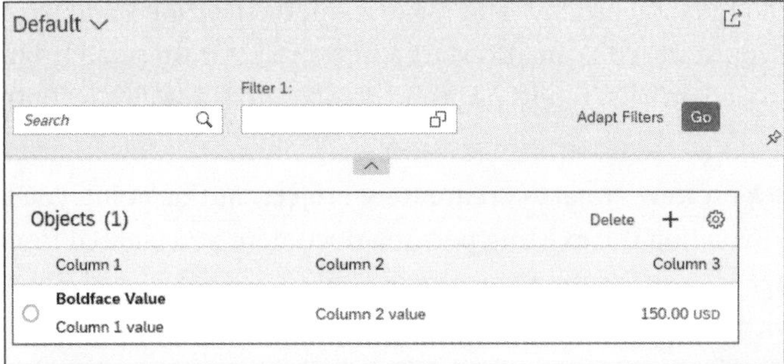

Figure 2.34 List Report Page Template

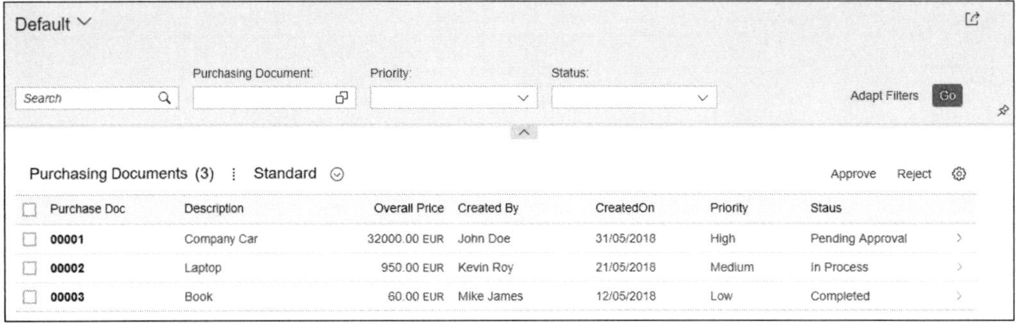

Figure 2.35 Completed Prototype of the List Report Page

Now, you'll need to build the object page for the details screen. You don't need to create another project; instead, you can add another page to the current project by clicking on the **+** icon next to the **Outline** option in the current project window, as shown in Figure 2.36, and selecting **Object Page**.

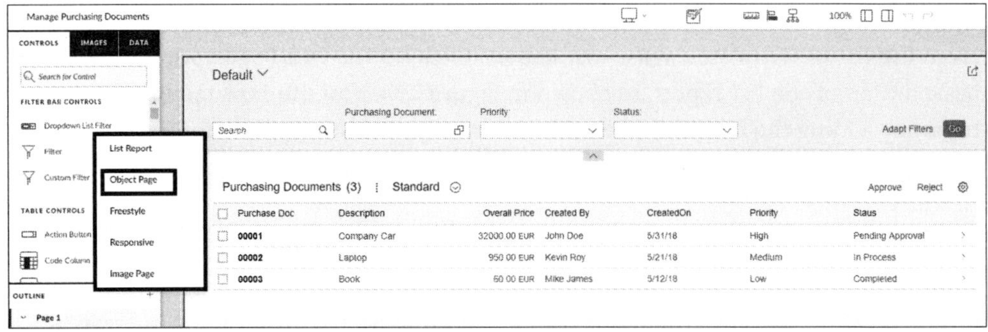

Figure 2.36 Adding an Object Page Template to the Project

At this point, you can start modifying the object page based on the sketch. As shown in Figure 2.37, the object page design is complete with the additional item details of the purchasing document. You can also add navigation actions to the table list in the list page to enable navigation to the object page.

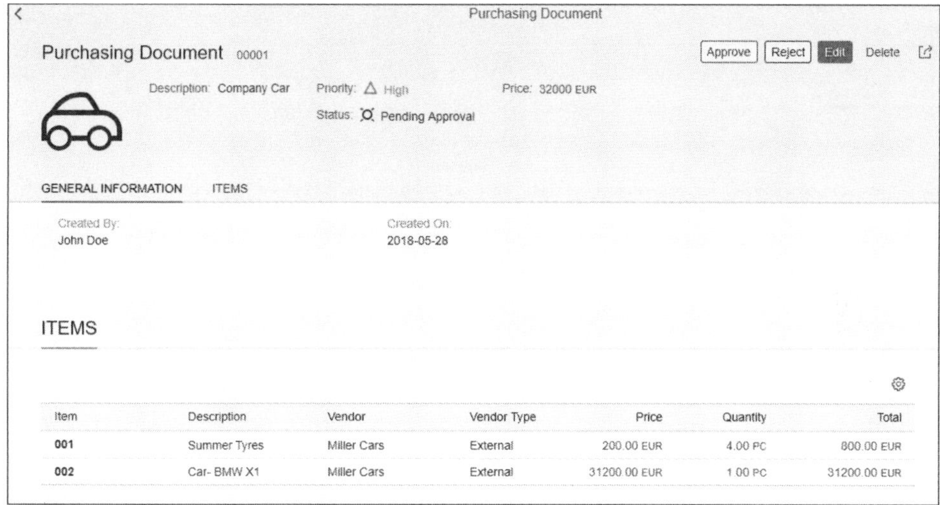

Figure 2.37 Object Page Prototype

Now, you can preview the prototype by clicking on the eye icon on the top-right corner of the UI editor, as shown in Figure 2.38.

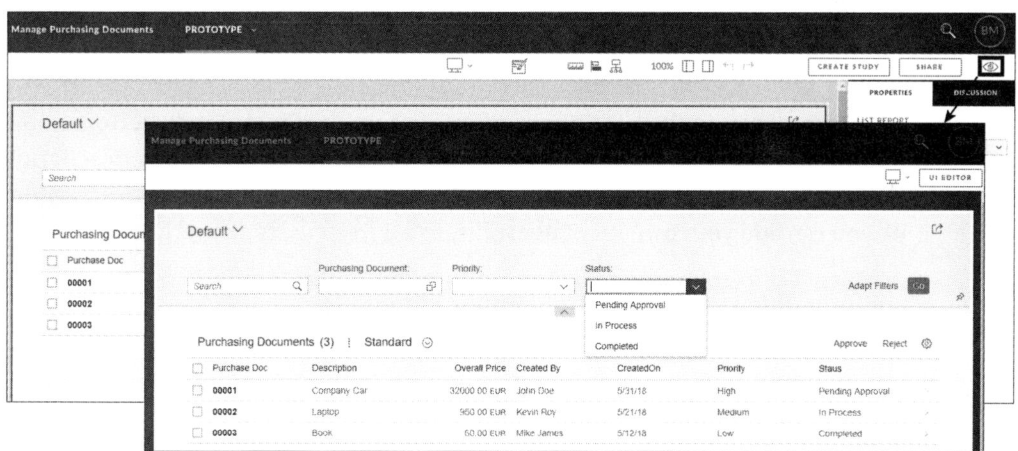

Figure 2.38 Previewing the Prototype

When you're happy with the preview, you can generate a sharable link to send to your users. Click on the **SHARE** button on the top-right toolbar of the UI editor, and a popup window with the URL link will open. Additionally, you can also download a ZIP file of the prototype, which can be imported into the SAP Web IDE, which can start generating the basic code required for the actual app, as shown in Figure 2.39.

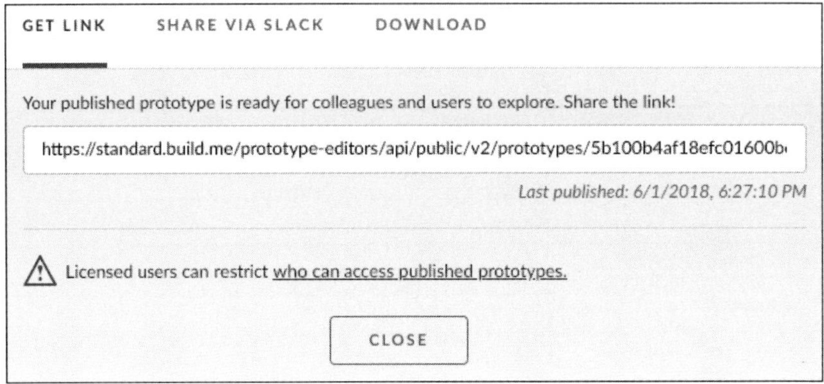

Figure 2.39 Generating a Sharable URL for the Prototype

Validate

After you're done prototyping, you can share the prototype with your users and wait for feedback to rectify any issues, which will ensure that your users are okay with the prototype before entering the development phase. To collect feedback, you can either use the template (available for download at *http://s-prs.co/498813*) and test the script link, or you can use the feedback tool within the layout editor of the app to generate a sharable interactive feedback URL that you can then share with your customer.

To create feedback, in the UI editor window, click on the **Create Study** button on the top-right side of the toolbar. In the popup window, provide a name and description for the study. Now, click on the **Create and Go to Feedback** button. As shown in Figure 2.40, you can add your own set of questions to ask your users about the app.

Now let's add a few questions. Click on the **NEW QUESTION** button, as shown in Figure 2.41, and select the prototype from the **Prototypes** tab. On this screen, you'll have multiple methods to create questions: You can ask users to complete certain actions, ask for opinions about a specific feature, give users multiple-choice options to select from, and give users the option of adding comments anywhere on the screen.

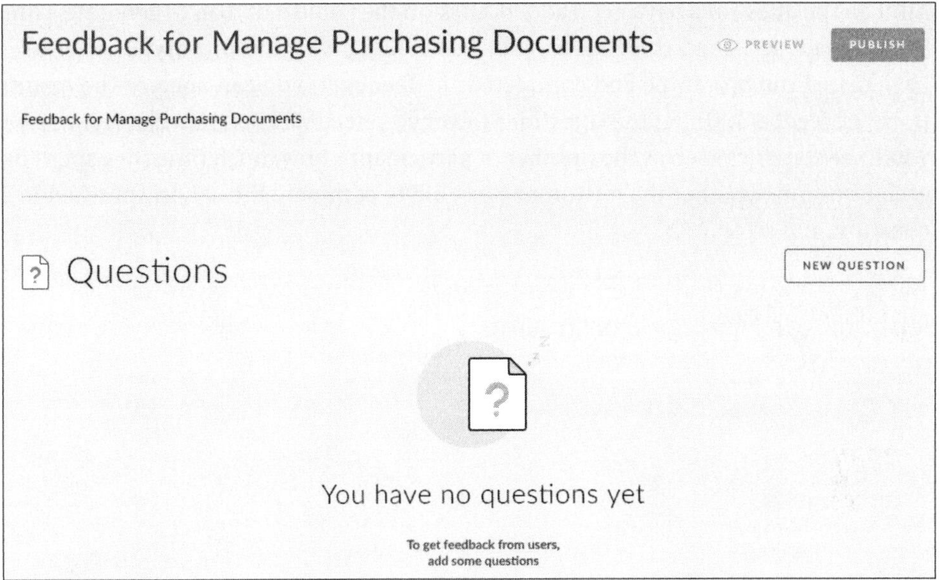

Figure 2.40 Feedback

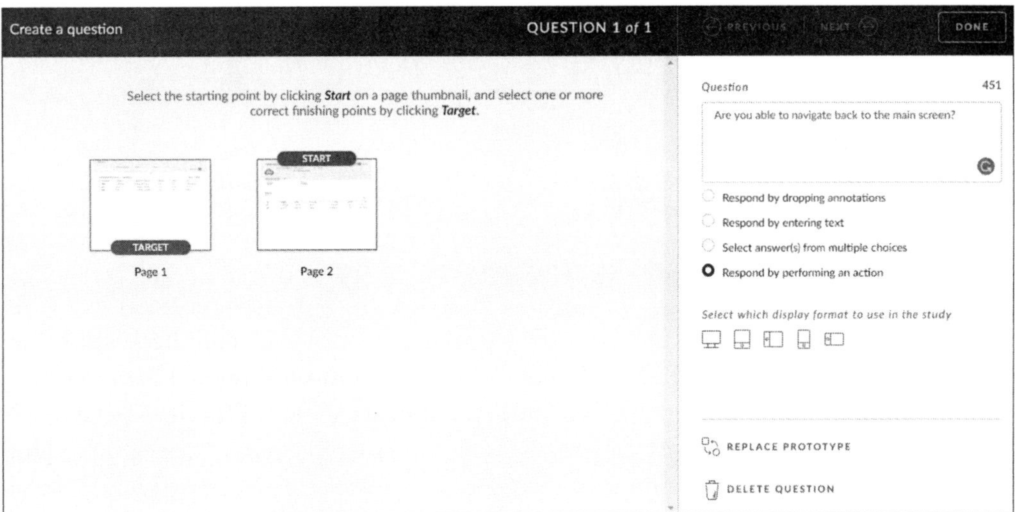

Figure 2.41 Prepare Questions for Feedback

After all the questions have been added, click on the **Publish** button to generate a link for the feedback. Send this link to your users along with the prototype. After user have tested the prototype and completed the feedback, you can analyze the results from the feedback. Under the **Questions** tab of your feedback, as shown in Figure 2.42, you'll see statistics such as the number of participants, how much time they spent on each question, whether the customer was able to complete the action specified in a question, and so on.

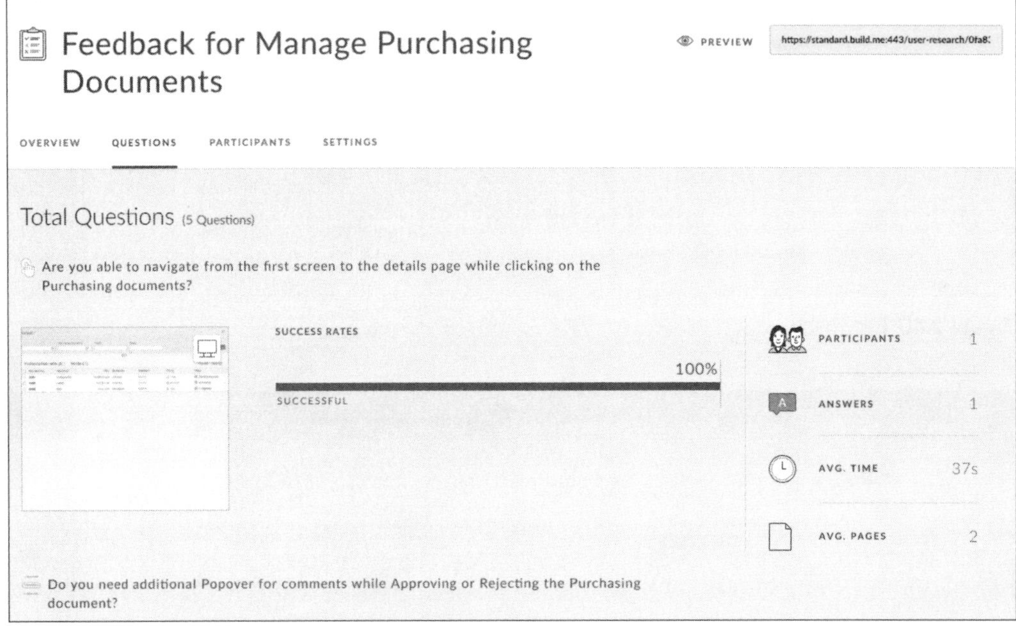

Figure 2.42 Analysis of Feedback from Customers

In addition, you can go through each question in the feedback and check which controls or areas on a page of the prototype users were most interested in by selecting the **Heatmap** checkbox in the questions window. As shown in Figure 2.43, you'll see the areas on the screen where the customer interacted the most. This feature is powerful because you'll see how a user uses the app, which might be completely different from how you might have used the app. Such insights will help you further tweak your prototype.

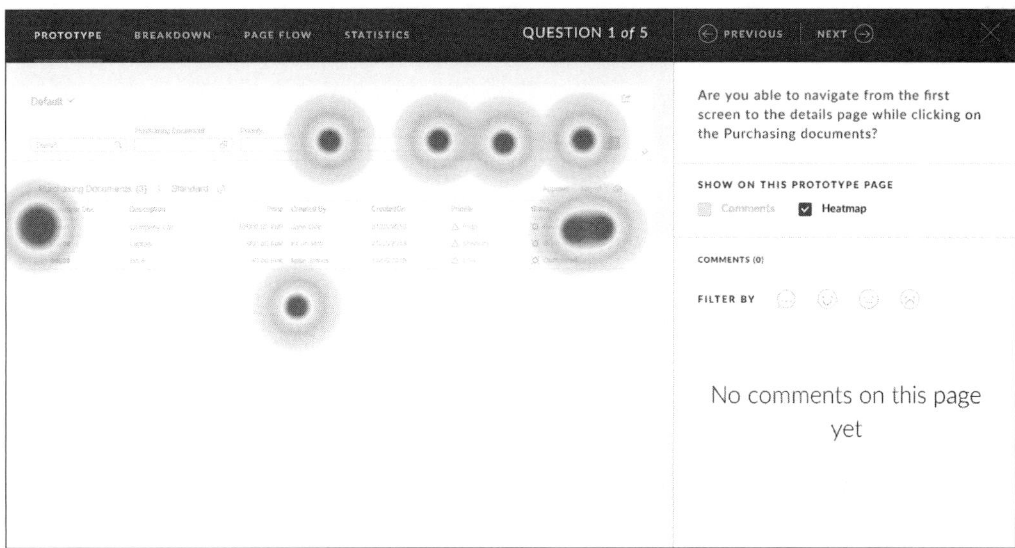

Figure 2.43 Heatmap Option in the Feedback Tool

2.5 Summary

SAP Fiori works seamlessly across desktops, tablets, and mobile devices to enable users to work on the go. SAP Fiori is the new UX for SAP software, so developers will need to understand its design principles and guidelines to develop new apps. Following these design guidelines is important and will ensure that your apps look and feel just as good as the standard suite of apps SAP Fiori offers.

In this chapter, we laid out the basic design principles of all SAP Fiori apps, discussed responsive and adaptive design, and explained the SAP Fiori launchpad and its components.

Then, we looked at the design-led development process and the different phases that are crucial for an SAP Fiori project. We considered the different app types offered by SAP Fiori to help developers with app development.

Finally, we discussed the different prototyping tools to help create beautiful design sketches and interactive prototypes for your final product.

In the next chapter, you'll learn about the ABAP RESTful programming model for SAP Fiori and its associated technologies.

Chapter 3
ABAP RESTful Programming Model

In this chapter, we'll introduce you to the ABAP RESTful programming model, which has been available on the SAP Cloud Platform since August 2018 and in on-premise installations since SAP S/4HANA 1909 in September 2019. The ABAP RESTful programming model is the standard development model for new SAP S/4HANA applications and reflects the SAP S/4HANA core architecture described in Chapter 1 and is the successor of the ABAP programming model for SAP Fiori, which we covered in the first edition of this book.

In general, like its predecessor, the ABAP RESTful programming model supports the development of SAP HANA-optimized OData services for SAP Fiori applications based on core data services (CDS) views and covers analytical, transactional, and search application processes. Two main scenarios exist when developing applications using the programming model: read-only applications and transactional applications. Read-only applications only require an underlying CDS data model and application-specific analytics or search annotations. The CDS data model and its annotations are then exposed as an OData service using the Service Adaptation Description Language (SADL) technology respectively the programming model's query runtime. Transactional applications, in addition to read-only applications, require the creation of a business object based on a behavior definition and implementation for the handling of create, read, update, and delete (CRUD) operations as well as additional business logic implemented in ABAP. In the following sections, we'll go through the different technologies associated with the RESTful programming model (CDS, SAP Gateway, and OData) before we dive into the model itself. We'll start with its design time development flow and its runtime stack before turning to queries, business objects, and service provisioning in detail. This chapter will provide you with the theoretical foundation of the ABAP RESTful programming model before we start developing SAP Fiori applications in the upcoming chapters.

3.1 Core Data Services

As mentioned in Chapter 1, core data services (CDS) are the foundation for all SAP S/4HANA application types. CDS can be deployed on top of legacy or new SAP ERP tables and enable the development of semantically rich data models that foster code pushdown to the SAP HANA database. CDS are developed on the ABAP stack in Eclipse and therefore use the standard lifecycle management of ABAP development objects; for instance, CDS are transported between systems using the standard ABAP Change and Transport System (CTS). The CDS view definition has the object repository entry `R3TR DDLS <CDS_DEFINITION_VIEW_NAME>`.

To cover different application scenarios, CDS views, which are defined using the data definition language (DDL) of CDS, can be enhanced using the following types of annotations:

- **Analytical annotations**
  To use a CDS view as a data cube or query within analytical application scenarios via the Analytical Engine, the CDS view must be annotated using `@Analytics` annotations.
- **UI annotations**
  CDS views can be annotated with user interface (UI) annotations (`@UI`) to define where certain entities, fields, and data will be placed within an SAP Fiori elements template application, which reduces the required JavaScript SAPUI5 frontend code drastically. UI annotations can be moved to a metadata extension file with object repository type `R3TR DDLX` in order not to clutter the core CDS view with loads of UI annotations.
- **Search annotations**
  CDS views can be configured for search scenarios using `@Search` annotations, for instance, as an Enterprise Search (ESH) model for the SAP Fiori launchpad search or for SAP Fiori in-app search by defining the SAP HANA text search scope and fuzziness.

To enable transactional processing for CDS entities, a business object structure needs to be modeled using special types of associations, which we'll cover in the section about the ABAP RESTful programming model. Previously, in the Business Object Processing Framework (BOPF), a business object could also be created using annotations. Figure 3.1 shows the importance of CDS technologies for application development within SAP S/4HANA. CDS data definitions are the basis for ESH search models generation, business object modeling and OData service provisioning. Business object modeling and the implementation of its corresponding behavior using as behavior definition and implementation are part of the ABAP RESTful programming model just like OData provisioning, which requires a service definition and a service binding. We'll look at the ABAP RESTful programming model in more detail later in Section 3.4. The whole development takes place in Eclipse except for developing the SAP Fiori app UI, which takes place in the SAP Web IDE.

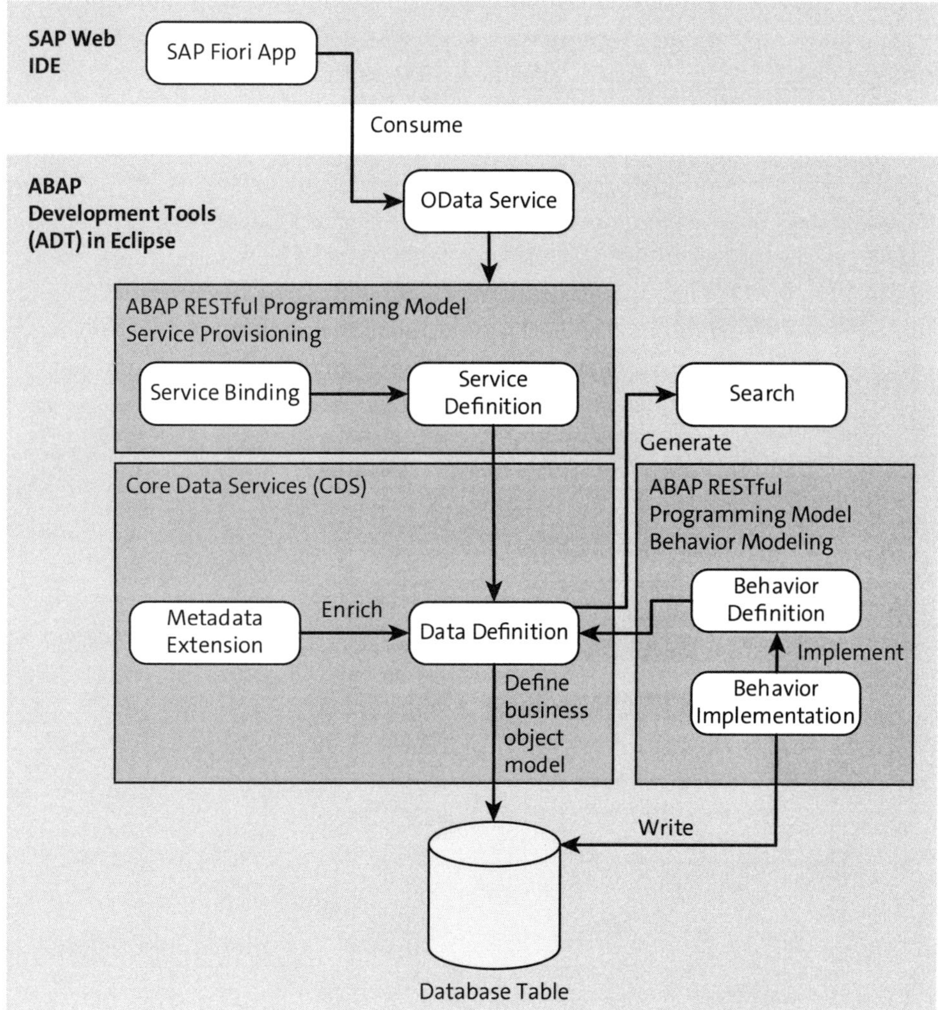

Figure 3.1 CDS as the Basis for Application Development in SAP S/4HANA Using the ABAP RESTful Programming Model

3.2 SAP Gateway

SAP Gateway plays a crucial role in providing an easy-to-use, non-ABAP-based access to business data stored in backend SAP NetWeaver systems. Access to business data is granted via REST-based OData services using HTTP as the underlying data transfer protocol. As of SAP NetWeaver version 7.40, the software component SAP_GWFND is installed with SAP NetWeaver standard and includes the full scope of functionality required for hub and backend enablement.

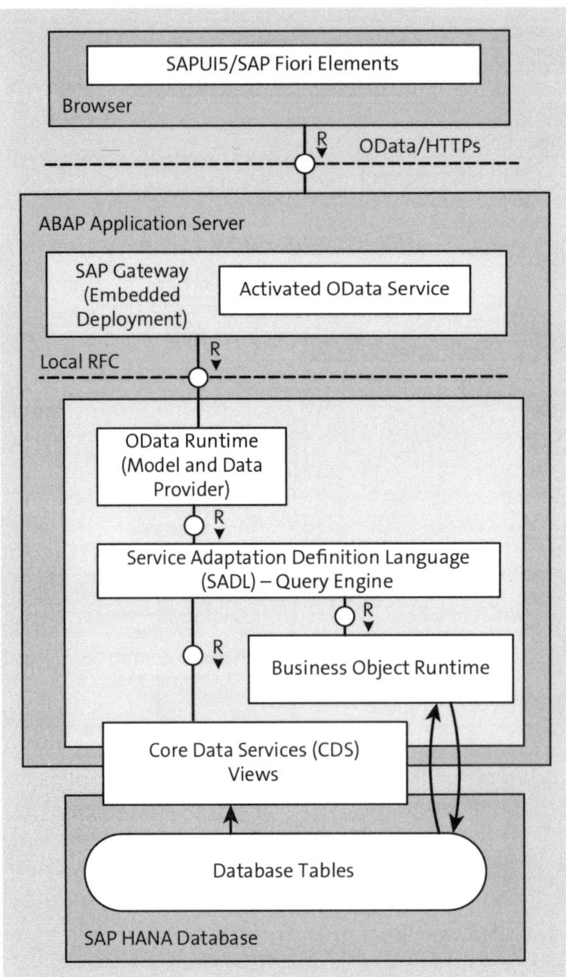

Figure 3.2 High-level Overview of a Typical SAP S/4HANA System Setup with SAP Gateway Provided as Embedded Deployment

In general, from an architectural perspective, there are two deployment approaches: embedded deployment or hub deployment. Hub deployments can be further split into development on the hub or development in the backend system. Currently, the best practice is to pursue embedded deployment. SAP no longer recommends an additional SAP Gateway frontend system, as recommended before SAP S/4HANA 1809. Figure 3.2 shows the setup for an SAP S/4HANA system. The OData service deployed on the embedded SAP Gateway and the backend communicate using a local remote function call (RFC) connection to forward requests. The RFC-enabled function module passing data from the frontend to the backend is `/IWBEP/FM_MGW_HANDLE_REQUEST`. The SAP Fiori app running in the browser sends OData HTTP `GET`, `POST`, `DELETE`, or `PUT` requests to the SAP Gateway system, which exposes all registered and activated OData services. The SAP Gateway passes the incoming OData requests to the backend via a local RFC connection. The OData runtime in the backend then delegates the actual data selection to the SADL framework layer. If the request is a read-only `GET` request, SADL will delegate the request to its query engine, which will generate an SQL `SELECT` statement to select the requested OData entity's data from the database tables via its corresponding CDS view. For write access, for instance, `POST` for create or `PUT` for update, the request will be delegated to the transactional business object runtime of the ABAP RESTful programming model, which will handle the database updates according to the defined and implemented behavior of the business objects.

3.3 OData

As you already know from Chapter 1, you can directly select data from a CDS view using Open SQL in ABAP, just as you could select data from a conventional database table. However, SAP Fiori apps require the exposure of data as an OData service using HTTP as the data transfer protocol. OData is a REST-based data protocol used for transferring business data as well as metadata between the ABAP backend system and client applications via the SAP Gateway. In SAP S/4HANA, client applications of OData services usually are SAP Fiori SAPUI5 applications running in the local browsers of end-user devices such as desktop PCs or tablets. Together with the SAP Gateway, OData provides access to the SAP backend business data in an easy-to-understand and well-defined way using HTTP as its data transfer protocol. An OData service organizes data in the form of entities that have a set of properties interconnected via associations. These elements resemble the elements of CDS data models, so CDS data models are the perfect candidates for exposure as OData services.

You can explore the structure of an OData service by looking at its service document and its service metadata document. The service document contains a list of entities or resources that can be accessed using this service and can be requested via /sap/opu/odata/sap/<OData_service_name>/. Additionally, you can see whether the service allows for CRUD operations on entities by looking at the sap:creatable, sap:updatable, and sap:deletable attributes of the <app:collection> tag, which also contains a relative reference to the entity set via its href attribute, as shown in Figure 3.3.

```
<app:service xml:lang="en"
xml:base="https://ldciuyt.wdf.sap.corp:44300/sap/opu/odata/sap/Z_PurchasingDocumentDDL_CDS/"
xmlns:app="http://www.w3.org/2007/app" xmlns:atom="http://www.w3.org/2005/Atom"
xmlns:m="http://schemas.microsoft.com/ado/2007/08/dataservices/metadata"
xmlns:sap="http://www.sap.com/Protocols/SAPData">
  <app:workspace>
    <atom:title type="text">Data</atom:title>
    <app:collection sap:creatable="false" sap:updatable="false" sap:deletable="false" sap:content-
    version="1" href="Z_PurchasingDocumentDDL">
      <atom:title type="text">Z_PurchasingDocumentDDL</atom:title>
      <sap:member-title>Purchase Document</sap:member-title>
    </app:collection>
    <app:collection sap:creatable="false" sap:updatable="false" sap:deletable="false" sap:content-
    version="1" href="Z_PurchasingDocumentItemDDL">
      <atom:title type="text">Z_PurchasingDocumentItemDDL</atom:title>
      <sap:member-title>Purchase Document Item</sap:member-title>
    </app:collection>
  </app:workspace>
  <atom:link rel="self"
  href="https://ldciuyt.wdf.sap.corp:44300/sap/opu/odata/sap/Z_PurchasingDocumentDDL_CDS/"/>
  <atom:link rel="latest-version"
  href="https://ldciuyt.wdf.sap.corp:44300/sap/opu/odata/sap/Z_PurchasingDocumentDDL_CDS/"/>
</app:service>
```

Figure 3.3 Service Document of a Simple Purchase Document and Purchase Document Item OData Service

The service metadata document is a lot more detailed than the service document and shows all metadata of the service. You can request the service metadata document using the $metadata option: /sap/opu/odata/sap/<OData_service_name>/$metadata. This document displays all entities of the service, including their properties and associations.

Figure 3.4 shows how the service metadata document will look for the simple scenario we introduced in Chapter 1. Recall that the purchase document CDS view (Z_PurchasingDocumentDDL) had an association to the purchase document items view (Z_PurchasingDocumentItemDDL). Both views now appear as OData entity types in the OData service's metadata document, including the information about the association between the two entities and their cardinalities. Which operations an entity supports is indicated by the `sap:creatable`, `sap:updatable`, and `sap:deletable` attributes of the `EntitySet` element. In the following example, notice that the service doesn't support any write access at all, as we haven't enabled the transactional runtime for our CDS model by modeling a business object and its behavior in the ABAP RESTful programming model. Thus, the service only supports read access via HTTP `GET` entity requests. As mentioned earlier, the metadata file of an OData service can be requested using the `$metadata` path `/sap/opu/odata/sap/<OData_service_name>/$metadata`.

```
- <EntityType sap:content-version="1" sap:label="Purchasing Document" Name="Z_PurchasingDocumentDDLType">
  - <Key>
      <PropertyRef Name="PurchasingDocument"/>
    </Key>
    <Property sap:label="Purchasing document" Name="PurchasingDocument" sap:quickinfo="Purchasing Document Number" sap:display-
      format="UpperCase" MaxLength="10" Nullable="false" Type="Edm.String"/>
    <Property sap:label="Purch. Organization" Name="PurchasingOrganization" sap:quickinfo="Purchasing Organization" sap:display-
      format="UpperCase" MaxLength="4" Type="Edm.String"/>
    <Property sap:label="Created On" Name="CreationDate" sap:quickinfo="Date on Which Record Was Created" sap:display-format="Date"
      Type="Edm.DateTime" Precision="0"/>
    <Property sap:label="Created By" Name="CreatedByUser" sap:quickinfo="Name of Person Who Created Object" sap:display-
      format="UpperCase" MaxLength="12" Type="Edm.String"/>
    <NavigationProperty Name="to_PurchasingDocumentItemDDL" ToRole="ToRole_assoc_3EDEE251A83223DE4BCA615BA622E7D2"
      FromRole="FromRole_assoc_3EDEE251A83223DE4BCA615BA622E7D2"
      Relationship="Z_PURCHASINGDOCUMENTDDL_CDS.assoc_3EDEE251A83223DE4BCA615BA622E7D2"/>
  </EntityType>
- <EntityType sap:content-version="1" sap:label="Purchase Document Item" Name="Z_PurchasingDocumentItemDDLType">
  - <Key>
      <PropertyRef Name="PurchasingDocument"/>
      <PropertyRef Name="PurchasPurchasingDocumentItem"/>
    </Key>
    <Property sap:label="Purchasing document" Name="PurchasingDocument" sap:quickinfo="Purchasing Document Number" sap:display-
      format="UpperCase" MaxLength="10" Nullable="false" Type="Edm.String"/>
    <Property sap:label="Item" Name="PurchasPurchasingDocumentItem" sap:quickinfo="Item Number of Purchasing Document"
      sap:display-format="NonNegative" MaxLength="5" Nullable="false" Type="Edm.String"/>
  </EntityType>
- <Association sap:content-version="1" Name="assoc_3EDEE251A83223DE4BCA615BA622E7D2">
    <End Type="Z_PURCHASINGDOCUMENTDDL_CDS.Z_PurchasingDocumentDDLType"
      Role="FromRole_assoc_3EDEE251A83223DE4BCA615BA622E7D2" Multiplicity="1"/>
    <End Type="Z_PURCHASINGDOCUMENTDDL_CDS.Z_PurchasingDocumentItemDDLType"
      Role="ToRole_assoc_3EDEE251A83223DE4BCA615BA622E7D2" Multiplicity="*"/>
  </Association>
- <EntityContainer Name="Z_PURCHASINGDOCUMENTDDL_CDS_Entities" sap:supported-formats="atom json xlsx"
  m:IsDefaultEntityContainer="true">
    <EntitySet sap:content-version="1" Name="Z_PurchasingDocumentDDL" sap:deletable="false" sap:updatable="false"
      sap:creatable="false" EntityType="Z_PURCHASINGDOCUMENTDDL_CDS.Z_PurchasingDocumentDDLType"/>
    <EntitySet sap:content-version="1" Name="Z_PurchasingDocumentItemDDL" sap:deletable="false" sap:updatable="false"
      sap:creatable="false" EntityType="Z_PURCHASINGDOCUMENTDDL_CDS.Z_PurchasingDocumentItemDDLType"/>
  - <AssociationSet sap:content-version="1" Name="assoc_3EDEE251A83223DE4BCA615BA622E7D2" sap:deletable="false"
    sap:updatable="false" sap:creatable="false"
    Association="Z_PURCHASINGDOCUMENTDDL_CDS.assoc_3EDEE251A83223DE4BCA615BA622E7D2">
      <End Role="FromRole_assoc_3EDEE251A83223DE4BCA615BA622E7D2" EntitySet="Z_PurchasingDocumentDDL"/>
      <End Role="ToRole_assoc_3EDEE251A83223DE4BCA615BA622E7D2" EntitySet="Z_PurchasingDocumentItemDDL"/>
    </AssociationSet>
  </EntityContainer>
```


Figure 3.4 XML Service Metadata Document of the Simple CDS Scenario from Chapter 1 Exposed as an OData Service

OData uses the REST HTTP commands `POST`, `GET`, `PUT`, and `DELETE` for CRUD operations on entities. Additionally, OData defines a simple but powerful query language for restricting the result set provided by the SAP Gateway. Table 3.1 lists the most common OData query options.

Operation	Query Option
Filtering	`$filter`, e.g., `$filter = PurchaseDocument eq '0005'`
Projecting or selecting properties	`$select`, e.g., `$select = PurchaseDocument, PurchasingOrganization,...`
Sorting	`$orderby`, e.g., `$orderby = CreationDate desc`
Client-side paging	`$top` and `$skip`, e.g., `$top = 10&$skip = 0`
Counting	`$count`
Formatting	`$format`, e.g., `$format = JSON`

Table 3.1 Most Important OData Query Options

Open access to backend business data via OData and SAP Gateway enables the use of modern non-ABAP UI technologies for displaying and interacting with business data. The UI of applications developed using the ABAP RESTful programming model is therefore completely based on the SAPUI5 framework, which implements SAP Fiori design principles. The UI part of applications is usually implemented using the cloud-based SAP Web IDE and is either based on SAP Fiori elements applications or on free-style applications. SAP Fiori elements applications, for instance, the list report and object page templates or floorplans, adapt their layouts based on the OData service's metadata and UI annotations defined in CDS views or their respective metadata extensions. Therefore, SAP Fiori elements templates significantly reduce the necessary frontend SAPUI5 JavaScript code to a minimum and increase developer productivity significantly by still providing flexibility using predefined extension points in the frontend.

Additionally, transparent to the developer, SAP Fiori elements applications implement the necessary CRUD request handling for read-only and transactional applications, depending on which business object operations have been defined and implemented in the behavior definition and implementation using the ABAP RESTful programming model. Freestyle applications, in contrast to SAP Fiori elements, provide the frontend developer with full flexibility over the UI design and logic but require a lot of effort in the development phase. The UI layout and its controls must be declared manually by the developer, and the necessary SAPUI5 JavaScript logic must be implemented. A risk when developing freestyle applications is the violation of SAP Fiori design principles. Consequently, we recommend only using freestyle applications when the required UI design isn't realizable using an existing SAP Fiori elements floorplan.

3.4 ABAP RESTful Programming Model

Now, let's look at the ABAP RESTful programming model in detail and get to know its various components. As SAP's latest programming model for ABAP, development had a strong focus on the cloud. The main purpose of the ABAP RESTful programming model is the development of RESTful OData services that can be consumed by SAP Fiori applications or any kind of OData clients. Unlike the previous ABAP programming model for SAP Fiori, the ABAP RESTful programming model has been integrated directly into the ABAP language core by introducing new transportable ABAP development object types for behavior definitions, service definitions, and service bindings as well as a new Entity Manipulation Language (EML). As a result, the programming model can be offered in the cloud as only the ABAP language core runtime without any additional libraries and tools (apart from SAP Gateway and the SADL orchestration framework dispatching requests to either the query or the business object runtime). With the previous ABAP programming model for SAP Fiori, this was not possible as it also relied on the BOPF for transactional processing, which is an ABAP framework and not part of the ABAP language. Additionally, now you can develop OData services end-to-end (E2E) in one tool environment (right now, Eclipse). SAP GUI access is no longer required in the development flow, which had also been a requirement for cloud development and was an annoying aspect of the previous programming model.

3.4.1 Introduction

The ABAP RESTful programming model is a rather opinionated framework that guides you through all steps required to develop a RESTful OData service. Classic freestyle ABAP Web Dynpro applications developed for SAP GUI enjoy a higher degree of freedom than developing with the ABAP RESTful programming model. However, as a result, applications developed with the ABAP RESTful programming model are more standardized and thus easier to maintain in the long run. In this subsection, we'll first look at the development flow that each developer is bound to when developing an OData service with the ABAP RESTful programming model. Additionally, we'll look at the components involved in processing OData requests from SAP Fiori UI requests (or any other OData clients) during runtime. As already mentioned, the E2E development of ABAP RESTful programming model services is completely Eclipse based and requires an installation of Eclipse with the ABAP development tools plug-in installed.

Note

Check out Chapter 4 of this book and the ABAP section on the SAP Development Tools website for more information on how to install the ABAP development tools: *https://tools.hana.ondemand.com/#abap.*

Development Flow

Figure 3.5 shows the basic development flow when developing RESTful OData services with the ABAP RESTful programming model. Let's walk through the flow, starting from the bottom.

Data Modeling and Behavior

The usual starting point of an ABAP RESTful programming model application is the data model with its foundation in classic database tables stored in the ABAP dictionary and created in the SAP HANA database. Independent of the application type, read-only or transactional, the next layer is formed by CDS views. CDS views provide a semantic view of the underlying database table structures and their relationships. Read-only data models are referred to as *queries* in the ABAP RESTful programming model whereas transactional data models are called *business objects*. To turn a CDS data model into a business object, the CDS model needs to define a compositional hierarchy. With the ABAP RESTful programming model, the definition of a compositional hierarchy has been fully integrated into the ABAP language core (replacing the use of annotations in the BOPF). To add the actual behavior to a business object (both CRUD operations and custom actions), a *behavior definition* with a corresponding *behavior implementation* is required. A behavior definition is a new ABAP development object that defines which actions each node of the business object supports using what's called the Behavior Definition Language (BDL), resembling the Data Definition Language (DDL) of CDS. The actual implementation of the operations is delegated to the *behavior implementation*, which is a standard ABAP global class (also called a *behavior pool*) that simply serves as a container and is empty while the actual behavior logic is implemented in local handler classes.

Business Service Provisioning

Following the ABAP RESTful programming model development flow, as of now, we've developed a CDS data model, and if transactional processing of data is a requirement

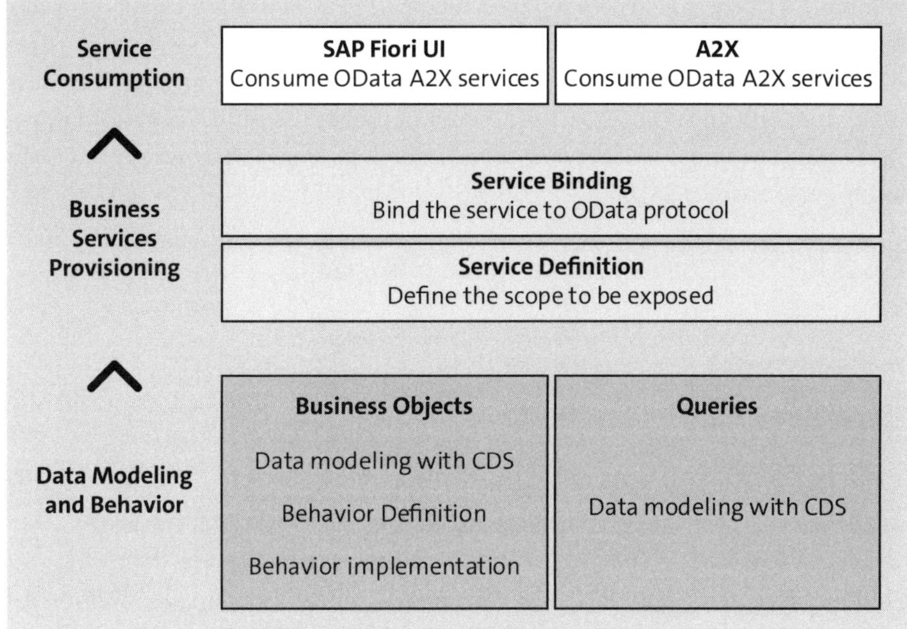

Figure 3.5 ABAP RESTful Programming Model: Development Flow

within our application, we'll create a business object with a behavior definition and one or more global ABAP classes (behavior pools) actually implementing the behavior (CRUD operations, etc.). So far, our data model is only consumable within the ABAP stack. To make our data model consumable by SAP Fiori applications or any other OData clients, we must expose it as an OData service. In the past, you would undertake a cumbersome process involving the creation of an SAP Gateway service builder project (Transaction SEGW), the mapping of the CDS entities to OData entities, and the deployment of the service on the SAP Gateway using Transaction /IWFND/MAINT_SERVICE. With the ABAP RESTful programming model, the definition of which CDS views to expose as OData entities has also been integrated into the ABAP language in the form of a *service definition*. Within a service definition, you can, in a declarative manner using a CDS-like syntax, define which CDS entities to expose with our OData service without the need for additional SAP GUI transactions or tools. With a new ABAP repository object called a *service binding*, you can finally actually expose an application model by binding the service definition to a specific client-server communication protocol such as OData. In this data model definition phase, SADL creates a mapping of CDS entities to an OData Entity Data Model (EDM).

Additionally, CDS view field data types are mapped to EDM primitive data types; for instance, the ABAP dictionary built-in type `DATS` is mapped to the `EDM.DateTime` data type. Moreover, if transactional processing is enabled for CDS entities, business object actions will appear as OData function imports in the service metadata document. Table 3.2 provides an overview of the mappings from CDS concepts to OData concepts performed by SADL.

CDS	OData
CDS view (DDL)	EDM entity
CDS associations	EDM association
CDS view field data type	EDM primitive data type
Business object actions	Function import

Table 3.2 Mappings between CDS Data Model Concepts and OData EDM Concepts

The binding type of the *service binding* currently supports two scenarios: a UI service or a web API. A UI service is an OData service that enables you to add an SAP Fiori elements UI or other UI clients to the service while also incorporating UI annotations, while a web API is a pure OData service used for unforeseen extensions of the SAP software.

Service Consumption

Now, the OData service is published and can, depending on the binding type, be consumed either by SAP Fiori element UIs, which will render their UI according to the provided UI annotations within the OData service's metadata, or by any kind of OData client, for instance, freestyle OpenUI5 applications that don't use UI annotations and purely rely on the service's data and metadata.

Runtime

Now, let's look at how the ABAP RESTful programming model handles OData client requests during runtime. After you've executed all steps of the previously described development flow, the service is deployed on the SAP Gateway and up and running. Then, the ABAP RESTful programming model's runtime environment takes over. Figure 3.6 shows the ABAP RESTful programming model's runtime and its various components. Incoming OData HTTP requests are first passed through the SAP Gateway OData standard runtime, which will forward the requests to the orchestration framework (in other words, to SADL). SADL will take care of transforming read-only queries into SQL statements as well as passing transactional requests to the business object's behavior implementation. Not only can business objects implemented with the ABAP RESTful programming model be consumed via the OData protocol but also programmatically in ABAP by using the Entity Manipulation Language (EML) syntax. We won't go into details about EML in this book, as the focus of the book is the usage of the ABAP RESTful programming model for creating OData services consumable in SAP Fiori applications, but you can refer to the SAP Help Portal for more details.

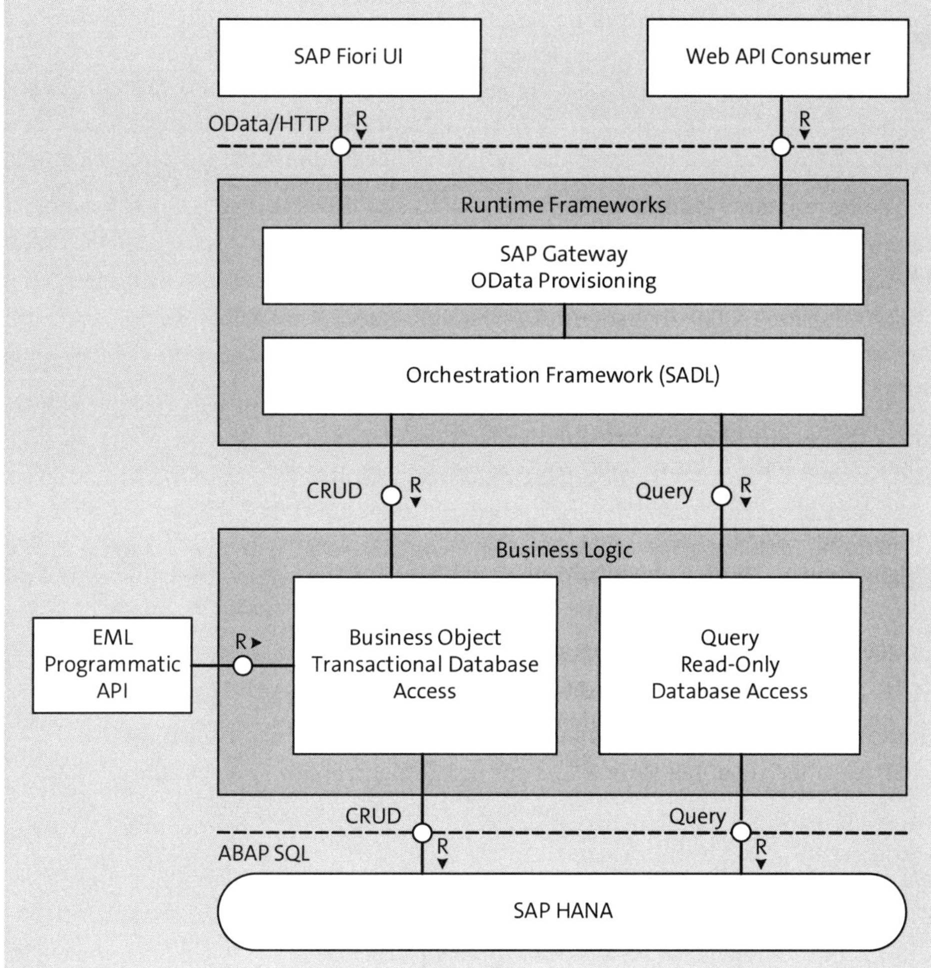

Figure 3.6 Runtime Components of the ABAP RESTful Programming Model

3.4.2 Query

In the ABAP RESTful programming model, *queries* provide read-only access to CDS data models. These non-transactional counterparts to *business objects* are thus based on CDS data models without behavior definition and implementation. Queries serve as the connecting interfaces between OData service requests, originating from SAP Fiori list report applications or analytical reports, and CDS data models. In general, we can distinguish between managed and unmanaged queries, which we'll look at in more detail next.

Managed Queries

The default choice for a query is a managed implementation. In this case, the query framework (SADL) takes care of transforming an incoming OData request to an Open SQL `SELECT` statement (or maybe also native SQL if certain native SAP HANA features like text search are required). The SAP Gateway OData runtime delegates OData requests to the generic SADL query engine, which generates SQL `SELECT` statements on CDS views based on the request parameters (`$select`, `$top`, `$filter`, etc.) and the requested OData entity.

An incoming HTTP OData `GET` request for the standard purchase order basic view entity might look like the code shown in Listing 3.1.

```
GET I_PurchaseOrderEntity?$select=
PurchaseOrder,PurchaseOrderType,PurchasingOrganization,PurchasingGroup,Purchas
eOrderDate&$top=10&$orderby=PurchaseOrderDate asc&$filter=
( PurchaseOrderDate ge datetime'2018-01-
01T00:00:00' and PurchaseOrderDate le datetime'2018-12-31T00:00:00')
```

Listing 3.1 OData GET Request for the I_PurchaseOrderEntity OData Entity

The SADL query framework will then transparently transform this request into an SQL `SELECT` statement on the `I_PurchaseOrder` CDS view, shown in Listing 3.2.

```
SELECT
PurchaseOrder,
PurchaseOrderType,
PurchasingOrganization,
PurchasingGroup,
PurchaseOrderDate
FROM
I_PurchaseOrder
```

```
WHERE
PurchaseOrderDate GE '20180601'
    AND PurchaseOrderDate LE '20180601'
ORDERBY
    PurchaseOrderDate ASCENDING
UP TO 10 ROWS
```

Listing 3.2 Generated SQL SELECT for the OData GET Request

When you compare the OData request and the generated SQL statement, notice how OData queries can easily be pushed down to a relational database. After all, OData already resembles SQL, and all OData parameters can be mapped to a certain part of the SQL `SELECT` statement. This property makes OData the perfect candidate for exposing business entities over HTTP because the easy transformation of HTTP requests to SQL `SELECT` statements promotes the use of SAP HANA's Code-to-Data paradigm and prevents unnecessary data processing on the ABAP server. Table 3.3 shows the mappings between OData parameters and SQL query parts. These capabilities for transforming standard OData request parameters to SQL are generally available and do not have to be explicitly modeled.

OData Parameter	SQL
`$select`	`SELECT`
`$top`	`UP TO n ROWS`
`$orderby`	`ORDERBY`
`$filter`	`WHERE`
`$count`	`COUNT()`

Table 3.3 Mapping between OData Parameters and Corresponding Parts of an SQL SELECT Statement

Other capabilities like search, aggregation, value help, or text provisioning need to be explicitly modeled in the CDS views using annotations and/or association relationships.

Unmanaged Queries

If data must be exposed as an OData service that can't be read directly from a CDS view and its underlying database table, you have the option of defining and implementing what's called an unmanaged query. Figure 3.7 shows the unmanaged query runtime (on the right) in contrast to the managed query runtime (on the left). Instead of pushing down the data selection via a CDS view to the database table, an unmanaged query relies on a custom CDS entity that delegates the data selection to an ABAP query implementation class. The ABAP query implementation class needs to implement the IF_A4C_RAP_QUERY_PROVIDER interface and implement whatever data selection is required, for instance, call an external OData service or some legacy ABAP code, which cannot be transformed into a CDS data model.

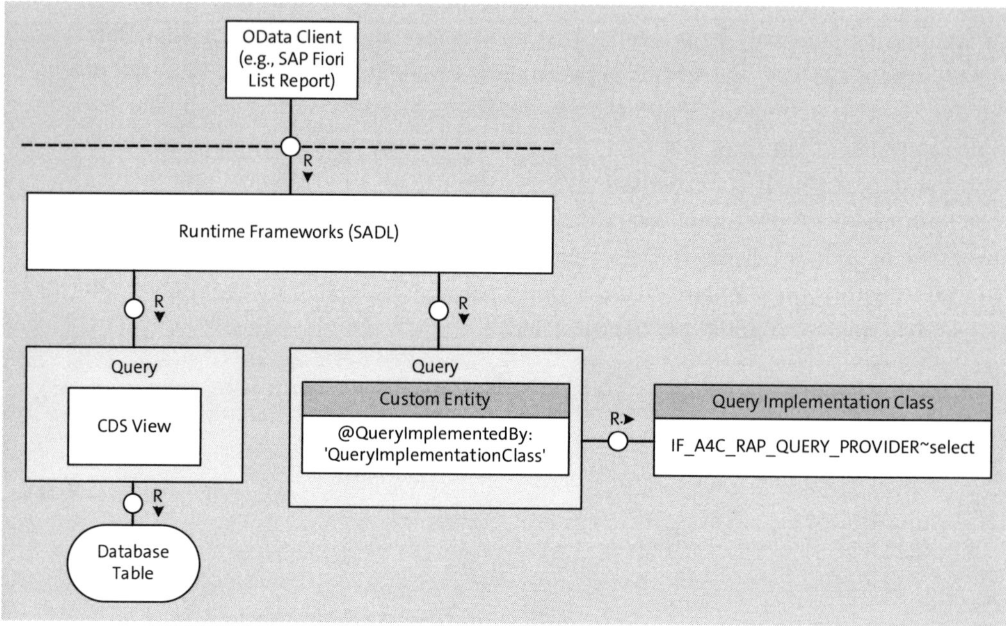

Figure 3.7 Managed and Unmanaged Query Runtime

Listing 3.3 shows the syntax for defining a CDS custom entity. The syntax must provide a typed element list as the type cannot be inferred from an underlying CDS entity or database table. Notice that, because of the ROOT keyword and the hierarchy associations (COMPOSITION, ASSOCIATION TO PARENT), the CDS entity can also be used within a business object. However, keep in mind, since no SQL artifact is generated for custom entities, they cannot be used like normal CDS views in SQL joins or SELECT statements. Additionally, all capabilities that are provided by the managed runtime out of the box need to be explicitly programmed here by the developer, e.g., $select, $filter, etc.

```
@EndUserText.label: 'EndUserText'
@QueryImplementedBy: 'QueryImplementationClass'

define [root] custom entity CustomEntityName

     [ with parameters
          ParamName : dtype [, ...]    ]

{
        [@element_annot]
   [key] ElemName : dtype;
         ElemName : dtype;
...
   [ _Assoc : association [cardinality] to TargetEntity on CondExp [
with default filter CondExp ]   ];

   [  _Comp : composition [cardinality] of TargetEntity   ];

   [  [@element_annot]
      _ParentAssoc : association to parent on CondExp   ];
}
```

Listing 3.3 Syntax for Defining a CDS Custom Entity

3.4.3 Business Objects

Business objects are the transactional counterparts of queries. Like queries, business objects are based on an underlying CDS data model but enhance the model with a hierarchical tree structure having a single root node with child nodes. Additionally, a behavior definition defines which actions the business object supports, and a behavior pool implements these specific operations in the form of one or several global ABAP classes having local handler classes for modifying and saving business objects.

Managed and Unmanaged Business Objects

The ABAP RESTful programming model considers several scenarios for transactional application development, but at the moment, primarily the unmanaged scenario is supported and also of interest for on-premise customers that already have existing data models and APIs for their applications. In an unmanaged scenario, you can make use of your existing application APIs, for instance, ABAP classes and/or function modules that write data to internal buffer tables or a save action that persists this buffered data to the database. This scenario is shown in Figure 3.8.

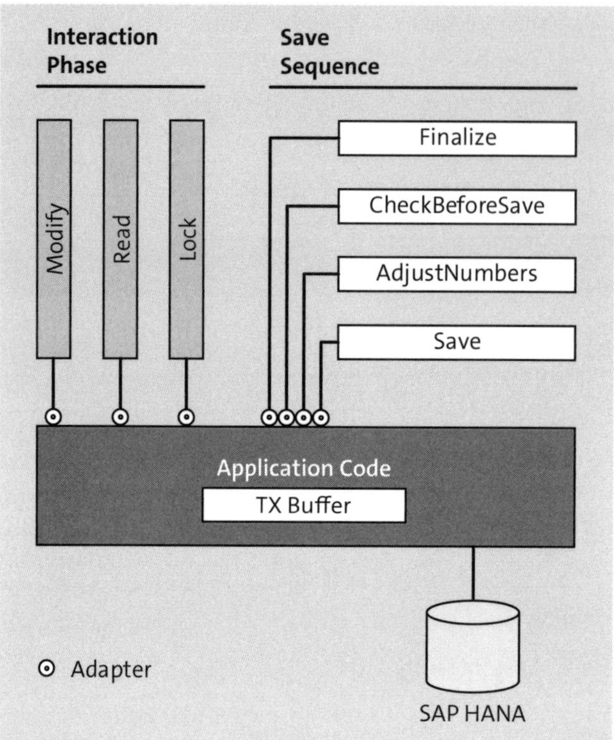

Figure 3.8 ABAP RESTful Programming Model: Unmanaged Application Scenario

In the interaction phase, data is written to transactional buffers (internal ABAP tables), and in the save sequence, the data is persisted on the database. Before the actual save method is called, the `finalize`, `check_before_save`, and `adjust_numbers` methods of the business object are called to finalize, validate and implement late numbering for business objects, if required. When using the late numbering feature, entities only get a temporary key on creation until the `adjust_numbers` method is called within the save sequence. The `adjust_numbers` method must then supply the actual keys to be persisted on the database.In a managed scenario, the technical implementation, for instance CRUD operations and the save operation, are taken over by the ABAP RESTful programming model's business object infrastructure. Developers can add business logic using determinations, validations, and actions (which should sound quite familiar if you've developed applications with BOPF). In the third unmanaged scenario, which is a hybrid scenario based on the previous two scenarios, the modifying operations are managed by the runtime because they were in the past too tightly coupled to old Web Dynpro UI technology (PAI/PBO) and cannot be reused. However, the available update-task function modules can be reused, in this case, in the save sequence to persist the data on the database. In the following sections, we'll focus on the unmanaged scenario, which is the most applicable for most applications and currently the only scenario available in SAP S/4HANA 1909.

Business Objects

As discussed earlier, creating a transactional business object is a two-step process. First, you'll define the structure of the business object and then specify and implement its behavior in ABAP. Let's say you want to expose your purchase document and purchase document item CDS views as a transactional business object. You must define the purchase document as the root node of the business object and the item as its child. The root node is of special importance as it serves as the representation of the business object that is indicated with the ROOT keyword. In our example, to define the purchase document CDS view as the root node of the business object, you must add the ROOT keyword to its view definition. To make the item view its child node, you must add the special COMPOSITION association to the item view inside the purchase document root view, as shown in Listing 3.4, and the ASSOCIATION TO PARENT, as shown in Listing 3.5, association in the item view pointing back to the purchase document root view.

```
@AbapCatalog.sqlViewName: 'CDS_DB_VIEW'
@[view_annotation_1]
...
@[view_annotation_n>]

DEFINE ROOT VIEW RootEntity
  [parameter_list]
  AS SELECT FROM data_source [AS alias]
  COMPOSITION [min..max] OF ChildEntity AS _childEntity ON condition_exp
  [additional_composition_list]
  [association_list]
{
   [element_list]
}
```

Listing 3.4 Syntax for Defining a Root Entity of a Business Object

```
@AbapCatalog.sqlViewName: 'CDS_DB_VIEW'
[@view_annotation_1]
...
[@view_annotation_n>]

DEFINE VIEW ChildEntity
   [parameter_list]
   AS SELECT FROM data_source [AS alias]
   ASSOCIATION TO PARENT ParentEntity AS _parentEntity ON condition_exp
   [additional_association_list]
{
  [element_list]
}
```

Listing 3.5 Syntax for Defining a Child Entity of a Business Object

Behavior Definition

Which transactions and business logic a business object supports is defined in a single behavior definition file. The behavior definition includes a behavior characteristic and a set of operations for each CDS entity of the business object's composition tree. The behavior definition is a new transportable ABAP repository object and is defined using a Behavior Definition Language (BDL), which is similar to the CDS DDL. Its syntax is shown in Listing 3.6. The behavior definition starts with the definition of the ABAP RESTful programming model scenario. In our case, we'll focus on the unmanaged scenario, which is the most common scenario. Then, you must define the behavior of each transactional CDS entity within your business object using the define behavior for CDSEntity...{...} statement (CDSEntity needs to be replaced with the actual CDS view name here). Next, you must provide the name of a global ABAP class that will actually implement the specified behavior of your business object node and define additional capabilities, like the field to be used as ETag (usually the last changed timestamp), locking, or whether late numbering should be active.

The ETag field enables optimistic concurrency control with the stateless HTTP protocol that OData is based on. On each request, the server sends the ETag field value inside the HTTP header of the OData response, and if a client wants to write data, first the ETag value of the requested resource is checked for changes (to determine if the current value matches the previously received value). If so, the client is not allowed to update the data, which would overwrite changes done by another client in the meantime. This issue is usually indicated by a HTTP 412 Precondition Failed Header response code. The lock master property indicates that the business object root node supports direct locking whereas lock dependent indicates that this business object node's lock status depends on its root or parent entity's lock status. When late numbering is activated, newly created instances get a temporary key $00000001, which must be transformed to a final key in the save sequence (in the adjust_numbers method) of the business object before the instance is persisted on the database.

Between the curly braces, you can then define a static field control, specify whether a field is read-only or mandatory, specify the operations supported by the business object node and additional actions. The internal keyword indicates that the operation should not be exported for external consumers. All associations (compositions) that form the business object's structure must also be declared in the behavior definition as associations. With the optional {create;} keyword entities of the associated entity can be created via the current parent entity.

```
/* Header of behavior definition */
implementation {unmanaged | managed | abstract};

/* Definition of entity behavior */
define behavior for CDSEntity [alias AliasName]
/* Entity properties */
[implementation in class ClASS_NAME unique]
[late numbering]
[etag (field)]
//Only supported for root entities
[lock {master | dependent (PropertyDependent = PropertyMaster)}] {
 /* Static field control */
 [field (read only | mandatory) field1[, field2, ..., fieldn];]

 /* Standard operations */
 [internal] create;
 [internal] update;
 [internal] delete;

 /* Actions */
 [static] action ActionName
                [parameter {InputParameterEntity | $self)}]
                [result [cardinality] {OutputParameterEntity | $self}];
```

```
/* Associations */
 association AssociationName [abbreviation AbbreviationName] {[create;]}
}
```

Listing 3.6 Syntax for Defining Transactional Behavior for a CDS Entity

> **Note**
>
> A behavior definition usually has the same name as the root CDS view of the business object structure but with the suffix _U for unmanaged.

Behavior Implementation

As you've seen, inside the behavior definition, the behavior implementation class is referenced using the `implementation in class ClASS_NAME unique` statement. The global ABAP class referenced in this case is just an empty container and is basically empty while the actual behavior logic is implemented in several local classes. These global ABAP classes referenced in the behavior definition are called behavior pools. Several behavior pools can exist for one behavior definition. You can create a behavior pool for each business object node, which is a best practice. Listing 3.7 shows the syntax of a global ABAP behavior pool class. Note that the behavior definition is referenced with the `FOR BEHAVIOR OF BehaviorDefinition` addition of the global class's definition.

```
CLASS class_name DEFINITION PUBLIC
ABSTRACT
FINAL
FOR BEHAVIOR OF BehaviorDefinition.
PUBLIC SECTION.
PROTECTED SECTION.
PRIVATE SECTION.
ENDCLASS.
CLASS class_name IMPLEMENTATION.
ENDCLASS.
```

Listing 3.7 Syntax of Global Behavior Pool ABAP Class

As mentioned earlier, the global behavior pool class is empty, and the actual behavior implementation takes place in local classes. Under the **Local Types** tab of Eclipse, two so-called handler classes must be implemented: one for the interaction phase (modifying operations) and one for the save sequence.For the interaction phase, the local class must be a subclass of `cl_abap_behavior_handler`,and for the save sequence of `cl_abap_behavior_saver`, the local class must override all of its methods (`finalize`, `check_before_save`, `adjust_numbers`, `save`). Only the implementation of the `save` method is mandatory. The implementation of all other methods is optional. However, the `finalize` and `check_before_save` methods can break the save sequence if an illegal state is detected in the business object, e.g., an invalid value. The interaction phase and save sequence handler classes reflect the two parts of the business object runtime, as shown in Figure 3.9. During the interaction phase, data is stored in a transactional buffer (one or more internal tables); in the save sequence, the data is persisted to the database. This separation also reflects the legacy of older programming models for SAP applications, for instance, Web Dynpro. Data was kept in internal buffer tables until a save was triggered, and then the data was persisted. If your legacy applications followed this paradigm, then the ABAP RESTful programming model is just another layer of abstraction on top of your existing APIs.

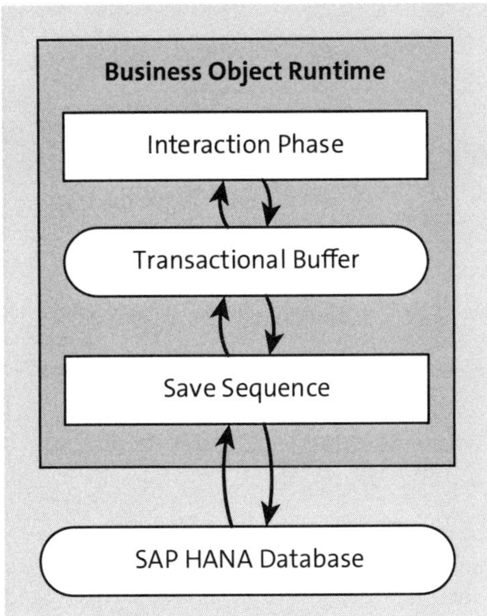

Figure 3.9 Parts of the Business Object Runtime: Interaction Phase and Save Sequence

Listing 3.8 shows the definition of a local handler class. This code contains methods for the modifying operations (CRUD operations and additional actions); a method for handling locking; and a read method for reading entities from the transactional buffers or, if not present in the buffers, from the database via the corresponding CDS view. A huge difference with the ABAP RESTful programming model compared to BOPF and other ABAP frameworks like the Service Provider Infrastructure (SPI) is that the parameters of the behavior implementation's methods are typed with the current CDS entity. The other frameworks rely on generic parameters that the developer had to type "cast" explicitly if required. The typed parameters in the ABAP RESTful programming model are a big advantage over other frameworks and make programming in the ABAP RESTful programming model a lot more convenient and safe.

```
CLASS lcl_handler DEFINITION INHERITING FROM cl_abap_behavior_
handler ABSTRACT FINAL.
  PRIVATE SECTION.
   METHODS <method_name> FOR MODIFY
     IMPORTING
       create_import_parameter    FOR CREATE entity
       update_import_parameter    FOR UPDATE entity
       delete_import_parameter    FOR DELETE entity
       action_import_parameter    FOR ACTION entity~action_name
                                      [RESULT action_export_parameter].

   METHODS <method_name> FOR LOCK IMPORTING lock_import_
parameter FOR LOCK entity.

   METHODS <method_name> FOR READ IMPORTING read_import_parameter
                                  FOR READ entity [RESULT read_export_parameter].

ENDCLASS.
```

Listing 3.8 Definition of the Local Handler Class

Listing 3.9 shows the definition of a local saver class. The `finalize` and `check_before_save` methods are called first and can break the save sequence by setting their `FAILED` parameter. The `adjust_numbers` method is called if late numbering has been activated in the behavior definition. Finally, the actual save of the entity occurs in the save method.

```
CLASS lsc_saver DEFINITION INHERITING FROM cl_abap_behavior_saver
  ABSTRACT FINAL.
```

```
  PROTECTED SECTION.

    METHODS finalize          REDEFINITION.
    METHODS check_before_save REDEFINITION.
    METHODS adjust_numbers    REDEFINITION.
    METHODS save              REDEFINITION.

ENDCLASS.
```

Listing 3.9 Definition of the Local Saver Class

Note

The name of the behavior pool (global ABAP class) usually ends with the suffix _U for unmanaged. The local handler class (lhc) usually has the `lhc_` prefix, while the local saver class (lsc) usually has the `lsc_` prefix.

Figure 3.10 shows the relationships between the CDS business object entities and the behavior definition and implementation.

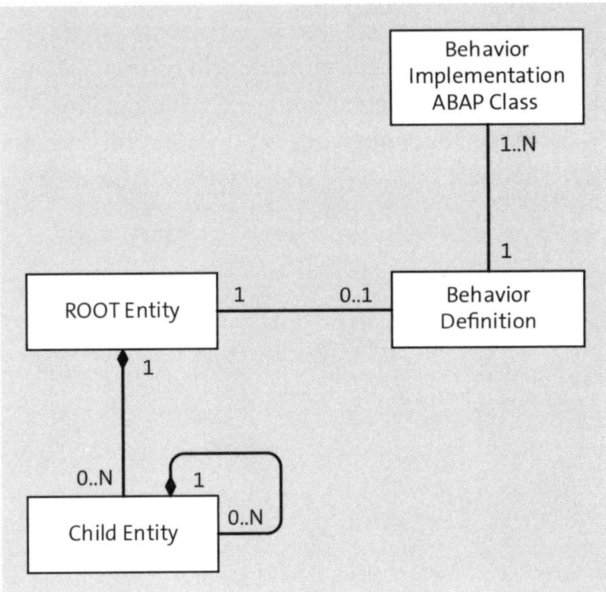

Figure 3.10 Relationship between the CDS Business Object Entities and the Behavior Definition and Implementation

Only one root business object entity can exist, but with several child entities, which in turn can also have their own child entities. For the whole business object or CDS root entity, only one behavior definition can exist (or none). The behavior definition implementation can be split into several behavior implementation classes (one for each business object node), but the whole implementation can also be put into a single class or behavior pool.

3.4.4 Business Service

So far, all the artifacts we've looked at reside purely in the ABAP stack and cannot be consumed by any SAP Fiori application. To make the business object model and its associated behavior consumable by SAP Fiori applications (or any other external client), it must be exposed as an OData service, which is where the new service definition and service binding objects come into play.

Service Definition

A service definition is a new transportable ABAP repository object type (`R3TR SRVD <SERVICE_DEFINITION_NAME>`), and just like the behavior definition, its syntax resembles the syntax of the CDS DDL, as shown in Listing 3.10. The content of a service definition is basically a list of CDS entities that will be exposed with an OData service. The entities listed inside the curly braces of the service definition will be transparently mapped to OData entities by the ABAP RESTful programming model design time. The service definition is not yet protocol specific, which means the definition does not require a certain OData version or protocol.

```
@EndUserText.label: 'text'
@<Annotation_1>
...
@<Annotation_n>

DEFINE SERVICE service_definition_name
{
EXPOSE cds_entity_1 [AS alias_1];
EXPOSE cds_entity_2 [AS alias_2];
EXPOSE ...
EXPOSE cds_entity_m [AS alias_m];
}
```

Listing 3.10 Syntax of a Service Definition

Note

A service definition is usually named according to the root node of the business object with the suffix _U for unmanaged.

Service Binding

The service binding then binds the previously defined service definition to a specific client communication protocol and deploys the OData service on the SAP Gateway. Like the service definition, a service binding is a new transportable ABAP repository object: R3TR SRVB <SERVICE_BINDING_NAME>. The benefit of separating service definition and service binding is so that the service definition can be reused and bound to several different service bindings, for example, different client-communication protocols. For instance, you could have a single service definition and service bindings for OData version 2, another for OData version 4, and another for SAP Fiori elements UIs without actually having to change the underlying implementation. Thus, the most important parameter of the service binding is the binding type. Currently two main groups are supported, UI service or web API. Additionally, the OData version can be configured.

Note

A service binding is usually named according to the root node of the business object with the suffix _U for unmanaged and an additional suffix for the OData version, e.g., _V2.

Figure 3.11 shows the relationship between the CDS data model, the service definition, and the service binding. Several service definitions can exist for a CDS data model consisting of at least one CDS view. In other words, you can create many different services, each exposing different parts (entities) of the same CDS data model.

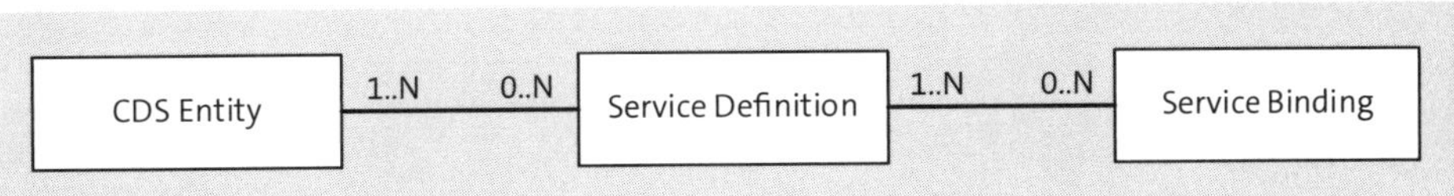

Figure 3.11 Relationship between CDS Data Model, Service Definition, and Service Binding

Service definitions can in turn also be exposed using different client communication protocols through different service binding. A service binding requires at least one service definition. As mentioned earlier, you could bind the same service definition to OData version 2, to OData version 4, and to a UI service.

3.4.5 Service Consumption

As mentioned in the previous section, an OData service can be either exposed as a UI service that can be consumed by an SAP Fiori application or a web API that can be consumed by any kind of OData client.

SAP Fiori UI

If an OData service is exposed as an SAP Fiori UI, additional UI annotations added to the underlying CDS data model will be exposed as OData UI annotations within the metadata of the service. These UI annotations will in turn be picked up by SAP Fiori elements applications, which will then configure their UI according to the UI annotations. The ABAP RESTful programming model also offers a preview of the SAP Fiori elements UI. However, this process does not replace actual UI development in the SAP Web IDE; it just mocks up the corresponding SAP Fiori elements UI for quick testing. You must still put the UI project under proper version control in Git and separately deploy it to the system.

Web API

If the consumer of the OData service is not an SAP Fiori elements application that will make use of UI annotations, the service should be exposed as a web API without any UI specific annotations in its service metadata file. The service is then generically consumable, for instance, by SAP or OpenUI5 freestyle applications or any other OData (HTTP) client. Figure 3.12 shows the two options for service consumption.

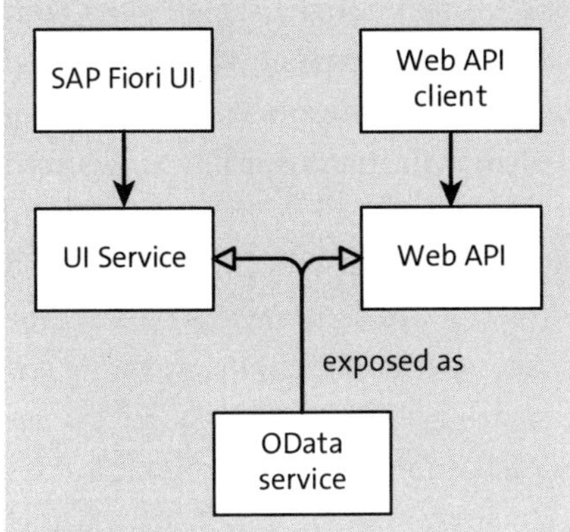

Figure 3.12 UI Service and Web API Service Binding Types and Their Consumers

3.5 Summary

In this chapter, we provided an overview of the ABAP RESTful programming model and its associated technologies. We started with CDS, which are at the center of all application development for SAP S/4HANA. CDS are the foundation for all application types and can be configured for different application types using domain-specific UIs, analytics, or search annotations. To turn a CDS data model into a transactional business object, new types of CDS associations are required to build a compositional hierarchy. Next, we looked at SAP Gateway and OData as technologies enabling easy network-based access to business data stored in SAP NetWeaver backend systems. Then, we turned to the ABAP RESTful programming model and explored how it supports the provision of model-based read and transactional access to CDS entities via OData. The ABAP RESTful programming model enhances the CDS data model with new, transportable ABAP repository objects for behavior modeling (behavior definition and implementation) and service provisioning (service definition and service binding), while also being a completely Eclipse-based E2E development experience. The ABAP RESTful programming model is currently the state-of-the-art programming model for developing applications for the SAP S/4HANA platform.

PART II
Developing Applications for SAP S/4HANA

Chapter 4

Developing an SAP Fiori Elements List Report and Object Page

In the previous chapter, you learned about the new ABAP RESTful programming model. Now, in this chapter, you'll learn to create an unmanaged transactional app based on SAP Fiori elements templates utilizing the ABAP RESTful programming model. We'll illustrate the end-to-end (E2E) development process in detail with step-by-step instructions. You'll create database tables and core data services (CDS) views, add an unmanaged implementation for enabling transactional processing in a business object, add user interface (UI) elements, and create a service definition and a service binding.

In this chapter, we'll use the business scenario and design developed in Chapter 2, Section 2.4.3, to create an application for managing purchase documents. As a reminder, the application design consisted of a list report displaying purchase documents in a table and an object page providing detailed information for a purchase document, including its individual purchase document items, which can be granted using a quick action.

Using this business scenario, this chapter will provide you with an E2E development guide for developing list report and object page applications based using the new ABAP RESTful programming model for SAP Fiori. In the first edition of this book, we covered creating an SAP Fiori elements application using Business Object Processing Framework (BOPF) concepts for transactional actions and created an OData service to consume the data from the backend using the SAP Gateway client. These two parts are the major difference when it comes to developing apps using the ABAP RESTful programming model. With the ABAP RESTful programming model, the BOPF concept is completely replaced, and instead of a normal OData Service generation using SAP Gateway, you'll create a service definition and a service binding in this chapter.

For creating our purchase document application, we'll first create a set of basic, composite, and consumption CDS views along with the necessary UI annotations, and then we'll take advantage of the service definition and service binding to register the OData service and expose the CDS view. Then, we'll add the transactional behavior via the behavior definition. (Refer to Chapter 3 for more about behavior definitions.)

Figure 4.1 shows the first part of our example app, where we'll create all the interface views and composite views. To these composite views, we'll later link our behavior definitions to add transactional operations like create, read, update, and delete (CRUD) and Quick Actions, and then we'll expose them as an OData service using the service definition and service binding feature.

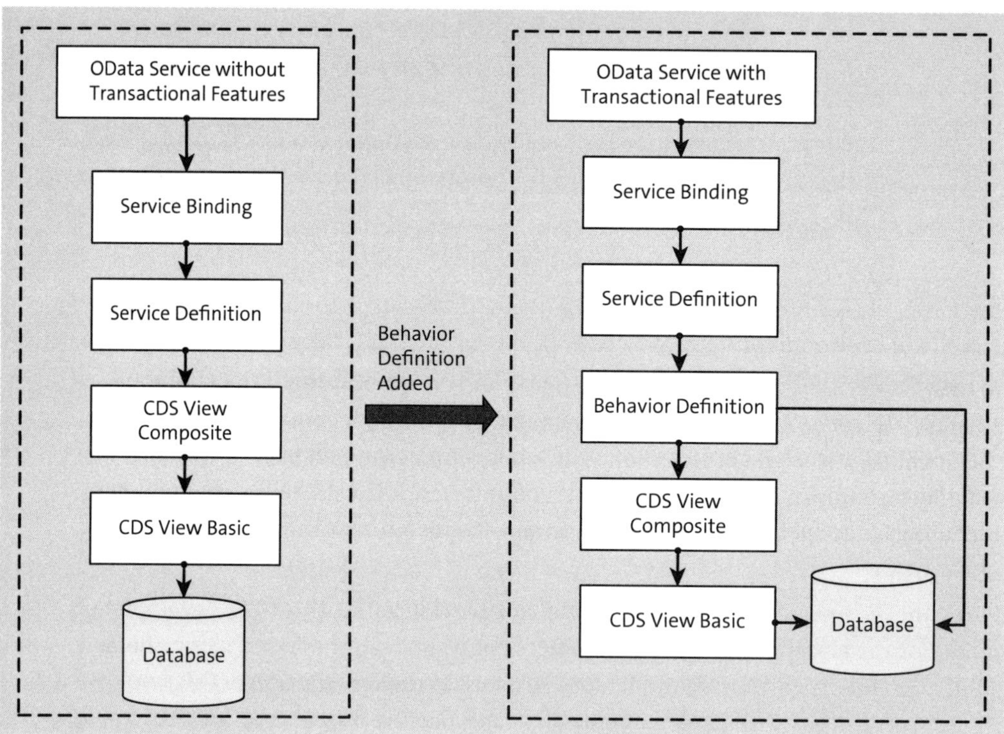

Figure 4.1 Building Basic Views and Then Adding Behavior Definitions to Enable Transactional Actions

In the second part, we'll create a projection view (the `VDM type` is `Consumption`) on top of the composite view with the necessary transactional capabilities added to them via the behavior definition. This practice will allow us to reuse our business objects (the views which to we'll enable CRUD functionalities using behavior definitions) across multiple applications. We'll also need to create a projection behavior definition so that we can reuse the underlying behavior definition linked to our business objects.

Figure 4.2 shows the how the projection views and projection behavior definitions come into picture and make the underlying business objects and behavior definitions reusable.

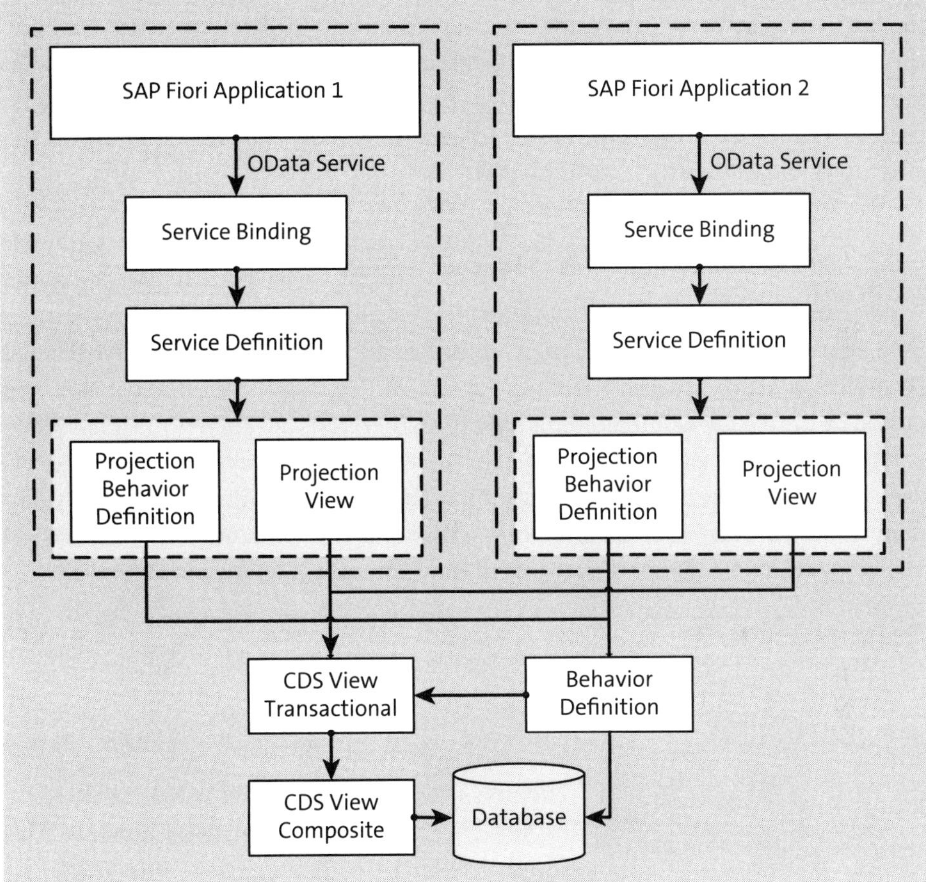

Figure 4.2 Projection CDS Views and Projection Behavior Definitions Enabling Reusability of the Business Objects and Behavior Definition

Now, let's begin with creating the necessary basic views for our example.

4.1 Core Data Services Views

In this section, you'll learn how to create a layered CDS data model according to the SAP S/4HANA Virtual Data Model (VDM) modeling guidelines, including unit tests for calculated field values using ABAP Unit and the CDS Test Double Framework. Before you can start developing, you first must install the ABAP development tools because Eclipse is the standard integrated development environment (IDE) for developing CDS views and modern ABAP code. You'll then start developing the app from the bottom up by first introducing the data model and its database tables. Based on this foundation, you'll create several layers of CDS views beginning with the basic interface layer as a simple projection layer on top of the database tables. Using the basic interface view layer as the base, you'll incrementally add more application-specific views and calculations, including tests.

4.1.1 ABAP Development Tools in Eclipse

For developing state-of-the-art ABAP applications based on the ABAP programming model for SAP Fiori, you can no longer use the classic ABAP Development Workbench (Transaction SE80) because the development of CDS-based data models isn't supported by the old development tools anymore. Therefore, developers must download and install a recent version of Eclipse, for instance, Eclipse Oxygen (the IDE for Java developers) from the Eclipse Foundation's website, and also install the ABAP development tools frontend as an Eclipse plug-in. To set up the environment, open Eclipse and, under the **Help** menu, choose **Install New Software**, as shown in Figure 4.3.

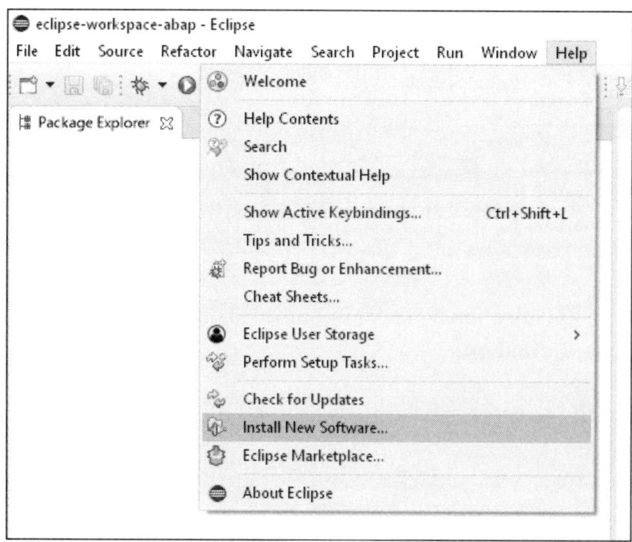

Figure 4.3 Starting the ABAP Development Tools Installation Procedure in Eclipse

The Eclipse installation dialog will open. Next, you must add the ABAP development tools update site as a new repository destination, as shown in Figure 4.4. The corresponding installation URL for the ABAP development tools for the current Eclipse version is available on the SAP Development Tools website at *http://s-prs.co/498814*.

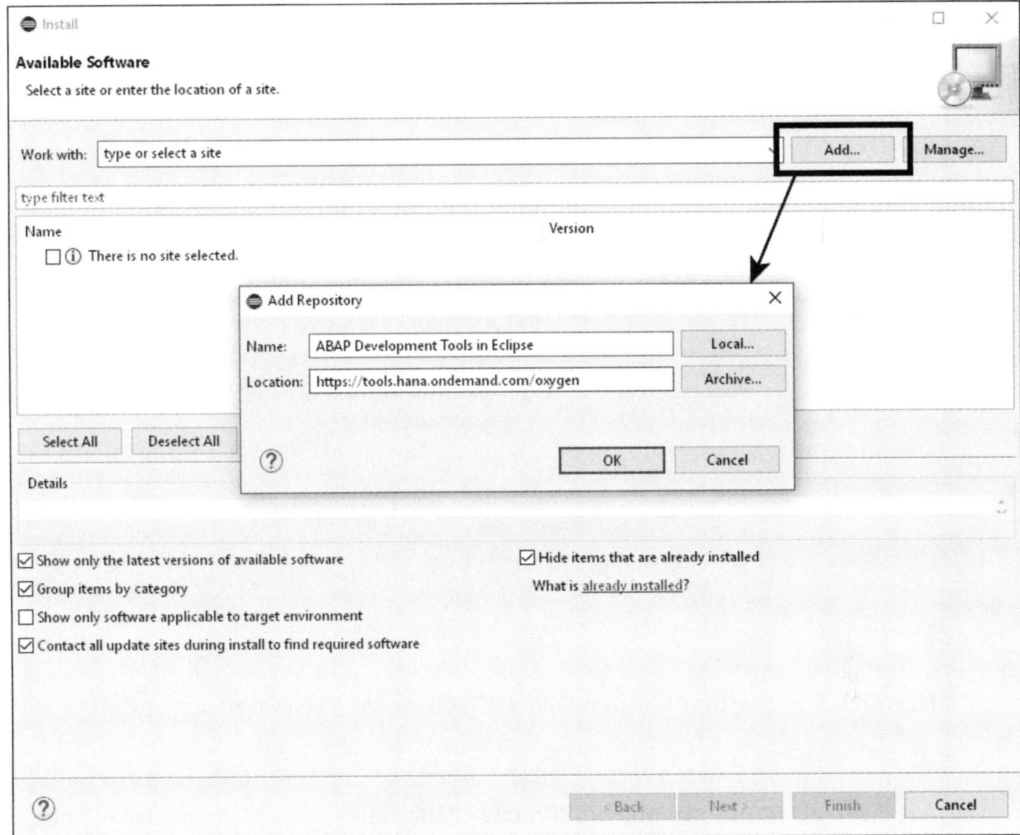

Figure 4.4 Adding the ABAP Development Tools in Eclipse Repository

To develop applications using the ABAP RESTful programming model for SAP Fiori, only the ABAP development tools for SAP NetWeaver are required, so only select this software package, as shown in Figure 4.5. Click **Next**, accept the terms of the license agreement, and click **Finish**. After the installation is complete, Eclipse will require a restart.

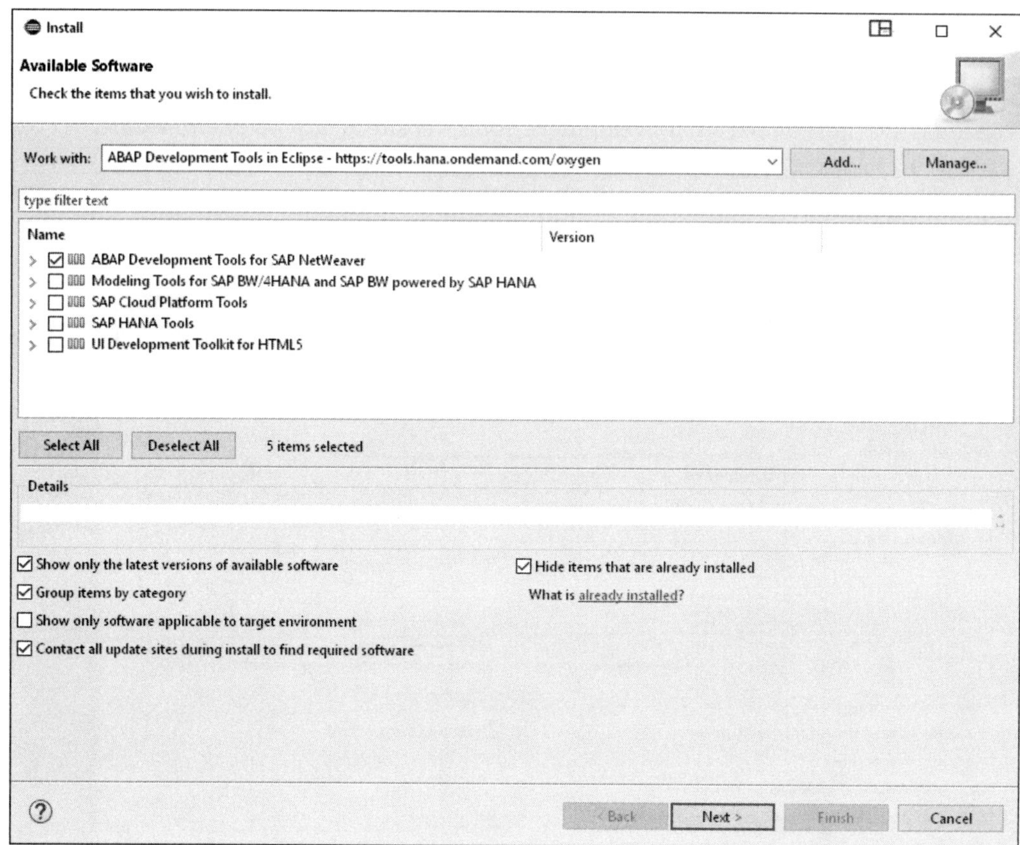

Figure 4.5 Selecting the ABAP Development Tools for SAP NetWeaver

To connect to an SAP NetWeaver ABAP backend server, first open the now available ABAP perspective by clicking on **Window • Perspective • Open Perspective • Other... • ABAP**. From this perspective, you'll create an ABAP project that will establish the connection to the backend server. Figure 4.6 shows how the ABAP project creation process can be started by clicking on **File • New • ABAP Project** in the Eclipse menu bar. A new project can be created in one of the following ways:

- From a predefined SAP Logon system connection
- By defining a manual system connection
- By duplicating an existing system connection

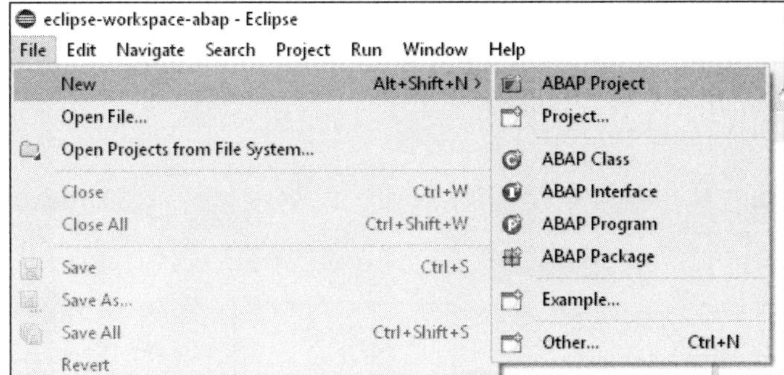

Figure 4.6 Creating an ABAP Project from the ABAP Perspective in Eclipse

> **Note**
>
> To enable your ABAP backend for using the ABAP development tools in Eclipse, see the "Configuring ABAP Back-end for ABAP Development Tools" guide provided by SAP at *http://s-prs.co/498815*.

4.1.2 Introduction to the Data Model

The first step to developing any app is the creation of a data model, followed by the creation of actual database tables for persisting transactional or master data. In the following sections, therefore, we'll introduce you to the underlying data model for the app and create the necessary database tables.

Entity Relationship Model

A conceptual data model of the app in the form of an Entity Relationship Model (ERM) is shown in Figure 4.7. This data model consists of a purchase document entity type and a purchase document item entity type. Purchase documents have a 0 to *n* relationship to items, and items have a 1 to 1 relationship to documents, which constitutes a parent-child relationship (purchase documents as the parent nodes and purchase document items as the child nodes).

The purchase document entity has several attributes, including the overall document status and priority of the purchase, as well as the responsible purchasing organization. The primary key of a purchase document is based on a single purchase document ID. The purchase document item entity represents the actual items of the purchase, including price and quantity. The primary key of a purchase document item entity consists of an item ID and the purchase document ID, which references the purchase document ID in the purchase document entity via a foreign key relationship.

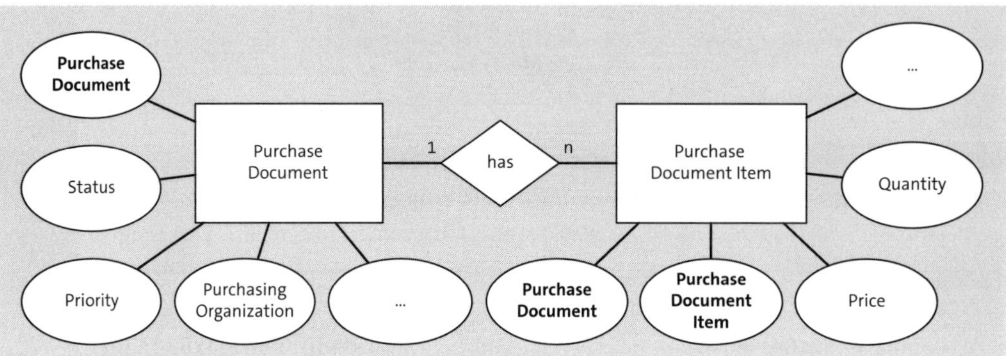

Figure 4.7 Conceptual Data Model of the Application Depicted in the Form of an ERM

Database Tables

The foundation of any application in SAP S/4HANA is made up of the database tables in which data is persisted in the SAP HANA database. New database tables can be created in Eclipse using a source code editor available since SAP NetWeaver Application Server for ABAP 7.52 SP 00 (SAP NetWeaver AS for ABAP). To persist the described purchase document and purchase document item entities and their values on the database, you'll need to create two separate database tables.

The following steps must be executed to create a transparent table in the ABAP Dictionary:

1. Open the ABAP perspective in the ABAP development tools in Eclipse.
2. In the ABAP project, select the package node in which you want to create the table via the **Project Explorer** view.
3. Open the context menu by right-clicking on the package and selecting **New • Other ABAP Repository Object • Dictionary • Database Table**.
4. The database table creation wizard will open. You must enter a **Name** and **Description**, as shown in Figure 4.8. In our case, we'll create a table for purchase documents called `ZPURCHDOCUMENT` and a table for purchase document items called `ZPURCHDOCITEM`.
5. Finally, the database table source code editor opens, where you can add fields to the table and configure its properties.

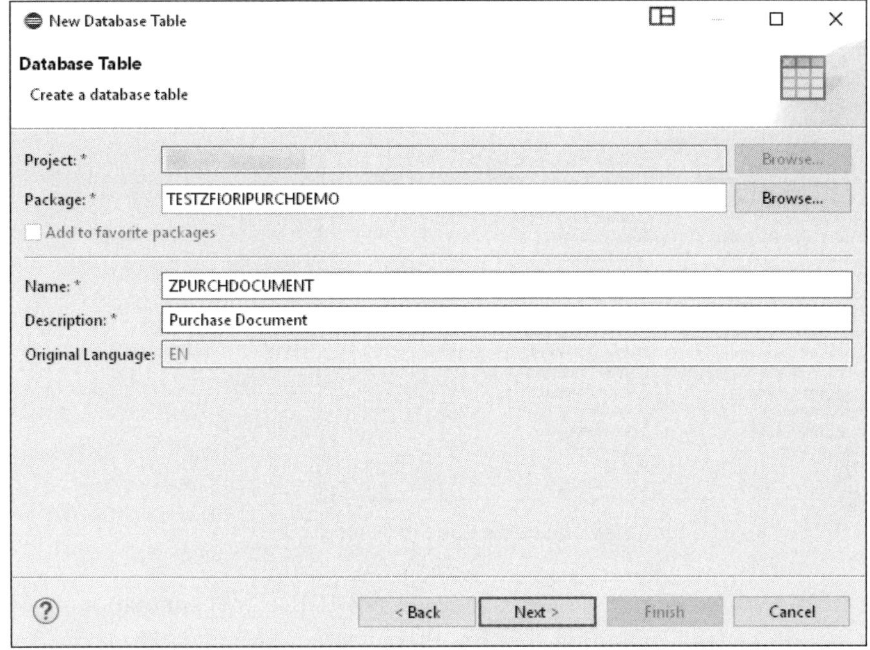

Figure 4.8 Database Table Creation Wizard

The programming language of the source code editor closely resembles the data definition language (DDL) of CDS. Metadata defined using annotations and technical properties, such as fields, is defined in an SQL-like syntax, as shown in Listing 4.1. On save or activation, the actual persistence is updated. The source code displayed in the editor isn't a new transportable development object. All information is stored and retrieved from the classic ABAP Dictionary. The source code definition of the database table for persisting purchase documents is shown in Figure 4.9 and Listing 4.1.

Using the editor based on source code in Eclipse, you can define technical as well as semantic attributes of the table with the help of annotations. For instance, with the `@EndUserText.label` annotation, you can provide meaningful and translatable labels and descriptions for objects and fields. For fields, this annotation will only be considered if the field has no data element assigned; otherwise, the field label is taken from the data element. For simplicity, we've only created a data element for the `purchasedocument` field (`zpurchasedocumentdtel`) since this data element is required for later referencing the field via a foreign key annotation in the purchase document items table. The other fields are typed using built-in ABAP types, for instance, `abap.char(4)`.

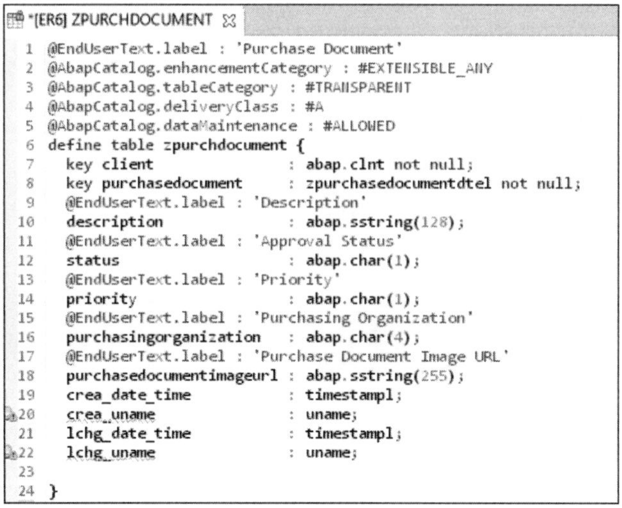

*[ER6] ZPURCHDOCUMENT

```
@EndUserText.label : 'Purchase Document'
@AbapCatalog.enhancementCategory : #EXTENSIBLE_ANY
@AbapCatalog.tableCategory : #TRANSPARENT
@AbapCatalog.deliveryClass : #A
@AbapCatalog.dataMaintenance : #ALLOWED
define table zpurchdocument {
  key client                 : abap.clnt not null;
  key purchasedocument       : zpurchasedocumentdtel not null;
  @EndUserText.label : 'Description'
  description                : abap.sstring(128);
  @EndUserText.label : 'Approval Status'
  status                     : abap.char(1);
  @EndUserText.label : 'Priority'
  priority                   : abap.char(1);
  @EndUserText.label : 'Purchasing Organization'
  purchasingorganization     : abap.char(4);
  @EndUserText.label : 'Purchase Document Image URL'
  purchasedocumentimageurl   : abap.sstring(255);
  crea_date_time             : timestampl;
  crea_uname                 : uname;
  lchg_date_time             : timestampl;
  lchg_uname                 : uname;

}
```

Figure 4.9 The Table Editor Based on Source Code in Eclipse

The technical `@AbapCatalog.enhancementCategory: #EXTENSIBLE_ANY` annotation in the header part of the table definition specifies that all structure and database components and their enhancements may contain components whose data type can be of any category. The `#TRANSPARENT` table category is the default category for database tables, and on activation, both a database table on the database and an identical variant in the classic ABAP Dictionary will be created. Delivery class `#A` indicates that the table is an application table holding either transactional or master data and is populated by application programs. The semantic data maintenance `#ALLOWED` annotation makes the table editable using the data browser in Transaction SE16.

```
@EndUserText.label : 'Purchase Document'
@AbapCatalog.enhancementCategory : #EXTENSIBLE_ANY
@AbapCatalog.tableCategory : #TRANSPARENT
@AbapCatalog.deliveryClass : #A
@AbapCatalog.dataMaintenance : #ALLOWED
define table zpurchdocument {
  key client                 : abap.clnt not null;
  key purchasedocument       : zpurchasedocumentdtel not null;
  @EndUserText.label : 'Description'
  description                : abap.sstring(128);
  @EndUserText.label : 'Approval Status'
  status                     : abap.char(1);
```

```
  @EndUserText.label : 'Priority'
  priority                  : abap.char(1);
  @EndUserText.label : 'Purchasing Organization'
  purchasingorganization    : abap.char(4);
  @EndUserText.label : 'Purchase Document Image URL'
  purchasedocumentimageurl : abap.sstring(255);
  crea_date_time            : timestampl;
  crea_uname                : uname;
  lchg_date_time            : timestampl;
  lchg_uname                : uname;

}
```

Listing 4.1 Database Table Definition for Purchase Documents

The database table definition for purchase document items is shown in Listing 4.2. In contrast to the purchase documents table, the database table definition has a compound primary key consisting of the `purchasedocumentitem` ID and the `purchasedocument` ID. Purchase document items and purchase documents tables are connected via a foreign key relationship on the `purchasedocument` ID field. The table contains fields for the price of an item and the quantity to purchase as well as fields for the corresponding currency and unit of measure. Those fields are connected using semantic annotations: `@Semantics.amount.currencyCode` for monetary values and `@Semantics.quantity.unitOfMeasure` for quantities.

```
@EndUserText.label : 'Purchase Document Item'
...
define table zpurchdocitem {
  key client                    : abap.clnt not null;
  @EndUserText.label : 'Purchase Document Item'
  key purchasedocumentitem      : abap.char(10) not null;
  @AbapCatalog.foreignKey.keyType : #KEY
  @AbapCatalog.foreignKey.screenCheck : true
  key purchasedocument          : zpurchasedocumentdtel not null
    with foreign key [1..*,1] zpurchdocument
      where client = zpurchdocitem.client
        and purchasedocument = zpurchdocitem.purchasedocument;
  @EndUserText.label : 'Description'
  description                   : abap.sstring(128);
  @EndUserText.label : 'Price'
```

```
  @Semantics.amount.currencyCode : 'zpurchdocitem.currency'
  price                          : abap.curr(13,2);
  @EndUserText.label : 'Currency'
  currency                       : abap.cuky;
  @EndUserText.label : 'Quantity'
  @Semantics.quantity.unitOfMeasure : 'zpurchdocitem.quantityunit'
  quantity                       : abap.quan(13,2);
  @EndUserText.label : 'Unit'
  quantityunit                   : abap.unit(3);
  @EndUserText.label : 'Vendor'
  vendor                         : abap.sstring(32);
  @EndUserText.label : 'Vendor Type'
  vendortype                     : abap.sstring(32);
  @EndUserText.label : 'Purchase Document Item Image URL'
  purchasedocumentitemimageurl : abap.sstring(255);
  crea_date_time                 : timestampl;
  crea_uname                     : uname;
  lchg_date_time                 : timestampl;
  lchg_uname                     : uname;
}
```

Listing 4.2 Database Table Definition for Purchase Document Items

Note

You can use the keyboard shortcut `Ctrl` + `Shift` + `A` to quickly open ABAP development objects in Eclipse, including packages, database tables, or CDS views.

4.1.3 Creating Basic Interface Core Data Services Views

In the previous section, we defined the data model and the underlying database tables of our application to persist purchase documents and their items. In this section, we'll put a semantic and reusable basic interface CDS layer on top of these previously created tables. We'll adhere to the standard development guidelines of the SAP S/4HANA VDM based on CDS views.

The basic interface layer is the foundation layer of CDS views and is directly deployed on top of the database tables. As described in Chapter 1, this layer isn't supposed to do any complex calculations or join large sets of data; instead, this interface layer simply projects the fields provided by the underlying database tables to foster the granular reuse of these views.

To create a CDS view using the ABAP development tools in Eclipse, follow these steps:

1. Open the ABAP perspective in the ABAP development tools in Eclipse.
2. In the ABAP project, select the package node into which you want to create the table via the **Project Explorer** view.
3. Open the context menu by right-clicking on the package and select **New • Other ABAP Repository • Core Data Services • Data Definition**.
4. In the CDS creation wizard that appears, enter a **Name** and **Description**. In our case, we'll call the purchase documents view `Z_I_PurchaseDocument` and the purchase document items view `Z_I_PurchaseDocumentItem`.
5. Select one of the provided templates to create a skeleton CDS view, for instance, **Define View**, which will create a simple projection view skeleton with one single data source and without any associations or joins.
6. Click the **Finish** button in the wizard, and the source code editor will open so you can add fields or associations to the view.

> **Note**
>
> You can use the shortcut [Ctrl]+[Space] inside the field selection section of the CDS view source code editor to trigger the Eclipse content assist popup window to easily select fields of the underlying database table or CDS view, as shown in Figure 4.10.

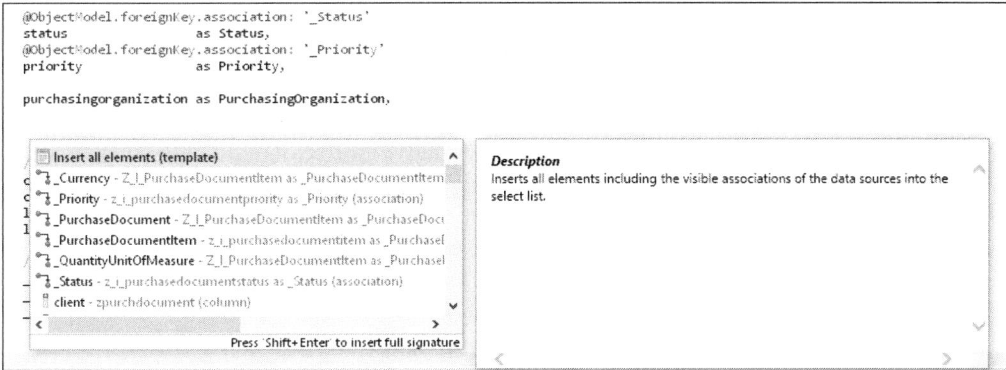

Figure 4.10 Triggering the Eclipse Content Assist for CDS Fields Using the Keyboard Shortcut

Listing 4.3 shows the basic interface view for purchase documents, which creates simple projection on the purchase document table (table zpurchdocument) to expose all table fields and provide camel case aliases for fields that are relevant to end users. To follow the naming conventions for interface layer views according to the SAP S/4HANA VDM development guidelines, we named the views using the following pattern: Z_I_<CDSViewName>. The Z_ indicates that a custom developed view in the customer namespace, and the I_ indicates that this view is an interface layer view. The view is also annotated with the @VDM.viewType: #BASIC annotation, which assigns the view to the basic interface view layer of the VDM.

In addition to the persistent database fields, the view also contains several associations that are propagated to potential consumers of this view at the end of the field selection list. By convention, associations start with an underscore, for instance, _PurchaseDocumentItem. Usually, most of the (key) fields contained in a view will have foreign key associations to other views because data is supposed to be stored in a normalized and redundancy-free form. In some cases, we omit this for the sake of simplicity, but, as an example, we've added associations to the Priority, Status, and PurchasingOrganization views. In the purchase document table, only the Priority, Status, and PurchasingOrganization keys will be stored; however, additional data, like texts, can be read via the foreign key associations to these views.

Another important annotation is the authorization check @AccessControl.authorizationCheck: #CHECK, which enables restricted access to a CDS view using a data control language (DCL) access control. We'll discuss access restrictions for CDS views in detail in Section 4.1.5.

The @ObjectModel.representativeKey annotation defines the field of the primary key that is specific for this view, and the @ObjectModel.semanticKey defines the primary key of this view. For the purchase document basic interface view, this field is the PurchaseDocument field in both cases. Fields containing descriptions or text should be annotated with @Semantics.text: true. The main description field of the entity can be linked to the entity key with the @ObjectModel.text.element: ['Description'] annotation.

```
@AbapCatalog.sqlViewName: 'ZIPURCHDOC'
@EndUserText.label: 'Purchase Document'
@AccessControl.authorizationCheck: #CHECK
@VDM.viewType: #BASIC
@ObjectModel.representativeKey: 'PurchaseDocument'
@ObjectModel.semanticKey: ['PurchaseDocument']
```

```
define view Z_I_PurchaseDocument
  as select from zpurchdocument
  association [0..*] to Z_I_PurchaseDocumentItem     as _PurchaseDocumentItem
on $projection.PurchaseDocument = _PurchaseDocumentItem.PurchaseDocument
  association [0..1] to Z_I_PurchaseDocumentPriority as _Priority
on $projection.Priority = _Priority.Priority
  association [0..1] to Z_I_PurchaseDocumentStatus   as _Status
on $projection.Status = _Status.Status
association [0..1] to Z_I_PurchasingOrganization   as _PurchasingOrganization
on $projection.PurchasingOrganization = _
PurchasingOrganization.PurchasingOrganization
{
      @ObjectModel.text.element: ['Description']
  key purchasedocument         as PurchaseDocument,
      @Semantics.text: true
      description              as Description,

      @ObjectModel.foreignKey.association: '_Status'
      status                   as Status,
      @ObjectModel.foreignKey.association: '_Priority'
      priority                 as Priority,
      @ObjectModel.foreignKey.association: '_PurchasingOrganization'
      purchasingorganization   as PurchasingOrganization,

      @Semantics.imageUrl: true
      purchasedocumentimageurl as PurchaseDocumentImageURL,

      crea_date_time,
      crea_uname,
      lchg_date_time,
      lchg_uname,

      // Associations
      _PurchaseDocumentItem,
      _Priority,
      _Status,
      _PurchasingOrganization
}
```

Listing 4.3 Basic Interface View on Top of the Purchase Documents Table (zpurchdocument)

The purchase document item basic interface view is shown in Listing 4.4. Its representative key is the PurchaseDocumentItem field, which is the most specific part of its primary key and defines this entity. The semantic key consists of the PurchaseDocument and PurchaseDocumentItem fields and reflects the primary key of the entity. The purchase document item basic interface view contains a foreign key association to the purchase document view as well as to reuse views for the currency (I_Currency) and the unit of measure (I_UnitOfMeasure) provided by the standard SAP S/4HANA basic interface view layer. As soon as views are explicitly released by SAP, you can use them in your own developments without the risk of introducing changes that break the view in future releases. The semantic currency and unit of measure annotations should be known from the table definition. We added the @DefaultAggregation:#NONE annotation to the Price and Quantity fields because all amount fields will be handled, by default, as measures and aggregated by SADL or the Analytical Engine. However, in our case, we explicitly want to suppress this default behavior.

```
@AbapCatalog.sqlViewName: 'ZIPURCHDOCITEM'
@EndUserText.label: 'Purchase Document Item'
@AccessControl.authorizationCheck: #NOT_REQUIRED
@VDM.viewType: #BASIC
@ObjectModel.representativeKey: 'PurchaseDocumentItem'
@ObjectModel.semanticKey: ['PurchaseDocumentItem','PurchaseDocument']

define view Z_I_PurchaseDocumentItem
  as select from zpurchdocitem
  association [1..1] to Z_I_PurchaseDocument as _PurchaseDocument      on
$projection.PurchaseDocument = _PurchaseDocument.PurchaseDocument
  association [0..1] to I_UnitOfMeasure      as _QuantityUnitOfMeasure on
$projection.QuantityUnit = _QuantityUnitOfMeasure.UnitOfMeasure
  association [0..1] to I_Currency           as _Currency              on
$projection.Currency = _Currency.Currency
{

      @ObjectModel.text.element: ['Description']
  key purchasedocumentitem as PurchaseDocumentItem,

      @ObjectModel.foreignKey.association: '_PurchaseDocument'
  key purchasedocument     as PurchaseDocument,
```

```
    @Semantics.text: true
    description          as Description,

    vendor               as Vendor,
    vendortype           as VendorType,

    @Semantics.amount.currencyCode: 'Currency'
    @DefaultAggregation: #NONE
    price                as Price,
    @Semantics.currencyCode: true
    @ObjectModel.foreignKey.association: '_Currency'
    currency             as Currency,

    @Semantics.quantity.unitOfMeasure: 'QuantityUnit'
    @DefaultAggregation: #NONE
    quantity             as Quantity,
    @Semantics.unitOfMeasure: true
    @ObjectModel.foreignKey.association: '_QuantityUnitOfMeasure'
    quantityunit         as QuantityUnit,

    @Semantics.imageUrl: true
    purchasedocumentitemimageurl as PurchaseDocumentItemImageURL,

    crea_date_time,
    crea_uname,
    lchg_date_time,
    lchg_uname,

    // Associations
    _PurchaseDocument,
    _QuantityUnitOfMeasure,
    _Currency
}
```

Listing 4.4 Basic Interface View on Top of the Purchase Document Items Table (zpurchdocitem)

4.1.4 Adding Calculated Fields

With the CDS DDL, you can dynamically calculate fields based on other persistent fields already present in the database. In the past, such calculated values might have been calculated on the application server or, worse, were precalculated and stored in redundant aggregate tables. However, with the launch of SAP HANA, this approach is obsolete because you can easily aggregate and calculate values on the fly now, which reduces the overall data footprint of the system and improves performance by pushing data-intensive calculations and aggregations to the database layer. In the following sections, we'll calculate several values for our application that don't have to be stored on the database, which would introduce redundancy. Instead, these values can be calculated dynamically using CDS views at runtime.

Calculating the Overall Item Price

A simple example of a calculated value is the overall price of a purchase document item. Let's say we've persisted the price of a single item and the requested quantity on the database but not the overall price. To calculate the overall price, you can simply multiply the requested quantity by the price of a single item and provide a new name for the field using an alias. For example, with an item price of 50 and a quantity of 10, the overall price of this item would be *50 * 10 = 500*. How you can implement this calculation in the `Z_I_PurchaseDoumentItem` basic view is shown in Listing 4.5:

```
...
@Semantics.amount.currencyCode: 'Currency'
@DefaultAggregation: #NONE
quantity  *  price  as OverallItemPrice,
...
```

Listing 4.5 Implementing Calculation in Purchase Document Item View

Although this field is a calculated field, you can also reference the already-persisted currency field.

Calculating Overall Purchase Document Price by Introducing a Composite Interface View and Using Test-Driven Development

Additionally, let's say we need the overall price of a purchase document. To calculate the overall price, you'll make use of the previously calculated overall item price since the overall price of a purchase document can be calculated by summing up all overall item prices of its assigned items. To perform this calculation, you must put an additional view on top of the basic purchase document view, which we'll name `Z_I_PurchDocOverallPrice` and assign to the composite interface layer of the VDM as this additional view will contain a calculation based on basic interface layer CDS views but is still intended for reuse. For now, simply add all fields of the basic purchase document view to the selection list of the new view.

Because the overall price calculation is already a calculation with moderate complexity, you should develop this calculation using test-driven development (TDD) to verify and safeguard your developed logic in an automated and repeatable way. Developing tests in a test-driven fashion means that, before you implement the actual calculations, you implement tests. TDD will allow you to incrementally implement calculations with the confidence that the already-implemented logic of previous steps isn't breaking subsequent steps or releases. This approach also has the advantage of introducing testing early in the development process so that test automation isn't simply omitted after a feature is working. In the end, you'll also have a safety net for future changes that might introduce regression bugs. Unit tests for CDS views are based on ABAP Unit and the CDS Test Double Framework. With the CDS Test Double Framework, you can dynamically create and configure test stubs or doubles for views or tables that the CDS view under test depends on.

Creating unit tests for CDS views is easy because the ABAP development tools in Eclipse already provide good unit test support. As shown in Figure 4.11, simply right-click on a CDS view and create a new global ABAP Unit test class for this view by choosing **New Test Class**.

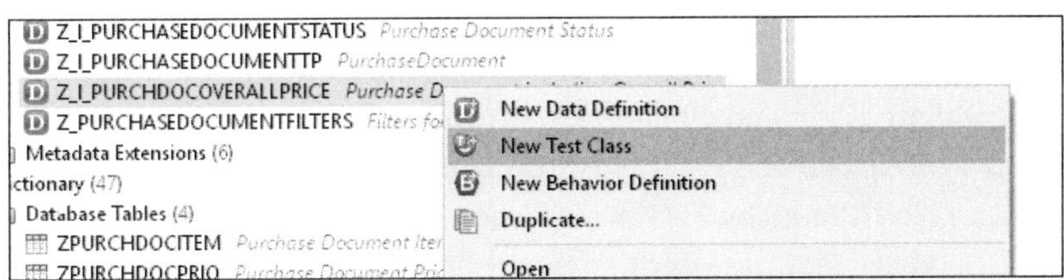

Figure 4.11 Generating a Unit Test Skeleton Class for a CDS View in the Eclipse Project Explorer

The test creation dialog wizard will open. On the first screen of the wizard, you must provide a name for the global ABAP test class, the package, and a description, as shown in Figure 4.12. The read-only **CDS Under Test** field indicates which CDS view you're creating the test for. A good practice is to keep the tests close to the tested code so that by default the tests are put into the same package as the CDS view under test.

After you've maintained these fields, go to the next screen of the wizard by clicking the **Next** button.

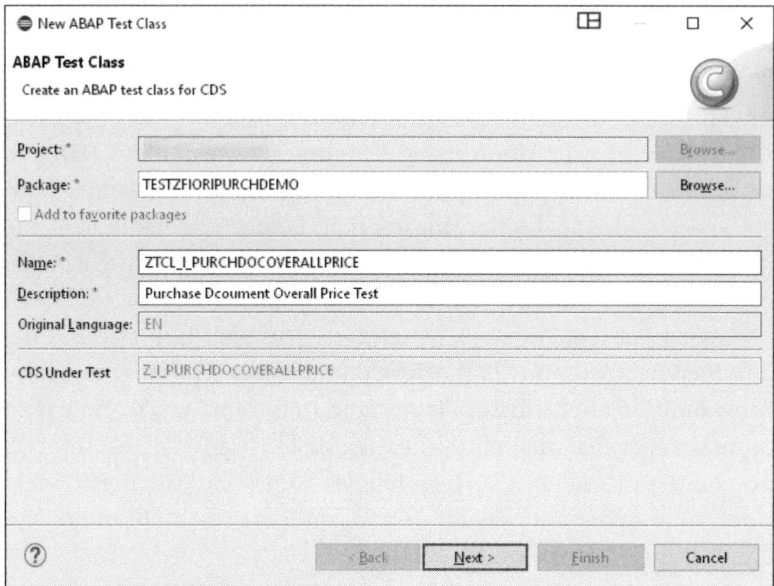

Figure 4.12 Creating a New Test Class for the Purchase Documents Overall Price CDS View (Z_I_PurchDocOverallPrice)

On the next screen, you'll select the CDS views or tables that your view under test depends on and that are required as test doubles for the test cases you want to implement, as shown in Figure 4.13. During test execution, the test doubles replace the actual views or database tables and dynamically provide different test data for different test cases. In general, two test types exist: **Unit Test**, which only considers first-level dependencies, and **Hierarchy Test**, which allows test double creation for the whole stack of CDS views that the view under test depends on. In our case, simply click **Next** because we're creating a unit test, and both basic interface views that our view under test depends on (`Z_I_PurchaseDocument` and `Z_I_PurchaseDocumentItem`) are already preselected and required as dependencies for double creation in our tests.

In addition to generating a global ABAP Unit test class and providing the required dependencies for test double creation, the test class creation wizard also supports test doubles with simple form-based test data creation, as shown in Figure 4.14. For our first test case, which we'll call `overall_price_no_items`, we won't create any test data for purchase document items, just a single table entry for purchase documents.

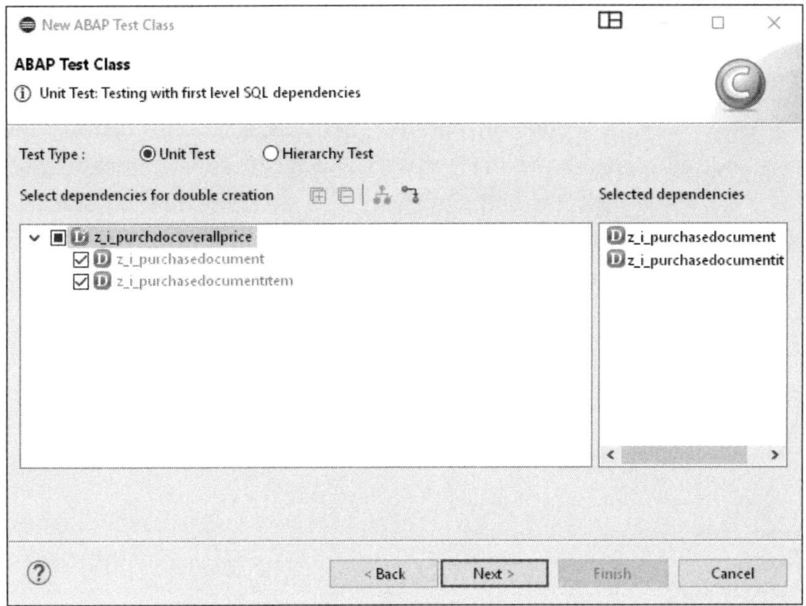

Figure 4.13 Dependency Selection Screen for the CDS Test

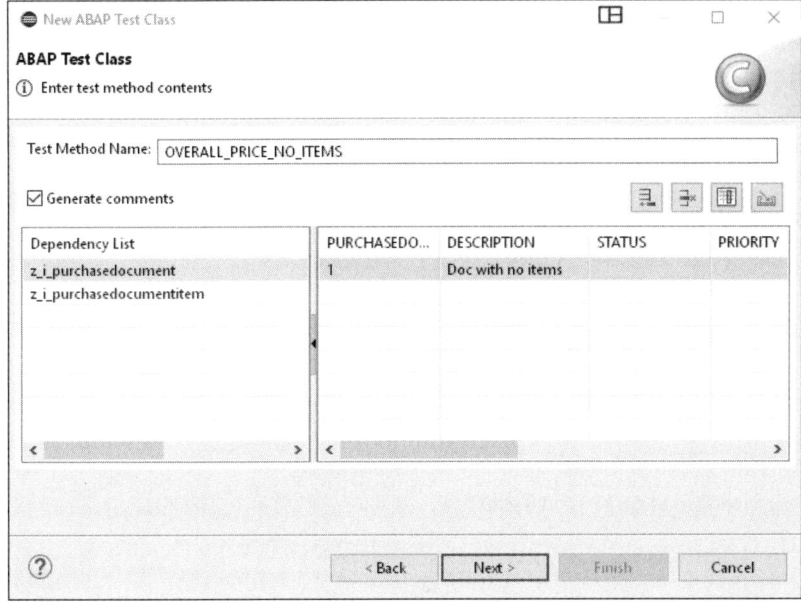

Figure 4.14 Form-Based Test Data Creation for CDS Test Doubles That the View Under Test Depends On

When you click **Next**, the newly generated global ABAP class will open in the Eclipse source code editor. However, in the global test class, you'll only find an empty class definition and implementation. To look at the generated local ABAP Unit test class containing the test fixture, data creation, and test methods, select the **Test Classes** tab in the source code editor, as shown in Figure 4.15, which contains our just-defined test method `overall_price_no_items` and a `prepare_test_data_set` method that will insert our previously specified purchase document test data into the purchase document test double of the test environment.

[ER9] ZTCL_I_PURCHDOCOVERALLPRICE

```

CLASS ltc_z_i_purchdocoverallprice IMPLEMENTATION.

  METHOD class_setup.
    environment = cl_cds_test_environment=>create( i_for_entity = 'Z_I_PURCHDOCOVERALLPRICE' ).
  ENDMETHOD.

  METHOD setup.
    environment->clear_doubles( ).
  ENDMETHOD.

  METHOD class_teardown.
    environment->destroy( ).
  ENDMETHOD.

  METHOD overall_price_no_items.
    prepare_testdata_set( ).
    SELECT * FROM z_i_purchdocoverallprice INTO TABLE @act_results.
    cl_abap_unit_assert=>fail( msg = 'Place your assertions here' ).
  ENDMETHOD.

  METHOD prepare_testdata_set.

    "Prepare test data for 'z_i_purchasedocument'
    lt_z_i_purchasedocument = VALUE #(
      (
        purchasedocument = '1'
        description = 'Doc with no items'
      ) ).
    environment->insert_test_data( i_data =  lt_z_i_purchasedocument ).

    "Prepare test data for 'z_i_purchasedocumentitem'
    "TODO: Provide the test data here
    lt_z_i_purchasedocumentitem = VALUE #(
      (
      ) ).
    environment->insert_test_data( i_data =  lt_z_i_purchasedocumentitem ).
```

Global Class | Class-relevant Local Types | Local Types | Test Classes | Macros

Figure 4.15 Generated Local ABAP Unit Test Class

Test data defined using the test data creation wizard won't be inserted in the original database tables of the *dependent on* views. Instead, the generated skeleton test class will set up a separate test environment in its `class_setup` method and won't affect any productive tables and their data. The stubbed *dependent on* views (these are copies of the original views that contain the predefined test data). and their data will only be available during the runtime of the test method and are by default cleared before each test execution in the `setup` test fixture method `environment->clear_doubles( )`.

For our first test case, we didn't create any item test data, only a single purchase document, which we inserted into the test environment. If a purchase document has no items, the overall purchase document price should be 0. We can verify this value by adapting the generated test method, which doesn't check for the correct value of the `overallprice` field yet. In general, the test procedure for CDS views always follows these steps:

1. Create test data for the views the view under test depends on (*arrange* or *given* step).
2. Select data from the CDS view under test (*act* or *when* step).
3. Ensure that a calculated value has the expected value (*assert* or *then* step).

To check values calculated by a CDS view, you can use the standard `CL_ABAP_UNIT_ASSERT` class, which provides many static methods for comparing expected and actual values. A simple test ensuring that purchase documents without items have an overall price of 0 is shown in Listing 4.6.

```
METHOD overall_price_no_items.
 prepare_testdata_set_no_items( ).
 SELECT * FROM z_i_purchdocoverallprice INTO TABLE    @act_results.
 cl_abap_unit_assert=>assert_equals( exp = 0 act = act_results[ 1 ]-
overallprice  ).
ENDMETHOD.
```

Listing 4.6 ABAP Unit Test for the Overall Price of a Purchase Document without Items

This listing follows the test procedure: First, we'll create test data in an analogous manner to the generated test data creation method, then we'll select the data from the CDS view under test using Open SQL. Finally, we'll check whether the selected data has the expected calculated value. Currently, the test will fail with a syntax error because we haven't yet added the field to the view. To fix the test, simply add the field to the view like this:

```
0 as as OverallPrice,
```

Note

You can either execute unit tests by right-clicking on the global class and selecting **Run As • ABAP Unit Test** or by using the shortcut [Ctrl]+[Shift]+[F10].

In our next test case, we'll create a new test data creation method that has two items with an overall item price of 10, as shown in Listing 4.7.

```
METHOD prepare_testdata_set.
 "Prepare test data for 'z_i_purchasedocument'
 lt_z_i_purchasedocument = VALUE #(
 (
  purchasedocument = '1'
  description = 'Doc with no items'
 ) ).
environment->insert_test_data( i_data =  lt_z_i_purchasedocument ).

 "Prepare test data for 'z_i_purchasedocumentitem'
  lt_z_i_purchasedocumentitem = VALUE #(
  ( purchasedocument = '1' purchasedocumentitem = '1'  overallitemprice = '10'
)
  ( purchasedocument = '1' purchasedocumentitem = '2' overallitemprice = '10'
) ).
  environment->insert_test_data( i_data =   lt_z_i_purchasedocumentitem ).
ENDMETHOD.
```

Listing 4.7 Test Double Creation for a Purchase Document with Two Purchase Document Items

Our second test method will thus look like the code shown in Listing 4.8.

```
METHOD overall_price.
 prepare_testdata_set( ).
 SELECT * FROM z_i_purchdocoverallprice INTO TABLE @act_results.
 cl_abap_unit_assert=>assert_equals( exp = 20 act =  act_results[ 1 ]-
overallprice  ).
  ENDMETHOD.
```

Listing 4.8 ABAP Unit Test for the Overall Price of a Purchase Document with Two Purchase Document Items

To fix this test, we must now actually aggregate the overall item prices of a purchase document's items. We'll first add the purchase document item overall price field to the view using the following path expression:

```
_PurchaseDocumentItem.OverallItemPrice
```

However, this expression will increase the cardinality of the data returned by the view from 1 purchase document to 2 purchase documents with different overall item prices. To reduce cardinality, you must group the overall item prices by their common purchase document fields and aggregate the overall item prices using a SUM aggregate function, assuming that all purchase document items use the same currency. Listing 4.9 shows an excerpt of the CDS view calculating the overall price of a purchase document.

```
@AbapCatalog.sqlViewName: 'ZIPURCHDOCPRICE'
@EndUserText.label: 'Purchase Document Item'
@VDM.viewType: #COMPOSITE

define view Z_I_PurchDocOverallPrice
as select from Z_I_PurchaseDocument
{
    key PurchaseDocument,

    @Semantics.amount.currencyCode: 'Currency'
    @DefaultAggregation: #NONE
    @ObjectModel.foreignKey.association: '_Currency'
    sum( _PurchaseDocumentItem.OverallItemPrice )as OverallPrice,

    @Semantics.currencyCode: true
    _PurchaseDocumentItem.Currency,
    ...
    // Associations
    ...
    _Currency
}
group by
 PurchaseDocument,
_PurchaseDocumentItem.Currency
...
```

Listing 4.9 Composite Interface View Calculating the Overall Price of a Purchase Document

Note

Field values calculated by a mathematical operator (+, -, /, etc.); an aggregate function (max, min, sum, etc.); or a CASE expression can't be used in the same view for additional calculations. In such cases, you always must create an additional view on top to make use of the calculated value or field.

Calculating the Overall Price Criticality by Introducing a Consumption View and Using Test-Driven Development

Another calculated field that you'll later need in the UI of our application is an indicator for the overall price criticality. We'll use the calculated criticality field to highlight overall prices we consider critical for the user checking purchase documents. The logic to be implemented is shown in Table 4.1; for instance, if the overall price of the document is below 1,000, the document shouldn't be considered critical and will be indicated by the number 3. On the other hand, if the price is higher than 10,000, we should consider this document very critical and indicate this criticality by the number 1.

Overall Price	Criticality
>= 0 and < 1,000	3 – Not critical
>= 1,000 and <= 10,000	2 – Medium criticality
> 10,000	1 – High criticality
Any other value	0 – Undefined

Table 4.1 Overall Price to Criticality Indicator Mappings

To implement this field, we'll put a final consumption view on top of the previous composite view, which we'll name Z_C_PurchaseDocumentLrp where C_ stands for consumption view. We'll again undertake the implementation in a test-driven manner and create a test case for each edge case before we implement the actual calculation logic inside the CDS view. Listing 4.10 shows the unit test implementation for an overall price of 1,000. In this case, we expect an output of 2 for the field, indicating a medium criticality.

```
METHOD price_1k_medium_critical.
 prepare_testdata_price( 1000 ).
 SELECT * FROM z_c_purchasedocumentlrp INTO TABLE  @act_results.
```

```
 cl_abap_unit_assert=>assert_equals( exp = 2 act =  act_results[ 1 ]-
overallpricecriticality ).
ENDMETHOD.
```

Listing 4.10 ABAP Unit Test for the Overall Price (1,000) to Criticality (2) Mapping

The other tests will look the same except for the price parameter and the expected value. The result of the overall price criticality field implementation in the CDS DDL then looks like Listing 4.11.

```
case when OverallPrice >= 0 and OverallPrice < 1000 then 3
 when OverallPrice >= 1000 and OverallPrice <= 10000 then 2
 when OverallPrice > 10000 then 1
 else 0 end as OverallPriceCriticality,
```

Listing 4.11 Calculation Logic for the OverallPriceCriticality Field in the Z_C_PurchaseDocumentLrp CDS Consumption View

Calculating Whether Approval Is Required or Not Using Test-Driven Development

Another simple indicator that we'll later need in the UI indicates whether the purchase document requires approval by the purchasing manager or not. We'll specify that a purchase document needs approval when the overall price exceeds 1,000. For this simple indicator, you'll just need two tests: one where the overall price is 1,000 and doesn't require approval and another where the overall price is 1,001 and does requires approval. The implementation result should look like Listing 4.12.

```
case when OverallPrice > 1000 then 'X' else '' end as IsApprovalRequired,
```

Listing 4.12 Calculation Logic for the IsApprovalRequired Field in the Z_C_PurchaseDocumentLrp CDS Consumption View

Figure 4.16 shows all successfully executed unit tests of the CDS view under test for the overall price criticality field as well as for the approval required field.

So far, after having added the calculated fields, the VDM of our purchasing app should look like the diagram shown in Figure 4.17. The database layer contains the transparent tables for the main entities of the application: purchase documents and items. Additionally, we created separate tables for document priorities, status, and purchasing organizations to store their keys and texts in a normalized and data redundancy-free way. On top of the database tables, we introduced a basic view layer with a basic interface view for each database table.

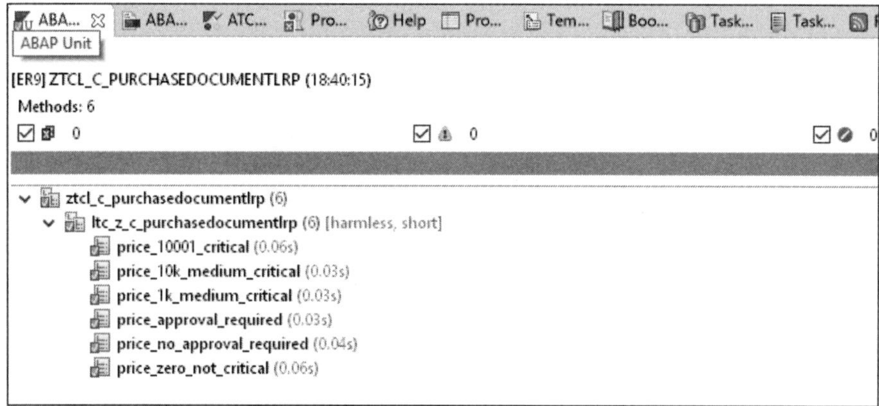

Figure 4.16 Successfully Executed Unit Tests for the Overall Price Criticality and Approval Required Fields

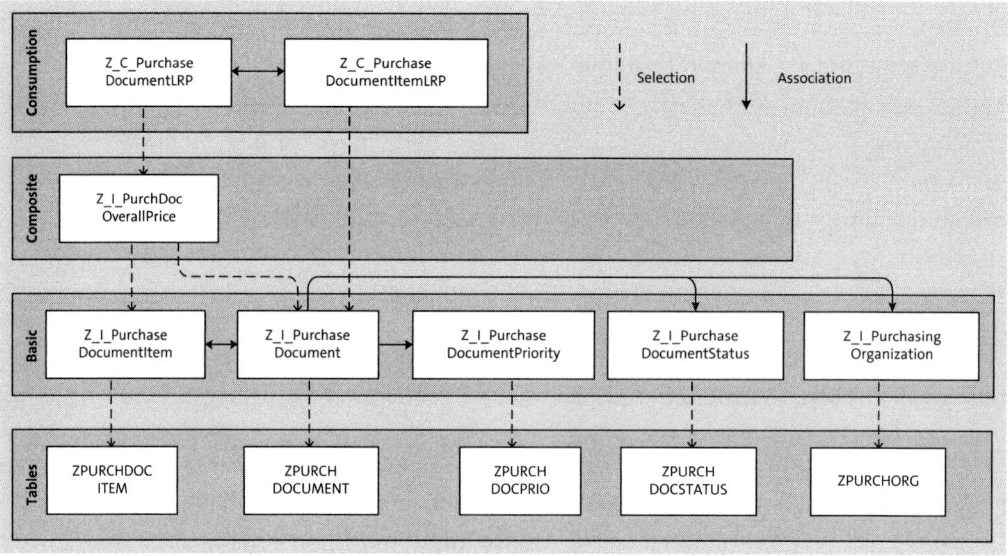

Figure 4.17 VDM of the Purchasing App Consisting of Four Different Layers

Priorities, statuses, and purchasing organizations are linked to the purchase document via foreign key associations. Documents and items also have associations to the other respective entity. On top of the purchase document and item views, we put a composite interface view to calculate the overall price for documents by aggregating the overall item prices of a document's items. Finally, the topmost layer consists of two consumption views for purchase documents and items. In the consumption view for purchase documents, we introduced two more calculated fields for the overall price criticality and whether approval of the document is required or not.

4.1.5 Adding Data Control Language Files

The access to data exposed by CDS views can be restricted using classic ABAP authorization objects and the DCL of CDS. To set up this restriction, you first must create an authorization field using Transaction SU20 and an authorization class and object using Transaction SU21. For our app scenario, we'll create an authorization object for the purchasing organization, which is also a field exposed by the purchase document CDS view. In our case, we only want to show the end users the purchase documents of the purchasing organizations they are assigned to since by default they shouldn't have access to all the purchase documents in the system. The authorization object for the purchasing organization is shown in Figure 4.18. The authorization object contains two authorization fields: one for the actual purchasing organization (ZPURCHORGA) and one for the allowed activity (ACTVT), for instance, "01" for create, "02" for change, and "03" for display.

To enforce access restrictions based on authorization objects, you must create an access control using the DCL of CDS and link it to the CDS view. You can create a CDS access control in Eclipse by carrying out the following steps:

1. Open the ABAP perspective in the ABAP development tools in Eclipse.
2. In the ABAP project, select the package node in which you want to create the table via the **Project Explorer** view.
3. Open the context menu by right-clicking on the package and select **New • Other ABAP Repository • Core Data Services • Access Control**.
4. When the creation wizard opens, enter a **Name** and **Description**. By convention, the DCL source name will be identical to the DCL source name. In our case, then, we'll name the DCL file *Z_I_PurchaseDocument*.
5. You can select one of the provided templates to create a skeleton DCL access control, for instance, **Define Instance Role,** which will create a simple DCL skeleton file.
6. Click the **Finish** button in the wizard, and the source code editor will open where you can now define access rules and conditions.

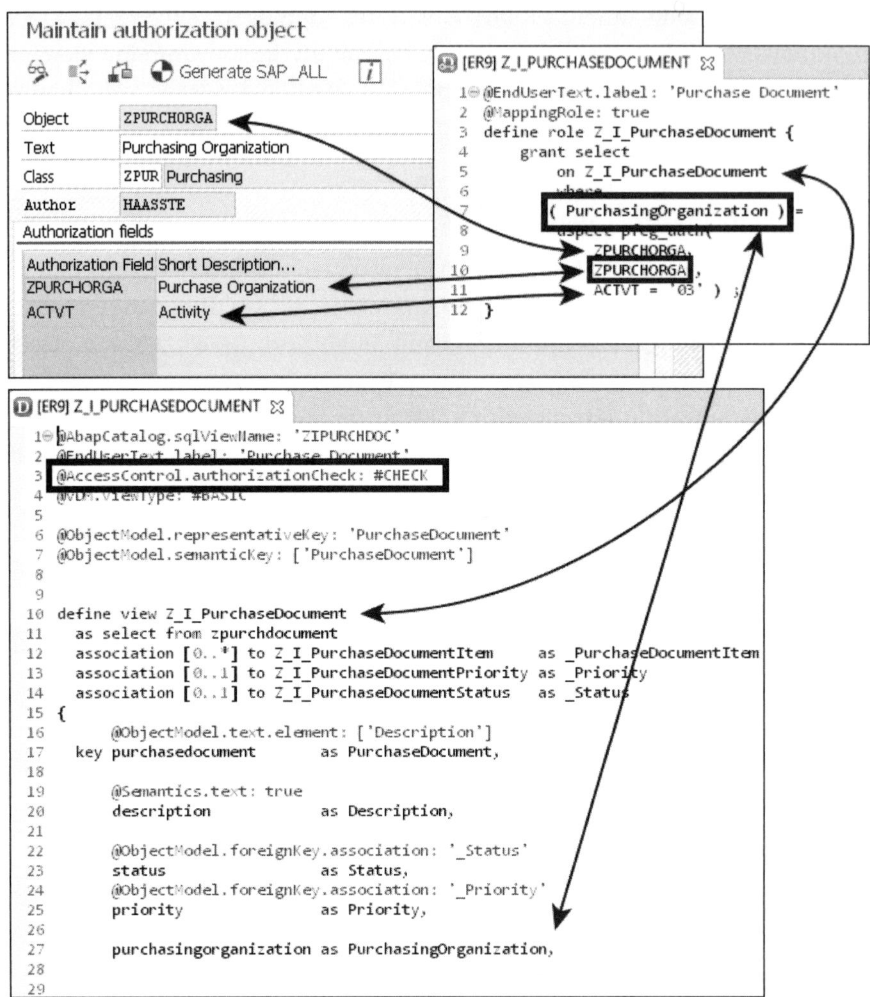

Figure 4.18 Overview of the Connections between Authorization Object, CDS View, and Access Control

Note

To enable the access control from the CDS view side, you also must add the `@AccessControl.authorizationCheck: #CHECK` annotation to the CDS view. This annotation will lead to implicit access control when data is selected from the CDS view using Open SQL.

The full access control definition for our purchase document basic interface view is shown in Listing 4.13. By convention, the name of the role inside the DCL will be identical to the CDS view name in camel case. The role definition contains a Transaction PFCG condition that will be evaluated each time the view is directly accessed using Open SQL. The left side of the condition consists of the PurchasingOrganization field of the CDS view where the right side consists of the name of the authorization object (ZPURCHORGA) as the first parameter followed by its authorization fields (ZPURCHORGA, ACTVT) to be evaluated.

```
@EndUserText.label: 'Role for Z_I_PurchaseDocument'
@MappingRole: true
define role Z_I_PurchaseDocument {
    grant select
        on Z_I_PurchaseDocument
        where
       ( PurchasingOrganization ) =
        aspect pfcg_auth(
            ZPURCHORGA, // Authorization object
            ZPURCHORGA , // Matched auth. object field
            ACTVT = '03' // Fixed auth. object field
             ) ;
}
```

Listing 4.13 Access Control Definition for the Z_I_PurchaseDocument CDS View Using the Data Control Language

During runtime, when performing an Open SQL select on the view, the user's assigned Transaction PFCG roles and authorizations will be fetched and compared with the data provided by the CDS view. In our example, the user might have been assigned to purchasing organization Org1, which will lead to the following transparent enhancement of the CDS SELECT statement:

```
SELECT * FROM Z_I_PurchaseDocument WHERE PurchaseOrganization = ‘Org1’;
```

Additionally, our Transaction PFCG condition also contains a hard-coded check (ACTVT=’03’), which will ensure that the user has display rights. If his assigned ACTVT value isn't equal to "03," the user won't see any data at all. Figure 4.18 summarizes the connections between the CDS view, the DCL role, and the authorization object.

To avoid repeating the same access rules and conditions for similar views, access controls can be inherited. You can also combine inherited and new access conditions. If you'd simply like to reuse the access control file created for the purchase document's basic interface view in our composite interface view introduced for calculating the overall price, you could create the access control shown in Listing 4.14 without having to repeat the Transaction PFCG condition.

```
@EndUserText.label: 'Purchase Document Overall Price'
@MappingRole: true
define role Z_I_Purchdocoverallprice {
    grant select
     on Z_I_PurchDocOverallPrice
     inherit Z_I_PurchaseDocument;
}
```

Listing 4.14 Example of an Inherited Access Control

To assign certain authorizations to users, you must create a Transaction PFCG role and include authorization objects and their values either manually or via an application having assigned authorization default values provided via Transaction SU22. Finally, for the authorizations to become effective, the user must be assigned to the Transaction PFCG role.

Note

DCL access controls are only considered on direct CDS view access. They are ignored when queried indirectly via other CDS views. Access controls can be tested using Transaction SACMSEL, which makes it possible to evaluate CDS access controls for different users.

4.2 Developing an Unmanaged Transactional Application Using the ABAP RESTful Programming Model

So far, our app consists of a VDM based on a CDS view that provides access to purchase documents and items using Open SQL, the query language of CDS. However, we can't create any documents or items yet. At this point, the application is completely read-only. If any transactional logic, for instance, using create, read, update, and delete (CRUD) operations on entities, is required, the new ABAP RESTful programming model would come into play because, since SAP S/4HANA 1909, you can generate an ABAP RESTful programming model-based business object and its node structure from a CDS data model. Consequently, in this section, you'll learn how to add transactional capabilities to a read-only CDS-based VDM with the help of behavior definitions.

4.2.1 Generating an Unmanaged Transaction Business Object from a CDS Model

Because we want to keep our basic interface views reusable for all application scenarios, we won't add the semantic business object associations required for modeling a transactional business object to existing basic interface views; instead, we'll create new composite interface views on top of the basic interface views. Then, we'll create an unmanaged business object for purchase documents as well as for purchase document items, which we'll name Z_I_PurchaseDocument_U and Z_I_PurchaseDocumentItem_U, where _U stands for unmanaged business object. (As described in Chapter 4, for SAP S/4HANA 1909, only the unmanaged version of the ABAP RESTful programming model has been released. The managed version is currently available on cloud, and the on-premise version will soon follow.) The naming convention we used to create the Z_I_PurchaseDocumentItem_U for the CDS view with the unmanaged implementation is not a mandatory naming practice; identifying these types of views with _U is just easier and more understandable. In both views, you'll add all fields of the underlying view to the selection field list to create a simple projection of the underlying view.

Similarly, we'll follow a few more naming conventions throughout this chapter. In general, development objects are named as [/<namespace>][<prefix>]_<object_name>_[<suffix>]. Following this rule of thumb, let's go through the naming practice for the various elements we'll be creating in this chapter:

- **Service bindings**
  For service bindings, the prefix should be UI_ or API_, depending on the type of OData service you wish to generate. The suffix will be _V2 or _V4 (depending on which OData protocol version you select). In this example, the additional Z_ before the names corresponds to most common customer namespace (which can also be exclusive customer-specific namespaces like /customername/).

  Example:

  Z_UI_PurchaseDocument_U_V2

- **Behavior pools or behavior implementation classes**
  Prefix would be BP_ (short for behavior pool).

Example:

`ZBP_I_PurchaeDocument_U`

- **Behavior handler and behavior saver classes**
  These classes are local classes within the behavior pool:
  - `LHC_` for the behavior handler class
  - `LSC_` for the behavior save class

  Example:

  ```
  lhc_Z_I_PurchaseDocument_U
  lsc_Z_I_PurchaseDocument_U
  ```

To add a behavior definition to a view, you must first define your new view as a root view. Let's call this root view, which will have transactional capabilities, `Z_I_PurchaseDocument_U`. This root view will serve as our purchase document header and will be a composite view.

The main annotations for this view are shown in Listing 4.15 on the header level.

```
@AbapCatalog.sqlViewName: 'ZIPURCHDOCU'
@AccessControl.authorizationCheck: #NOT_REQUIRED
@EndUserText.label: 'PurchaseDocument'
@AbapCatalog.preserveKey: true
@VDM.viewType: #COMPOSITE
define root view Z_I_PurchaseDocument_U
```

Listing 4.15 Business Object Root Node Header Annotations

A business object is represented as a hierarchical tree of nodes, and by adding the `define root view` syntax, the view is characterized as the root view of the node hierarchy. The `@AbapCatalog.preserveKey: true` must be added when a view is set are root view. Additionally, to build up the business object node hierarchy, you must also annotate the association to the purchase document items view as composite, as shown in Listing 4.16.

```
define root view Z_I_PurchaseDocument_U
  as select from Z_I_PurchDocOverallPrice
composition [0..*] of Z_I_PurchaseDocumentItem_U as _PurchaseDocumentItem,
```

Listing 4.16 BOPF Business Object Root Node Child Association

Furthermore, you must add several annotations on the header level in the purchase document item view (Z_I_PurchaseDocumentItemTP), as shown in Listing 4.17.

```
@AbapCatalog.sqlViewName: 'ZIPURCHDOCITEMU'
@AccessControl.authorizationCheck: #NOT_REQUIRED
@EndUserText.label: 'Purchase Document Item'
@AbapCatalog.preserveKey: true
@VDM.viewType: #COMPOSITE
...
```

Listing 4.17 Business Object Child Node Header Annotations

As we did earlier for purchase documents, you'll also need to enable all transactional operations for this business object node. The association back to the purchase document must be annotated as a parent association. Moreover, views that don't represent the root node of the hierarchy must also specify their root node association, which, in our case, is equivalent to the parent association, as shown in Listing 4.18.

```
define view Z_I_PurchaseDocumentItem_U
  as select from Z_I_PurchaseDocumentItem
  association to parent Z_I_PurchaseDocument_U as _PurchaseDocument on
$projection.PurchaseDocument = _PurchaseDocument.PurchaseDocument
```

Listing 4.18 Business Object Child Node Parent Association

4.2.2 Service Definition

After activating the transactional or business object views, you can directly go into creating a behavior definition that adds the CRUD functionality to the views. But first, let's register our views using the service definition and service binding and see how the OData service should look. To create a new service definition, right-click on the package name in the project folder then select **New • Other ABAP repository Object**. Then, expand the **Business Services** folder and select **Service Definition**, as shown in Figure 4.19.

Now, enter a name and description for the service definition. Service definitions don't follow any special naming conventions since they are part of the business service and don't have types or specifications, unlike the service binding. Enter the details for the service definition, as shown in Figure 4.20, and click **Next.**

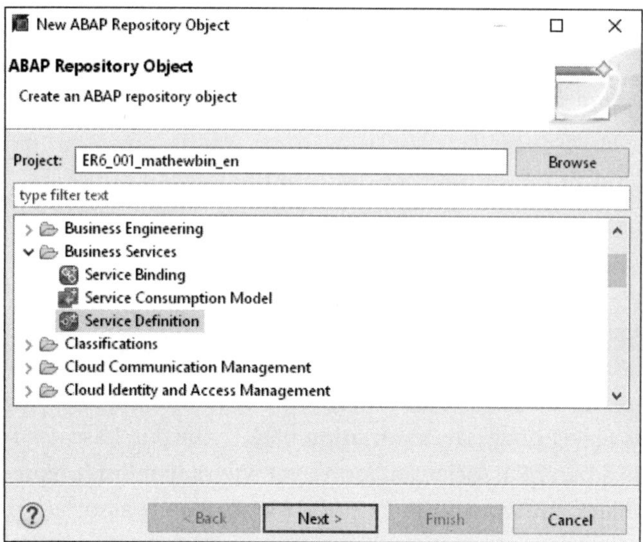

Figure 4.19 Creating a New Service Definition for Unmanaged Views

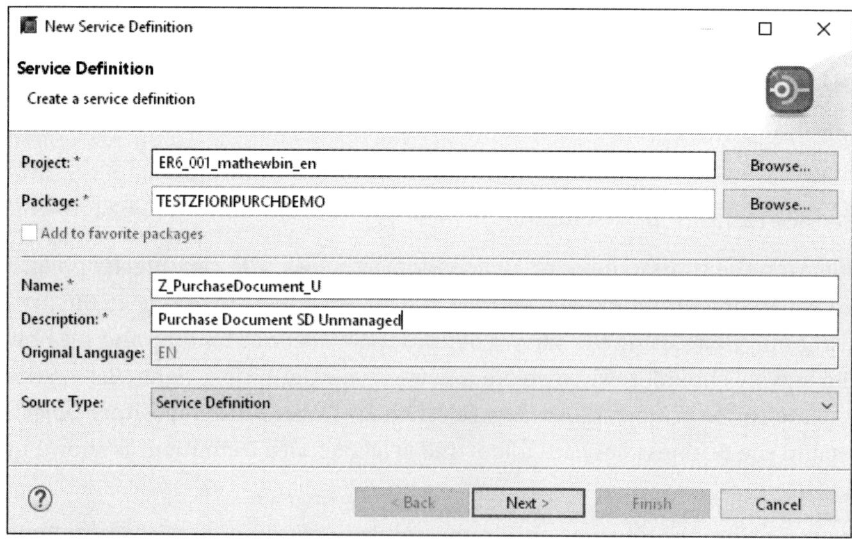

Figure 4.20 Service Definition Details

Once the service definition is created, you'll see an empty service definition, which is where you'll be exposing all the CDS views as entities. If you're familiar with Transaction SEGW for creating the OData projects (or if you've read the first edition of this book), you'll notice the same set of entities being exposed under **Data Model • Data Source References • Exposures via SADL • CDS-Entity Exposures • Entity Types** inside any of the Transaction SEGW projects you create based on a CDS view. While almost exactly the same, in this case, we won't use the SAP GUI to access Transaction SEGW but instead manually expose the CDS views and its associations required for our project. With this approach, you'll never have to open SAP GUI for any part of development. For our scenario, to ensure that all the value helps and foreign key associations are properly picked up, we'll expose all the main `_U` views, the underlying `I_` views, and the relevant value help views as shown in Figure 4.21.

[ER6] Z_PURCHASEDOCUMENT_U

```
@EndUserText.label: 'Purchase Document SD Unmanaged'
define service Z_PurchaseDocument_U {
  expose Z_I_PurchaseDocument_U as PurchaseDocument_U;
  expose Z_I_PurchaseDocumentItem_U as PurchaseDocumentItem_U;
  expose I_Indicator as ApprovalRequired;
  expose I_Currency as Currency;
  expose I_UnitOfMeasure as QuantityUnitofMeasure;
  expose Z_I_VendorType as VendorType;
  expose Z_C_StatusVH as StatusVH;
  expose Z_C_VendorTypeVH as VendorTypeVH;
  expose Z_C_PriorityVH as PriorityVH;
  expose Z_I_PurchaseDocumentPriority as Priority;
  expose Z_I_PurchaseDocumentStatus as Status;
  expose Z_I_PurchDocOverallPrice as PurchDocOveralPrice;
  expose Z_I_PurchaseDocument as PruchasDocumentBase;
  expose Z_I_PurchaseDocumentItem as PurchaseDocumentItemBase;
}
```

Figure 4.21 Exposing the Required CDS View Fields via the Service Definition

4.2.3 Service Binding

Now that we've defined which CDS views must be exposed as the OData service, let's register this as an OData service by creating a service binding. This process is same when you activated your SAP Gateway service builder project (Transaction SEGW) for the first time, and your OData service is activated in the background. To create a new service binding, right-click on the package name in the project folder and then select **New • Other ABAP repository Object**. Then, expand the **Business Services** folder and select **Service Binding**, as shown in Figure 4.22.

In the next screen, give the service binding a name (following the naming convention, the prefix should be `UI_` since we're registering the OData to use it within SAPUI5 apps, and the suffix should be `_V2` since we're using OData V2 protocol).

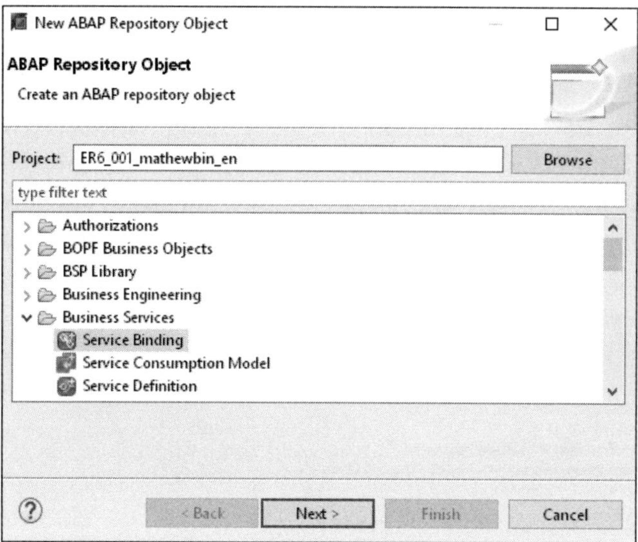

Figure 4.22 Service Binding for Registering the OData Service

Also, you must give the service definition name, as shown in the Figure 4.23, so that the service binding can refer the service definition and expose the CDS views accordingly in the resulting OData service.

New Service Binding

Service Binding

Create Service Binding

Project: * ER6_001_mathewbin_en Browse...

Package: * TESTZFIORIPURCHDEMO Browse...

Add to favorite packages

Name: * Z_UI_PURCHASEDOCUMENT_U_V2

Description: * Purchase Document SB Unmanaged

Original Language: EN

Binding Type: * ODATA V2 (UI - User Interface: Consumed in SAPUI5 Apps)

Service Definition: * Z_PURCHASEDOCUMENT_U Browse...

< Back Next > Finish Cancel

Figure 4.23 Service Binding Details

As shown in Figure 4.24, multiple options are available when creating the service definitions. In addition to the OData V2 and V4 options, you can also see a subcategory for UI services and web APIs. (Web APIs are normal CDS views exposed as OData services without UI annotations, which are generally used for template-based SAP Fiori apps such as SAP Fiori elements.)

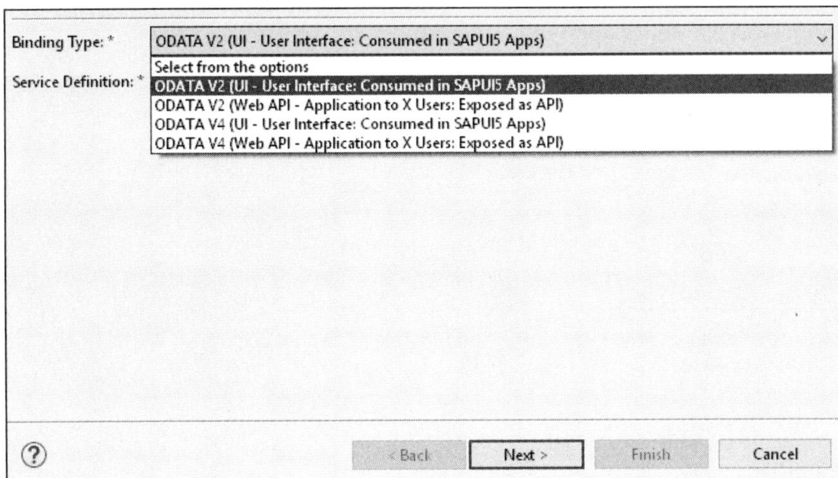

Figure 4.24 Service Binding Types

Once you've completed the service binding wizard, you'll see the **Name** and **Version** for your service definition. Now, you must activate your service binding. Click the **Activate** button, shown in Figure 4.25, which will register your OData service in the system.

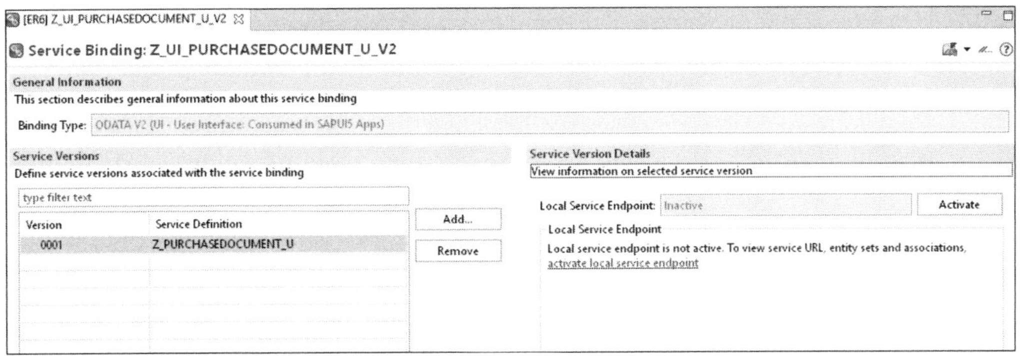

Figure 4.25 Activating the Service Binding

Now, you'll see the OData service in the **Service URL** field. You can click on the **Service URL** link to see the OData service call. But the ABAP RESTful programming model provides an even more interesting and powerful option: You can preview your service within an actual SAP Fiori elements app that is automatically generated based on the annotations provided in our CDS views. Right-click on the top CDS view entity set `PurchaseDocument_U`, which we exposed from `Z_I_PurchaseDocument_U` CDS view, and click on **Open Fiori Elements App Preview**, as shown in Figure 4.26.

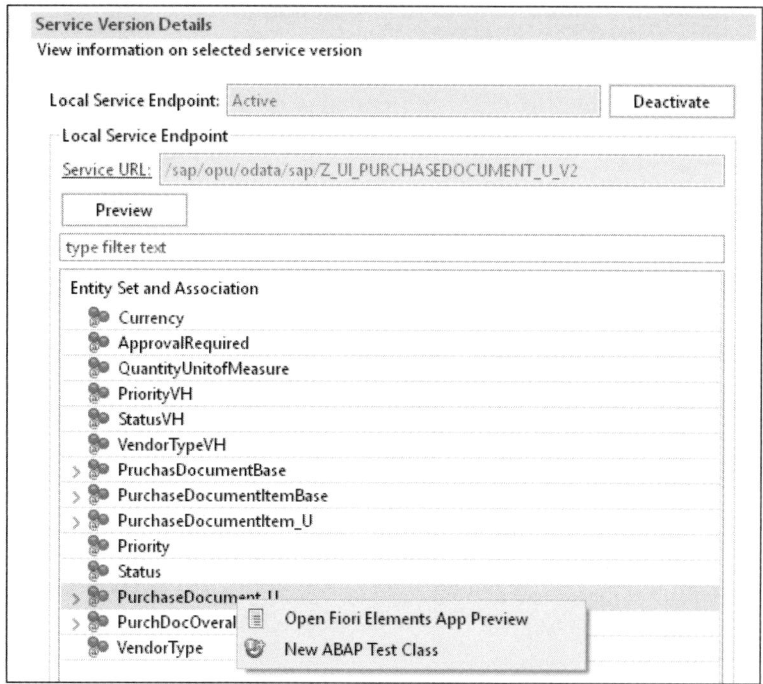

Figure 4.26 Open SAP Fiori Elements App Preview Feature in the Service Definition

Now, your SAP Fiori elements app will open in the browser automatically. By default, no columns will be selected in the table of the app. (Because we didn't add UI annotations to specify columns and corresponding UI properties, we'll add these later in this chapter in Section 4.4.4). To see the result of your CDS view, click on the settings icon to the top right of the table, select the required columns, and click the **Go** button, as shown in Figure 4.27. In this preview, notice that you still don't have any transactional functions enabled. We'll add these to our `_U` views in the next section.

Standard *
Adapt Filters
Go
Standard *
Delete
Create
Purchase Document
Description
OverallPrice
Priority
Status
PurchasingOrganization
Company Car Purchase (1) | Company Car Purchase | 41,200.00 EUR | High (1) | Approved (2) | Purchasing Organization 1 (ORG1)
Hardware Purchase (2) | Hardware Purchase | 1,050.00 EUR | Medium (2) | Closed (3) | Purchasing Organization 2 (ORG2)
Book Purchase (3) | Book Purchase | 100.00 EUR | Low (3) | Approved (2) | Purchasing Organization 3 (ORG3)
Company Car Purchase for Mike (4) | Company Car Purchase for Mike | 59,410.00 EUR | High (1) | Approved (2) | Purchasing Organization 1 (ORG1)
New Office Laptop (5) | New Office Laptop | 3,750.00 EUR | Low (3) | Created (1) | Purchasing Organization 3 (ORG3)

Figure 4.27 SAP Fiori Elements App Preview

4.2.4 Entity Manipulation Language (EML)

Before you start adding transactional operations using behavior definitions, let's first get familiar with the Entity Manipulation Language (EML) that forms the basis of behavior definition. The EML controls a business object's behavior, and in the ABAP RESTful programming model, EML is a part of the ABAP language. EML enables CRUD access to the data found within transactional objects.

The EML has the following three main properties: modify entities, read entities, and commit entities.

Modify Entities

This property covers operations that allow data changes in entities and supports the following operations:

- Create: Create new entries in the entity.
- Create by Association: Creates new entries in the child entity by passing the key of the parent entity.
- Update: Updating/modifying the data in the entity.
- Delete: Deletion of data from the entity.

- Actions: Custom logic that under normal scenarios cannot be achieved by create, read, update, and delete (CRUD) operations. (In our example, we're using this custom logic to approve or reject purchase documents.)

All CRUD operations have input parameters as a table of instances. All the CRUD operation methods have input parameters which are of the *table* type. Also, for actions, a `RESULT` parameter can be added in case the action is supposed to return some result. `MODIFY` also has response parameters named `FAILED`, `MAPPED`, and `REPORTED`, these result parameters can be used to pass responses for each operation. You'll learn about result parameters in more detail in Section 4.2.6.

Read Entities

This property allows all operations that don't involve data changes/modifications in entities and supports the following operations:

- Read: Retrieves data from entity via key.
- Read by Association: Retrieves data from the child entities based on parent child association by passing the key.

The read operation has a `RESULT` property that must be used to specify the returning result. The Read by Association operation has a property called `LINK`, which contains only a list of keys, the key of the source entity, and the key of the target entity. This `LINK` property is used to ensure the read by association process is valid based on the key.

Commit Entities

All the operations mentioned under `MODIFY` (which are executed within the behavior implementation class or behavior pool) do not save data to the database. Instead, this data is stored in an intermediate buffer (internal tables), and the contents of these buffers are valid until the end of that ABAP session. Therefore, the data must be saved towards the end of the session.

These save sequences are triggered using the `COMMIT ENTITIES` statement. During runtime, these save sequences are divided into the following methods executed in this order:

- `finalize`: All the final calculations are done in this method.
- `check_before_save`: All final validations and checks are done here.

- save: Final commit is done to the database. In case the late numbering feature is being used (to replace the temporary key with the actual key before saving the data), then a call to the adjust_numbers method is also triggered at this stage.

4.2.5 Behavior Definitions to Add Transactional Features

As mentioned in the previous chapter, a behavior definition is used to describe the behavior of business object via the Behavior Definition Language (BDL). The behavior definition adds capabilities like CRUD operations and modeling aspects, such as the lock concept between parent and child views. In addition to the standard CRUD operations, a behavior definition also allows custom actions to be added a business object. A business object can only have one behavior definition, and the business object should be defined as a root view.

Now, let's create a behavior definition view to enable transactional actions in the above views. To create a behavior definition, right-click on your package and select **New • Other ABAP repository Object**. Then, expand the **Core Data Services** folder and select **Behavior Definition**, as shown in Figure 4.28.

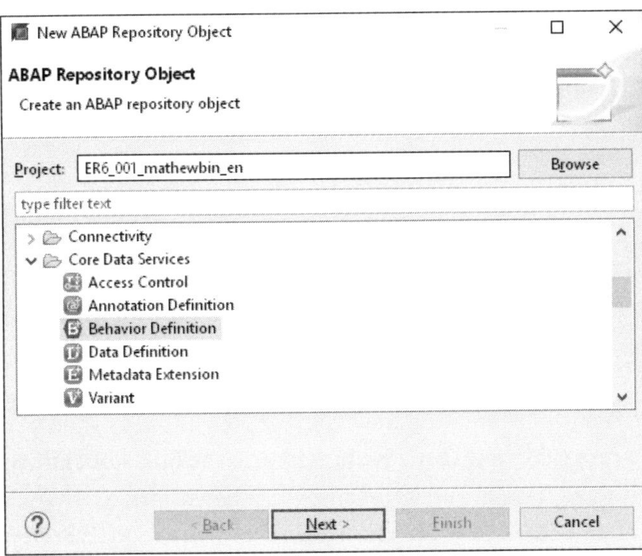

Figure 4.28 Create a New Behavior Definition

On the next screen, provide the behavior definition details. In this step, you can't provide your own name for the behavior definition. Instead, you can only specify the root entity name of the CDS view for which the behavior definition is being created. We'll enter the name of our root view `Z_I_PurchaseDocument_U`, as shown in Figure 4.29, and then click **Next** and **Finish**. In Figure 4.29, you might have noticed the **Implementation Type** field. You won't see this field unless you're on a cloud-based system. Currently, only unmanaged implementations are supported on on-premise systems.

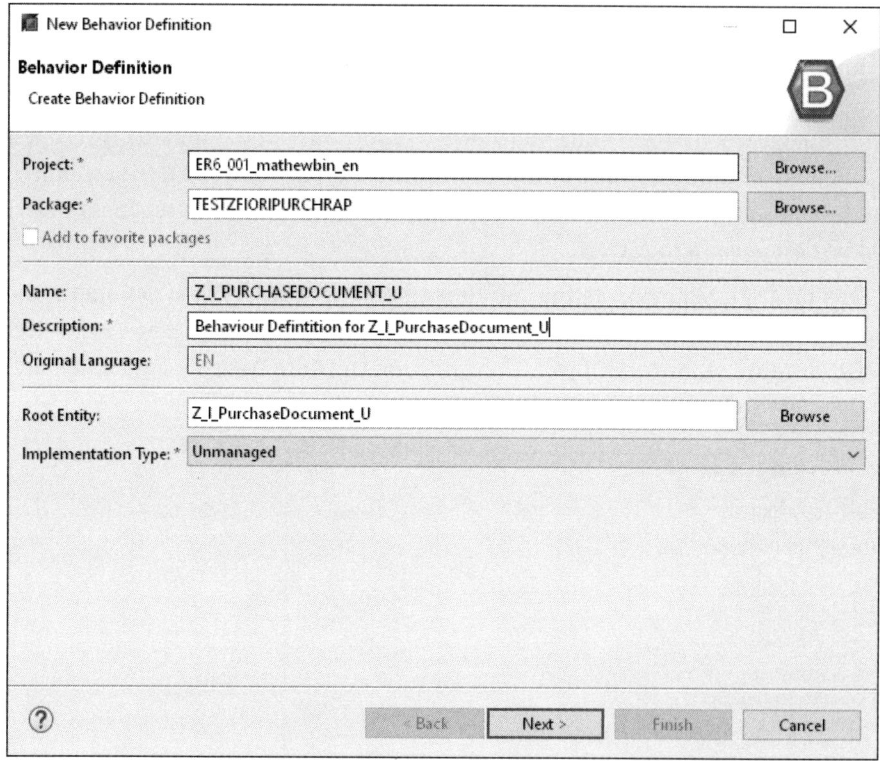

Figure 4.29 Behavior Definitions Details

The root CDS view you specified when creating the behavior definition, as shown in Figure 4.29. You can see the root CDS view name is entered into the field **Root Entity**, and the behavior definition itself have a 1:1 relationship. In other words, a behavior definition can only have once CDS root view, and vice versa. This root CDS view should handle all the necessary associations with other views.

As shown in Figure 4.30. the behavior definition wizard has automatically created code to implement CRUD actions. The wizard also identified a parent-child association between `Z_I_PurchaseDocument_U` and `Z_I_PurchaseDocumentItem_U` and created the Create by Association feature, also implemented automatically. This association is important if you want to create deep entities like the purchase document header item. In the next step, when you create the behavior definition implementation, the framework will automatically create the class methods for all the actions and associations (Create by Association, Read by Association, etc.). On the header line of the behavior definition, you'll see an implementation class name has been automatically suggested by the framework, as shown in Figure 4.30. We'll create this class as part of the behavior implementation in the next section. Also, in the header area, you can see the property `unique` defined after the class name. This declaration means that each operation is implemented exactly once. In other words, the same behavior global class defined in this step applies to all the entities defined within the definition, in this case, to `Z_I_Purchasedocument_u` and `Z_PurchaseDocumentItem`. If you need different global behavior implementation classes, then you must remove the class name and the unique declaration from the header line and define the individual class names next to the entities, for example, `implementation in class <class name> [unique]` or the syntax shown in Listing 4.19.

```
define behavior for Z_I_PurchaseDocument_U alias PurchaseDocument
implementation in class zbp_i_purchasedocument_u unique
define behavior for Z_I_PurchaseDocumentItem_U alias PurchaseDocumentItem
implementation in class zbp_i_purchasedocumentItem_U unique
```

Listing 4.19 Behavior Implementation Class Syntax

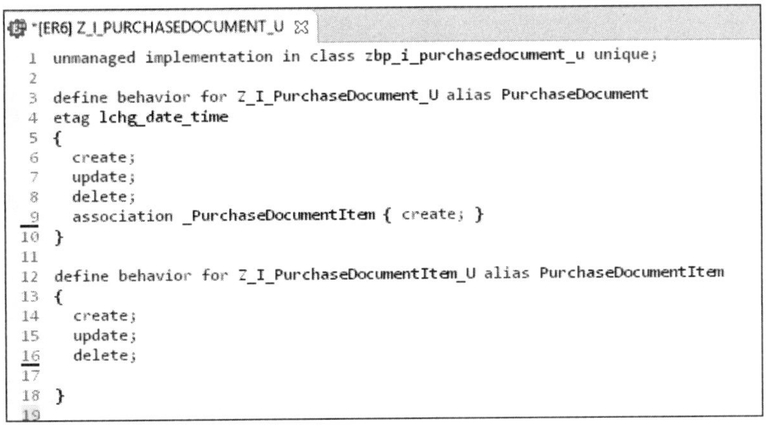

*[ER6] Z_I_PURCHASEDOCUMENT_U

```
unmanaged implementation in class zbp_i_purchasedocument_u unique;

define behavior for Z_I_PurchaseDocument_U alias PurchaseDocument
etag lchg_date_time
{
  create;
  update;
  delete;
  association _PurchaseDocumentItem { create; }
}

define behavior for Z_I_PurchaseDocumentItem_U alias PurchaseDocumentItem
{
  create;
  update;
  delete;

}
```

Figure 4.30 Behavior Definition Implementation

The behavior definition is like a BOPF implementation. If you're used to BOPF concepts, notice that the behavior definition is replicating BOPF steps in a similar sequence. A BOPF also has a part to define actions and then a part to implement the logic for those actions via classes. Behavior definitions are replacing the BOPF concept with a different approach.

Looking at the entity-level definitions shown in Figure 4.30, notice an `etag` definition as well (which we described in detail in Chapter 3, Section 3.4.3). The ETag is used to handle concurrency following the same concept in SAP Gateway where the framework fires a `READ` request from the backend with the client side before performing an update/modify action. You can also take advantage of other entity-level definitions based on the application requirements such as *lock* (lock master and lock dependent) or *late numbering* (assigns a temporary key to the field which, based on the business logic, might only get the actual key just before commit/save of the data in the backend). Detailed explanation of these concepts were provided in Chapter 3.

Another part of the behavior definition are its supported operations. The operations supported by behavior definitions are:

- Create
- Update
- Delete
- Create by Association (example: `association _PurchaseDocumentItem {create}`, as shown in Figure 4.30)

The `{create;}` keyword is used to declare that this association is create enabled, which can be used for deep entity creations like purchase document and item creation.

Another feature supported by the behavior definitions is actions, which are operations that not part of the standard behavior definition offering like CRUD operations. Actions can be defined in the following way:

```
[static] action ActionName [external 'ExternalActionName'] [parameter
InputParameterEntity] [result[cardinality] ResultParameterEntity]
```

This statement consists of the following elements:

- `static`: is optional (these action do not reference to any entity).
- `external`: keyword is optional, used to provide an alias name for internal actions.
- `parameter`: is optional which is used to handle inputs.

- `result`: is an optional output parameter for an action.
- `cardinality`: defines the cardinality of the resulting entity.
- `ResultParameterEntity`: defines the return type of the result parameter, this will be a CDS entity, if the result entity of the action is the same, then the keyword `$self`, as shown in Figure 4.31, can be used instead of a result parameter.

Sample syntax:

```
action ChangePriority parameter proirity result [0..1] $self
static action CancelOrder;
static action GetAlternateVendor result [0..*] I_Vendor;
```

Now, let's add two custom actions called `Approve_Order` and `Reject_Order` to our behavior definition since our app needs an option to approve or reject orders, as shown in Figure 4.31. We also need to make a few fields read-only and mandatory. In this case, we don't want the user to assign a purchase document number, so we'll make the `PurchaseDocument` field read-only, the same applies for the `Created By`, `Created Date`, `Last Changed By`, and `Last Changed Date` fields.

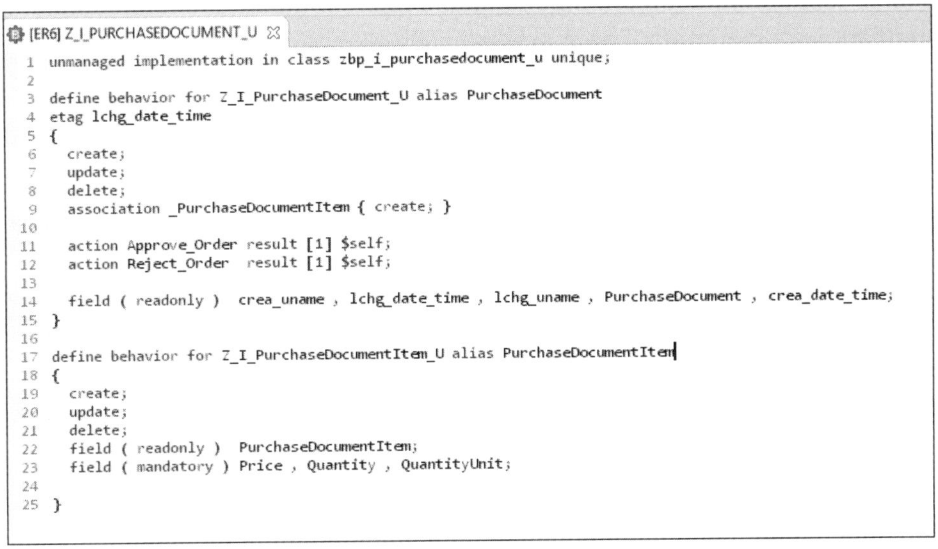

[ER6] Z_I_PURCHASEDOCUMENT_U

```
unmanaged implementation in class zbp_i_purchasedocument_u unique;

define behavior for Z_I_PurchaseDocument_U alias PurchaseDocument
etag lchg_date_time
{
  create;
  update;
  delete;
  association _PurchaseDocumentItem { create; }

  action Approve_Order result [1] $self;
  action Reject_Order  result [1] $self;

  field ( readonly ) crea_uname , lchg_date_time , lchg_uname , PurchaseDocument , crea_date_time;
}

define behavior for Z_I_PurchaseDocumentItem_U alias PurchaseDocumentItem
{
  create;
  update;
  delete;
  field ( readonly ) PurchaseDocumentItem;
  field ( mandatory ) Price , Quantity , QuantityUnit;

}
```

Figure 4.31 Adding Custom Action Buttons via Behavior Definition

Listing 4.20 shows the full code of the behavior definition with properties like `mandatory` and `readonly` for certain fields (which will automatically get picked up and added to the fields in the SAP Fiori app).

```
unmanaged implementation in class zbp_i_purchasedocument_u unique;

define behavior for Z_I_PurchaseDocument_U alias PurchaseDocument

{
  create;
  update;
  delete;
  association _PurchaseDocumentItem { create; }

  action Approve_Order result [1] $self;
  action Reject_Order  result [1] $self;

  field ( readonly )  crea_uname , lchg_date_time , lchg_uname ,
PurchaseDocument , crea_date_time;
}

define behavior for Z_I_PurchaseDocumentItem_U alias PurchaseDocumentItem

{
  create;
  update;
  delete;
  field ( readonly )  PurchaseDocumentItem;
  field ( mandatory ) Price , Quantity , QuantityUnit;

}
```

Listing 4.20 Behavior Definition

4.2.6 Behavior Implementation Language (BIL)

The behavior implementation implements the features/properties defined in the behavior definition and is itself defined using the Behavior Implementation Language (BIL), which is just a fancy way of saying it is using ABAP object-oriented classes to implement the logic. Implementation is done with the help of one or more global classes. Within these global classes, multiple local classes handle the behavior. In general, two local classes generated by the implementation framework:

- The behavior handler local class
- The behavior save local class

4.2.7 Behavior Handler Local Class

This local class is defined as an abstract final class that inherits from the `CL_ABAP_BEHAVIOR_HANDLER` class. The main methods within this class are `MODIFY`, `LOCK`, and `READ`. These methods are also defined based on which entity should have these methods by the keyword `FOR <OPERATION>`.

MODIFY

This method handles all the CRUD operations and actions on an entity. The create operation is defined by `MODIFY` using the syntax:

```
METHODS <method_name> FOR MODIFY IMPORTING <import_parameter>
FOR CREATE <entity_name>.
```

Modify Import Parameters

The `<import_parameter>` is a table type contains the structure shown in Figure 4.32. All the entity fields and its values:

- **`%cid`**
  Content ID, provided by the SADL framework but generally only useful for the late numbering feature. This field is also useful for deep entity creation, where the import parameter of the child entity will have another field `%cid_ref` that contains the same value as the `%cid` field of the parent entity, thus enabling the linking of records between both entities during runtime.

ENTITIES	[1x16(172)]Standard Table	\BDEF=Z_I_PURCHASEDOCUME...	Standard Table	0
[1]	Structure: deep	\BDEF=Z_I_PURCHASEDOCUME...	Structure: deep	172
%CID	%SADL_CID__1	ABP_BEHV_CID	CString	13
PURCHASEDOCUMENT		ZPURCHASEDOCUMENTDTEL	C	10
DESCRIPTION	Test	\TYPE=%_T00004S00000575O00...	CString	4
STATUS		\TYPE=%_T00004S00000575O00...	C	1
PRIORITY	3	\TYPE=%_T00004S00000575O00...	C	1
ISAPPROVALREQUIRED		\TYPE=%_T00004S00000575O00...	C	1
OVERALLPRICECRITICALITY	0	\TYPE=%_T00004S00000575O00...	INT1	1
OVERALLPRICE	0.0000	\TYPE=%_T00004S00000575O00...	P	14
CURRENCY		\TYPE=%_T00004S00000575O00...	C	5
PURCHASINGORGANIZATION	ORG1	\TYPE=%_T00004S00000575O00...	C	4
PURCHASEDOCUMENTIMAGEURL		\TYPE=%_T00004S00000575O00...	CString	0
CREA_DATE_TIME	0.0000000	TIMESTAMPL	P	11
CREA_UNAME		UNAME	C	12
LCHG_DATE_TIME	0.0000000	TIMESTAMPL	P	11
LCHG_UNAME		UNAME	C	12
%CONTROL	Structure: flat, not charlike	\TYPE=%_T00004S00000573O00...	Structure: flat, not charlike	14

Figure 4.32 Import Parameter for Create Operation under MODIFY

- **`%control`**
  A structure that contains the name of all the properties of the entity and an

additional property flag field that indicates whether the value of property field of the entity was changed by the user or not. This field is essential when carrying out updates on the underlying table in the database. The data type of this flag field is ABP_BEHV_FLAG, as shown in Figure 4.33.

(x)= Variables ⛝ Breakpoints

Name	Value	Actual Type	Technical Type	Length
<Enter variable>				0
ENTITIES[1]-%CONTROL	Structure: flat, not charlike	\TYPE=%_T00004S00000573O00...	Structure: flat, not charlike	14
PURCHASEDOCUMENT	00	ABP_BEHV_FLAG	X	1
DESCRIPTION	01	ABP_BEHV_FLAG	X	1
STATUS	01	ABP_BEHV_FLAG	X	1
PRIORITY	01	ABP_BEHV_FLAG	X	1
ISAPPROVALREQUIRED	01	ABP_BEHV_FLAG	X	1
OVERALLPRICECRITICALITY	01	ABP_BEHV_FLAG	X	1
OVERALLPRICE	01	ABP_BEHV_FLAG	X	1
CURRENCY	01	ABP_BEHV_FLAG	X	1
PURCHASINGORGANIZATION	01	ABP_BEHV_FLAG	X	1
PURCHASEDOCUMENTIMAGEURL	01	ABP_BEHV_FLAG	X	1
CREA_DATE_TIME	00	ABP_BEHV_FLAG	X	1
CREA_UNAME	00	ABP_BEHV_FLAG	X	1
LCHG_DATE_TIME	00	ABP_BEHV_FLAG	X	1
LCHG_UNAME	00	ABP_BEHV_FLAG	X	1

Figure 4.33 The CONTROL Table within the Return Parameter of the Create Operation

Modify Export Parameters

The `<export/Changing_Parameters>`: by default, when you look at the generated code of the behavior implementation class, you won't see any `CHANGING` parameters, which exist as implicit parameters. You can pass values to the parameters within these methods at runtime without having to declare them manually. This concept is also shown in Figure 4.27.

Now, let's look at each of the export parameter tables:

- `FAILED`
  This export table is a nested table with a table for every entity that is defined within the behavior definition. The advantage to filling in this export table is that, if an error arises and you want to cancel the save sequence, all you need to do is to return a key via this table, and the save sequence will be canceled by the framework automatically. As shown in Figure 4.34, the fields of this table are as follows:
  - `%cid`: Content ID.
  - `%pid`: The preliminary ID is provided by the application when an entity set is created. This attribute is used as replacement when a temporary number is not used. This attribute is only valid when `LATE NUMBERING` is defined that isn't followed by an `IN PLACE` definition.

- ID: This attribute can be one or several fields for an entity and are basically CDS field properties masked as key fields.
- %fail: The reason for error is specified in this attribute.

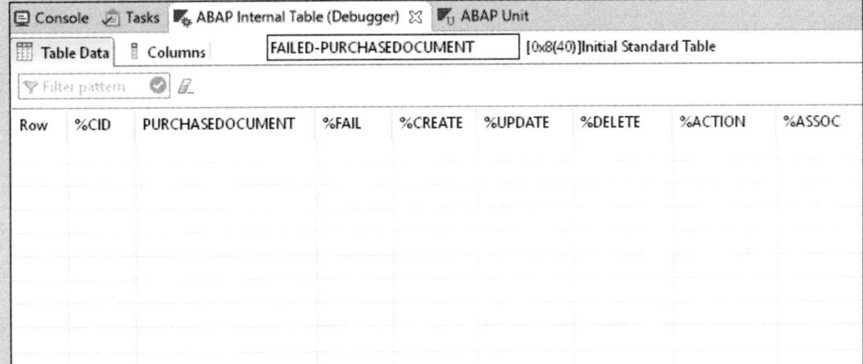

Figure 4.34 The Export Parameter Table for FAILED

- MAPPED
  This export table is also a nested table with one table for every entity set defined in the behavior definition. This parameters in this table provide ID mapping information back to the frontend when the LATE NUMBERING feature is being used. Basically, as shown in Figure 4.35, this table stores objects that were created:
  - %cid: Content ID
  - %pid: Preliminary ID
  - ID: Key field values

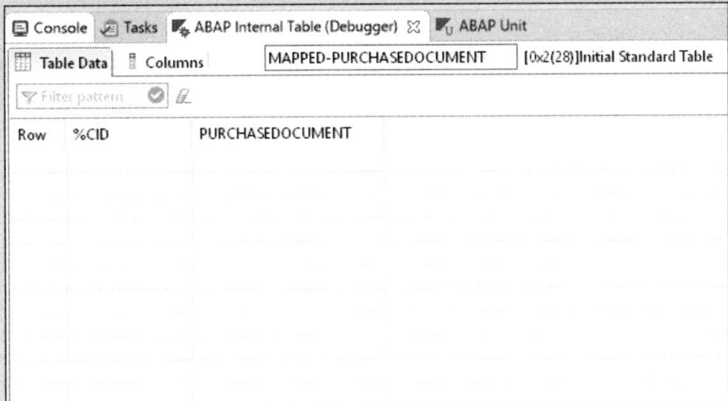

Figure 4.35 The Export Parameter Table for MAPPED

- **REPORTED**
  This table is also an export table with one table for every entity set defined in the behavior definition. The parameters in this table can be used to pass messages specific to an entity or can be passed with the %OTHERS table in it to pass messages that are not specific to an entity set. For entity-specific messages, as shown in Figure 4.36, the following parameters are used:
  - %CID: Content ID.
  - %PIDC: Preliminary ID.
  - ID: Key field values.
  - %MSG: This field is an instance of the interface IF_ABAP_BEHV_MESSAGE.
  - %ELEMENT: This optional field is of the data type ABP_BEHV_FLAG (which is the same as the %control field of the CHANGING parameter).

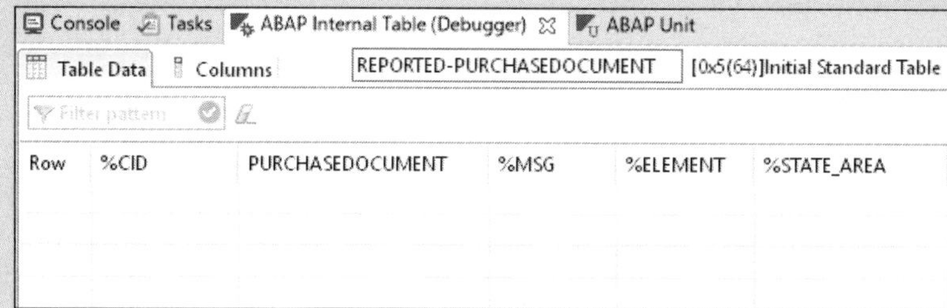

Figure 4.36 The Export Parameter Table for REPORTED

For general messages, the table inside the REPORTED table REPORTED-%OTHERS are used. This table line type is a reference of the interface IF_ABAP_BEHV_MESSAGE, as shown in Figure 4.37.

(x)= Variables | Breakpoints

Name	Value	Actual Type	Technical Type	Length
<Enter variable>				0
REPORTED	Structure: deep	\BDEF=Z_I_PURCHASEDOCUME...	Structure: deep	24
PURCHASEDOCUMENT	[0x5(64)]Initial Standard ...	\BDEF=Z_I_PURCHASEDOCUME...	Standard Table	0
PURCHASEDOCUMENTITEM	[0x7(104)]Initial Standard...	\BDEF=Z_I_PURCHASEDOCUME...	Standard Table	0
%OTHER	[0x1(8)]Initial Standard T...	Type TT_MESSAGE in IF_ABAP_B...	Standard Table	0

Figure 4.37 The Export Parameter Table for REPORTED-%OTHERS

Create by Association

Create by Association is a subset of the create operation and is used to create instances of child entities by making use of the association property. The importing parameter for this operation will contain the key field of the parent entity and a table containing the data for the child entity, as follows:

```
METHODS <method_name> FOR MODIFY IMPORTING <import_parameter>
FOR CREATE <entity_name>\<association_name>.
```

Create by Association Import Parameters

The Create by Association fields of the `<import_parameter>` table contain the following parameters, shown in Figure 4.38:

- All key fields of the parent entity.
- `%cid_ref`: Reference to the content ID in the child entity.
- `%target`: Another table that contains the data for the child entity, as shown in Figure 4.39.
- `%cid`: All the properties of the child entity.
- `%control`: Another structure that contains all the properties of the CDS view field in the first column and a property flag (that indicates whether the value of property field of the entity has been changed by the user or not) in the second column of the data type ABP_BEHV_FLAG.

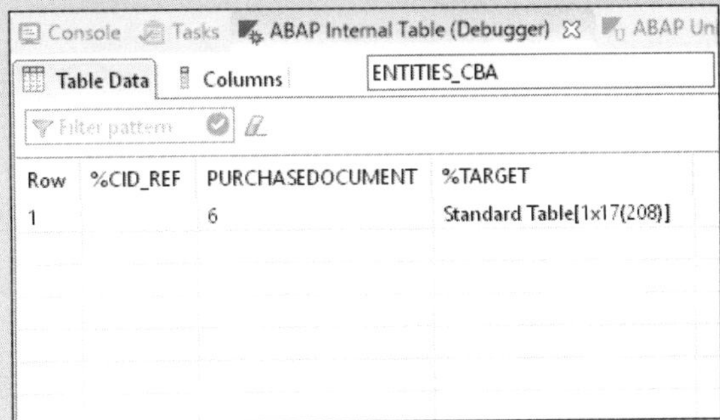

Figure 4.38 The Import Parameter Table for Create by Association

Console | Tasks | ABAP Internal Table (Debugger) | ABAP Unit

Table Data | Columns | ENTITIES_CBA[1]-%TARGET | [1x17(208)]Standard Table

Row	%CID	PUR...	PURCHASE...	DESCRIPTI...	VENDOR	VENDORTYPE	PRICE	CURRENCY	QUANTITY	QUA...	OVERALL...	P...	%CONTROL
1	%SADL_CID_1			Macbook ...	ABC Vendor	E	2800.00	EUR	1.00	PC	2800.0000		Structure: flat, not charlike

Figure 4.39 TARGET Table inside the Import Parameter Table for Create by Association

Create by Association Export Parameters

Like the other operations of the `MODIFY` statement, the update operation also has the following `CHANGING` fields:

- `FAILED`: Same table as the create operation export parameter.
- `REPORTED`: Same table as the create operation export parameter.
- `MAPPED`: Same table as the create operation export parameter.

Update

The update operation is defined using `MODIFY` method via the following syntax:

```
METHODS <method_name> FOR MODIFY IMPORTING <import_parameter>
FOR UPDATE <entity_name>.
```

Update Input Parameters

The update fields of the `<import_parameter>` table contain the following fields, also shown in Figure 4.40:

- All the entity properties.
- `%cid_ref`: Reference to the content ID in the child entity.
- `%pid`: Preliminary ID.
- `%key`: All the key fields of the underlying CDS view.
- `%data`: Contains the data of all the CDS view fields.

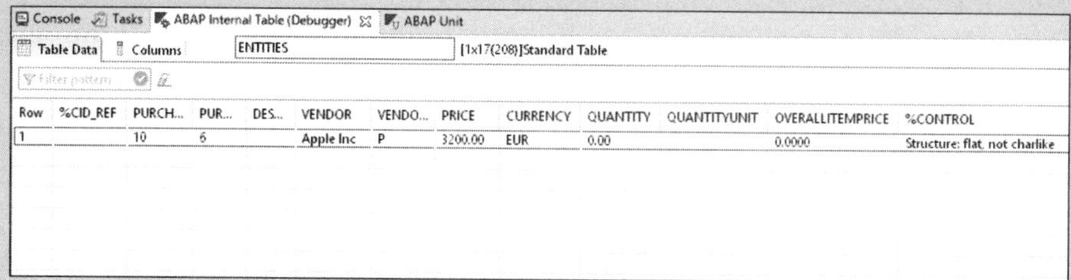

Figure 4.40 The Import Parameter Table for Update

`%control` is another structure that contains all the properties of the CDS view field in the first column and a property flag, which indicates whether the value of property field of the entity was changed by the user or not (columns with new values are marked with the value "01," and the unchanged field values are marked with the value "00" by default) in the second column of the data type ABP_BEHV_FLAG, as shown in Figure 4.41.

Name	Value	Actual Type	Technical Type	Length
<Enter variable>				0
ENTITIES[1]-%CONTROL	Structure: flat, not charlike	\TYPE=%_T00004S00000578O00...	Structure: flat, not charlike	15
PURCHASEDOCUMENTITEM	00	ABP_BEHV_FLAG	X	1
PURCHASEDOCUMENT	00	ABP_BEHV_FLAG	X	1
DESCRIPTION	00	ABP_BEHV_FLAG	X	1
VENDOR	01	ABP_BEHV_FLAG	X	1
VENDORTYPE	01	ABP_BEHV_FLAG	X	1
PRICE	01	ABP_BEHV_FLAG	X	1
CURRENCY	01	ABP_BEHV_FLAG	X	1
QUANTITY	00	ABP_BEHV_FLAG	X	1
QUANTITYUNIT	00	ABP_BEHV_FLAG	X	1
OVERALLITEMPRICE	00	ABP_BEHV_FLAG	X	1
PURCHASEDOCUMENTITEMIMAGEURL	00	ABP_BEHV_FLAG	X	1
CREA_DATE_TIME	00	ABP_BEHV_FLAG	X	1
CREA_UNAME	00	ABP_BEHV_FLAG	X	1
LCHG_DATE_TIME	00	ABP_BEHV_FLAG	X	1
LCHG_UNAME	00	ABP_BEHV_FLAG	X	1

Figure 4.41 CONTROL Table inside the Import Parameter Table for Update

Like the other operations of the MODIFY statement, the update operation also has the CHANGING fields:

- FAILED: Same table as the create operation export parameter
- REPORTED: Same table as the create operation export parameter

Delete

The delete operation is defined using MODIFY method via the following syntax:

```
METHODS <method_name> FOR MODIFY IMPORTING <import_parameter>
FOR DELETE <entity_name>.
```

Delete Import Parameters

The delete fields of the <import_parameter> table contain the following fields, as shown in Figure 4.42:

- ID fields: All the key fields of the underlying CDS view
- %cid_ref: Reference to the content ID in the child entity
- %pid: Preliminary ID

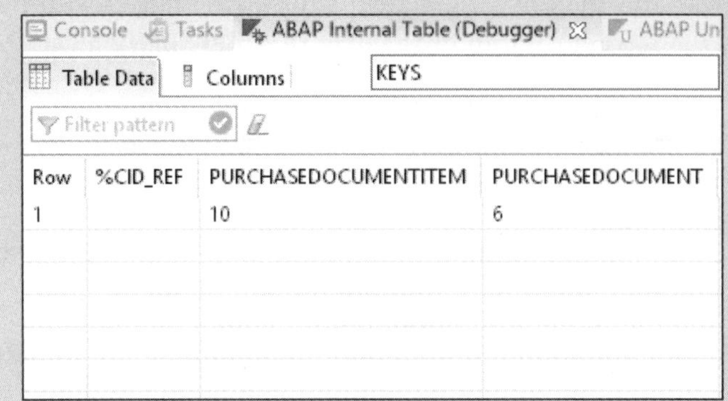

Figure 4.42 The Import Parameter Table for Delete

Delete Export Parameters

Like the other operations of the MODIFY statement, the update operation also has the following CHANGING fields:

- FAILED: Same table as the create operation export parameter
- REPORTED: Same table as the create operation export parameter

Action

An action is defined using MODIFY method via the following syntax:

```
METHODS <method_name> FOR MODIFY IMPORTING <import_parameter>
FOR ACTION <entity_name> RESULT <result_parameter>.
```

Action Import Parameters

The action import fields of the <import_parameter> table contain the following fields, as shown in Figure 4.43:

- ID fields: All the key fields of the underlying CDS view
- %cid_ref: Reference to the content ID in the child entity
- %pid: Preliminary ID
- %param: An optional field used if any import parameters are defined

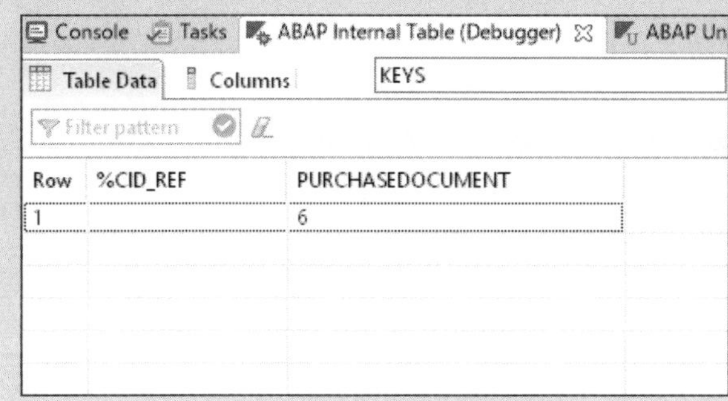

Figure 4.43 The Import Parameter Table for Action

Action Export Parameters

Like the other operations of the `MODIFY` statement, the update operation also has the following `CHANGING` fields:

- `FAILED`: Same table as the create operation export parameter
- `REPORTED`: Same table as the create operation export parameter

An optional parameter, `<result_parameter>`, can contain the resulting data from the action if defined in the behavior definition.

LOCK

This method is defined using the following syntax:

```
METHODS <method_name> FOR LOCK <import_parameter>
FOR LOCK <entity_name>.
```

Lock Import Parameters

The lock import fields of the `<import_parameter>` table contain the following parameters:

- ID fields: All the key fields of the underlying CDS view
- `%cid_ref`: Reference to the content ID in the child entity
- `%pid`: Preliminary ID

Lock Export Parameters

For the `<export_parameters>` table, like the other operations of the `MODIFY` statement, the lock operation also has the following `CHANGING` fields:

- `FAILED`: Same table as the create operation export parameter
- `REPORTED`: Same table as the create operation export parameter

READ

This method is for read-only access. This method has two variants: Read by Key and Read by Association. Let's look at each variant in depth next.

Read by Key

This method has the following syntax:

```
MTEHODS <read> FOR READ IMPORTING <keys> FOR READ <entity_name> RESULT
<exporting_parameter>
```

Read Import Parameters

The read import fields of the `<import_parameter>` table contain the following parameters:

- ID fields: All the key fields of the underlying CDS view.
- `%pid`: Preliminary ID.
- `%control`: Structure that contains all the properties of the CDS view field in the first column and a property flag in the second column of the data type ABP_BEHV_FLAG.

Read Export Parameters

Like the other operations of the `MODIFY` statement, the update operation also has the following `CHANGING` fields:

- `FAILED`: Same table as the create operation export parameter.
- `REPORTED`: Same table as the create operation export parameter.
- `<export_parameter>`: Data from the read statement.
- `%pid`: Preliminary ID.
- All properties of the target entity with their values.

Read by Association

Read by Association has the following syntax:

```
METHODS <read> FOR READ IMPORTING <import_parameter> FOR READ <parent_entity_
name>\<_association> FULL <result_requested> RESULT RESULT <exporting_
parameter> LINK <association_links>
```

Read by Association Import Parameters

The Read by Association fields of the `<import_parameter>` table contain the following parameters:

- ID fields: All the key fields of the underlying CDS view.
- `%pid`: Preliminary ID.
- `<parent_entity_name>\<_association>`: Name of the parent entity and the child entity or any other association with the parent entity.
- `<result_requested>`: An indicator. If `<result_requested>` is `INITIAL`, then only the return table associated with the `LINK` (check the above syntax for Read by Association) is returned. If the `<result_requested>` is not `INITIAL`, then the return tables associated with both `LINK` and `RESULT` are returned.

Read by Association Export Parameters

Like the other operations of the `MODIFY` statement, the update operation also has the following `CHANGING` fields:

- `FAILED`: Same table as the create operation export parameter.
- `REPORTED`: Same table as the create operation export parameter.
- `<association_links>`: This return table type contains the parent and child/association keys.
- `<exporting_parameter>`: This parameter returns the data from the read request. As mentioned earlier, the `RESULT`'s return parameter will only be filled if the `<result_requested>` is not initial.
  - `%pid`: Preliminary ID.
  - All the target entities fields with its values.

MODIFY, LOCK, and READ Syntax

The following examples syntax cover all operations based on `MODIFY`, `LOCK`, and `READ` (refer also to Section 4.2.7, subsection "MODIFY"):

```
METHODS <create> FOR MODIFY IMPORTING <entities> FOR CREATE <entity_name>.
METHODS <update> FOR MODIFY IMPORTING <entities> FOR UPDATE <entity_name>.
METHODS <delete> FOR MODIFY IMPORTING <keys> FOR DELETE <entity_name>.
METHODS <approve_order> FOR MODIFY IMPORTING <keys> FOR ACTION <approve_order>
RESULT <result_parameter>.
METHODS <lock> FOR LOCK IMPORTING <import_parameter> FOR LOCK <entity_name>.
METHODS <read> FOR MODIFY IMPORTING <keys> FOR CREATE <entity_name>
<entity_name\_association_name>. - (for Create by Association)
METHODS <read> FOR READ IMPORTING <keys> FOR READ
<entity_name\_association_name> FULL <result_requested> RESULT LINK <result_
parameter> LINK association_links
METHODS read FOR MODIFY IMPORTING <import_parameter> FOR FUNCTION <entity_
name~action_name> RESULT <result_parameter>
```

Note

Data passed into the MODIFY operations are not really saved in the database, as shown earlier in Figure 4.27. In reality, this data is stored in intermediate buffer tables. The data will be saved into the database via the transactional methods in the behavior saver local classes, which we'll discuss in the next section.

4.2.8 Behavior Saver Local Class

This class (a concept discussed earlier and shown in Figure 4.27) is implemented as a local class within the behavior definition pool to enable the transactional methods such as finalize, check_before_save, save, etc. This class is defined as an abstract final class and inherits from CL_ABAP_BEHAVIOR_SAVER, as shown in Listing 4.21.

```
CLASS lcl_behavior_saver DEFINITION INHERITING FROM cl_abap_behavior_saver
ABSTRACT FINAL.

PROTECTED SECTION.
    METHODS finalize REDEFINITION.
    METHODS check_before_save REDEFINITION.
    METHODS adjust_numbers REDEFINITION.
    METHODS save REDEFINITION.
    METHODS cleanup REDEFINITION.
ENDCLASS.
```

Listing 4.21 Local Behavior Saver Class

Let's briefly look at each of the methods in the local behavior saver class:

- `Finalize`
  The data is finalized before saving into the database. This method also has export parameters `FAILED` and `REPORTED`, which is of the same type as the export parameters for CRUD operations we discussed earlier in Section 4.2.7 about the behavior handler local class, the only difference is that `%cid` is not part of these tables.
- `check_before_save`
  Checking the data in the buffer table for consistency, this method is the last point where the `COMMIT` of data to the database can be rolled back. In case of error, the next method in the sequence, `save`, can be skipped by filling the export parameter `FAILED`. Also, the method `cleanup` can be called to clear the buffer tables. This method has the following export parameters:
  - `FAILED`: Same table as the CRUD operations export parameter minus the `%cid` field.
  - `REPORTED`: Same table as the CRUD operations export parameter minus the `%cid` field.
  - `Save`: With this method, the values from the buffer tables are retrieved, and the final commit of the data to the database is performed.
- `cleanup`
  This method contains the logic to clear all the buffer tables and other related variables that needs to be initialized. This method can be called by any of the above methods in the saver class. For example, the `finalize` and `check_before_save` methods will call the `cleanup` method in case of any errors found in the data that warrants a rollback of the operation. You can also call this method after the `save` to cleanup everything.

4.2.9 Behavior Implementation

A behavior implementation will create the relevant handler classes for the transactional operations logic by referring to the corresponding operations defined in the behavior definition.

Creating a New Behavior Implementation

Now, let's create a behavior implementation. Right-click on a behavior definition. Then, select **New Behavior Implementation** folder, as shown in Figure 4.44.

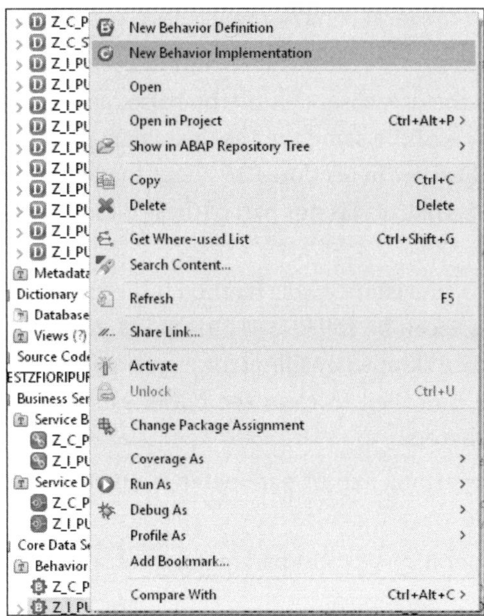

Figure 4.44 Creating Behavior Implementation

Provide the same name for the behavior implementation class that was automatically generated in the behavior definition by the framework, as shown in Figure 4.45. Enter information into the **Description** field and click **Next.**

New Behavior Class

ABAP Class

Create an ABAP class

Project: * ER6_001_mathewbin_en

Package: * TESTZFIORIPURCHRAP

Add to favorite packages

Name: * ZBP_I_PURCHASEDOCUMENT_U

Description: * Behavior Implementation for Z_I_PURCHASEDOCUMENT_U

Original Language: EN

Behavior Definition: Z_I_PURCHASEDOCUMENT_U

< Back | Next > | Finish | Cancel

Figure 4.45 Behavior Implementation Class Details

A behavior definition pool or global class, shown in Figure 4.46, will have a subsequent implementation of behavior handler local classes to handle the logic for CRUD operations, for locks, etc. This global class also has a local saver class to commit the changes from CRUD operations.

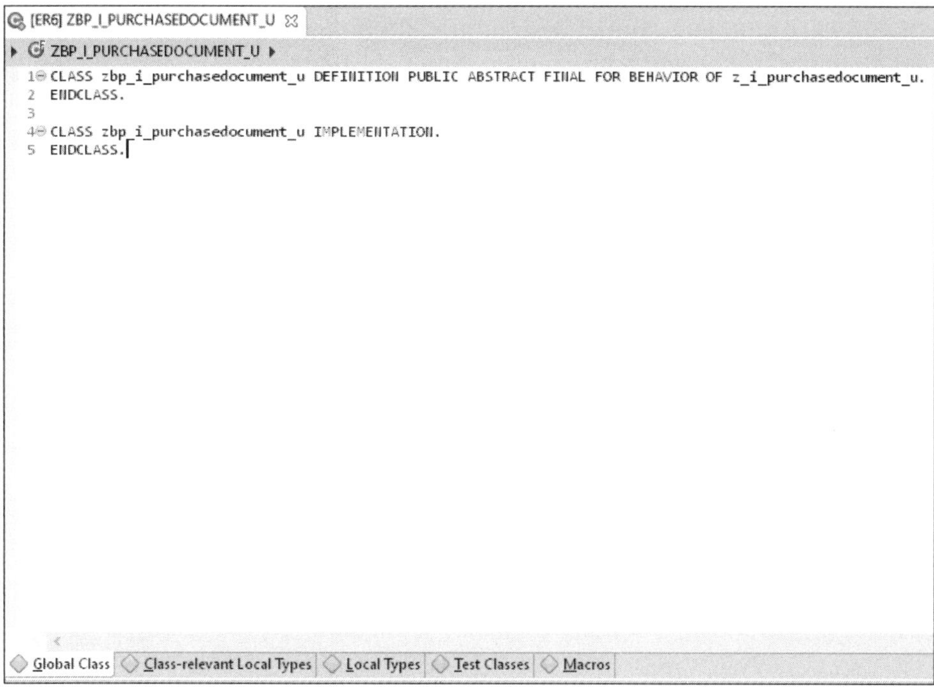

Figure 4.46 Behavior Definition Pool or Global Class

Once the behavior class is implemented, click on the **Local Types** tab on the bottom of the class. You'll see two sets of local classes were generated. The first, `lhc_purchaseDocument`, shown in Figure 4.47, is inheriting from `CL_ABAP_BEHAVIOR_HANDLER` (which handles the actions on the business object defined by the behavior definition, such as CRUD operations or custom actions). Here the methods used typed parameters, unlike the previous development model (the ABAP programming model for SAP Fiori) and thus are much easier to work with since the parameter types are direct references to the entity types the parameters are based on.

The second local class `lsc_Z_I_PurchaseDocument_U`, shown in Figure 4.48, inherits from `CL_ABAP_BEHAVIOR_SAVER` (to handle the save/commit part of the transaction). The complete code for the class is shown in Listing 4.22.

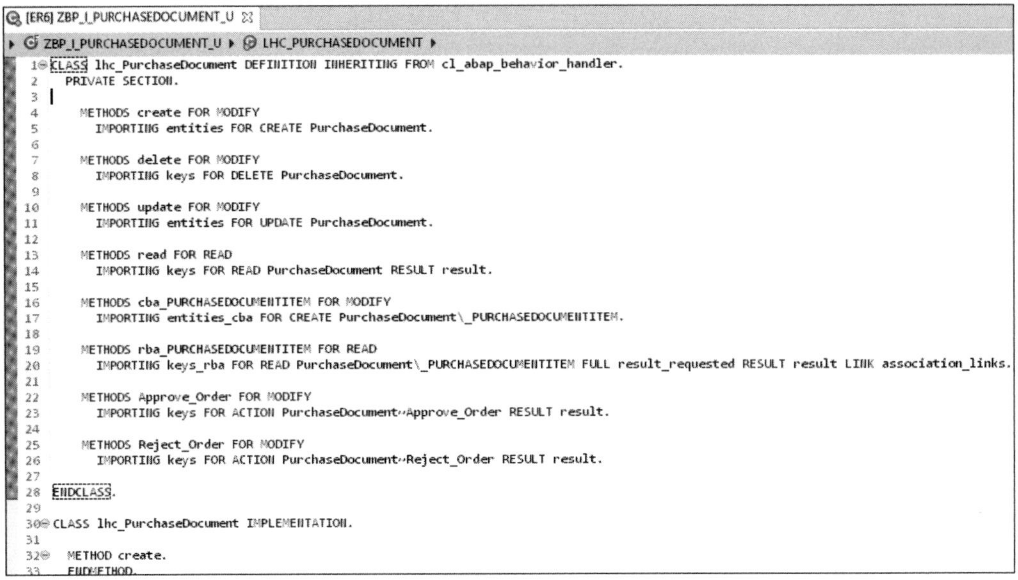

[ER6] ZBP_I_PURCHASEDOCUMENT_U

ZBP_I_PURCHASEDOCUMENT_U ▸ LHC_PURCHASEDOCUMENT ▸

```
CLASS lhc_PurchaseDocument DEFINITION INHERITING FROM cl_abap_behavior_handler.
  PRIVATE SECTION.

    METHODS create FOR MODIFY
      IMPORTING entities FOR CREATE PurchaseDocument.

    METHODS delete FOR MODIFY
      IMPORTING keys FOR DELETE PurchaseDocument.

    METHODS update FOR MODIFY
      IMPORTING entities FOR UPDATE PurchaseDocument.

    METHODS read FOR READ
      IMPORTING keys FOR READ PurchaseDocument RESULT result.

    METHODS cba_PURCHASEDOCUMENTITEM FOR MODIFY
      IMPORTING entities_cba FOR CREATE PurchaseDocument\_PURCHASEDOCUMENTITEM.

    METHODS rba_PURCHASEDOCUMENTITEM FOR READ
      IMPORTING keys_rba FOR READ PurchaseDocument\_PURCHASEDOCUMENTITEM FULL result_requested RESULT result LINK association_links.

    METHODS Approve_Order FOR MODIFY
      IMPORTING keys FOR ACTION PurchaseDocument~Approve_Order RESULT result.

    METHODS Reject_Order FOR MODIFY
      IMPORTING keys FOR ACTION PurchaseDocument~Reject_Order RESULT result.

ENDCLASS.

CLASS lhc_PurchaseDocument IMPLEMENTATION.

  METHOD create.
  ENDMETHOD.
```

Figure 4.47 Behavior Implementation Local Class for Handling User Actions

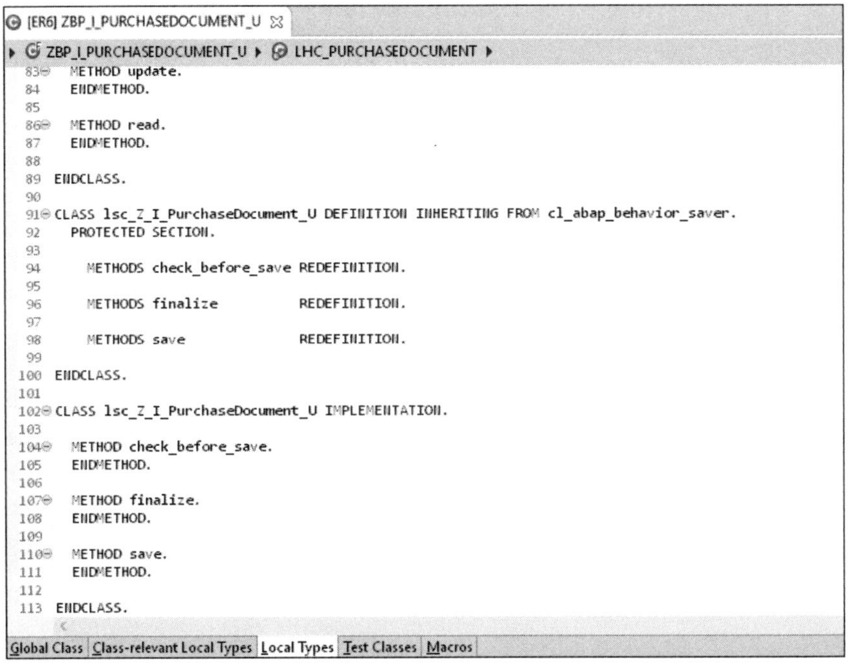

[ER6] ZBP_I_PURCHASEDOCUMENT_U

ZBP_I_PURCHASEDOCUMENT_U ▸ LHC_PURCHASEDOCUMENT ▸

```
  METHOD update.
  ENDMETHOD.

  METHOD read.
  ENDMETHOD.

ENDCLASS.

CLASS lsc_Z_I_PurchaseDocument_U DEFINITION INHERITING FROM cl_abap_behavior_saver.
  PROTECTED SECTION.

    METHODS check_before_save REDEFINITION.

    METHODS finalize          REDEFINITION.

    METHODS save              REDEFINITION.

ENDCLASS.

CLASS lsc_Z_I_PurchaseDocument_U IMPLEMENTATION.

  METHOD check_before_save.
  ENDMETHOD.

  METHOD finalize.
  ENDMETHOD.

  METHOD save.
  ENDMETHOD.

ENDCLASS.
```

Global Class | Class-relevant Local Types | Local Types | Test Classes | Macros

Figure 4.48 Behavior Implementation Local Class for Handling Saving Data into Database

Listing 4.22 is a complete listing for the local handler class implementation for a purchase document.

```
CLASS lhc_PurchaseDocument DEFINITION INHERITING FROM cl_abap_behavior_
handler.
  PRIVATE SECTION.
    METHODS create FOR MODIFY
      IMPORTING entities FOR CREATE PurchaseDocument.

    METHODS delete FOR MODIFY
      IMPORTING keys FOR DELETE PurchaseDocument.

    METHODS update FOR MODIFY
      IMPORTING entities FOR UPDATE PurchaseDocument.

    METHODS read FOR READ
      IMPORTING keys FOR READ PurchaseDocument RESULT result.

    METHODS cba_PURCHASEDOCUMENTITEM FOR MODIFY
      IMPORTING entities_cba FOR CREATE PurchaseDocument\_
purchasedocumentitem.

    METHODS rba_PURCHASEDOCUMENTITEM FOR READ
      IMPORTING keys_rba FOR READ PurchaseDocument\_purchasedocumentitem FULL
result_requested RESULT result LINK association_links.

    METHODS Approve_Order FOR MODIFY
      IMPORTING keys FOR ACTION PurchaseDocument~Approve_Order RESULT result.

    METHODS Reject_Order FOR MODIFY
      IMPORTING keys FOR ACTION PurchaseDocument~Reject_Order RESULT result.
ENDCLASS.

CLASS lhc_PurchaseDocument IMPLEMENTATION.

  METHOD create.
  ENDMETHOD.
  METHOD delete.
```

```
  ENDMETHOD.
  METHOD update.
  ENDMETHOD.
  METHOD read.
  ENDMETHOD.
  METHOD cba_PURCHASEDOCUMENTITEM.
  ENDMETHOD.
  METHOD rba_PURCHASEDOCUMENTITEM.
  ENDMETHOD.
  METHOD Approve_Order.
  ENDMETHOD.
  METHOD Reject_Order.
  ENDMETHOD.
ENDCLASS.

CLASS lhc_PurchaseDocumentItem DEFINITION INHERITING FROM cl_abap_behavior_
handler.
  PRIVATE SECTION.

    METHODS create FOR MODIFY
      IMPORTING entities FOR CREATE PurchaseDocumentItem.

    METHODS delete FOR MODIFY
      IMPORTING keys FOR DELETE PurchaseDocumentItem.

    METHODS update FOR MODIFY
      IMPORTING entities FOR UPDATE PurchaseDocumentItem.

    METHODS read FOR READ
      IMPORTING keys FOR READ PurchaseDocumentItem RESULT result.
    DATA et_messages        TYPE zif_prchdc_logic=>tt_if_t100_message.

ENDCLASS.

CLASS lhc_PurchaseDocumentItem IMPLEMENTATION.
  METHOD create.
  ENDMETHOD.
```

```
  METHOD delete.
  ENDMETHOD.
  METHOD update.
  ENDMETHOD.
  METHOD read.
  ENDMETHOD.
ENDCLASS.

CLASS lsc_Z_I_PurchaseDocument_U DEFINITION INHERITING FROM cl_abap_behavior_
saver.
  PROTECTED SECTION.
    METHODS check_before_save REDEFINITION.
    METHODS finalize          REDEFINITION.
    METHODS save              REDEFINITION.
    METHODS cleanup           REDEFINITION.
ENDCLASS.

CLASS lsc_Z_I_PurchaseDocument_U IMPLEMENTATION.
  METHOD check_before_save.
  ENDMETHOD.
  METHOD finalize.
  ENDMETHOD.
  METHOD save.
  ENDMETHOD.
  METHOD cleanup.
  ENDMETHOD.
ENDCLASS.
```

Listing 4.22 Behavior Pool Implementation Class for the PurchaseDocument App

Behavior Implementation Class Coding Overview

Before going into the coding to implement in these local classes, let's look at an overview of the dependent classes and methods that we'll be using in our example, as shown in Figure 4.49, to implement our behavior pool.

The local behavior handler classes `lhc_PurchaseDocument` and `lhc_PurchaseDocumentItem` (which belongs to the main global class `zpb_i_purchasedocument_u` will have its) for the purchase document and purchase document item, respectively. The corresponding behavior save class `lsc_Z_I_PurchaseDocument_U` will depend on the following classes to handle the transactional logic in their respective methods.

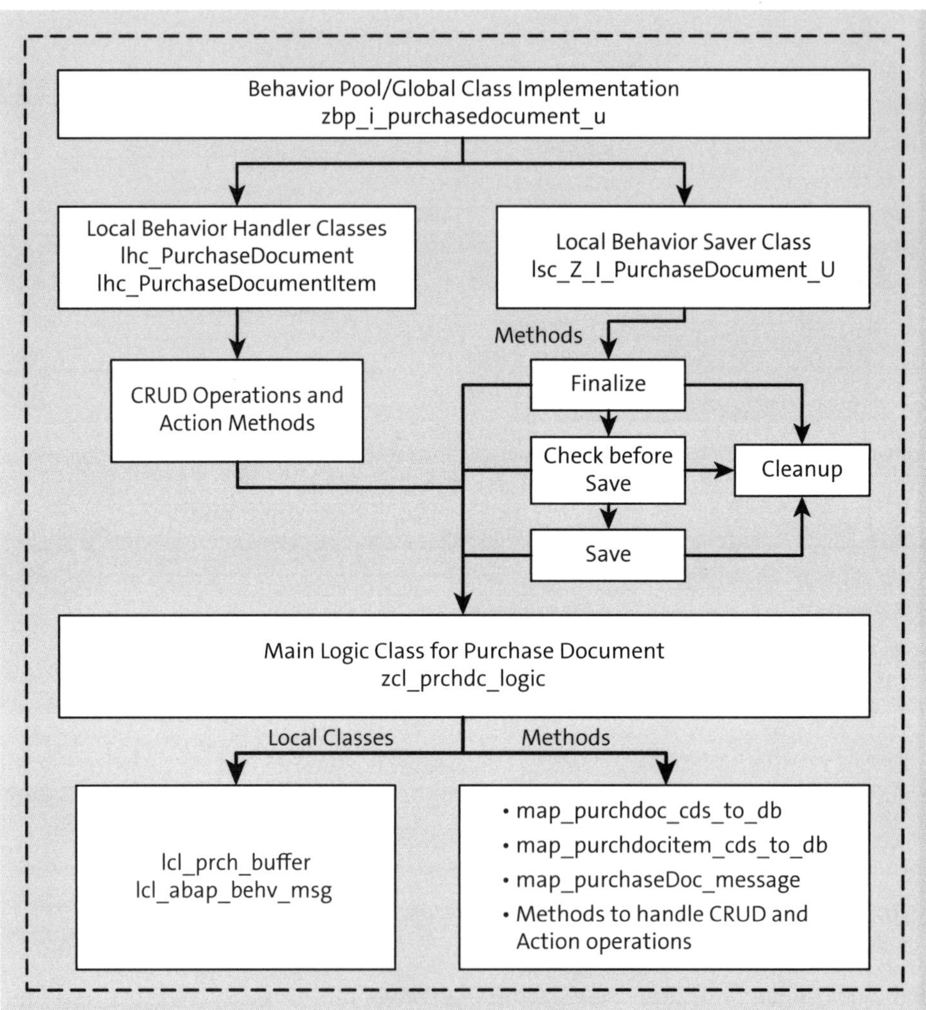

Figure 4.49 Behavior Pool Implementation Logic for the PurchaseDocument Management App

To handle the logic in CRUD and action methods within the behavior handler class, we'll create a new class called `zcl_prchdc_logic` to act as a bridge to store and pass the data between the local handler class and the saver class. The `zcl_prchdc_logic` has a few methods and local classes to handle our apps logic:

- **map_purchdoc_cds_to_db**
  As mentioned earlier in Section 4.2.6, the import parameters of the CRUD operations and the action methods have multiple fields in addition to the actual data we need to save into the corresponding database table. So, we need to map the relevant fields to a compatible structure, and then we can store them in the buffer table to be saved later in the saver class. In the following methods, you can see that the incoming structure from the PurchaseDocument entity's operations are mapped to the corresponding structure of the database table for the purchase document, which helps with storing the data in the buffer table for later saving the data directly to the corresponding database table (see Listing 4.23).

```
CLASS-METHODS map_purchdoc_cds_to_db
      IMPORTING is_i_purchdoc_u     TYPE Z_I_PurchaseDocument_U
      RETURNING VALUE(rs_purchdoc) TYPE zif_prchdc_logic=>ts_purchasedocument.

   METHOD map_purchdoc_cds_to_db.
   rs_purchdoc = CORRESPONDING #( is_i_purchdoc_u MAPPING purchasedocument
= PurchaseDocument
                          crea_date_time            = crea_date_time
                          crea_uname                = crea_uname
                          description               = Description
                          lchg_date_time            = lchg_date_time
                          lchg_uname                = lchg_uname
                          priority                  = Priority
                          purchasedocumentimageurl = PurchaseDocumentImageURL
                          purchasingorganization   = PurchasingOrganization
                          status                    = status ).
  ENDMETHOD.
```

Listing 4.23 Purchase Document CDS to Database Mapping Method

- **map_purchdocitem_cds_to_db**
  Same purpose as the previous method, this method is used for mapping purchase document items to the corresponding database table structure instead of the purchase document, as shown in Listing 4.24.

```
CLASS-METHODS map_purchdocitem_cds_to_db
      IMPORTING is_i_purchdocitem_u    TYPE z_i_purchasedocumentitem_u
      RETURNING VALUE(rs_purchdocitem) TYPE zif_prchdc_logic=>ts_purchasedocitem.
```

```
  METHOD map_purchdocitem_cds_to_db.
    rs_purchdocitem = CORRESPONDING #( is_i_purchdocitem_u MAPPING
purchasedocument                   = PurchaseDocument
                  crea_date_time                = crea_date_time
                  crea_uname                    = crea_uname
                  description                   = Description
                  lchg_date_time                = lchg_date_time
                  lchg_uname                    = lchg_uname
                  purchasedocumentitem          = PurchaseDocumentItem
                  quantity                      = Quantity
                  quantityunit                  = QuantityUnit
                  vendor                        = Vendor
                  vendortype                    = VendorType
                  price                         = Price
                  purchasedocumentitemimageurl = PurchaseDocumentItemImageURL
                  currency                      = Currency ).
  ENDMETHOD.
```

Listing 4.24 Purchase Document Item CDS to Database Mapping Method

- **map_purchaseDoc_message**
  Just as you need to map the incoming fields for saving the data to the database, the same type of mapping is required to fill in the contents of the export tables such as FAILED, MAPPED, and REPORTED. This method maps the data back to the corresponding fields of those exporting parameters based on the requirement. For example, Listing 4.25 is used to map the response back to the REPORTED table structure of the PurchaseDocument entity's export parameter.

```
    CLASS-METHODS map_purchaseDoc_message
      IMPORTING iv_cid               TYPE string OPTIONAL
                iv_purchasedocument TYPE zpurchasedocumentdtel OPTIONAL
                is_message          TYPE LINE OF zif_prchdc_logic=>tt_if_
t100_message
                is_messageType      TYPE symsgty
      RETURNING VALUE(rs_report)    TYPE LINE OF zif_prchdc_logic=>tt_
purchasedocumet_reported.

  METHOD map_purchaseDoc_message.
    DATA: ls_message TYPE LINE OF tt_message.
    MOVE-CORRESPONDING is_message->t100key TO ls_message.
    ls_message-msgty = is_messageType.
```

```
    ls_message-msgv1 = iv_purchasedocument.
    DATA(lo) = new_message( id        = ls_message-msgid
                            number    = ls_message-msgno
                            severity  = if_abap_behv_message=>severity-error
                            v1        = ls_message-msgv1
                            v2        = ls_message-msgv2
                            v3        = ls_message-msgv3
                            v4        = ls_message-msgv4 ).
    rs_report-%cid      = iv_cid.
    rs_report-PurchaseDocument = iv_purchasedocument.
    rs_report-%msg      = lo.
  ENDMETHOD.
```

Listing 4.25 Purchase Document Message Mapping Method

Now, let's cover the local classes:

- **lcl_abap_behv_msg**
  This class creates exception messages and passes these messages to the corresponding return parameter tables of the relevant operations as needed.
- **lcl_prch_buffer**
  This local class is responsible for storing all the data that is passed from the behavior class and to store this data in relevant buffer tables. This same buffer table will be accessed later by the saver class for the final commit of the data to the database tables. As shown in Listing 4.26, we've declared the buffer tables based on the corresponding database table structures. We also defined methods to handle the different transactional functions of the behavior handler class as well as the methods of the behavior saver class.

```
CLASS lcl_prch_buffer DEFINITION FINAL CREATE PRIVATE.
  PUBLIC SECTION.

    " Buffer Tables
    DATA: mt_create_buffer_PurchDoc     TYPE zif_prchdc_logic=>tt_
purchasedocument,
          mt_update_buffer_PurchDoc     TYPE zif_prchdc_logic=>tt_
purchasedocument,
          mt_delete_buffer_PurchDoc     TYPE zif_prchdc_logic=>tt_
purchasedocumentKey,
          mt_create_buffer_PurchDocItem TYPE zif_prchdc_logic=>tt_
purchdocumentitem,
```

```
          mt_update_buffer_PurchDocItem TYPE zif_prchdc_logic=>tt_
purchdocumentitem,
          mt_delete_buffer_PurchDocItem TYPE zif_prchdc_logic=>tt_
purchdocitem_key.

    CLASS-METHODS: get_instance RETURNING VALUE(ro_instance) TYPE REF TO
lcl_prch_buffer.


    METHODS buffer_PurchDoc_for_Create     IMPORTING it_purchaseDocument
TYPE zif_prchdc_logic=>tt_purchasedocument
                                           EXPORTING et_purchaseDocument
TYPE zif_prchdc_logic=>tt_purchasedocument
                                                     et_messages
TYPE zif_prchdc_logic=>tt_if_t100_message.

    METHODS buffer_purchdoc_for_delete     IMPORTING it_purchaseDocumentkey
TYPE zif_prchdc_logic=>tt_purchasedocumentkey
                                                     it_purchaseDocitemtkey
TYPE zif_prchdc_logic=>tt_purchdocitem_key
                                           EXPORTING et_messages
TYPE zif_prchdc_logic=>tt_if_t100_message.

    METHODS buffer_purchdoc_for_update     IMPORTING it_purchaseDocument
TYPE zif_prchdc_logic=>tt_purchasedocument
                                           EXPORTING et_messages
TYPE zif_prchdc_logic=>tt_if_t100_message.

    METHODS buffer_PurchDocItem_for_create IMPORTING it_purchaseDocItem
TYPE zif_prchdc_logic=>tt_purchdocumentitem
                                           EXPORTING et_messages
TYPE zif_prchdc_logic=>tt_if_t100_message.

    METHODS buffer_purchdocitem_for_update IMPORTING it_purchaseDocItem
TYPE zif_prchdc_logic=>tt_purchdocumentitem
                                           EXPORTING et_messages
TYPE zif_prchdc_logic=>tt_if_t100_message.

    METHODS buffer_purchdocitem_for_delete IMPORTING it_purchaseDocItemKey
TYPE zif_prchdc_logic=>tt_purchdocitem_key
```

```
                                                    EXPORTING et_messages
  TYPE zif_prchdc_logic=>tt_if_t100_message.


      METHODS save.
      METHODS initialize.

    PRIVATE SECTION.

      CLASS-DATA go_instance TYPE REF TO lcl_prch_buffer.

      TYPES:
        BEGIN OF ts_purchasedocument_id,
          purchasedocument TYPE zpurchasedocumentdtel,
        END OF ts_purchasedocument_id,

        tt_purchasedocument_id TYPE SORTED TABLE OF ts_purchasedocument_id
  WITH UNIQUE KEY purchasedocument.

      DATA lt_purchasedocument_id TYPE tt_purchasedocument_id.

  ENDCLASS.
```

Listing 4.26 Buffer Class Definition

As shown in Listing 4.27, for the buffer class, the implementation of the corresponding methods for handling the different transactional functions and the methods of the saver class. For example, if you check the `buffer_purchDoc_for_Create` method, we're checking for different scenarios, for example, if the incoming purchase document number is already present in the database or not, whether the purchase document field is initial or not, etc. These checks will help us with basic validations before storing the data in the buffer tables. If any of these basic validations fair, then we'll generate a response with the corresponding exception message and call the `initialize` method to clear the buffer tables. If all the checks are valid, then the message table will be left empty, and the data will be stored into the corresponding buffer table.

In the save method, when it's called, we'll retrieve the values from the buffer table and stores the data into the corresponding database table. You'll see these class methods getting called by the behavior handler and the behavior saver class in the upcoming sections.

```
CLASS lcl_prch_buffer IMPLEMENTATION.

  METHOD get_instance.
    go_instance = COND #( WHEN go_instance IS BOUND THEN go_instance ELSE NEW
#( ) ).
    ro_instance = go_instance.
  ENDMETHOD.

  METHOD buffer_PurchDoc_for_Create.
    CLEAR: et_purchaseDocument,
           et_messages,
           lt_purchasedocument_id.

    CHECK it_purchaseDocument IS NOT INITIAL.

    SELECT FROM zpurchdocument
    FIELDS                                   purchasedocument
    FOR ALL ENTRIES IN                       @it_purchaseDocument
    WHERE                                    purchasedocument = @it_
purchaseDocument-purchasedocument
    INTO CORRESPONDING FIELDS OF TABLE @lt_purchasedocument_id.

    LOOP AT it_purchaseDocument INTO DATA(ls_purchdoc_create) ##INTO_OK.
      " Check Purchase Document number is initial or not
      IF ls_purchdoc_create-purchasedocument IS INITIAL.
        "add exception to message class if purchase document ID is initial
        APPEND NEW zcx_purchdoc_excptns( textid = zcx_purchdoc_excptns=>
purchasedocintial  mv_purchasedocument = ls_purchdoc_create-purchasedocument )
        TO et_messages.
        initialize( ).
        RETURN.
      ENDIF.

      " Check if the Purchase Document ID already Exists
      IF line_exists( lt_purchasedocument_id[ purchasedocument = ls_purchdoc_
create-purchasedocument ] ).
        "add exception to message class if Purchase Do  cument ID exists
        APPEND NEW zcx_purchdoc_excptns( textid = zcx_purchdoc_excptns=>
purchasedocexists  mv_purchasedocument = ls_purchdoc_create-purchasedocument )
```

```
        TO et_messages.
        initialize( ).
        RETURN.
      ENDIF.

      " Check in buffer table if the Purchase Document ID already exists or
not
      IF line_exists( mt_create_buffer_PurchDoc[ purchasedocument = ls_
purchdoc_create-purchasedocument ] ).
        "add exception to message class if Purchase Document ID exists in
buffer table
        APPEND NEW zcx_purchdoc_excptns( textid = zcx_purchdoc_excptns=>
purchasedocexitsinbuffer  mv_purchasedocument = ls_purchdoc_create-
purchasedocument )
        TO et_messages.
        initialize( ).
        RETURN.
      ENDIF.

      INSERT ls_purchdoc_create INTO TABLE mt_create_buffer_PurchDoc.
    ENDLOOP.

    et_purchaseDocument = mt_create_buffer_PurchDoc.
  ENDMETHOD.

  METHOD buffer_purchdoc_for_delete.
    CLEAR: et_messages.
    CHECK it_purchaseDocumentkey IS NOT INITIAL.

    MOVE-CORRESPONDING it_purchasedocumentkey TO mt_delete_buffer_PurchDoc.
    MOVE-CORRESPONDING it_purchasedocitemtkey TO mt_delete_buffer_
purchdocitem.

  ENDMETHOD.

  METHOD buffer_purchdoc_for_update.
    CLEAR: et_messages.
    CHECK it_purchasedocument IS NOT INITIAL.
```

```
    MOVE-CORRESPONDING it_purchasedocument TO mt_update_buffer_purchdoc.
  ENDMETHOD.


  METHOD buffer_PurchDocItem_for_create.
    CLEAR et_messages.
    CHECK it_purchasedocitem IS NOT INITIAL.
    MOVE-CORRESPONDING it_purchasedocitem TO mt_create_buffer_PurchDocItem.
  ENDMETHOD.

  METHOD buffer_purchdocitem_for_update.
    CLEAR: et_messages.
    CHECK it_purchasedocitem IS NOT INITIAL.
    MOVE-CORRESPONDING it_purchasedocitem TO mt_update_buffer_purchdocitem.
  ENDMETHOD.

  METHOD buffer_purchdocitem_for_delete.
    CLEAR: et_messages.
    CHECK it_purchasedocitemkey IS NOT INITIAL.
    MOVE-CORRESPONDING it_purchasedocitemkey TO mt_delete_buffer_purchdocitem.
  ENDMETHOD.


  METHOD save.
    "Here in the save method, the corresponding buffer tables are read
    "and the relevant data is updated,deleted or created in the
    "PurchaseDocument and PurchasedocumentItem tables
    INSERT zpurchdocument FROM TABLE @mt_create_buffer_PurchDoc.
    UPDATE zpurchdocument FROM TABLE @mt_update_buffer_PurchDoc.
    DELETE zpurchdocument FROM TABLE @( CORRESPONDING #( mt_delete_buffer_
PurchDoc ) ).
    "Same logic is applied to the PurchaseDocument Table
    INSERT zpurchdocitem  FROM TABLE @mt_create_buffer_PurchDocItem.
    UPDATE zpurchdocitem  FROM TABLE @mt_update_buffer_PurchDocItem.
    DELETE zpurchdocitem  FROM TABLE @( CORRESPONDING #( mt_delete_buffer_
PurchDocItem ) ).
  ENDMETHOD.
```

```
  METHOD initialize.
    CLEAR: mt_create_buffer_PurchDoc,
           mt_update_buffer_purchdoc,
           mt_delete_buffer_purchdoc,
           mt_delete_buffer_PurchDocItem,
           mt_update_buffer_PurchDocItem.
  ENDMETHOD.
ENDCLASS.
```

Listing 4.27 Buffer Class Implementation

Implementing Local Behavior Handler Class Methods for Purchase Document

Now let's get into coding our local behavior handler class methods for handling the CRUD operations and actions logic for the PurchaseDocument. (We'll only add logic to the methods that we need for our example.)

Create

In the create method, shown in Listing 4.28, the incoming data (import parameters of the create entity definition from the behavior definition) is looped and the corresponding fields are extracted. In this case, we'll also fill in some fields that users don't maintain through the UI, such as the created data time, last changed data time, created by username, last changed by username, the initial status of the created purchased document, etc. Once all the required data is filled in and sorted accordingly, we'll call the corresponding zcl_purchdc_logic class method to store our PurchaseDocument data in the buffer table. The method create_purchasedocument has an importing parameter et_messages (which will be filled in the case of any exceptions or validation failures). If this returning parameter is INITIAL, then we'll fill a success message into the REPORTED table (which is an exporting parameter for the method CREATE), so that success messages will be displayed in the app. (Instead of filling in the REPORTED table at this point, we can also do the same thing with the check_before_save method of the local behavior saver class; the developer can decide how and where to fill these returning table parameters based on the application's complexity.)

Similarly, if the et_messages table is not initial, something went wrong while validating the data in the buffer class. Therefore, we'll need to fill in the FAILED table (as explained earlier, every FAILED, REPORTED, and MAPPED table has a dedicated table within its line item for all the entity sets defined in the behavior definition). Since this CREATE method is for the PurchaseDocument entity, the relevant table for FAILED will be FAILED-PurchaseDocument) with the corresponding message in the et_messages table. Filling in the FAILED table also prevents the save method from being triggered in the local behavior saver class, thereby ensuring the data is not saved into the database.

```
  METHOD create.
    TYPES tt_message TYPE STANDARD TABLE OF symsg.
    CLEAR et_messages.
    DATA: ls_purchdocument      TYPE zpurchdocument,
          lt_purchdocument      TYPE zif_prchdc_logic=>tt_purchasedocument,
          lv_purchasedocument   TYPE ZPURCHASEDOCUMENTDTEL,
          lv_cid                TYPE string.
* Selecting the highest PurchaseDocument number from the DB table to assign
the next PurchaseDocument Number
    SELECT FROM zpurchdocument FIELDS MAX( purchasedocument ) INTO @lv_
purchasedocument.
* Loop at the importing parameter of the method to retrieve the
PurchaseDocument details for creation
    LOOP AT entities ASSIGNING FIELD-SYMBOL(<fs_PurchaseDocument_Create>).
      CLEAR ls_purchdocument.
*The incoming PurchaseDocument structure is not an 1:1 match with the DB table
structure for PurchaseDocument
*Hence, we need to map the relevant fields of the incoming structure to the
compatible DB Structure.
      ls_purchdocument = CORRESPONDING #( zcl_prchdc_logic=>get_instance( )->
map_purchdoc_cds_to_db( CORRESPONDING #( <fs_PurchaseDocument_Create> ) ) ).
      lv_cid = <fs_PurchaseDocument_Create>-%cid.
      if <fs_PurchaseDocument_Create>-PurchaseDocument > lv_purchasedocument .
      lv_purchasedocument = <fs_PurchaseDocument_Create>-PurchaseDocument.
      ENDIF.
      lv_purchasedocument = lv_purchasedocument + 1.
      condense lv_purchasedocument.
      ls_purchdocument-purchasedocument = lv_purchasedocument.
* Setting the Time Stamp Field for Created Date Time and Last Changed Date
Time
      GET TIME STAMP FIELD ls_purchdocument-crea_date_time.
      GET TIME STAMP FIELD ls_purchdocument-lchg_date_time.
* Details of the Created and Last changed User name is also added
      ls_purchdocument-crea_uname               = sy-uname.
      ls_purchdocument-lchg_uname               = sy-uname.
      ls_purchdocument-status                   = 1.
* You can make the ImageURL dynamic for your example, For this example.
```

```
* We're giving a hard-coded value of one of the existing MIME objects in the
BSP application source code of this project
      ls_purchdocument-purchasedocumentimageurl = './images/book.jpg'.
      APPEND ls_purchdocument TO lt_purchdocument.
    ENDLOOP.
* Calling up the relevant method from the ZCL_PRCHDC_LOGIC class to store the
PurchaseDocument details in the Buffer Table,
* This Class method will also do some validations on the incoming Purchase
Document data and it will will its Exporting Parameter
* et_messages with the relevant error message
    zcl_prchdc_logic=>get_instance( )->create_purchasedocument( EXPORTING it_
purchasedocument = lt_purchdocument
                                                                  IMPORTING et_
messages = et_messages ).
    IF et_messages IS INITIAL.
* If there is no errors returned by the create_purchasedocument method, then
we set the success message to the REPORTED
* Parameter with new purchaseDocument number to be displayed as a Toast
message in the Application
      INSERT VALUE #(   purchasedocument = ls_purchdocument-purchasedocument
                        %msg = new_message( id = 'ZPURCHDOC_EXCEPTIONS' number
= '000' v1 = ls_purchdocument-purchasedocument
                                            severity = if_abap_behv_message=>
severity-success )
                        %element-purchasedocument = cl_abap_behv=>flag_changed
                        %cid = lv_cid    )
                        INTO TABLE reported-PurchaseDocument.
    ELSE.
      LOOP AT et_messages INTO DATA(ls_message).
* In case of a Failed Scenario, the FAILED Parameter is filled with the
relevant PurchaseDocument number, This will stop any further execution of the
Class methods
        INSERT VALUE #( %cid = lv_cid  purchasedocument = ls_purchdocument-
purchasedocument )
             INTO TABLE failed-purchasedocument.
* We will also push the relevant error message to REPORTED parameter so that
it is displayed in the front-end application as a toast message
        INSERT zcl_prchdc_logic=>map_purchasedoc_message(
                                            iv_purchasedocument = ls_
purchdocument-purchasedocument
```

```
                                                  is_message     = ls_message
                                                  is_messagetype = 'E' ) INTO TABLE
reported-purchasedocument.
      ENDLOOP.
    ENDIF.

  ENDMETHOD.
```

Listing 4.28 Method Implementation for Create Operation

Delete

In the delete method, the incoming parameter is looped, and the corresponding values of the key fields are extracted (in our case, the purchase document is the only key). Since the deletion is at the header level (purchase document), we'll have to fetch all the items from the purchase document item table as well, as shown in Listing 4.29. Once both the corresponding table structure for purchase documents and purchase document items is filled in, we'll pass these tables into the `delete_purchasedocument` method of the class `zcl_purchdc_logic`. As a result, the data will be passed to the local buffer table class for storage in the corresponding buffer table. In this method, the `et_messages` table will also be checked to determine whether the `REPORTED` table needs to be filled in or not.

```
  METHOD delete.
    DATA: ls_purchdocument     TYPE zpurchdocument,
          lv_purchasedocumentItem TYPE ZPURCHASEDOCUMENTDTEL,
          ls_purchdocumentkey     TYPE zif_prchdc_logic=>ts_purchdocitem_key,
          lt_purchdocumentKey TYPE zif_prchdc_logic=>tt_purchasedocumentkey,
          lt_purchdocitemKey TYPE zif_prchdc_logic=>tt_purchdocitem_key.
    CLEAR et_messages.

    LOOP AT keys ASSIGNING FIELD-SYMBOL(<fs_PurchaseDocument_Delete>).
      MOVE-CORRESPONDING <fs_PurchaseDocument_Delete> TO ls_purchdocument.
* The relevant PurchaseDocument number for deletion is retrieved
      APPEND VALUE #( purchasedocument =  ls_purchdocument-purchasedocument )
TO lt_purchdocumentKey.
    ENDLOOP.
    IF lt_purchdocumentKey is NOT INITIAL.
* If any PurchaseDocument Items exists for this Document, those items will be
fetched and passed to the relevant delete method as well.
      SELECT  * FROM zpurchdocitem into CORRESPONDING FIELDS OF TABLE lt_
```

```
purchdocitemKey
      FOR ALL ENTRIES IN lt_purchdocumentKey
      where purchasedocument =  lt_purchdocumentKey-purchasedocument.
* The delete_purchasedocument method is called by passing the relevant
PurchaseDocument and PurchaseDocument Item numbers
      zcl_prchdc_logic=>get_instance( )->delete_purchasedocument( EXPORTING
it_purchasedocumentkey = lt_purchdocumentKey

it_purchdocitemkey     = lt_purchdocitemKey
                                                                 IMPORTING et_
messages = et_messages ).
      IF  et_messages IS INITIAL.
* If no errors are returned, then the REPORTED parameter is filled with the
relevant success message
        APPEND VALUE #(  purchasedocument = ls_purchdocument-purchasedocument
                           %msg = new_message( id = 'ZPURCHDOC_EXCEPTIONS'
number = '004' v1 = ls_purchdocument-purchasedocument severity = if_abap_behv_
message=>severity-success )
                          %element-purchasedocument = cl_abap_behv=>flag_
changed ) TO reported-PurchaseDocument.
      ENDIF.
    ENDIF.
  ENDMETHOD.
```

Listing 4.29 Method Implementation for Delete Operation

Update

In the update method, when looping the import parameters, we'll need to consider the `%control` field in the import parameter table to identify which fields of the entity has been modified by the user. Whether a change has occurred is represented by the value in the `%control` structure against the respective property names of the entity. For example, if the field `%control-status` is "00," this field is unchanged; if the value was "01," then the status field value has been changed. To simplify this check, we can take advantage of the Boolean function `xsdbool` (which will return "X" for true and blank for false), as shown in Listing 4.30. The corresponding values of this check is stored in the internal table `lt_purchasedocumentControl`, which will be passed onto the `update_purchasedocument` method of the class `zcl_purchdc_logic` for storing the data in the buffer table. In the `update_purchasedocument` method, the table `lt_purchasedocumentControl` will be used as a flag to create the final table structure (which will have the corresponding field values updated with the new values) for the data before it is stored in the buffer table. (You can check the logic in the source code provided with this book on the SAP PRESS website at *www.sap-press.com/4988*.)

```
  METHOD update.

    DATA: ls_purchdocument             TYPE zpurchdocument,
          ls_purchdocumentControl      TYPE zif_prchdc_logic=>ts_
purchdocumentControl,
          lt_purchasedocument          TYPE zif_prchdc_logic=>tt_
purchasedocument,
          lt_purchasedocumentControl TYPE zif_prchdc_logic=>tt_
purchdocumentcontrol.

* The incoming structure containing the PurchaseDocument Details to be updated
is looped
    LOOP AT entities ASSIGNING FIELD-SYMBOL(<fs_PurchaseDocument_Create>).
* Here the relevant fields of the incoming Structure is mapped to the
compatible structure of the PurchaseDocument DB table.
      ls_purchdocument = CORRESPONDING #( zcl_prchdc_logic=>get_instance( )->
map_purchdoc_cds_to_db( CORRESPONDING #( <fs_PurchaseDocument_Create> ) ) ).
* As mentioned in chapter 4, the incoming Structure also has some column
%CONTROL which contains the
* flag against all the fields of the PurchaseDocuments that were modified by
the user and hence we need to store them in a separate structure so that it
can be used as
* a reference later to determine which fields from the DB needs to be updated
      ls_purchdocumentControl-action                    = 'U'.
      ls_purchdocumentControl-purchasedocument          = ls_purchdocument-
purchasedocument.
      ls_purchdocumentControl-description               = xsdbool( <fs_
PurchaseDocument_Create>-%control-Description             = cl_abap_behv=>
flag_changed ).
      ls_purchdocumentControl-status                    = xsdbool( <fs_
PurchaseDocument_Create>-%control-Status                  = cl_abap behv=>
flag_changed ).
      ls_purchdocumentControl-priority                  = xsdbool( <fs_
PurchaseDocument_Create>-%control-Priority                = cl_abap_behv=>
flag_changed ).
```

```
      ls_purchdocumentControl-purchasingorganization      = xsdbool( <fs_
PurchaseDocument_Create>-%control-PurchasingOrganization      = cl_abap_behv=>
flag_changed ).
      ls_purchdocumentControl-purchasedocumentimageurl    = xsdbool( <fs_
PurchaseDocument_Create>-%control-PurchaseDocumentImageURL    = cl_abap_behv=>
flag_changed ).
      ls_purchdocumentControl-crea_date_time              = xsdbool( <fs_
PurchaseDocument_Create>-%control-crea_date_time              = cl_abap_behv=>
flag_changed ).
      ls_purchdocumentControl-crea_uname                  = xsdbool( <fs_
PurchaseDocument_Create>-%control-crea_uname                  = cl_abap_behv=>
flag_changed ).
      ls_purchdocumentControl-lchg_date_time              = 'X'.
      ls_purchdocumentControl-lchg_uname                  = 'X'.
* The last change date time needs to be updated as well
      GET TIME STAMP FIELD ls_purchdocument-lchg_date_time.
* Also the details about the user who made the changes needs to be stored
      ls_purchdocument-lchg_uname       = sy-uname.
      APPEND ls_purchdocument         TO lt_purchasedocument.
      APPEND ls_purchdocumentControl TO lt_purchasedocumentControl.
    ENDLOOP.
    IF lt_purchasedocument IS NOT INITIAL.
* The method update_purchasedocument is called to update the relevant
PurchaseDocument Buffer table
* which will be later referred to update the relevant DB table
      zcl_prchdc_logic=>get_instance( )->update_purchasedocument(  EXPORTING
it_purchasedocument     =  lt_purchasedocument
                         it_purchdocumentcontrol = lt_purchasedocumentcontrol
                         IMPORTING et_messages = et_messages ).
      IF  et_messages IS INITIAL.
* If no error messages are returned from the update_purchasedocument method,
then the relevant success message is pushed to the REPORTED parameter
        APPEND VALUE #(  purchasedocument = ls_purchdocument-purchasedocument
                          %msg = new_message( id = 'ZPURCHDOC_EXCEPTIONS'
number = '011' v1 = ls_purchdocument-purchasedocument severity = if_abap_behv_
message=>severity-success )
                         %element-purchasedocument = cl_abap_behv=>flag_
changed ) TO reported-PurchaseDocument.
```

```
      ENDIF.
    ENDIF.
  ENDMETHOD.
```

Listing 4.30 Method Implementation for the Update Operation

Read (Read by Key)

In the read method, data from the buffer will be returned. If the buffer tables are empty, then the data will be read from the database. Read queries are pushed down by the SADL framework to the database automatically.

However, the read method logic is usually implemented when ETag handling is required/enabled. When data needs to be modified, SADL framework locks the data, and then the read method is triggered to retrieve the current ETag value. When the data is matched, and only then, will the corresponding modification methods be called. But in our example, we're not utilizing the ETag feature nor is the data we're fetching critical enough to be compared against the buffer table entry. (You can add the logic to read from buffer tables which you can create for read method just like we created for the CRUD operations.) Thus, this method is left unchanged.

cba_PurchaseDocumentItem (Create by Association)

In the Create by Association method, the data from the importing parameter is looped to get the value of the key field purchase document and then the structure %target (as described earlier, the %target field within the import parameter of a Create by Association method will be containing a structure with the data for the child/association entity) is looped into to retrieve the corresponding data for creating purchase document items. The PurchaseDocument item table is passed into the method create_purchasedocitem of the class zcl_prchdc_logic.

```
  METHOD cba_PURCHASEDOCUMENTITEM.
    DATA: ls_purchdocument       TYPE zpurchdocument,
          ls_purchdocumentItem TYPE zpurchdocitem,
          lt_purchdocumentItem TYPE zif_prchdc_logic=>tt_purchdocumentitem,
          lv_purchdocitem        TYPE zpurchasedocumentdtel.
* In this Create By Association method for creating the PurchaseDocument Item
in relation with the parent PurchaseDocument,
* The highest value of the current PurchaseDocumentItem for the respective
PurchaseDocument is retrieved to determine the next number
 SELECT FROM zpurchdocitem FIELDS MAX( purchasedocumentitem ) INTO @lv_
```

```
purchdocitem.
* The incoming parameter is looped to retrieve the PurchaseDocumentItem details
    LOOP AT entities_cba ASSIGNING FIELD-SYMBOL(<fs_PurchaseDocument>).
        ls_purchdocument-purchasedocument          = <fs_PurchaseDocument>-
PurchaseDocument.
* As explained in Chapter 4, the incoming parameter also has a field %TARGET
which contains the Parent View Key fields,
* We need these key field values to create the Items in the
PurchaseDocumentItem DB table with the correct PurchaseDocument Number
      LOOP AT <fs_PurchaseDocument>-%target ASSIGNING FIELD-SYMBOL(<fs_
PurchaseDocumentItem>).
        MOVE-CORRESPONDING <fs_PurchaseDocumentItem> TO ls_purchdocumentItem.
      if <fs_PurchaseDocumentItem>-Purchasedocumentitem > lv_purchdocitem .
        lv_purchdocitem = <fs_PurchaseDocumentItem>-Purchasedocumentitem.
      ENDIF.
        lv_purchdocitem = lv_purchdocitem + 1.
        condense lv_purchdocitem.
        ls_purchdocumentItem-purchasedocumentitem         = lv_purchdocitem.
        ls_purchdocumentItem-purchasedocument             = ls purchdocument-
purchasedocument.
        ls_purchdocumentItem-lchg_uname                   = sy-uname.
        ls_purchdocumentItem-crea_uname                   = sy-uname.
* You can make the ImageURL dynamic for your example, For this example.
* We are giving a hard-coded value of one of the existing MIME objects in the
BSP application source code of this project
        ls_purchdocumentItem-purchasedocumentitemimageurl = './images/book.jpg'.
* Setting the Time Stamp Field for Created Date Time and Last Changed Date Time
        GET TIME STAMP FIELD ls_purchdocumentItem-lchg_date_time.
        GET TIME STAMP FIELD ls_purchdocumentItem-crea_date_time.
        APPEND ls_purchdocumentItem to lt_purchdocumentItem.
      ENDLOOP.
    ENDLOOP.
    IF lt_purchdocumentItem IS NOT INITIAL.
* The create_purchasedocitem method of the ZCL_PRCHDC_LOGIC is called to store
the relevant PurchaseDocument Items in the buffer table
    zcl_prchdc_logic=>get_instance( )->create_purchasedocitem( EXPORTING it_
purchasedocItem = lt_purchdocumentItem IMPORTING et_messages = et_messages ).
```

```
    ENDIF.
  ENDMETHOD.
```

Listing 4.31 Method Implementation for Create by Association for Creating the Purchase Document Item Based on the Key from the Header Purchase Document

Approve_Order (Action)

In the custom action method `Approve_Order`, as shown in Listing 4.32, we decided to update the database table directly instead of passing changes into a buffer table, which works but is admittedly a bit lazy. You can also always pass these values into a buffer table and make the update later in the `save` method in the local behavior saver class Passing the values of an action to a buffer table depends on its use case. Ideally an action is supposed to be immediate, for example, approving an order or booking a ticket. In such cases, passing the action to a buffer might not be the best approach.

```
  METHOD Approve_Order.
    DATA ls_purchdocument TYPE zpurchdocument.
    CLEAR result.
* In the custom Action method for Approving a PurchaseDocument,
* The incoming parameter is looped and the relevant PurchaseDocument status is
set as approved and details of the Action is store in the RESULT parameter of
the method
    LOOP AT keys ASSIGNING FIELD-SYMBOL(<fs_PurchaseDocument>).
      UPDATE zpurchdocument SET status = 2 WHERE purchasedocument = <fs_
PurchaseDocument>-PurchaseDocument.
      if sy-subrc eq 0.
      APPEND VALUE #(   purchasedocument         = <fs_PurchaseDocument>-
PurchaseDocument
                        %param-purchasedocument = <fs_PurchaseDocument>-
PurchaseDocument
                        %param-status           = '2')
                TO result.
      endif.
    ENDLOOP.
* The relevant Success Message is mapped to the REPORTED parameter of the method
    APPEND VALUE #(  purchasedocument = ls_purchdocument-purchasedocument
                    %msg = new_message( id = 'ZPURCHDOC_EXCEPTIONS' number =
'002' v1 = <fs_PurchaseDocument>-PurchaseDocument    severity = if_abap_behv_
message=>severity-success )
```

```
                    %element-purchasedocument = cl_abap_behv=>flag_changed )
TO reported-PurchaseDocument.
  ENDMETHOD.
```

Listing 4.32 Method Implementation for Approve_Order Action

Reject_Order (Action)

The Reject_Order action button also has a similar logic of the Approve_Order method, as shown in Listing 4.33. The importing parameter is looped, and the corresponding purchase document status is updated. A success message will be sent back to the UI by filling in the REPORTED export parameter table.

```
  METHOD Reject_Order.
    DATA ls_purchdocument TYPE zpurchdocument.
* In the custom Action method for Rejecting a PurchaseDocument,
* The incoming parameter is looped and the relevant PurchaseDocument status is
set as rejected and details of the Action is store in the RESULT parameter of
the method
    LOOP AT keys ASSIGNING FIELD-SYMBOL(<fs_PurchaseDocument>).
      UPDATE zpurchdocument SET status = 3 WHERE purchasedocument = <fs_
PurchaseDocument>-PurchaseDocument.
    ENDLOOP.
* The relevant Success Message is mapped to the REPORTED parameter of the
method
    APPEND VALUE #(  purchasedocument = ls_purchdocument-purchasedocument
                     %msg = new_message( id = 'ZPURCHDOC_EXCEPTIONS' number =
'003' v1 = <fs_PurchaseDocument>-PurchaseDocument  severity = if_abap_behv_
message=>severity-success )
                     %element-purchasedocument = cl_abap_behv=>flag_changed )
TO reported-PurchaseDocument.

  ENDMETHOD.
```

Listing 4.33 Method Implementation for Reject_Order Action

Implementing Local Behavior Handler Class Methods for Purchase Document Item

Now, let's look at the coding part of our local behavior handler class methods for the PurchaseDocumentItem.

Delete

The logic of the delete method in the purchase document item is similar to the PurchaseDocument entity's delete operation, as shown in Listing 4.34. We'll loop into the importing parameter, retrieve the key field value, and call the delete_PurchaseDocItem method of the class zcl_purchdoc_logic class. If the et_messages return parameter of the delete_PurchaseDocItem is initial, we'll map the success message back to the REPORTED exporting parameter of the delete operation.

```
  METHOD delete.
    DATA: ls_purchdocItem     TYPE zpurchdocitem,
          lt_purchdocItemKey TYPE zif_prchdc_logic=>tt_purchdocitem_key.
    CLEAR et_messages.
* The relevant PurchaseDocumentItem number for deletion is retrieved
    LOOP AT keys ASSIGNING FIELD-SYMBOL(<fs_PurchaseDocItem_Delete>).
      MOVE-CORRESPONDING <fs_PurchaseDocItem_Delete> TO ls_purchdocItem.
      APPEND VALUE #( purchasedocument =  ls_purchdocItem-purchasedocument
purchasedocumentItem =  ls_purchdocItem-purchasedocumentitem ) TO lt_
purchdocItemKey.
    ENDLOOP.
    IF lt_purchdocItemKey IS NOT INITIAL.
* The delete_purchasedocumentItem method is called by passing the relevant
PurchaseDocument Item numbers
      zcl_prchdc_logic=>get_instance( )->delete_PurchaseDocItem( EXPORTING it_
purchasedocitemkey = lt_purchdocItemKey
                                                                  IMPORTING et_
messages = et_messages ).
      IF  et_messages IS INITIAL.
* If no errors are returned by the delete_PurchaseDocItem method, then the relevant
Success Message is mapped to the REPORTED parameter of the method
        APPEND VALUE #(  purchasedocumentItem = ls_purchdocItem-purchasedocumentitem
                         %msg = new_message( id = 'ZPURCHDOC_EXCEPTIONS' number =
'015' v1 = ls_purchdocItem-purchasedocument  severity = if_abap_behv_message=>
severity-success )
                         %element-purchasedocument = cl_abap_behv=>flag_changed )
TO reported-purchasedocumentitem.
      ENDIF.
    ENDIF.
  ENDMETHOD.
```

Listing 4.34 Method Implementation for Delete Operation

Update

The update operation also has a similar logic of the update operation for the PurchaseDocument entity. As shown in Listing 4.35, we'll loop at the import parameter of the Update method table. In Listing 4.35, you can see that the import parameter named entities is been looped. This import parameter contains PurchaseDocumentItem details and we will loop them to determine the data that needs to be updated. Then, we'll and pass the structure to the map_purchdocitem_cds_to_db method to get a structure like the database table of the purchase document item. We'll also loop in the %control field within the importing parameter table to retrieve the flags to identity which properties of the entity has been modified by the user. This structure within the importing parameter contains the details of which fields in the PurchaseDocumentItem has been updated by the user. We'll then pass both the mapped table (lt_purchasedocumentItem) and the table containing the fields retrieved from the %control field (lt_purchasedocItemControl) to the update_purchasedocitem method of the class zcl_prchdc_logic.

```
  METHOD update.
    DATA: ls_purchdocumentItem        TYPE zpurchdocitem,
          ls_purchdocumentItemControl TYPE zif_prchdc_logic=>ts_
purchdocumentitemControl,
          lt_purchasedocumentItem     TYPE zif_prchdc_logic=>tt_
purchdocumentitem,
          lt_purchasedoctItemControl  TYPE zif_prchdc_logic=>tt_
purchdocumentitemcontrol.
* The incoming structure containing the PurchaseDocumentItem Details to be
updated is looped
    LOOP AT entities ASSIGNING FIELD-SYMBOL(<fs_PurchaseDocItem_Create>).
* Here the relevant fields of the incoming Structure is mapped to the
compatible structure of the PurchaseDocumentItem DB table.
      ls_purchdocumentItem = CORRESPONDING #( zcl_prchdc_logic=>get_instance(
)->map_purchdocitem_cds_to_db( CORRESPONDING #( <fs_PurchaseDocItem_Create> )
) ).
* As mentioned in chapter 4, the incoming Structure also has a column %CONTROL
which contains the
* flag against all the fields of the PurchaseDocumentItems that were modified
by the user and hence we need to store them in a separate structure so that it
can be used as
* a reference later to determine which fields from the DB needs to be updated
      ls_purchdocumentItemControl-action                    = 'U'.
```

```
        ls_purchdocumentItemControl-purchasedocument                  = ls_
purchdocumentItem-purchasedocument.
        ls_purchdocumentItemControl-purchasedocumentitem              = ls_
purchdocumentItem-purchasedocumentitem.
        ls_purchdocumentItemControl-crea_date_time                    = xsdbool(
<fs_PurchaseDocItem_Create>-%control-crea_date_time                     = cl_abap_
behv=>flag_changed ).
        ls_purchdocumentItemControl-crea_uname                        = xsdbool(
<fs_PurchaseDocItem_Create>-%control-crea_uname                         = cl_abap_
behv=>flag_changed ).
        ls_purchdocumentItemControl-currency                          = xsdbool(
<fs_PurchaseDocItem_Create>-%control-Currency                           = cl_abap_
behv=>flag_changed ).
        ls_purchdocumentItemControl-description                       = xsdbool(
<fs_PurchaseDocItem_Create>-%control-Description                        = cl_abap_
behv=>flag_changed ).
        ls_purchdocumentItemControl-lchg_date_time                    = 'X'.
        ls_purchdocumentItemControl-lchg_uname                        = 'X'.
        ls_purchdocumentItemControl-price                             = xsdbool(
<fs_PurchaseDocItem_Create>-%control-Price                              = cl_abap_
behv=>flag_changed ).
        ls_purchdocumentItemControl-purchasedocumentitemimageurl      = xsdbool(
<fs_PurchaseDocItem_Create>-%control-PurchaseDocumentItemImageURL       = cl_abap_
behv=>flag_changed ).
        ls_purchdocumentItemControl-quantity                          = xsdbool(
<fs_PurchaseDocItem_Create>-%control-Quantity                           = cl_abap_
behv=>flag_changed ).
        ls_purchdocumentItemControl-quantityunit                      = xsdbool(
<fs_PurchaseDocItem_Create>-%control-QuantityUnit                       = cl_abap_
behv=>flag_changed ).
        ls_purchdocumentItemControl-vendor                            = xsdbool(
<fs_PurchaseDocItem_Create>-%control-Vendor                             = cl_abap_
behv=>flag_changed ).
        ls_purchdocumentItemControl-vendortype                        = xsdbool(
<fs_PurchaseDocItem_Create>-%control-VendorType                         = cl_abap_
behv=>flag_changed ).
        ls_purchdocumentItemControl-lchg_uname                        = xsdbool(
<fs_PurchaseDocItem_Create>-%control-lchg_uname                         = cl_abap_
behv=>flag_changed ).
```

```
* Time Stamp Field for Last Changed Date Time and last changed user name needs
to be updated
      GET TIME STAMP FIELD ls_purchdocumentItem-lchg_date_time.
      ls_purchdocumentItem-lchg_uname      = sy-uname.
      APPEND ls_purchdocumentItem        TO lt_purchasedocumentItem.
      APPEND ls_purchdocumentItemControl TO lt_purchasedoctItemControl.
    ENDLOOP.
    IF lt_purchasedoctItemControl IS NOT INITIAL.
* The method update_purchasedocument is called to update the relevant
PurchaseDocument Buffer table
* which will be later referred to update the relevant DB table
      zcl_prchdc_logic=>get_instance( )->update_purchasedocitem(  EXPORTING
it_purchasedocitem =  lt_purchasedocumentItem

it_purchdocitemcontrol = lt_purchasedoctItemControl
                                                                 IMPORTING
et_messages = et_messages ).
      IF  et_messages IS INITIAL.
* If no error messages are returned from the update_purchasedocument method,
then the relevant success message is pushed to the REPORTED parameter
        APPEND VALUE #(   purchasedocumentItem = ls_purchdocumentItem-
purchasedocumentitem
                %msg = new_message( id = 'ZPURCHDOC_EXCEPTIONS' number = '001'
v1 = ls_purchdocumentItem-purchasedocumentitem    severity = if_abap_behv_
message=>severity-success )
                %element-purchasedocument = cl_abap_behv=>flag_changed ) TO
reported-purchasedocumentitem.
      ENDIF.
    ENDIF.
  ENDMETHOD.
```

Listing 4.35 Method Implementation for Update Operation

Implementing Local Behavior Saver Class Methods

Now, let's look at the implementation logic of the local behavior saver class, as shown in Listing 4.36. For our example, we aren't handling `finalize` (since we aren't using the late numbering feature, there isn't much need for the `finalize` method in our app) or `check_before_save` (because our example app doesn't need any additional validation of the data before save). This might be different for other scenarios. For example, if you are using a booking system that might require other operations to be completed prior to making the final booking, then this final check will help you to either roll back the changes or commit the changes.Furthermore, in our example, we've already handled exception messages during the saving of the data into the buffer class. To make the implementation more streamlined, you could move the exception message handling logic to the `check_before_save` method, as shown in Listing 4.36.

```
CLASS lsc_Z_I_PurchaseDocument_U IMPLEMENTATION.
* These methods are executed in the below listed Sequence, except for the
cleanup method,
* which is called within any of the other three methods in case the execution
logic is aborted
  METHOD check_before_save.
  ENDMETHOD.
  METHOD finalize.
  ENDMETHOD.
  METHOD save.
* The final method where all the data from the relevant buffer tables are used
to either created, updated or deleted
* the records in the relevant DB tables based on the execution logic
    zcl_prchdc_logic=>get_instance( )->save( ).
  ENDMETHOD.
  METHOD cleanup.
* This method is used to cleanup all the buffer tables in case the Execution
flow is terminated
    zcl_prchdc_logic=>get_instance( )->initialize( ).
  ENDMETHOD.
ENDCLASS.
```

Listing 4.36 Behavior Saver Class Implementation

Preview the SAP Fiori Elements Application in Service Binding

Now, if you open the service binding and click on the **Open Fiori Elements App Preview** of the entity `PurchaseDocument` after you've reactivated it, as shown in Figure 4.26. You'll see the app preview with **Create** and **Delete** functions on top of the table, as shown in Figure 4.50. But, even after specifying the custom actions in the behavior definition, these actions still won't be visible because the corresponding UI annotations for the views are missing (which we'll add later in Section 4.4).

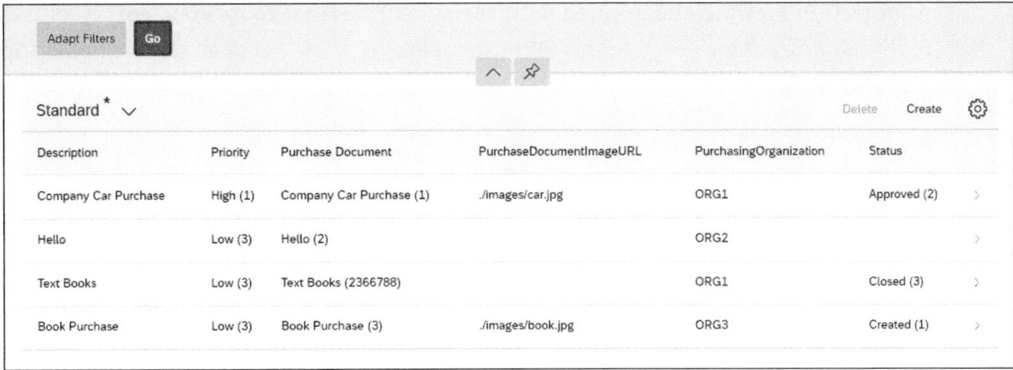

Adapt Filters
Go
Standard *
Delete
Create
Description
Priority
Purchase Document
PurchaseDocumentImageURL
PurchasingOrganization
Status
Company Car Purchase
High (1)
Company Car Purchase (1)
./images/car.jpg
ORG1
Approved (2)
Hello
Low (3)
Hello (2)
ORG2
Text Books
Low (3)
Text Books (2366788)
ORG1
Closed (3)
Book Purchase
Low (3)
Book Purchase (3)
./images/book.jpg
ORG3
Created (1)

Figure 4.50 App Preview with Transactional Actions Enabled

4.2.10 Creating Projection Views

As mentioned at the beginning of this chapter and as shown in Figure 4.2, we now need to create projection views on top of these "_U" views so that these underlying views are reusable. By taking this approach of adding all our custom UI annotations directly to the "_U" views, then any other team/person who wants to use these views will end up getting the UI interface that we customized for our requirement. So, in an ideal development environment, every SAP Fiori app should have its own final consumption view so that we can customize them for our app specific requirement without tampering with the underlying business object. For this same reason, we had created two final CDS consumption views `C_PurchaseDocumentLRP` and `C_PurchaseDocumentItemLRP` earlier in Section 4.1.4.

But we won't be able to fetch from our underlying "_U" views without modifying these consumption views first. This limitation occurs because the ABAP RESTful programming model doesn't allow normal consumption views to fetch from CDS views associated with the ABAP RESTful programming model. Thus, we need to convert our current consumption views into projection views, as shown in Listing 4.37. Projection views are a special type of view developed for the ABAP RESTful programming model that can reuse the transaction views created with the ABAP RESTful programming model. Projection views don't have SQL tables associated to them because they are projections of the actual underlying CDS views. Projection views have some limitations; for instance, case statements can't be used directly in a project view. Therefore, we'll need to push these statements down to our "_U" views.

A projection view can be defined with the syntax, **define root view entity** <view_name> **as projection on** <underlying_transactional_view_name> as shown in Listing 4.37 and Listing 4.38.

```
@EndUserText.label: 'Purchase Document'
@AccessControl.authorizationCheck: #NOT_REQUIRED
@Search.searchable: true
@Metadata.allowExtensions:true
@VDM.viewType: #CONSUMPTION

define root view entity Z_C_PurchaseDocumentLrp
  as projection on Z_I_PurchaseDocument_U

{
      @EndUserText.label: 'Purchase Document'
      @Consumption.semanticObject: 'PurchasingDocument'
  key PurchaseDocument,
      @EndUserText.label: 'Overall Price'
      OverallPrice,
      @EndUserText.label: 'Approval Required'
      @ObjectModel.foreignKey.association: '_IsApprovalRequired'
      @Consumption.valueHelpDefinition: [{entity:{name:'I_Indicator' ,
element: 'IndicatorValue'}}]
      IsApprovalRequired,
      OverallPriceCriticality,
      @EndUserText.label: 'Status'
      @Consumption.valueHelpDefinition: [{entity:{name:'Z_C_StatusVH' ,
element: 'Status'}}]
      Status,
      @EndUserText.label: 'Priority'
      @Consumption.valueHelpDefinition: [{entity:{name:'Z_C_PriorityVH' ,
element: 'Priority'}}]
      Priority,
      @Search.defaultSearchElement : true
      @Search.fuzzinessThreshold : 0.8
      @Semantics.text: true
      @EndUserText.label: 'Description'
      Description,
      @EndUserText.label: 'Purchasing Organization'
      @Consumption.valueHelpDefinition: [{entity:{name:'Z_I_
PurchasingOrganization' , element: 'PurchasingOrganization'}}]
```

```
      PurchasingOrganization,
      @EndUserText.label: 'Currency'
      Currency,
      @EndUserText.label: 'Created at'
      @Consumption.filter.hidden: true
      crea_date_time,
      @EndUserText.label: 'Created by'
      crea_uname,
      @EndUserText.label: 'Last changed at'
      @Consumption.filter.hidden: true
      lchg_date_time,
      @EndUserText.label: 'Last changed by'
      lchg_uname,
      @EndUserText.label: 'Image'
      @Consumption.filter.hidden: true
      PurchaseDocumentImageURL,
      /* Associations */
      _PurchaseDocumentItem : redirected to composition child Z_C_
PurchaseDocumentItemLrp,
      _Currency,
      _IsApprovalRequired,
      _Priority,
      _Status,
      _PurchasingOrganization
}
```

Listing 4.37 Projection View Z_C_PurchaseDocumentLRP

The consumption view Z_C_PurchaseDocumentItemLRP view also needs to be modified so that it can fetch from the Z_I_PurchaseDocumentItem_U view, as shown in Listing 4.38. In the next section, we'll add a virtual element field into this CDS view for the vendor rating calculation. Adding a virtual field to a projection view is also slightly different when compared to a normal CDS view.

```
@EndUserText.label: 'Purchase Document'
@AccessControl.authorizationCheck: #NOT_REQUIRED
@Search.searchable: true
@Metadata.allowExtensions:true
@VDM.viewType: #CONSUMPTION

define view entity Z_C_PurchaseDocumentItemLrp
```

```
  as projection on Z_I_PurchaseDocumentItem_U
{
      @EndUserText.label: 'Purchase Document Item'
      @Search: {defaultSearchElement: true, ranking: #HIGH,
fuzzinessThreshold: 0.8}
  key PurchaseDocumentItem,
      @ObjectModel.foreignKey.association: '_PurchaseDocument'
      @EndUserText.label: 'Purchase Document'
  key PurchaseDocument,
      @EndUserText.label: 'Price'
      Price,
      @EndUserText.label: 'Quantity'
      Quantity,
      @EndUserText.label: 'Overall Item Price'
      OverallItemPrice,
      @Search: {defaultSearchElement: true, ranking: #HIGH,
fuzzinessThreshold: 0.8}
      @EndUserText.label: 'Vendor Name'
      Vendor,
      @EndUserText.label: 'Vendor Type'
      @Consumption.valueHelpDefinition: [{entity:{name:'Z_C_VendorTypeVH' ,
element: 'VendorType'}}]
      VendorType,
      @Search: {defaultSearchElement: true, ranking: #HIGH,
fuzzinessThreshold: 0.8}
      @EndUserText.label: 'Item Description'
      Description,
     @Consumption.valueHelpDefinition: [{entity:{name:'I_Currency' , element:
'Currency'}}]
      Currency,
      @Consumption.valueHelpDefinition: [{entity:{name:'I_UnitOfMeasure' ,
element: 'UnitOfMeasure'}}]
      QuantityUnit,
      @EndUserText.label: 'Image'
      @Consumption.filter.hidden: true
      PurchaseDocumentItemImageURL,
      @EndUserText.label: 'Created at'
      crea_date_time,
      @EndUserText.label: 'Created by'
```

```
        crea_uname,
        @EndUserText.label: 'Last changed at'
        lchg_date_time,
        @EndUserText.label: 'Last changed by'
        lchg_uname,
        /* Associations */
        _PurchaseDocument  : redirected to parent Z_C_PurchaseDocumentLrp,
        _QuantityUnitOfMeasure,
        _VendorType

}
```

Listing 4.38 Projection View Z_C_PurchaseDocumentItemLRP

After converting our consumption views into projection views, now the final VDM of our application is shown in Figure 4.51. The composite layer is being consumed by the projection views, and therefore, the transactional features from the composite views are now passed on to these reusable consumption view layers.

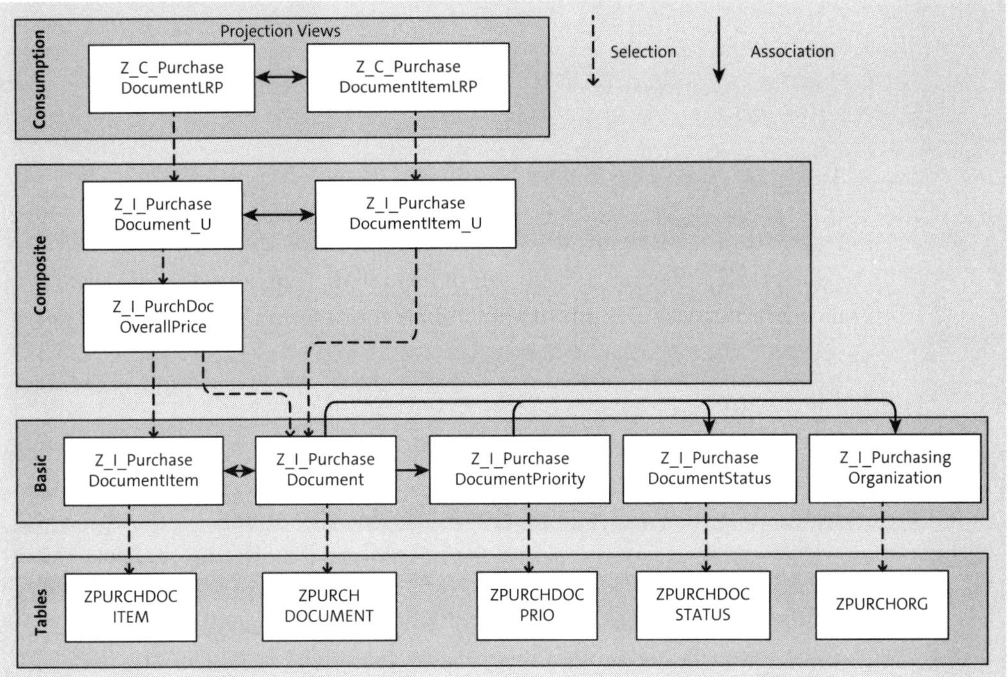

Figure 4.51 Final VDM of the Application

4.2.11 Creating Projection Behavior Definition

The same rule for creating a projection view to consume from the ABAP RESTful programming model-enabled business objects applies for behavior definitions as well. Since only one behavior definition is allowed for a view, our new projection view needs its own dedicated projection behavior definition view as well. The steps for creating a projection behavior definition is the same as for a normal behavior definition. Only difference is to provide the projection view name in the **Root View** name field in the behavior definition creation wizard window. The projection behavior definition will look like the code shown in Listing 4.39. If you check the coding, the first line shows that it's a `projection`, and the CRUD and action operations are defined using **use** keyword before the actual operation/action names.

```
projection;
define behavior for Z_C_PurchaseDocumentLrp //alias <alias_name>
{
  use create;
  use update;
  use delete;
  use action Approve_Order as Approve;
  use action Reject_Order  as Reject;
  use association _PURCHASEDOCUMENTITEM { create; }
}

define behavior for Z_C_PurchaseDocumentItemLrp //alias <alias_name>
{
  use create;
  use update;
  use delete;
}
```

Listing 4.39 Projection Behavior Definition

4.3 Virtual Elements in Core Data Services

In Section 4.1.4, you learned that the expressive CDS data DDL enables us to push down calculations to SAP HANA, which reduces calculations on the ABAP server and fosters code pushdown and the Code-to-Data paradigm to exploit the SAP HANA database and its capabilities. In some cases, however, you might still need to call some ABAP coding to calculate values that aren't part of a persistent model, for instance, legacy ABAP logic that can't be migrated to CDS views easily. In such cases, virtual elements can come into play and are defined on the CDS consumption view level but are calculated using ABAP code exits.

4.3.1 Adding a Virtual Element to a Core Data Services View

The annotations required for defining a CDS field as a virtual element are shown in Listing 4.40. On the CDS level, the virtual element field is simply an empty field. However, SADL will parse the annotations and, when the CDS view is queried via its corresponding OData entity, delegate the data calculation to an ABAP exit class (`@ObjectModel.virtualElementCalculatedBy`).

If you can also filter and sort the OData entity's provided data by the virtual element field, the filter (`@ObjectModel.filter.transformedBy`) and sort (`@ObjectModel.sort.transformedBy`) annotations and exits must be implemented.

```
@ObjectModel.virtualElementCalculatedBy: 'ABAP:<ABAP_class>'
@ObjectModel.filter.transformedBy: 'ABAP:<ABAP_class>'
@ObjectModel.sort.transformedBy: 'ABAP:<ABAP_class>'
Virtual <field_name> : <datatype>
```

Listing 4.40 Declare a Field as a Virtual Element in the CDS Field Selection List

4.3.2 Implementing an ABAP Code Exit to Populate the Virtual Element

To calculate, sort, and filter virtual elements, the relevant ABAP exit classes must implement the interfaces and methods listed in Table 4.2.

For the virtual element calculation, the `GET_CALCULATION_INFO` method is called before the actual database `SELECT` is performed. This method is supposed to return all fields that are required for the virtual element field to be calculated. SADL will then make sure that those fields are also selected from the database using its generic query engine. In the `CALCULATE` method, which is called after the database `SELECT`, the calculation of the virtual element field value must be implemented and can make use of the before specified and selected fields. The respective mapping methods of the filter (`MAP_ATOM`) and sort (`MAP_ELEMENT`) exits are called before the actual database `SELECT` takes place. Sort or filter conditions defined for the virtual element must in this case be mapped onto other fields that are available in the persistent database table and can be included in the database `SELECT` statement the SADL query engine generates.

Interface	Method
Calculate	IF_SADL_EXIT_CALC_ELEMENT_READ
Filter	IF_SADL_EXIT_FILTER_TRANSFORM
Sort	IF_SADL_EXIT_SORT_TRANSFORM

Table 4.2 Interfaces to Be Implemented for the Different Virtual Element Exits

In our CDS view, we'll utilize this virtual element feature to determine vendor ratings on the fly. (In the previous ABAP programming model for SAP Fiori, these virtual fields were simply part of the annotations, but they've been integrated into the ABAP language.) Virtual fields can be added to the projection view, as shown in Listing 4.41. The logic for vendor calculation is implemented in the class ZCL_VENDOR_RATING_CALC_EXIT.

```
@ObjectModel.virtualElementCalculatedBy: 'ABAP:ZCL_VENDOR_RATING_CALC_EXIT'
virtual VendorRating :abap.int1 ( 0  ),
```

Listing 4.41 Virtual Element Implementation for Vendor Rating

4.4 Adding User Interface Annotations to Projection Views

The UI of our application will be based on the SAP Fiori elements list report and object page templates. In contrast to SAP Fiori freestyle applications, the layout of SAP Fiori elements apps is relatively fixed, and UI controls can't be placed at will anywhere on the page. However, when using SAP Fiori elements template-based apps, you must specify which fields will be displayed at which predefined positions of the template using CDS @UI annotations. In the following subsections, we'll walk you through the steps for specifying the UI annotations required for our purchasing application. Additionally, we'll also introduce some non-UI annotations that will also influence the layout and functionality of the UI, for instance, @Search annotations.

4.4.1 Creating a Metadata Extension File

You can either add UI annotations directly into the CDS DDL file or create a metadata extension file. If you create a lot of UI annotations, which is normally the case when using SAP Fiori elements template-based apps, we recommend moving those annotations to a separate file to avoid cluttering the core CDS view with loads of UI annotations. You can create a metadata extension file by following these steps:

1. Open the ABAP perspective in the ABAP development tools in Eclipse.
2. In the ABAP project, select the **package** node in which you want to create the table via the **Project Explorer** view.
3. Right-click on the package and select **New • Other ABAP Repository • Core Data Services • Metadata Extension**.
4. The metadata extension creation wizard appears where you'll enter a **Name** and **Description**. We'll call the purchase document's metadata extension `Z_C_PurchaseDocumentLrp` and the purchase document items metadata extension `Z_C_PurchaseDocumentItemLrp`. By convention, metadata extension files will have the same names as their annotated DDL sources.
5. Click **Finish**, and the source code editor will open.

In the metadata extension file, you must define which CDS view you want to annotate. In our case, we first want to annotate the purchase document view `Z_C_PurchaseDocumentLRP` to configure the list report. Additionally, you must specify the priority of the metadata extension by assigning it to a layer. The `#CORE` layer has the lowest priority, whereas the `#CUSTOMER` layer has the highest priority. We'll simply go with the `#CORE` layer so that we can overwrite our UI annotations later without having to change the core extension file, as shown in Listing 4.42.

```
@Metadata.layer: #CORE
annotate view Z_C_PurchaseDocumentLRP with{…}
```

Listing 4.42 Metadata Extension File Header for the Z_C_PurchaseDocumentLRP CDS View

To enable metadata extensions from the CDS DDL side, the following annotation must be added on the header level: `@Metadata.allowExtensions:true`. All UI annotations we'll introduce in the following sections will be added to the metadata extensions we just created for the purchase document and purchase document item CDS consumption views (`Z_C_PurchaseDocumentLrp` and `Z_C_PurchaseDocumentItemLrp`).

4.4.2 User Interface-Relevant Annotations for the List Report

In this section, we'll go through the most important UI annotations of the list report template and configure the UI of our purchase document list report. Figure 4.52

shows an overview of the most important list report CDS UI annotations and how they are reflected on the UI. These include:

❶ `@Search.searchable: true`

❷ `@UI.selectionField`

❸ `@UI.headerInfo`

❹ `@UI.lineItem`

To configure the UI of the list report, we must annotate the `Z_C_PurchaseDocumentItemLrp` CDS view because the corresponding purchase document OData entity will be bound to the list report screen.

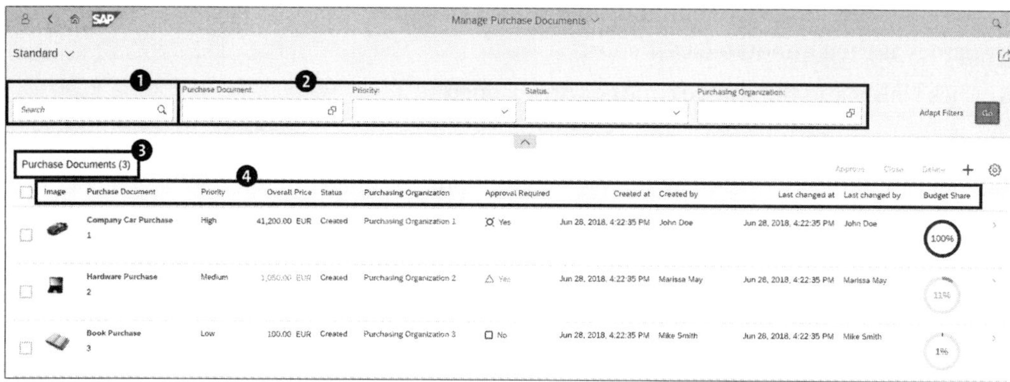

Figure 4.52 Most Important List Report CDS UI Annotations and How They Will Be Reflected in the List Report Template

Line Item Annotation

To specify which fields of the `Z_C_PurchaseDocumentLRP` OData entity will initially be displayed as columns in the table of the list report, we must annotate these fields with the `@UI.lineItem` annotation. How this looks for the `PurchaseDocument` field, which we want to display as the second column in the table, is shown in Listing 4.43.

```
@UI.lineItem: [{ importance: #HIGH, position: 20 }]
PurchaseDocument;
```

Listing 4.43 Line Item Annotation for the PurchaseDocument Field

We must specify the `position` of the field by which the columns of the table are sorted. Additionally, we can also define the `importance` of the field. Fields annotated with `importance: #HIGH` will always be displayed even, for instance, when the table is rendered on small displays. If no importance is specified, the line item is treated as having #LOW importance.

Header Info Annotation

The header of the table can be set using the header-level UI annotation @UI.headerInfo. For the list report, the value specified for typeNamePlural will be used as the title of the table, as shown in Listing 4.44.

```
@UI.headerInfo: {
 ...
 typeNamePlural: 'Purchase Documents',
 ... }
```

Listing 4.44 Header Info typeNamePlural Annotation for Purchase Documents

Image Annotation

The @UI.headerInfo annotation also contains an imageUrl annotation to define a field containing URLs for images to display in the application. In our case, we'll reference the PurchaseDocumentImageURL field, as shown in Listing 4.45.

```
@UI.headerInfo: {
 ...
 imageUrl: 'PurchaseDocumentImageURL'
 ... }
```

Listing 4.45 Header Info imageUrl Annotation for Purchase Documents

Additionally, the PurchaseDocumentImageURL field must also be annotated with @Semantics.imageUrl: true. If we then add the field as the first column in our table using the @UI.lineItem annotation introduced previously, the template will automatically render an HTML <img> tag with the src property set to the image URL provided by the field value.

Criticality Annotation

We'll use the OverallPriceCriticality field value calculated in the backend CDS layer to indicate the criticality of the OverallPrice column, as shown in Listing 4.46. Depending on the overall price criticality value, the overall price field value will be displayed in a certain color, as listed in Table 4.3. The criticality annotation is also part of the @UI.lineItem annotation.

```
@UI.lineItem: [{ importance: #HIGH, position: 40, criticality:
'OverallPriceCriticality', value: 'OverallPrice'  }]}
OverallPrice;
```

Listing 4.46 Line Item Criticality Annotation for the OverallPrice Field

Criticality Value	Color
3 – Not critical	Green
2 – Medium criticality	Yellow
1 – High criticality	Red
0 – Undefined	No color

Table 4.3 Mappings between Criticality Value and Color

We also use the `OverallPriceCriticality` field value in the same way to indicate the criticality of the `IsApprovalRequired` field.

Contact Quick View

You can also display contact information in a quick view for a field by adding the `type: #AS_CONTACT` annotation, as shown in Listing 4.47, which is also part of the `@UI.lineItem` annotation, as shown in Figure 4.53.

The data of the quick view, as shown in Listing 4.48, must be provided via an association `value: '_PurchasingOrganization'` where the associated view must contain several semantically annotated fields, as shown earlier in Figure 4.49.

```
@UI.lineItem: [{ importance: #MEDIUM, position: 60, type: #AS_CONTACT, value:
'_PurchasingOrganization', label: 'Purchasing Organization' }]
PurchasingOrganization;
```

Listing 4.47 Contact Quick View Annotation for the PurchasingOrganization Field

```
...
@Semantics.text: true
@Semantics.name.fullName: true
description            as Description,

@Semantics: {
eMail.address: true,
```

```
eMail.type:  [ #WORK ]
}
emailaddress              as Email,
@Semantics.telephone.type:  [ #WORK ]
phonenumber               as Phone,
@Semantics.telephone.type:  [ #FAX ]
faxnumber                 as Fax
...
```

Listing 4.48 Required Annotations for the Contact Quick View in the Associated View

Figure 4.53 Contact Quick View for the Purchasing Organization

Selection Field Annotation

To make certain fields appear in the expanded filter bar area of the list report as selection fields, we must annotate those fields with the `@UI.selectionField` annotation. As with the line item annotation, we also must specify the `position` annotation to sort the selection fields. As shown in Listing 4.49, the `PurchaseDocument` and `Priority` fields must be annotated to appear in sequence.

```
...
@UI.selectionField: [{ position: 10 }]
PurchaseDocument;
@UI.selectionField: [{ position: 20 }]
Priority;
...
```

Listing 4.49 Selection Field Annotation for the Filter Bar

The other selection fields, shown earlier in Figure 4.52, must be annotated accordingly with increasing `position` values.

Searchable Annotation

The @Search.searchable: true header-level annotation marks a CDS view entity relevant for search scenarios. Additionally, by annotating certain fields with @Search.defaultSearchElement: true, those elements will be considered in freestyle searches and form the search scope. In our case, we'll annotate the purchase document Description field with search annotations in the main CDS view. We'll do this directly in the main view, not in the metadata extension, as we only want to move UI annotations to the metadata extension file. We'll also introduce an @Search.fuzzinessThreshold to make our search somewhat error tolerant. The value can vary between 0 and 1, where 1 means that only exact matches will be returned by the search. We'll use the recommended value 0.7, which introduces some fuzziness but not too much:

```
...
@Search.defaultSearchElement : true
@Search.fuzzinessThreshold : 0.7
@Semantics.text: true
Description,
...
```

@Search annotations don't belong to the UI annotation category, but annotating the purchase document CDS view entity with @Search annotations will render a freestyle search field in the list report template, as shown earlier in Figure 4.52. When generating an OData service metadata document, SADL will consider search annotations and set the EntitySet property sap:searchable to true, indicating to the UI or consuming clients that the entity supports freestyle search. When sending a search query for a certain entity, SADL will trigger an SAP HANA text search (transparent to the developer) considering the fuzziness indicator and the search scope formed by the @Search.defaultSearchElement: true annotated fields of the CDS view.

The OData search request GET Z_C_PurchaseDocumentLrp?search=<SEARCH_TERM>&... will be transformed by SADL to an SAP HANA fuzzy text search SELECT statement making use of the SAP HANA CONTAINS predicate:

```
SELECT ... FROM Z_C_PurchaseDocumentLRP WHERE CONTAINS(Description, <SEARCH_TERM>,
FUZZY(0.7))...;
```

Value Helps

The value help for a field must be defined with the annotation @Consumption.valueHelpDefinition. If a field is annotated with @Consumption.valueHelpDefinition: [{entity:{name:'<valueHelp_View_Name>' , element: '<field_name>'}}] and the field is used in the behavior definition, then during service binding activation, the SADL will take this information into account when generating the OData service and will create value help annotations for the key field of the associated view. Listing 4.50 shows the value help definition for `Status` in the `Z_C_PurchaseDocumentLRP` CDS view.

```
@Consumption.valueHelpDefinition: [{entity:{name:'Z_C_StatusVH' , element:
'Status'}}]
Status
```

Listing 4.50 Value Help Odata Annotation for Status field

The corresponding CDS view that is used as the value help view also needs a few value help-specific annotations defined. The annotation `@ObjectModel.resultSet.sizeCategory: #XS` will make the value help for `Status` accessible through a multiselect dropdown list in the UI, unlike a normal value help. The annotation `@ObjectModel.dataCategory: #VALUE_HELP` classifies this CDS view as a value help view, as shown in Listing 4.51.

```
...
@VDM.viewType: #CONSUMPTION
@ObjectModel.resultSet.sizeCategory: #XS
@ObjectModel.dataCategory: #VALUE_HELP
define view Z_C_StatusVH as select from Z_I_PurchaseDocumentStatus {
@ObjectModel.text.element: ['StatusText']
key Status,
@Search: { defaultSearchElement: true, ranking: #HIGH, fuzzinessThreshold: 0.7
}
    StatusText
}
```

Listing 4.51 Value Help CDS View for Status

Enabling Quick Actions

The quick actions we've added to the purchase document root (`Z_I_PurchaseDocument_U`) node of our unmanaged business objects can be enabled on the list report UI by adding the `@UI.lineItem` annotations shown in Listing 4.52 to the `PurchaseDocument` field.

```
@UI: {
lineItem: [
...
   { type: #FOR_ACTION, dataAction: 'Approve', position: 10, label: 'Approve'  },
```

```
    { type: #FOR_ACTION, dataAction: 'Reject',  position: 20, label: 'Close' }]
…
 ]
}
PurchaseDocument;
```

Listing 4.52 Line Item Annotation to Enable BOPF Quick Actions on the List Report UI

4.4.3 User Interface Annotations for the Object Page

To configure the object page, shown later in Figure 4.55, we must mainly annotate the Z_C_PurchaseDocumentLRP CDS view as the data we want to display in the header in the **Purchase Document** section provided by this CDS view. The Z_C_PurchaseDocumentItemLRP must be annotated with @UI.lineItem annotations to configure the items table contained in the **Purchase Document Items** section of the object page.

Header Info Annotation

The object page title and subtitle can be configured using the @UI.headerInfo.title and description annotations. In our case, we want to display the Description and PurchaseDocument fields of the Z_C_PurchaseDocumentLRP entity in these positions of the template layout, as shown in Listing 4.53.

```
@UI: {
    headerInfo: {
        description: {
            value: 'Description',
            type: #STANDARD
        },
        title: {
            value: 'PurchaseDocument',
            type: #STANDARD
        },
        …
    }
}
```

Listing 4.53 Header Info Description and Title Annotation

In Figure 4.54, you can see:

❶ @UI.headerInfo

❷ @UI.facet (purpose: #HEADER, type: #DATAPOINT_REFERENCE)

Figure 4.54 CDS UI Annotations for the Object Page Header

Data Point Header Facet Annotation

Furthermore, we want to add several data points to the header section of the object page to highlight several values: `Status`, `OverallPrice`, `IsApprovalRequired`, and `Priority`, as shown in Figure 4.54. Therefore, we must create several header facets using the `@UI.facet` annotation with `purpose: #HEADER` and `type: #DATAPOINT_REFERENCE`. Via the `targetQualifier` annotation, the facets reference corresponding fields annotated with the `@UI.dataPoint` annotation. As an example, Listing 4.54 shows the required annotations for displaying the `OverallPrice` field as a data point header facet.

```
@UI.facet: [
   ...
         {
           id:          'OverallPriceDataPointFacet',
           purpose:     #HEADER,
           type:        #DATAPOINT_REFERENCE,
           targetQualifier: 'OverallPrice'
          },
   ...
    ]
}
PurchaseDocument;
...
@UI.dataPoint: { title: 'Overall Price', criticality:
```

```
'OverallPriceCriticality' }
OverallPrice;
...
```

Listing 4.54 Data Point Header Facet Annotations for the OverallPrice Field

Facet Annotation

The different sections of an object page are defined using `@UI.facet` annotations, as shown in Figure 4.55. These include:

❶ `@UI.facet (type: #COLLECTION)`

❷ `@UI.facet (type: #LINEITEM_REFERENCE)`

❸ `@UI.fieldGroup`

❹ `@UI.facet (type:#FIELDGROUP_REFERENCE)`

❺ `@UI.lineItem`

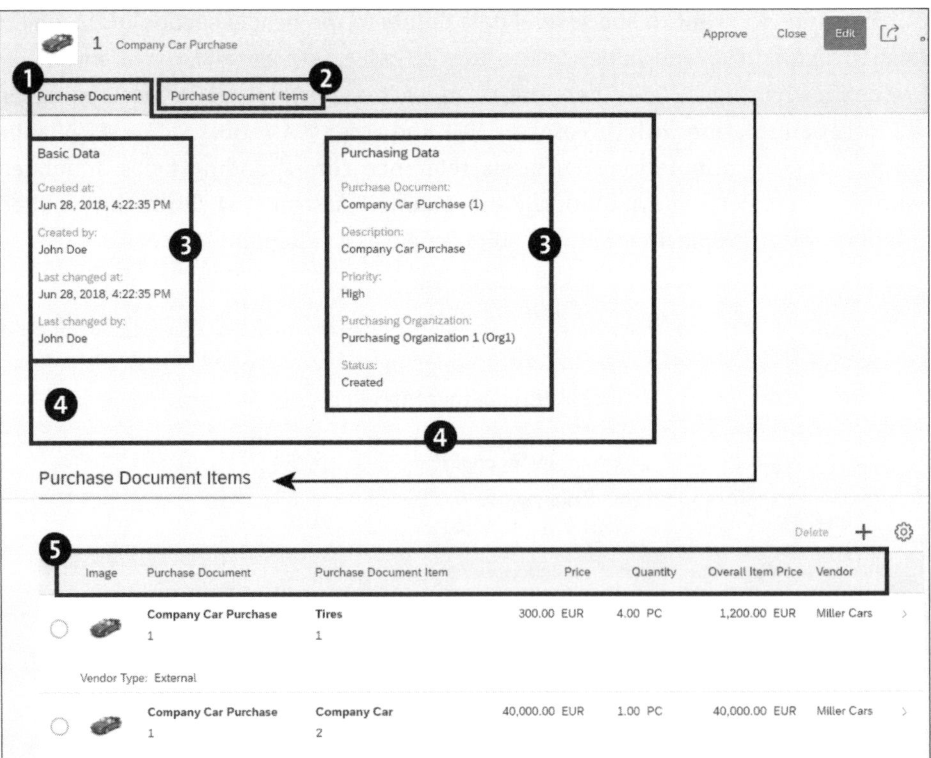

Figure 4.55 Sections of an Object Page and Their Corresponding UI Annotations

The **Purchase Document** section is defined as a collection facet using the `@UI.facet.type: #COLLECTION` annotation. The section includes two field groups, **Basic Data** and **Purchasing Data**, which are defined using reference facets (`@UI.facet.type: #FIELDGROUP_REFERENCE`). In turn, reference field groups are defined with the `@UI.fieldGroup` annotation. To group reference facets into the same collection facet, reference facets must provide the `@UI.facet.parentId` annotation pointing to the ID annotation of the collection facet. Fields with the same field group `qualifier` annotation, in our case, `PurchasingDocumentFieldGroup` or `BasicDataFieldGroup`, are assigned to the same field groups. The **Purchase Document Items** section is defined using the `@UI.facet.type: #LINEITEM_REFERENCE` annotation and references the `_PurchaseDocumentItem` association. The columns of the items table are defined using `@UI.lineItem` annotations. Listing 4.55 shows an excerpt of the required annotations for defining the UI shown in Figure 4.55.

```
@UI: {
facet:[
...
// Purchase Document Section
{
    label: 'Purchase Document',
    type: #COLLECTION,
    id: 'PurchaseDocumentCollectionFacet',
    purpose: #STANDARD
},
// Basic Data field group
{
    label: 'Basic Data',
    type: #FIELDGROUP_REFERENCE,
    id: 'BasicDataFieldGroupReferenceFacet',
    parentId: 'PurchaseDocumentCollectionFacet',
    purpose: #STANDARD,
    targetQualifier: 'BasicDataFieldGroup'
},
// Purchasing Data field group
{
    label: 'Purchasing Data',
    type: #FIELDGROUP_REFERENCE,
    id: 'PurchasingDocumentFieldGroupReferenceFacet',
    parentId: 'PurchaseDocumentCollectionFacet',
    purpose: #STANDARD,
```

```
    targetQualifier: 'PurchasingDocumentFieldGroup'
},
// Items Section
{
    label: 'Purchase Document Items',
    type: #LINEITEM_REFERENCE,
    id: 'PurchaseDocumentItemsLineItemReferenceFacet',
    purpose: #STANDARD,
    targetElement: '_PurchaseDocumentItem'
}
],
fieldGroup: [{ qualifier: 'PurchasingDocumentFieldGroup',
position: 10, importance: #HIGH }]
}
PurchaseDocument;
...
@UI.fieldGroup: [{ qualifier: 'BasicDataFieldGroup', position: 10, importance:
#HIGH }]
crea_date_time;
...
```

Listing 4.55 Excerpt of the Required CDS UI Annotations for Defining Object Page Sections and Field Groups

Line Item Annotation

The columns of the purchase document items table on the object page are defined via `@UI.lineItem` annotations, as shown in Listing 4.56. In this case, the annotations must be added to the metadata extension file of the `Z_C_PurchaseDocumentItemLRP` CDS view.

```
...
@UI.lineItem: [{ importance: #HIGH, position: 10, }]
PurchaseDocumentItemImageURL;
@UI.lineItem: [{ importance: #HIGH, position: 20 }]
PurchaseDocument;
@UI.lineItem: [{ importance: #HIGH, position: 30 }]
PurchaseDocumentItem;
...
```

Listing 4.56 LineItem Annotation to Determine Columns and Position in the Table for Purchase Document Item

Enabling Quick Actions

To enable the **Approve** and **Close** status quick actions on the object page, you must add the `@UI.identification` annotation to the `PurchaseDocument` field, as shown in Listing 4.57.

```
@UI: {
 identification: [
{ type: #FOR_ACTION, dataAction: 'Approve', position: 10, importance: #HIGH,
label: 'Approve' },
{ type: #FOR_ACTION, dataAction: 'Reject',  position: 20, importance: #HIGH,
label: 'Close' }],
...
}
PurchaseDocument;
```

Listing 4.57 Identification Annotation to Enable the Approve and Close Quick Actions in the Object Page

4.4.4 Preview of the SAP Fiori Elements App with UI Annotations Using Service Binding

Just as we created the service definition and service binding for the `Z_I_PurchaseDocument_U` earlier in Sections Section 4.2.2 and Section 4.2.3, now we'll create those same objects for the new projection view `Z_C_PurchaseDocumentLRP` as well. In this example, we called our service definition `Z_PurchaseDocumentLRP`. As shown in Listing 4.58, make sure you expose `Z_C_PurchaseDocumentLrp`, `Z_C_PurchaseDocumentItemLrp`, and `Z_I_PurchasingOrganization` in the service definition if you're copying the code from the service binding you created for the `Z_I_PurchaseDocument_U`. We called the service binding `Z_UI_PURCHASEDOCUMENT_V2`.

```
@EndUserText.label: 'Purchase Document SD Unmanaged'
define service Z_PurchaseDocumentLRP {
  expose Z_C_PurchaseDocumentLrp as PurchaseDocument;
  expose Z_C_PurchaseDocumentItemLrp as PurchaseDocumentItem;
  expose Z_I_PurchaseDocument_U as PurchaseDocument_U;
  expose Z_I_PurchaseDocumentItem_U as PurchaseDocumentItem_U;
  expose I_Indicator as ApprovalRequired;
  expose I_Currency as Currency;
  expose I_UnitOfMeasure as QuantityUnitofMeasure;
  expose Z_I_VendorType as VendorType;
```

```
  expose Z_C_StatusVH as StatusVH;
  expose Z_C_VendorTypeVH as VendorTypeVH;
  expose Z_C_PriorityVH as PriorityVH;
  expose Z_I_PurchaseDocumentPriority as Priority;
  expose Z_I_PurchaseDocumentStatus as Status;
  expose Z_I_PurchDocOverallPrice as PurchDocOveralPrice;
  expose Z_I_PurchaseDocument as PruchasDocumentBase;
  expose Z_I_PurchaseDocumentItem as PurchaseDocumentItemBase;
  expose Z_I_PurchasingOrganization as PurchasingOrganization;
}
```

Listing 4.58 Service Binding for Z_C_PurchaseDocumentLRP

Now, if you right-click on the activated service binding's `PurchaseDocument` entity, you'll be able to see the custom action buttons as well as all the UI annotations we added to the consumption views via the metadata extension. As shown in Figure 4.56, you can now see the SAP Fiori elements app complete with custom action buttons and the CRUD operations.

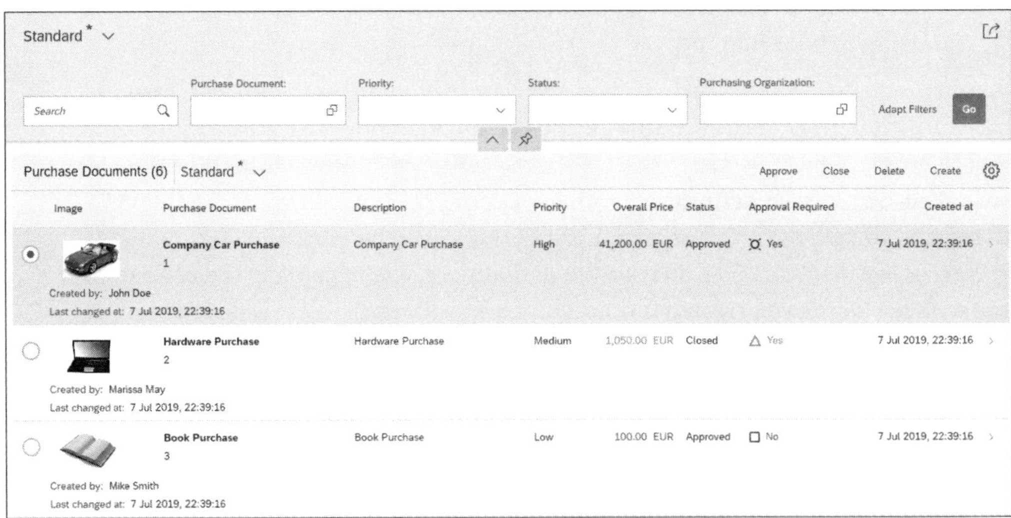

Figure 4.56 Purchase Document App Preview with Custom Action Buttons and Other UI Elements Enabled by UI Annotations Defined in the Metadata Extension

If you click on the line items of the purchase document table, you'll be navigated to the second screen where you'll see all the UI annotations that we created in the metadata extensions, as shown in Figure 4.57. You could also see the UI annotations for the purchase document item's CDS view in effect in the form of the table.

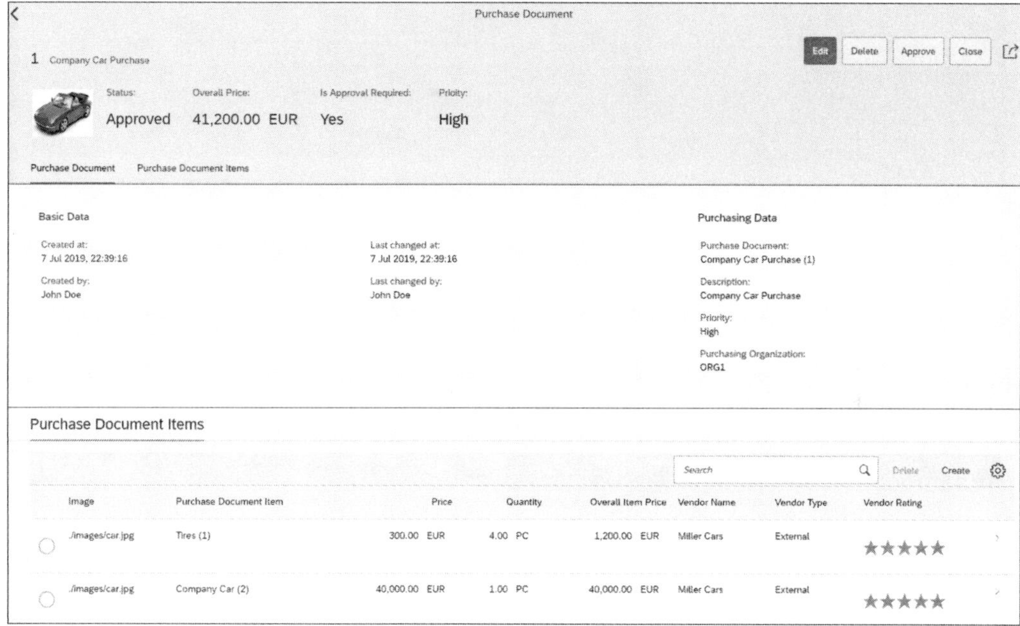

Figure 4.57 Purchase Document Object Page with Purchase Document Item Table Enabled with UI Annotations

Now, if you go back to the main screen of the purchase document and click on the create action button, you'll be navigated automatically to the object page of the purchase documents, as shown in Figure 4.58. On this page, only the **Description**, **Priority**, and **Purchase Organization** fields are editable. (We defined the other fields as read only in the behavior definition for our CDS view, as shown earlier in Figure 4.31.) Also, you can see the value help definition in the CDS view for the **Priority** field in effect. If you put the debugger in the `Create` method of the behavior implementation class `zbp_i_purchasedocument_u`, you'll see all the import and export parameters we discussed earlier in Section 4.2.9, Create.

Similarly, if you click the create action button for the purchase document item in the object page, you'll be navigated to a create page for purchase document items, as shown in Figure 4.59. On this page, you can create the corresponding items for the purchase document, and the ABAP RESTful programming model will trigger the Create by Association method in the behavior implementation class when you click the **SAVE** button.

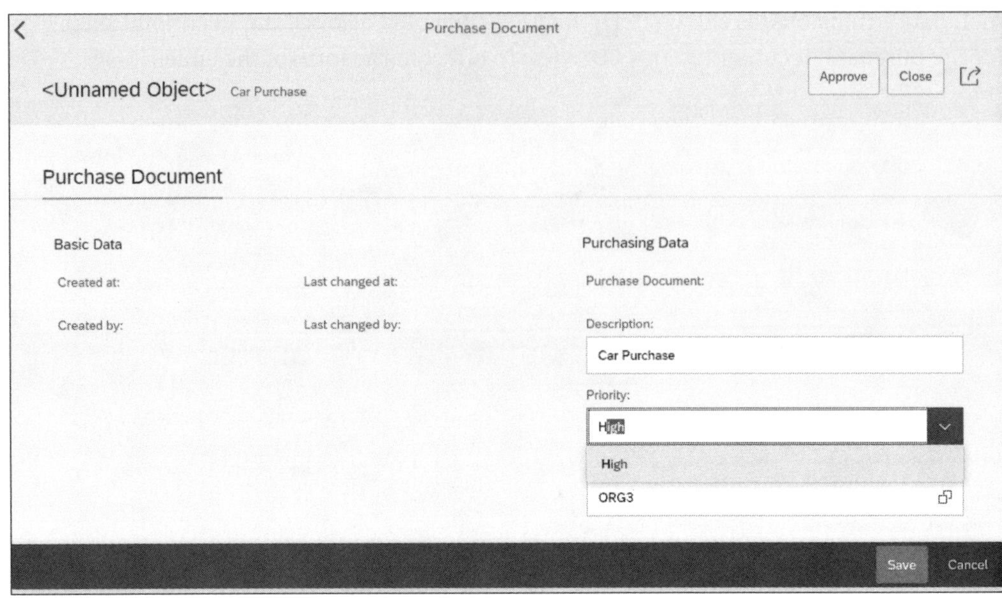

Figure 4.58 Create Operation of the Purchase Document Defined in the Behavior Definition

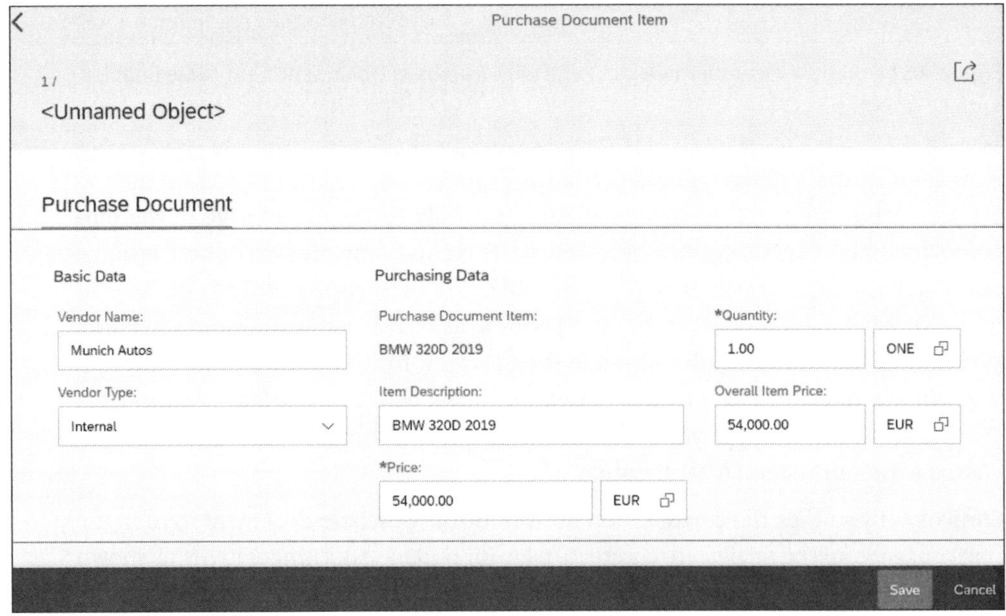

Figure 4.59 Create Operation of the Purchase Document Item Defined in the Behavior Definition (Triggers Create by Association Method)

If you click the **Edit** button on the purchase document object page, as shown in Figure 4.60, all the fields related to purchase document and its line items will become editable (except for the fields that are defined as read only in the behavior definition). Edits are tracked in the `%control` table, which is part as the import parameter for the update operation comes into the picture. For every field that you change, the `%control` structure will mark those fields with "01" in it. And thereby, in the `UPDATE` method, you'll be able to identify which fields needs to be updated in the backend. Up to this point of the development, you haven't even touched the SAP Web IDE to create the SAP Fiori elements application nor you have opened the SAP GUI to register the OData services. This ease of use is the advantage or power of the new ABAP RESTful programming model. If you're an ABAP developer who isn't much into SAPUI5 development, you can still control almost every aspect of the application using the SAP HANA Studio. When you're happy with the functionality of the app and look and feel of the UI, you can then hand over the OData service name to the UI developer to polish up the final app based on app-specific UI requirements. This level of control was not possible until the introduction of the ABAP RESTful programming model.

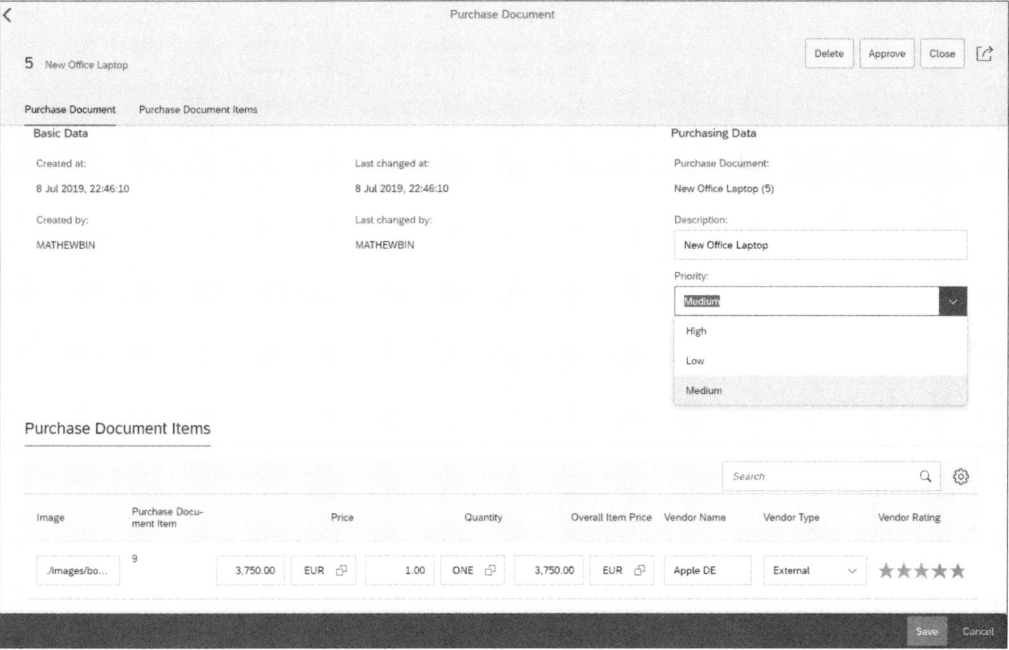

Figure 4.60 Update Operation of the Purchase Document and Purchase Document Item Defined in the Behavior Definition

4.5 Generating a List Report Template in SAP Web IDE Full-Stack

The SAP Web IDE full-stack is the recommended IDE for developing state-of-the-art SAP Fiori applications based on the SAPUI5 framework. This cloud-based IDE is accessible via browser, and because it's a service of the SAP Cloud Platform, you can easily subscribe to it. SAP Web IDE full-stack provides excellent support for creating frontend project skeletons for freestyle SAP Fiori applications as well as for SAP Fiori elements applications. In the following subsections, we'll use the SAP Web IDE to generate our SAP Fiori elements-based list report and object page UI using the previously generated OData service of our app.

To create a list report and object page SAP Fiori elements app, select **File • New • Project from Template** and then select the list report application template within the **SAP Fiori Elements** template category, as shown in Figure 4.61.

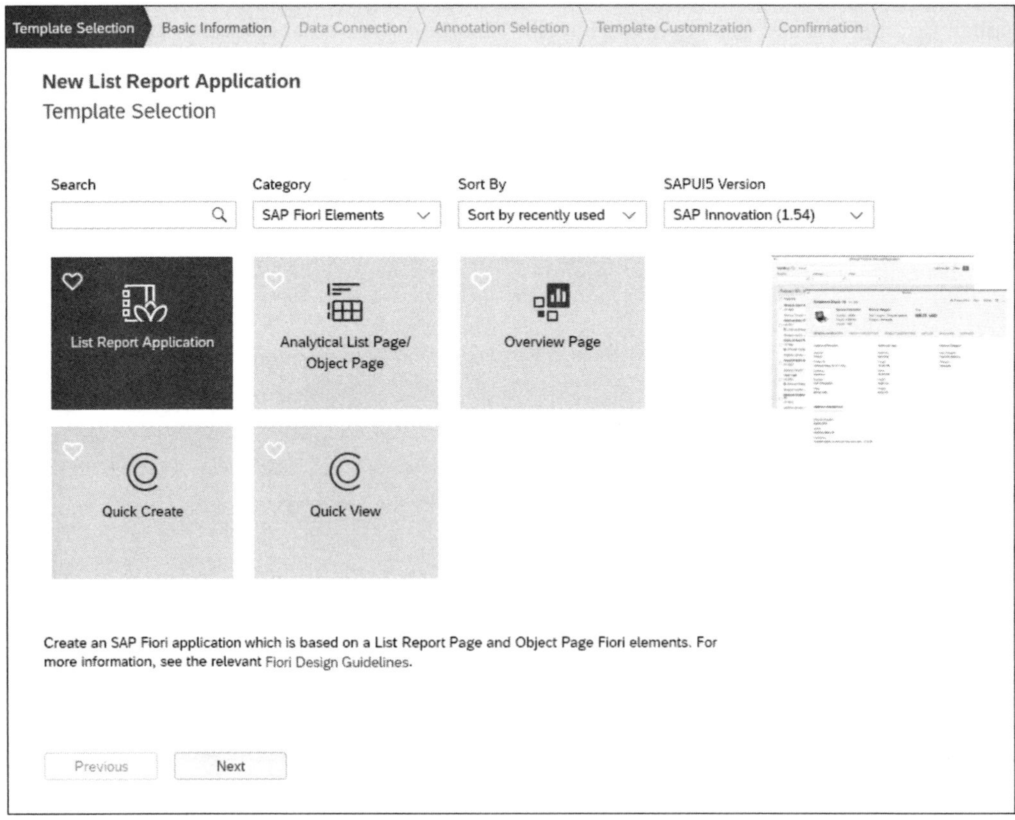

Figure 4.61 SAP Fiori Elements Templates Provided by the SAP Web IDE Full-Stack

Next, provide a name for the project and some additional data that will be written to the app descriptor of the application, as shown in Figure 4.62. You can later find this information in the *manifest.json* file of the project. Click **Next**.

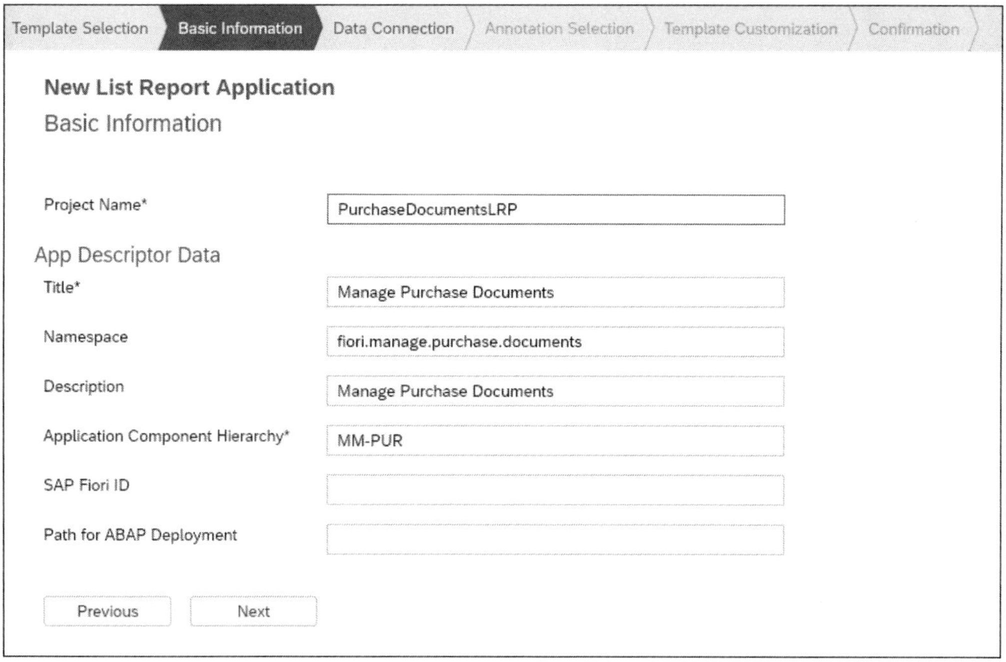

Figure 4.62 Basic Information and App Descriptor Data When Creating a New Template-Based List Report

On the next screen of the creation wizard, select the OData service of the app which was generated using the service binding (`zbp_i_purchasedocument_u`), as shown in Figure 4.63. For our example, we must first choose an SAP Gateway hub system where our service has been activated. Subsequently, we can search for the service by its technical name. Select the service and click **Next**.

Our service provides two annotation files: the service metadata document, which can be requested using the `$metadata` URL parameter, and an additional annotation file containing our UI annotations, as shown in Figure 4.64. This annotation file is provided by the Catalog Service of the SAP Gateway hub system. You can also find this OData annotation service in the `dataSources` object of the app descriptor (*manifest.json* file):

```
/sap/opu/odata/IWFND/CATALOGSERVICE;v=2/Annotations(TechnicalName='Z_C_
PURCHASEDOCUMENTLRP_CDS_VAN',Version='0001')/$value/
```

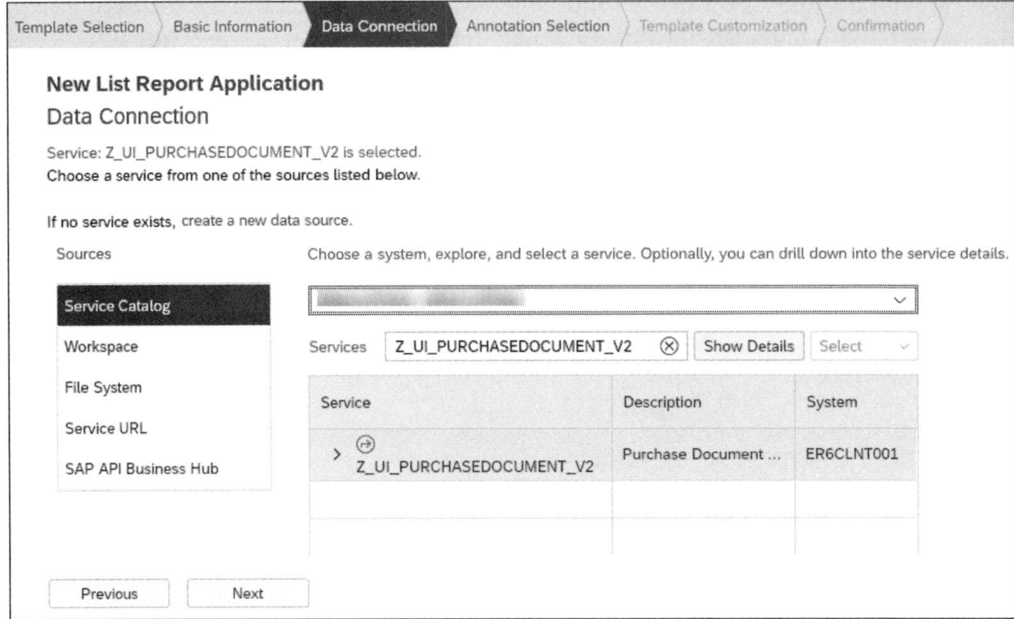

Figure 4.63 Selecting the OData Service for the App

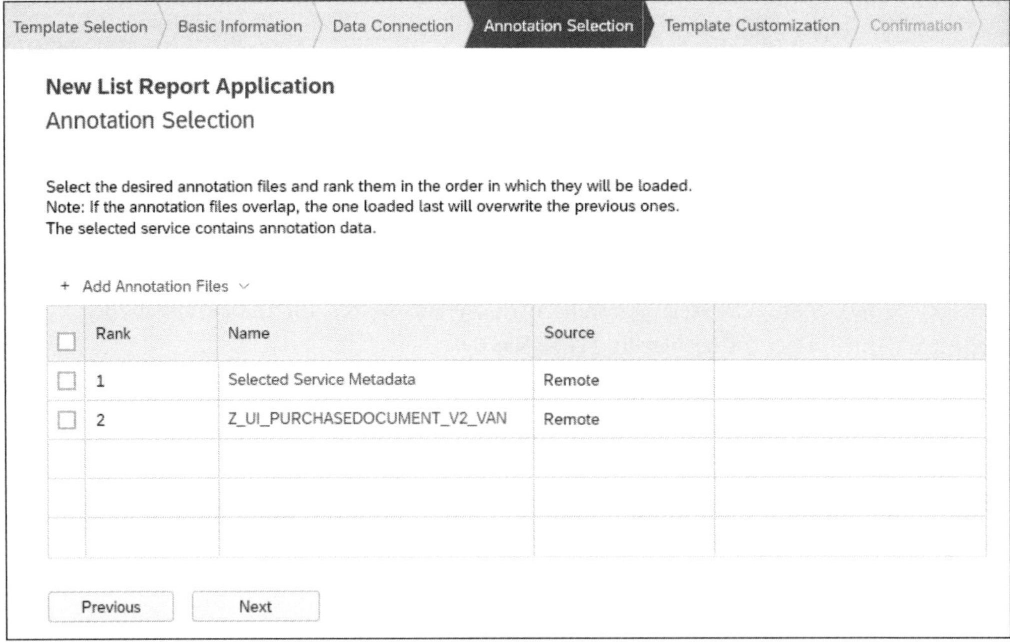

Figure 4.64 Annotation Files Provided by the Service

On the last screen of the wizard, we must customize the template and provide our two main entities as **OData Collection** and **OData Navigation**. Click **Finish**, as shown in Figure 4.65. To run the application, right-click on the root folder of the project in the files pane and select **Run • Run As • Web Application** from the context menu.

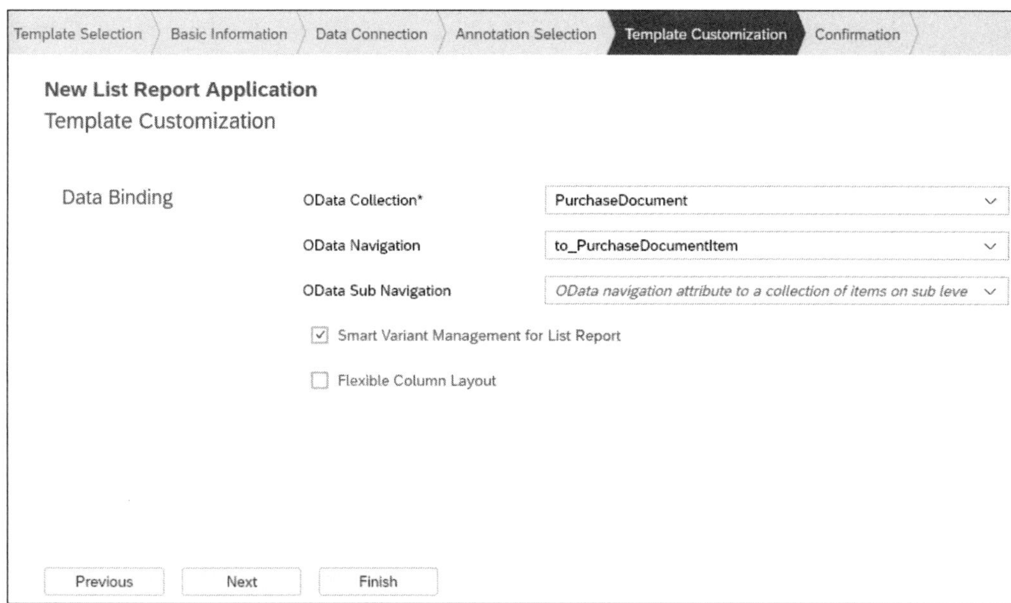

Figure 4.65 Customizing the Template by Choosing the Purchase Document Entity and the Purchase Document Item Entity

Note

In general, OData annotations can be provided from three sources: the service metadata document, the Catalog Service using the annotation model of the OData service, and local annotations. By default, the SAP Web IDE will create a local annotation file when generating the list report SAP Fiori elements application to render default facets on the object page. However, as we could provide all UI annotations via CDS annotations, we must comment out or remove these annotations because they will otherwise overwrite our CDS annotations.

Nevertheless, if certain annotations can't be provided via CDS, the local annotation file and its annotation modeler tool can be used instead. However, note that the OData annotation also must be supported and interpreted by the respective SAP Fiori elements template application.

4.6 Extending the User Interface

You can further extend the generated list report and object page layout on the UI side by using several predefined extension points; for instance, the list report defines an extension point for adding additional table columns and the object page for adding additional sections. In this case, UI parts aren't defined using annotations but instead using actual XML fragment declarations and JavaScript SAPUI5 code as if you were developing a freestyle SAPUI5 app. However, these coded extensions live within strictly defined extension boundaries, which aren't supposed to break the overall design and structure of the SAP Fiori elements template. In the following section, we'll illustrate the concept of UI extension points by adding a custom column to the purchase documents table. The column extension will visualize the budget share of a purchase document using a radial micro chart control.

Note

UI extensions should be used with caution and only if the functionality can't be achieved by other means, for instance, annotations and app descriptor changes. UI extensions are a greater intervention into the frontend project and increase the risk of bugs and violations of the SAP Fiori design guidelines. For a full overview of all extension possibilities, check the SAPUI5 SDK online documentation at *http://s-prs.co/498816.*

4.6.1 Implementing User Interface Extensions via Breakout

The SAP Web IDE provides an extension wizard that you can open either from the top-level menu bar by choosing **File • New • Extension** or from the context menu of the project by choosing **New • Extension**. However, you can also add extensions manually by modifying the *manifest.json* app descriptor file and creating the necessary SAPUI5 controls and logic.

We'll do the latter and manually create two SAPUI5 fragment declarations in a newly created *ext* folder for extending the table columns, as shown in Figure 4.66. The *ListReportResponsiveTableColumns.fragment.xml* contains the definition of the new column, whereas the *ListReportResponsiveTableCells.fragment.xml* contains the definition of the content, in our case, the `RadialMicroChart` control. Additionally, we'll create a *ListReportExtension.controller.js* file and a *formatter.js* file because we want to calculate the properties of the chart control dynamically based on the `OverallPrice` field of the purchase document.

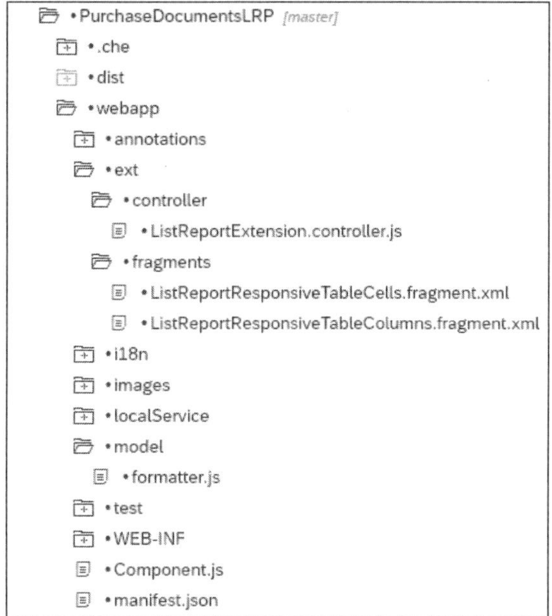

Figure 4.66 Overview of the Folder Structure and the Required Files for Implementing the Column Extension

The column definition defined in the `ListReportResponsiveTableColumns.fragment.xml` fragment consists of the code shown in Listing 4.59:

```
<core:FragmentDefinition xmlns:core="sap.ui.core" xmlns="sap.m">
 <Column>
  <Text text="Budget Share"/>
   <customData>
    <core:CustomData key="p13nData" value='\{"columnKey":  "TestKey",
"columnIndex" : "200"}'/>
   </customData>
 </Column>
</core:FragmentDefinition>
```

Listing 4.59 Column Definition in Responsive Table Columns Fragment Declaration

Using the `CustomData` tag and the `p13nData` attribute, we'll enable the column for personalization, which enables users to configure the user interface through the personalization dialog of the table, like the other fields provided by the backend. The cell definition defined in the ListReportResponsiveTableCells.fragment.xml fragment consists of the code shown in Listing 4.60:

```
<core:FragmentDefinition xmlns:core="sap.ui.core" xmlns="sap.m" xmlns:micro=
"sap.suite.ui.microchart"
xmlns:app="http://schemas.sap.com/sapui5/extension/sap.ui.core.CustomData/1">
    <FlexBox height="70px" width="70px">
        <layoutData>
            <FlexItemData maxHeight="70px"/>
        </layoutData>
        <micro:RadialMicroChart percentage="{ path: 'OverallPrice',
        formatter: '.formatter.calculatePercentage' }"  app:name="radial"
        press="press" valueColor="{ path: 'OverallPrice', formatter:
        '.formatter.calculateCriticality' }"/>
    </FlexBox>
</core:FragmentDefinition>
```

Listing 4.60 Cell Definition in Responsive Table Cells Fragment Declaration

We'll define the RadialMicroChart as the content of the new extension column and calculate the percentage and valueColor properties of the control using the formatter's calculatePercentage and calculateCritcality functions. The implementation of the formatter is shown in Listing 4.61. In the calculatePercentage function, we'll calculate what percentage of the total budget the current purchase document would consume. In the calculateCritcality function, we'll once again calculate the criticality of the OverallPrice value; however, this time, the calculation is performed on the UI side.

```
sap.ui.define([], function () {
"use strict";
var TOTAL_BUDGET = 10000;
return {
    calculatePercentage: function (nOverallPrice) {
        var percentage = Math.round((nOverallPrice / TOTAL_BUDGET) * 100);
        return percentage > 100 ? 100 : percentage;
    },
```

```
    calculateCriticality: function (nOverallPrice) {
        if (nOverallPrice <= 1000) {
            return "Good";
        } else if (nOverallPrice > 1000 && nOverallPrice < 5000) {
            return "Critical";
        } else {
            return "Error";
        }
    }
};
});
```

Listing 4.61 Implementation of the Formatter for Dynamically Calculating the Percentage and Criticality Based on the OverallPrice Field

To enable the formatter to use within the cell content definition fragment, we must add the formatter to the extension controller as an object property, as shown in Listing 4.62.

```
sap.ui.define([
    "fiori/manage/purchase/documents/purchasedocumentslrp/model/formatter"
], function (formatter) {
    "use strict";
    return sap.ui.controller(
    "fiori.manage.purchase.documents.purchasedocumentslrp.ext.controller.
    ListReportExtension", {
        formatter: formatter
});
});
```

Listing 4.62 Controller Implementation Including the Formatter as an Object Property to Enable Usage within the Content Definition of the Extension Column

Finally, to enable the extension implementation, we must define the column extension and the custom controller in the app descriptor (*manifest.json*) file, as shown in Figure 4.67.

```
"extends": {
    "extensions": {
        "sap.ui.viewExtensions": {
            "sap.suite.ui.generic.template.ListReport.view.ListReport": {
                "ResponsiveTableColumnsExtension|PurchaseDocument": {
                    "type": "XML",
                    "className": "sap.ui.core.Fragment",
                    "fragmentName": "fiori.manage.purchase.documents.purchasedocumentslrp.ext.fragments.ListReportResponsiveTableColumns"
                },
                "ResponsiveTableCellsExtension|PurchaseDocument": {
                    "className": "sap.ui.core.Fragment",
                    "fragmentName": "fiori.manage.purchase.documents.purchasedocumentslrp.ext.fragments.ListReportResponsiveTableCells",
                    "type": "XML"
                }
            }
        },
        "sap.ui.controllerExtensions": {
                "sap.suite.ui.generic.template.ListReport.view.ListReport": {
                    "controllerName": "fiori.manage.purchase.documents.purchasedocumentslrp.ext.controller.ListReportExtension"
                }
            }
    }
},
```

Figure 4.67 App Descriptor (manifest.json) Changes to Enable the Column and Controller Extension

Now, if you open the app by creating a new configuration by right-clicking on the project and selecting **RUN • Run Configurations,** you can then create a new configuration as **Run as SAP Fiori Launchpad Sandbox**. You should be able to preview the app, as shown in Figure 4.68.

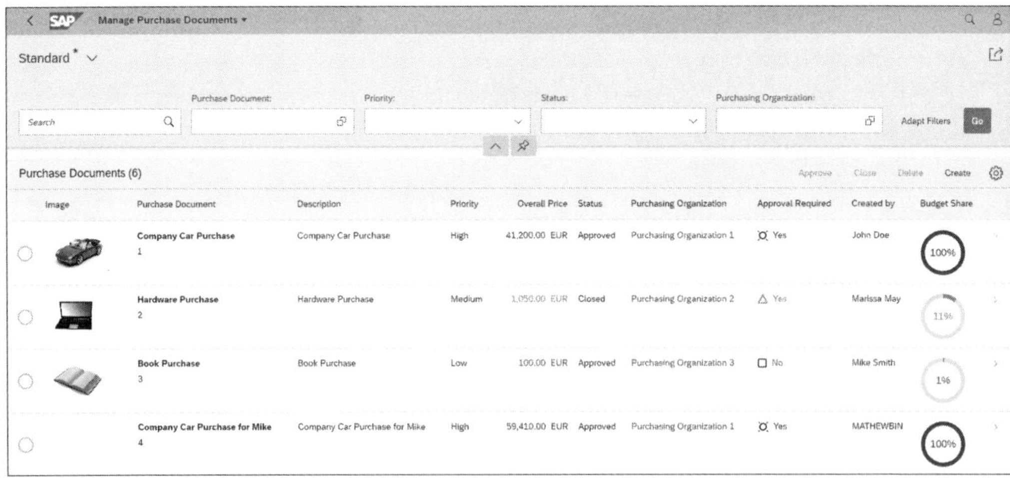

Figure 4.68 SAP Fiori Elements Application Created in SAP Web IDE

4.6.2 Adding a QUnit Unit Test

When implementing UI extensions and introducing logic implemented in JavaScript and SAPUI5, you should always cover this logic with a unit test. QUnit is the recommended unit testing framework for implementing unit tests for SAPUI5 applications because it's a powerful and easy-to-use unit testing framework included with the SAPUI5 SDK. To add unit tests for our formatter, we first will add a unit test folder below the already existing *test* folder which we'll name *unit*, as shown in Figure 4.69.

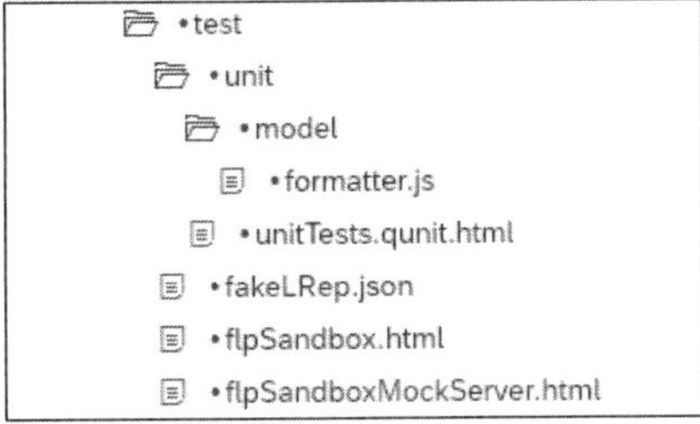

Figure 4.69 Folder Structure for Unit Tests

Additionally, we'll add a folder called *model* to reflect the folder structure of the actual implementation and the corresponding test file, which we'll also call *formatter.js*. The formatter unit test will create several test cases covering the corner cases of our logic implemented in `calculateCriticality` and `calculatePercentage`. You can see an excerpt of the unit test in Listing 4.63.

```
sap.ui.define(["fiori/manage/purchase/documents/purchasedocumentslrp/model/
formatter"],
    function (formatter) {
        "use strict";

QUnit.module("Calculate Criticality");

QUnit.test("If the overall price is less than or equal to 1000 the criticality
is formatted to Good", function (assert) {
    assert.strictEqual(formatter.calculateCriticality(1000),  "Good");
});
...
QUnit.module("Calculate Percentage");

QUnit.test("With an overall price of 10000 and a total budget of 10000 the
```

```
budget utilization should be 100%", function (assert) {
    assert.strictEqual(formatter.calculatePercentage(10000), 100);
});
...
```

Listing 4.63 Excerpt of the Formatter Unit Test

In the *unit* folder, we'll create an HTML file called *unitTests.qunit.html*, which will start the tests and display the test results.

The content of the *unitTests.qunit.html* file is shown in Listing 4.64. We'll set the `data-sap-ui-resourceroots` property in our example to link the namespaces to the relevant implementation and test root folders and include the `formatter` test case. The test result will be inserted dynamically at runtime in the body part of the HTML document. The tests can be run by choosing **Run • Runs As • Unit Test** from the context menu of the *unitTests.qunit.html* file. The output of a test run is shown in Figure 4.70.

```
<html>
   <head>
      <meta http-equiv="X-UA-Compatible" content="IE=edge">
      <script id="sap-ui-bootstrap"
         src="../../resources/sap-ui-core.js"
         data-sap-ui-theme="sap_belize"
         data-sap-ui-noConflict="true"
         data-sap-ui-resourceroots='{
   "fiori.manage.purchase.documents.purchasedocumentslrp"      :"../../",
         "test.unit": "./"
         }'></script>
      <script language="javascript">
         jQuery.sap.require("sap.ui.qunit.qunit-css");
         jQuery.sap.require("sap.ui.thirdparty.qunit");
         jQuery.sap.require("sap.ui.qunit.qunit-junit");
         jQuery.sap.require("sap.ui.qunit.qunit-coverage");
         sap.ui.require(["test/unit/model/formatter"]);
      </script>
   </head>
   <body>
      <div id="qunit"></div>
   </body>
</html>
```

Listing 4.64 QUnit Test File That Will Display the Results of the Test

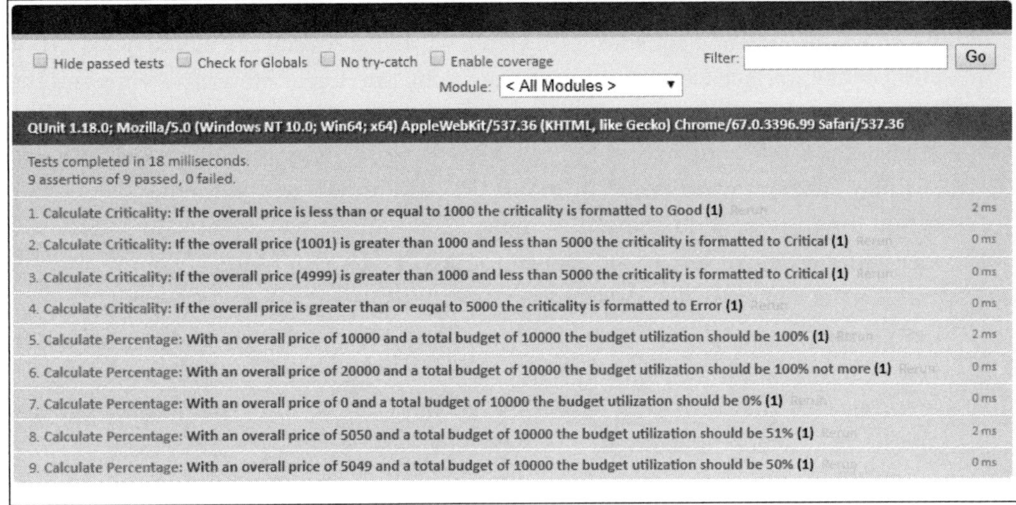

Figure 4.70 Output of the QUnit Unit Test Run

4.7 List Report Application versus Worklist Application

At first sight, the SAP Fiori elements list report and worklist templates look quite similar. Both templates have a table on their start page, and both offer navigation to an object page to inspect the table entries in detail. Therefore, we could easily reuse our OData service to create a worklist application instead. However, the main difference is that the list report template provides a powerful filter bar that allows searching, filtering, and acting on large data sets unlike the worklist template, which doesn't have a separate filter bar at all. Consequently, the worklist application will only display the items a certain user must process and therefore doesn't require sophisticated filtering of table entries because the work items should already be prefiltered based on the user's tasks.

4.8 Summary

In this chapter, we developed an SAP Fiori elements list report application from scratch. We started the development from the bottom up by creating the database tables for our main entities: the purchase document and the purchase document item. On top of the database tables, we put up a VDM according to the SAP S/4HANA development guidelines, starting with reusable basic interface views over to composite interface views and consumption views. We added several calculated fields to our composite interface views and tested the calculation logic using ABAP Unit and the CDS Test Double Framework. Additionally, we added transactional capabilities to our application by with the help of the new ABAP RESTful programming model (by using the new behavior definitions) from our CDS data model and implemented a quick action for approving purchase documents. Subsequently, we created an OData service with the help of service binding and added CDS UI annotations to our projection view's metadata extension files to configure the list report template according to our design. Finally, we generated the list report and object page applications using the SAP Web IDE. As a last step, we extended the standard list report template by implementing a calculated column extension. We used QUnit unit tests to safeguard the JavaScript calculation logic. In the next chapter, you'll learn how to work with another SAP Fiori elements application type called an overview page (OVP).

Chapter 5
Developing an Overview Page

In this chapter, you'll learn about building an overview page (OVP) application and about how different types of cards can be used in an overview page to represent data in different formats.

For this OVP application, we'll build a set of core data services (CDS) views on top of the purchase document and purchase document item tables we used in Chapter 4 to build a list report application. Because we went with using the automatic generation of OData services using CDS view annotations in the previous chapter, we'll create the OData service manually in this chapter. We'll also create individual consumption views in the backend and use those CDS views in the OVP template in the SAP Web IDE to generate multiple types of cards for the OVP.

5.1 Core Data Services Views

As in the previous chapter, we'll take a bottom-up approach to build several layers of CDS views with a basic interface layer on top of database tables. Because we've already created the database tables in the previous chapter, we won't start from the beginning.

Before we start building our views, let's decide what we need to display in our overview page (OVP). If you recall the guidelines mentioned in Chapter 2, an OVP is used to visually represent information from multiple applications, you should only use OVPs for certain scenarios. So, our plan is to design an OVP that will have multiple cards to provide the end user an overall view into the different aspects of the underlying data, which should help the user in decision-making. The app should show the underlying data in different formats, such as charts or tables, so that the user can easily analyze the information. The following cards that should fit those requirements:

- **Analytical card**
  Displays the overall number of documents based on priority and status in the form of a chart.

- **Table card**
  Gives a summary of pending documents at the item level.
- **List card (standard type)**
  Gives the approver an overview of the number of documents pending for approval.
- **List card (bar type)**
  Gives a summarized view of whether the purchasing documents are within the allowed budget or not.

5.1.1 Creating a Simple Core Data Services View

Now that we have an idea of what information is needed to be displayed on the app, let's discuss the CDS views that we'll need to build the app. An OVP requires separate CDS views for each card as well as a dedicated CDS view for the filter bar. As shown in Figure 5.1, we've followed a design approach that includes the number of consumption views required to generate the OVP and the cards.

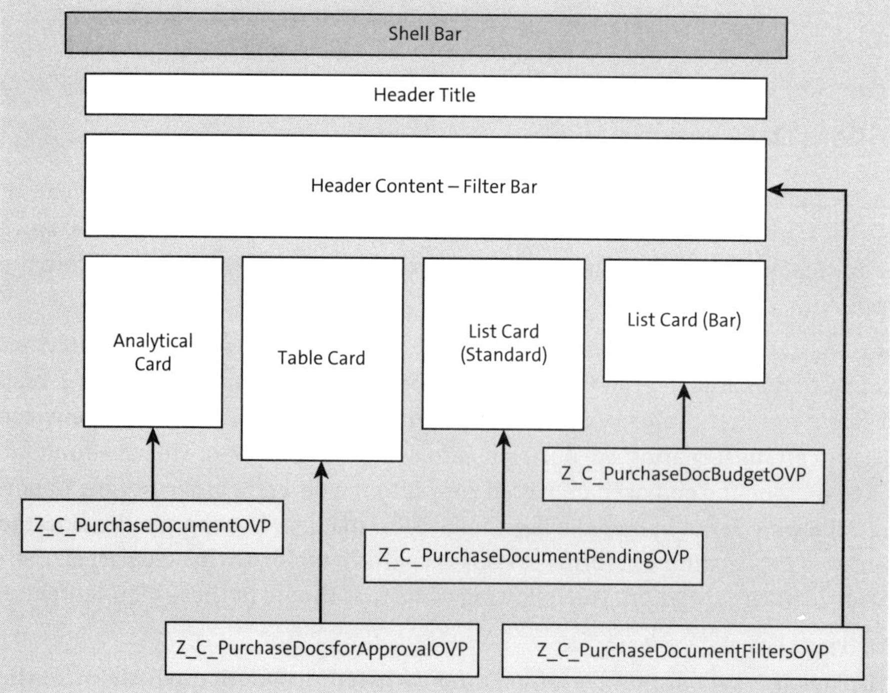

Figure 5.1 CDS Views Required for the OVP

We'll need a total of five main consumption views for the app. Each CDS view needs to fetch the required data for the corresponding cards:

- Z_C_PurchaseDocumentOVP for the analytical card
- Z_C_PurchaseDocsforApprovalOVP for the list card (standard)
- Z_C_PurchaseDocBudgetOVP for the list card (bar)
- Z_C_PurchaseDocumentPendingOVP for the table card
- Z_C_PurchaseDocumentFiltersOVP for the filter bar

In this section, we'll build all the necessary CDS views for fetching the required data for the different type of cards and the basic filter consumption view for the filter bar of the OVP. Then, in Section 5.2, we'll concentrate on building metadata extensions for these CDS views with the same name (like we did in Chapter 4) where we'll use UI annotations for generating the different types of cards.

Build a Consumption View for the Analytical Card

Now let's move on to the first consumption CDS view, Z_C_PurchaseDocumentOVP for the analytical card.

Listing 5.1 shows the consumption view code for the analytical card. For the analytical card, we're planning to show a donut chart. A donut chart will require some key data to act as dimensions and measure attributes. Our plan is to create an analytical card that can display the chart based on priority and status, so we'll need the Priority, PriorityText, Status, and StatusText fields to be present in our consumption view. In addition to these fields, we'll need one field to act as measure to count the number of rows based on the priority or status for the chart. So, we'll add a custom column called TotalNumberofDocuments with a default value of 1, and we'll also need to aggregate the sum of the column using @DefaultAggregation: #SUM annotation.

```
@AbapCatalog.sqlViewName: 'ZCPURCHDOCOVP'
@AccessControl.authorizationCheck: #NOT_REQUIRED
@EndUserText.label: 'Purchasing Document Overview Page'

@VDM.viewType: #CONSUMPTION
@Metadata.allowExtensions: true

define view Z_C_PurchaseDocumentOVP
  as select from Z_I_PurchaseDocument
  association [0..1] to Z_I_PurchaseDocumentPriority as _
```

```
Priority on $projection.Priority = _Priority.Priority
  association [0..1] to Z_I_PurchaseDocumentStatus   as _
Status   on $projection.Status = _Status.Status
{
  key PurchaseDocument,
  Priority,
 _Priority.PriorityText,
  Status,
 _Status.StatusText,
...
      @DefaultAggregation: #SUM
      cast( 1 as eam_num_orders_outstanding ) as TotalNumberofDocuments,
...
}
```

Listing 5.1 Z_C_PurchaseDocumentOVP Consumption View for the Analytical Card

Build a Basic Interface View for the List Card

For most of these consumption views, we already created the required basic interface views in the previous chapter, except for the `Z_C_PurchaseDocsforApprovalOVP` view, which needs a new interface view to fetch some fields that aren't within the other existing interface views. We can also slightly modify one of the existing interface views to adapt it for our purposes, but let's just make one interface view for this consumption view. Because the interface view is for the approval consumption view, we'll name it `Z_I_PurchaseDocAprovalStat`.

Let's start with building our interface view. To create a CDS view in the ABAP development tools in Eclipse/SAP HANA Studio, you can follow the same steps as described in Chapter 4, Listing 5.2 shows the composite interface view for purchase documents that require approval. The `@VDM.viewType:` is set as `#COMPOSITE` because the view is fetching it from an underlying basic interface view. The underlying composite view `Z_I_PurcDocOverallPrice` will provide the necessary information required for our consumption view and the `Approval` field that is calculated based on the `case` statement to determine whether the document exceeds the threshold of `1000` euros and sets the value as `Approval Required` or `No Approval Required`. This view also provides other key information such as the creation date of the document, priority of the document, status, and so on. Press [Ctrl]+[F3] to activate the view.

```
@AbapCatalog.sqlViewName: 'ZIPRCHDOCAPRSTAT'
@AccessControl.authorizationCheck: #NOT_REQUIRED
@EndUserText.label: 'Purchasing Docs with Approval Status'

@VDM.viewType: #COMPOSITE
define view Z_I_PurchaseDocAprovalStat
  as select from Z_I_PurchDocOverallPrice
{
  key PurchaseDocument,
...
      Priority,
      OverallPrice,
...
      case
      when OverallPrice > 1000
      then 'Approval Required'
      else 'No Approval Required' end as Approval,
      _Priority,
      _Status

}
```

Listing 5.2 Composite Interface View Z_I_PurchaseDocAprovalStat to Fetch from the Underlying Composite View

Build a Consumption View for the List Card (Standard)

Now that our composite view is ready, let's build the consumption view Z_C_PurchaseDocAprovalStat. As shown in Listing 5.3, the @VDM.viewType is set to #CONSUMPTION because the view is fetching data from a COMPOSITE interface view. For our example, we must set a where condition to fetch only the records with the Status value 1 (Created) and the purchasing documents with an OverallPrice more than 1000 euros. In addition, we'll need to add the @Metadata.allowExtensions:true annotation to enable metadata extensions for the consumption view.

```
@AbapCatalog.sqlViewName: 'ZCPURHPNDNGAPRVL'
@AccessControl.authorizationCheck: #NOT_REQUIRED
@EndUserText.label: 'Purchase orders Pending for Approval'
@Metadata.allowExtensions:true
@VDM.viewType: #CONSUMPTION
```

```
define view Z_C_PurchaseDocsforApprovalOVP
  as select from Z_I_PurchaseDocAprovalStat
{
      @ObjectModel.foreignKey.association: '_PurchaseDocument'
      @Consumption.semanticObject: 'PurchasingDocument'
  key PurchaseDocument,
      Description,
      OverallPrice,
      Priority,
      crea_uname,
…
}
where
      Status        = '1'
  and OverallPrice > 1000
```

Listing 5.3 Z_C_ PurchaseDocsforApprovalOVP Consumption View for Pending Approvals List Card in the OVP

Now, press F8 on the keyboard to view the output of the consumption view. Figure 5.2 shows the output of the view; notice how the **Approval** field value only shows results with **Approval Required**.

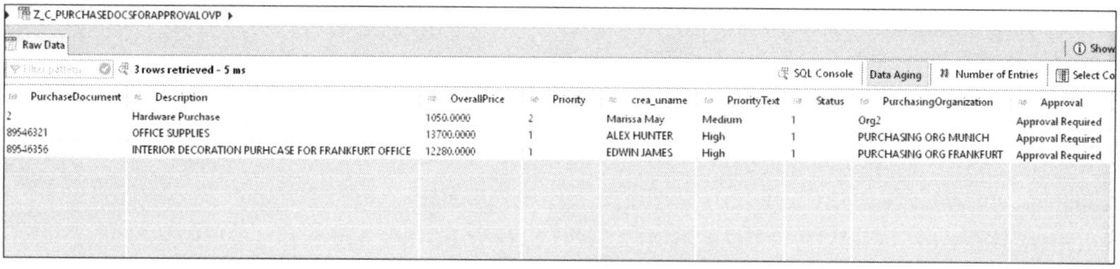
Z_C_PURCHASEDOCSFORAPPROVALOVP
Raw Data
3 rows retrieved - 5 ms
SQL Console | Data Aging | Number of Entries | Select Co

PurchaseDocument	Description	OverallPrice	Priority	crea_uname	PriorityText	Status	PurchasingOrganization	Approval
2	Hardware Purchase	1050.0000	2	Marissa May	Medium	1	Org2	Approval Required
89546321	OFFICE SUPPLIES	13700.0000	1	ALEX HUNTER	High	1	PURCHASING ORG MUNICH	Approval Required
89546356	INTERIOR DECORATION PURHCASE FOR FRANKFURT OFFICE	12280.0000	1	EDWIN JAMES	High	1	PURCHASING ORG FRANKFURT	Approval Required

Figure 5.2 Pending Approval Consumption View Output

Build a Consumption View for the List Card (Bar)

Next, let's create the consumption view `Z_C_PurchaseDocBudgetOVP` for the bar list card, as shown in Listing 5.4. This view provides information regarding the percentage of the total budget used by each purchasing document. In this view, we're doing two main things. The first is the calculation of the budget used under the `BudgetUtilization` field and the declaration of % as a unit of measure via the `@Semantics.quantity.unitofMeasure:true` for the field `Percentage`. The `Percentage` field is bound to the

BudgetUtilization as its unit of measure via @Semantics.quantity.unitOfMeasure: annotation. Second, the budget utilization is calculated by dividing the overall price of the purchasing document with the budget limit set to 10000 euros.

```
@AbapCatalog.sqlViewName: 'ZPUCHDOCBUDGT'
@AccessControl.authorizationCheck: #NOT_REQUIRED
@EndUserText.label: 'OVP card for Overall Budget'
@VDM.viewType: #CONSUMPTION
@Metadata.allowExtensions:true

define view Z_C_PurchaseDocBudgetOVP
  as select from Z_I_PurchaseDocumentTP
{
  key PurchaseDocument,
…
      @Semantics.quantity.unitOfMeasure: 'Percentage'
      division(OverallPrice * 100, 10000, 2) as BudgetUtilization,
…
      @Semantics.unitOfMeasure: true
      cast(' % ' as abap.unit(3))            as Percentage
}
```

Listing 5.4 Z_C_PurchaseDocBudgetOVP Consumption View for the Bar List Card

Build a Consumption View for the Table Card

Finally, we'll need to create the consumption view Z_C_PurchaseDocumentPendingOVP for the table card, as shown in Listing 5.5. This view shows purchasing documents at the item level with a status of Created. So, let's keep a where condition at the end of the select with Status as 1. Because the table card can be resized in the UI, we can choose to display several fields from the items table. You can specify which fields to display via UI annotations in the metadata extension of this view.

```
@AbapCatalog.sqlViewName: 'ZCPURCHDOCITMOVP'
@AccessControl.authorizationCheck: #CHECK
@EndUserText.label: 'Pending Purchase Documents item list'
@VDM.viewType: #CONSUMPTION
@Metadata.allowExtensions: true

define view Z_C_PurchaseDocumentPendingOVP
  as select from Z_I_PurchaseDocumentItem
```

```
{
  key PurchaseDocument,
  key PurchaseDocumentItem,
  _PurchaseDocument.Description as PurchaseDocumentDescription,
      Description,
      OverallItemPrice,
...
      _PurchaseDocument.Priority,
      _PurchaseDocument.Status,
...

}
where
  _PurchaseDocument.Status = '1'
```

Listing 5.5 Z_C_PurchaseDocumentPendingOVP Consumption View for the Table Card

Build a Consumption View for the Filter Bar

We've now built all the necessary CDS views for all five cards. At this point, we still need to build a CDS view for the filter bar with filters common across all the CDS views. This step is important because when you set/choose a filter from the filter bar, the corresponding OData call to the backend system from the OVP will automatically add those filters to all the OData services bound to the cards. If one of the card's CDS views behind the OData service call is missing this filter, then that card won't load results. Therefore, you'll need to choose the filters accordingly. Because the basic idea of the cards for this OVP-based application is based on the priority of the purchasing documents and for the documents with an open status (neither approved nor closed), you can use the **Priority** and **Status** fields as the common filter for all the cards.

Let's create the consumption view for the filter bar CDS view. Listing 5.6 shows the code for the `Z_C_PurchaseDocumentFiltersOVP` consumption view. The fields for the filters should not be linked from the CDS views from the cards directly; instead, you can `cast` an empty value with reference to its corresponding ABAP type. In addition, to make the filters visible by default and in the correct required order, we'll need to use the UI annotation `@UI.SelectionField`. The property `exclude:false` will make the field visible by default, and the property `Position` sets the order in which the filters should be displayed.

```
@AbapCatalog.sqlViewName: 'ZCPRCHDOCFILTERS'
@AccessControl.authorizationCheck: #NOT_REQUIRED
@EndUserText.label: 'Filters for Purchasing Document OVP'

@VDM.viewType: #CONSUMPTION
define view Z_C_PURCHASEDOCUMENTFILTERSOVP
  as select from Z_I_PurchaseDocument
{
...
      @UI: {
          selectionField: { exclude: false, position: 10 }
        }
      @Consumption: {
        valueHelpDefinition: [{ entity: { name: 'Z_C_
PriorityVH', element: 'Priority'  }}]
        }
      cast('' as abap.char(1)) as Priority,
      @UI: {
         selectionField: { exclude: false, position: 20 }
       }
      @Consumption: {
        valueHelpDefinition: [{ entity: { name: 'Z_C_
StatusVH', element: 'Status'  }}]
        }
      cast('' as abap.char(1)) as Status

}
```

Listing 5.6 Z_C_PurchaseDocumentFiltersOVP Consumption View for the Filter Bar

As shown in Listing 5.6, the `Priority` and `Status` fields have one additional annotation named `@Consumption.valueHelpDefinition`. This annotation sets the value help for the fields that will act as [F4] helps in the UI of the app. However, we could have used the normal interface views, `Z_I_PurchaseDocumentPriority` and `Z_I_PurchaseDocumentStatus`, via the foreign key association `@ObjectModel.foreignKey.association` annotation. You can also create and add custom value helps using a CDS view with the UI annotation `@ObjectModel.dataCategory: #VALUE_HELP`. This annotation will help the OData project identify such views as value helps (discussed later in Section 5.3 when we create the OData service using the CDS views, where the value helps will be automatically recognized by the framework). With this new approach, more enhanced modeling options are available compared to an annotation-based on a foreign key, so we've created two new CDS views as value helps for `Priority` and `Status`. The naming format of a value help should end with `VH` to identify those CDS views as value helps. For our purposes, we named them `Z_C_PriorityVH` and `Z_C_StatusVH`.

Listing 5.7 shows the coding for the value help CDS view `Z_C_PriorityVH`. The annotation `@ObjectModel.dataCategory: #VALUE_HELP` helps the framework identify the CDS view as a value help view. In addition, we wanted the filters to be a dropdown list instead of a regular value help because the values for `Priority` are `High`, `Medium`, and `Low`, so using these as fixed values in F4 help doesn't make sense. Normally, a value help will be a blank input field with an icon on the right side where you click on it to bring the available values for that field. For our example, we must use the annotation `@ObjectModel.resultSet.sizeCategory:#XS` to make them appear in a dropdown list. The value help for `Status` is also set up in the same way.

```
@AbapCatalog.sqlViewName: 'ZPRIOVH'
@AccessControl.authorizationCheck: #NOT_REQUIRED
@EndUserText.label: 'Value Help for Priority'
@Search.searchable: true
@ObjectModel.semanticKey:  [ 'priority' ]
@ObjectModel.representativeKey: ['priority']
@VDM.viewType: #CONSUMPTION

@ObjectModel.resultSet.sizeCategory: #XS
@ObjectModel.dataCategory: #VALUE_HELP

define view Z_C_PriorityVH as select from Z_I_PurchaseDocumentPriority {
@ObjectModel.text.element: ['PriorityText']
key Priority,
@Search: { defaultSearchElement: true, ranking: #
HIGH, fuzzinessThreshold: 0.7 }
    PriorityText
}
```

Listing 5.7 Value Help CDS View for Priority

Note

For more information about value helps, visit *http://s-prs.co/498819*.

5.1.2 Adding a Data Control File

Like the previous chapter, we've created a data control language (DCL) file for our CDS view to restrict access to the CDS view via ABAP authorization objects.

For our app, we'll reuse the authorization object for the purchase organization. By using the purchase organization for DCL, we can restrict the results displayed to end users by their purchasing organization.

Listing 5.8 shows the DCL for the CDS view `Z_C_Purchasedocumentpendingovp`. After you've created the access control file, you'll need to update the corresponding CDS view's annotation as shown in `@AccessControl.authorizationCheck:#CHECK`. Similarly, you can restrict unauthorized access to the other CDS views.

```
@EndUserText.label: 'ACL Pending Purchase Documents Item List'
@MappingRole: true
define role Z_C_Purchasedocumentpendingovp {
    grant
        select
            on
                Z_C_PurchaseDocumentPendingOVP
        where
       ( PurchasingOrganization ) =
        aspect pfcg_auth(
            ZPURCHORGA,
            ZPURCHORGA ,
            ACTVT = '03' ) ;
}
```

Listing 5.8 Access Control File for the View Z_C_Purchasedocumentpendingovp

5.2 Adding User Interface Annotations

None of the CDS views we've created so far (except for the filter bar CDS view) contain any of the UI-specific annotations that are required to generate the cards in the OVP. The CDS view guidelines recommend putting all UI-related annotations in a separate metadata extension file with the same name of its corresponding consumption CDS view to separate the UI from functional aspects.

5.2.1 Creating Annotations for an Analytical Card

Now, let's create a metadata extension for the consumption view of our analytical card. Right-click on the **Metadata Extension** folder in the **Project Explorer** tab of your project and then click **New Metadata Extension,** as shown in Figure 5.3. Use the same name as your consumption view (in our case `Z_C_PurchaseDocumentOVP`) and enter a description to create the metadata extension view.

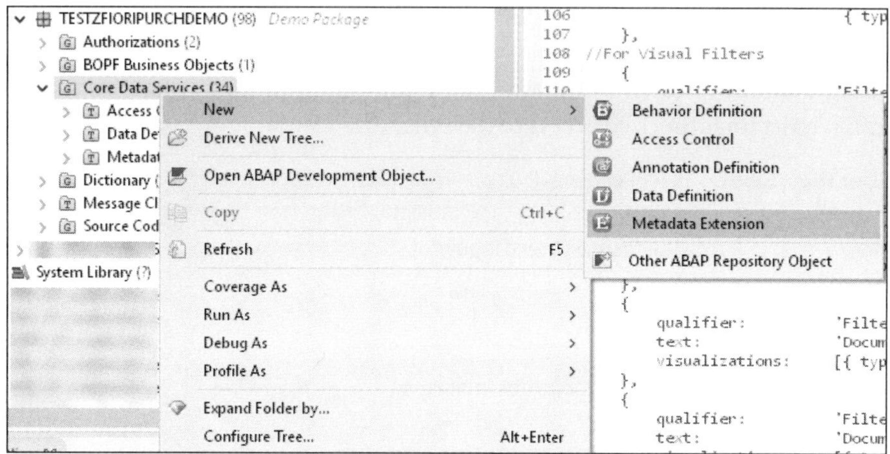

Figure 5.3 Creating a Metadata Extension for the Z_C_PurchaseDocumentOVP Consumption View

Listing 5.9 shows the code for the metadata extension for `Z_C_ PurchaseDocumentOVP`. Because this metadata extension is for an analytical card, and our plan is to display a chart, we'll need to use the `@UI.chart` annotation. We'll also need a `qualifier` to make each chart unique. (You'll see how this qualifier comes into use when we create the OVP via the SAP Web IDE template later in Section 5.4.) Because the charts need to display the values `By Priority` and `By Status`, let's name the first qualifier `ByPurchaseDocumentPriority` and the second qualifier `ByPurchaseDocumentStatus`. We must set the `chartType` as `#DONUT`. The dimensions to be shown are the `Priority` and the `PriorityText`. The `measures` attribute will be our custom field `TotalNumberofDocuments`, created in the `Z_C_PurchaseDocumentOVP` consumption view, and the `measures` attribute will be used by the chart to determine the total number of purchasing documents that belongs to each `Priority` and `Status` category. In addition, we'll have to assign the UI annotation `@UI.dataPoint.visualization: #NUMBER` to the `TotalNumberofDocuments` fields to indicate that this field is a number. Like the first chart, we'll use the same annotations, but this time, the dimensions are `Status` and `StatusText`. We've also assigned a UI annotation `@UI.identification:` with type `#FOR_INTENT_BASED_NAVIGATION` and `semanticObjectAction:` for the `PurchaseDocument` field to enable navigation to the list report application from the chart. We'll look at cross-app navigation in detail in Chapter 8.

```
@Metadata.layer: #CORE

@UI.chart: [
  {
    qualifier:  'ByPurchaseDocumentPriority',
    title: 'Purchasing documents by Priority',
    chartType:  #DONUT,
    dimensions: [  'Priority', 'PriorityText' ] ,
    measures:   [ 'TotalNumberofDocuments'    ],
    dimensionAttributes: [
      {dimension: 'Priority', role: #CATEGORY},
      {dimension: 'PriorityText', role: #CATEGORY}

    ],
    measureAttributes: [
      {measure: 'TotalNumberofDocuments', role: #AXIS_1, asDataPoint: true}
    ]
  },
  {
    qualifier:  'ByPurchaseDocumentStatus',
    title: 'Purchasing documents by Status',
    chartType:  #DONUT,
    dimensions: [  'Status', 'StatusText' ] ,
    measures:   [ 'TotalNumberofDocuments'    ],
…

annotate view Z_C_PurchaseDocumentOVP
    with
{
  @UI.identification: [{
    type: #FOR_INTENT_BASED_NAVIGATION,
    semanticObjectAction: 'PurchasingDocument',
    label: 'Display Purchasing Document Information'
  }]
```

```
  PurchaseDocument;
    @UI.dataPoint.visualization: #NUMBER
    TotalNumberofDocuments;
    @UI.textArrangement: #TEXT_FIRST
    Priority;
    @UI.textArrangement: #TEXT_FIRST
    Status;
}
```

Listing 5.9 Metadata Extension for Consumption View Z_C_PurchaseDocumentOVP

5.2.2 Creating Annotations for a List Card

As mentioned earlier in Section 5.1, two types of list cards exist: a standard list card and a bar list card. We'll create the annotation for a standard list card to display the list of purchasing documents pending for approval and an annotation for a bar list card to display the percentage of budget used by each purchasing document. In addition, we'll create a table card. A table card is slightly different from a list card in that it shows the column header name and can show more columns than a list card.

Create Annotations for a Standard List Card

Listing 5.10 is the metadata extension for the consumption view. Notice that we're using the annotation `@UI.lineItem` with properties such as `position`, `importance`, and `label`. These annotations are specific to line items and, because we're building this CDS view for a list card, will help us control the properties of the list in the card. Using this annotation, we can specify at which order a field should appear in the list via the `position` property starting with `10` as the first position of the table columns. The `label` property will set the text for the column in the table. The `importance` property will set the field values to appear as bold.

```
@Metadata.layer: #CORE
annotate view Z_C_PurchaseDocsforApprovalOVP with
{
  @UI.lineItem: [{
      position: 10,
      importance: #HIGH,
      label: 'Document',
      type: #FOR_INTENT_BASED_NAVIGATION,
      semanticObjectAction: 'manage'
```

```
    }]
  PurchaseDocument;

  @UI.lineItem: [{
    position: 20,
    importance: #HIGH,
    label: 'Description'
  }]
  Description;
...

  @UI.lineItem: [{
     position: 60,
     importance: #HIGH,
     label: 'Quantity'
      }]
  Approval;

}
```

Listing 5.10 Metadata Extension for Consumption View Z_C_PurchaseDocsforApprovalOVP

Create Annotations for a Bar List Card

Listing 5.11 shows the metadata extension for the bar list card CDS view. In this view, our plan is to generate a bar list with a criticality calculation annotation that will visually represent whether a purchasing document is within the allowed budget or not. To achieve this functionality, we'll need to use the `@UI.datapoint.criticalityCalculation` annotation. The annotations that belong to the `UI.dataPoint` are used for the visualization of a single point of data that is usually a number although sometimes even text. In this CDS view, we're declaring the `BudgetUtilization` field, which is a calculated field, as `datapoint`. The `datapoint` has some other features as listed here:

- **`valueFormat.numberOfFractionalDigits`**
  This annotation sets the number of fractional digits to be displayed.
- **`minimumValue`**
  This annotation acts as an indicator for the minimum threshold value.
- **`maximumValue`**
  This annotation acts as an indicator for the maximum threshold value.

- **criticalityCalculation**
  This annotation, which is a part of the @UI annotation, acts as an alternative to the usual way of setting criticality for a field. This annotation has the following further properties:
  - deviationRangeHighValue: Specifies the maximum deviation a field can have before it reaches a negative value. If the value crosses the deviationRangeHighValue threshold, the field turns yellow as a warning.
  - toleranceRangeHighValue: Specifies the maximum tolerance range for a field. If the value crosses the tolreanceRangeHighValue, the field turns red to indicate that you've exceeded the allowed limit.
  - improvementDirection: The improvement direction is critical to how the visualization will react to the field value. For example, if improvementDirection is set to #MINIMIZE, and if the value of the respective field goes under toleranceRangeHighValue, then the field is displayed in green (to indicate a positive value). The values between toleranceRangeHighValue and deviationRangeHighValue will be displayed in yellow (indicating a critical value), and values above deviationRangeHighValue are displayed in red (indicating a negative value). The other values of improvementDirection are #MAXIMIZE (which is the opposite of #MINIMUM) and #TARGET. For our scenario, #MINIMIZE is the better fit because the visualization is supposed to be green whenever the overall price for a purchasing document is below 40% of the budget, should start moving to yellow when the utilization is between 80% and 100%, and should be red when the utilization is above 100%.

```
@Metadata.layer: #CORE
annotate view Z_C_PurchaseDocBudgetOVP with
{
...
  @UI: {
  lineItem: [{
  type: #AS_DATAPOINT,
  importance: #HIGH,
  position: 10
  }],
  dataPoint: {
  title: 'Overall Price',
  valueFormat.numberOfFractionalDigits: 2,
  minimumValue: 0,
```

```
  maximumValue: 100,
  criticalityCalculation: {
      improvementDirection: #MINIMIZE,
      toleranceRangeHighValue: 80,
      deviationRangeHighValue: 100      }
  }
  }
  BudgetUtilization;
}
```

Listing 5.11 Metadata Extension for Consumption View Z_C_PurchaseDocBudgetOVP

Create Annotations for a Table Card

Listing 5.12 is for the metadata extension for the table card CDS view. The UI annotations for a list card and a table card are the same. The only difference is that the list card won't show column names, only values with a maximum number of six columns, whereas a table card will show column names. So, like the list card metadata extension we created earlier, in this extension, we'll also specify the order of the columns via the `@UI.lineItem` UI annotation.

```
@Metadata.layer: #CORE
annotate view Z_C_PurchaseDocumentPendingOVP with
{
  @UI.lineItem: [{
    position: 10,
    importance: #HIGH,
    label: 'Document'
  }]
  PurchaseDocumentDescription;
…
  @UI.lineItem: [{
    position: 80,
    importance: #HIGH,
    label: 'Currency'
  }]
  Currency;
}
```

Listing 5.12 Metadata Extension View for Z_C_PurchaseDocumentPendingOVP

5.3 Creating an OData Service Using the ABAP RESTful Programming Model

Now that we've created all the required CDS views, let's create our OData service using the service definition. In the first edition of this book, we created an OData service using a Transaction SEGW project, but this time, we'll be using the ABAP RESTful programming model's service definition and service binding feature to register our OData service (as we did in Chapter 4).

5.3.1 Creating a New Service Definition

To create a new service definition, right-click on the package name in the project folder then select **New • Other ABAP Repository Object**. Then, expand the **Business Services** folder and select **Service Definition,** as shown in Figure 5.4.

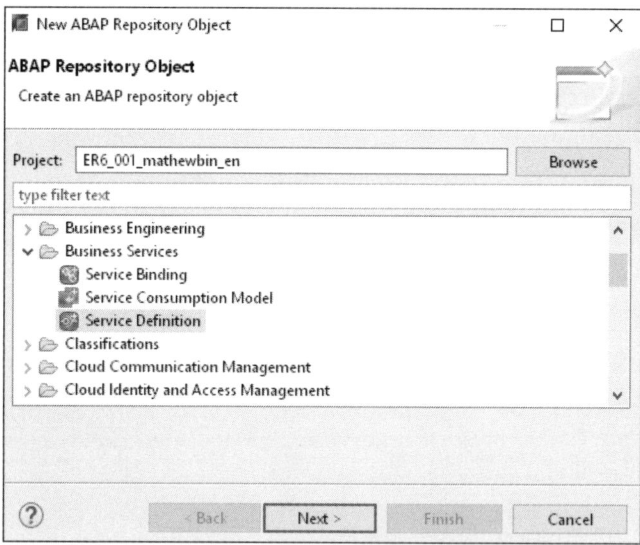

Figure 5.4 Creating a New Service Definition

In the next screen of the wizard, provide the service definition's details, as shown in Figure 5.5.

In the service definition file that was just created, we need expose all the relevant CDS views for our OVP, including all the CDS views for the different types of cards, the CDS view for the filters, and all the other relevant CDS views for value helps, which we created earlier in Section 5.1.1 as shown in Figure 5.6.

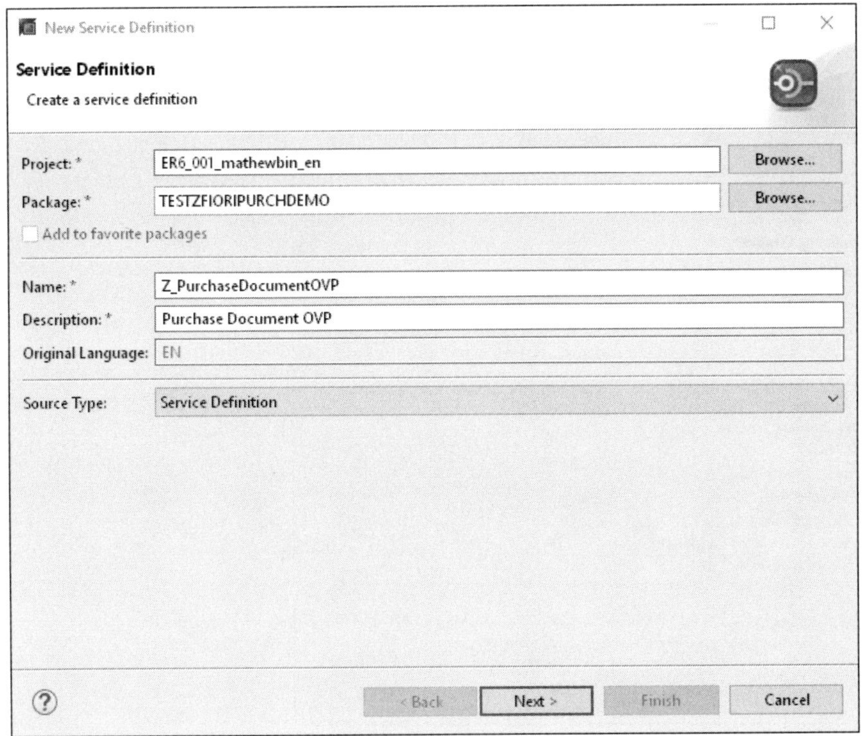

Figure 5.5 Service Definition Details

[ER6] Z_PURCHASEDOCUMENTOVP

```
@EndUserText.label: 'Purchase Document OVP'
define service Z_PurchaseDocumentOVP {
  expose Z_C_PurchaseDocumentOVP;
  expose Z_C_PURCHASEDOCUMENTFILTERSOVP;
  expose Z_C_PurchaseDocBudgetOVP;
  expose Z_C_PurchaseDocsforApprovalOVP;
  expose Z_C_PurchaseDocumentPendingOVP;
  expose Z_C_PriorityVH;
  expose Z_C_StatusVH;
}
```

Figure 5.6 Exposing Card CDS Views and Other Related Views for Creating the Final OData Service

5.3.2 Creating a New Service Binding

To create a new service binding, right-click on the package name in the project folder then select **New • Other ABAP Repository Object.** Then, expand the **Business Services** folder and select **Service Binding**, as shown in Figure 5.7.

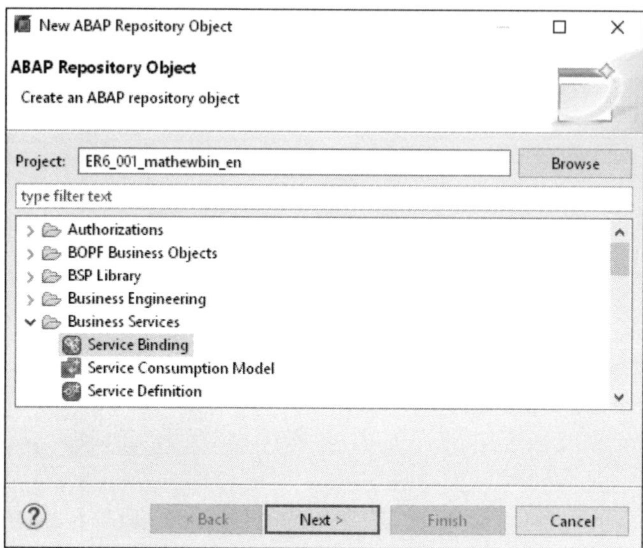

Figure 5.7 Creating a New Service Binding

In the next screen of the wizard, provide details for the service binding, as shown in Figure 5.8. You should follow the same naming conventions for the service binding as described in Chapter 4. Enter the service definition name (Z_PURCHASEDOCUMENTOVP), which we created earlier in Section 5.1.1, in the field **Service Definition**. The **Binding Type** should be **ODATA V2 (UI – User Interface: Consumed in SAPUI5 Apps)** since we're building a UI using this app.

Once you finish the wizard, activate the binding.Refer to Chapter 4 to see in detail on how to activate the service binding. You should then see the **Service URL** (click on the link to see the OData service preview in the browser) and the exposed **Entity Sets and Associations**, as shown in Figure 5.9.

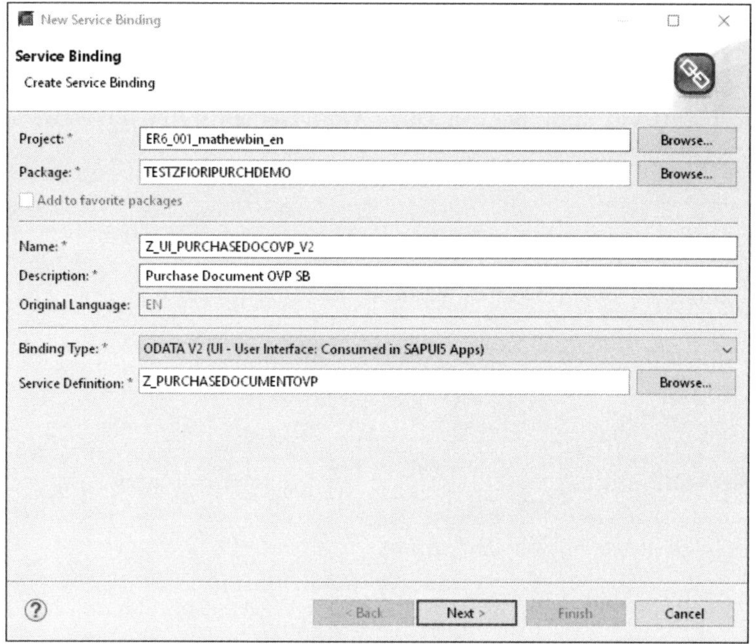

Figure 5.8 Service Binding Details

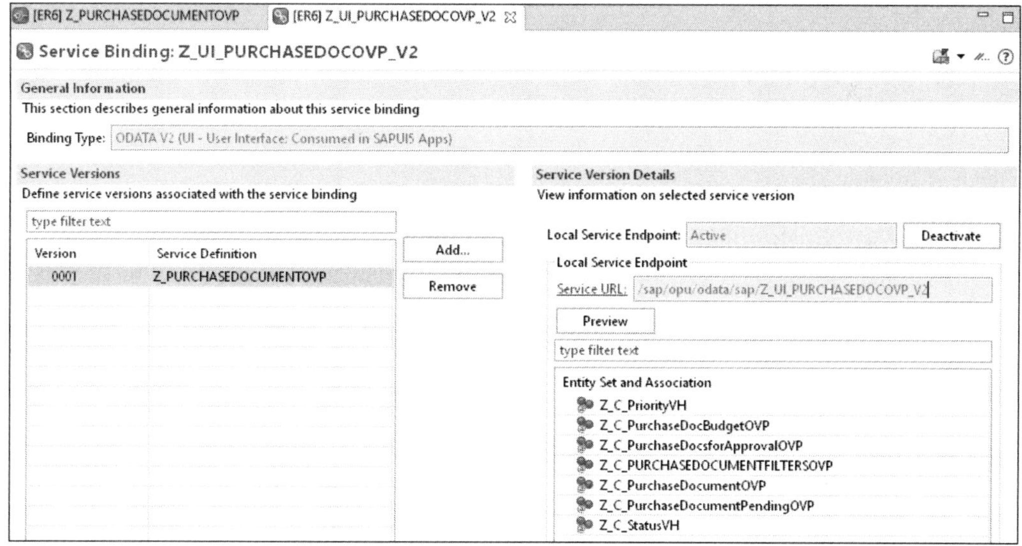

Figure 5.9 Activated Service Binding

Now, we can preview this app in an SAP Fiori elements template just to make sure the service is working and check whether the data is coming properly from the OData service. To preview the app, right-click on one of our card CDS view entities (for example, **Z_C_PurchaseDocumentOVP**) and click on **Open Fiori Elements App Preview**, as shown in Figure 5.10.

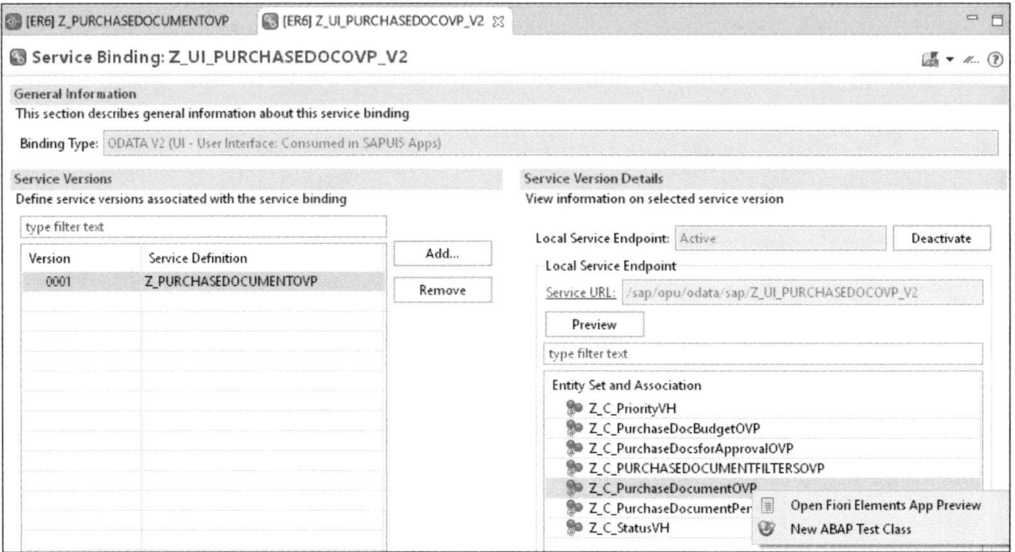

Figure 5.10 App Preview from Service Binding

As shown in Figure 5.11, the OData service is returning data for our analytical card CDS view. However, this preview uses an SAP Fiori elements-based list report template. The template we need is of the type OVP.

Notice how the filter bar field isn't exactly how we specified; this discrepancy is because we haven't used our filter CDS view yet. This information will be displayed when we create the overview page.

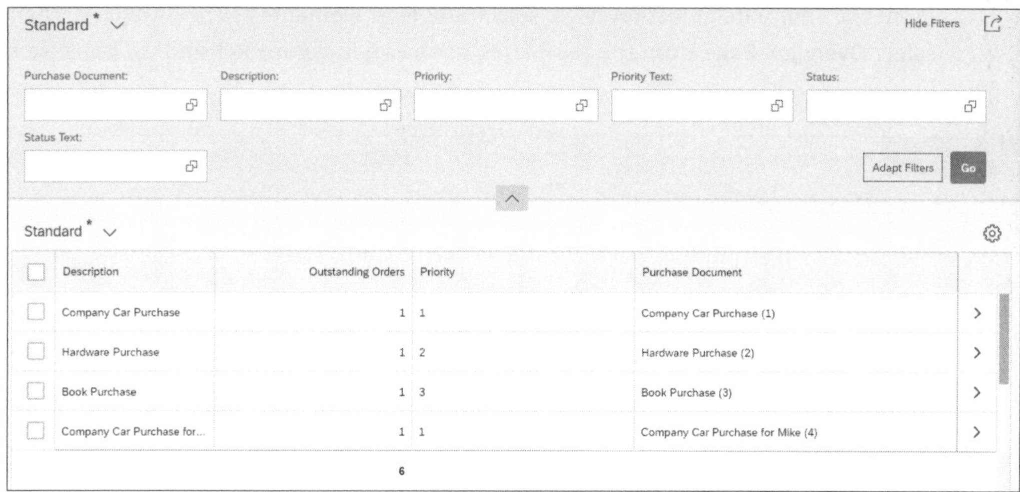

Figure 5.11 SAP Fiori Elements App Preview via Service Binding Preview Feature

5.4 Generating an Overview Page Template Project in SAP Web IDE

Now that our CDS view is exposed via the OData service, we can start developing our frontend application using the SAP Web IDE.

5.4.1 Generating the Basic Overview Page Layout

The SAP Web IDE offers multiple application templates to choose from. To create an OVP, open the SAP Web IDE and select **File • Project from Template**, as shown in Figure 5.12.

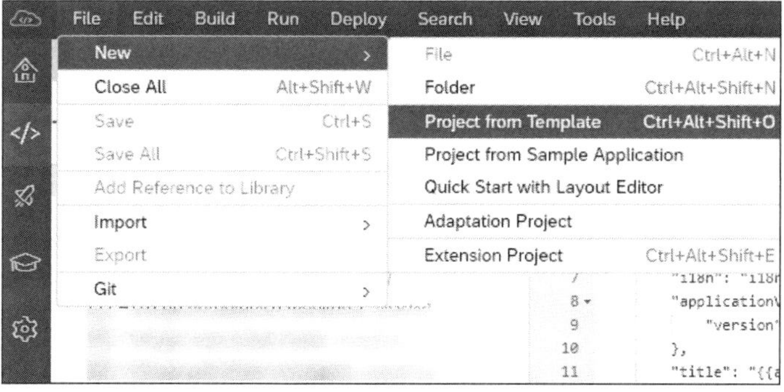

Figure 5.12 Creating a New Project from Template in SAP Web IDE

From the **Template Selection** page, select **SAP Fiori Elements** as the **Category**. Then, select **Overview Page** from the templates, as shown in Figure 5.13, and click the **Next** button.

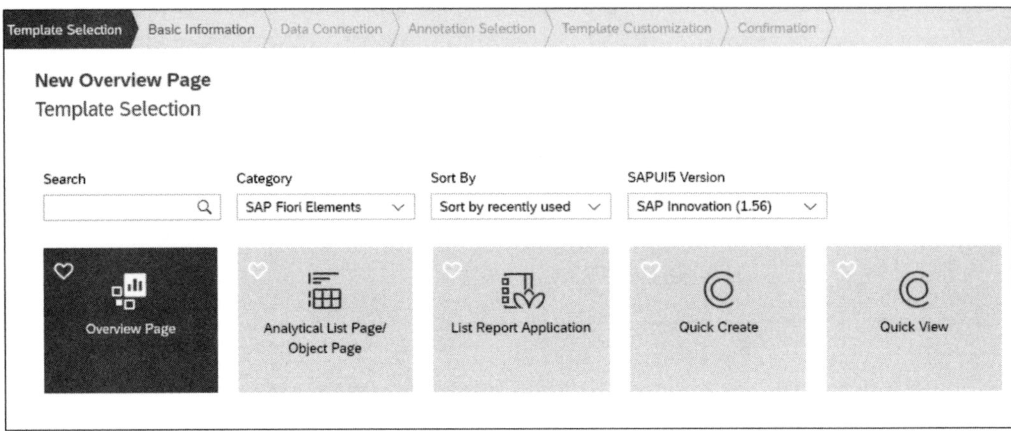

Figure 5.13 Selecting the Overview Page Template

Under the **Basic Information** tab, shown in Figure 5.14, enter the details as listed in Table 5.1, and click the **Next** button.

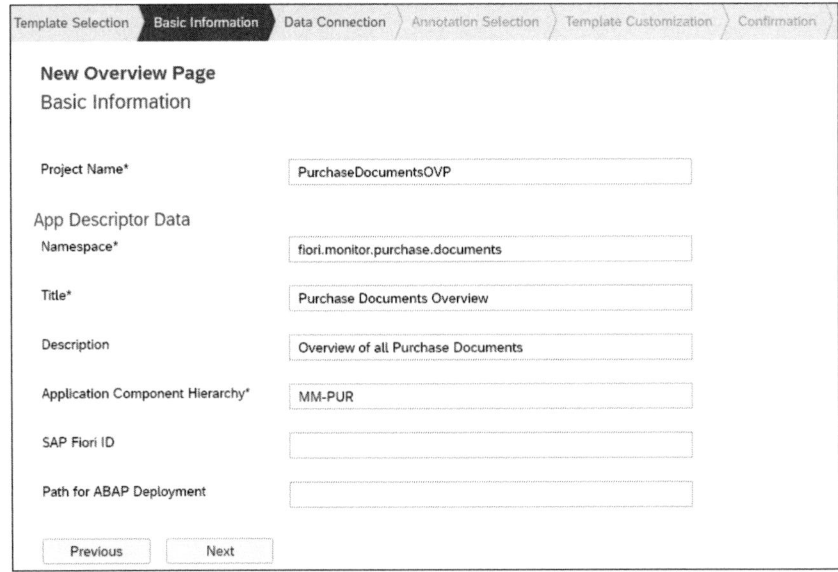

Figure 5.14 Basic Information Tab for the Overview Page Template

Field	Parameter
Project Name	"PurchaseDocumentsOVP"
Namespace	"fiori.monitor.purchase.documents"
Title	"Purchasing Documents Overview"
Description	"Overview of all purchase Documents"
Application Component Hierarchy	"MM-PUR"

Table 5.1 Values for Basic Information Overview Template Creation

Under the **Data Connection** tab, in the **Service Catalog** section, as shown in Figure 5.15, select the system in which you created the OData service using the ABAP RESTful programming model. After selecting the system, enter the OData service name (in our case Z_UI_PURCHASEDOCOVP_V2) and click the **Next** button.

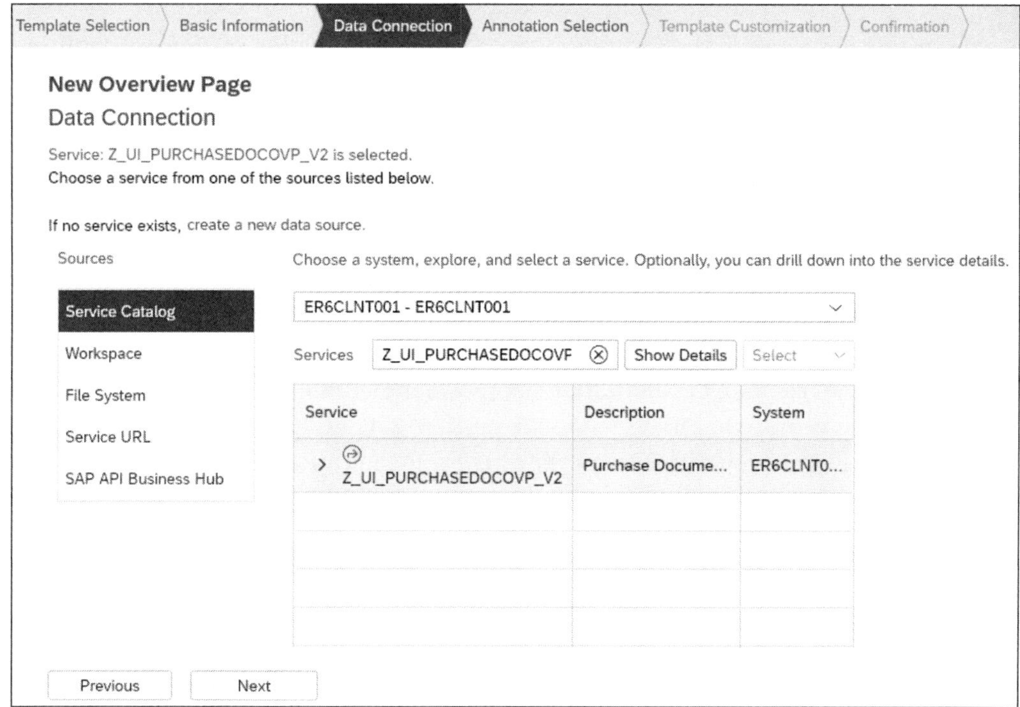

Figure 5.15 Selecting the OData Service from the SAP Gateway System

In the **Annotation Selection** section, the wizard will list the annotation model and the service metadata that the framework detected from the OData service. Select both services, as shown in Figure 5.16, and click the **Next** button.

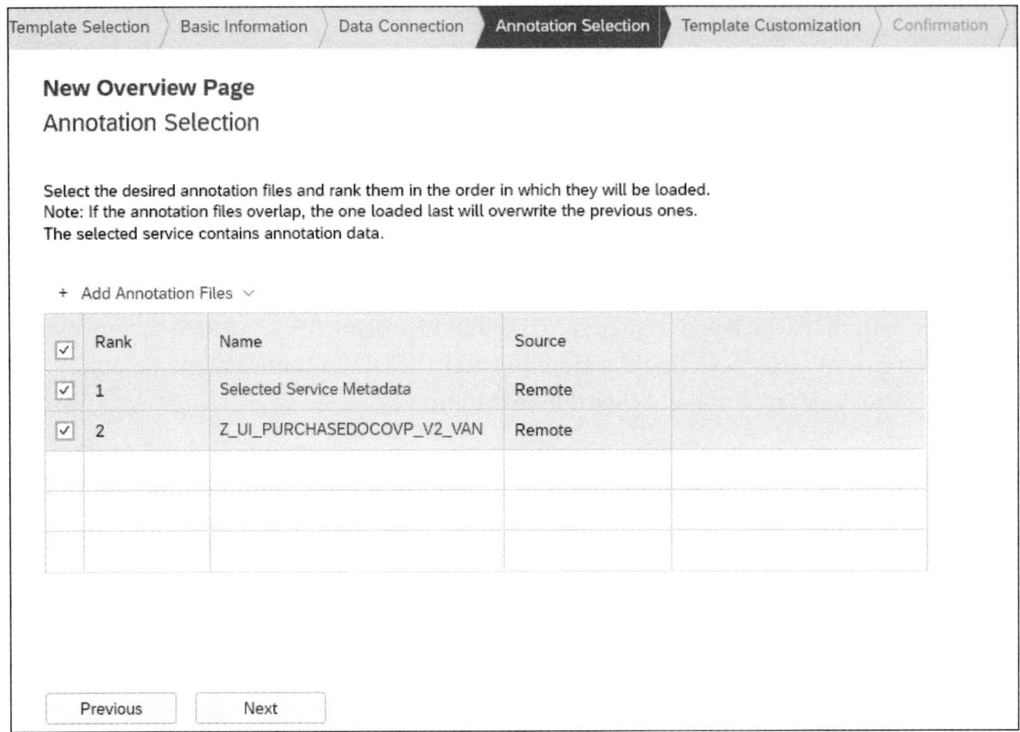

Figure 5.16 Annotation Model and Service Metadata File List from the OData Service

Under the **Template Customization** tab, shown in Figure 5.17, select the **EntityType for Filter** name from the OData service (in our case **Z_C_PURCHASEDOCUMENTFILTERS-OVPType**). This step will generate the filter bar in the OVP.

At this point, we've created a basic template for the OVP along with a default filter. Let's create a `Run Configuration` for the app so that we can test the output. Right-click on the project and select **Run • Run Configurations,** as shown in Figure 5.18.

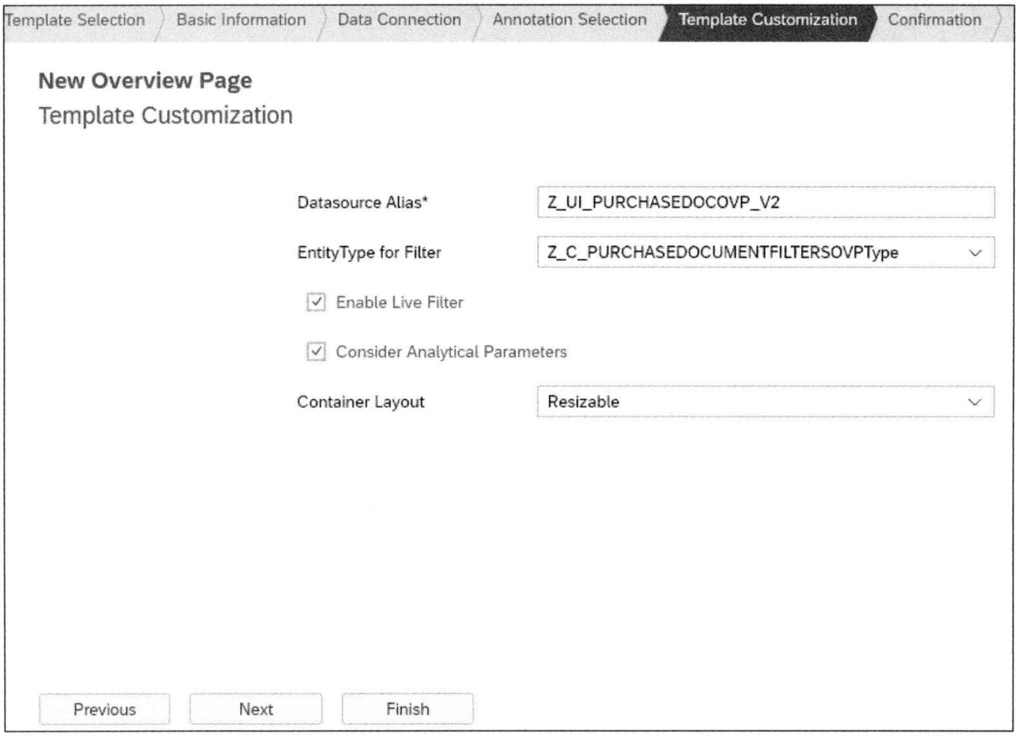

Template Selection 〉 Basic Information 〉 Data Connection 〉 Annotation Selection 〉 Template Customization 〉 Confirmation

New Overview Page

Template Customization

Datasource Alias* Z_UI_PURCHASEDOCOVP_V2

EntityType for Filter Z_C_PURCHASEDOCUMENTFILTERSOVPType

☑ Enable Live Filter

☑ Consider Analytical Parameters

Container Layout Resizable

Previous Next Finish

Figure 5.17 Selecting the Entity Type for Filter the OVP Filter Bar

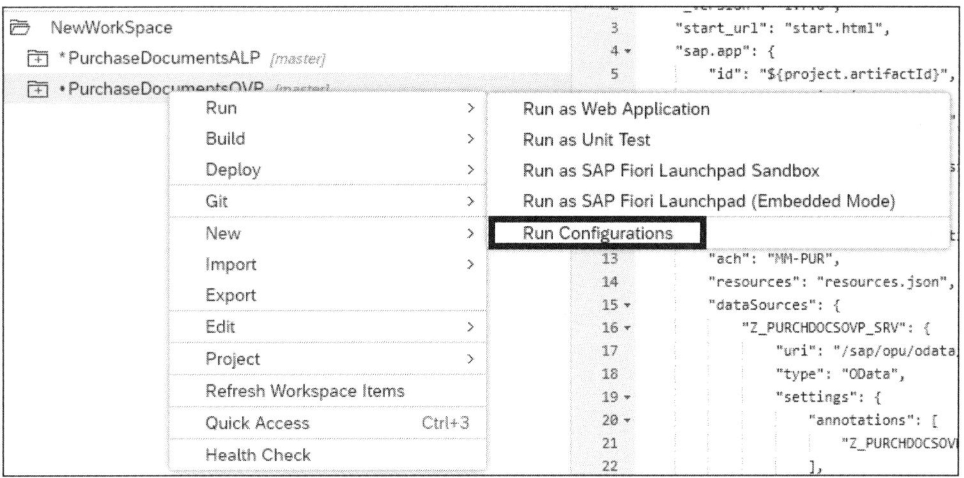

Figure 5.18 Create Run Configurations for the OVP App

In the **Run Configurations for PurchasingDocuments** wizard screen, click on the **+** symbol on the top-left side, as shown in Figure 5.19 ❶, and select **SAP Fiori Launchpad Sandbox**. Now, click the **Save and Run** button ❷.

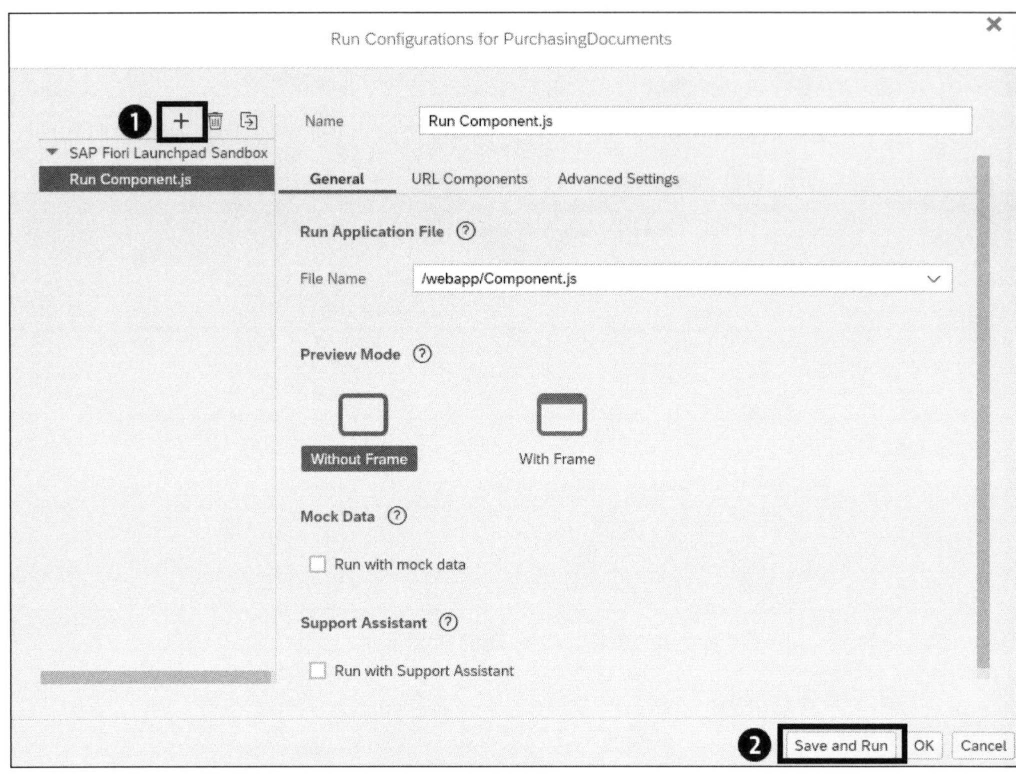

Figure 5.19 Running the Configuration Wizard

At this point, you'll see the output of our app. Notice how the filter bar has been generated with the **Priority** and **Status** fields and has picked up the UI annotation from the CDS views accordingly and converted the regular filter fields into a dropdown list, as shown in Figure 5.20. However, no cards appear in the app yet because we still need to configure each card for the app one by one.

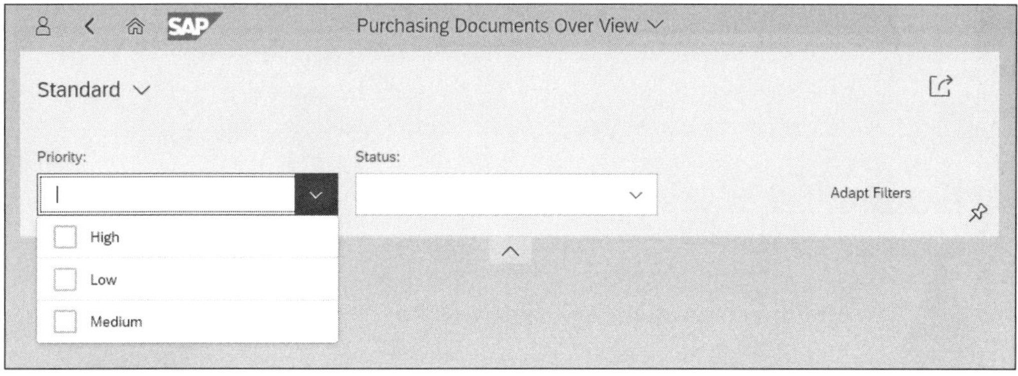

Figure 5.20 OVP Output with Filter Bar

5.4.2 Adding the List Analytical Card

Now, let's start adding the cards, as shown in Figure 5.21. First, we'll add the analytical card, which contains our donut chart for **Priority** and **Status**. Right-click on the project and select **New • Card**.

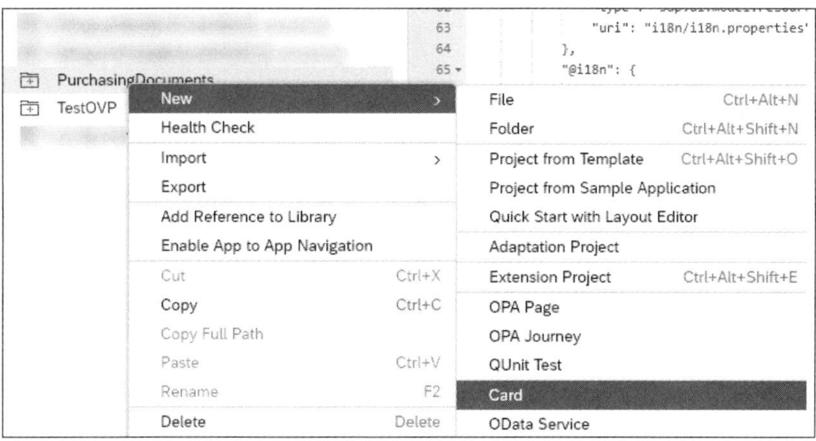

Figure 5.21 Adding Cards to the OVP Project

In the wizard, select the **Analytic Card** and then select the **Select to enable view switch for this card.** checkbox, as shown in Figure 5.22. This checkbox is required because we're planning to show the chart for **Priority** and **Status**. If you don't check this checkbox, then in the next screen, you'll get the option to only add one of the values for the chart.

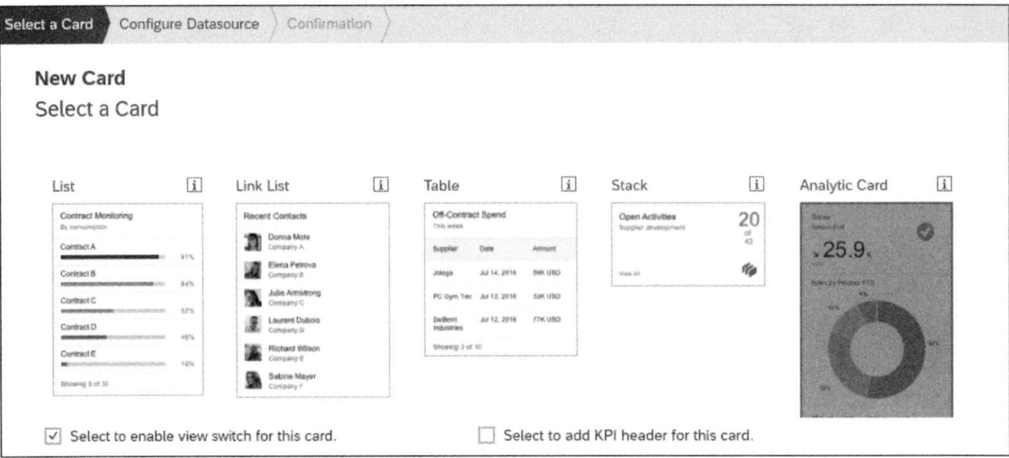

Figure 5.22 Selecting the Analytic Card from the Wizard

Under the **Configure Datasource** tab, shown in Figure 5.23, select the **Use existing Datasource** radio button, which will be listed with our default OData service for the app.

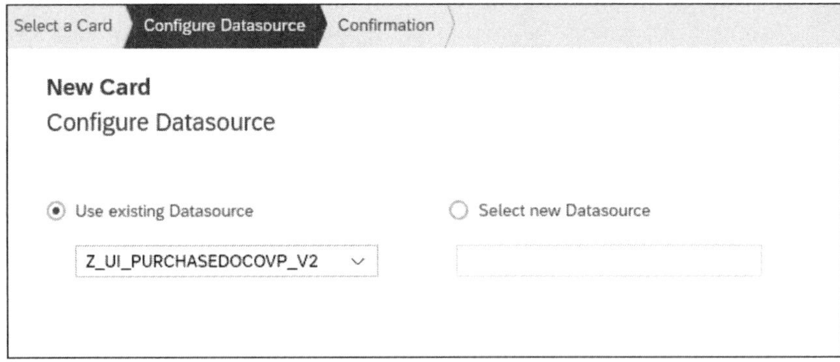

Figure 5.23 Configuring the Data Source for the Analytic Card

Under the **Template Customization** tab, shown in Figure 5.24, enter the values as listed in Table 5.2. Notice how we have the **Annotation: First View** and **Annotation: Second View** options. The second option was enabled because the **Select to enable view switch for this card.** checkbox was selected in the **Select a card** tab. In the **Value** fields for each annotation view, enter "Priority" and "Status" as the values. The **Chart Annotation Path** is a dropdown list with the qualifiers we've created via UI annotations earlier in Section 5.2.1.

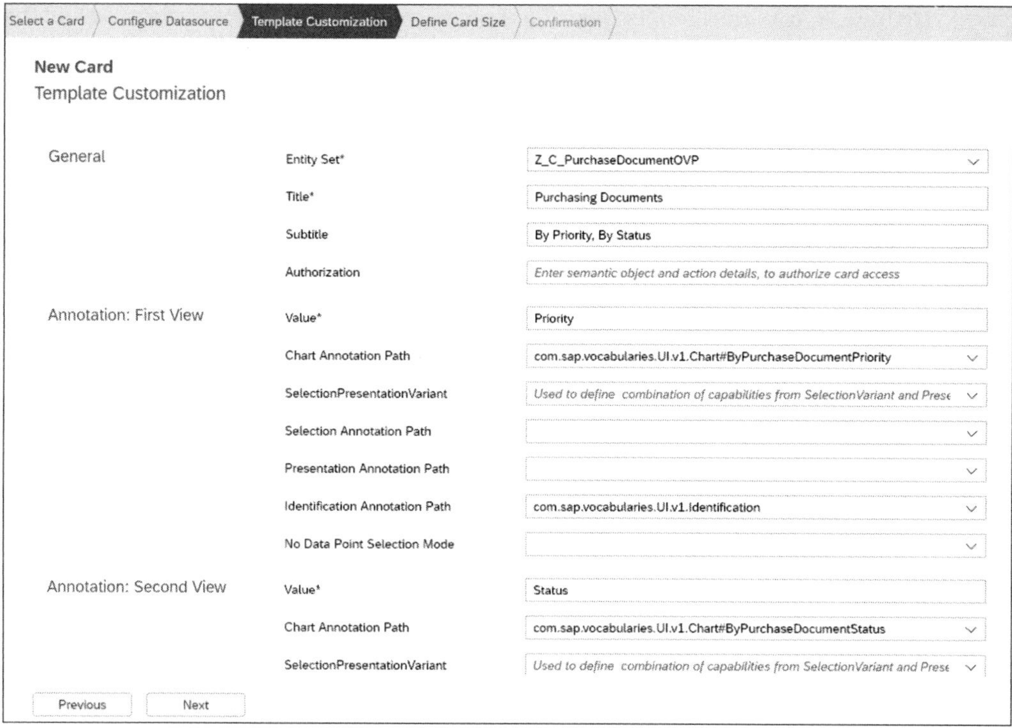

Figure 5.24 Template Customization for the Analytic Card

Field	Parameter
Entity Set	"Z_C_PurchaseDocumentOVP"
Title	"Purchasing Documents"
Subtitle	"By Priority, By Status"
Annotation: First View Value	"Priority"
Chart Annotation Path	"com.sap.vocabularies.UI.v1.Chart#ByPurchaseDocumentPriority"
Annotation: Second View Value	"sap"
Chart Annotation Path	"com.sap.vocabularies.UI.v1.Chart#ByPurchaseDocumentStatus"

Table 5.2 Values for Template Customization: Analytic Card

Listing 5.13 from the *manifest.json* file shows what the app generates when we add the analytical card using the wizard.

```
"card00": {
"model": "Z_UI_PURCHASEDOCOVP_V2",
"template": "sap.ovp.cards.charts.analytical",
"settings": {
"title": "{{card00_title}}",
"subTitle": "{{card00_subTitle}}",
"entitySet": "Z_C_PurchaseDocumentOVP",
"tabs": [{
"value": "Priority",
"chartAnnotationPath": "com.sap.vocabularies.UI.v1.Chart#
ByPurchaseDocumentPriority",
"identificationAnnotationPath": "com.sap.vocabularies.UI.v1.Identification",
"navigation": "dataPointNav"
},
{
"value": "Status",
"chartAnnotationPath": "com.sap.vocabularies.UI.v1.Chart#
ByPurchaseDocumentStatus",
"identificationAnnotationPath": "com.sap.vocabularies.UI.v1.Identification",
"navigation": "dataPointNav"
}]
}
},
```

Listing 5.13 The manifest.json Entry for the Analytical Card

5.4.3 Adding the Standard List Card

Next, let's add the standard list card, as shown in Figure 5.25. The first step to open the **Select a Card** wizard, just like we did in Section 5.4.2. Select the **List** card from the wizard and click **Next**.

Under the **Template Customization** tab for the **List** card, as shown in Figure 5.26, select the **Entity Set Z_C_PurchaseDocsforApprovalOVP**. To display the maximum number of fields for the list card, you'll need to set the **List Type** as **Extended** so that it will display the maximum six fields (enter the values listed in Table 5.3). We'll also specify the **List Flavor** as **Standard** and specify that the list should be sorted by **OverallPrice** in **Descending** order.

Select a Card
Configure Datasource
Template Customization
Define Card Size
Confirmation
New Card
Select a Card
List
Link List
Table
Stack
Analytic Card
Open Activities
20
25.9
Select to enable view switch for this card.
Select to add KPI header for this card.

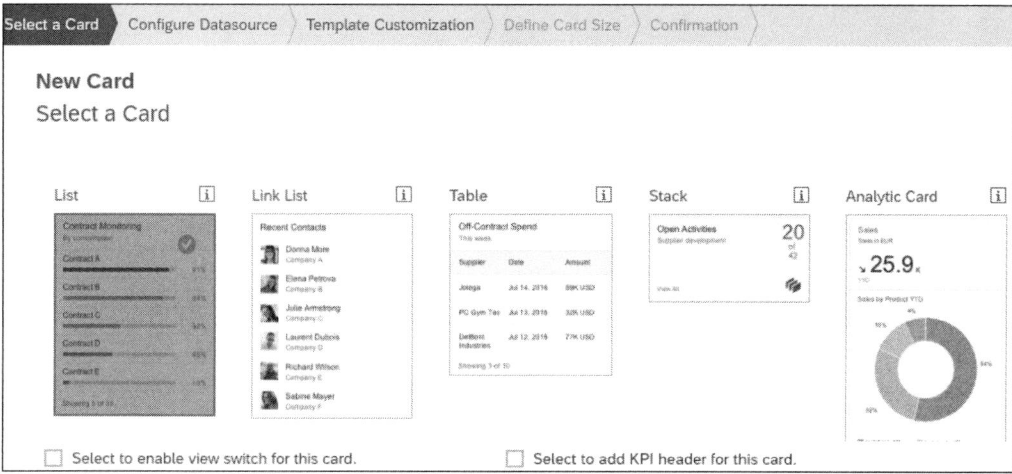

Figure 5.25 Selecting the List Card from the Wizard

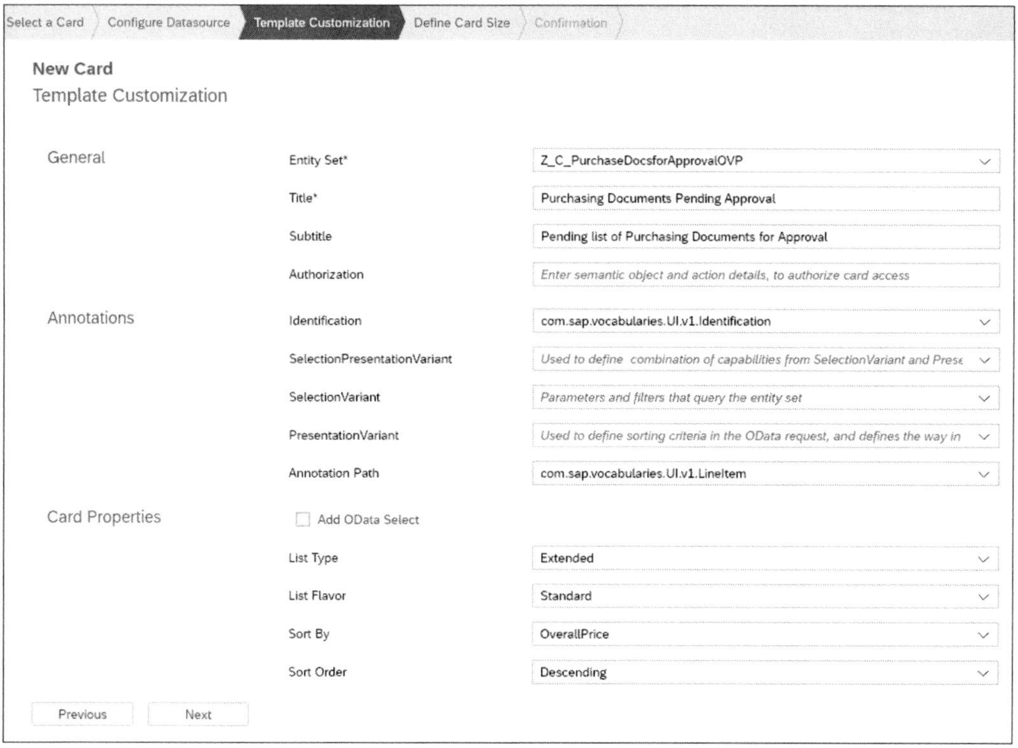

Select a Card
Configure Datasource
Template Customization
Define Card Size
Confirmation
New Card
Template Customization
General
Entity Set*
Z_C_PurchaseDocsforApprovalOVP
Title*
Purchasing Documents Pending Approval
Subtitle
Pending list of Purchasing Documents for Approval
Authorization
Enter semantic object and action details, to authorize card access
Annotations
Identification
com.sap.vocabularies.UI.v1.Identification
SelectionPresentationVariant
Used to define combination of capabilities from SelectionVariant and Prese
SelectionVariant
Parameters and filters that query the entity set
PresentationVariant
Used to define sorting criteria in the OData request, and defines the way in
Annotation Path
com.sap.vocabularies.UI.v1.LineItem
Card Properties
Add OData Select
List Type
Extended
List Flavor
Standard
Sort By
OverallPrice
Sort Order
Descending
Previous
Next

Figure 5.26 Template Customization for the Standard List Card

Field	Parameter
Entity Set	Z_C_PurchaseDocsforApprovalOVP
Title	"Purchasing Documents Pending Approval"
Subtitle	"Pending List of Purchasing Documents for Approval"
List Type	Extended
List Flavor	Standard
Sort By	OverallPrice
Sort Order	Descending

Table 5.3 Values for Template Customization: Standard List Card

Listing 5.14 from the *manifest.json* file shows what the app generates when we add the standard list card using the wizard.

```
"card01": {
"model": "Z_UI_PURCHASEDOCOVP_V2",
"template": "sap.ovp.cards.list",
"settings": {
"title": "{{card01_title}}",
"subTitle": "{{card01_subTitle}}",
"entitySet": "Z_C_PurchaseDocsforApprovalOVP",
"listType": "extended",
"listFlavor": "standard",
"sortBy": "OverallPrice",
"sortOrder": "descending",
"addODataSelect": false,
"identificationAnnotationPath": "com.sap.vocabularies.UI.v1.Identification",
"annotationPath": "com.sap.vocabularies.UI.v1.LineItem"
}
},
```

Listing 5.14 The manifest.json Entry for the Standard List Card

5.4.4 Adding the Bar List Card

Now, let's add the bar list card, as shown in Figure 5.27. The first step to get to the **Select a Card** wizard, just like we did in Section 5.4.2. The card to be selected is a list card, as shown earlier in Figure 5.25. Under the **Template Customization** tab for the card, select the **Entity Set Z_C_PurchaseDocBudgetOVP**, which contains the data point for `criticalityCalculation`, which will populate the bar list card. In addition, let's set the **List Flavor** as **Bar**. Enter the values as listed in Table 5.4.

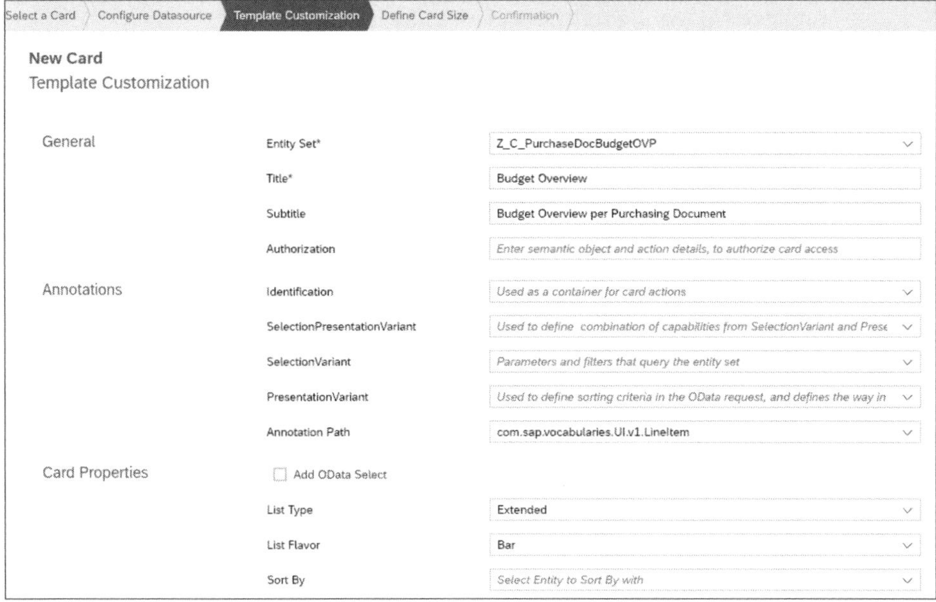

Figure 5.27 Template Customization for the Bar List Card

Field	Parameter
Entity Set	**Z_C_PurchaseDocBudgetOVP**
Title	"Budget Overview"
Subtitle	"Budget Overview per Purchasing Document"
List Type	**Extended**
List Flavor	**Bar**

Table 5.4 Values for Template Customization: Bar List Card

Listing 5.15 from the *manifest.json* file shows what the app generates when we add the bar list card using the wizard.

```
"card02": {
    "model": "Z_UI_PURCHASEDOCOVP_V2",
    "template": "sap.ovp.cards.list",
    "settings": {
        "title": "{{card02_title}}",
        "subTitle": "{{card02_subTitle}}",
        "entitySet": "Z_C_PurchaseDocBudgetOVP",
        "listType": "extended",
        "listFlavor": "bar",
        "addODataSelect": false,
        "annotationPath": "com.sap.vocabularies.UI.v1.LineItem"
        }
},
```

Listing 5.15 The manifest.json Entry for the Bar List Card

5.4.5 Adding the Table Card

Finally, let's add the table card, as shown in Figure 5.28. Select the **Table Card** from the wizard and click **Next**.

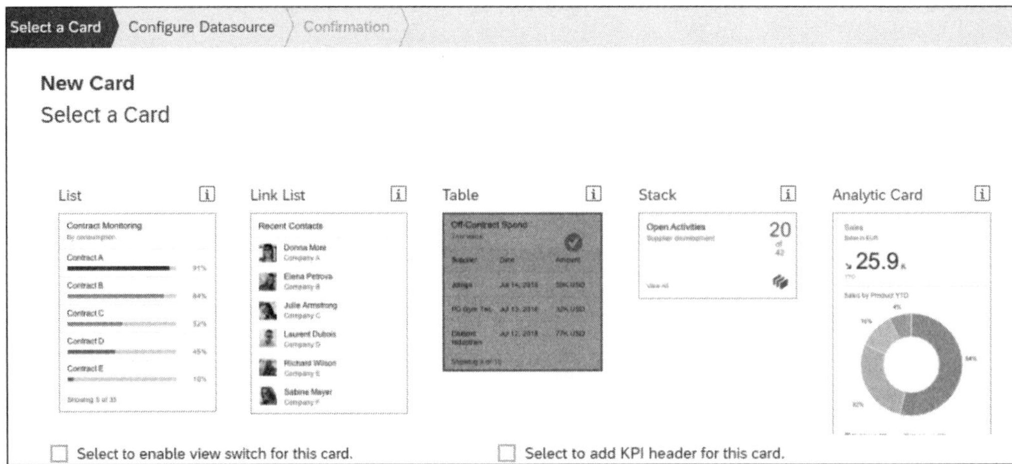

Figure 5.28 Selecting the Table Card from the Wizard

Under the **Template Customization** tab, shown in Figure 5.29, select the **Entity Set Z_C_PurchaseDocumentPendingOVP** and enter the values as listed in Table 5.5.

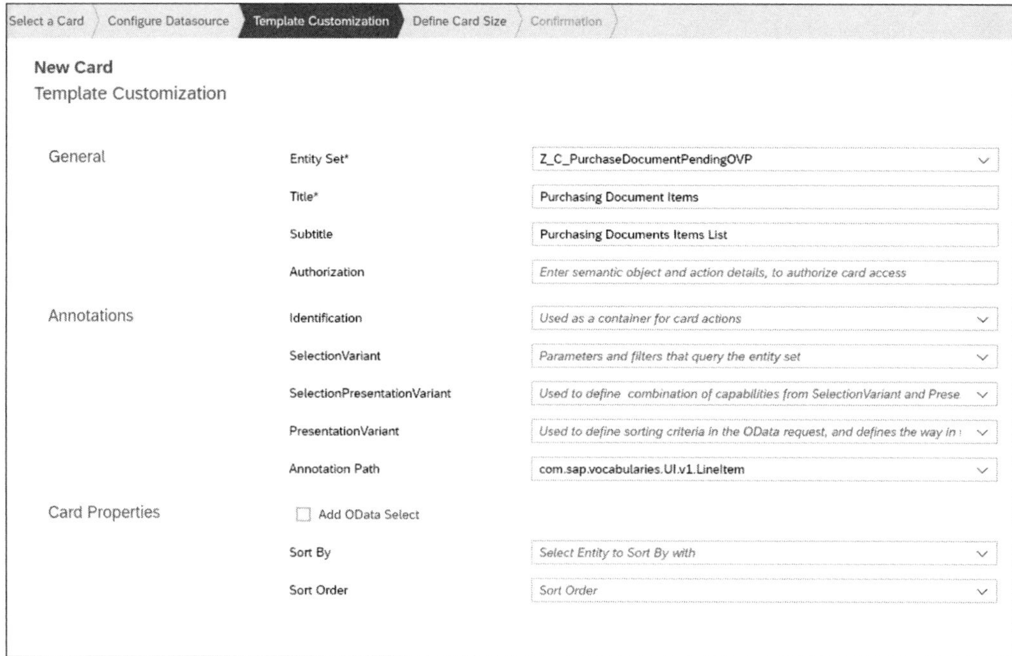

Figure 5.29 Template Customization for the Table Card

Field	Parameter
Entity Set	**Z_C_PurchaseDocumentPendingOVP**
Title	"Purchasing Document Items"
Subtitle	"Purchasing Documents Items List"

Table 5.5 Values for Template Customization: Table Card

Listing 5.16 from the *manifest.json* file shows what the app generates when we add the table card using the wizard.

```
"card03": {
"model": "Z_UI_PURCHASEDOCOVP_V2",
"template": "sap.ovp.cards.table",
```

```
"settings": {
"title": "{{card03_title}}",
"subTitle": "{{card03_subTitle}}",
"entitySet": "Z_C_PurchaseDocumentPendingOVP",
"addODataSelect": false,
"annotationPath": "com.sap.vocabularies.UI.v1.LineItem"
}
}
```

Listing 5.16 The manifest.json Entry for the Table Card

5.4.6 Overview Page Output

Now that we've added all the cards, let's run the application again to confirm that all the cards are visible in our app, as shown in Figure 5.30. The cards are resizable, so if we want the table card (**Purchasing Document Items**) to show all the fields, then we can increase the width of the card by dragging the card's edge with the mouse.

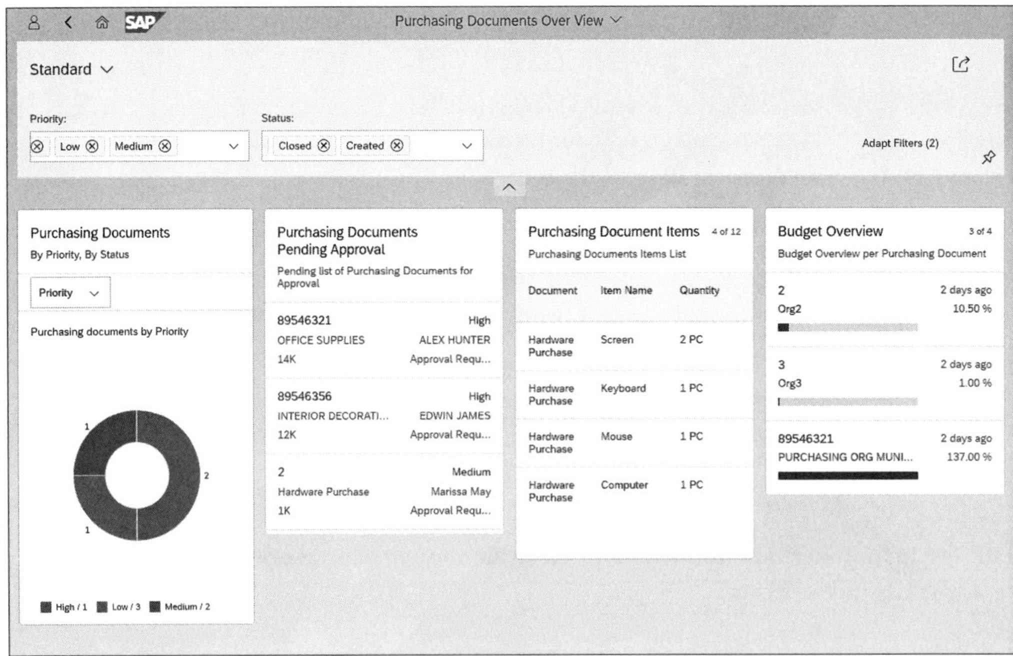

Figure 5.30 Purchase Documents OVP Output

Note

To further modify any of the cards' properties, navigate to **projectname • webapp • manifest.json** under the **sap.ovp • Cards** section.

5.5 Summary

In this chapter, we discussed OVPs. We created the CDS views required for OVP cards and covered the required CDS view annotations for generating different OVP cards. Then, we talked about using the new ABAP RESTful programming model to create the OData service using the business services which replaced the earlier concepts of ABAP programming model for SAP Fiori. Later, we used the SAP Web IDE to generate an OVP from the OData services and explored configuring different OVP cards (e.g., list card, analytical card, and table card). In the next chapter, you'll learn about creating an analytical list report page.

Chapter 6
Developing an Analytical List Page

In this chapter we'll cover the basics of building an SAP Fiori elements-based analytical list report application and explore some of its features like key performance indicators (KPIs), visual filters, charts, and more.

In this chapter, you'll learn all about building an analytical list page (ALP) application. We'll cover the different core data services (CDS) views required and the annotations you'll use to build ALPs for building KPIs, visual filters, and default charts and tables. Finally, we'll generate the ALP from our CDS views using the SAP Web IDE analytical list template.

6.1 Introduction

As described in Chapter 2, an ALP is a type of SAP Fiori elements app created to serve as a dashboard consisting of different KPIs, visual filters, charts, and tables. This type of application is suitable for users who need to go through a lot of transactional data and need some form of visualization to gain useful insights. For our example, we'll use all the data from our purchase documents to create a dashboard for the end user that will provide all the relevant information. We'll use a combination of charts, tables, and visual filters to build this application.

6.2 Building the Required CDS Views

To build our ALP, we'll need to build an analytical CDS view with the help of the `@Analytics.query: true` annotation. This view will be the topmost or root view of Virtual Data Model (VDM) type `CONSUMPTION`. But for this analytical CDS view to get all the relevant information, we'll need child views with the data categories `DIMENSION` and `CUBE`. Let's build these views and then build our main view on top of them. The following analytical view data categories might be used when building views for analytics:

- **Fact**
  Views containing just transactional data as well as measures. Syntax: `@Analytics.dataCategory: #FACT`.
- **Cube**
  Views containing transactional data with all relevant fields for data aggregation (associations to master data elements, dimensions, etc.). Syntax: `@Analytics.dataCategory: #CUBE`.
- **Dimension**
  Views containing business documents, configurations, and master data. These views also contain associations to attributes and texts. Syntax: `@Analytics.dataCategory: #DIMENSION`.
- **Text**
  Views with language-dependent texts. Syntax: `@Analytics.dataCategory: #CUBE`.
- **Hierarchy**
  Views with hierarchy notes containing keys of the hierarchy directory. Syntax: `@Analytics.dataCategory: #HIERARCHY`.

Figure 6.1 shows how the different analytical view categories are related to each other for the application scenario in this chapter.

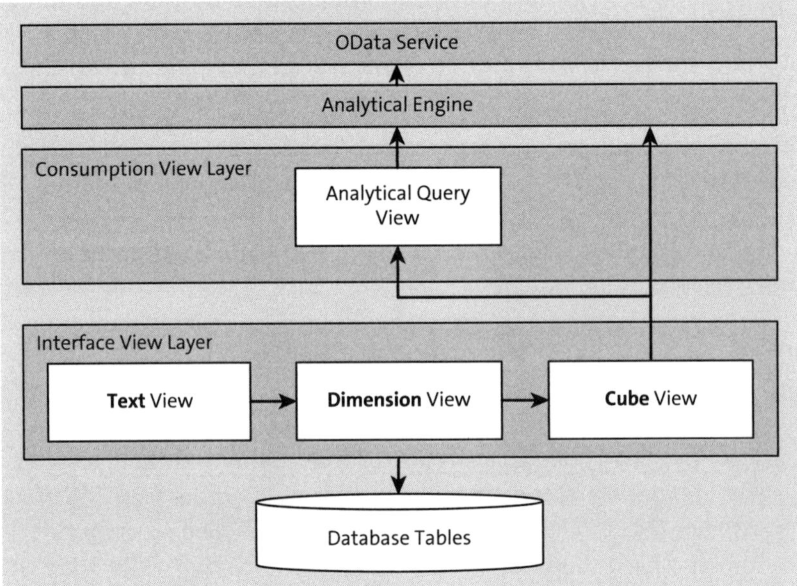

Figure 6.1 Analytical View Relationships

Note

You can learn more about analytics annotations at *http://s-prs.co/498817*. In this chapter, we won't use the service binding feature of the ABAP RESTful programming model to generate the OData service because the current version for the ABAP RESTful programming model does not support analytical CDS view-specific annotations such as @Analytics.query:true. The ABAP RESTful programming model will be updated in a future release to support analytical views. For now, you'll need to use the @ODATA.publish:true annotation to generate the OData service.

6.2.1 Building Dimension Views

As described in Section 6.1, the dimension view contains master data, business documents, and configurations including associations to attributes and texts. The annotation for the dimension view is @Analytics.dataCategory: #DIMENSION. As shown in Listing 6.1, the CDS view has annotated the analytics data category as DIMENSION and has fields such as Priority, PriorityText, and so on that fit the classification. You must annotate all the relevant CDS views that we've created so far with #DIMENSION. (The sample source codes for this book will have all the relevant CDS views annotated accordingly.)

```
@AbapCatalog.sqlViewName: 'ZIPURCHDOCPRIO'
...
@Analytics.dataCategory: #DIMENSION
define view Z_I_PurchaseDocumentPriority
  as select from zpurchdocprio
{

      @ObjectModel.text.element: ['PriorityText']
      @EndUserText.label: 'Priority'
  key priority     as Priority,

      @Semantics.text: true
      @EndUserText.label: 'Priority Text'
      prioritytext as PriorityText
}
```

Listing 6.1 Z_I_PurchaseDocumentPriority Dimension View to Be Used in the Analytical Query View

6.2.2 Building Cube Views

Cube views contain the transactional data required for data aggregations and analysis. For our scenario, we'll need a cube view to collect data from the `DIMENSION` CDS views of purchase documents and items. The annotation for a cube view is `@Analytics.dataCategory:#CUBE`. As shown in Listing 6.2, the CDS view is categorized as a `CUBE` view. This view fetches from `Z_I_PurchaseDocumentItem`, and because this view deals with transactional data, the classification `CUBE` is appropriate for the data it's displaying. In the cube view, you can take advantage of aggregation annotations, such as the `@DefaultAggregation: #SUM` for fields like `OverallItemPrice`, so we can use them to display aggregated values in the table for our ALP.

```
@AbapCatalog.sqlViewName: 'ZIPURCHDOCCUBEVW'
...
@EndUserText.label: 'Purchase Document Cube View'
@Analytics: { dataCategory: #CUBE }

@VDM.viewType: #COMPOSITE

define view Z_I_PurchaseDocumentCube
  as select from Z_I_PurchaseDocumentItem
{
      @ObjectModel.text.element: ['PurchaseDocumentName']
  key PurchaseDocument,
      @ObjectModel.text.element: ['Description']
  key PurchaseDocumentItem,
      @Semantics.text: true
      _
PurchaseDocument.Description      as                    PurchaseDocumentName,
...
      @Semantics.amount.currencyCode: 'Currency'
      @DefaultAggregation: #SUM
      OverallItemPrice,
...
...
```

Listing 6.2 Z_I_PurchaseDocumentCube Cube View to Be Used in the Analytical Query

Listing 6.3 shows the CDS view Z_I_PurchaseDocumentItem annotated with data category DIMENSION. This view has business document data, such as the purchase document items, which makes the classification DIMENSION appropriate for this view.

```
@AbapCatalog.sqlViewName: 'ZIPURCHDOCITEM'
...
@Analytics: { dataCategory: #DIMENSION }

define view Z_I_PurchaseDocumentItem
  as select from zpurchdocitem
  association [1..1] to Z_I_PurchaseDocument as _
PurchaseDocument      on $projection.PurchaseDocument = _
PurchaseDocument.PurchaseDocument
...
{

      @ObjectModel.text.element: ['Description']
  key purchasedocumentitem as PurchaseDocumentItem,
...
      @Semantics.amount.currencyCode: 'Currency'
      @DefaultAggregation: #NONE
      price                as Price,
      @Semantics.currencyCode: true
      @ObjectModel.foreignKey.association: '_Currency'
      currency             as Currency,
...
      @Semantics.quantity.unitOfMeasure: 'QuantityUnit'
      @DefaultAggregation: #NONE
      quantity             as Quantity,
...



      @Semantics.amount.currencyCode: 'Currency'
      @DefaultAggregation: #NONE
      quantity  *   price  as OverallItemPrice,


...
```

Listing 6.3 Z_I_PurchaseDocumentItem Dimension View to Be Used in the Analytical Query

6.2.3 Building the Main Query View

After we've built all the required underlying views, we'll now make our final consumption view for the analytical query. This CDS view needs to be annotated with @Analytics.query: true. We'll separate this view into a normal view with all the required fields and a metadata extension view to which we'll add all the necessary annotations that will build the different areas of the ALP. Listing 6.4 shows our view, which is annotated as an analytical query view. This view doesn't have any @UI annotations, which will be added to the metadata extension of this CDS view. But some other annotations are specific to analytical queries, such as @AnalyticsDetails.query.display: #KEY_TEXT. This annotation specifies that the field will show its key value along with its text in the user interface (UI).

```
@AbapCatalog.sqlViewName: 'ZCPRCHDOCCUBE'
...
@Metadata.allowExtensions:true
@Analytics.query: true
@OData.publish: true
@VDM.viewType: #CONSUMPTION
define view Z_C_PurchaseDocumentALP as select from Z_I_PurchaseDocumentCube
{
  @AnalyticsDetails.query.display: #KEY_TEXT
  @ObjectModel.text.element:'PurchaseDocumentName'
key  PurchaseDocument,
  @AnalyticsDetails.query.display: #KEY_TEXT
  @EndUserText.label: 'Purchase Document Item'
  @ObjectModel.text.element:'Description'
key  PurchaseDocumentItem,
...
  Price,
  @AnalyticsDetails.query.display: #KEY_TEXT
  @EndUserText.label: 'Priority'
  Priority,
...
```

Listing 6.4 The Main Consumption View Used for the Analytical Query

In the next section, we'll start building the different parts of our analytical app via the metadata extension view.

6.3 Configuring the Title Area

Let's start by adding KPIs for purchase documents to the page's title area. The title area can hold a maximum of three KPIs, but our example only needs two KPIs. The first KPI will show the overall item price per purchase document, and the second KPI will show the quantity of total items per purchase document. Figure 6.2 shows the KPIs in both a minimized look and an expanded look. When minimized, the KPI will only show the data points assigned to it via the annotations. When expanded, the KPI shows further details based on the data point via charts.

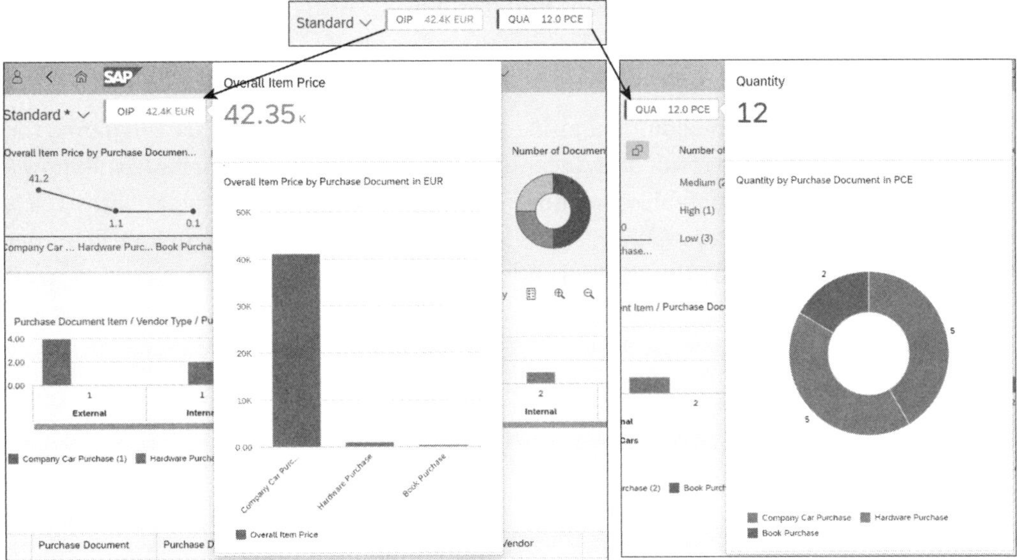

Figure 6.2 Overall Item Price and Quantity KPIs

Listing 6.5 shows a UI annotation named `@selectionVariant` with properties such as a `qualifier` (acts as a unique identifier for the variant) with the value `KPIDocumentsByOverallItemPrice`. The `UI.selectionVariant` is used to represent a group of parameters and filters, which will be translated by the Service Adaptation Definition Language (SADL) framework into the corresponding OData annotations to query the related entity sets that are annotated in the CDS view. Basically, these parameters and filters are identifiers for the different UI components, such as the KPIs, visual filters, default charts, and so on. For our first KPI, we named its qualifier `KPIDocumentsByOverallItemPrice` so that the relevant KPI can be referenced by the UI via this unique name.

```
@UI.selectionVariant: [{
        qualifier:       'KPIDocumentsByOverallItemPrice',
        text:            'KPI Documents By Overall Price'
    }]
```

Listing 6.5 SelectionVariant Annotation for KPIs

Next, we'll need to create a UI.presentationVariant annotation for our first KPI. This annotation defines what should be the result of the query from the SADL framework for the annotated entities via the UI.selectionVariant and in what form the result should be displayed. We'll connect both the variants using the same qualifier name KPIDocumentsByOverallItemPrice so that the query can find the corresponding UI.presentationVariant.

Listing 6.6 shows an additional property named visualizations that will define the form or shape of the result of an incoming query from the UI. Our first KPI will show a chart for the main content, so we must specify the type as #AS_CHART along with a qualifier named ChartDocumentsByOverallItemPrice (which will act as a unique identifier for our chart's annotation later). However, KPIs require data points; therefore, we'll need to specify an additional type as #AS_DATAPOINT and specify a qualifier, which in this case is the name of the field in the CDS view that should be holding that value.

```
@UI.presentationVariant: [{
  qualifier:     'KPIDocumentsByOverallItemPrice',
  text:          'Number of Documents per OverallItemPrice',
  visualizations:     [{ type: #AS_
CHART, qualifier: 'ChartDocumentsByOverallItemPrice'},
 { type: #AS_DATAPOINT, qualifier: 'OverallItemPrice'}]
    },…]
```

Listing 6.6 presentationVariant Annotation for KPIs

We've specified our selection variant and the presentation variant. Next, we need to create annotations for sending the response for the queries in the shape we've specified in our UI.presentationVariant. Listing 6.7 shows a @UI.chart annotation, which is required because we've specified that our KPIs will be showing charts. With the qualifier property of the chart, we'll link this chart with the corresponding presentationVariant. In this case, we must also specify the dimensions and measures required for our chart. We'll also have to specify the type of chart to display, in this case, a #COLUMN type chart.

```
@UI.chart: [ {
    qualifier: 'ChartDocumentsByOverallItemPrice',
    chartType: #COLUMN,
    dimensions: ['PurchaseDocument'],
    measures:   [ 'OverallItemPrice' ],
    dimensionAttributes: [{ dimension: 'PurchaseDocument', role: #CATEGORY}],
    measureAttributes: [{ measure: 'OverallItemPrice', role: #AXIS_1}]
    }...]
```

Listing 6.7 UI Chart Annotations for KPIs

We want our first KPI for overall item price per purchase document to show a warning if its value reaches a certain upper limit per purchase order. The KPI should be highlighted in red if it crosses the threshold. Therefore, we'll use the `criticalityCalculation` annotation like the one we used in the budget utilization card in Chapter 5 when we created an overview page (OVP) app. Listing 6.8 shows the `minimumValue` as `0` and the `maximumValue` as `100000`. We've also set `improvementDirection` to `#MINIMIZE`, `toleranceRangeHighValue` to `40000`, and the `deviationRangeHighValue` to `100000`. With this configuration, our KPI will turn yellow if its value crosses `40000` (as shown in Figure 6.2 and Figure 6.3) and red if it crosses `100000`.

```
@UI: {
        dataPoint: {
            title: 'Overall Item Price',
            valueFormat.numberOfFractionalDigits: 2,
            minimumValue: 0,
            maximumValue: 100000,
            criticalityCalculation: {
                improvementDirection: #MINIMIZE,
                toleranceRangeHighValue: 40000,
                deviationRangeHighValue: 100000
            }
          }
        }
  OverallItemPrice;
```

Listing 6.8 Data Point Annotation for KPIs for criticalityCalculation

For our second KPI showing the purchase document based on the total quantity of its items, we'll follow the same steps. As shown in Figure 6.3, the `@UI.selectionVariant`,

@UI.presentationVariant, and the corresponding @UI.chart are all interlinked together by the qualifier property.

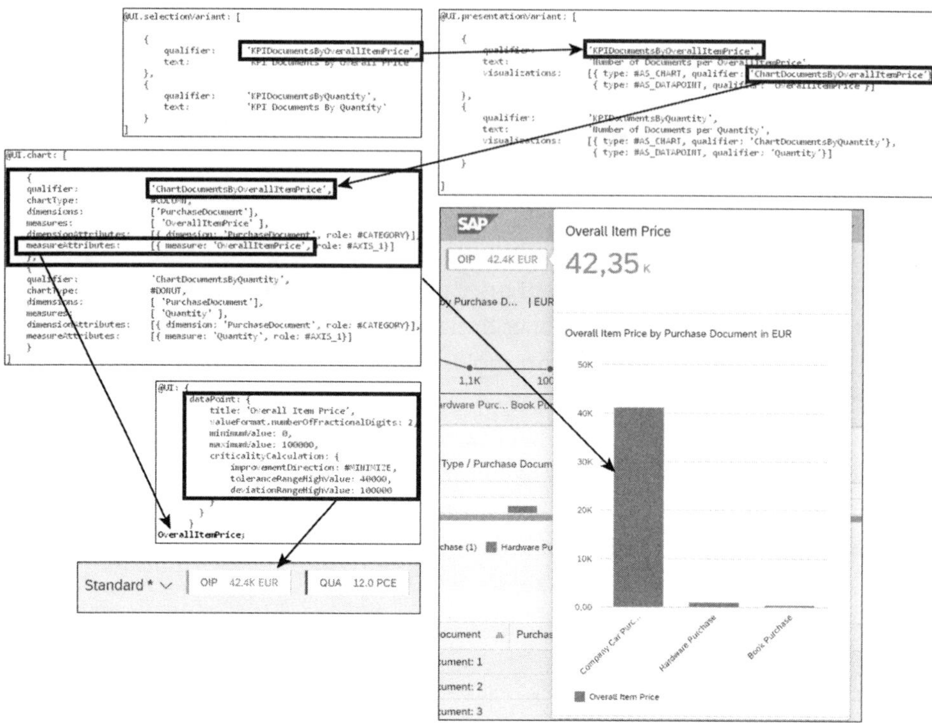

Figure 6.3 Linking Selection Variant, Presentation Variant, and Charts for KPIs

6.4 Configuring the Filter Area

In the header area, you can add visual filters, which behave like normal filters but with visually represented values. Because our app is about purchase documents, we'll create five visual filters relevant to our scenario. Figure 6.4 shows how our five different visual filters will look in the app:

- Overall Item price by Purchase Documents
- Document Items by Priority
- Document Items by Vendor
- Document Items by Vendor Type
- Document Items by Purchasing Organization

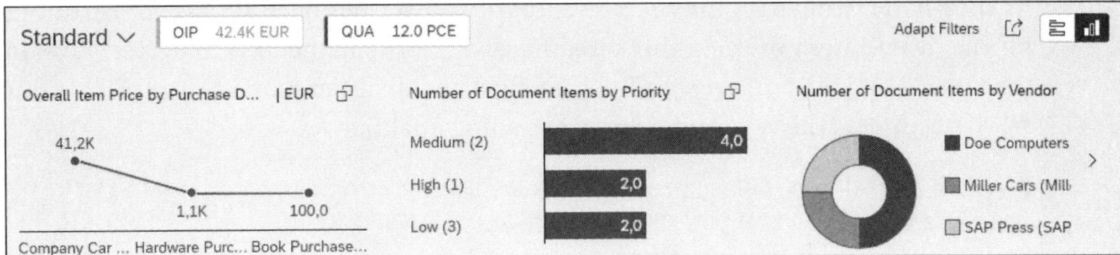

Figure 6.4 ALP Visual Filters

Just like the KPI annotations, our visual filter annotations have the same set of configurations, but you'll have to manually add the visual filters in the annotation modeler of the app in the UI. As shown in Listing 6.9, we'll create the `@UI.selectionVariant` references with the corresponding `qualifier` for each visual filter.

```
@UI.selectionVariant: [
//For Visual Filters
    {
        qualifier:          'FilterByItemPrice',
        text:               'Documents By Item Price'
    },
    {
        qualifier:          'FilterByPriority',
        text:               'Documents By Priority'
    },
    {
        qualifier:          'FilterByVendor',
        text:               'Documents By Vendor'
    },
    {
        qualifier:          'FilterByVendorType',
        text:               'Documents By VendorType'
    },
    {
        qualifier:          'FilterByPurchasingOrganization',
        text:               'Documents By Purchase Org'
    }
]
```

Listing 6.9 selectionVariant Annotations for Visual Filters

As shown in Listing 6.10, the @UI.presentationVariant has been set for our first filter for the overall item price. In this case, the qualifier is named FilterByItemPrice. In the visualizations property, we'll set the type and qualifier name as well as pass our #AS_Datapoint as the type and its corresponding qualifier.

```
@UI.presentationVariant: [{
 qualifier:           'FilterByItemPrice',
 text:                ' Documents By Item Price',
 visualizations:      [{ type: #AS_
CHART, qualifier: 'ChartDocumentsByItemPrice'},
{ type: #AS_DATAPOINT, qualifier: 'Price'}]
},
...
{
 qualifier:           'FilterByPurchasingOrganization',
 text:                'Documents By Purchase Org',
 visualizations:      [{ type: #AS_CHART, qualifier: 'ChartPurchaseOrg'}]}]
```

Listing 6.10 presentationVariant Annotations for Visual Filters

Listing 6.11 shows the @UI.chart annotation where we'll specify the chart type as #LINE chart. The dimensions and measures are set as PurchaseDocument and OverallItemPrice, respectively.

```
@UI.chart: [{
    qualifier:              'ChartDocumentsByItemPrice',
    chartType:              #LINE,
    dimensions:             [ 'PurchaseDocument'],
    measures:               [ 'OverallItemPrice' ],
    dimensionAttributes:    [{ dimension: 'PurchaseDocument', role: #
CATEGORY}],
    measureAttributes:      [{ measure: 'OverallItemPrice', role: #AXIS_1}]
    },
... }]
```

Listing 6.11 UI Chart Annotations for Visual Filters

You'll have to create similar annotations for the remaining four visual filters, as shown in Figure 6.5.

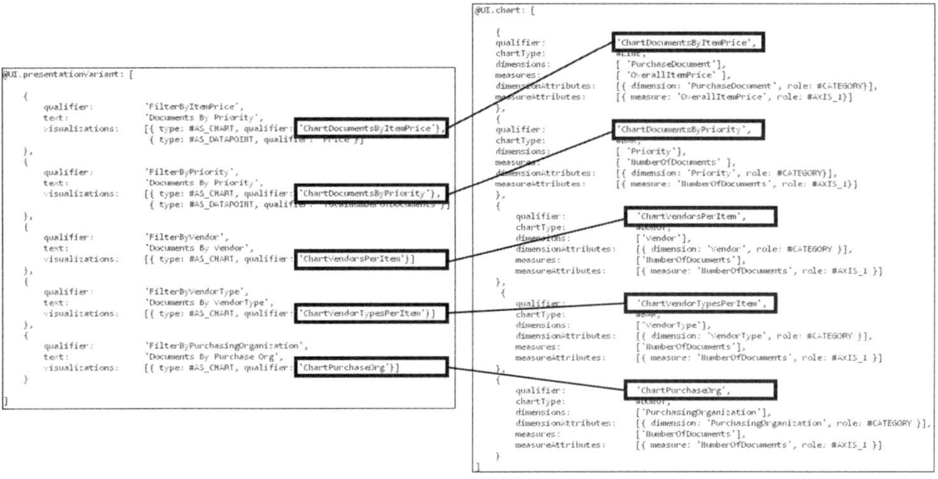

Figure 6.5 Visual Filter Presentation Variant and Chart Annotations

6.5 Configuring the Content Area

In the page content, we'll add a chart and a table. The chart will be a column chart that will show the quantity of each purchase document item with the associated vendor type. The table will show the aggregation of overall item price along with the purchase document, document item, vendor, vendor type, status, and priority.

6.5.1 Configuring the Default Chart

Our plan is to use the content area to display a hybrid combination of a default chart and a table. The chart is supposed to display the purchase documents based on different vendors and vendor types, as shown in Figure 6.6.

The default chart requires the `@UI.selectionVariant`, as shown in Listing 6.12, to be specified for use in the template customizing area of SAP Web IDE's **Create Application from Template** wizard section. We'll give the `qualifier` the name `Default` because it's the default chart.

```
@UI.selectionVariant: [{
        qualifier:       'Default',
        text:            'Default'
    }]
```

Listing 6.12 selectionVariant Annotation for Default Chart

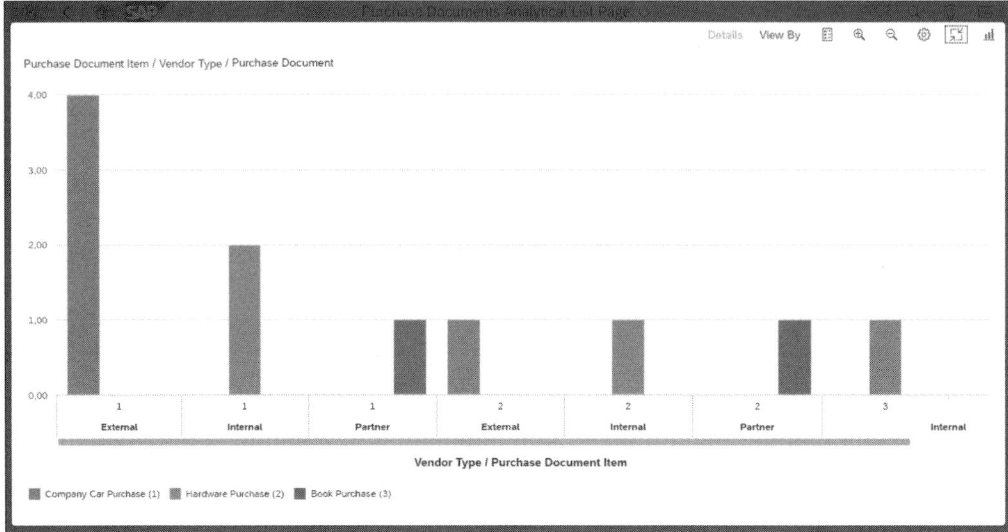

Figure 6.6 Default Chart for Main Content Area of the ALP

In @UI.presentationVariant, we'll give the qualifier and visualizations property values accordingly. We'll also use the same property to pass the type and qualifier for the default table, as shown in Listing 6.13. In addition to these two properties, the sortOrder and groupBy properties can be used for the default table. We'll explain the behavior of these properties in the next section when we create annotations for the table.

```
@UI.presentationVariant: [{
 qualifier:'Default',
 sortOrder:[{ by: 'PurchaseDocument', direction: #ASC}],
 groupBy:  [ 'PurchaseDocument','PurchaseDocumentItem'],
 visualizations: [{ type: #AS_CHART,
                    qualifier: 'ChartDefault'},
{ type: #AS_LINEITEM, qualifier: 'Default' }]…}]
```

Listing 6.13 Presentation Variant Annotation for Default Chart

Listing 6.14 shows the @UI.chart configurations for our default chart. In our case, the chart is set as a #COLUMN type, and we've specified the corresponding dimensions and measures for the chart.

```
@UI.chart: [{
    qualifier:  'ChartDefault',
    title:      'Costs by PurchaseDoc / Items',
```

```
    description:'Costs by PurchaseDoc / Items',
    chartType:    #COLUMN,
    dimensions:  [
 'PurchaseDocument','PurchaseDocumentItem','VendorType','Vendor' ],
    measures:    [ 'Quantity'],
    dimensionAttributes:
    [{ dimension: 'PurchaseDocument', role: #SERIES},
    { dimension: 'PurchaseDocumentItem', role: #CATEGORY},
    { dimension: 'VendorType', role: #CATEGORY},
    { dimension: 'Vendor', role: #CATEGORY}],
    measureAttributes: [{ measure: 'Quantity', role: #AXIS_1}]
    }…]
```

Listing 6.14 UI Chart Annotations for Default Chart

As shown in Figure 6.7, the `selectionVariant`, `presentationVariant`, and the `chart` are interlinked via the annotations.

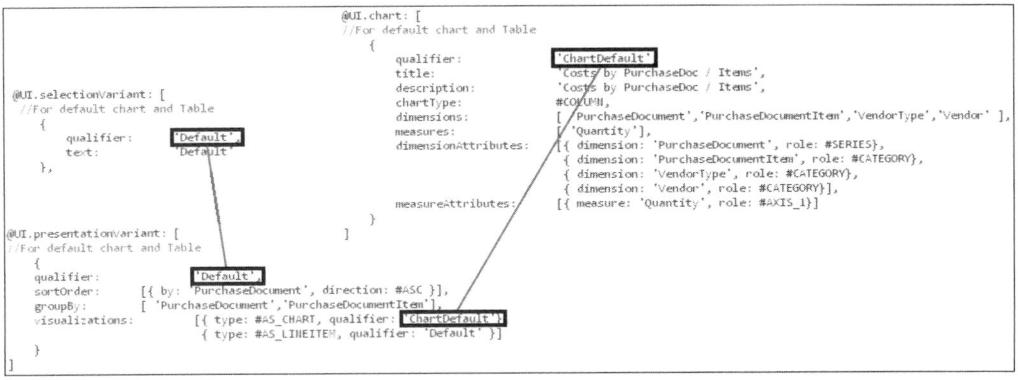

```
@UI.selectionVariant: [
 //For default chart and Table
    {
        qualifier:        'Default',
        text:             'Default'
    },

@UI.presentationVariant: [
//For default chart and Table
    {
    qualifier:                 'Default',
    sortOrder:        [{ by: 'PurchaseDocument', direction: #ASC }],
    groupBy:          [ 'PurchaseDocument','PurchaseDocumentItem'],
    visualizations:         [{ type: #AS_CHART, qualifier: 'ChartDefault' },
                             { type: #AS_LINEITEM, qualifier: 'Default' }]
    }
]

@UI.chart: [
//For default chart and Table
    {
        qualifier:              'ChartDefault'
        title:                  'Costs by PurchaseDoc / Items',
        description:            'Costs by PurchaseDoc / Items',
        chartType:              #COLUMN,
        dimensions:             [ 'PurchaseDocument','PurchaseDocumentItem','VendorType','Vendor' ],
        measures:               [ 'Quantity'],
        dimensionAttributes:    [{ dimension: 'PurchaseDocument', role: #SERIES},
                                 { dimension: 'PurchaseDocumentItem', role: #CATEGORY},
                                 { dimension: 'VendorType', role: #CATEGORY},
                                 { dimension: 'Vendor', role: #CATEGORY}],
        measureAttributes:      [{ measure: 'Quantity', role: #AXIS_1}]
    }
]
```

Figure 6.7 UI Annotations for the Default Chart

6.5.2 Configuring the Table

In our table, shown in Figure 6.8, we'll take advantage of the aggregations we implemented in our `CUBE` views, and we'll also use the `sortBy` and `groupBy` annotations used in the `@UI.chart` (as shown earlier in Listing 6.13).

As shown in Figure 6.9, `@UI.presentationVariant` is interlinked at the field level via the `@UI.lineItem` annotation using the `qualifier`. Notice also how the `groupBy` property is influencing the table layout.

	Purchase Document	Purchase Document Item	Priority	Status	Vendor	Quantity	Price	Overall Item Price
∨ Purchase Document: 1								
∨ Purchase Document Item: 1								
	Company Car Purc...	1	High (1)	Created (1)	Miller Cars	4.00 PCE	300.00 EUR	1,200.00 EUR
∨ Purchase Document Item: 2								
	Company Car Purc...	2	High (1)	Created (1)	Miller Cars	1.00 PCE	40,000.00 EUR	40,000.00 EUR
1						**5.00 PCE**	**40,300.00 EUR**	**41,200.00 EUR**
∨ Purchase Document: 2								
› Purchase Document Item: 1						2.00 PCE	200.00 EUR	400.00 EUR
› Purchase Document Item: 2						1.00 PCE	100.00 EUR	100.00 EUR
› Purchase Document Item: 3						1.00 PCE	50.00 EUR	50.00 EUR
› Purchase Document Item: 4						1.00 PCE	500.00 EUR	500.00 EUR
2						**5.00 PCE**	**850.00 EUR**	**1,050.00 EUR**
› Purchase Document: 3						2.00 PCE	100.00 EUR	100.00 EUR
						12.00 PCE	**41,250.00 EUR**	**42,350.00 EUR**

Figure 6.8 Table for Purchase Documents with Aggregated Values

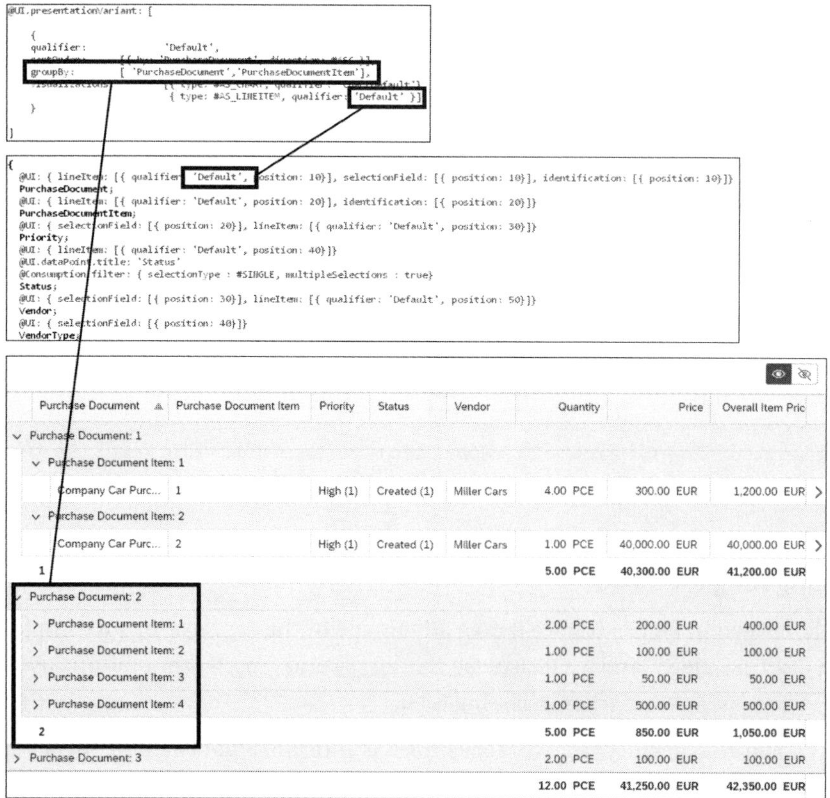

Figure 6.9 UI Annotations for the Main Content Area Table

6.6 Combining All the UI Annotations in the Metadata Extension View

At this point, we've covered the individual annotations for the various parts of the ALP's main CDS view (Z_C_PurchaseDocumentALP). Let's combine these annotations together into its metadata extension CDS view. Figure 6.10 shows how the @UI.selectionPresentationVariant annotations for the different UI elements are grouped together.


```
@UI.selectionPresentationVariant: [
 //For KPIs
    {
        qualifier:                       'KPIDocumentsByOverallItemPrice',
        presentationVariantQualifier:    'KPIDocumentsByOverallItemPrice',
        selectionVariantQualifier:       'KPIDocumentsByOverallItemPrice'
    },
    {
        qualifier:                       'KPIDocumentsByQuantity',
        presentationVariantQualifier:    'KPIDocumentsByQuantity',
        selectionVariantQualifier:       'KPIDocumentsByQuantity'
    },
 //For default chart and Table
    {
        qualifier:                       'Default',
        presentationVariantQualifier:    'Default',
        selectionVariantQualifier:       'Default'
    },
 //For Visual Filters
    {
        qualifier:                       'FilterByItemPrice',
        presentationVariantQualifier:    'FilterByItemPrice',
        selectionVariantQualifier:       'FilterByItemPrice'
    },
    {
        qualifier:                       'FilterByPriority',
        presentationVariantQualifier:    'FilterByPriority',
        selectionVariantQualifier:       'FilterByPriority'
    },
    {
        qualifier:                       'FilterByVendor',
        presentationVariantQualifier:    'FilterByVendor',
        selectionVariantQualifier:       'FilterByVendor'
    },
    {
        qualifier:                       'FilterByVendorType',
        presentationVariantQualifier:    'FilterByVendorType',
        selectionVariantQualifier:       'FilterByVendorType'
    },
    {
        qualifier:                       'FilterByPurchasingOrganization',
        presentationVariantQualifier:    'FilterByPurchasingOrganization',
        selectionVariantQualifier:       'FilterByPurchasingOrganization'
    }
]
```

Figure 6.10 Grouping Together the selectionPresentationVariant and selectionVariant UI Annotations for the Different UI Elements

Note

The @UI.selectionPresentationVariant annotations are used as placeholders to group together all the different @UI.selectionVariant and @UI.presentationVariant annotations. You can learn more about UI annotations at *http://s-prs.co/498818*.

Figure 6.11 shows how all the @UI.selectionVariant annotations for the different UI elements are grouped together.

```
@UI.selectionVariant: [
 //For KPIs
    {
        qualifier:      'KPIDocumentsByOverallItemPrice',
        text:           'KPI Documents By Overall Price'
    },
    {
        qualifier:      'KPIDocumentsByQuantity',
        text:           'KPI Documents By Quantity'
    },
 //For default chart and Table
    {
        qualifier:      'Default',
        text:           'Default'
    },
 //For Visual Filters
    {
        qualifier:          'FilterByItemPrice',
        text:               'Documents By Item Price'
    },
    {
        qualifier:          'FilterByPriority',
        text:               'Documents By Priority'
    },
    {
        qualifier:          'FilterByVendor',
        text:               'Documents By Vendor'
    },
    {
        qualifier:          'FilterByVendorType',
        text:               'Documents By VendorType'
    },
    {
        qualifier:          'FilterByPurchasingOrganization',
        text:               'Documents By Purchase Org'
    }
]
```

Figure 6.11 Grouping Together All selectionVariant Annotations for the Default Chart, Table, KPIs, and Visual Filters

Figure 6.12 shows how all the @UI.presentationVariant annotations for our different UI elements, such as the KPIs, visual filters, and default charts and tables, are grouped together.

```
@UI.presentationVariant: [
//For default chart and Table
    {
    qualifier:                  'Default',
    sortOrder:          [{ by: 'PurchaseDocument', direction: #ASC }],
    groupBy:            [ 'PurchaseDocument','PurchaseDocumentItem'],
    visualizations:             [{ type: #AS_CHART, qualifier: 'ChartDefault'},
                                 { type: #AS_LINEITEM, qualifier: 'Default' }]

    },
//For KPIs
    {
        qualifier:              'KPIDocumentsByOverallItemPrice',
        text:                   'Number of Documents per OverallItemPrice',
        visualizations:         [{ type: #AS_CHART, qualifier: 'ChartDocumentsByOverallItemPrice'},
                                 { type: #AS_DATAPOINT, qualifier: 'OverallItemPrice'}]
    },
    {
        qualifier:              'KPIDocumentsByQuantity',
        text:                   'Number of Documents per Quantity',
        visualizations:         [{ type: #AS_CHART, qualifier: 'ChartDocumentsByQuantity'},
                                 { type: #AS_DATAPOINT, qualifier: 'Quantity'}]
    },
//For Visual Filters
    {
        qualifier:              'FilterByItemPrice',
        text:                   'Documents By Item Price',
        visualizations:         [{ type: #AS_CHART, qualifier: 'ChartDocumentsByItemPrice'},
                                 { type: #AS_DATAPOINT, qualifier: 'Price'}]
    },
    {
        qualifier:              'FilterByPriority',
        text:                   'Documents By Priority',
        visualizations:         [{ type: #AS_CHART, qualifier: 'ChartDocumentsByPriority'},
                                 { type: #AS_DATAPOINT, qualifier: 'TotalNumberofDocuments'}]
    },
    {
        qualifier:              'FilterByVendor',
        text:                   'Documents By Vendor',
        visualizations:         [{ type: #AS_CHART, qualifier: 'ChartVendorsPerItem'}]
    },
    {
        qualifier:              'FilterByVendorType',
        text:                   'Documents By VendorType',
        visualizations:         [{ type: #AS_CHART, qualifier: 'ChartVendorTypesPerItem'}]
    },
    {
        qualifier:              'FilterByPurchasingOrganization',
        text:                   'Documents By Purchase Org',
        visualizations:         [{ type: #AS_CHART, qualifier: 'ChartPurchaseOrg'}]
    }

]
```

Figure 6.12 Grouping Together All presentationVariants for the Default Chart, Table, KPIs, and Visual Filters

Now, let's group all the `@UI.chart` annotations (including annotations for the default table and the KPIs). Figure 6.13 and Figure 6.14 show all the corresponding annotations to build the different charts for the ALP.

```
@UI.chart: [
 //For KPIs
    {
        qualifier:                 'ChartDocumentsByOverallItemPrice',
        chartType:                 #COLUMN,
        dimensions:                ['PurchaseDocument'],
        measures:                  [ 'OverallItemPrice' ],
        dimensionAttributes:       [{ dimension: 'PurchaseDocument', role: #CATEGORY}],
        measureAttributes:         [{ measure: 'OverallItemPrice', role: #AXIS_1}]
    },
    {
        qualifier:                 'ChartDocumentsByQuantity',
        chartType:                 #DONUT,
        dimensions:                [ 'PurchaseDocument'],
        measures:                  [ 'Quantity' ],
        dimensionAttributes:       [{ dimension: 'PurchaseDocument', role: #CATEGORY}],
        measureAttributes:         [{ measure: 'Quantity', role: #AXIS_1}]
    },
 //For default chart and Table
    {
        qualifier:                 'ChartDefault',
        title:                     'Costs by PurchaseDoc / Items',
        description:               'Costs by PurchaseDoc / Items',
        chartType:                 #COLUMN,
        dimensions:                [ 'PurchaseDocument','PurchaseDocumentItem','VendorType','Vendor' ],
        measures:                  [ 'Quantity'],
        dimensionAttributes:       [{ dimension: 'PurchaseDocument', role: #SERIES},
                                    { dimension: 'PurchaseDocumentItem', role: #CATEGORY},
                                    { dimension: 'VendorType', role: #CATEGORY},
                                    { dimension: 'Vendor', role: #CATEGORY}],
        measureAttributes:         [{ measure: 'Quantity', role: #AXIS_1}]
    },
```

Figure 6.13 Grouping Together All UI Chart and Table Annotations for the Default Chart, Table, and KPIs

```
//For Visual Filters
    {
        qualifier:                 'ChartDocumentsByItemPrice',
        chartType:                 #LINE,                                                         }
        dimensions:                [ 'PurchaseDocument'],                                       ]
        measures:                  [ 'OverallItemPrice' ],
        dimensionAttributes:       [{ dimension: 'PurchaseDocument', role: #CATEGORY}],
        measureAttributes:         [{ measure: 'OverallItemPrice', role: #AXIS_1}]
    },
    {
        qualifier:                 'ChartDocumentsByPriority',
        chartType:                 #BAR,
        dimensions:                [ 'Priority'],
        measures:                  [ 'NumberOfDocuments' ],
        dimensionAttributes:       [{ dimension: 'Priority', role: #CATEGORY}],
        measureAttributes:         [{ measure: 'NumberOfDocuments', role: #AXIS_1}]
    },
    {
        qualifier:                 'ChartVendorsPerItem',
        chartType:                 #DONUT,
        dimensions:                ['Vendor'],
        dimensionAttributes:       [{ dimension: 'Vendor', role: #CATEGORY }],
        measures:                  ['NumberOfDocuments'],
        measureAttributes:         [{ measure: 'NumberOfDocuments', role: #AXIS_1 }]
    },
     {
        qualifier:                 'ChartVendorTypesPerItem',
        chartType:                 #BAR,
        dimensions:                ['VendorType'],
        dimensionAttributes:       [{ dimension: 'VendorType', role: #CATEGORY }],
        measures:                  ['NumberOfDocuments'],
        measureAttributes:         [{ measure: 'NumberOfDocuments', role: #AXIS_1 }]
    },
    {
        qualifier:                 'ChartPurchaseOrg',
        chartType:                 #DONUT,
        dimensions:                ['PurchasingOrganization'],
        dimensionAttributes:       [{ dimension: 'PurchasingOrganization', role: #CATEGORY }],
        measures:                  ['NumberOfDocuments'],
        measureAttributes:         [{ measure: 'NumberOfDocuments', role: #AXIS_1 }]
```

Figure 6.14 Grouping Together All UI Chart and Table Annotations for the Visual Filters

Figure 6.15 shows that all the UI annotations of all the table-level fields are grouped together.

```
annotate view Z_C_PurchaseDocumentALP with
{
  @UI: { lineItem: [{ qualifier: 'Default', position: 10}], selectionField: [{ position: 10}], identification: [{ position: 10}]}
  PurchaseDocument;
  @UI: { lineItem: [{ qualifier: 'Default', position: 20}], identification: [{ position: 20}]}
  PurchaseDocumentItem;
  @UI: { selectionField: [{ position: 20}], lineItem: [{ qualifier: 'Default', position: 30}]}
  Priority;
  @UI: { lineItem: [{ qualifier: 'Default', position: 40}]}
  @UI.dataPoint.title: 'Status'
  @Consumption.filter: { selectionType : #SINGLE, multipleSelections : true}
  Status;
  @UI: { selectionField: [{ position: 30}], lineItem: [{ qualifier: 'Default', position: 50}]}
  Vendor;
  @UI: { selectionField: [{ position: 40}]}
  VendorType;
  @UI: { selectionField: [{ position: 50}]}
  PurchasingOrganization;
  @UI: { lineItem: [{ qualifier: 'Default', position: 60}]}
  @UI.dataPoint.title: 'Quantity'
  Quantity;
  @UI: { lineItem: [{ qualifier: 'Default', position: 70}], identification: [{ position: 40}]}
  Price;
  @UI: { lineItem: [{ qualifier: 'Default', position: 80}], identification: [{ position: 50}]}
//Data Point with Criticality Calculation for the KPIs to highlight values based on the threshold limiit
  @UI: {
        dataPoint: {
            title: 'Overall Item Price',
            valueFormat.numberOfFractionalDigits: 2,
            minimumValue: 0,
            maximumValue: 100000,
            criticalityCalculation: {
                improvementDirection: #MINIMIZE,
                toleranceRangeHighValue: 40000,
                deviationRangeHighValue: 100000
            }
          }
        }
  OverallItemPrice;
}
```

Figure 6.15 Grouping Together All UI Annotations for the Default Table

6.7 Generating an Analytical List Page from SAP Web IDE

Finally, we have all the required CDS views in place along with their UI annotations, so let's create the ALP using the template feature of the SAP Web IDE. Navigate to **File • New • Template from Project** in the SAP Web IDE and select **Analytical List Page/ Object Page,** as shown in Figure 6.16.

In the next window, shown in Figure 6.17, enter basic information for our ALP as listed in Table 6.1.

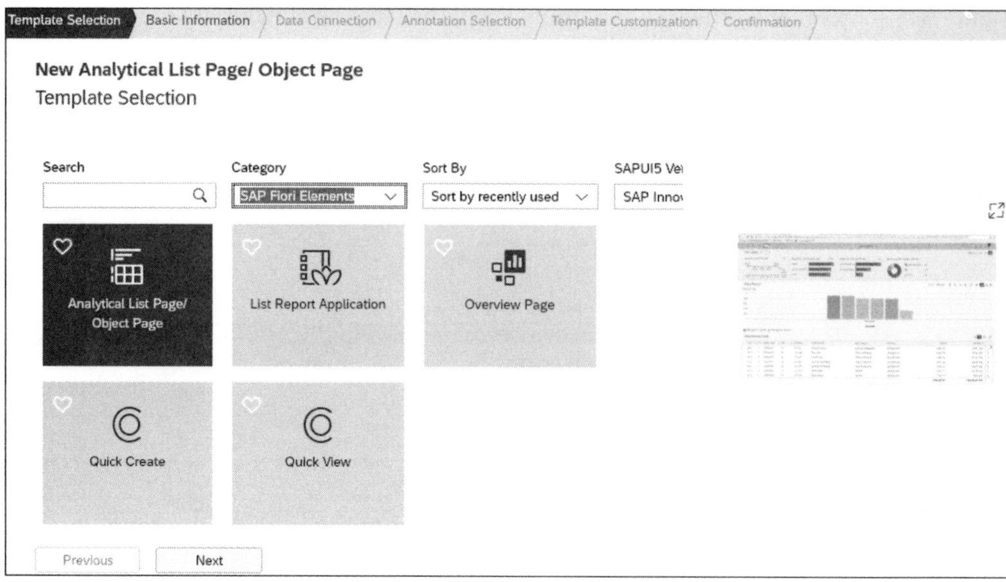

Figure 6.16 Selecting the ALP Template in SAP Web IDE

Template Selection | **Basic Information** | Data Connection | Annotation Selection | Template Customization | Confirmation

New Analytical List Page/ Object Page

Basic Information

Project Name*	PurchaseDocumentsALP

App Descriptor Data

Title*	Purchase Documents Analytical List Page
Namespace*	fiori.display.purchase.documents
Description	Analyze Purchase Documents
Application Component Hierarchy*	MM-PUR
SAP Fiori ID	

Previous | Next

Figure 6.17 Basic Information for the ALP Template

Field	Parameter
Project Name	"PurchaseDocumentsALP"
Title	"Purchase Documents Analytical List Page"
Namespace	"fiori.display.purchase.documents"
Description	"Analyze Purchase Documents"
Application Component Hierarchy	"MM-PUR"

Table 6.1 Basic Information Values for the ALP

Next, select our OData service, which is generated from the CDS view annotation `@OData.publish:true` directly, as shown in Figure 6.18. For our example, the **Service** name is **Z_C_PURCHASEDOCUMENTALP_CDS**.

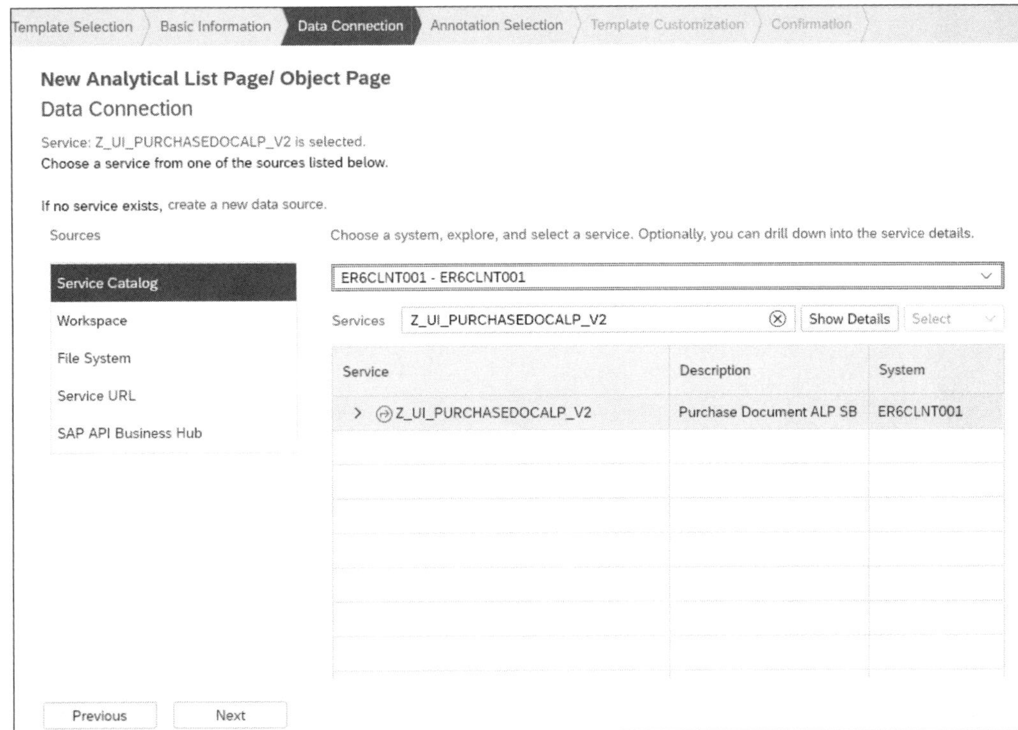

Figure 6.18 Selecting the OData Service from SAP Gateway for the Project

Under the **Annotation Selection** tab, you'll see the service metadata and the annotation model, as shown in Figure 6.19. Select both services and click **Next**.

> **Note**
>
> Remember our `qualifier` annotation for the default chart we discussed earlier in this chapter? This annotation is how the app can link the main content area with the corresponding chart annotations from the CDS view.

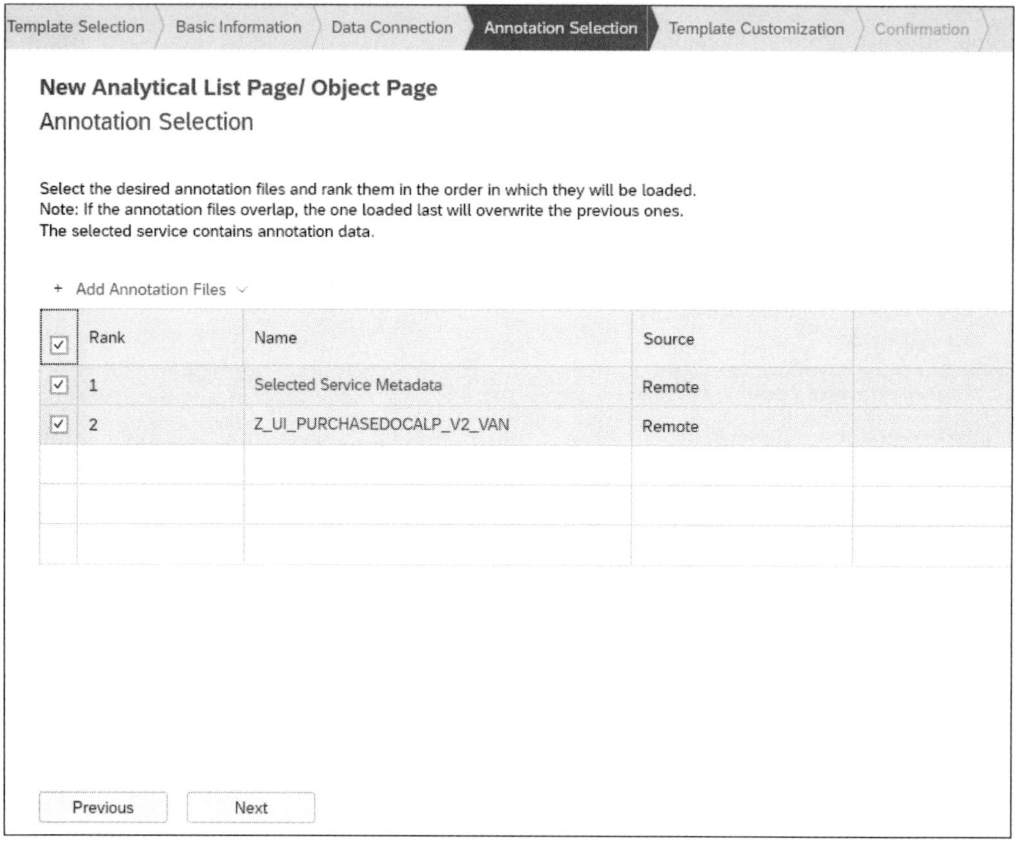

Figure 6.19 Annotation Model and Service Metadata File List from the OData Service

Under the **Template Customization** tab shown in Figure 6.20, select **Z_C_PURCHASEDOCUMENTALP** from the **OData Collection** field and enter the value "Default" for the

Qualifier (content area) as listed in Table 6.2. Select the **Table Type** as **Responsive** and click **Finish**.

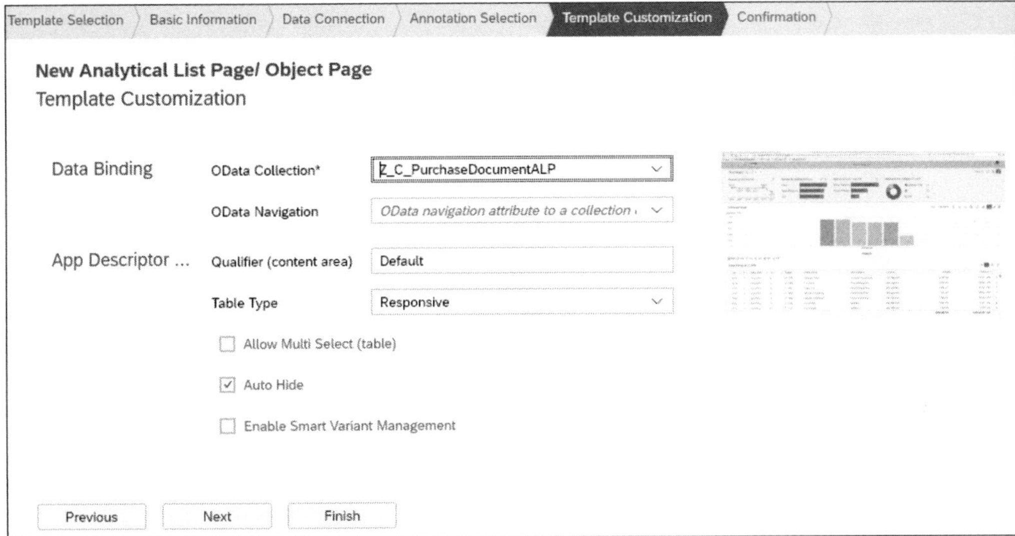

Figure 6.20 Selecting the OData Binding and App Descriptor Values for the ALP

Field	Parameter
OData Collection	**Z_C_PURCHASEDOCUMENTALP**
Qualifier (content area)	**Default**
Table Type	**Responsive**

Table 6.2 Values for ALP Template Customization

6.7.1 Adding Key Performance Indicators to the Project

After the project is created, navigate in the project folder structure to **PurchaseDocumentsALP • webapp • manifest.json** ❶ and click on the **Descriptor Editor** ❷ from the bottom side of the *manifest.json* file area, as shown in Figure 6.21. Click on the **+** button ❸ on the screen under the **Models** tab.

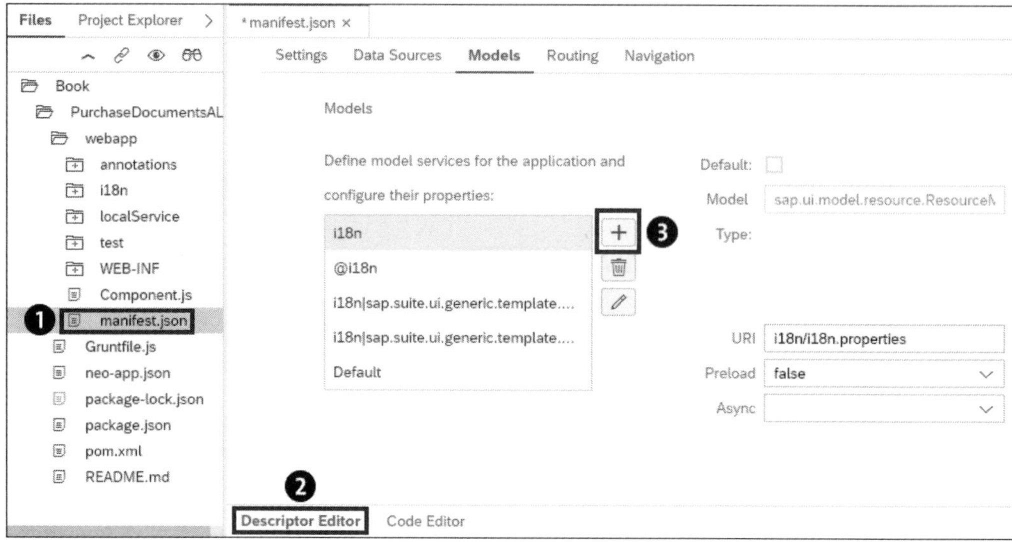

Figure 6.21 Descriptor Editor for the manifest.json File

In the popup window, create a new model with the name "KPIModel" and set the **Model Source** as **mainService**, as shown in Figure 6.22. Then, click **OK**.

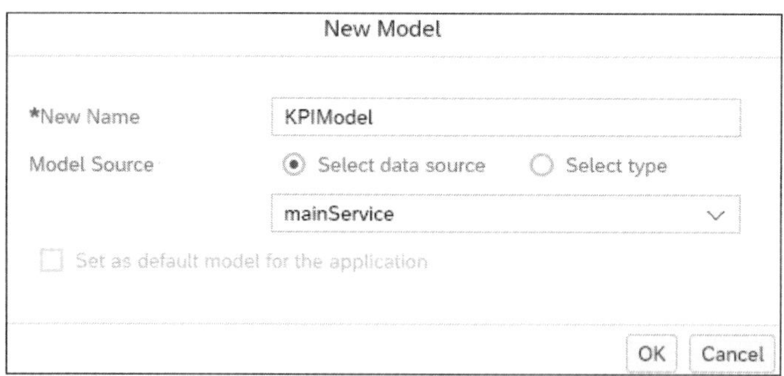

Figure 6.22 Creating a New Model for KPIs in manifest.json

After creating the model, you'll need to add our KPI details to the *manifest.json* file. For this step, you must switch from the **Descriptor Editor** tab to the **Code Editor** tab. Now, add the values, as listed in Table 6.3, to the `keyPerformanceIndicators` JavaScript Object Notation (JSON) structure, as shown in Figure 6.23.

Values for KPIs	
DocumentsByOverAllItemPrice	
model	KPIModel
enititySet	Z_C_PURCHASEDOCUMENTALP
qualifier	KPIDocumentsByOverallItemPrice
DocumentsByQuantity	
model	KPIModel
enititySet	Z_C_PURCHASEDOCUMENTALP
qualifier	KPIDocumentsByQuantity

Table 6.3 Values for KPIs to Be Added in the manifest.json File

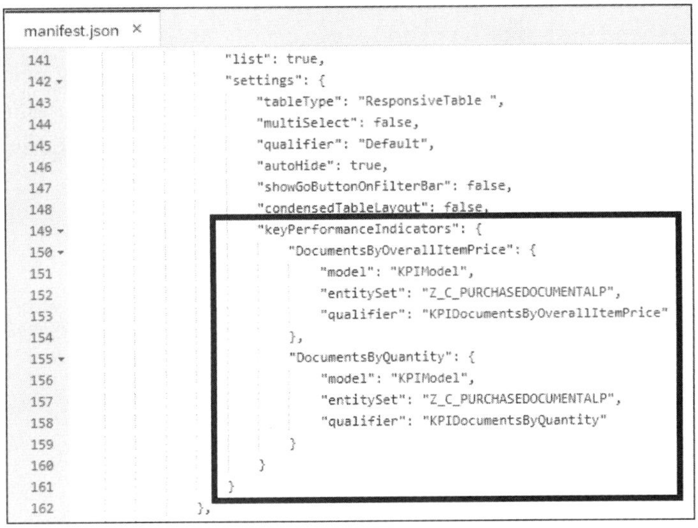

```
manifest.json ×
                "list": true,
                "settings": {
                    "tableType": "ResponsiveTable ",
                    "multiSelect": false,
                    "qualifier": "Default",
                    "autoHide": true,
                    "showGoButtonOnFilterBar": false,
                    "condensedTableLayout": false,
                    "keyPerformanceIndicators": {
                        "DocumentsByOverallItemPrice": {
                            "model": "KPIModel",
                            "entitySet": "Z_C_PURCHASEDOCUMENTALP",
                            "qualifier": "KPIDocumentsByOverallItemPrice"
                        },
                        "DocumentsByQuantity": {
                            "model": "KPIModel",
                            "entitySet": "Z_C_PURCHASEDOCUMENTALP",
                            "qualifier": "KPIDocumentsByQuantity"
                        }
                    }
                }
            },
```

Figure 6.23 Adding KPI Details to the manifest.json File

6.7.2 Adding Visual Filters to the Project

Now that we've added our KPIs, we can turn to adding our visual filters. Navigate in the project folder structure to **PurchaseDocuments • ALP • webapp • annotations • annotations.xml** ❶ and click on the **Annotation Modeler** tab ❷. Then, click on the **Select Targets** button ❸ in the **Annotation Structure** window, as shown in Figure 6.24.

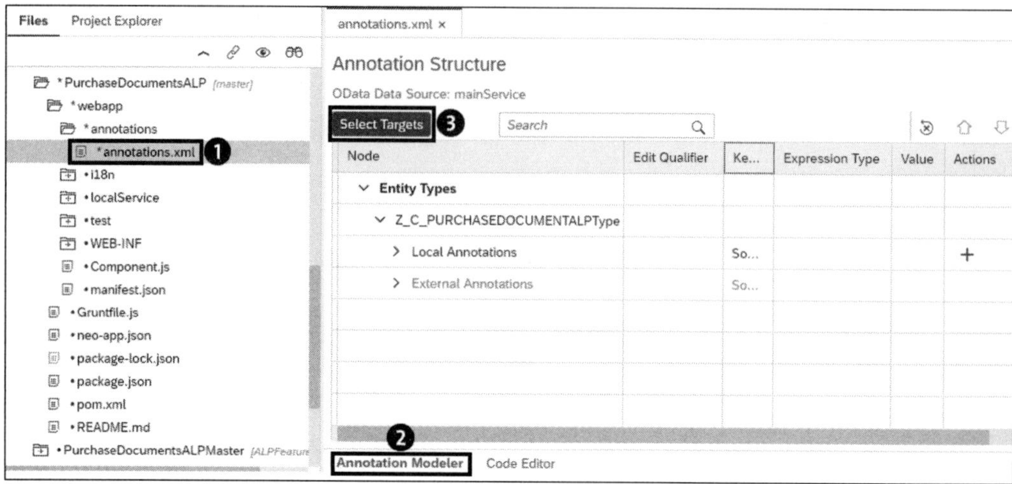

Figure 6.24 Select Targets Button from the Annotation Modeler

In the popup window, expand the **Entity Types** and select **Z_C_PURCHASEDOCUMENTALPType**, as shown in Figure 6.25. Under **Properties,** select the corresponding field names that we used as measures for our visual filter charts in the CDS view annotations. For our scenario, the fields to select are **Priority**, **PurchaseDocument**, **PurchasingOrganization**, **Vendor**, and **VendorType**.

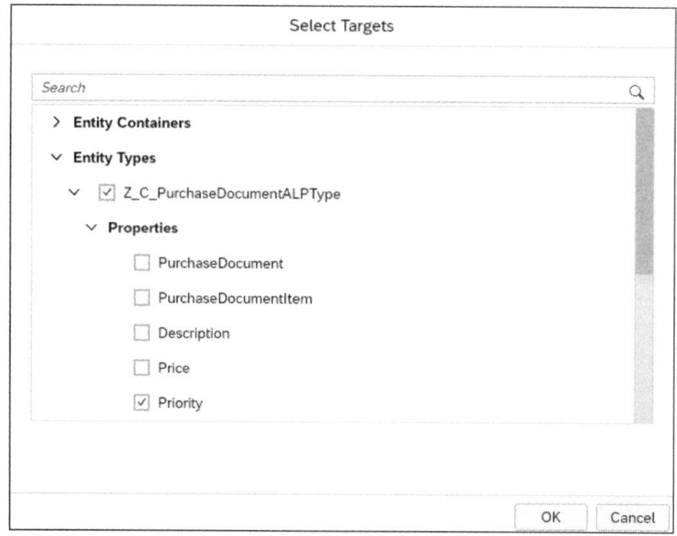

Figure 6.25 Selecting the Properties for Visual Filters

After adding the properties, click on the **+** icon next to all the added properties, as shown in Figure 6.26.

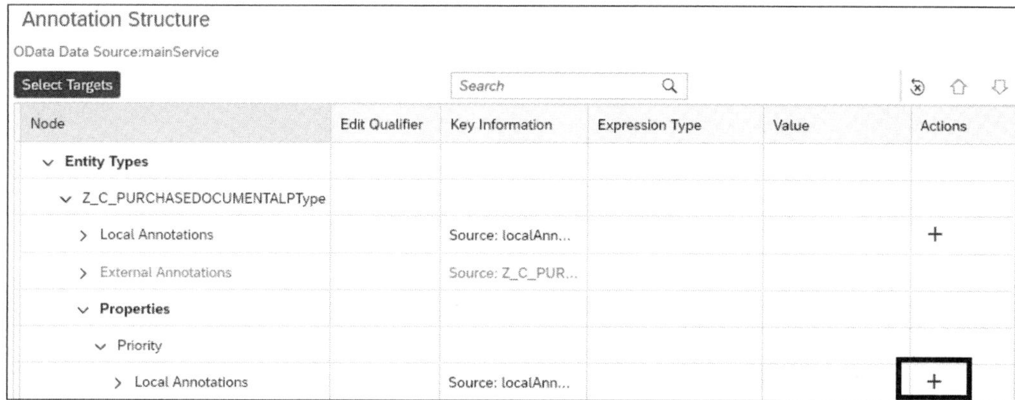

Figure 6.26 Adding Subnodes to the Visual Filter Properties

In the popup window, expand the annotation **Common Vocabulary** and select the property **ValueList,** as shown in Figure 6.27.

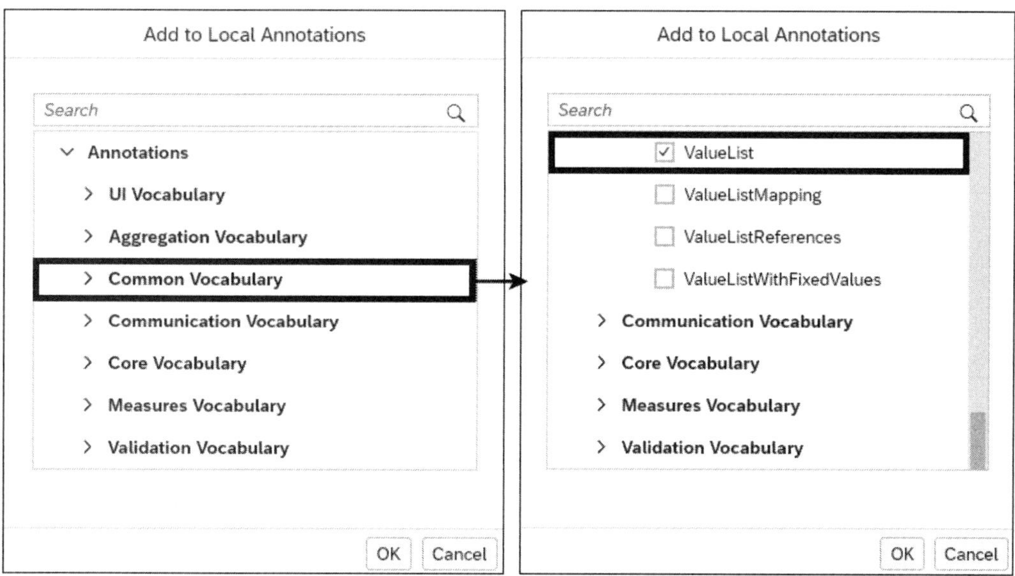

Figure 6.27 Adding the ValueList Annotation to the Visual Filter Properties

After the `ValueList` property is added for all the visual filter property fields, click on the **+** icon on the row with the `ValueList` and select the `PresentationVariantQualifier` annotation, as shown in Figure 6.28. Repeat this step for all five of our visual filter properties.

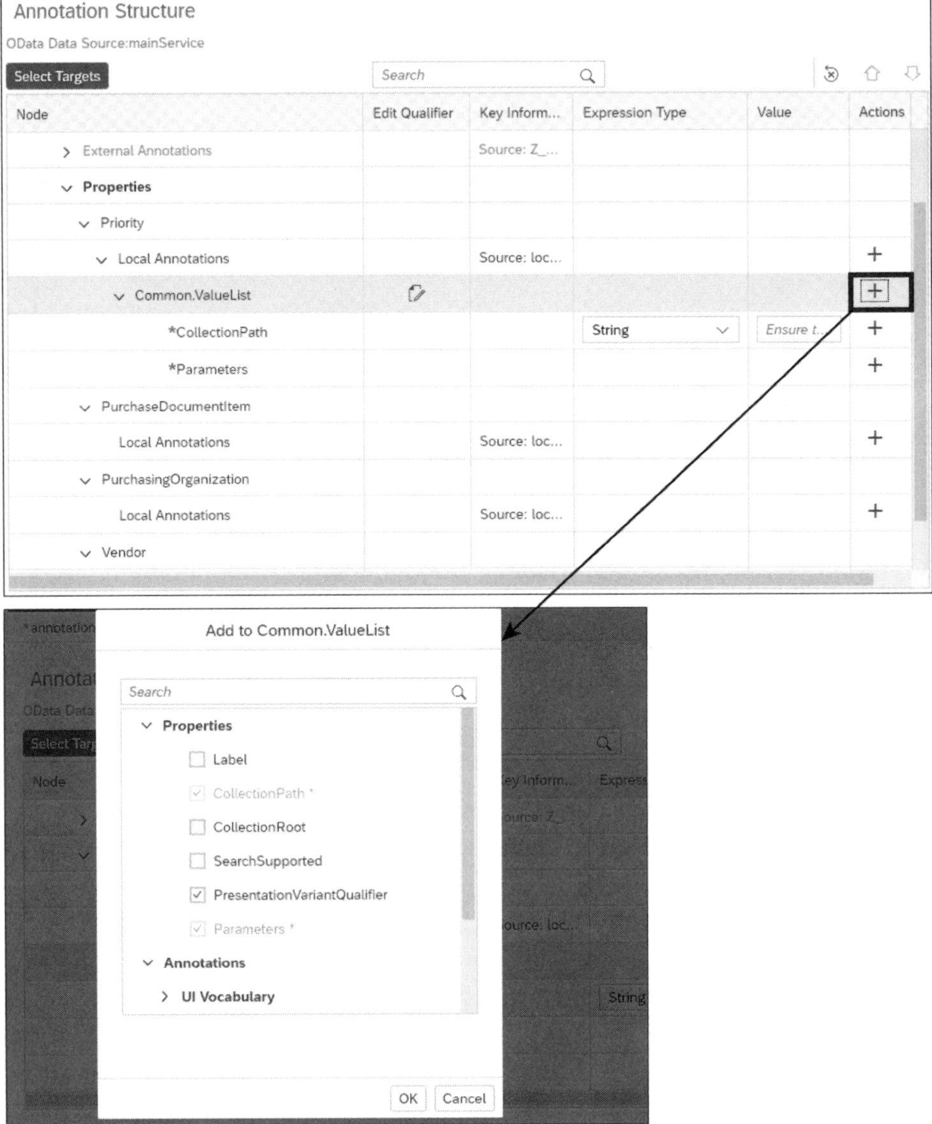

Figure 6.28 Adding PresentationVariantQualifier for the Visual Filter Properties

Now, as shown in Figure 6.29, you'll see the properties for our visual filters. The value for `CollectionPath` will be the same for all properties because this value coming from the same CDS view. The value for `PresentationVariantQualifier` is the same value we used as a qualifier under the `PresentationVariant` annotation in the CDS view for the visual filters (as shown earlier in Figure 6.3 and Listing 6.10). Table 6.4 lists the values that need to be entered for the properties.

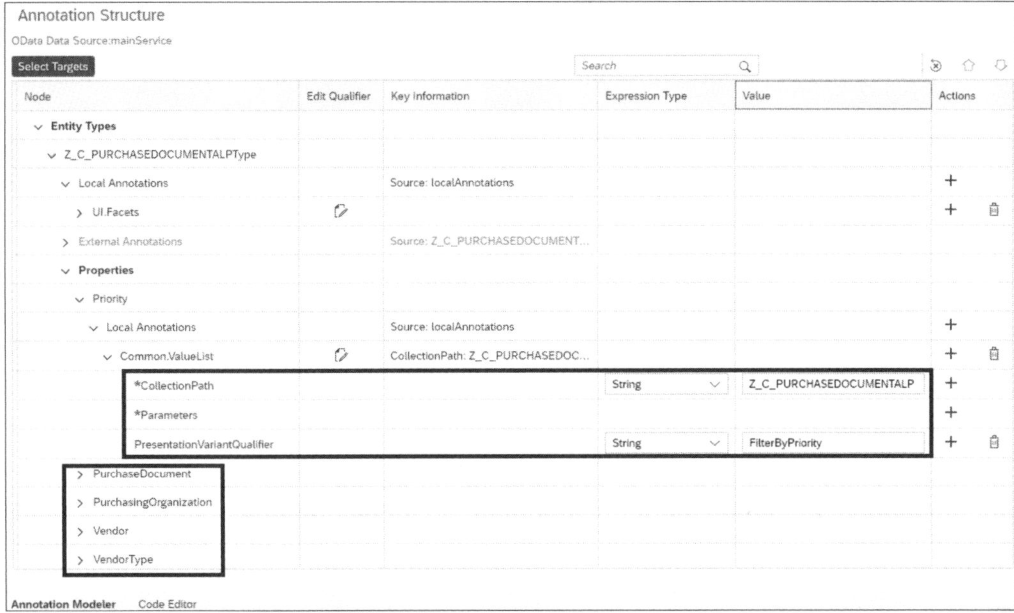

Figure 6.29 Adding CollectionPath and PresentationVariantQualifier for Visual Filter Properties

Values to Enter	
`Priority`	
`CollectionPath`	`Z_C_PURCHASEDOCUMENTALP`
`Parameters`	`FilterByPriority`
`PurchaseDocument`	

Table 6.4 Values for CollectionPath and PresentationVariantQualifier

Values to Enter	
CollectionPath	Z_C_PURCHASEDOCUMENTALP
Parameters	FilterByItemPrice
Vendor	
CollectionPath	Z_C_PURCHASEDOCUMENTALP
Parameters	FilterByVendor
VendorType	
CollectionPath	Z_C_PURCHASEDOCUMENTALP
Parameters	FilterByVendorType
PurchasingOrganization	
CollectionPath	Z_C_PURCHASEDOCUMENTALP
Parameters	FilterByPurchasingOrganization

Table 6.4 Values for CollectionPath and PresentationVariantQualifier (Cont.)

Now we've made all the required modifications to the project. Let's create a `Run Configuration` for the app so that we can test the output. Right-click on the project and select **Run • Run Configurations**. In the **Run Configuration** wizard screen, click on the + symbol on the top left and select **SAP Fiori Launchpad Sandbox**. Click the **Save and Run** button.

Figure 6.30 shows all the KPIs, visual filters, default charts, and tables generated via CDS view annotations.

Now, in the title area, our KPI based on overall item price is displaying its value in orange because our tolerance value of `40000`, set via the `criticalityCalculation` annotation in the CDS view, has been crossed. In addition, the table in the content area shows the `sortBy` and `groupBy` annotations that we added via UI annotations in the CDS view in effect.

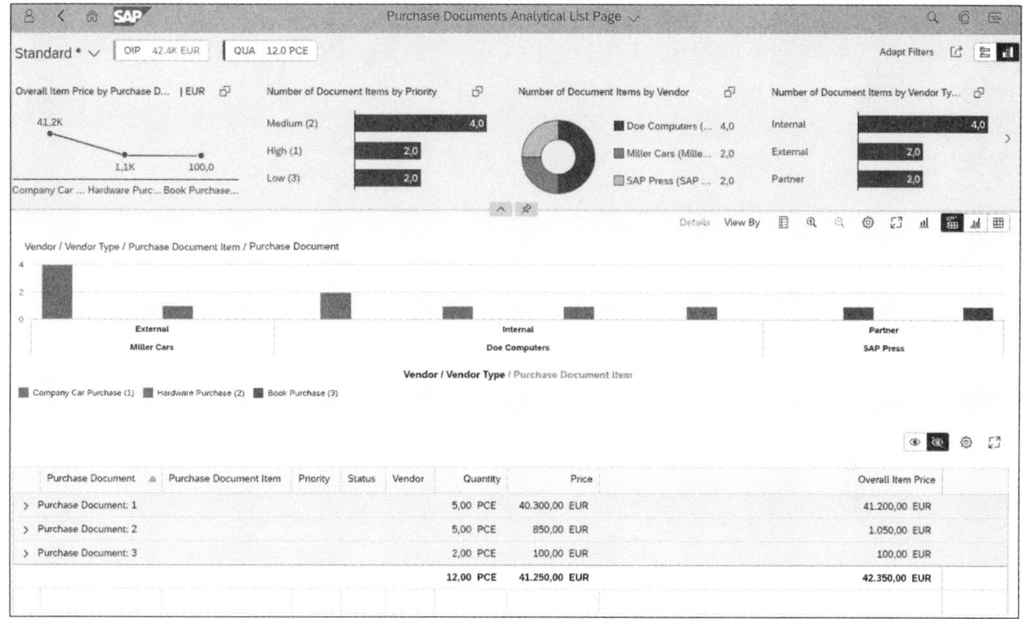

Figure 6.30 ALP Application Output

6.8 Summary

In this chapter, you learned how to create ALP applications. First, we added all required analytical annotations (dimensions) to the basic interface CDS views, and then we created an analytical cube view as the data provider for our analytical query. Subsequently, we started building UI annotations for each area of the ALP, showing you how to create KPI annotations for the title area, visual filter annotations for the filter area, and default chart and table annotations for the main content area. Then, we combined all the annotations into the metadata extension to make the main consumption view complete. We created the app from an SAP Web IDE template using the CDS view and made the necessary modifications, such as creating a model for KPIs in the manifest file, modifying the annotation modeler to include the visual filters, and finally running the application to see the ALP output. In the next chapter, you'll learn how to create a freestyle application using SAP Web IDE full-stack.

Chapter 7
Developing a Freestyle Application

In this chapter, you'll learn how to develop a freestyle SAPUI5 application using smart controls and the SAP Web IDE full-stack. Developing a freestyle application might be required if no SAP Fiori elements application type fits your specific use case and UI design.

In previous chapters, you learned how to implement several different SAP Fiori element template applications. These template-based applications significantly decrease the amount of required frontend JavaScript and SAPUI5 code and provide several generically configurable and extendable templates for different application scenarios. However, in some scenarios, the templates may not fit the UI design and mockups you developed in the design phase. In this case, you must develop a freestyle SAPUI5 application. Luckily, with the introduction of the SAP Fiori elements application templates, several *smart controls* were introduced to implement the SAP Fiori elements concept on a lower level while also being used inside the SAP Fiori element templates. Smart controls use OData annotations to reduce the required JavaScript frontend code but still provide the flexibility to use a freestyle application layout. In this chapter, you'll get to know the most common smart controls. After an introduction to each control, we'll demonstrate their usage by developing a simple freestyle application for creating and displaying purchase documents. Additionally, you'll learn how to set up an SAPUI5 freestyle application project in the SAP Web IDE full-stack, how to establish the backend OData service connection, how to configure navigation between different views, and how to write a One-Page Acceptance (OPA5) user interface (UI) integration test to test the whole application scenario.

7.1 Smart Controls

Smart controls are part of the `sap.ui.comp` SAPUI5 library, which contains composite SAPUI5 controls. As its name suggests, controls in this library are a combination of several SAPUI5 basis controls, for instance, from the `sap.m` library, and are bundled together in a new reusable control. Moreover, apart from combining several controls, controls starting with the *smart* prefix analyze OData metadata or UI annotations to reduce the necessary XML and JavaScript SAPUI5 frontend code. For instance, if a SmartField detects a value help OData annotation in the service metadata document for the property it's bound to, the SmartField will automatically render a value help. In the following sections, we'll introduce the most common smart controls and their main annotations.

7.1.1 SmartField

The `sap.ui.comp.smartfield.SmartField` SAPUI5 control is a wrapper around several other controls that are rendered based on the provided OData annotations of the respective bound OData entity type property. The purpose of the SmartField is to display or edit field values of an underlying OData entity. Listing 7.1 shows an example of how a SmartField can be used inside an SAPUI5 XML view definition. In this example, the SmartField is bound to the `PurchasingOrganization` property via its `value` property. The `smartField` prefix is defined for the `"sap.ui.comp.smartfield"` XML namespace (`xmlns:smartField="sap.ui.comp.smartfield"`).

```
<smartField:SmartField value="{PurchasingOrganization}"/>
```

Listing 7.1 SmartField Bound to the PurchasingOrganization Property of the Z_C_PurchaseDocumentLrp Entity

At runtime, the `SmartField` is rendered as an input field with a corresponding label and value help. What controls are rendered exactly depends on the attributes of the bound entity type property of annotations in the OData service metadata document. In our example, the field is rendered as an editable input field because its property element doesn't contain the `sap:creatable="false"` and `sap:updatable="false"` XML attributes, and it has the Entity Data Model (EDM) type `Edm.String`, as shown in Figure 7.1. Moreover, the label of the field is automatically displayed without having to explicitly define a label control and is taken from the `sap:label` attribute of the relevant property element. The origin of the `sap:label` attribute's value is usually its data element's field label or the `@EndUser.textLabel` annotation on the core data services (CDS) level. Additionally, it's also possible to overwrite field labels in an SAP Gateway service builder project (Transaction SEGW). The `sap:value-list` attribute indicates that a standard value help is available and will be displayed.

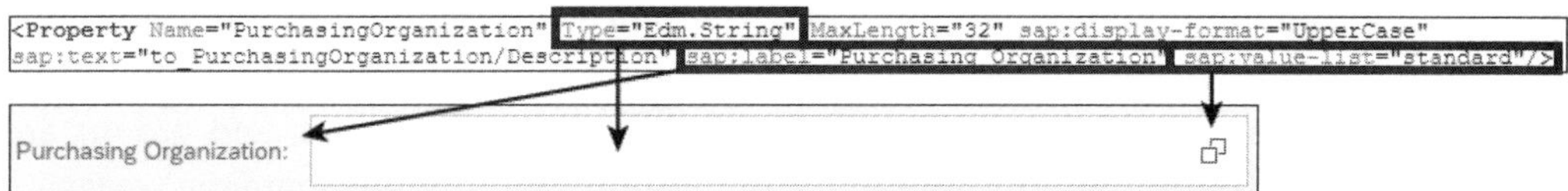
<Property Name="PurchasingOrganization" Type="Edm.String" MaxLength="32" sap:display-format="UpperCase"
sap:text="to_PurchasingOrganization/Description" sap:label="Purchasing Organization" sap:value-list="standard"/>
Purchasing Organization:

Figure 7.1 OData Service Metadata Document Annotations Interpreted by the SmartField Control

Figure 7.2 shows the required OData annotations for rendering the generic standard value help. The value help is based on the value help definition to the `Z_I_PurchasingOrganization` CDS view; it takes the `PurchasingOrganization` field as an in-and-out argument and additionally displays the `Description` of the purchasing organization. An in-and-out argument is when the `PurchasingOrganization` field is taken as an input for filtering the value help data by `PurchasingOrganizations` and is additionally also displayed in the output table of the value help.

```
<Annotations Target="cds_z_purchasedocumentlrp.PurchaseDocumentType/PurchasingOrganization" xmlns="http://docs.oasis-open.org/odata/ns/edm">
    <Annotation Term="Common.ValueList">
        <Record>
            <PropertyValue Property="Label" String="Purchasing Organization"/>
            <PropertyValue Property="CollectionPath" String="PurchasingOrganization"/>
            <PropertyValue Property="SearchSupported" Bool="false"/>
            <PropertyValue Property="Parameters">
                <Collection>
                    <Record Type="Common.ValueListParameterInOut">
                        <PropertyValue Property="LocalDataProperty" PropertyPath="PurchasingOrganization"/>
                        <PropertyValue Property="ValueListProperty" String="PurchasingOrganization"/></Record>
                    <Record Type="Common.ValueListParameterDisplayOnly"><PropertyValue Property="ValueListProperty" String="Description"/></Record>
                    <Record Type="Common.ValueListParameterDisplayOnly"><PropertyValue Property="ValueListProperty" String="Email"/></Record>
                    <Record Type="Common.ValueListParameterDisplayOnly"><PropertyValue Property="ValueListProperty" String="Phone"/></Record>
                    <Record Type="Common.ValueListParameterDisplayOnly"><PropertyValue Property="ValueListProperty" String="Fax"/></Record>
                </Collection>
            </PropertyValue>
        </Record>
    </Annotation>
</Annotations>
```

Figure 7.2 Value Help Annotations for the PurchasingOrganization Field

7.1.2 Smart Link

The `sap.ui.comp.navpopover.SmartLink` control renders a link for a field and provides a popup window containing navigation links to other related applications, as shown in Figure 7.3. To generate these links, this control analyzes the `SemanticObject` OData annotation of the bound OData entity type property and collects all navigation targets of the user containing the respective semantic object—in this case, PurchasingDocument. In our example, the user has access to the `PurchasingDocument - create` (**Create Purchase Document**), `monitor` (**Purchase Documents Overview Page**), and `analyzeKPIDetails` (Purchasing Documents) applications. The possible navigation targets are restricted to the targets contained in the assigned frontend Transaction PFCG business roles of the user. In an SAP Gateway hub scenario, frontend Transaction PFCG roles containing the relevant business catalogs, target mappings, and groups are assigned to the user on the frontend or on the hub system. To generate the `SemanticObject` OData annotation, the field must be annotated with `@Consumption.semanticObject:<SEMANTIC_OBJECT>` on the CDS data definition language (DDL) level. Like the UI annotations, the annotation is part of the separate annotation model provided by the SAP Gateway Catalog Service when generating an OData service using Auto-Exposure or the Reference Data Source (RDS) scenario.

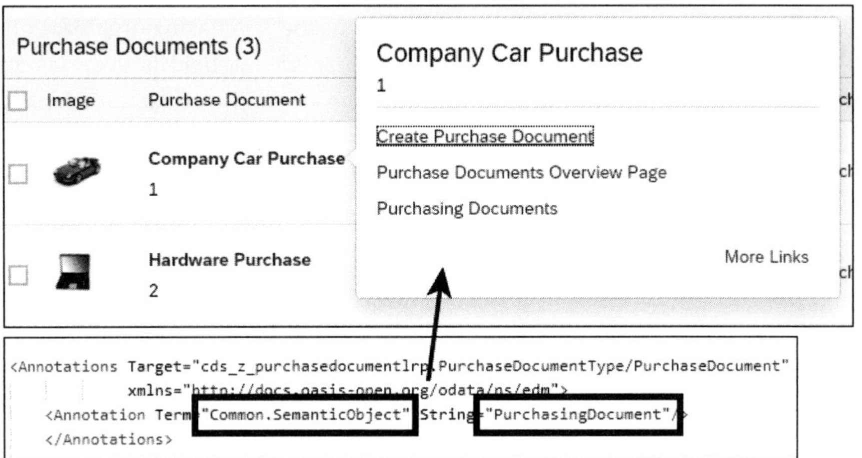

Figure 7.3 Smart Link and Its Navigation Popup Window Containing Links to Related Applications with the Annotated Semantic Object

Note

The `sap.ui.comp.navpopover.SmartLink` control will only work in the SAP Fiori launchpad and not when testing the application locally in the SAP Web IDE. The user will only see navigation links and get access to applications that are part of his assigned frontend Transaction PFCG business roles and whose semantic object defined in their target mappings match the semantic object defined for the field. The available target mappings for a user, containing the semantic objects and actions a user has authorization for, are fetched while SAP Fiori launchpad is starting up.

7.1.3 SmartForm

The sap.ui.comp.smartform.SmartForm control, in combination with SmartField controls, lets you create a form with minimal effort. This control contains a group (sap.ui.comp.smartform.Group) aggregation that contains a GroupElements (sap.ui.comp.smartform.GroupElement) aggregation. A GroupElement is a combination of a label and different controls associated with this label, usually a SmartField. Listing 7.2 shows the general structure of a SmartForm definition, including the Group, GroupElement, and SmartField controls.


```
<SmartForm title="Smart Form Title">
 <Group label="Group Label">
  <GroupElement>
   <SmartField value="{ODATA_ENTITY_TYPE_PROPERTY}"/>
  </GroupElement>
 </Group>
 <Group>
  ...
 </Group>
</SmartForm>
```

Listing 7.2 Element Structure of a SmartForm Consisting of Group, GroupElement, and SmartField Controls

Moreover, the SmartForm contains a layout aggregation that you can use to configure the ResponsiveGridLayout, which is internally used by the SmartForm to align its controls in a responsive way, depending on the available space. The layout organizes its child controls in a 12-column row. Using the properties of the control, you can specify how many columns the controls should consume based on the available screen size. Listing 7.3 shows an example on how the sap.ui.comp.smartform.Layout control can be used with the layout aggregation to configure the layout of the SmartForm.

```
<SmartForm>
 <layout>
<Layout emptySpanL="1" emptySpanM="0" labelSpanL="3"   labelSpanM="3"/>
 </ layout>
</SmartForm>
```

Listing 7.3 Layout Example for the SmartForm

The emptySpanL="1" attribute specifies that, on a large screen, one grid cell at the end of each line will be empty. On a medium size screen, you'll need all the space, so set it to emptySpanM="0". On large and medium size screens, the label control should not take up more than 3 columns of the 12-column grid space (labelSpanL="3" and labelSpanM="3").

Another feature of the SmartForm control is the possibility to enable a check button for the form by setting checkButton="true". If you click this button, the values of the SmartFields contained in the form will be checked against their OData metadata annotations. Figure 7.4 shows an example of a validation triggered by the Check button. The PurchaseDocument property is marked as mandatory by the Nullable="false" attribute in the OData metadata annotations. Therefore, if the check determines that a SmartField is empty, that field will be marked in red. When the user clicks on the field, the corresponding error message is shown. But since we've already made the PurchaseDocument field a read-only field (because we're generating its value in the backend), we'll make this field hidden.

```
<Key><PropertyRef Name="PurchaseDocument"/></Key>
<Property Name="PurchaseDocument" Type="Edm.String" Nullable="false" MaxLength="10" sap:text="Description" sap:label="Purchase Document"
    sap:creatable="false" sap:updatable="false"/>
```

Figure 7.4 Example Validation of a Mandatory Field Triggered by Clicking the Check Button

7.1.4 Smart Table

The sap.ui.comp.smarttable.SmartTable control is a wrapper containing SAPUI5 tables. Like the other smart controls, it analyzes the OData service's metadata annotations ($metadata) and the UI annotations provided by a separate annotation model and the Catalog Service of the SAP Gateway hub (/sap/opu/odata/IWFND/CATALOGSERVICE;v=2/Annotations(TechnicalName='<ANNOTATION_MODEL>',Version='0001')/$value/). UI annotations for Smart Controls and SAP Fiori elements applications are not exposed via the app's standard OData service but via a separate annotation model that is exposed via a separate OData service called CATALOGSERVICE;v=2. You will find this service in the set of available services on the SAP Gateway system. The SmartTable control renders a table for a specific OData entity set and can create tables with just a view lines of XML. Because the SmartTable control is also used in the SAP Fiori elements list report template, the same UI annotations can be used for both cases.

Figure 7.5 shows some `UI.LineItem` annotations and how they are interpreted by the `SmartTable` control. As in an SAP Fiori elements list application, the `@UI.lineItem` annotation must be used on the CDS DDL level to specify the default visible columns of the table and their sequence. The criticality of the `OverallPrice` and `ApprovalRequired` columns is indicated by the `OverallPriceCriticality` field. This information is also provided by the line item annotation.

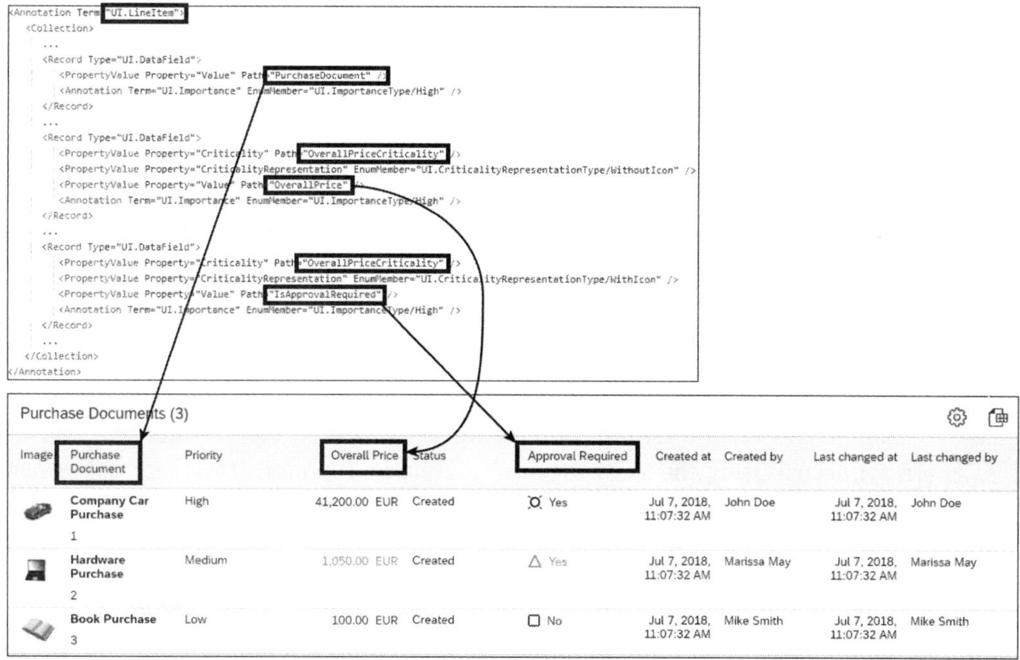

Figure 7.5 Example of How the UI.LineItem Annotations Are Interpreted by the SmartTable Control

You can hide certain fields from the UI but not completely from the entity type. In this way, for instance, you can use these fields as a criticality indicator, you must annotate these fields with the `@UI.hidden` annotation. Listing 7.4 shows how to add the annotation to the `OverallPriceCriticality` field since we don't want to make this field available in the table field catalog but instead need it as a technical field to indicate the criticality.

```
@UI.hidden: true
OverallPriceCriticality;
```

Listing 7.4 Hide a Field from the UI but Not from the OData Entity Type

Defining a smart table in an SAPUI5 XML view is quite simple. Listing 7.5 shows the minimal property values required for rendering the table. The smartTable prefix is defined for the sap.ui.comp.smarttable namespace (xmlns:smartTable="sap.ui.comp.smarttable"). The entitySet defines the OData entity set that the table will be bound to. The header attribute sets the text of the table header, and the tableType attribute specifies the table type to be used—in our case, a ResponsiveTable. By setting the enableAutoBinding attribute to true, data for the specified entity set will be requested immediately from the OData service deployed on the SAP Gateway hub system when the table is rendered.

```
<smartTable:SmartTable entitySet="Z_C_PurchaseDocumentLrp" header=
"Purchase Documents" enableAutoBinding="true" tableType="ResponsiveTable" />
```

Listing 7.5 SmartTable Definition inside an SAPUI5 XML View

Usually, a SmartTable is used in combination with a SmartFilterBar. The two controls are connected using the id of the SmartFilterBar. Therefore, the SmartTable must define the SmartFilterBar's id using its smartFilterId attribute.

7.1.5 Smart Filter Bar

The sap.ui.comp.smartfilterbar.SmartFilterBar control analyzes OData metadata and UI annotations and renders a FilterBar control that can be used to filter a SmartTable. Figure 7.6 shows some of the metadata and UI annotations interpreted by the SmartFilterBar control. The initial displayed fields in the expanded filter bar must be annotated with the OData UI.SelectionField annotation (@UI.selectionField on the CDS DDL level). In the example, the PurchaseDocument, Priority, Status, and PurchasingOrganization fields were annotated as selection fields. Which kind of value help is rendered for a selection field depends on the sap:value-list attributes of the relevant entity type property; for instance, a dropdown list-style value help will be rendered for the Priority field because its sap:value-list attribute has a fixed-values value. The PurchasingOrganization property's sap:value-list attribute is set to standard, so a standard value help will be rendered.

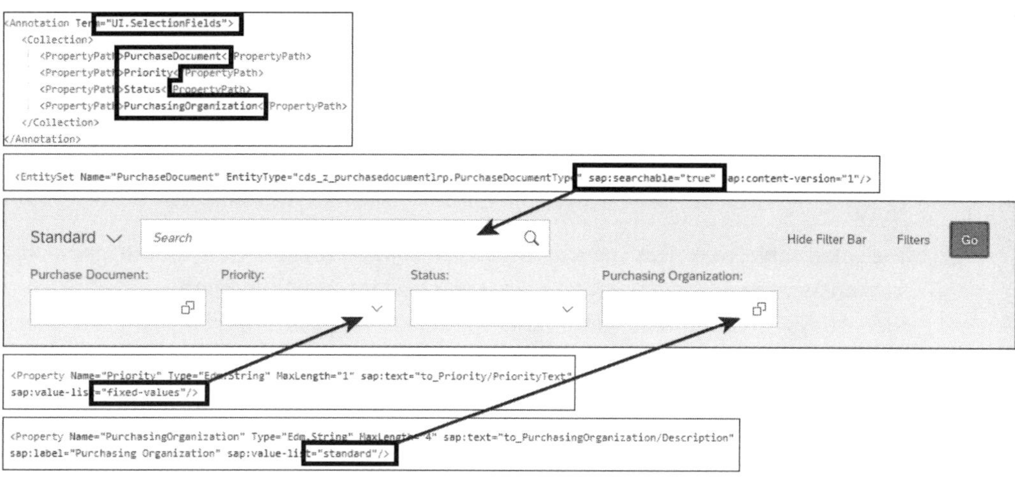

Figure 7.6 Some Metadata and UI Annotations Analyzed by the Smart Filter Bar

In an SAPUI5 XML view, the `SmartFilterBar` control can be declared as shown in Listing 7.6. The `smartFilterBar` prefix is defined for the `sap.ui.comp.smartfilterbar` namespace (`xmlns:smartFilterBar=" sap.ui.comp.smartfilterbar"`). The `entitySet` attribute defines the OData entity set whose metadata is used to render the smart filter bar. The `persistencyKey` specifies that the key that is used for storing personalization data, for instance, a filter variant that must be used periodically. Although the entity set might support free text search, as indicated by the `sap:searchable="true"` attribute, a free text search field isn't rendered automatically. To be enabled in the smart filter bar, the `enableBasicSearch` attribute must be set to `true` explicitly.

```
<smartFilterBar:SmartFilterBar id="purchaseDocumentsSmartFilterBar" entitySet=
"PurchaseDocument " persistencyKey=
"purchaseDocumentsFilterBarKey" enableBasicSearch="true" />
```

Listing 7.6 SmartFilterBar Definition inside an SAPUI5 XML View

To completely remove a field from the smart filter bar's set of selection fields, you'll annotate the field with `@Consumption.filter.hidden: true` on the CDS DDL level, as shown in Listing 7.7. On the OData service level, this configuration will generate the OData UI annotation `UI.HiddenFilter` for the respective field.

```
@Consumption.filter.hidden: true
PurchaseDocumentImageURL
```

Listing 7.7 Hiding a Field from the Set of Available Selection Fields in the Smart Filter Bar

Note

The smart table, as well as the smart filter bar control, support variant management as soon as you provide a unique key via their `persistencyKey` property under which the settings can be stored. The variants will be stored in the layered repository of the SAP Gateway hub frontend system. To store smart table and filter bar settings in a single variant, you can use the smart variant management control to enable page variant management. You can find further information under **Smart Variant Management** in the documentation for SAPUI5 Software Development Kit (SDK) at *http://s-prs.co/498820*.

7.2 Application Development with the SAP Web IDE Full-Stack

In this section, we'll develop a small SAPUI5 freestyle application consisting of a SmartForm for creating purchase documents and a smart filter bar and table for displaying purchase documents. We'll develop the frontend part of the application in the SAP Web IDE full-stack and reuse the OData service developed in Chapter 4 for the SAP Fiori elements list report and object page. We'll guide you through all of the necessary steps for developing the application, including setting up the OData service connectivity and navigation in the app descriptor (*manifest.json*) as well as creating an OPA5 integration test covering the whole create and display scenario.

7.2.1 Setting Up an OData Service

We'll start developing our app by first creating the initial project structure and setting up the OData service connection to the backend. To create a new freestyle SAPUI5 project in the SAP Web IDE full-stack, choose **File • New • Project from Template** from the top-level menu bar. In the initial **Template Selection** step of the project creation wizard shown in Figure 7.7, select the **SAPUI5 Application** template, which is contained in the **SAP Fiori Application Category.** The **SAPUI5 Application** template is an empty SAPUI5 project skeleton that includes a start view and its corresponding controller. Click **Next**.

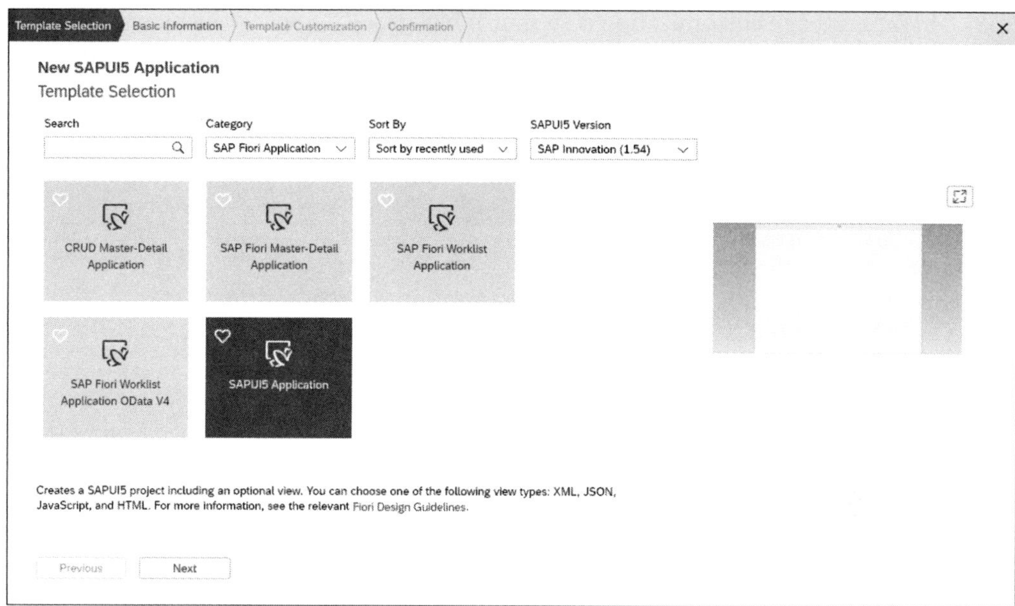

Figure 7.7 Creating a New SAPUI5 Application in the SAP Web IDE Full-Stack

On the next screen of the project creation wizard shown in Figure 7.8, provide the **Project Name** and the **Namespace** with which to prefix the SAPUI5 artifacts. Click **Next**.

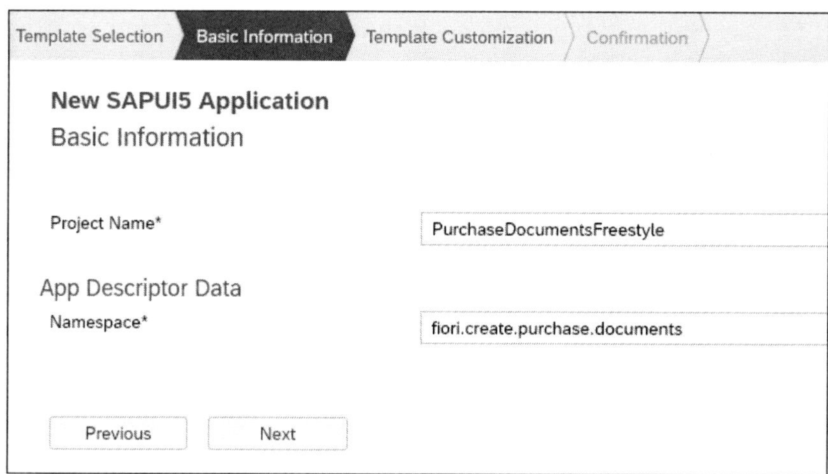

Figure 7.8 Providing a Project Name and Namespace for the Freestyle SAPUI5 Project

In the template customization step shown in Figure 7.9, specify the **View Type** and a **View Name** for the initial view. **XML** view type is the recommended view type for defining SAPUI5 views. For our example, let's call the initial view "CreatePurchase-Document." Click **Finish**.

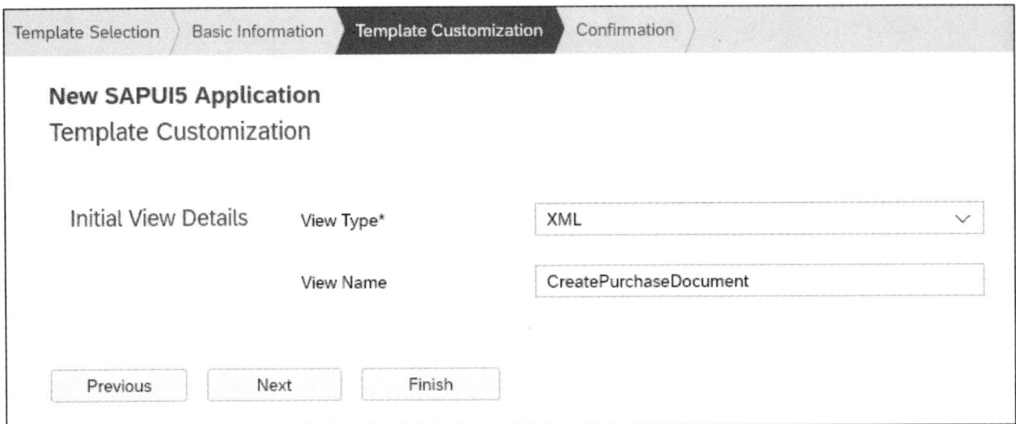

Figure 7.9 Selecting the View Type and Defining a View Name for the Initial View

To set up the connection to the backend OData service we developed in Chapter 4, open the app descriptor *manifest.json* file. The app descriptor is the central repository containing all application-relevant configurations, including the app's data sources, models, and routing settings. To enable the OData service, including its UI annotation model, for usage within the application, add the service to the data sources of the application, as shown in Figure 7.10. In general, you can edit the app descriptor in two ways: using the form-based descriptor editor or the JavaScript Object Notation (JSON)-based code editor. Use the descriptor editor and click on the OData service's **Add** (+) button.

A dialog wizard, shown in Figure 7.11, will open, where you'll configure the **Data Connection**. First, enter the SAP Gateway hub system where the service was registered. Then, choose the service by searching for it using the **Services** search field. When you've found and selected the service, click **Next**.

In the **Model Selection** step shown in Figure 7.12, provide the model name for the previously defined OData service connection or set it as the default model of the application. In our example, we want to set the data connection as the default model because it's the primary OData service of the application and therefore its default data source. Click **Next** and then **Finish**.

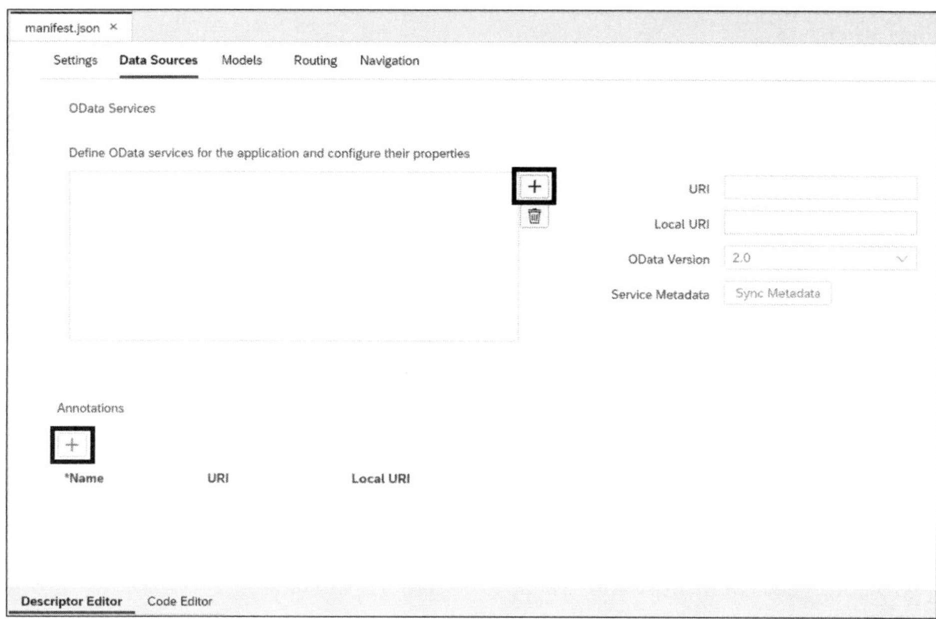

Figure 7.10 Descriptor Editor to Edit the App Descriptor manifest.json File's Data Sources

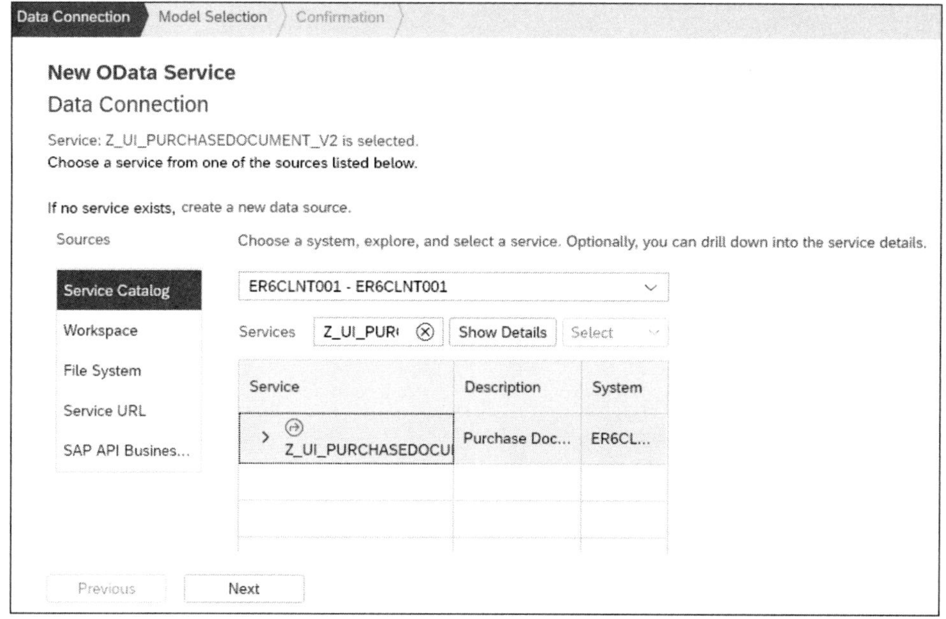

Figure 7.11 Selecting the OData Service to Add as a Data Source to the App Descriptor

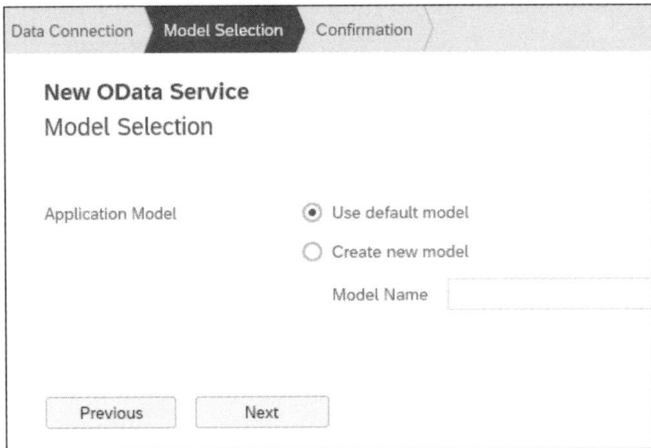

Figure 7.12 Setting the Previously Created Data Connection as the Default Model of the App

Now that the OData service has been selected and assigned to the default model, you'll configure the annotation source to enable the use of smart controls, as shown in Figure 7.13.

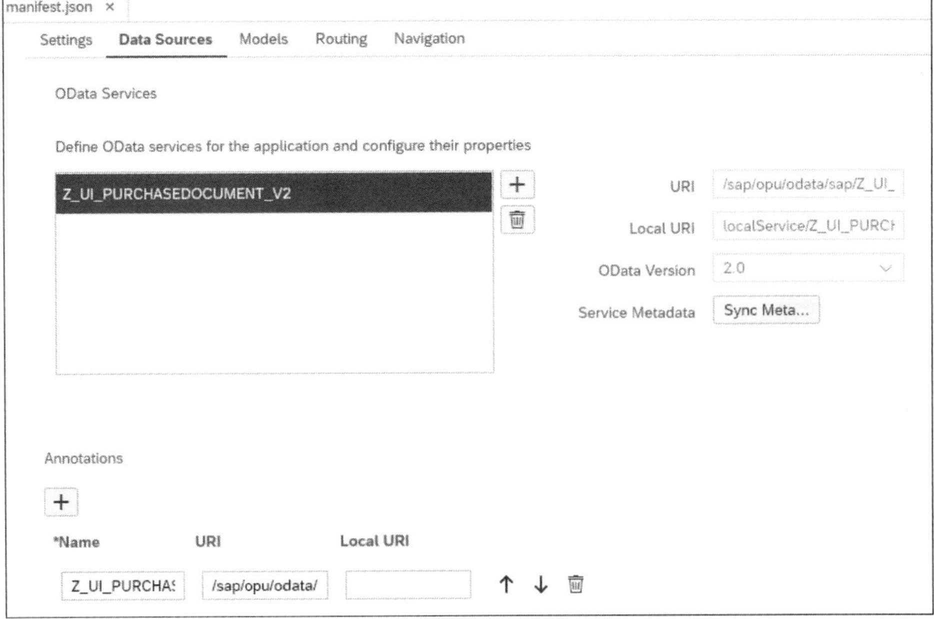

Figure 7.13 Added OData Service and Corresponding Annotation File

Click the **Add New Annotation** (+) button in the **Annotations** section of the screen, below the **OData Services** section. Let's call the annotation data source "Z_UI_PURCHASEDOCUMENT_V2_VAN" like the actual OData annotation model in the backend and set its **URI** to "/sap/opu/odata/IWFND/CATALOGSERVICE;v=2/Annotations(TechnicalName='Z_UI_PURCHASEDOCUMENT_V2_VAN',Version='0001')/$value/" because the annotations must be downloaded via the Catalog Service of the SAP Gateway hub system.

To write data back to the OData model and service, you'll need to set the binding mode of the model to *two-way*. Select the **Models** tab of the descriptor editor and then select **TwoWay** from the **Default Binding Mode** dropdown list, as shown in Figure 7.14.

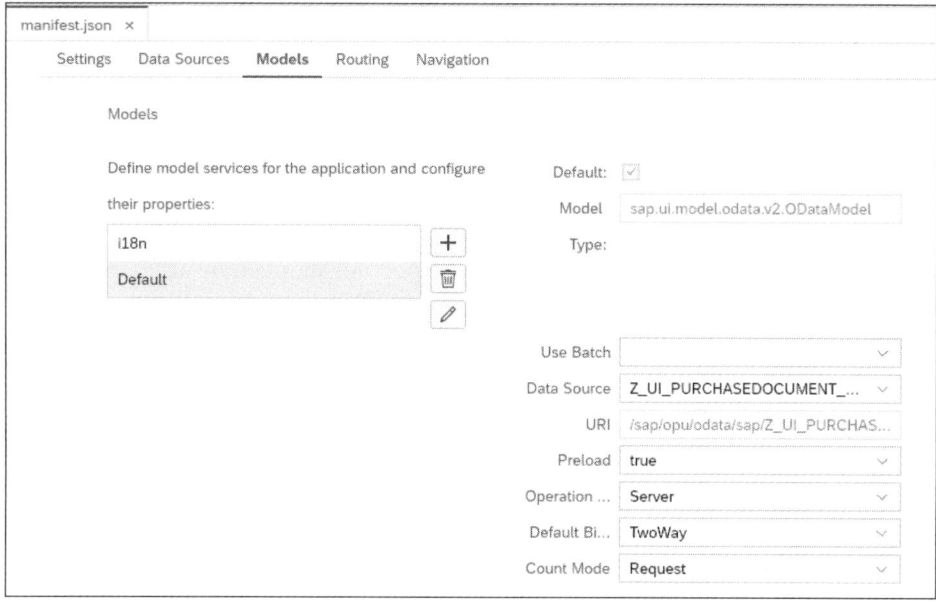

Figure 7.14 Setting the Default Model's Binding Mode to TwoWay

Figure 7.15 and Figure 7.16 summarize the changes made so far. Figure 7.15 shows the data sources of the application in the JSON code editor of the *manifest.json* app descriptor file. We've added the `Z_UI_PURCHASEDOCUMENT_V2` OData and `Z_UI_PURCHASEDOCUMENT_V2_VAN` annotations services as data sources to the app. The OData service references its UI annotations via the `annotations` property that points to the annotation service.

```
    "dataSources": {
        "Z_UI_PURCHASEDOCUMENT_V2": {
            "uri": "/sap/opu/odata/sap/Z_UI_PURCHASEDOCUMENT_V2/",
            "type": "OData",
            "settings": {
                "localUri": "localService/Z_UI_PURCHASEDOCUMENT_V2/metadata.xml",
                "annotations": ["Z_UI_PURCHASEDOCUMENT_V2_VAN"]
            }
        },
        "Z_UI_PURCHASEDOCUMENT_V2_VAN": {
            "uri": "/sap/opu/odata/IWFND/CATALOGSERVICE;v=2/Annotations(TechnicalName='Z_UI_PURCHASEDOCUMENT_V2_VAN',Version='0001')/$value/",
            "type": "ODataAnnotation",
            "settings": {
                "localUri": ""
            }
        }
    }
},
```

Figure 7.15 OData and OData Annotation Data Sources for the App in the App Descriptor Code Editor (manifest.json)

Figure 7.16 shows the models of the applications. The default model of the app references the `Z_UI_PURCHASEDOCUMENT_V2` OData service and configures the OData service using additional properties, for instance, the binding and count mode. The model that will be instantiated by the UI component file (*Component.js*) on app startup is an `sap.ui.model.odata.v2.ODataModel` model. The i18n model provides language-dependent texts stored locally in *i18n-*.properties* files, for instance, *i18n-en.properties* for English. Texts stored as properties in *i18n-*.properties* files can be accessed in XML views via the `i18n` model using relative bindings (`{i18n>PROPERTY}`). For simplicity, we'll hard-code the UI texts and not fetch them from language dependent *i18n-*.properties* files.

```
    "models": {
        "i18n": {
            "type": "sap.ui.model.resource.ResourceModel",
            "settings": {
                "bundleName": "fiori.create.purchase.documents.PurchaseDocumentsFreestyle.i18n.i18n"
            }
        },
        "": {
            "dataSource": "Z_UI_PURCHASEDOCUMENT_V2",
            "preload": true,
            "type": "sap.ui.model.odata.v2.ODataModel",
            "uri":"/sap/opu/odata/sap/Z_UI_PURCHASEDOCUMENT_V2/",
            "settings": {
                "defaultOperationMode": "Server",
                "defaultBindingMode": "TwoWay",
                "defaultCountMode": "Request"
            }
        }
    },
```

Figure 7.16 Default OData and i18n Models of the App in the App Descriptor Code Editor (manifest.json)

7.2.2 Object Creation Page Using SmartFields and Forms

Our app is now connected to an OData model, and you can start with the actual application development. Recall that, when we created the project in the previous section, the SAP Web IDE already created a view for us, which we called `CreatePurchaseDocument.view.xml`. As the next step, we'll need to insert a SmartForm for creating purchase documents into the currently empty view definition that contains several SmartFields for entering the initial data of a purchase document. Additionally, we'll add a save button to the footer of the page to trigger the submission of the purchase document to the backend OData service. The final SmartForm definition is shown in Figure 7.17. You'll need to set the `editable` attribute of the `SmartForm` to `true` to render `sap.m.Input` fields instead of `sap.m.Text` fields for the different `SmartFields`. You'll also set the `checkButton` attribute to `true` to enable the evaluation of the input data against the OData metadata of the relevant bound OData entity type property.

CreatePurchaseDocument.view.... ×

```
<mvc:View controllerName="fiori.create.pruchase.documents.PurchaseDocumentsFreestyle.controller.CreatePurchaseDocument"
    xmlns:html="http://www.w3.org/1999/xhtml" xmlns:mvc="sap.ui.core.mvc" displayBlock="true" xmlns="sap.m"
    xmlns:smartForm="sap.ui.comp.smartform" xmlns:smartField="sap.ui.comp.smartfield">
        <Page title="Create Purchase Document">
            <content>
                <smartForm:SmartForm editable="true" checkButton="true" id="createPurchaseDocumentSmartForm" title="Purchase Document">
                    <smartForm:layout>
                        <smartForm:Layout emptySpanL="1" emptySpanM="0" labelSpanL="3" labelSpanM="3"/>
                    </smartForm:layout>
                    <smartForm:Group id="createPurchaseDocumentSmartFormGroup">
                        <smartForm:GroupElement id="descriptionSmartFormGroupElement">
                            <smartField:SmartField value="{Description}" id="descriptionSmartField"/>
                        </smartForm:GroupElement>
                        <smartForm:GroupElement id="prioritySmartFormGroupElement">
                            <smartField:SmartField value="{Priority}" id="prioritySmartField" />
                        </smartForm:GroupElement>
                        <smartForm:GroupElement id="purchasingOrganizationSmartFormGroupElement">
                            <smartField:SmartField value="{PurchasingOrganization}" id="purchasingOrganizationSmartField" />
                        </smartForm:GroupElement>
                        <smartForm:GroupElement id="purchasingDocumentImageURLSmartFormGroupElement">
                            <smartField:SmartField value="{PurchaseDocumentImageURL}" id="purchasingDocumentImageURLSmartField" />
                        </smartForm:GroupElement>
                    </smartForm:Group>
                </smartForm:SmartForm>
            </content>
            <footer>
                <OverflowToolbar>
                    <ToolbarSpacer/>
                    <Button type="Default" text="Navigate to List" press="onNavToList"/>
                    <Button type="Emphasized" text="Save" press="onSave" id="savePurchaseDocumentButton"/>
                </OverflowToolbar>
            </footer>
        </Page>
</mvc:View>
```

Figure 7.17 SmartForm Definition for Creating a Purchase Document

Inside the `SmartForm`, you can only define one `Group` without a `label`, but you can add several `GroupElement` controls, including `SmartFields` to the `Group`'s default `groupElements` aggregation. More specifically, you'll add SmartFields fields for the PurchaseDocument ID, Description, Priority, PurchasingOrganization, and PurchaseDocumentImageURL properties of the Z_C_PurchaseDocumentLRP OData entity and bind their values to the respective value attribute of the SmartField control.

However, to render the UI based on OData metadata and UI annotations, the SmartForm and its child controls require bindings to OData entity properties to obtain their metadata information. The binding to a newly created purchase document entity can be established via the respective view controller. When the initial *CreatePurchaseDocument.view.xml* file was created by the SAP Web IDE, a corresponding *CreatePurchaseDocument.controller.js* file was also generated to serve as the controller of this view. As we've added the OData service as the default model to the app descriptor, the sap.ui.model.odata.v2.ODataModel will be instantiated automatically by the SAPUI5 framework. Automatically instantiated models can be retrieved in controllers by calling this.getView().getModel(). Having to retrieve a model from a controller happens quite frequently, so moving this functionality to a BaseController.js module from which other view controllers inherit, as shown in Listing 7.8, makes sense. You can then get the OData model inside view controllers by simply calling this.getModel().

```
sap.ui.define([
    "sap/ui/core/mvc/Controller"
], function (Controller) {
"use strict";
return Controller.extend("…/BaseController", {
 …
 getModel: function (sName) {
  var oModel = this.getView().getModel(sName);
  if (!oModel) {
   oModel = this.getOwnerComponent().getModel(sName);
  }
  return oModel;
 }
 …
 });
});
```

Listing 7.8 BaseController.js Module Containing a Convenience getModel Method for Retrieving the View's Model inside the View Controller

Creating a new empty purchase document in the controller and binding it to the view is shown in Listing 7.9. In the `onInit` method of the `CreatePurchaseDocument` controller, you'll attach to the route-matched event, which is fired every time the `CreatePurchaseDocument` route is displayed (more specifically, whenever the URL hash matches the pattern defined for the route). When the event is fired, the `_createPurchaseDocument` callback function is called. Inside the function, you'll wait until the `metdataLoaded` promise is resolved, and if the model has no pending changes, you'll create a new purchase document entity by calling the `createEntry` method of the OData model with the entity set name `PurchaseDocument` as a parameter. The new purchase document isn't immediately sent to the backend, but instead a request is stored in a request queue so that we can later manually sent it to the backend when we have finished editing the document.

```
sap.ui.define([
    ".../BaseController"
], function (BaseController) {
"use strict";
 return BaseController.extend(".../CreatePurchaseDocument",
 {
  onInit: function () {
   this.getRouter().getRoute("CreatePurchaseDocument").
   attachMatched(this._createPurchaseDocument, this);
  },

  _createPurchaseDocument: function () {
   this.getModel().metadataLoaded().then(function () {
    if (!this.getModel().hasPendingChanges()) {
     var oPurchaseDocumentBindingContext =
     this.getModel().createEntry("/PurchaseDocument ");
     this.getView().bindElement(oPurchaseDocumentBindingContext.getPath());
    }
   }.bind(this));
  }
 });
});
```

Listing 7.9 Create a New Purchase Document Entry and Bind It to the View

To run the app from the **Files** pane in the SAP Web IDE full-stack, simply right-click on the root folder of the app and choose **Run • Run As • Web Application** from its context menu. At runtime, the **Create Purchase Document** view will resemble the screen shown in Figure 7.18.

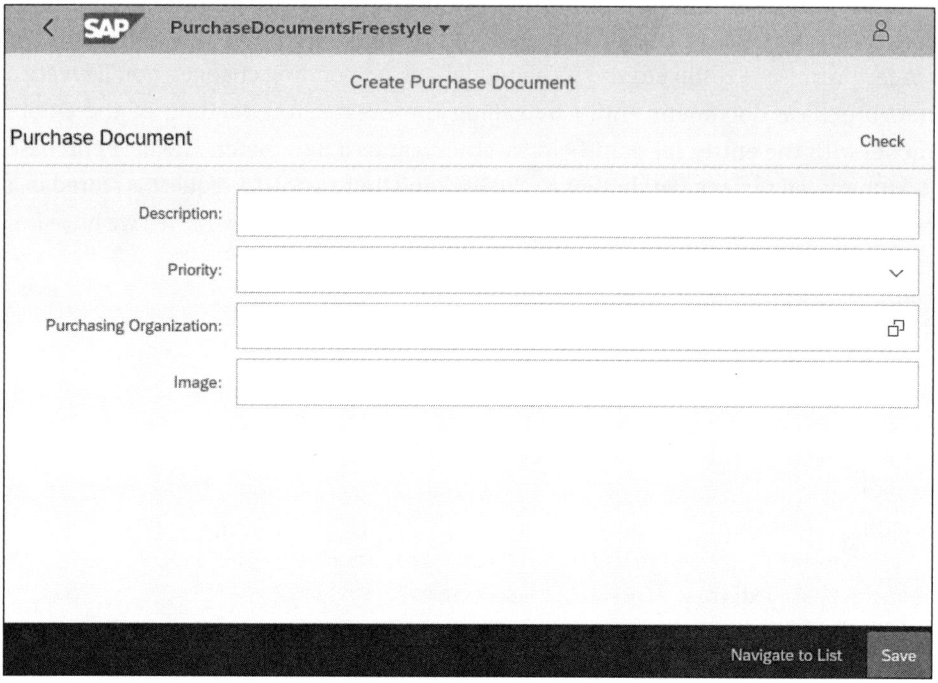

Figure 7.18 Create Purchase Document View at Runtime

Finally, to send the newly created purchase document entity to the backend when the **Save** button is clicked and its onSave event handler function is triggered inside the controller, you must call the submitChanges method of the sap.ui.model.odata.v2.ODataModel instance as shown in Listing 7.10. Its parameter object contains a success callback function that is called on success and an error callback function that is called on error. If submitting the changes to the backend was successful, you'll also unbind the entity from the view so that you can create and bind a new entity.

```
sap.ui.define([
    "./BaseController"
], function (BaseController) {
"use strict";
```

```
return BaseController.extend("...CreatePurchaseDocument",
{
 onSave: function () {
  ...
  this.getModel().submitChanges({
   success: function () {
   this.getView().unbindElement();
   }.bind(this),
   error: function () {...}.bind(this)
  });
 ...
 }
 });
});
```

Listing 7.10 Submit the Collected Changes to the Backend in the onSave Method of the CreatePurchaseDocument.controller.js Module

Before submitting the new purchase document to the backend, you should first evaluate its values against the metadata of the service to detect any obvious client errors by calling the SmartForm's `check` method. As shown in Listing 7.11, we must first fetch the SmartForm instance by its ID and then call its `check` method. The check method then returns an array of fields having errors in relation to the fields' OData metadata, for instance, the field is too long (`MaxLength`) or is an empty mandatory field (`Nullable="false"`).

```
onSave: function () {
var oSmartForm = this.getView().byId("createPurchaseDocumentSmartForm");
 var aSmartFieldsWithErrors = oSmartForm.check();
 if (aSmartFieldsWithErrors.length !== 0) {
  return;
 }
 ...
}
```

Listing 7.11 Call the SmartForm's Check Method to Check for Client Errors before Submitting Changes to the Backend

After submitting a newly created purchase document to the backend, you'll need to navigate to a new view that will display all purchase documents created so far. To display and filter the purchase documents, you'll use a smart table and smart filter bar control. For the moment, let's create a new empty view called DisplayPurchase-Documents.view.xml. You'll first need to set up the navigation between the CreatePurchaseDocument.view.xml and the DisplayPurchaseDocuments.view.xml view before implementing the view definition. Additionally, you'll create another view called App.view.xml that will serve as the root view of the application, as shown in Listing 7.12. Inside the view, you'll only put a single sap.m.App control with the ID app as the root container for all the views.

Other views will then be dynamically inserted into the pages aggregation of the instantiated sap.m.App control at runtime. The sap.m.App control inherits its navigation capabilities from the sap.m.NavContainer and additionally adds some header tags to the HTML page that are considered useful for mobile applications.

```
<mvc:View xmlns="sap.m" xmlns:mvc="sap.ui.core.mvc" displayBlock="true" >
 <App id="app" busy="{app>/isBusy}" busyIndicatorDelay="0"/>
</mvc:View>
```

Listing 7.12 Root View of the Application

The navigation routes and targets of the application are defined in the sap.ui5 namespace of the app descriptor *manifest.json* file. However, the first thing you must do now is to make the newly created App.view.xml the root view of the application. Figure 7.19 shows how the App.view.xml can be defined as the root view of the application inside the *manifest.json* app descriptor file.

```
"sap.ui5": {
    "rootView": {
        "viewName": "fiori.create.pruchase.documents.PurchaseDocumentsFreestyle.view.App",
        "type": "XML",
        "async": true,
        "id": "app"
    },
```

Figure 7.19 Defining the Root View of the Application in the App Descriptor manifest.json File

The navigation configuration for our application is shown in Figure 7.20. In the config object of the routing configuration, define some default configuration relevant for routes and targets, for instance, the viewType or transition. The controlId and controllAggregation properties are relevant for sap.m.routing.Targets and define that new views accessed using navigation will be inserted into the `pages` aggregation of the `sap.m.App` container control inside the root view (`App.view.xml`) with the ID `app`. The `CreatePurchaseDocument` route is mapped to the `CreatePurchaseDocument` view via the `CreatePurchaseDocument` target. The `pattern` of the route is empty because it's the start page of the application. The `DisplayPurchaseDocuments` route is mapped to the `DisplayPurchaseDocuments` view via the `DisplayPurchaseDocuments` target.

```
"routing": {
    "config": {
        "routerClass": "sap.m.routing.Router",
        "viewType": "XML",
        "viewPath": "fiori.create.purchase.documents.PurchaseDocumentsFreestyle.view",
        "controlId": "app",
        "controlAggregation": "pages",
        "transition": "show",
        "async": true
    },
    "routes": [{
        "name": "CreatePurchaseDocument",
        "pattern": "",
        "target": "CreatePurchaseDocument"
    }, {
        "name": "DisplayPurchaseDocuments",
        "pattern": "DisplayPurchaseDocuments",
        "target": "DisplayPurchaseDocuments"
    }],
    "targets": {
        "CreatePurchaseDocument": {
            "viewName": "CreatePurchaseDocument"
        },
        "DisplayPurchaseDocuments": {
            "viewName": "DisplayPurchaseDocuments"
        }
    }
}
```

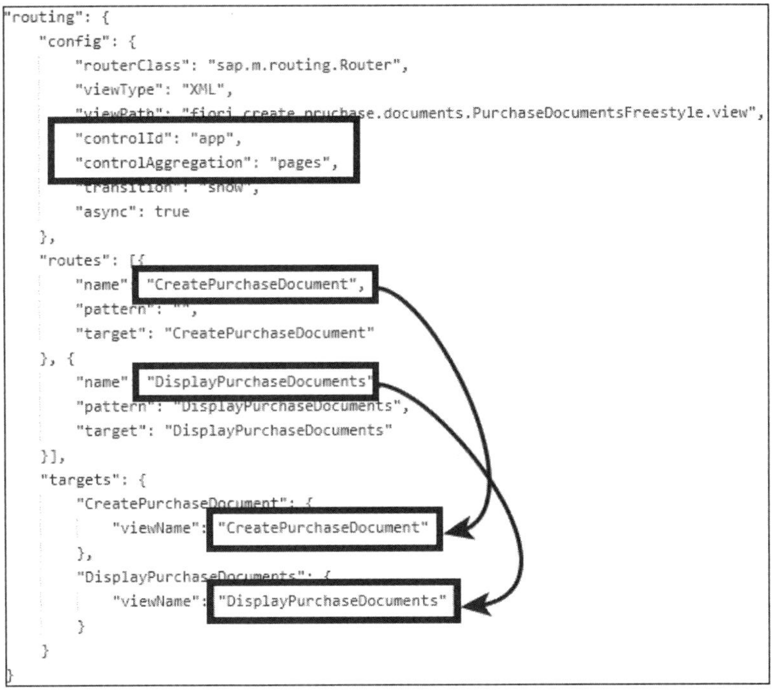

Figure 7.20 Mapping from Routes to Target Views in the App Descriptor manifest.json File

You can directly navigate to the `DisplayPurchaseDocuments` view by appending the fragment identifier `#/DisplayPurchaseDocuments` to the application URL as its route `pattern` is `DisplayPurchaseDocuments`.

To programmatically navigate in controllers from one view to another, you first must retrieve an instance of the `sap.m.routing.Router` defined in the app descriptor *manifest.json* file, which can be achieved inside a controller, as shown in Listing 7.13. We'll define a new convenience function in the base controller from which all other controllers inherit since most controllers will need this functionality.

```
sap.ui.define([
    "sap/ui/core/mvc/Controller"
], function (Controller) {
"use strict";
 return Controller.extend("../BaseController", {
 ...
  getRouter: function () {
   return sap.ui.core.UIComponent.getRouterFor(this);
  }
 ...
 });
});
```

Listing 7.13 Function Definition for Obtaining an Automatically Instantiated sap.m.routing.Router Instance via the sap.ui.core.UIComponent

To navigate from the create view to the display view after the new purchase document has been submitted to the backend, you'll simply execute the code shown in Listing 7.14. The route name of the view you want to navigate to (DisplayPurchaseDocuments) is simply passed as a parameter to the navTo function of the sap.m.routing.Router object.

```
this.getRouter().navTo("DisplayPurchaseDocuments");
```

Listing 7.14 Navigate from the Create View to the Display View

This navigation is triggered inside the success callback of the submitChanges call shown earlier in Listing 7.10.

7.2.3 List Report Page Using Smart Table and Filter Bar

So far, we haven't defined the content of the DisplayPurchaseDocuments.view.xml, which is our next step. As mentioned earlier, our goal is to display all available purchase documents in a table and enable filtering. Thus, we'll use a smart table to display the purchase documents and a smart filter bar to filter the table data. Figure 7.21 shows the view definition containing a smart filter bar and smart table. Both controls are bound to the PurchaseDocument entity set, and the smart table and filter bar are connected by the smart filter bar ID purchaseDocumentsSmartFilterBar.

DisplayPurchaseDocuments.vie... ×

```
<mvc:View xmlns:html="http://www.w3.org/1999/xhtml" xmlns:mvc="sap.ui.core.mvc" displayBlock="true" xmlns="sap.m"
    xmlns:smartFilterBar="sap.ui.comp.smartfilterbar" xmlns:smartTable="sap.ui.comp.smarttable"
    controllerName="fiori.create.pruchase.documents.PurchaseDocumentsFreestyle.controller.DisplayPurchaseDocuments">
    <Page title="Display Purchase Documents" showNavButton="true" navButtonPress="onNavBack">
        <content>
            <smartFilterBar:SmartFilterBar id="purchaseDocumentsSmartFilterBar" entitySet="PurchaseDocument"
                persistencyKey="purchaseDocumentsFilterBarKey" enableBasicSearch="true"/>
            <smartTable:SmartTable entitySet="PurchaseDocument" header="Purchase Documents" smartFilterId="purchaseDocumentsSmartFilterBar"
                enableAutoBinding="true" tableType="ResponsiveTable" persistencyKey="purchaseDocumentsFilterBarKey" demandPopin="true"
                id="purchaseDocumentsSmartTable"/>
        </content>
    </Page>
</mvc:View>
```

Figure 7.21 Definition of the DisplayPurchaseDocuments.view.xml View Containing a Smart Table and Filter Bar Control

If you run the app now and create a purchase document, you should automatically be forwarded to the **Display Purchase Documents** view, which will display all available purchase documents in a smart table, as shown in Figure 7.22. To create purchase document items, you could simply navigate to the created object page (discussed throughout Chapter 4) by clicking on the **Purchase Documents Manage** link. From the object page, you could add items to the purchase document.

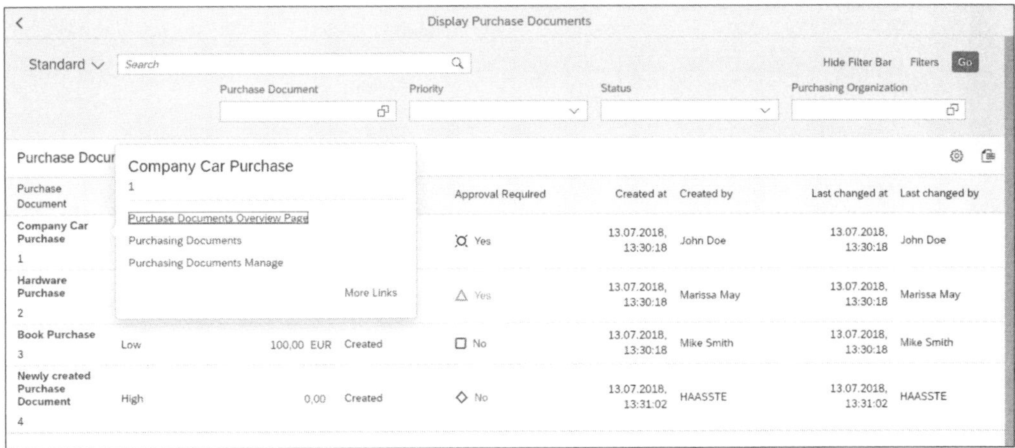

Figure 7.22 Display Purchase Documents View at Runtime

7.2.4 Add a One-Page Acceptance Integration Test

To test and safeguard the creation and display of purchase documents with the application, including the navigation between the create and display views, you should write a UI integration test, with the help of the One-Page Acceptance (OPA5) test for the SAPUI5 framework, which is part of the SAPUI5 SDK. This framework provides an API for SAPUI5 controls and eases testing user interactions and navigations by hiding asynchronicity. OPA5 can be used with any JavaScript unit test framework, but, in our case, we'll use QUnit as the basic test runner and unit test framework. You can easily set up a default test structure for an SAPUI5 application project in the SAP Web IDE full-stack by right-clicking on the project root folder and choosing **New • Test Structure**, as shown in Figure 7.23.

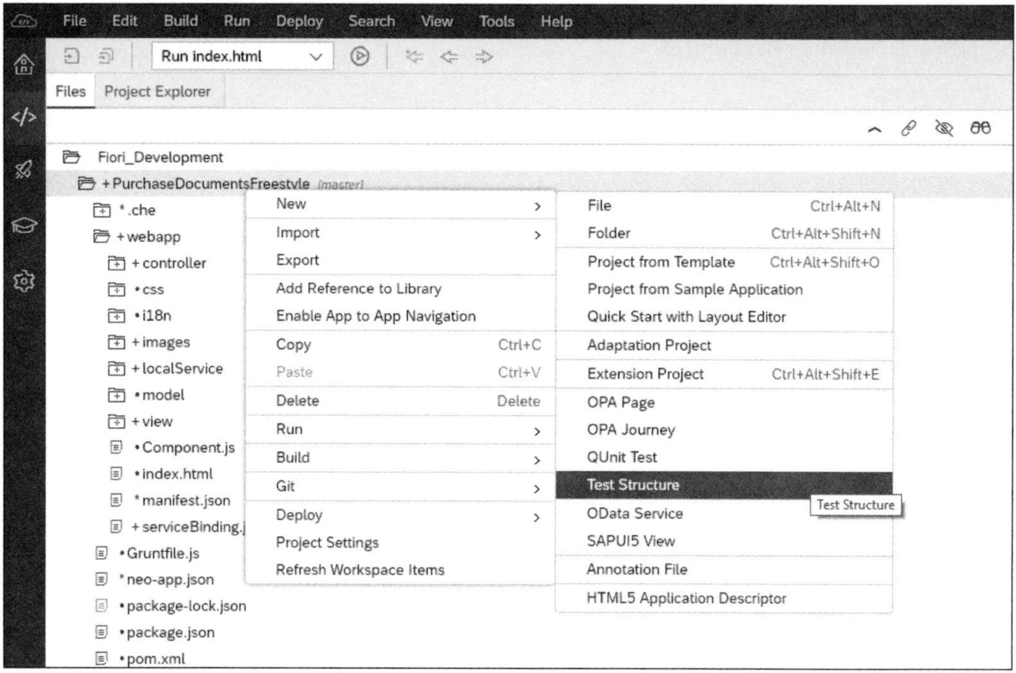

Figure 7.23 Creating a Test Structure for an SAPUI5 Application Project in the SAP Web IDE Full-Stack

A *test* folder with *unit* and *integration* test subfolders will be generated. The *unit* subfolder will contain QUnit test skeletons, and the *integration* subfolder will contain OPA5 integration test skeletons. The generated structure is shown in Figure 7.24. We'll ignore unit testing for now and focus on UI integration testing in the following section. The SAP Web IDE has also generated a default OPA5 journey (`navigationJourney.js`), which we'll also ignore and delete because we'll create our own journey.

Nevertheless, getting this test structure generated is quite convenient; for instance, we now have a test runner (`opaTests.qunit.html`) for running the OPA5 journeys we'll develop and a module collecting all our journeys (`AllJourneys.js`). We'll later adapt the files contained in the *pages* folder to our specific needs. OPA5 tests are organized in *journeys* and *pages*. A journey contains all test cases for a specific use case and structures its test cases according to high-level given-when-then sentences hiding the actual test case implementation. Journeys use pages that implement the necessary arrangements, actions, and assertions used within the high-level journey definition and are usually related to a single view.

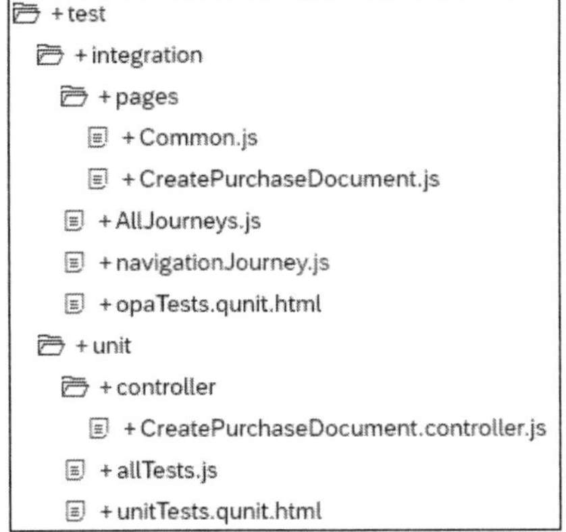

Figure 7.24 Generated Test Structure for the SAPUI5 Application Project

Setting Up a Mock Server

When testing the purchase document creation, navigation, and display process in the UI, you should use a mock server because you don't want to depend on any backend OData service or data being available. The mock server will intercept the OData requests the application sends to the backend and return local mock data instead. The mock server supports create, read, update, and delete (CRUD) requests and stores changes locally during a session. To set up a mock server, create a `mockserver.js` module in the *localService* folder of the project where you'll set up and configure the server. Listing 7.15 shows how you can instantiate the mock server with the root URI of the OData service and simulate the service by specifying the local service metadata document (*metadata.xml*) and the base folder for mock data (*mockdata*). By setting the `bGenerateMissingMockData` property to `true`, the mock server will automatically generate mock data for entities that don't have dedicated mock data in the *mockdata* folder.

```
sap.ui.define([
"sap/ui/core/util/MockServer"
], function (MockServer) {
"use strict";
 return {

  init: function () {
   var oMockServer = new MockServer({
    rootUri: "/sap/opu/odata/sap/ Z_UI_PURCHASEDOCUMENT_V2/"
   });

   oMockServer.simulate("../localService/metadata.xml", {
    sMockdataBaseUrl: "../localService/mockdata",
    bGenerateMissingMockData: true
   });

   oMockServer.start();
  }
 };
});
```

Listing 7.15 Instantiating the sap.ui.core.util.MockServer with the OData Service's Root URI and Simulating the OData Service by Specifying the Metadata XML File and the Base Folder of the Mock Data

Create Mock Data

You can easily create proper mock data for entities by right-clicking on the local *metadata.xml* file in the *localService* folder and choosing **Edit Mock Data**. The **Edit Mock Data** dialog box, shown in Figure 7.25, will open where you'll select entities in the **Entity Sets** pane and create mock data by clicking on the **Add Row** button in the upper-right corner.

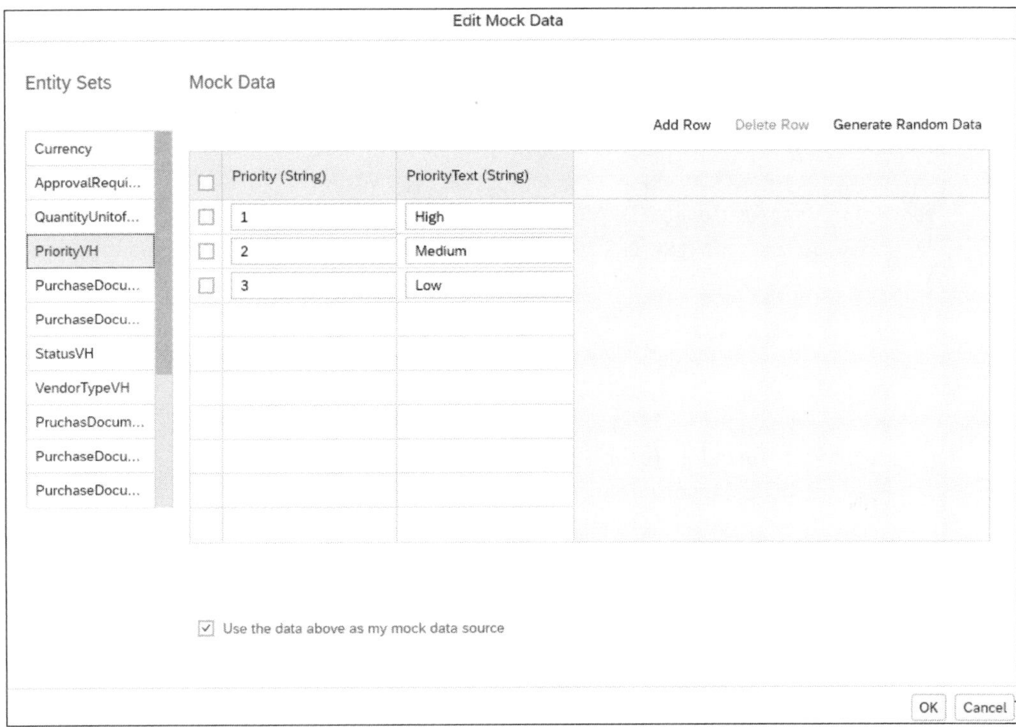

Figure 7.25 Creating Mock Data for the OData Service Defined in the Local Service Metadata Document (metadata.xml)

After you click **OK**, mock data JSON files will be created in the *mockdata* folder containing the previously defined data, as shown in Figure 7.26.

localService
mockdata
PriorityVH.json
PurchaseDocument.json
PurchasingOrganization.json
StatusVH.json

Figure 7.26 Created Mock Data JSON Files

Because you're using smart controls, the application also heavily depends on the UI annotation model for rendering the controls. To completely isolate the application from the backend, you also must mock the Catalog Service, which is providing the UI annotation model of the OData service, as shown in Listing 7.16. For the UI annotation mock server, you'll define an additional request, matching all GET requests sent to the service that will simply return the local annotation file *Z_C_PURCHASEDOCUMENTLRP_CDS_VAN.xml*.

```
...
var oAnnotationMockServer = new MockServer({
rootUri: "/sap/opu/odata/IWFND/CATALOGSERVICE;v=2/Annotations(TechnicalName=
'Z_C_PURCHASEDOCUMENTLRP_CDS_VAN',Version='0001')/$value/"
});

oAnnotationMockServer.setRequests([{
    method: "GET",
    path: new RegExp(".*"),
    response: function (oXhr) {
        var oLocalAnnotations = jQuery.sap.sjax({
            url: sAnnotationURL,
            datatype: "XML"
        }).data;
        oXhr.respondXML(200, {}, jQuery.sap.serializeXML
            (../localService/Z_UI_PURCHASEDOCUMENT_V2_VAN.xml));
        return true;
}
}]);

oAnnotationMockServer.start();
...
```

Listing 7.16 Create Local Mock Server for the UI Annotations

Note

To update the local metadata file in the SAP Web IDE full-stack, simply right-click on the file and choose **Sync Metadata**.

Creating an OPA5 UI Integration Test

The journey we want to implement and test is shown in Listing 7.17 and should almost read like a manual test case description or user story. This approach is called *behavior-driven development (BDD)*. The general idea behind BDD is that requirements are defined in the form of high-level given-when-then sentences and later executed as automated tests, which eases the definition of requirements and test scenarios by nontechnical stakeholders. With our journey, we'll test the creation, saving, and correct display in the smart table of the purchase document after the automatic navigation to the display view took place.

```
sap.ui.define([
    "sap/ui/test/opaQunit"
], function (opaTest) {
"use strict";

QUnit.module("Create Purchase Document Journey");

opaTest("Should see the newly created Purchase Document in the Smart Table",
    function (Given, When, Then) {

    Given.iStartTheApp();

    var oPurchaseDocument = {
        Description: "OPA5 Test Description",
        Priority: "1",
        PurchasingOrganization: "ORG1",
        PurchaseDocumentImageURL: "../images/book.jpg"
    };

    When.onTheCreatePurchaseDocumentPage
    .iEnterPurchaseDocumentData(oPurchaseDocument)
    .and
    .iSavePurchaseDocument();

    Then.onTheDisplayPurchaseDocumentsPage
    .iCheckPurchaseDocumentIsInTable(oPurchaseDocument)
    .and.iTeardownMyUIComponent();
    });
});
```

Listing 7.17 An OPA5 Journey for Creating and Displaying a Purchase Document (createPurchaseDocumentJourney.js)

The Given object provided as a parameter to the opaTest function contains the arrangements of all loaded pages, the When object in turn contains all actions, and the Then object contains all assertions. In our journey, we're calling one arrangement method (iStartTheApp), which will start the app's UI component (Component.js) and the mock servers defined in the mockserver.js module by calling its init method. The arrangement is implemented in the Common.js module, which serves as the base class for all the page objects we'll implement, as shown in Figure 7.27.

Common.js ×

```
sap.ui.define([
    "sap/ui/test/Opa5",
    "fiori/create/pruchase/documents/PurchaseDocumentsFreestyle/localService/mockserver"
], function (Opa5, mockserver) {
    "use strict";

    return Opa5.extend("fiori.create.pruchase.documents.PurchaseDocumentsFreestyle.test.integration.pages.Common", {
        iStartTheApp: function (oOptions) {
            mockserver.init();

            this.iStartMyUIComponent({
                componentConfig: {
                    name: "fiori.create.pruchase.documents.PurchaseDocumentsFreestyle"
                }
            });
        }
    });
});
```

Figure 7.27 Common.js Base Object for OPA5 Pages Containing the iStartApp Arrangement

The iEnterPurchaseDocumentData and iSavePurchaseDocument actions are implemented in the CreatePurchaseDocument.js page. Figure 7.28 shows some of the implementation of the iEnterPurchaseDocumentData action. We're using the waitFor method of sap.ui.test.Opa5 to wait until the control we want to select using its view and SmartField ID has been rendered. As soon as the control is selected, we're calling the predefined sap.ui.test.actions.EnterText action to enter text into the input fields, which will enable us to fill out the purchase document creation form.

After you've filled out the form, the iSavePurchaseDocument action will be called from the createPurchaseDocumentJourney.js journey. In this action, shown in Listing 7.18, simply click the **Save** button using the predefined sap.ui.test.actions.Press action as soon as the button has been found by its ID inside the CreatePurchaseDocument view.

```
CreatePurchaseDocument.js ×
sap.ui.define([
    "sap/ui/test/Opa5",
    "fiori/create/pruchase/documents/PurchaseDocumentsFreestyle/test/integration/pages/Common",
    "sap/ui/test/actions/Press",
    "sap/ui/test/actions/EnterText",
    "sap/ui/test/matchers/Ancestor",
    "sap/ui/test/matchers/Properties"
], function (Opa5, Common, Press, EnterText, Ancestor, Properties) {
    "use strict";
    var sCreatePurchaseDocumentView = "CreatePurchaseDocument";
    Opa5.createPageObjects({
        onTheCreatePurchaseDocumentPage: {
            baseClass: Common,
            actions: {
                iEnterPurchaseDocumentData: function (oPurchaseDocument) {
                    // Enter Description
                    this.waitFor({
                        viewName: sCreatePurchaseDocumentView,
                        id: "descriptionSmartField",
                        actions: new EnterText({
                            text: oPurchaseDocument.Description
                        })
                    });
                    // Choose Priority
                    this.waitFor({
                        viewName: sCreatePurchaseDocumentView,
                        id: "prioritySmartField",
                        matchers: [
                            function (oPrioritySmartFIeld) {
                                return oPrioritySmartFIeld.getInnerControls()[0];
                            }
                        ],
                        actions: new Press(),
                        success: function (oComboBox) {
                            oComboBox.setSelectedKey(oPurchaseDocument.Priority);
                        },
                        errorMessage: "Could not find Priority Smart Field"
                    });
```

Figure 7.28 The CreatePurchaseDocument.js OPA5 Page Object Containing the iEnterPurchaseDocumentData Action

```
iSavePurchaseDocument: function () {
 // Press Save Button
 return this.waitFor({
  viewName: sCreatePurchaseDocumentView,
  id: "savePurchaseDocumentButton",
  actions: new Press()
 });
}
```

Listing 7.18 iSavePurchaseDocument Action also Implemented in the CreatePurchaseDocument.js OPA5 Page Object

For the `iCheckPurchaseDocumentIsInTable` assertion, checking the presence of the newly created purchase document in the smart table, we'll create a new page called `DisplayPurchaseDocuments.js` as the assertion logically belongs to the `DisplayPurchaseDocuments.view.xml`. In the assertion shown in Figure 7.29, the smart table is first selected by its view and ID. On top of that, two custom matchers are implemented to find the newly created purchase document inside the smart table.

DisplayPurchaseDocuments.js ×

```
sap.ui.define([
    "sap/ui/test/Opa5",
    "fiori/create/pruchase/documents/PurchaseDocumentsFreestyle/test/integration/pages/Common"
], function (Opa5, Common) {
    "use strict";

    function purchaseDocumentsAreEqual(oExpectedPurchDoc, oActualPurchDoc) {
        return oExpectedPurchDoc.Description === oActualPurchDoc.Description &&
            oExpectedPurchDoc.Priority === oActualPurchDoc.Priority &&
            oExpectedPurchDoc.PurchasingOrganization === oActualPurchDoc.PurchasingOrganization &&
            oExpectedPurchDoc.PurchaseDocumentImageURL === oActualPurchDoc.PurchaseDocumentImageURL;
    }

    Opa5.createPageObjects({
        onTheDisplayPurchaseDocumentsPage: {
            baseClass: Common,
            actions: {},
            assertions: {
                iCheckPurchaseDocumentIsInTable: function (oPurchaseDocument) {
                    return this.waitFor({
                        viewName: "DisplayPurchaseDocuments",
                        id: "purchaseDocumentsSmartTable",
                        matchers: [function (oSmartTable) {
                            return oSmartTable.getTable();
                        }, function (oTable) {
                            return oTable.getItems().some(function (oItem) {
                                var oPurchaseDocumentTableEntry = oItem.getBindingContext().getObject();
                                return purchaseDocumentsAreEqual(oPurchaseDocument, oPurchaseDocumentTableEntry);
                            });
                        }],
                        success: function () {
                            Opa5.assert.ok("true", "New Purchase Document is displayed in the Smart Table");
                        },
                        errorMessage: "Could not find the new Purchase Document in the Smart Table"
                    });

                }
            }
        }
    });
});
```

Figure 7.29 Assertion (iCheckPurchaseDocumentIsInTable) Checking the Display of the Newly Created Purchase Document in the Smart Table on the DisplayPurchaseDocuments View

The first matcher function extracts the table contained inside the smart table; in our case, this extracted table will be an `sap.m.Table`. The second matcher function fetches the items of the table and iterates over them using the JavaScript `some` function, which checks whether any element in an array fulfills a certain condition. We'll return `true` in the callback function if one purchase document table item is equal to the expected purchase document. We can check the equality of the actual and expected purchase document by using a naïve comparison function (`purchaseDocumentsAreEqual`) that simply compares the purchase document properties used for creation of two purchase document objects. If the second matcher returns `true`, the `success` function will be called, and the test is executed successfully. If a time out occurs because the purchase document isn't found, the `errorMessage` property will be displayed, and the test will fail.

When we created the test structure for our project, the SAP Web IDE full-stack had created an *AllJourneys.js* module file and an *opaTests.qunit.html* file for loading and executing the OPA5 integration tests. To run the new integration tests, we must load our journey (`createPurchaseDocumentJourney`) and the corresponding pages (`CreatePurchaseDocument` and `DisplayPurchaseDocuments`) inside the *AllJourneys.js* module file shown in Figure 7.30. Using the *opaTests.qunit.html* file, we can then directly execute the journey because it's already loading the *AllJourneys.js* module file. Run the tests by right-clicking on the *opaTests.qunit.html* file and selecting **Run • Run As • Web Application**.

AllJourneys.js ×

```
/* global QUnit*/
sap.ui.define([
    "sap/ui/test/Opa5",
    "fiori/create/pruchase/documents/PurchaseDocumentsFreestyle/test/integration/pages/Common",
    "sap/ui/test/opaQunit",
    "fiori/create/pruchase/documents/PurchaseDocumentsFreestyle/test/integration/pages/CreatePurchaseDocument",
    "fiori/create/pruchase/documents/PurchaseDocumentsFreestyle/test/integration/pages/DisplayPurchaseDocuments",
    "fiori/create/pruchase/documents/PurchaseDocumentsFreestyle/test/integration/createPurchaseDocumentJourney"
], function (Opa5, Common) {
    "use strict";
    Opa5.extendConfig({
        arrangements: new Common(),
        viewNamespace: "fiori.create.pruchase.documents.PurchaseDocumentsFreestyle.view.",
        autoWait: true
    });
});
```

Figure 7.30 AllJourneys.js Module: Central Module for Loading All OPA5 Journeys and Pages Needed for Testing the App

Similar to the QUnit unit tests, the *opaTests.qunit.html* file is a QUnit runner and executes all integration tests defined in the *AllJourneys.js* module file, as shown in Figure 7.31. Additionally, this file displays its result in a readable format as a web page.

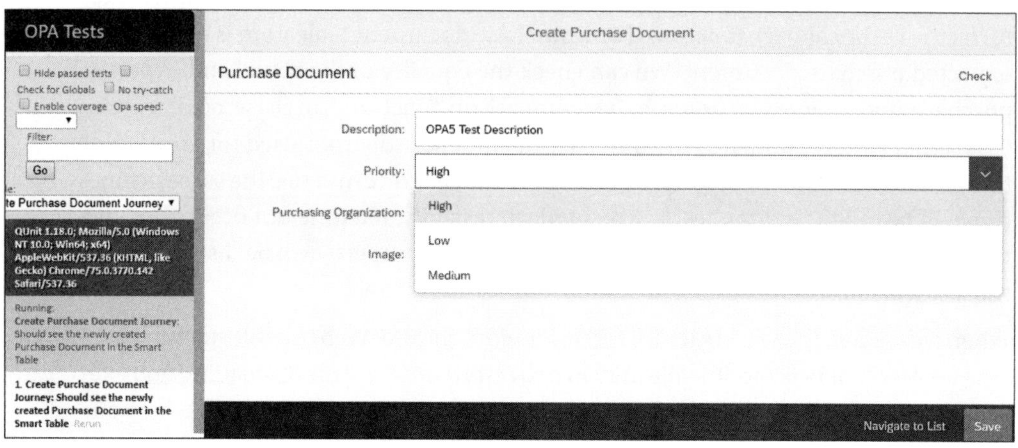

Figure 7.31 Running the OPA5 Test Using the opaTests.qunit.html File as a QUnit Test Runner

7.3 Summary

In this chapter, you learned about the most common smart controls: SmartField, smart link, SmartForm, smart table, and smart filter bar. We discussed the annotations they analyze to adapt their appearance and how they significantly reduce the amount of required frontend SAPUI5 XML and JavaScript code by still providing flexibility in terms of the overall layout and design of the application. We demonstrated all the smart controls described in this chapter by developing a small freestyle SAPUI5 application for creating and displaying purchase documents. Additionally, you learned how to set up a freestyle SAPUI5 project in SAP Web IDE full-stack, configure data sources and models, set up navigation between views, and create a UI integration test, including a mock server for the whole create and display scenario using the OPA5 framework included with the SAPUI5 SDK. In the next chapter you'll learn how to deploy all applications developed so far to the SAP Fiori launchpad.

Chapter 8
Deploying Applications to the SAP Fiori Launchpad

In this chapter, we'll cover different ways you can deploy your applications to the frontend server, including SAP Fiori launchpad admin configurations for application tiles.

Let's look at how you can deploy SAP Fiori applications, like the ones we've created in the previous chapters, into the ABAP frontend server. We'll consider two options for deploying the applications to the frontend server: directly from the SAP Web IDE or via an SAP transaction in the frontend server. Then, you'll learn how to create catalogs using the SAP Fiori launchpad admin page and how to configure tiles for your applications. We'll also cover how you can create groups in the launchpad admin so that the apps will appear as a custom group in the end user's home page.

8.1 Uploading a User Interface to the ABAP Frontend Server

In the previous chapters, we created four types of SAP Fiori applications: a list report page (LSP), an overview page (OVP), an analytical list page (ALP), and a freestyle application. Now, let's see these apps in action in the SAP Fiori launchpad. You'll also need to enable cross-application navigation between the apps.

When deploying SAP Fiori applications to the ABAP frontend server, two different methods are available:

- Deploying applications from the SAP Web IDE
- Uploading the applications directly to the frontend server

8.1.1 Deploying Applications from the SAP Web IDE

The SAP Web IDE has the option deploying applications directly from the project workspace. To deploy an application, right-click on the project and select **Deploy • Deploy to SAPUI5 ABAP Repository**, as shown in Figure 8.1.

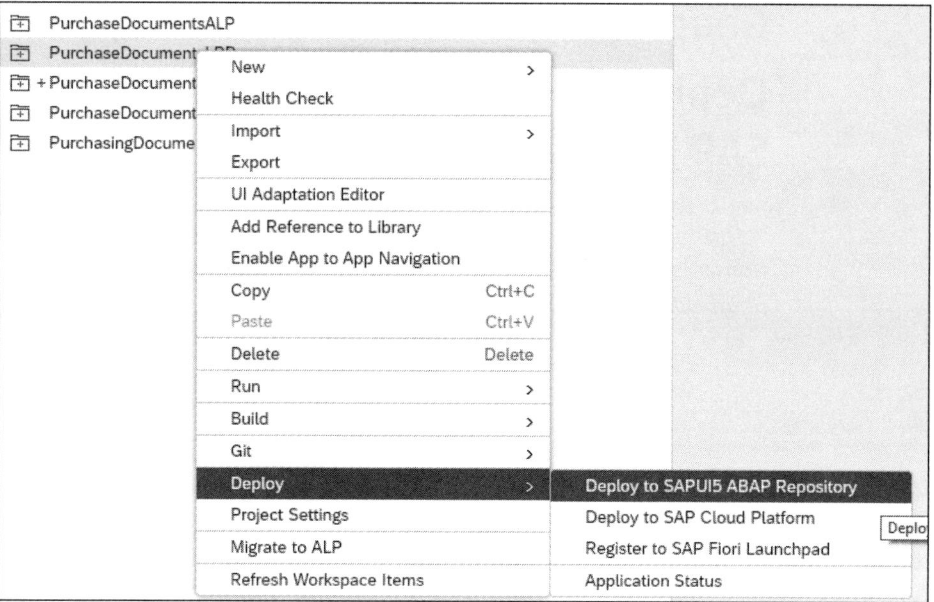

Figure 8.1 Deploying Applications from the SAP Web IDE Workspace

In the next popup window, you must select the relevant frontend system, as shown in Figure 8.2. In addition, make sure the **Deploy a new application** radio button is selected. Then, click on the **Next** button.

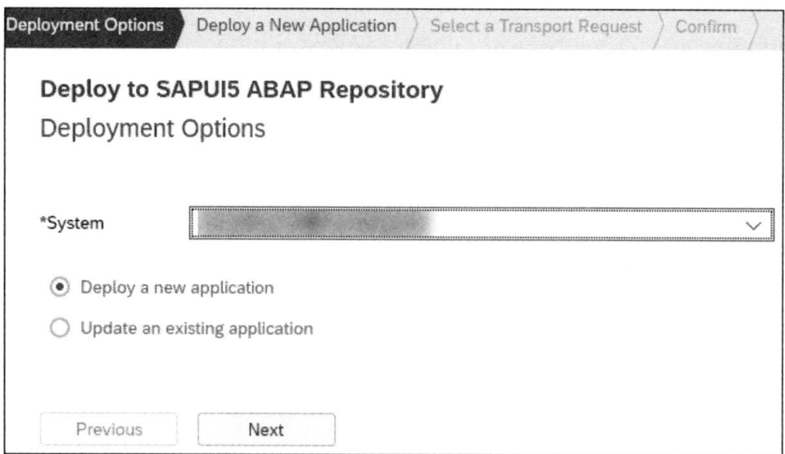

Figure 8.2 Deployment Options for SAPUI5 Applications

In the next window, as shown in Figure 8.3, you'll need to enter a **Name**, a **Description**, and a **Package** name, as listed in Table 8.1, for the business server page (BSP) application.

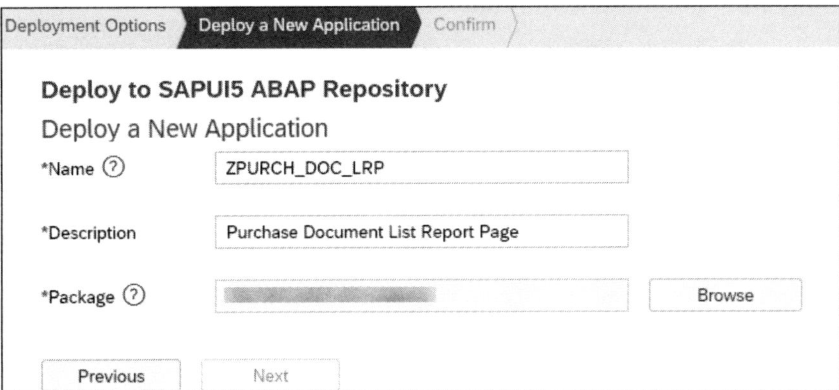

Figure 8.3 Deploying a New Application

Field	Parameter
Name	"ZPURCH_DOC_LRP"
Description	"Purchase Document List Report Page"
Package	"*<Your Package Name>*"

Table 8.1 Values for Deploying a New Application

> **Note**
>
> In a productive environment, you'll also see the additional option for specifying the **Transport Request Number** when you click **Next** from this window. Because we're saving our application into a local package, we won't see the tab for **Select a Transport Request**.

In the next window, click on the **Finish** button, as shown in Figure 8.4, and the SAP Web IDE will start the uploading process for your application. The SAP Web IDE is basically the second method for deploying applications directly on the ABAP frontend server. The advantage of the first method is that you're presented with a wizard instead of having to take the manual steps required in the second method.

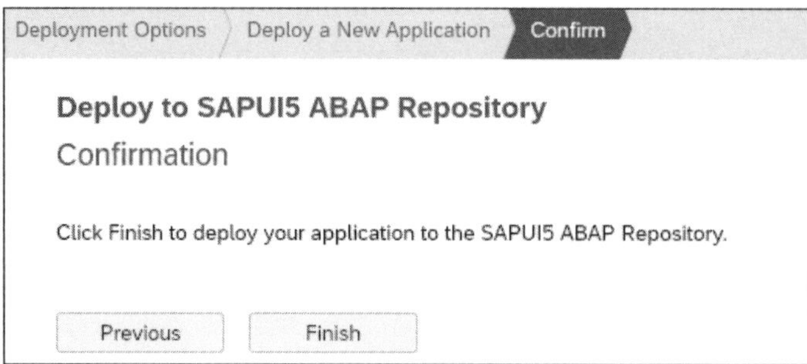

Figure 8.4 Confirming Deployment of the Application to the SAPUI5 ABAP Repository

8.1.2 Uploading Applications Directly into the Frontend Server

The SAP Web IDE has the option of exporting the source code of the projects into a ZIP file. To export your project as a ZIP file, right-click on the project name and click **Export**, as shown in Figure 8.5. Unzip the file into a folder; we'll use this unzipped file later in the chapter to upload the projects back directly into the ABAP frontend server.

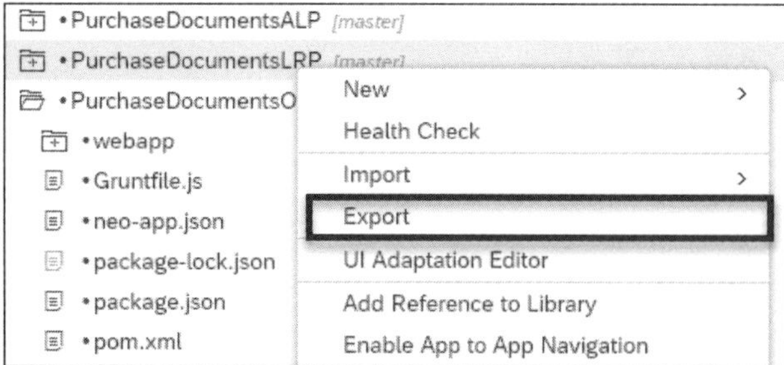

Figure 8.5 Exporting Applications from SAP Web IDE into ZIP Files

Next, log in to the ABAP frontend server via SAP Logon, execute Transaction SE38, and run the program named **/UI5/UI5_REPOSITORY_LOAD**, as shown in Figure 8.6.

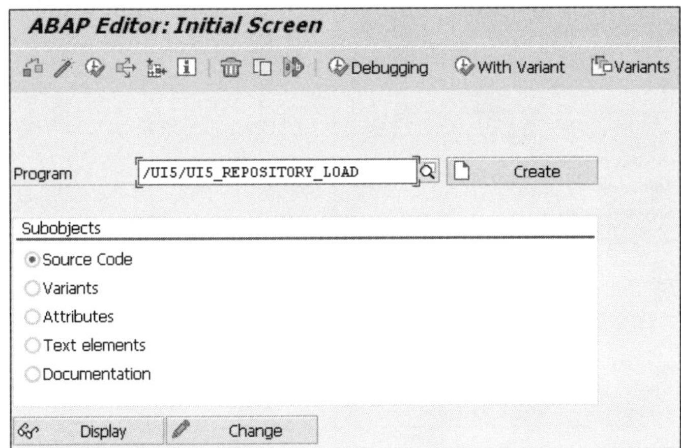

Figure 8.6 ABAP Repository Upload Program from the ABAP Frontend Server

Assign a name for your application in the input field. Make sure that the **Upload** radio button is selected, as shown in Figure 8.7, and press F8.

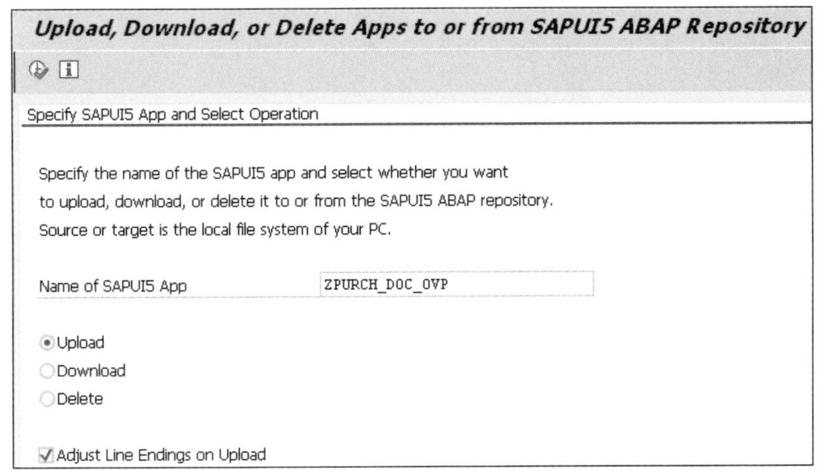

Figure 8.7 Assigning a Name for the BSP Application

Select the folder named **webapp** from the folder structure of the unzipped application source code and click on the **OK** button, as shown in Figure 8.8.

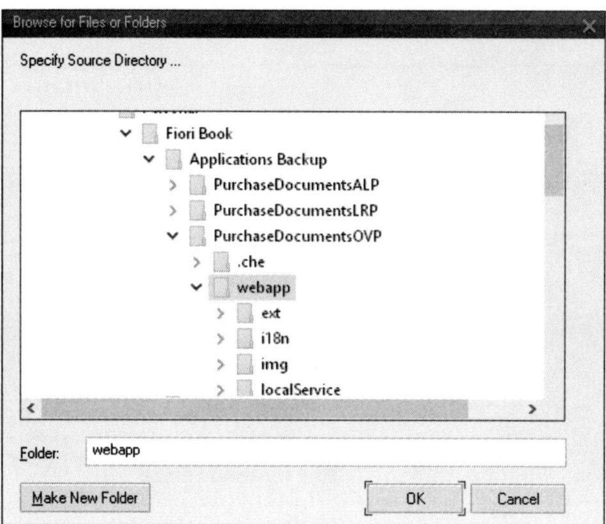

Figure 8.8 Selecting the webapp Folder of the Source Code

Now, the program will list the number of files it will be uploading to the server. Click on the green highlighted **Click here to upload** link, as shown in Figure 8.9.

```
Load SAPUI5 Application from File System to the SAPUI5 ABAP Repository

This is going to happen when you confirm at the end of this list ...

*  Create SAPUI5 Application    ZPURCH_DOC_OVP  *

Upload File     :  C:\Users\D067402\Desktop\Images\Personal\Fiori Book\Applications Backup\PurchaseDocumentsOVP\webapp\Component.js  ( Text )
Upload File     :  C:\Users\D067402\Desktop\Images\Personal\Fiori Book\Applications Backup\PurchaseDocumentsOVP\webapp\manifest.json  ( Text )
Create Folder   :  C:\Users\D067402\Desktop\Images\Personal\Fiori Book\Applications Backup\PurchaseDocumentsOVP\webapp\ext
Upload File     :  C:\Users\D067402\Desktop\Images\Personal\Fiori Book\Applications Backup\PurchaseDocumentsOVP\webapp\ext\readme.txt  ( Text )
Create Folder   :  C:\Users\D067402\Desktop\Images\Personal\Fiori Book\Applications Backup\PurchaseDocumentsOVP\webapp\i18n
Upload File     :  C:\Users\D067402\Desktop\Images\Personal\Fiori Book\Applications Backup\PurchaseDocumentsOVP\webapp\i18n\i18n.properties  ( Text )
Create Folder   :  C:\Users\D067402\Desktop\Images\Personal\Fiori Book\Applications Backup\PurchaseDocumentsOVP\webapp\img
Upload File     :  C:\Users\D067402\Desktop\Images\Personal\Fiori Book\Applications Backup\PurchaseDocumentsOVP\webapp\img\readme.txt  ( Text )
Create Folder   :  C:\Users\D067402\Desktop\Images\Personal\Fiori Book\Applications Backup\PurchaseDocumentsOVP\webapp\localService
Upload File     :  C:\Users\D067402\Desktop\Images\Personal\Fiori Book\Applications Backup\PurchaseDocumentsOVP\webapp\localService\mockserver.js  ( Text )
Create Folder   :  C:\Users\D067402\Desktop\Images\Personal\Fiori Book\Applications Backup\PurchaseDocumentsOVP\webapp\localService\Z_PURCHDOCSOVP_SRV
Upload File     :  C:\Users\D067402\Desktop\Images\Personal\Fiori Book\Applications Backup\PurchaseDocumentsOVP\webapp\localService\Z_PURCHDOCSOVP_SRV\metadata.xml  ( Text )
Upload File     :  C:\Users\D067402\Desktop\Images\Personal\Fiori Book\Applications Backup\PurchaseDocumentsOVP\webapp\localService\Z_PURCHDOCSOVP_SRV\Z_PURCHDOCSOVP_ANNO_MDL.xml  ( Text )
Create Folder   :  C:\Users\D067402\Desktop\Images\Personal\Fiori Book\Applications Backup\PurchaseDocumentsOVP\webapp\test
Upload File     :  C:\Users\D067402\Desktop\Images\Personal\Fiori Book\Applications Backup\PurchaseDocumentsOVP\webapp\test\fakeLRep.json  ( Text )
Upload File     :  C:\Users\D067402\Desktop\Images\Personal\Fiori Book\Applications Backup\PurchaseDocumentsOVP\webapp\test\testOVP.html  ( Text )
Upload File     :  C:\Users\D067402\Desktop\Images\Personal\Fiori Book\Applications Backup\PurchaseDocumentsOVP\webapp\test\testOVPwithMock.html  ( Text )
Create Folder   :  C:\Users\D067402\Desktop\Images\Personal\Fiori Book\Applications Backup\PurchaseDocumentsOVP\webapp\WEB-INF
Upload File     :  C:\Users\D067402\Desktop\Images\Personal\Fiori Book\Applications Backup\PurchaseDocumentsOVP\webapp\WEB-INF\web.xml  ( Text )

*  Items to be ignored have been determined from the built-in standard settings.  *
*  Text files have been identified from standard settings.  *
*  Binary files have been identified from standard settings.  *
*  The adjustment of line endings has been requested.  *

[  Click here to Upload  ]
```

Figure 8.9 Preview Window for Uploading Application Files

A popup window will appear where you'll need to specify a **Description**, **Package** name, and **Transport Request** number. Leave the **External Codepage** field blank, as shown in Figure 8.10.

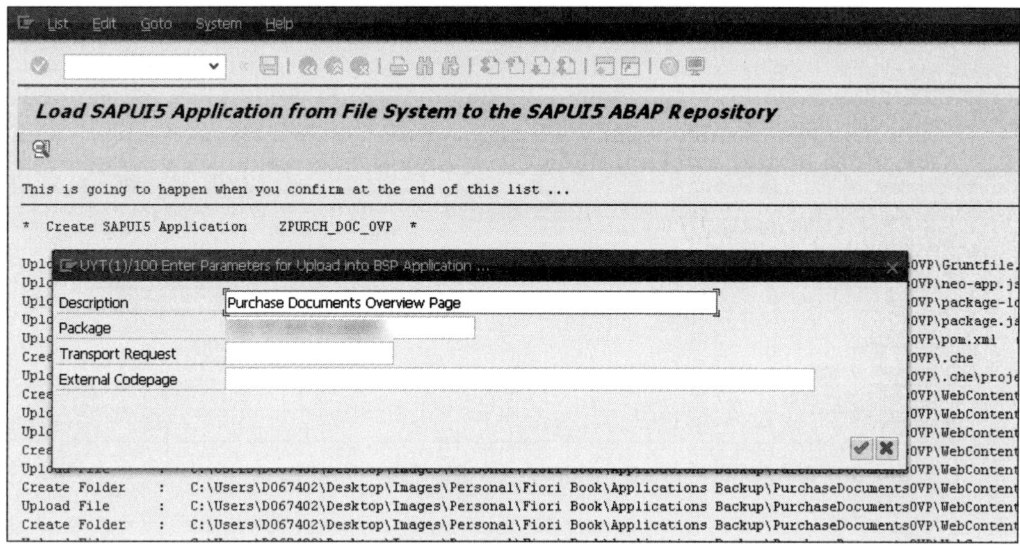

Figure 8.10 Specifying the BSP Application Properties

After the upload is complete, execute Transaction SE80 to open the Object Navigator and open the package that you entered during the upload step. Navigate to **BSP Library • BSP Applications • ZPURCH_DOC_OVP** (or the name of the BSP application you entered during the upload) to see the files, as shown in Figure 8.11. Alternatively, you can select **BSP Application** and enter the app's name directly on the **Repository Browser** of the Object Navigator page. Note down the path mentioned in the *Component.js* file within `sap.ovp.app.Component.extend` as shown in Listing 8.1. In our example, the value is `fiori.monitor.purchase.documents.PurchaseDocumentsOVP`, which is the path we'll be using while configuring the application tile so that the SAP Fiori launchpad can locate the *Component.js* file of the relevant app to launch the application. We'll use this path later in Section 8.4.

```
sap.ovp.app.Component.extend("fiori.monitor.purchase.documents.PurchaseDocumen
tsOVP.Component", {
    metadata: {
      manifest: "json"
    }
```

Listing 8.1 Path for the Component File of the Application

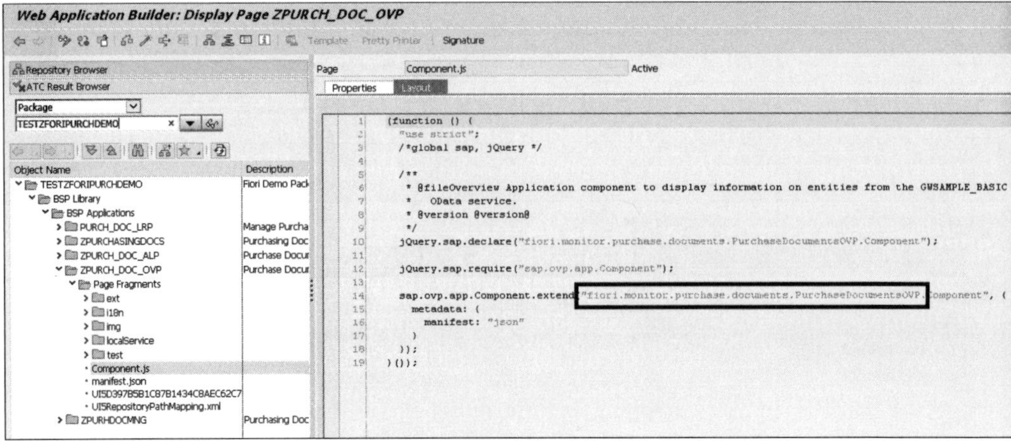

Figure 8.11 BSP Applications Uploaded to the ABAP Frontend Server

Note

When you upload your application source code into the ABAP frontend repository, the application is converted into a BSP application. Make sure that you select the **webapp** folder from the unzipped source code of your application instead of the root folder to which you unzipped the files. This step is important because, if you select the root folder instead of the **webapp** folder, then the launchpad won't be able to navigate to the *component.js* file of your application because the **webapp** folder is no longer directly under the BSP application's folder structure. Otherwise, you'll have to update the reference path of the *component.js* file in the tile configuration of your app accordingly. If you also want the app to load independently without the launchpad, then you'll have to add an *index.html* file in the folder containing a code to redirect to the *component.js* file so that the browser can start the app from the *index.html* file.

8.2 SAP Fiori Launchpad Admin Page

This page is different from the regular SAP Fiori launchpad home page. The SAP Fiori launchpad admin page is where you configure all the tiles that will show up in the SAP Fiori launchpad home page. Using this admin page, you can control which tiles should be displayed on the home page and who will have access to which tile.

The launchpad admin page URL is in the following format:

https://<host>/sap/bc/ui5_ui5/sap/arsrvc_upb_admn/main.html?scope=CONF&sap-client=<systemClient>&sap-language=<languageKey>

To access this admin page, the user ID to log in to this page requires the role assigned as listed in Table 8.2.

Role	Description
SAP_UI2_ADMIN	Composite role for launchpad administrator
SAP_UI2_USER_700	Role for accessing the SAP Fiori launchpad home page

Table 8.2 Roles for SAP Fiori Launchpad

Note

For detailed steps on how to assign these roles to the user, visit *http://s-prs.co/498821*.

On the SAP Fiori launchpad admin page, you'll need to understand three concepts before creating application tiles: catalogs, groups, and roles. Let's look at each next.

8.2.1 Catalogs

A catalog is a collection of apps that you can use to assign apps to a specific role. When you create a catalog in the SAP Fiori launchpad admin page, you must specify which apps belong to that catalog. Users with roles in this catalog can browse through the applications available within the catalog and choose which applications to add to their home pages.

Catalogs are divided into two categories:

- **Technical catalog (TC)**
  TCs are collections of SAP Fiori applications based on specific roles or areas. TCs acts as a master copy of a set of SAP Fiori applications. For example, a TC can be created for a specific area such as production and planning, and this catalog will hold all the SAP Fiori apps related to that area.

- **Business catalog (BC)**
This catalog is a child catalog inheriting from one or more TCs, as shown in Figure 8.12. For example, let's say you create a catalog that takes a few apps from the production and planning area and then a few apps from the demand-driven replenishment area. You can open the TC and specify which apps should be passed on to a BC. Then, these selected apps and their relevant tile configurations will be automatically copied from the TC to the BC. Thus, the process is sped up because you'll only need to create one TC with all the app tile configurations for a certain category, and after that, you can just create references of these app tiles from the TC to any number of BCs.

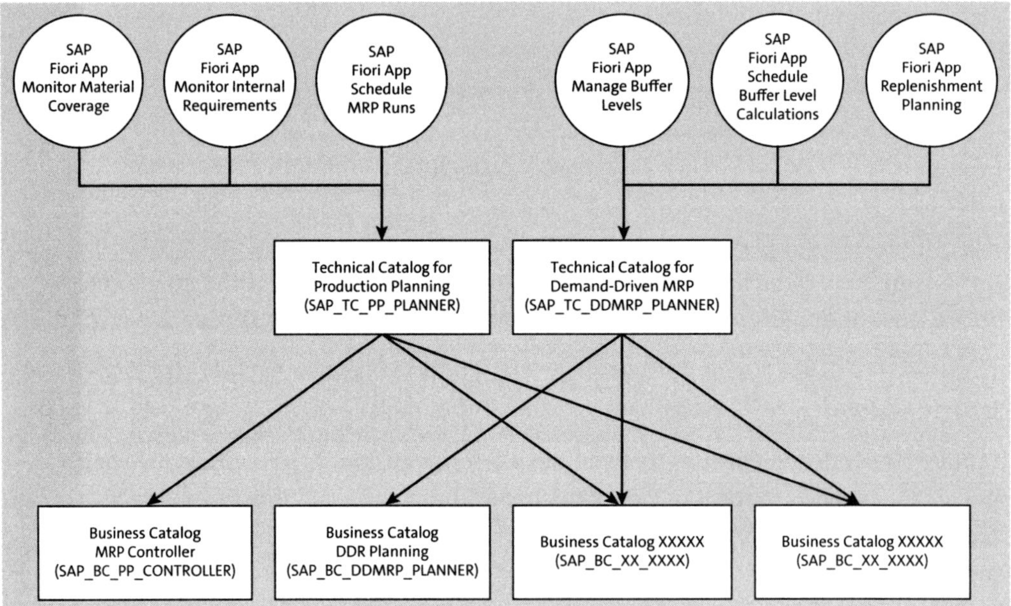

Figure 8.12 SAP Fiori Launchpad Catalog Concepts

8.2.2 Groups

Groups acts like a set of default apps that should be visible to the user's SAP Fiori home page. When you create a group and assign the SAP Fiori applications to that group, the administrator can assign this group to a user, and then the user see those groups of apps by default in his home page. With this approach, the user doesn't need to edit his home page and manually add the app tiles to the home page.

8.2.3 Roles

Roles are created in the frontend server rather than on the SAP Fiori admin page. Roles help administrators provide or restrict access to SAP Fiori applications based on the user's role. For example, if a user is in production planning and doesn't need access to SAP Fiori apps in other areas, the administrator can restrict that user's access to those other apps because the necessary roles for access won't be assigned to that user role.

Here's how catalogs, groups, and roles fit together:

1. Create catalogs for apps based on area/role.
2. Create default groups for the apps from a catalog or a group of catalogs.
3. Assign the groups to a role in the frontend server.
4. Map the users to their relevant roles.

8.2.4 SAP Fiori Launchpad Content Manager Tool for ABAP

A new offering for SAP S/4HANA 1709 (SAPUI5 version 1.52, SAP NetWeaver 7.52 and SP07) and above, this tool allows you to configure your SAP Fiori launchpad content directly from ABAP as an alternative to the SAP Fiori launchpad admin page. As a result, you can create/modify catalogs. However, you cannot create new tiles/target mappings; instead, you can add/remove existing ones to a catalog. To access the Launchpad Content Manager tool, use Transaction /UI2/FLPCM_CONF (for client-independent launchpad content management). For client-specific launchpad management, use the Transaction /UI2/FLPCM_CUST, which will also give you access to client-specific roles under a new tab in the transaction.

For our example, open up the Launchpad Content Manager tool and check the technical catalog that we created earlier in Section 8.2.1 via Transaction ZSAP_TC_MM_PUR_DOCUMENTS. As shown in Figure 8.13, the launchpad content manager has two tabs. The first tab is for managing the catalogs, and the second tab is for managing tiles and target mappings. Under the **Catalogs** tab, as shown in Figure 8.13, our technical catalog is open, showing all the Tiles and Target Mappings assigned to it. You can add or remove tiles from the catalog or even create a new catalog using this transaction.

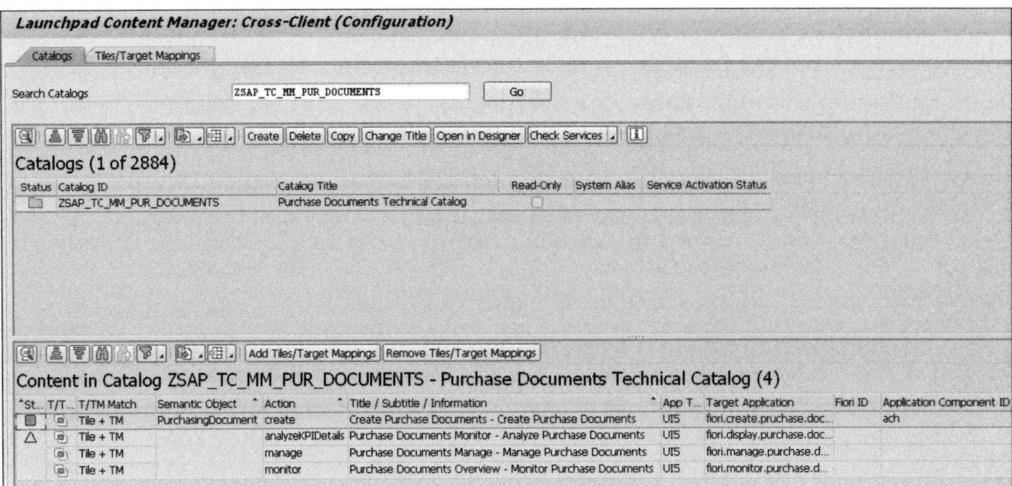

Figure 8.13 Launchpad Content Manager Catalogs Tab

Under the **Tiles/Target Mappings** tab, as shown in Figure 8.14, you'll see the search results for our applications. You can also add references to a catalog directly for a tile/ target mapping directly from this tab. You can even open the SAP Fiori launchpad designer from this transaction.

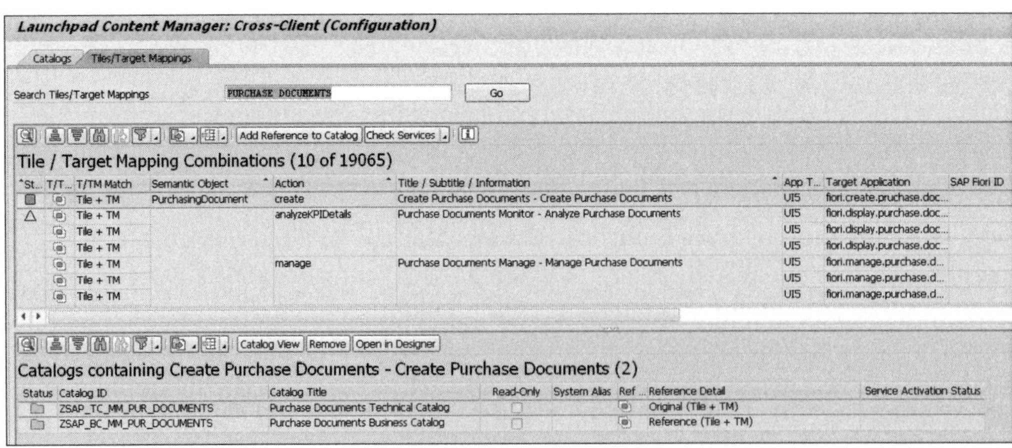

Figure 8.14 Launchpad Content Manager Tiles/Target Mappings Tab

8.3 Creating the Technical Catalog and Business Catalog

As described earlier in Section 8.2.1, BCs are different sets of SAP Fiori applications grouped together based on roles, business areas, and so on. To configure the tiles for the SAP Fiori apps we created in previous chapters, you'll need to create a catalog to configure the app tiles and assign them to end users.

To create a catalog, click on the + icon ❶ on the bottom-left of the SAP Fiori admin page. Select the **Standard** radio button and enter the **Title** ❷ and **ID** ❸ values, as shown in Figure 8.15. The naming style shown in Table 8.3 for the catalogs isn't mandatory, but we recommend including "TC" within the name so that you can more easily differentiate between technical catalogs and business catalogs.

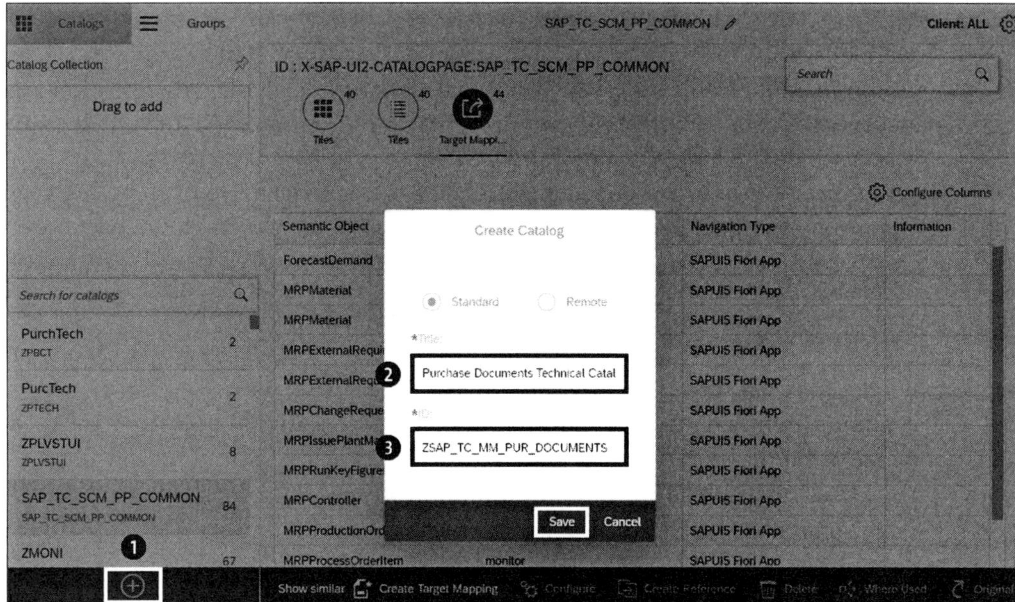

Figure 8.15 Creating a Technical Catalog

Field	Parameter
Title	"Purchase Documents Technical Catalog"
ID	"ZSAP_TC_MM_PUR_DOCUMENTS"

Table 8.3 Values for Technical Catalog Creation

Before you start configuring tiles in the TC, let's create the BC as well. To create the BC, the steps are basically identical to TC. Click on the + sign and enter the values shown in Figure 8.16 and Table 8.4. In this step, the naming style includes "BC" within the name to differentiate the catalog as a BC. We won't create or add any tiles manually into the BC because it inherit the right tiles from the TC. We'll see how the TC creates a reference of its tiles to the BC later in Section 8.4.

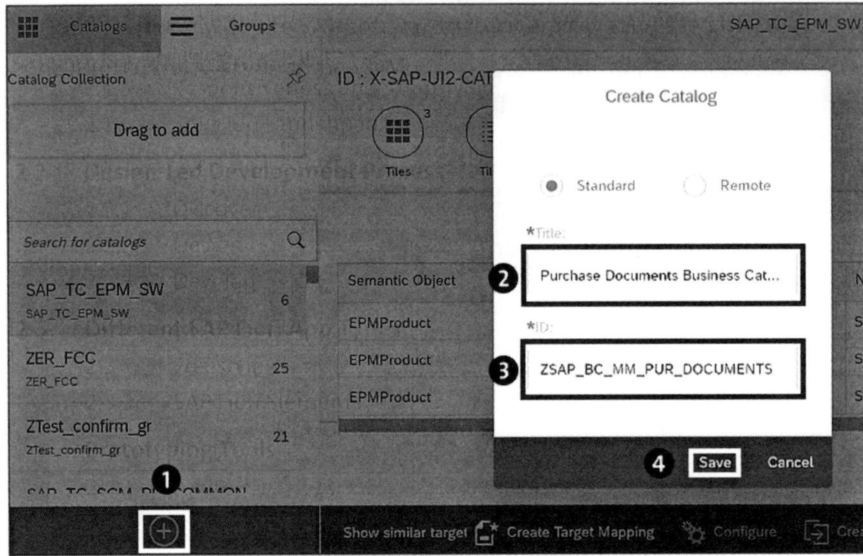

Figure 8.16 Creating a Business Catalog

Field	Parameter
Title	"Purchase Documents Business Catalog"
ID	"ZSAP_BC_MM_PUR_DOCUMENTS"

Table 8.4 Values for Creating a Business Catalog

8.4 Creating the Application Tiles

Now that we've created a TC and BC, let's start configuring our tiles. Open the TC (**Purchase Documents Technical Catalog**) that we created earlier, and then, click on the + icon, found on the left under **Tiles,** as shown in Figure 8.17.

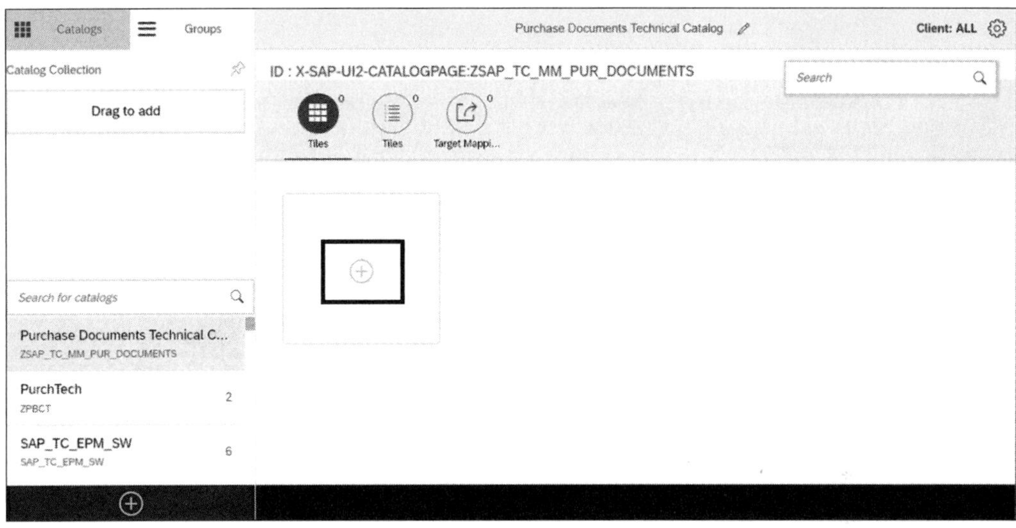

Figure 8.17 Adding Tiles for the Technical Catalog

In the next window, you'll be presented with three app tile templates to select from:

- **App Launcher – Dynamic**
  This app type is used when the tile needs to show a dynamic counter, such as a pending number of items, that is relevant for the use case of the application.
- **News Tile**
  This app type is used for tiles that show multiple pieces of information via sliding information from different data sources. For example, if the company wants a tile in SAP Fiori launchpad to show internal company announcements or news for every user, news tiles could be created with dynamic content linked to article feeds. A news tile can have a maximum of 10 feeds per tile. You can also configure the refresh intervals for each article feed and the cycle intervals between feeds.
- **App Launcher – Static**
  This app type is like the dynamic app launcher, without a dynamic counter on the tile.

For our example, we'll be using the last option: static app launcher. To create the first tile for the Purchase Document list report page (LRP) application, click on the **App Launcher – Static** tile from the tile templates, as shown in Figure 8.18.

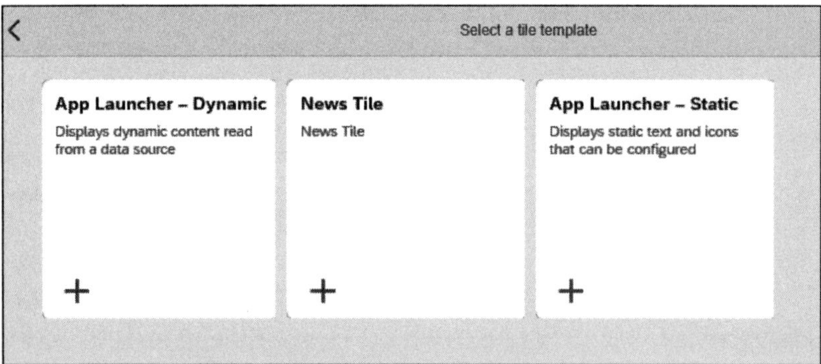

Figure 8.18 Selecting the Application Tile Template

In the window shown in Figure 8.19, configure the properties of the tile by entering the values as listed in Table 8.5. Select an icon from the **Icon** input field that would best suit the application you're building. On the right side of the image, you'll see the **Semantic Object** and **Action** fields. For our app, choose **PurchasingDocument** as the semantic object and **manage** as the action.

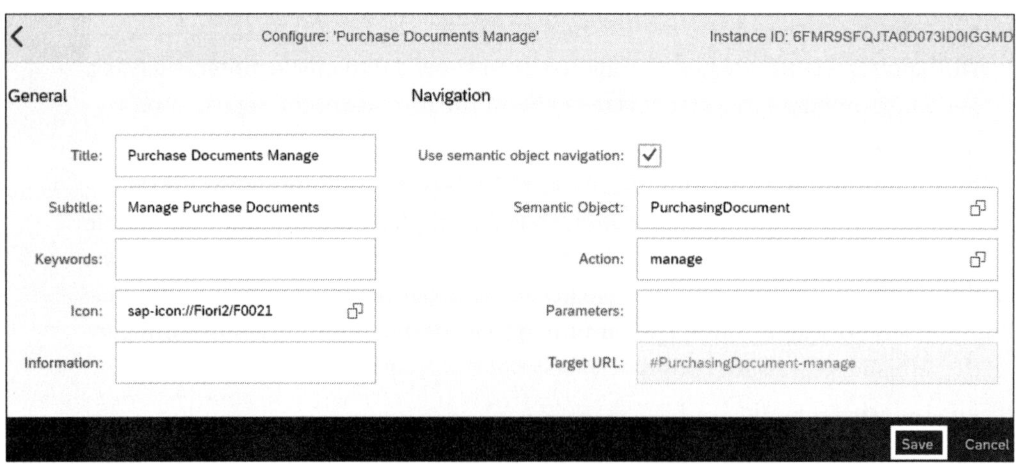

Figure 8.19 Purchase Document LRP App Static Tile Configurations

Every app that you configure in the catalogs has two main parts: tiles and target mappings. In the tile configuration, you'll specify properties such as the name, description, icons, semantic objects, and actions. In the target mapping, you'll configure properties specific to the application type you're using, such as semantic object and action.

Field	Parameter
Title	"Purchase Documents Manage"
Subtitle	"Manage Purchase Documents"
Icon	"sap-icon://Fiori2/F0021"
Semantic Object	"PurchasingDocument"
Action	"manage"

Table 8.5 Values for Purchase Document List Report Page Static Tile

In both tiles and target mappings, common properties like **Semantic Object** and **Action** are how tiles are linked to their corresponding target mappings. A semantic object represents the application area, and the action represents the type of usage with the app (display, manage, monitor, analyze key performance indicators [KPIs] in detail, etc.).

After the tile is configured for the Purchase Document list report page (LRP) tile, you can create a target mapping to link with the application tile. Click on the **Create Target Mapping** button on the lower left side of the page, as shown in Figure 8.20.

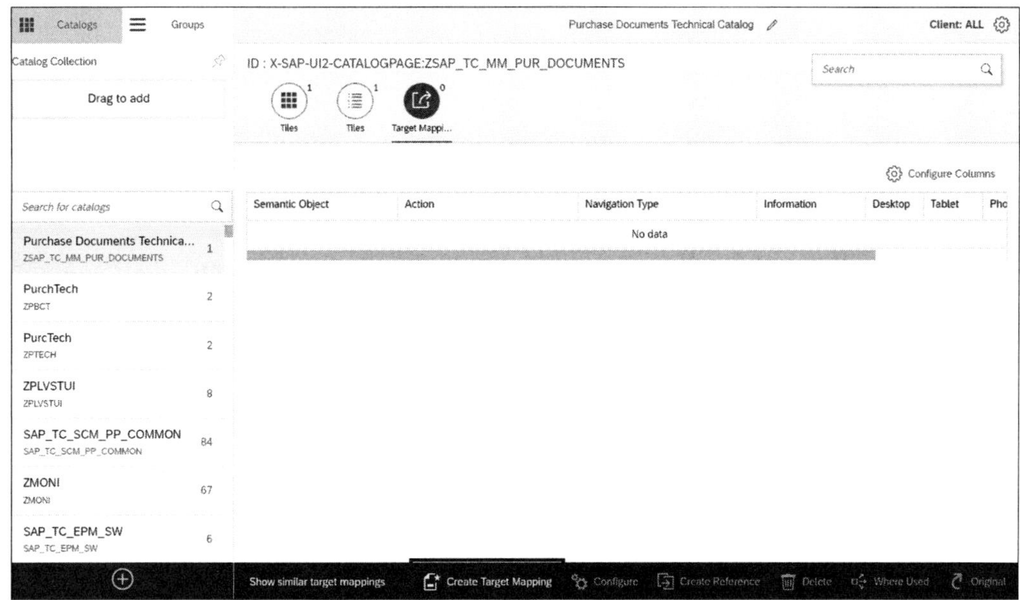

Figure 8.20 Creating a Target Mapping for the Purchase Document LRP App

In the target mapping configuration, you can link the configuration with the tile by specifying the same **Semantic Object** and **Action** as used for the Purchase Document LRP app. In the **Application Type** field, select **SAPUI5 Fiori App**. In older versions of the SAP Fiori launchpad admin page, you previously had to create custom launchpad configurations in the frontend server via Transaction LPD_CUST, select the application type as **Fiori App using LPD_CUST,** and enter the properties you created in the frontend server using Transaction LPD_CUST. This method is no longer recommended.

In the **URL** field, provide the path of the BSP application service, which is registered in the server. You can check the service path of your BSP application in the frontend server via Transaction SICF. The default path for all the BSP applications deployed from the SAP Web IDE or uploaded directly in the frontend server via the `/UI5/UI5_REPOSITORY_LOAD` is `/sap/bc/ui5_ui5/sap/<name_of_your_bsp_app>`.

For the **ID** field, provide the path for the *Component.js* file of the application, as shown in Figure 8.21 and Table 8.6. The path can be found within the *Component.js* file of the application folder, as shown earlier in Figure 8.11.

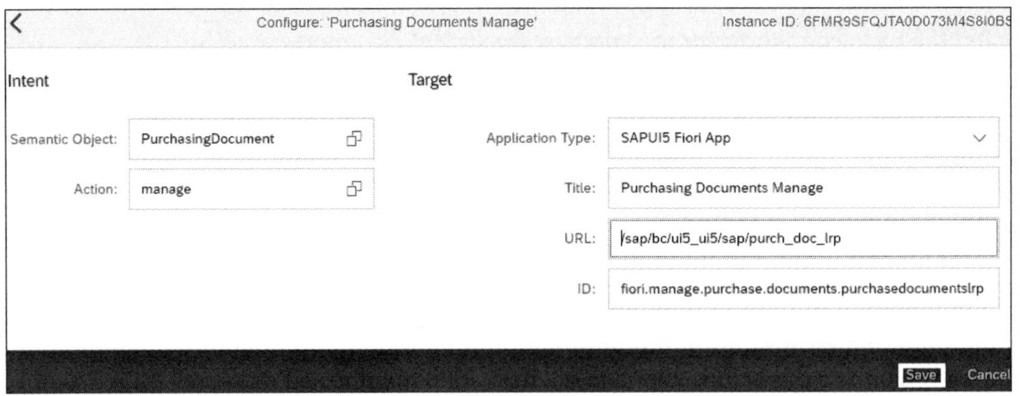

Figure 8.21 Purchase Document LRP App Target Mapping Configurations

Field	Parameter
Semantic Object	"PurchasingDocuments"
Action	"manage"
Application Type	**SAPUI5 Fiori App**
Title	"Purchasing Documents Manage"

Table 8.6 Values for Purchase Document LRP App Target Mapping

Field	Parameter
URL	"/sap/bc/ui5_ui5/sap/zpurch_doc_lrp"
ID	"fiori.manage.purchase.documents.purchasedocumentslrp"

Table 8.6 Values for Purchase Document LRP App Target Mapping (Cont.)

Now, you can configure the tile for the Purchase Document overview page (OVP) application by entering the values as listed in the Table 8.7. The main difference in this step is with the **Action** linked with the **Semantic Object**. The **Semantic Object** is the same because the app is still about purchase documents, but the **Action** will be set to **monitor**, as shown in Figure 8.22 because the purpose of the OVP is to monitor the purchase documents.

Field	Parameter
Title	"Purchase Documents Overview"
Subtitle	"Monitor Purchase Documents"
Icon	"sap-icon://Fiori2/F0102"
Semantic Object	"PurchasingDocument"
Action	"monitor"

Table 8.7 Values for Purchase Document OVP Static Tile

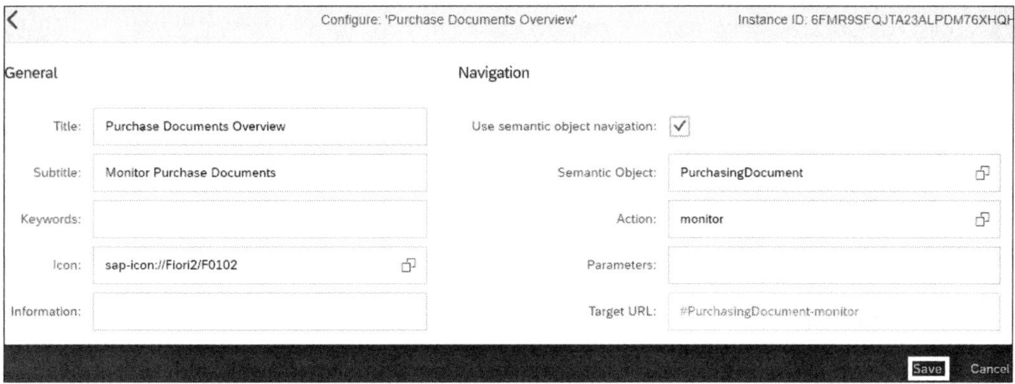

Figure 8.22 Purchase Document OVP Target Static Tile Configurations

The Purchase Document OVP app's target mapping is also not that much different from the previous app. In the target mapping window, enter the values as listed in Table 8.8. In this step, the main difference is with the URL and the ID, as shown in Figure 8.23. The **URL** has the BSP application name of the Purchase Document OVP, and the **ID** is taken from the *Component.js* file of the respective BSP application.

Field	Parameter
Semantic Object	"PurchasingDocuments"
Action	"monitor"
Application Type	**SAPUI5 Fiori App**
Title	"Purchasing Documents Manage"
URL	"/sap/bc/ui5_ui5/sap/zpurch_doc_ovp"
ID	"fiori.monitor.purchase.documents.PurchaseDocumentsOVP"

Table 8.8 Values for Purchase Document OVP App Target Mapping

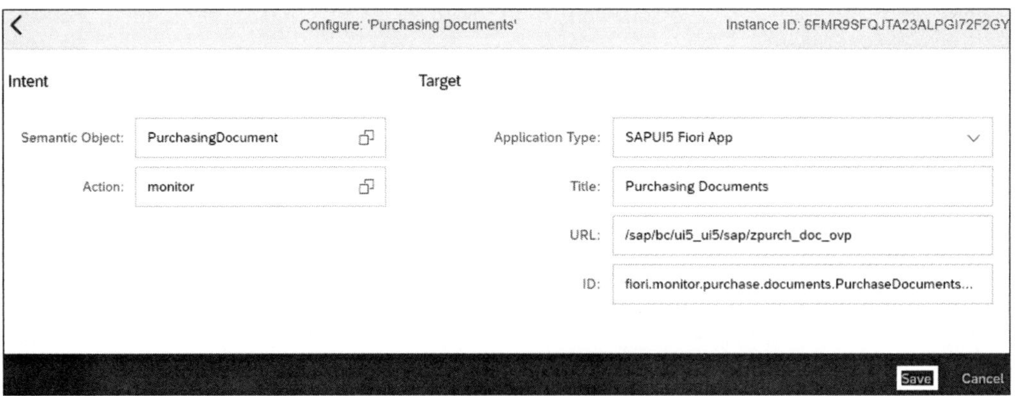

Figure 8.23 Purchase Document OVP App Target Mapping Configurations

To configure the Purchase Document analytical list page (ALP) app's static tile, enter the values as listed in Table 8.9. In this step, the **Semantic Object** stays the same, but the **Action** is set to **analyzeKPIDetails**, as shown in Figure 8.24.

Field	Parameter
Title	"Purchase Documents Monitor"
Subtitle	"Analyze Purchase Documents"
Icon	"sap-icon://Fiori2/F0101"
Semantic Object	"PurchasingDocument"
Action	"analyzeKPIDetails"

Table 8.9 Values for Purchase Document ALP Static Tile

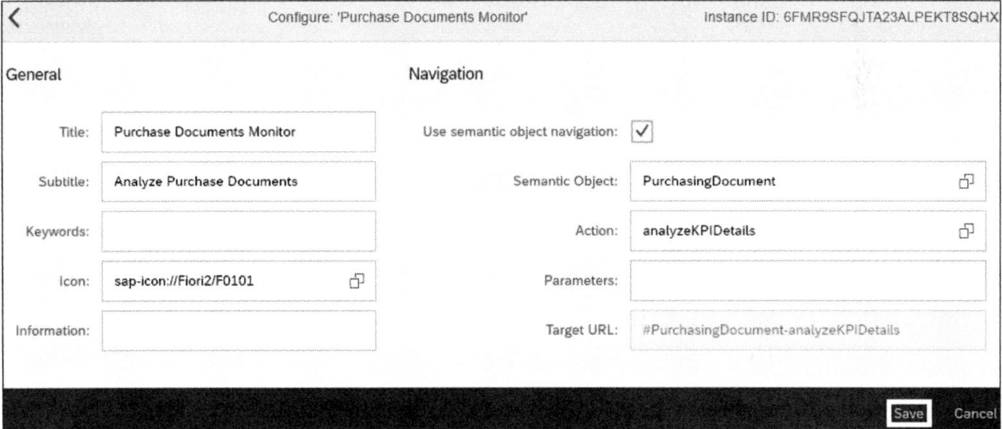

Figure 8.24 Purchase Document ALP Static Tile Configuration

Note

If you don't find a relevant **Semantic Object** name from the list of standard SAP-delivered semantic objects for your app, you can create your own semantic objects using Transaction /UI2/SEMOBJ.

You can also create your own semantic objects via Customizing by following these steps:

1. Choose the SAP Reference IMG.
2. Go to **SAP NetWeaver • UI Technologies • SAP Fiori • Configuring Launchpad Content • Adding Apps to SAP Fiori Launchpad • Define Semantic Objects for Navigation.**

In the target mapping configuration for the Purchase Document ALP, enter the values as listed in Table 8.10. In this step, you'll see that the **URL** and **ID** field values should be changed according to the BSP application of the app, as shown in Figure 8.25.

Field	Parameter
Semantic Object	"PurchasingDocuments"
Action	"analyzeKPIDetails"
Application Type	**SAPUI5 Fiori App**
Title	"Purchase Document ALP"
URL	"/sap/bc/ui5_ui5/sap/zpurch_doc_alp"
ID	"fiori.display.purchase.documents.PurchaseDocumentsALP"

Table 8.10 Values for Purchase Document ALP Target Mapping

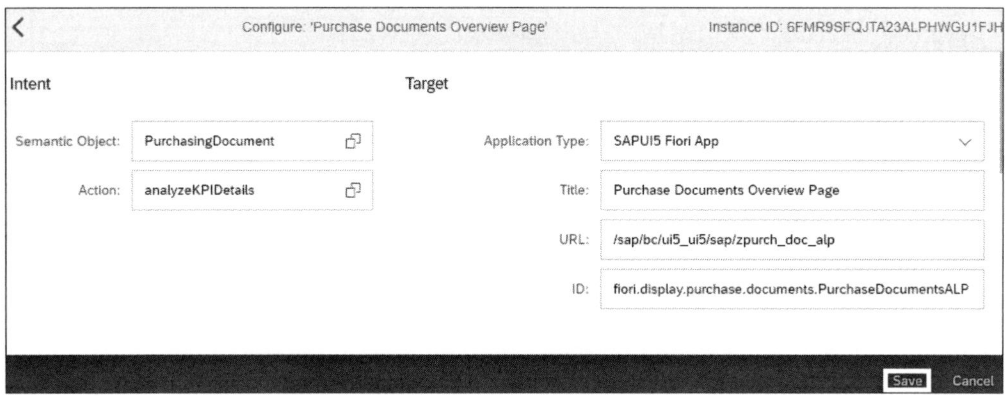

Figure 8.25 Purchase Document ALP Target Mapping Configurations

To configure the static tile for Create Purchase Documents freestyle app, enter the values as listed in Table 8.11. For this application, the **Action** is set to **Create**, as shown in Figure 8.26, because the application is used for creating purchase documents.

Fields	Parameter
Title	"Create Purchase Documents"
Subtitle	"Create Purchase Documents"

Table 8.11 Values for Create Purchase Documents Freestyle Static Tile

Fields	Parameter
Icon	"sap-icon://Fiori2/FBL5N"
Semantic Object	"PurchasingDocument"
Action	"Create"

Table 8.11 Values for Create Purchase Documents Freestyle Static Tile (Cont.)

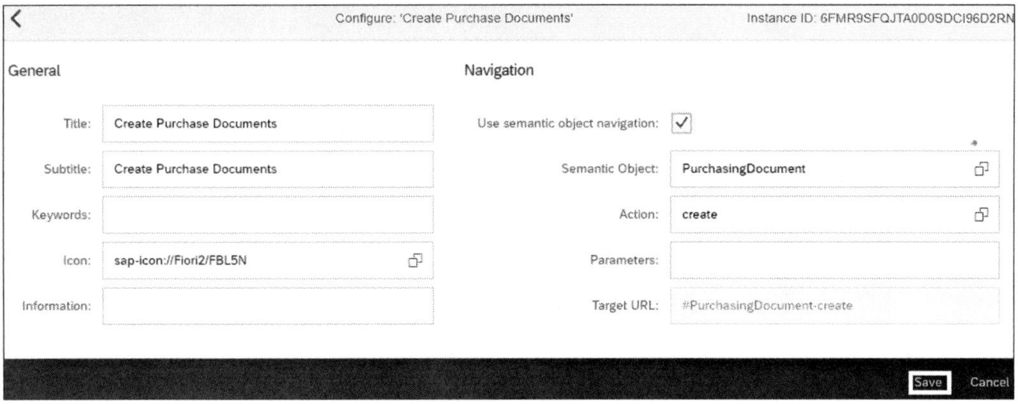

Figure 8.26 Create Purchase Documents Freestyle Static Tile Configuration

In the target mapping configuration for the Create Purchase Documents freestyle app, enter the following values as listed in Table 8.12. The **URL** and **ID** for the freestyle app needs to be updated accordingly, as shown in Figure 8.27.

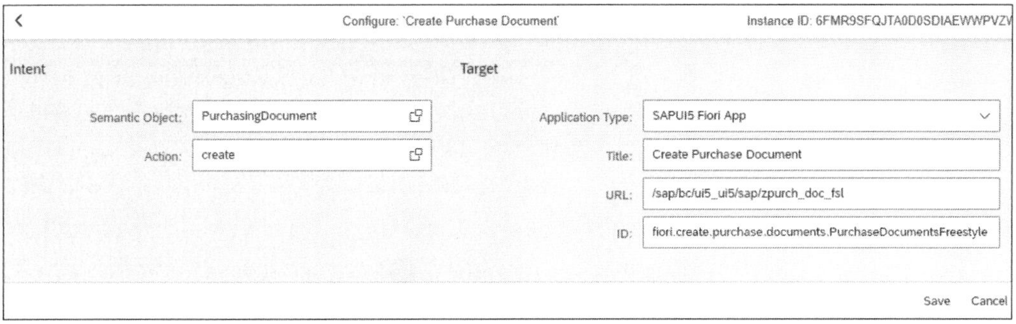

Figure 8.27 Create Purchase Documents Freestyle App Target Mapping Configuration

Field	Parameter
Semantic Object	"PurchasingDocuments"
Action	"create"
Application Type	**SAPUI5 Fiori App**
Title	"Create Purchase Document"
URL	"/sap/bc/ui5_ui5/sap/zpurch_doc_fsl"
ID	"fiori.create.purchase.documents.PurchaseDocumentsFreestyle"

Table 8.12 Values for Create Purchase Documents Freestyle Target Mapping

Now that you're done creating the tiles for TC, you can map the TC's tiles and target mappings to the BC. Click on the **Tiles** icon ❶ above the table, as shown in Figure 8.28. Then, select the tile for **Purchase Documents Manage** and click on the **Create Reference** button ❷ at the bottom.

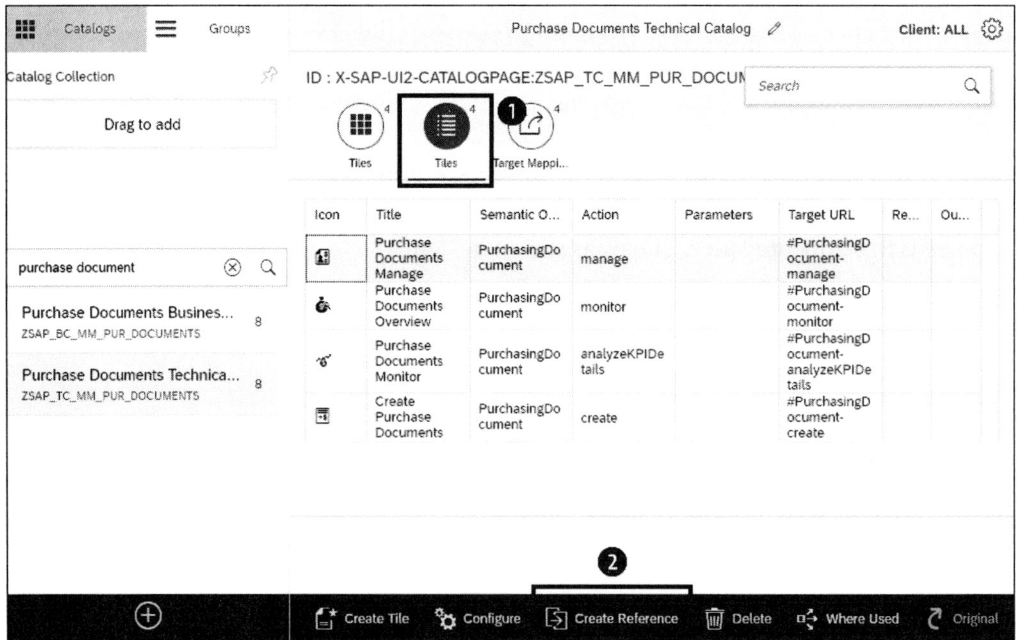

Figure 8.28 Creating a Tile Reference from a Technical Catalog to a Business Catalog for the Purchase Document LRP App

In the popup window shown in Figure 8.29, select the BC called **Purchase Documents Business Catalog**, which we created earlier.

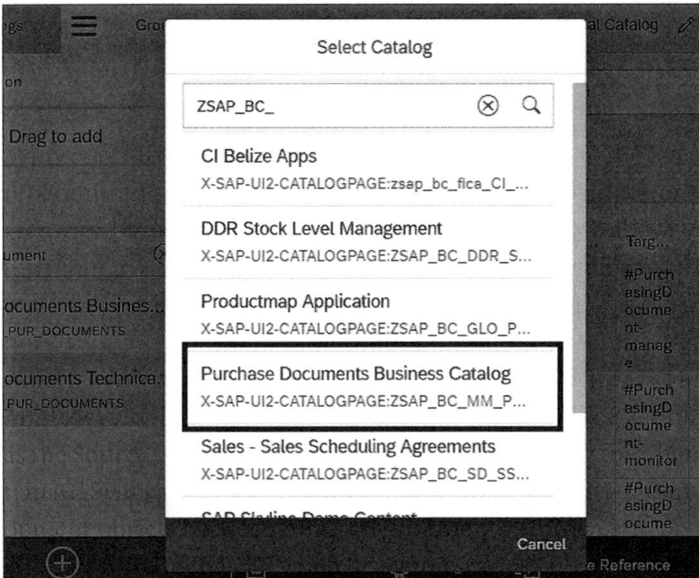

Figure 8.29 Selecting the Business Catalog for Creating a Tile Reference from the Technical Catalog

Now, let's create the reference for the target mapping of the Purchase Document LRP app from the TC to the BC. Click on the **Target Mappings** tab ❶ above the table, as shown in Figure 8.30, and then click on the **Create Reference** button ❷.

From the popup window, select the BC named **Purchase Documents Business Catalog**, as shown in Figure 8.31. Now, repeat the steps for the tile and target mapping for the other two apps and assign them to the same BC. After this step, if you open and check the BC in the launchpad admin page, you'll see all the tiles, and the relevant target mappings are now automatically created in the catalog. The advantage of this approach is that, if you need to create a separate catalog in the future with only a few apps from the TC, then you can create a new empty BC and follow the same steps as you did for the apps previously but with only the apps you need. All the configurations will be set automatically for you.

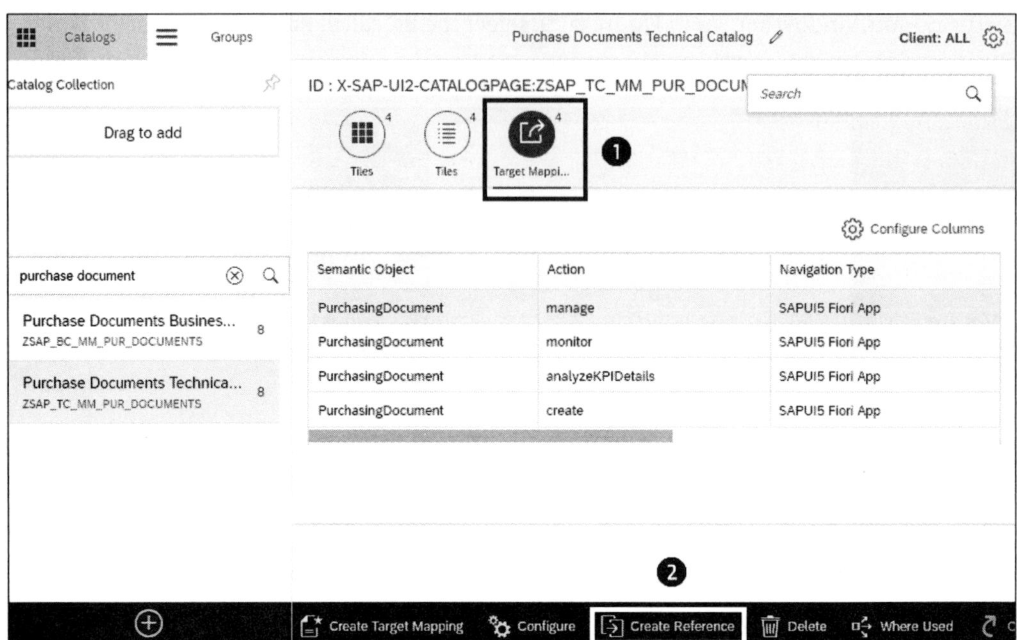

Figure 8.30 Creating the Target Mapping Reference from the Technical Catalog to the Business Catalog for the Purchase Document LRP App

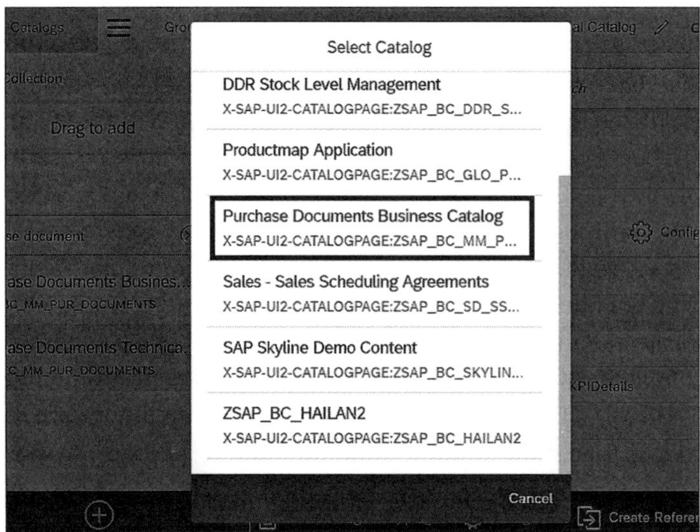

Figure 8.31 Selecting the Business Catalog for Creating the Target Mapping Reference from the Technical Catalog

8.5 Creating Groups for Application Tiles

Now, we need to create a group for the BC. As shown earlier in Figure 8.12, groups are used to help end users access apps without requiring users to manually add the tiles to their home pages. To create a group, click on the **Groups** tab ❶ on the top-left side of the pane and then click on the + icon ❷ on the bottom-left side of the pane. In the popup window, as shown in Figure 8.32, enter the values as listed in Table 8.13 and click on the **Save** button ❸.

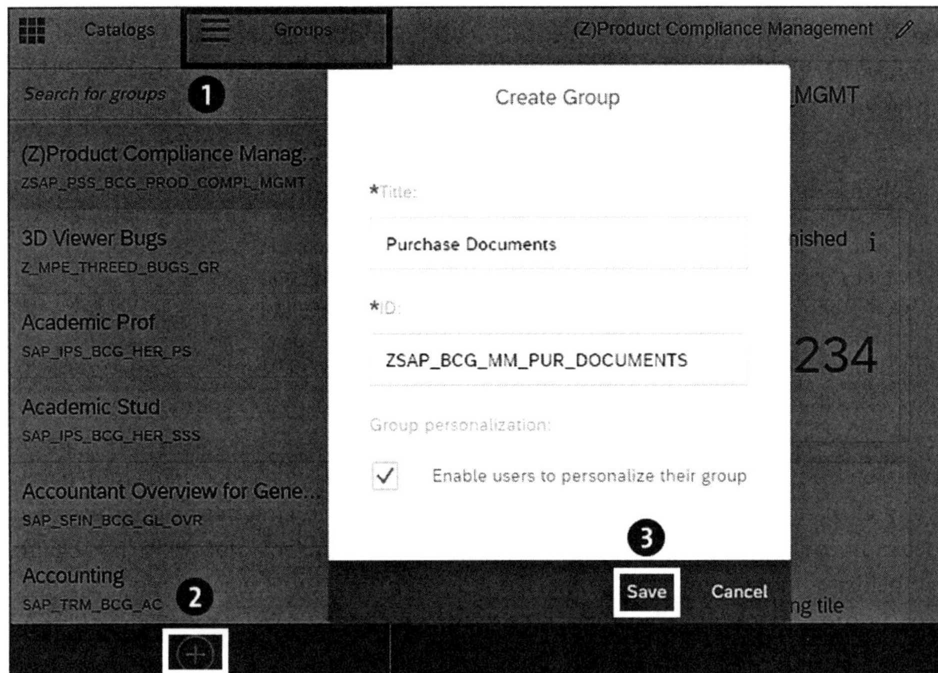

Figure 8.32 Creating a New Group for the Tiles

Field	Parameter
Title	"Purchase Documents"
ID	"ZSAP_BCG_MM_PUR_DOCUMENTS"

Table 8.13 Values for Group Creation in the SAP Fiori Admin Page

Now, click on the + icon on the right to add the tiles from the BC, as shown in Figure 8.33. Because we already created a reference from the TC to the BC, the tiles will be visible inside the BC already.

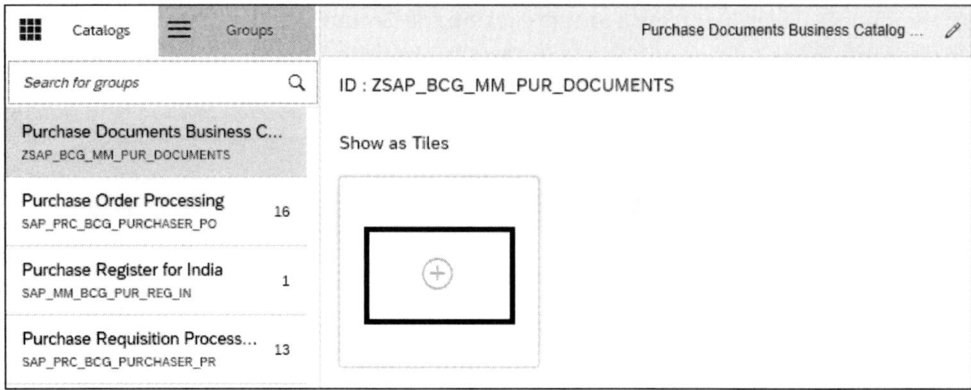

Figure 8.33 Adding Tiles into the Group for the Purchase Documents Business Catalog

In the next window, enter the BC name in the search window and select all four apps from the BC list, as shown in Figure 8.34. If you need to remove one of the apps from the group in the future, you can simply open this group and uncheck the apps you don't need.

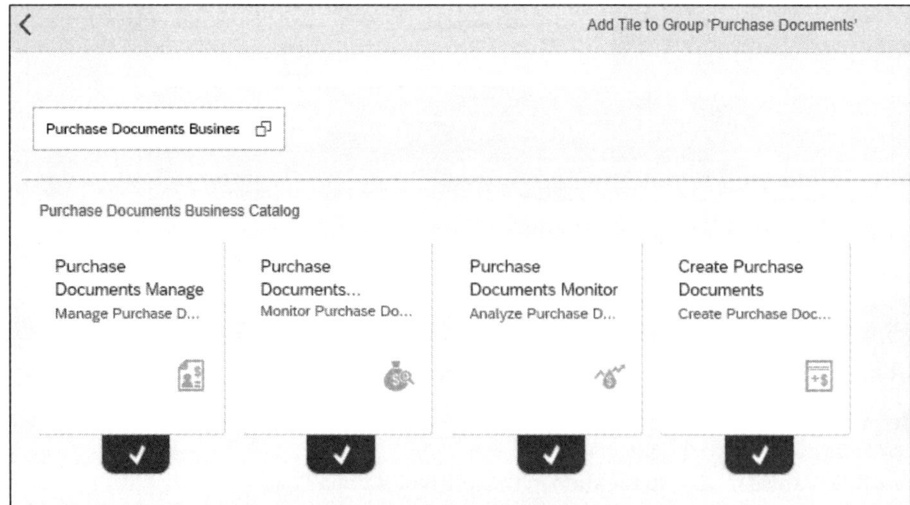

Figure 8.34 Assigning Tiles from the Business Catalog into the Group

8.6 Creating and Assigning a Transaction PFCG Role to Users

At this point, although all the catalogs and groups have been created, they still don't have any links to the users who will use the apps. To link the catalogs and groups with the users, you must first create a role. To create a role, execute Transaction PFCG; enter a name for the **Role** (for our example, the role name is "ZPURCHDOCSROLE"); and then click on the **Single Role** button, as shown in the Figure 8.35.

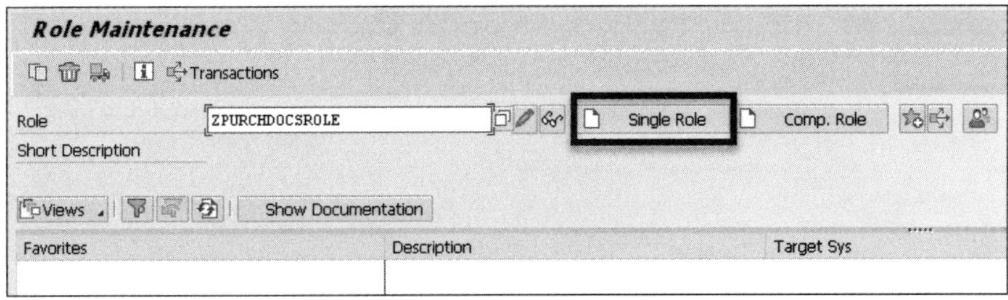

Figure 8.35 Creating a Role for Assigning Catalogs and Groups

> **Note**
>
> Transaction PFCG roles must be created on the SAP Gateway hub system.

Now, click on the **Transaction** button and select **SAP Fiori Tile Catalog**, as shown in Figure 8.36.

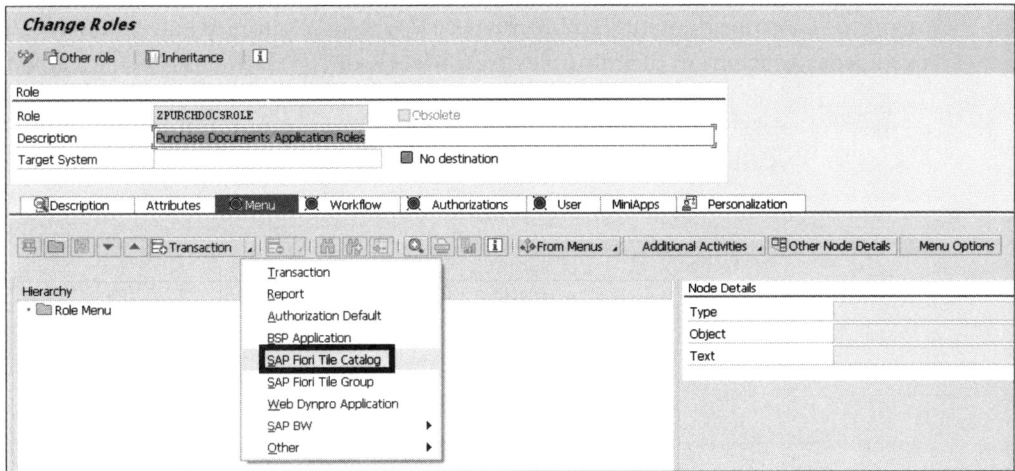

Figure 8.36 Adding the SAP Fiori Tile Catalog to the Role

Enter the BC name "ZSAP_BC_MM_PUR_DOCUMENTS" in the **Catalog ID** field, as shown in Figure 8.37.

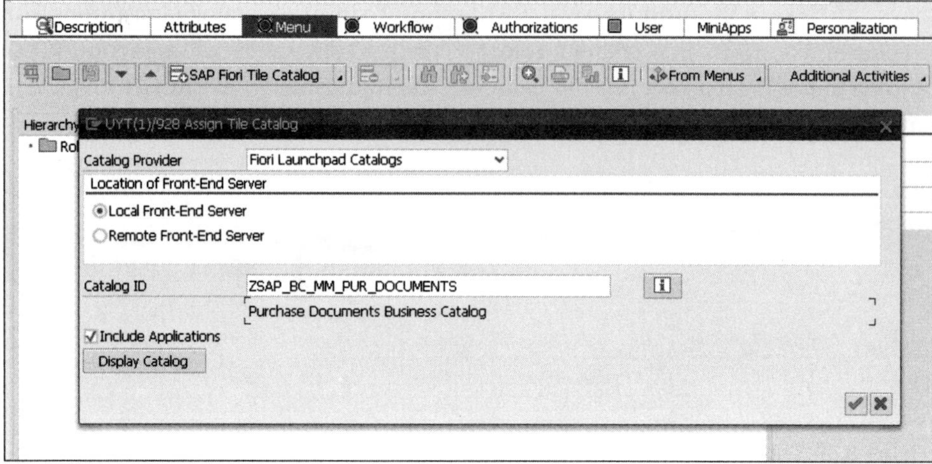

Figure 8.37 Assigning the Business Catalog to the Role

Next, you'll need to add the group to the role. Click on the **Transaction** button, and select **SAP Fiori Tile Group**, as shown in Figure 8.38.

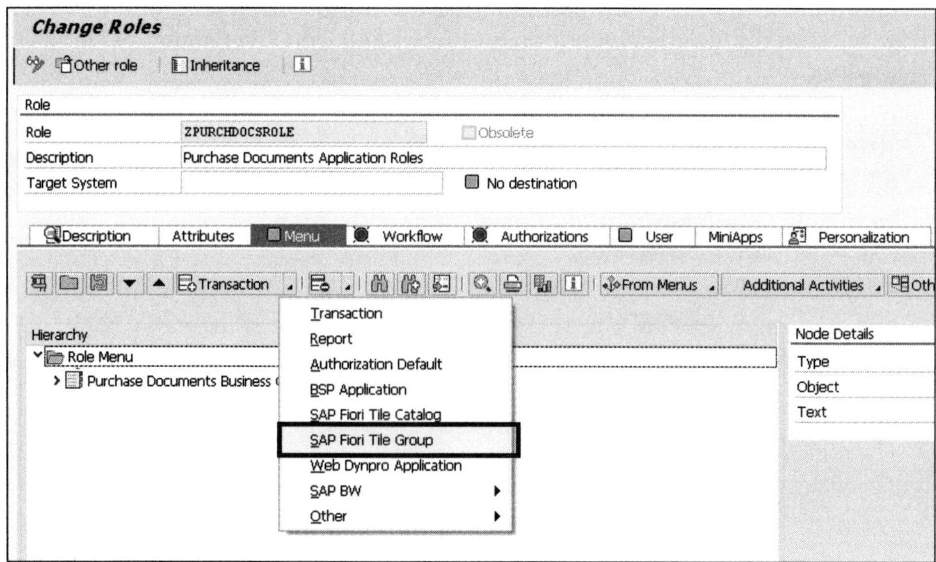

Figure 8.38 Adding the SAP Fiori Tile Group to the Role

Enter "ZSAP_BCG_MM_PUR_DOCUMENTS" in the **Group ID** field. Now, the role is linked to both the BC and the group, as shown in Figure 8.39.

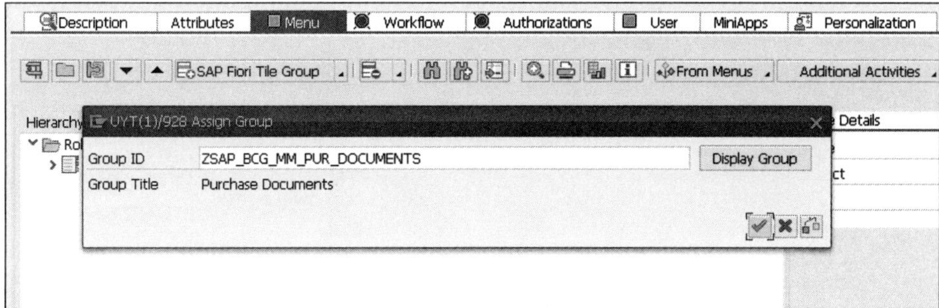

Figure 8.39 Assigning the Group to the Role

However, we still haven't linked the role to the user of the SAP Fiori launchpad. To create this link, click on the **User** tab in Transaction PFCG, as shown in Figure 8.40, or execute Transaction SU01 and assign the role to the user in that transaction.

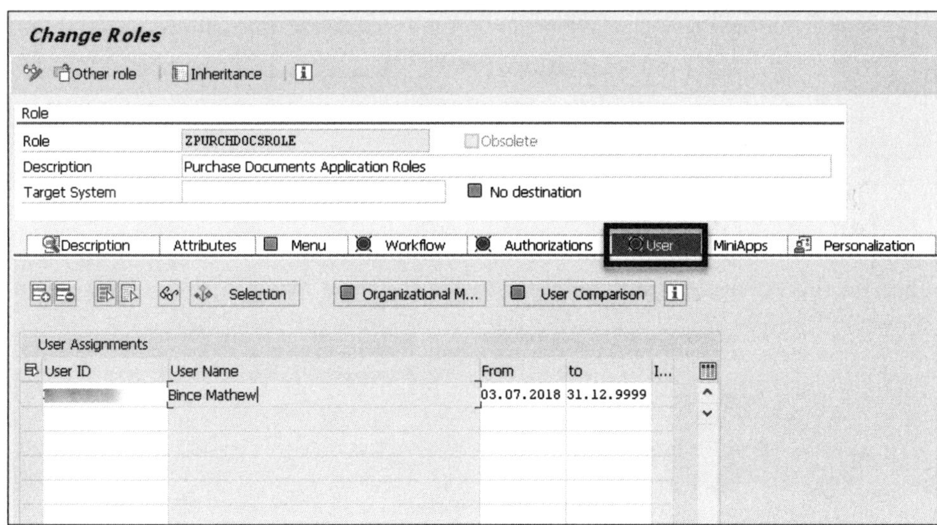

Figure 8.40 Mapping the Role with Users

After this step, log in to the SAP Fiori home page with your user. The URL for the SAP Fiori home page is as follows:

https://<host>/sap/bc/ui5_ui5/ui2/ushell/shells/abap/FioriLaunchpad.html?sap-language=<languageKey>&sap-client=<systemclient>#Shell-home

After you log in to the SAP Fiori launchpad, you'll the group as one of the tabs in the launchpad, as shown in Figure 8.41.

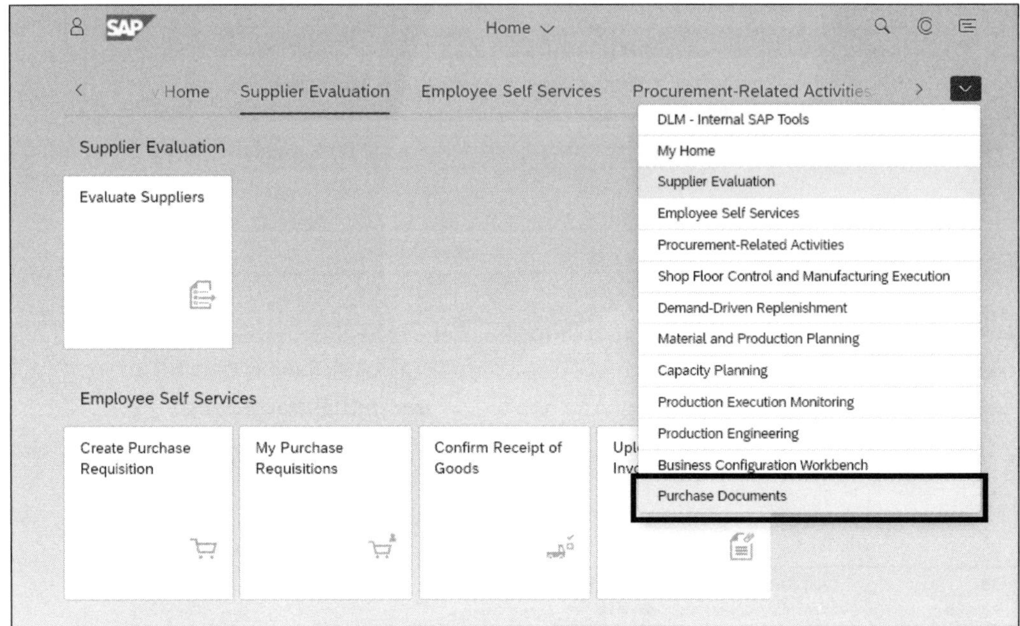

Figure 8.41 Accessing the Tiles via the Tile Group in the SAP Fiori Launchpad Home Page

Click on the **Purchase Documents** tab to see the apps listed in the home page, as shown in Figure 8.42.

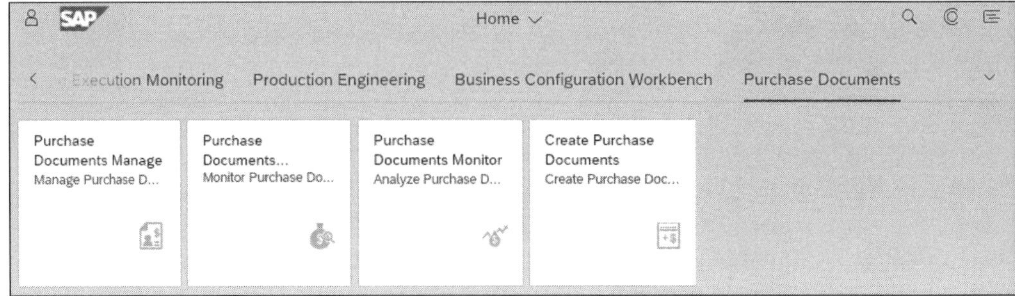

Figure 8.42 Purchase Document Application Tiles in the Home Page

In addition, if users want to add or remove tiles manually, they can click on the left side of the SAP Fiori launchpad to show the settings pane and then click on the **Edit Home Page** icon, as shown in Figure 8.43.

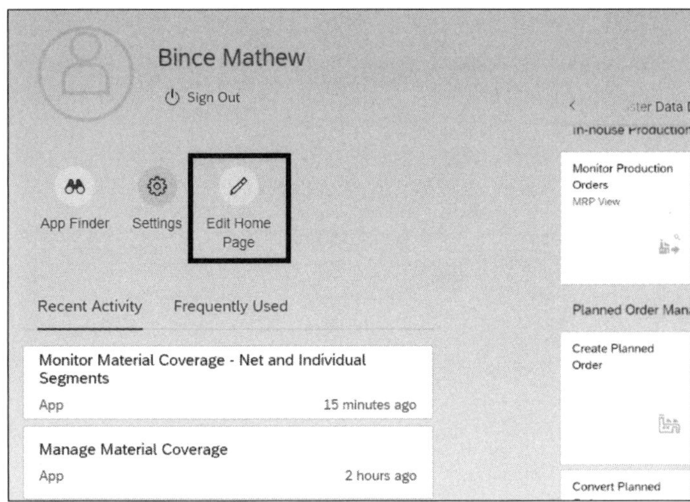

Figure 8.43 Editing the SAP Fiori Launchpad Home Page

Now that the home page is in editable mode, the **+** icon can be used to add or remove the tiles from the home page, as shown in Figure 8.44. The apps are added to the **My Home** tab, which acts as a placeholder for the user's favorite list of apps.

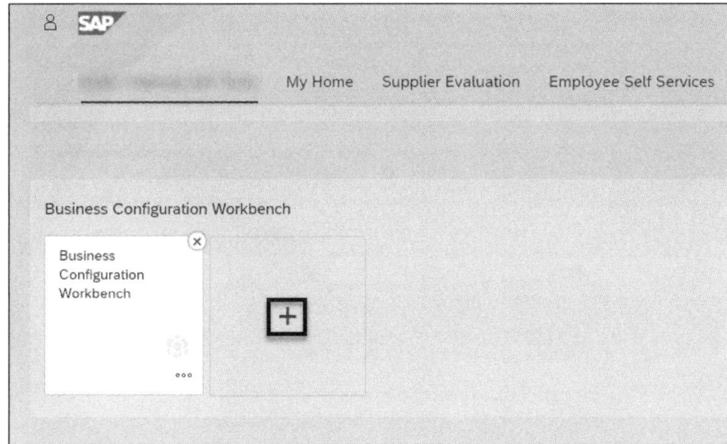

Figure 8.44 Manually Adding the Tiles into the Home Page

8

As shown in Figure 8.45, the BC listed on the left pane of the launchpad. Click and add the relevant app tiles.

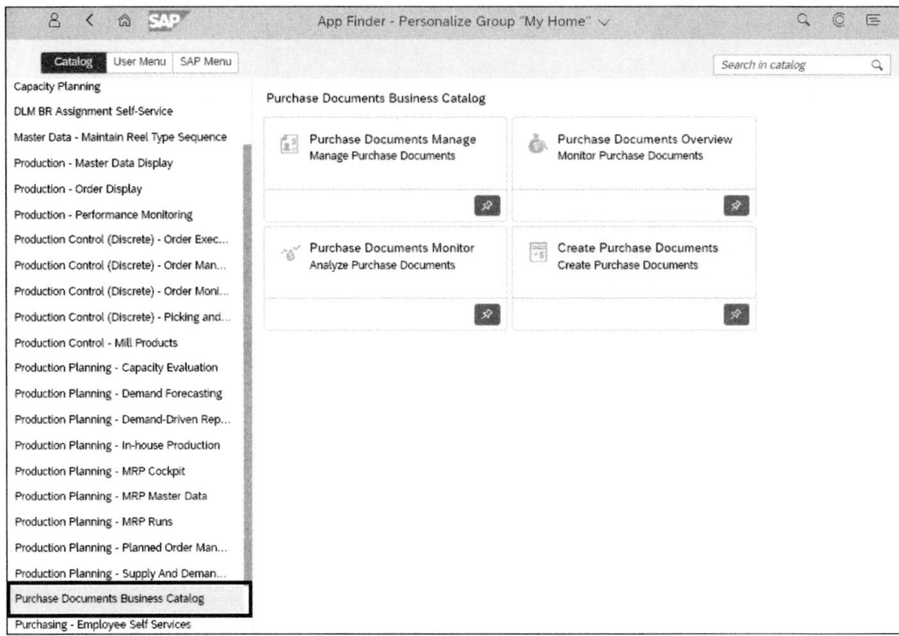

Figure 8.45 Add or Remove Tiles from the Launchpad from the BC

Now, you can see that the Purchase Document apps have been added to the **My Home** tab, as shown in Figure 8.46.

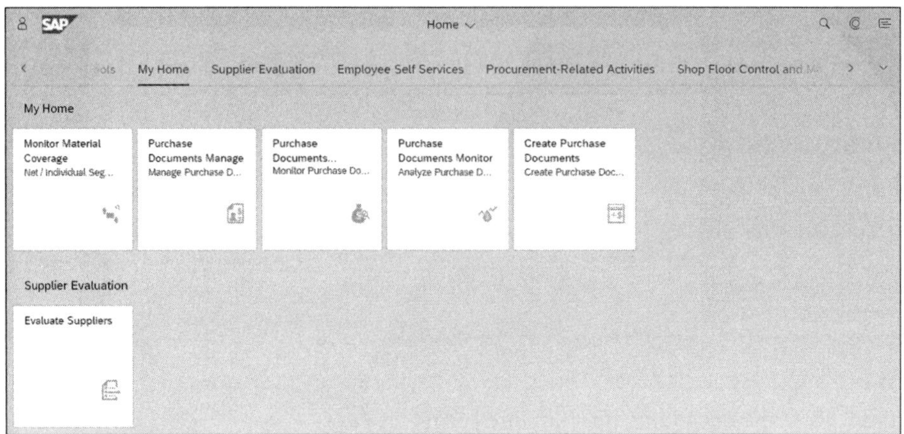

Figure 8.46 My Home Tab with the Purchase Document App Tiles

8.7 Setting Up Intent-Based Cross-Application Navigation from OVP to LRP

So far, we've deployed all the apps into the SAP Fiori launchpad, but the apps aren't interconnected, especially the Purchase Document OVP app, which you'll primarily use for monitoring pending purchase documents for approvals. Therefore, we'll need to set up the navigation from the Pending for Approvals OVP card to the Purchase Document LRP app. This navigation will help users directly navigate to the right purchase documents and take appropriate action without the need to open the Purchase Document LRP application separately. To create this navigation, you'll need to slightly modify the core data services (CDS) views. In the CDS view for the Purchase Documents Pending Approval list card (`Z_C_PurchaseDocAprovalStat`), add the annotation `@Consumption.semanticObject: 'PurchasingDocument'`, as shown in Listing 8.2, for the field `PurchaseDocument`.

8

```
...
define view Z_C_PurchaseDocsforApprovalOVP
  as select from Z_I_PurchaseDocAprovalStat
{
      @ObjectModel.foreignKey.association: '_PurchaseDocument'
      @Consumption.semanticObject: 'PurchasingDocument'
  key  PurchaseDocument,
...
```

Listing 8.2 Annotation for Navigation Based on the Semantic Object

In addition, you'll need to add another annotation `@UI.lineItem: [{type: #FOR_INTENT_BASED_NAVIGATION, semanticObjectAction: 'manage'}]` in the metadata annotation of the CDS view, as shown in Listing 8.3.

The annotation type: `#FOR_INTENT_BASED_NAVIGATION` will cause the SAP Fiori elements application to recognize that the field `PurchaseDocument` now has an active navigation property. The SAP Fiori elements application will also recognize which semantic object and action are required to navigate based on the annotations provided to the field. After the annotations are added, activate the CDS views and then reload the application in the SAP Fiori launchpad. Now, you should be able to navigate from the list card by clicking the pending document to the Purchase Document LRP application, as shown in Figure 8.47.

```
...
annotate view Z_C_PurchaseDocsforApprovalOVP with
{
  @UI.lineItem: [{
      position: 10,
      importance: #HIGH,
      label: 'Document',
      type: #FOR_INTENT_BASED_NAVIGATION,
      semanticObjectAction: 'manage'
    }]
  PurchaseDocument;
```

Listing 8.3 Setting semanticObjectAction and Navigation Type

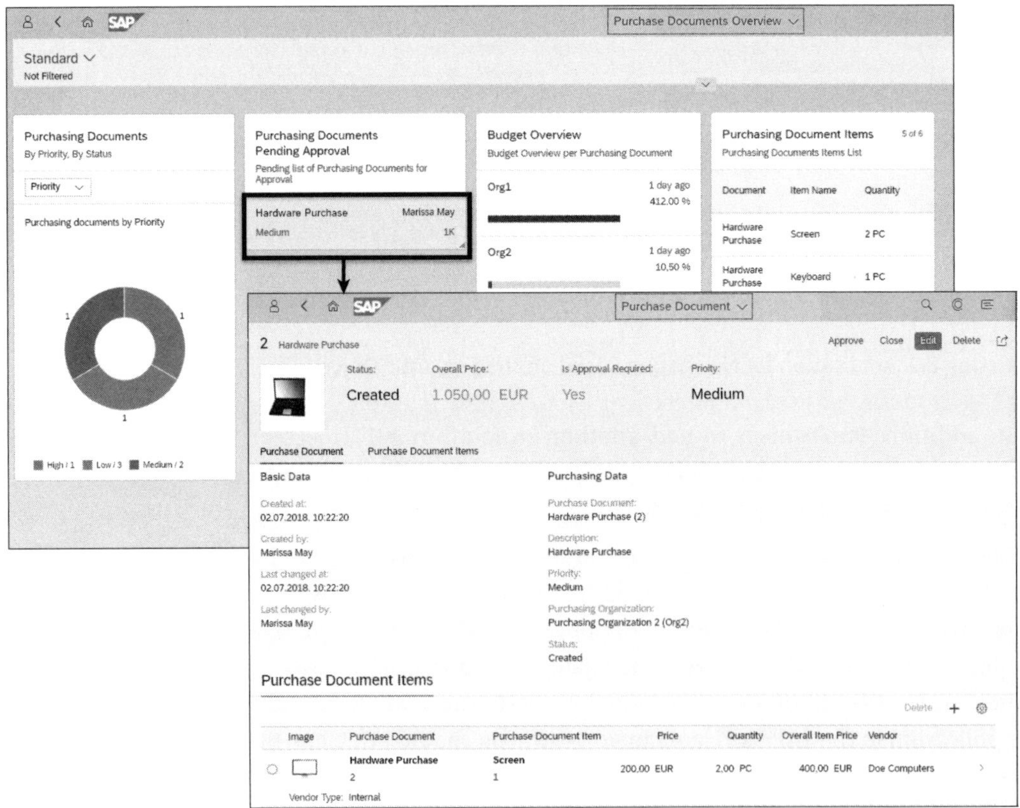

Figure 8.47 Navigation in Action from the Purchase Document OVP App to the Purchase Document LRP App

8.8 Summary

In this chapter, you learned how to deploy SAP Fiori applications from the SAP Web IDE into the ABAP frontend server. You also learned how to upload applications directly into the frontend server via SAP GUI. Then, we covered various concepts for using the SAP Fiori launchpad admin page, including catalogs, groups, and roles. We discussed how to create technical catalogs and business catalogs, how to create application tiles in the SAP Fiori admin launchpad, and how to create groups for adding application tiles from the BC. Then, we created Transaction PFCG roles in the ABAP frontend server and assigned the relevant groups and catalogs to the roles. Finally, we updated our CDS views to enable navigation from the Purchase Document OVP app to the Purchase Document LRP app. In the next chapter, we'll learn about version control in the SAP Web IDE using GitHub.

PART III

Operating Applications

Chapter 9
Version Control in SAP Web IDE Using Git

In this chapter, we'll introduce you to the basic concepts behind using Git as a Source Code Management (SCM) system and how to work with Git repositories using the SAP Web IDE.

Git is the version control system (VCS) most commonly used for SAPUI5 development. In this chapter, we'll cover the most important Git workflows and commands used for SAPUI5 development in the SAP Web IDE. You'll also learn how to link the Git repository with the SAP Web IDE projects and the concepts about working with different Git repository branches.

9.1 Git Introduction

A source code management (SCM) system helps you keep track of all the changes to your project files. The SAP Web IDE has integrated support for Git, so we'll use Git for our projects. However, instead of setting up a standalone Git repository on a system, we'll create project repositories using GitHub (a popular service that extends Git) and then link these repositories to their projects in the SAP Web IDE. In a project environment, using an SCM is useful when multiple developers are working on the same project. By adding SCM to your project, you can keep track of who modified a file in the project, compare the source code with its earlier versions, reverse changes, or even track who made that last commit that created a bug or issue in the project, and more. Because we're using Git as the SCM for the SAP Web IDE, let's start with some basics.

9.2 Git Basics

Git will serve as a central repository that will contain the most up-to-date version of a project. All developers working on this project will clone the central repository to their SAP Web IDE and work on the copy of the code in a local repository. Developers can submit the code back to the central repository and commit their changes. These changes can be synchronized by other developers into their local repository where they can continue working on their parts independently, as shown in Figure 9.1.

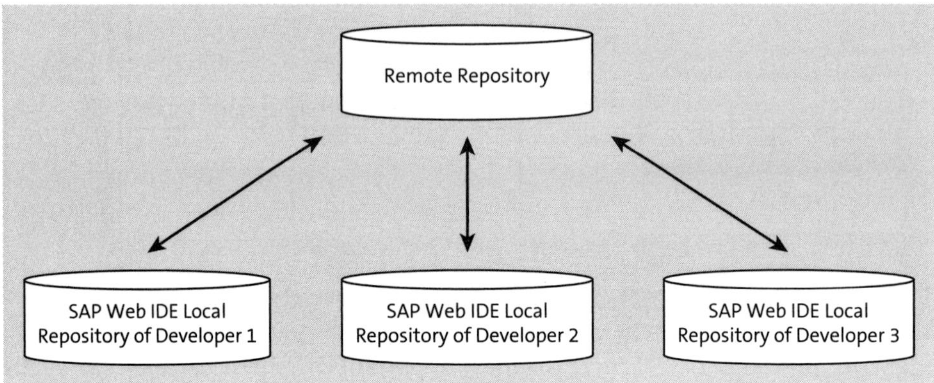

Figure 9.1 Shared Repository Concept for Projects Using Git

Unlike other VCSs, Git tracks changes as snapshots. In other words, not only does Git track new file changes in each version, it stores a snapshot of the entire project status every time a new change is pushed to its repository. Figure 9.2 shows how Git stores the snapshots; the rectangles with dotted lines signify files that haven't changed in that version, so Git references the file in its previous version.

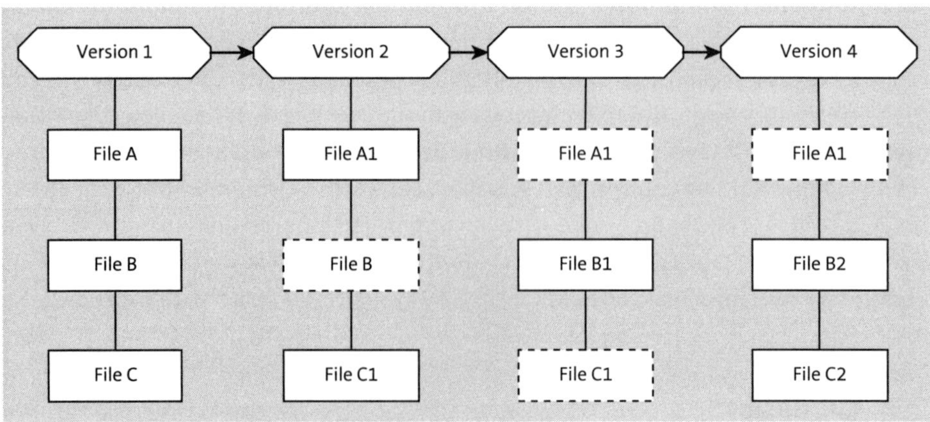

Figure 9.2 Git Snapshots Approach for Project Status

Now that you have a basic understanding of Git, let's start building a repository and linking it with our previously created projects. An alternative approach would be to create Git repositories prior to the creation of the actual apps in the previous chapters, but for our examples, we decided to link the apps in SAP Web IDE with a Git repository after completing the apps. You can take either approach. If you'll be the user setting up the initial version of the app, then you can create repositories later. If multiple developers are involved from the start of the project, then you'll need to set up the initial remote repository first, then clone the blank repositories to the SAP Web IDE for each developer of the project, and start working on the app. Figure 9.3 shows a high-level overview of the steps to setting up the Git repository for your projects.

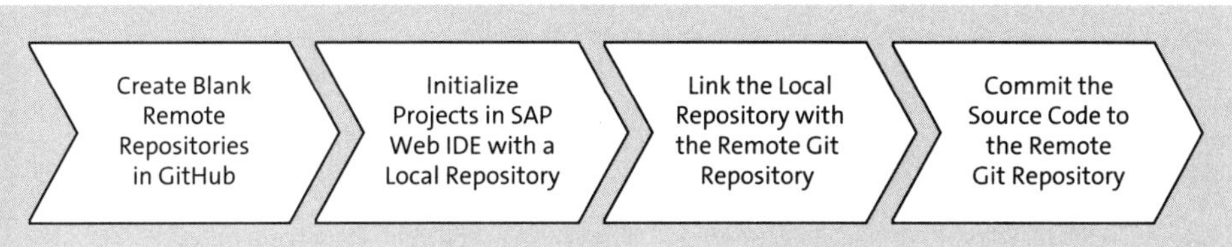

Figure 9.3 Git Project Repository Setup Plan

9.2.1 Creating Initial Project Repositories Using GitHub

First, you'll need to set up an account at *https://github.com*. On the GitHub home page, click on the **New Repository** button on left side of the page, as shown in Figure 9.4, to set up an initial blank repository for the project.

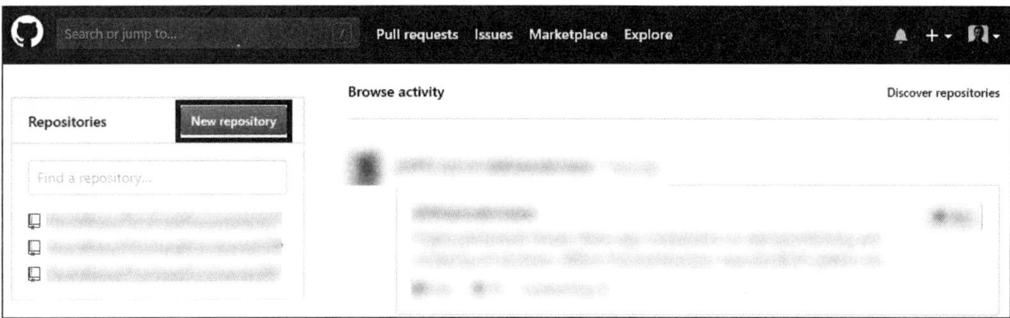

Figure 9.4 Creating a New Repository in GitHub

On the next screen, give the repository a name (for our example, enter "Purchase-DocumentsALPRepo") and a description. Select the **Initialize this repository with a README** checkbox and click on **Create repository**, as shown in Figure 9.5.

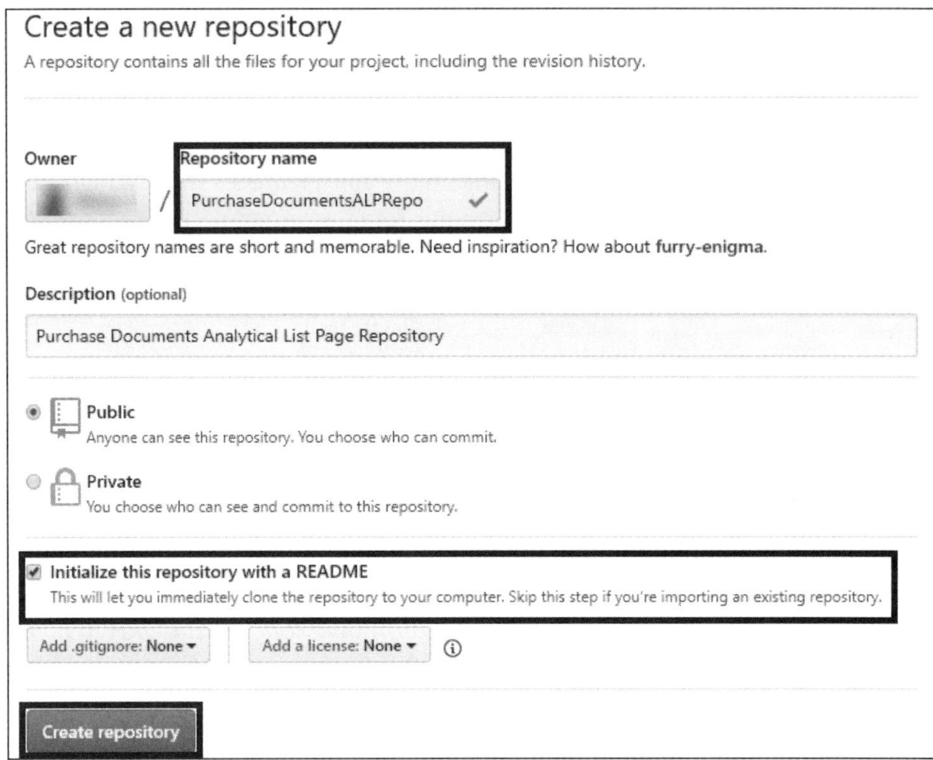

Figure 9.5 Setting Up and Initializing the New Repository

On the next screen, you'll see that the repository has been set up. Now, click on the **Clone or download** button and then click on the **Copy** icon to copy the URL, as shown in Figure 9.6.

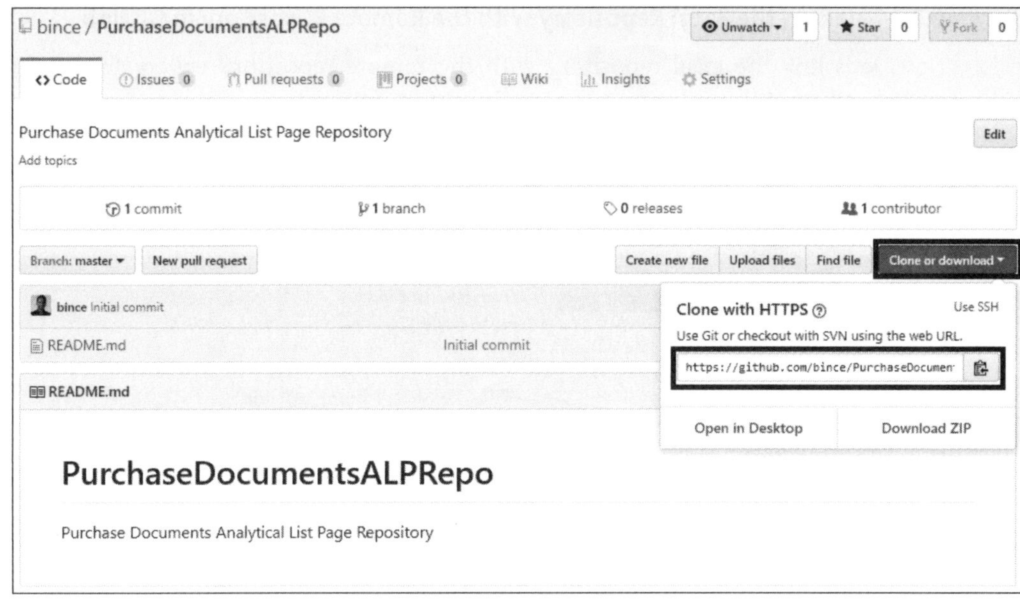

Figure 9.6 Copying the URL for the Git Repository

9.2.2 Initializing the Local Repository for the Projects in SAP Web IDE

After you've set up the initial remote repository, open the SAP Web IDE and right-click on the project. Then, go to **Git • Initialize Local Repository**, as shown in Figure 9.7. A local Git repository will be created with a default master branch for the project. This repository will act as your primary repository for further developments until you push changes back to the remote repository.

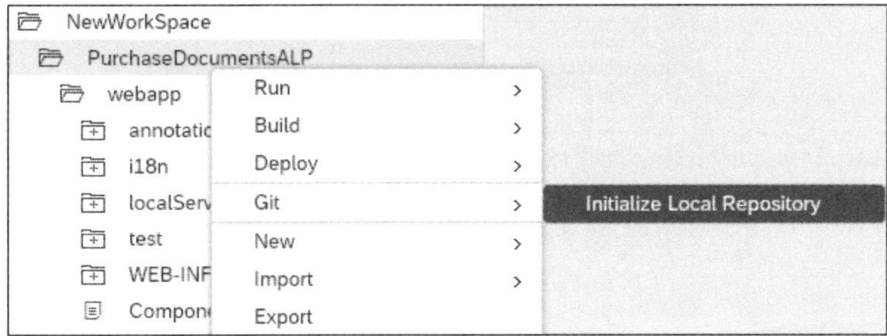

Figure 9.7 Initializing a Local Repository for the Project in SAP Web IDE

9.2.3 Linking the Local Repository with the Remote Repository in GitHub

Now, let's link the local repository with the remote repository we created using GitHub. Right-click on the project and go to **Git • Set Remote**, as shown in Figure 9.8.

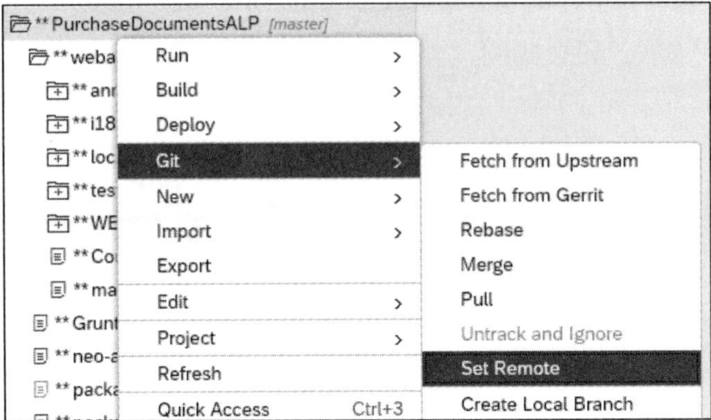

Figure 9.8 Linking Local Repository with the Remote Git Repository

In the next popup window, enter the **URL** of the remote repository, which we copied from the GitHub project earlier, and then click **OK**, as shown in Figure 9.9.

Configure Git Repository

You can now connect your local repository to a remote repository. You can make changes later from: Project Settings > Git Repository Configuration

Remote Repository

Name: origin

URL: https://github.com/bince/PurchaseDocumentsALPRepo.git

Advanced Configuration

☐ Add configuration for Gerrit

OK Cancel

Figure 9.9 Configuring the Git Repository Using the Git URL in SAP Web IDE

In the next window, as shown in Figure 9.10, click **OK** to confirm the changes fetched from the remote repository branch.

Changes Fetched

Summary	Author	Date	Change ID
master (origin/master)			
Initial commit	bincemathew	8/23/2018, 8:35:58 PM	5e79516

OK

Figure 9.10 Changes Fetched from the Remote Branch in Git

9.2.4 Submitting Code to Repository (Stage, Commit, Push)

Before committing changes to the Git repository, you'll need to understand some basic concepts in the SAP Web IDE related to Git integration. Let's take a quick look at certain parts of the SAP Web IDE that you'll need later in this chapter to work with our repositories.

As shown in Figure 9.11, when you click on the **Git Pane** icon on the right side of the SAP Web IDE project, a bunch of icons related to Git will appear.

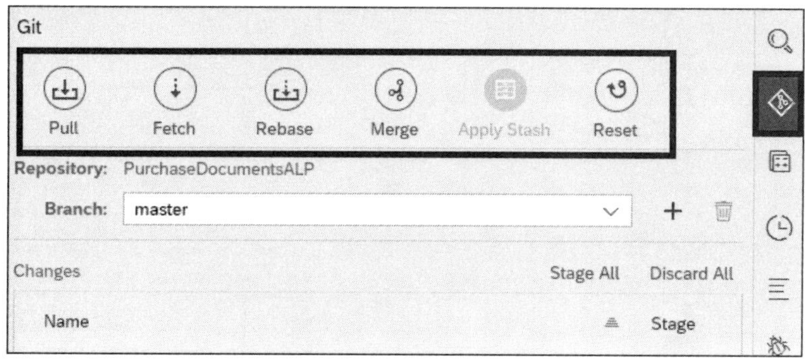

Figure 9.11 Git Pane in the SAP Web IDE

Let's look at each of these icons briefly:

- **Pull**
  As a combination of fetch and rebase Git actions, this icon fetches any changes from your remote repository branch and combines those changes with your local branch in the SAP Web IDE.

- **Fetch**
  This option fetches changes detected in the remote repository and lists those changes for you; however, those changes won't be applied to your local branch.
- **Rebase**
  In addition to the remote/master branch, you might have to create additional local branches based on project requirements, which often leads to conflicting code in the different branches. In this situation, the **Rebase** option can be helpful, as this option will make Git temporarily discard the changes in the local branch, update the code from the remote branch, and then try to apply the local changes again in the correct order. This option will help when your local changes are in conflict with the remote repository or when you want a new change in the remote branch to be added to your local branch without losing local changes on the project. **Rebase** will also rewrite the project commit history for a cleaner project history, as shown in Figure 9.12, in which the different commits in remote and local branches are represented by squares and triangles, respectively.

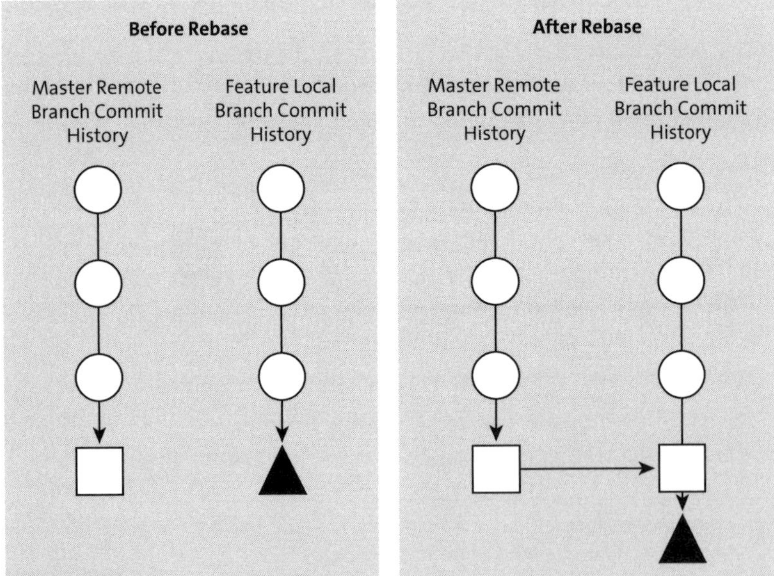

Figure 9.12 Git Rebase Concept

- **Merge**
  This option works like the **Rebase** option but in a slightly different way. Let's say you need some new changes submitted to the remote branch from a local repository for

a new feature. For instance, you might have opted to create a new feature branch in your local SAP Web IDE to work on this feature and need some of the changes from the master/remote branch to be incorporated into your local branch. The **Merge** option creates a merge commit to your local branch by combining the history of both branches together and thereby merging the commit history of both branches, as shown in Figure 9.13.

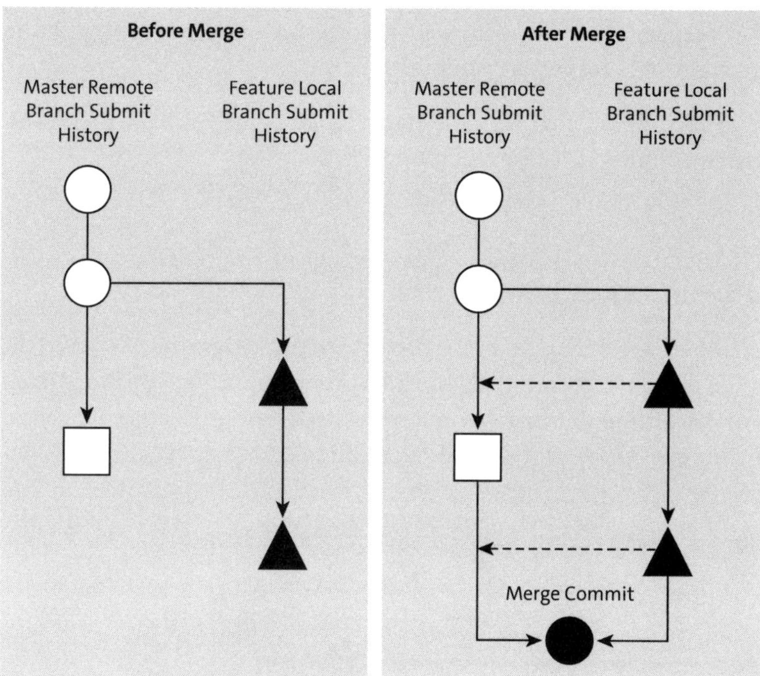

Figure 9.13 Git Merge Concept

- **Apply Stash**
  This option is useful when you're working on your local branch on a file and decide to switch to another local branch to work on a separate feature for your project, but you don't want to commit the current unfinished changes back to the remote branch. Instead of submitting changes to the remote branch, the developer can use the **Stash** option to temporarily store uncommitted changes and then switch to a different local branch without losing those changes. After the developer is done working in the other local branch and switches back to the local branch of the uncommitted code, the code can be retrieved using **Apply Stash** button from the Git pane.

- **Reset**
  As the name suggests, this option resets all the uncommitted changes from the local branch in the SAP Web IDE. Resets have two variations: a mixed reset or a hard reset. A mixed reset resets your files from the staging area and reverts your local repository back to the original commit history of your remote branch, but your local changes are still available in files. A hard reset resets the commit history, removes files from the staging area, and removes all the local changes you've made in your workspace. Basically, your workspace is put back into sync with the last committed state of its respective remote branch.

Next, you'll need to become familiar with the staging area of the Git pane in the SAP Web IDE, as shown in Figure 9.14. These include the:

❶ Staging area

❷ Staging options

❸ Uncommitted files in the local branch

The staging area is where local changes in the project are tracked by the SAP Web IDE, and the user has the option of committing the files into the remote repository from the staging area or discarding the changes and revert to the original code. By checking or unchecking the checkboxes for each file, you can select which files are committed or not.

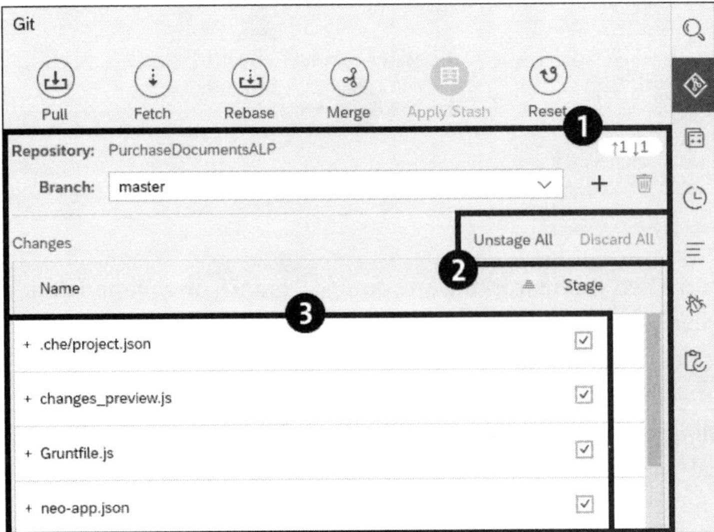

Figure 9.14 Staging Area in SAP Web IDE Full-Stack

Just below the staging area's list of tracked changes, a text area is available for entering a comment to describe the commit as well as some options to **Commit**, **Commit and Push**, **Push**, or **Stash** the changes, as shown in Figure 9.15. If you've already pushed a change, and you need to amend a new change to the previous push, then you must select the **Amend** checkbox before clicking the **Push** button.

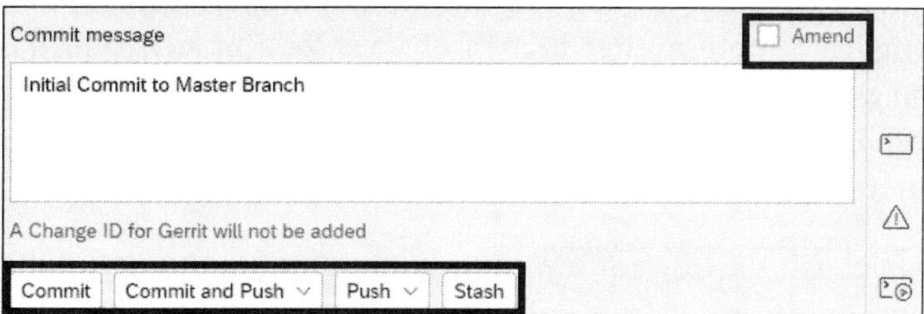

Figure 9.15 Staging Area Amend, Commit, Commit and Push, Push, and Stash Options

Now that we've covered the concepts related to the Git pane, let's get back to the step where we linked the local branch with the remote branch in the GitHub. After linking with the remote branch, click on the **Pull** button ❶, as shown in Figure 9.16, to sync the remote branch with the local branch (the remote branch didn't have any code in it other than a *Readme* file, so it shouldn't create any conflicts).

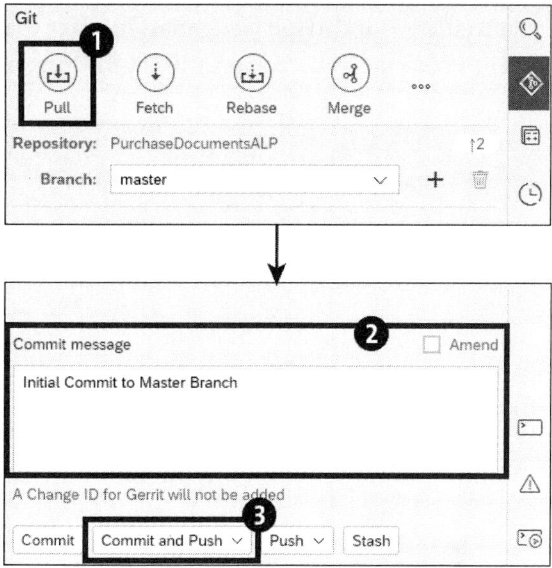

Figure 9.16 Making the Initial Commit to the Master Branch

After this step, you can submit all the code in your local branch for the project back to the remote branch and make the first commit. Enter your commit message ❷, as shown in Figure 9.16, and then click on the **Commit and Push** button ❸. All the code from your local branch will be submitted to the remote branch.

When you click **Commit and Push**, notice that the SAP Web IDE will offer you two options for the branch to commit, as shown in Figure 9.17. The **origin/master** option points toward the original remote master branch of your local branch, and the **Remote Branch** option gives you a list of available remote branches to choose from. For our scenario, select **origin/master** from the list, and the SAP Web IDE will create this branch in the remote repository.

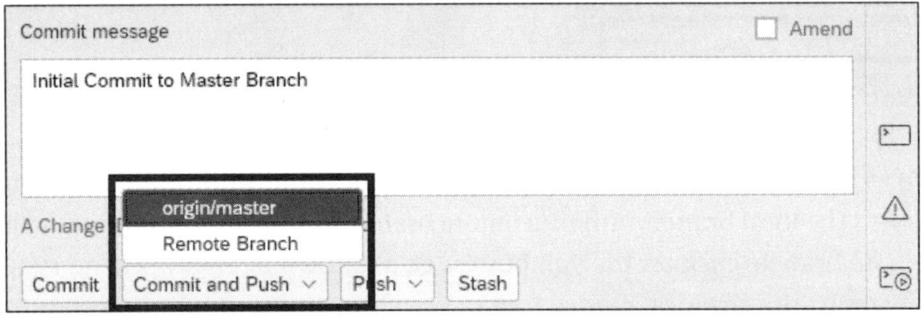

Figure 9.17 SAP Web IDE Creating a New Remote Repository for the Initial Commit

A popup window will appear where you'll enter your GitHub credentials to make the commit. Enter the details of your GitHub account and click on the **OK** button, as shown in Figure 9.18.

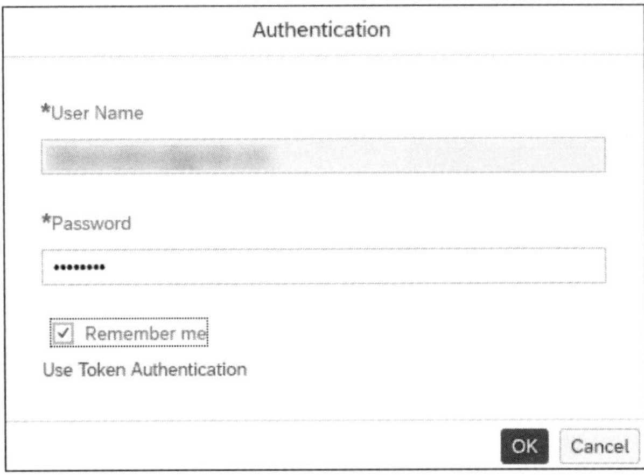

Figure 9.18 Entering the GitHub Account Credentials to Commit the Code

Now, if you log in to your GitHub account, you should see all your code committed from the SAP Web IDE in your local repository, as shown in Figure 9.19.

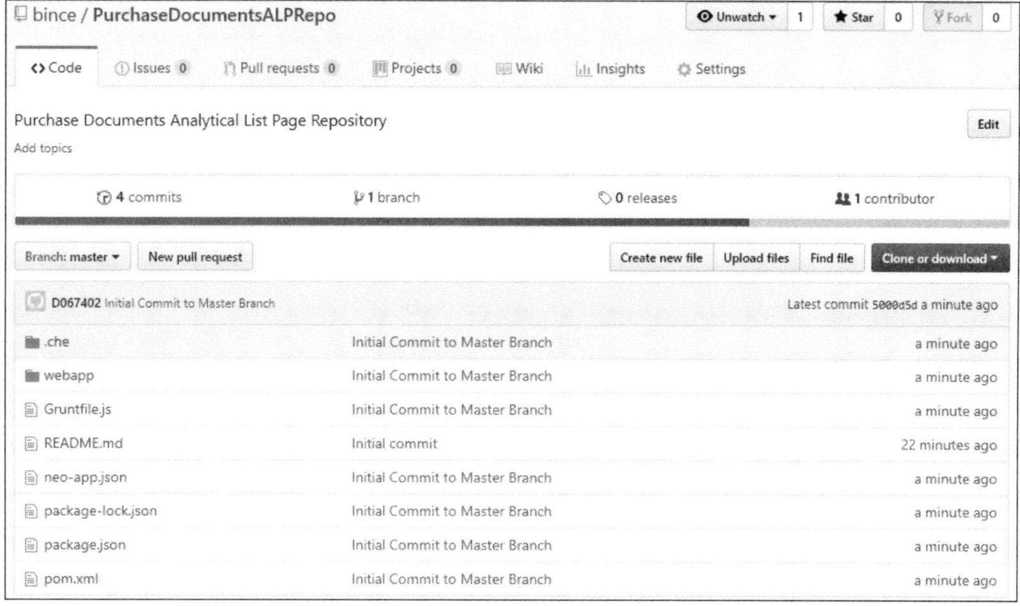

Figure 9.19 Committed Code Now Visible in GitHub

9.2.5 Cloning the Project into SAP Web IDE

To explore the **Fetch**, **Merge**, and **Pull** options from the perspective of another developer working on the same project in the SAP Web IDE, let's clone our newly created remote branch from GitHub into our SAP Web IDE. To replicate a scenario where two developers are working on the same project, this additional cloned project into the SAP Web IDE will act as the second developer. We'll then submit code from the original project (in which we initialized a local repository and then later linked with the GitHub remote repository) and retrieve/merge codes into the cloned project in the same SAP Web IDE to simulate the scenario.

To clone projects from Git, go to **File • Git • Clone Repository**, as shown in Figure 9.20.

In the popup window, enter the Git repository **URL** (the same URL we copied earlier in this chapter when creating the initial repository in GitHub) and click the **Clone** button, as shown in Figure 9.21.

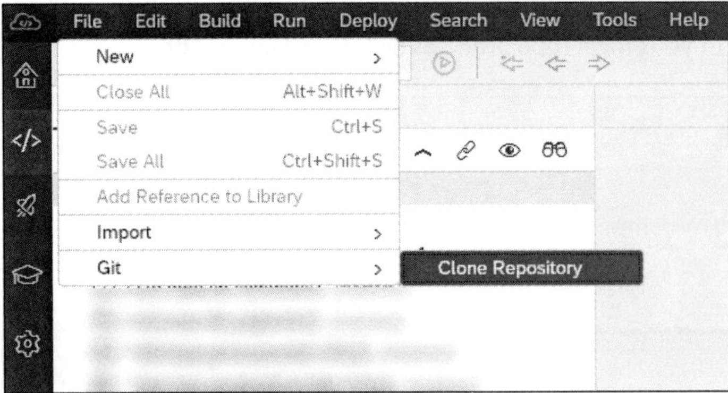

Figure 9.20 Cloning the Git Repository in SAP Web IDE

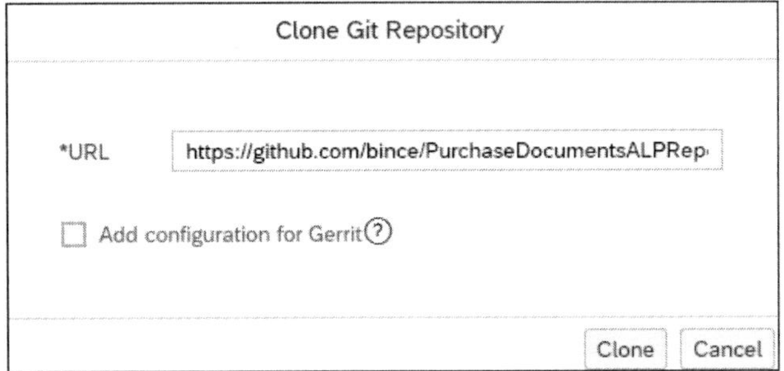

Figure 9.21 Entering the Git Repository URL to Clone the Project

Now, let's create a new local branch within the SAP Web IDE. Click on the **+** icon, as shown in the Figure 9.22.

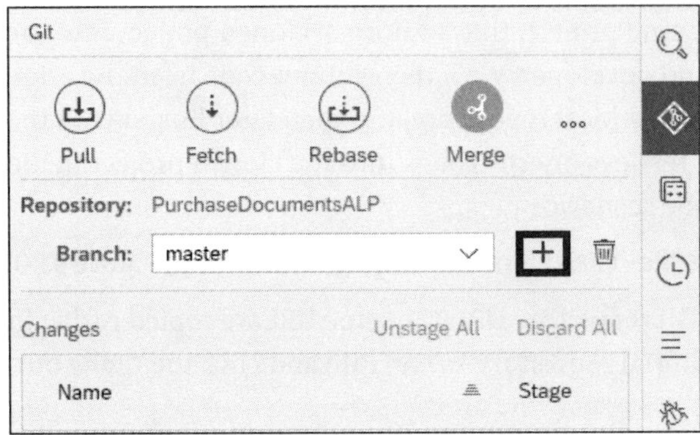

Figure 9.22 Adding a New Local Branch

Let's name the new branch "ALPFeatureBranch" and the **Source Branch** "master," as shown in Figure 9.23, because we need a copy of the master branch to the new local branch. Click **OK**.

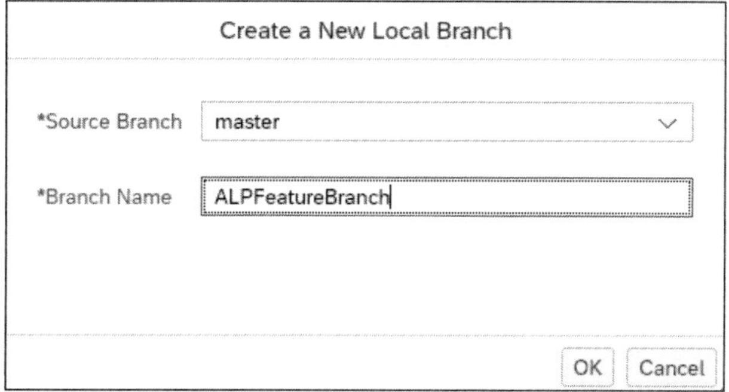

Figure 9.23 Creating the New Local Branch

Now, the new local branch has been created, and you can see that the new branch is selected in the Git pane, as shown in Figure 9.24.

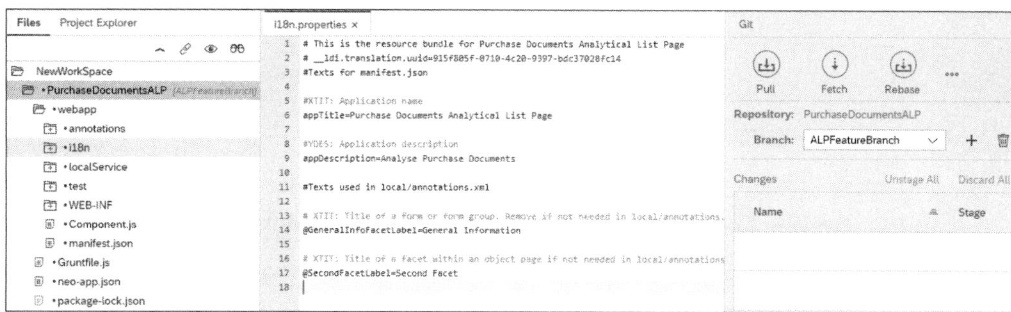

Figure 9.24 The New Local Branch Added to the Cloned Project in SAP Web IDE

Next, let's open the project that has only one local branch (master branch) and push some changes to the remote branch. For example, let's say one of our developers made a few changes in the *i18n* file and committed the changes to the master branch. As shown in Figure 9.25, the files that have been changed appear in the staging area. These include:

❶ Files selected to be committed from staging area

❷ Files excluded from staging area for commit

A developer can select or deselect files accordingly and then commit the changes. Notice that the developer has selected the *project.json* and *i18n.properties* files to be staged. The *extended_runnable_file.html* file was unselected and therefore won't be pushed to the remote branch. When you commit the changes to the remote repository, the code will be updated in the `master` branch to which the SAP Web IDE had made the initial commit.

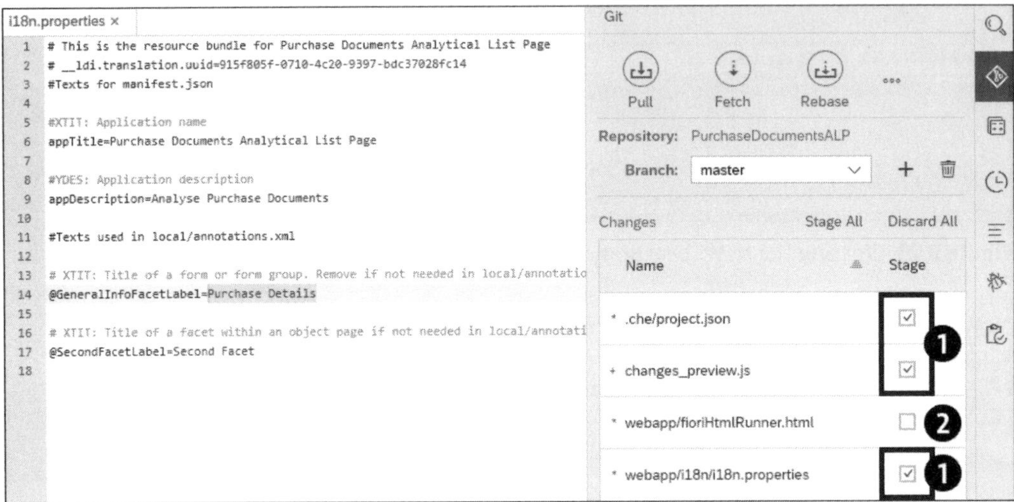

Figure 9.25 Staging Area in the SAP Web IDE for the Git Pane

9.2.6 Getting Code from the Remote Branch (Fetch, Merge, Pull)

Now, let's fetch the new changes from the remote branch that were pushed from the other project to the new local branch and then merge the changes from the remote branch to the new local branch. In this case, however, the second developer was also editing the same *i18n.properties* file. But first the developer needs to check whether any new changes have been pushed to the remote branch recently by another team member or not, so the developer clicks on the **Fetch** icon, as shown in Figure 9.26.

The `Fetch` action detected changes in the remote branch and lists the changes in a popup window, as shown in the Figure 9.27.

Now, the developer attempts a `Merge` action by clicking on the **Merge** button, as shown in Figure 9.28, which will try to merge the code from the master branch to the new local feature branch.

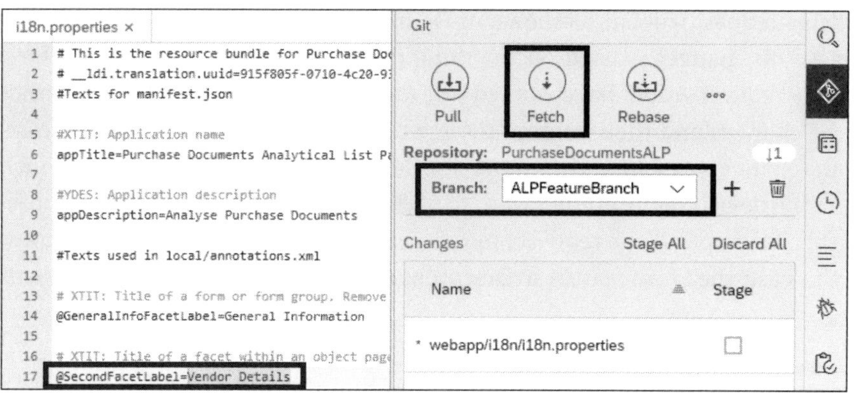

Figure 9.26 Initiating a Fetch to Look for Changes in the Remote Branch

Changes Fetched

Summary	Author	Date	Change ID
ALPFeatureBranch (origin/master)			
FacetLabel heading change	D067402	8/24/2018, 4:42:54 PM	d2ac7ba
ReleaseVersion1.0 (origin/ReleaseVersion1.0)			
ReleaseVersion2.0 (origin/ReleaseVersion2.0)			
master (origin/master)			

Figure 9.27 Fetch Action Detecting Changes from the Remote Branch

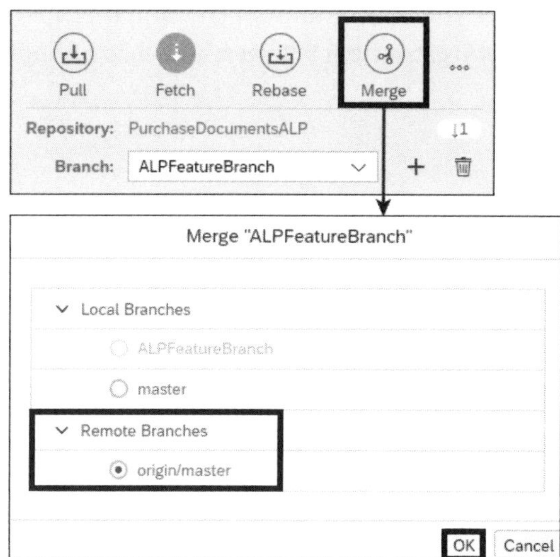

Figure 9.28 Merging the New Local Branch with the Remote Branch

But the `Merge` request will fail, as shown in Figure 9.29, because changes exist in the same file. (If no changes existed on the same file in this new local branch, then a `Merge/Rebase` request would have worked just fine.) Now, the developer must either discard the changes and then attempt a `Merge` or use the **Stash** option. In this case, because the change was minor, no issue arises. But let's assume the changes are much larger, and the developer just didn't want to back up the codes manually into a notepad and then attempt a `Merge` request after discarding the changes in the local repository. In this case, the **Stash** feature in Git comes is particularly handy for developers.

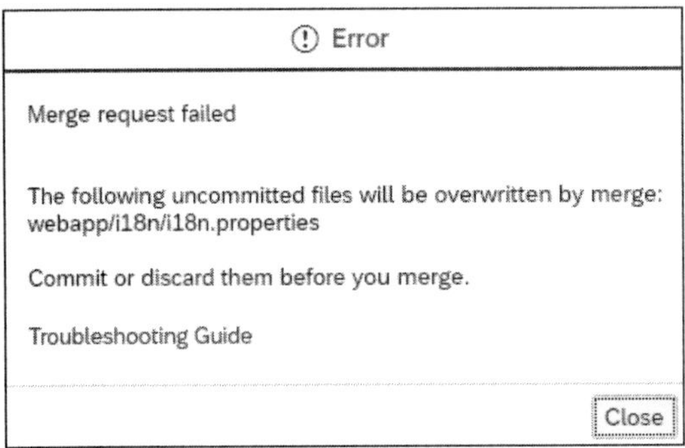

Figure 9.29 Merge Request Failure Due to File Conflicts

Toward the bottom of the staging area, notice that the **Stash** button is now active. Click on the **Stash** button, as shown in Figure 9.30. As mentioned earlier in Section 9.2.4, **Stash** serves as temporary storage for your uncommitted codes that enables you to retrieve these changes later so that you can switch between branches without losing changes.

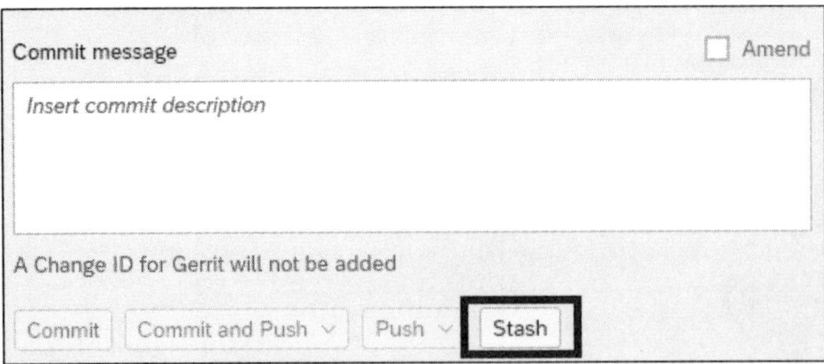

Figure 9.30 Stash Option in the Git Pane

In the next window, you must give a description for your stashed code so that you can identify it later when trying to retrieve it. Enter the required **Description** (in this case, "i18n File Changes backup") and click on the **Stash** button, as shown in Figure 9.31.

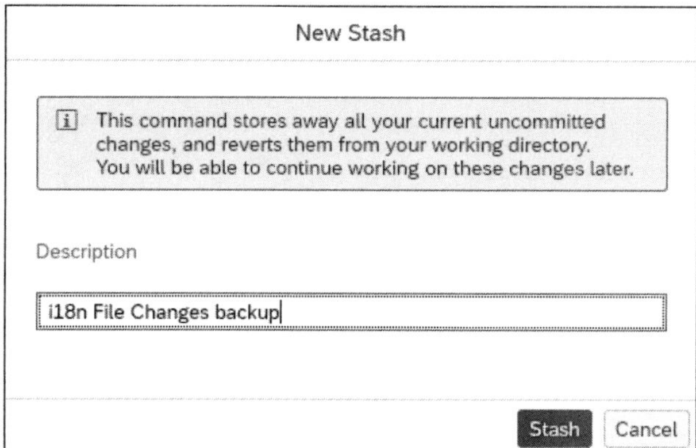

Figure 9.31 Naming the New Stash File

After local changes have been stashed, the developer can initiate the **Merge** action ❶, as shown in Figure 9.32. This time, the action will be successful without any conflicts. New changes from the master branch will be visible in the new local branch as well. Now, the developer can retrieve the stashed codes back into the project. Click on the **Apply Stash** button ❷ in the Git pane as shown in Figure 9.32. Codes that have been merged from the master branch with the new local branch after clicking on the **Merge** button ❸.

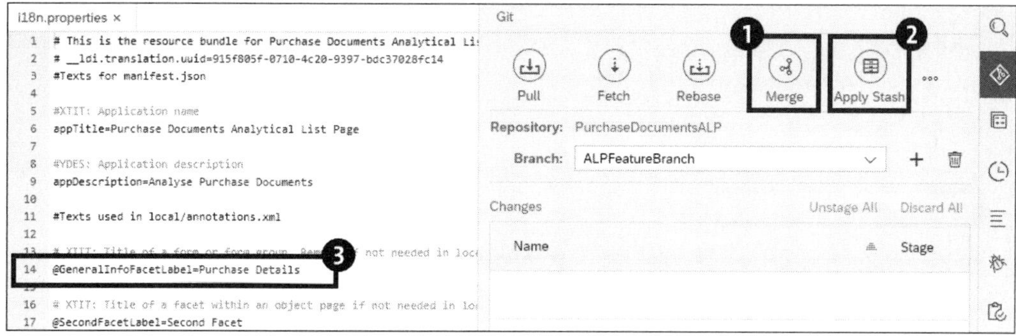

Figure 9.32 Merging and Applying Stash in the Git Pane

A new window will appear with the list of saved stash files. Select the **Stash** file; click on the second radio button (the developer can choose whether to keep the stashed files for future use or discard them); and click **Continue**, as shown in Figure 9.33.

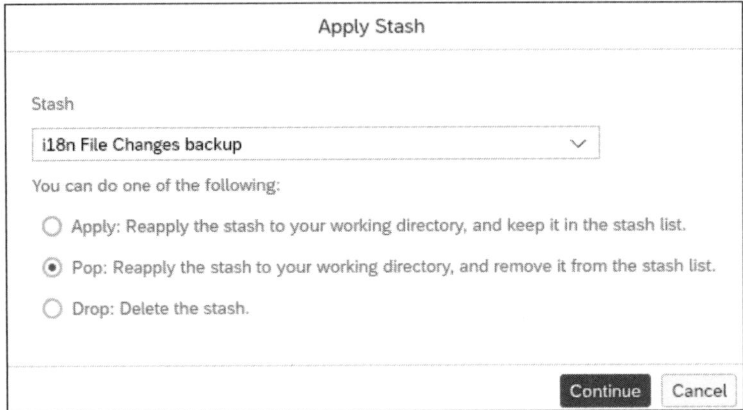

Figure 9.33 Selecting the Saved Stash from the Popup Window

Now, the previously uncommitted codes will reappear in the files, as shown in Figure 9.34. The developer can commit these changes back to the master branch after development in the local branch has been completed.

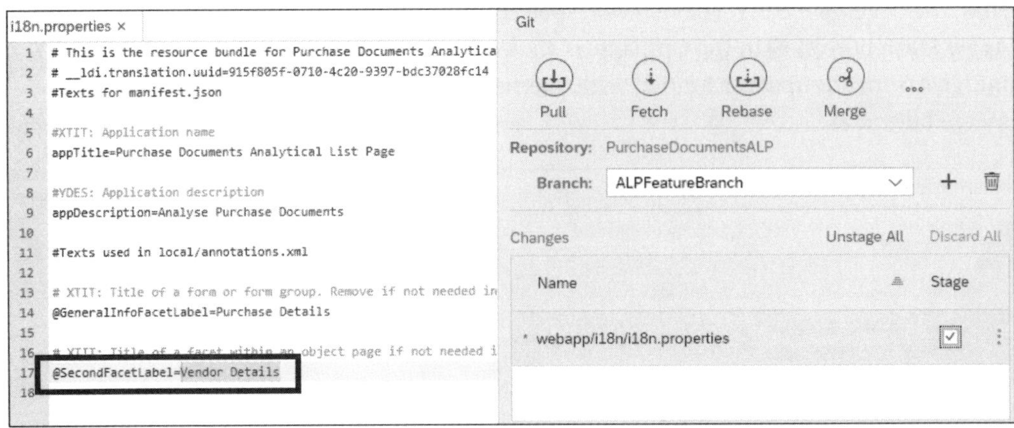

Figure 9.34 The Stashed Codes Now Restored to the Local Branch

Let's assume these new changes in the local branch have been completed by the second developer, and he has committed it back to the master branch. The other team members can now get the latest code from the central repository by clicking on the **Pull** button from the Git pane, and all the local branches will be synchronized with the remote branch, as shown in Figure 9.35.

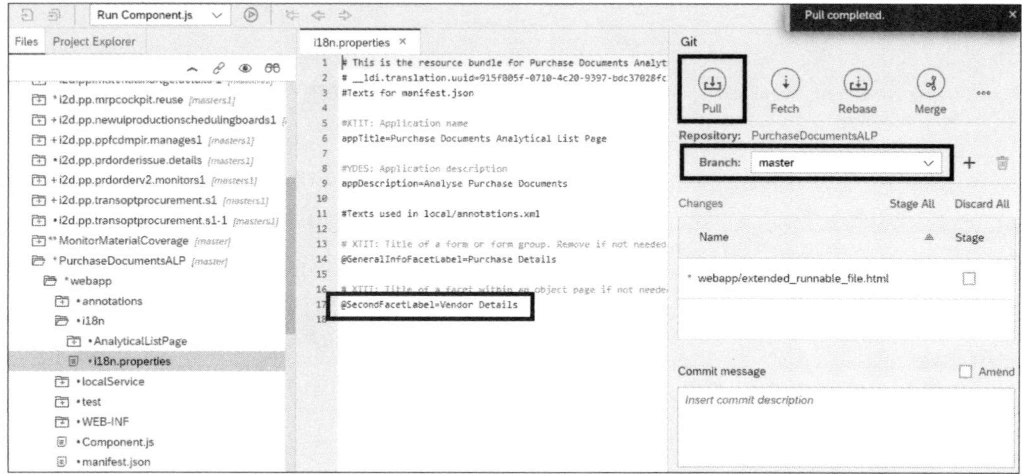

Figure 9.35 Initiating a Pull Request to Retrieve the Latest Code from the Remote Master Branch

9.2.7 Working with Branches

When your development project needs to deliver multiple versions of the product over time, dividing your remote repositories into different iterations based on the features or versions of the product makes sense. But you'll always need a master/infinity branch to contain the latest code. Different version branches of your application are created periodically from this master branch. Figure 9.36 shows a scenario with multiple remote and local branches. Each remote branch may have *n* number of local branches, depending on project requirements. This approach using multiple remote branches helps you separate what each version of a product will deliver, and developers can continue to provide support to older versions to address bugs within the product, issuing patches, and so on. Developers could even choose to downport a certain feature to older version of the product if necessary.

In this section, we'll create two additional remote branches: one branch using GitHub and one remote branch directly from the SAP Web IDE. Then, we'll create local branches in the SAP Web IDE from those remote branches.

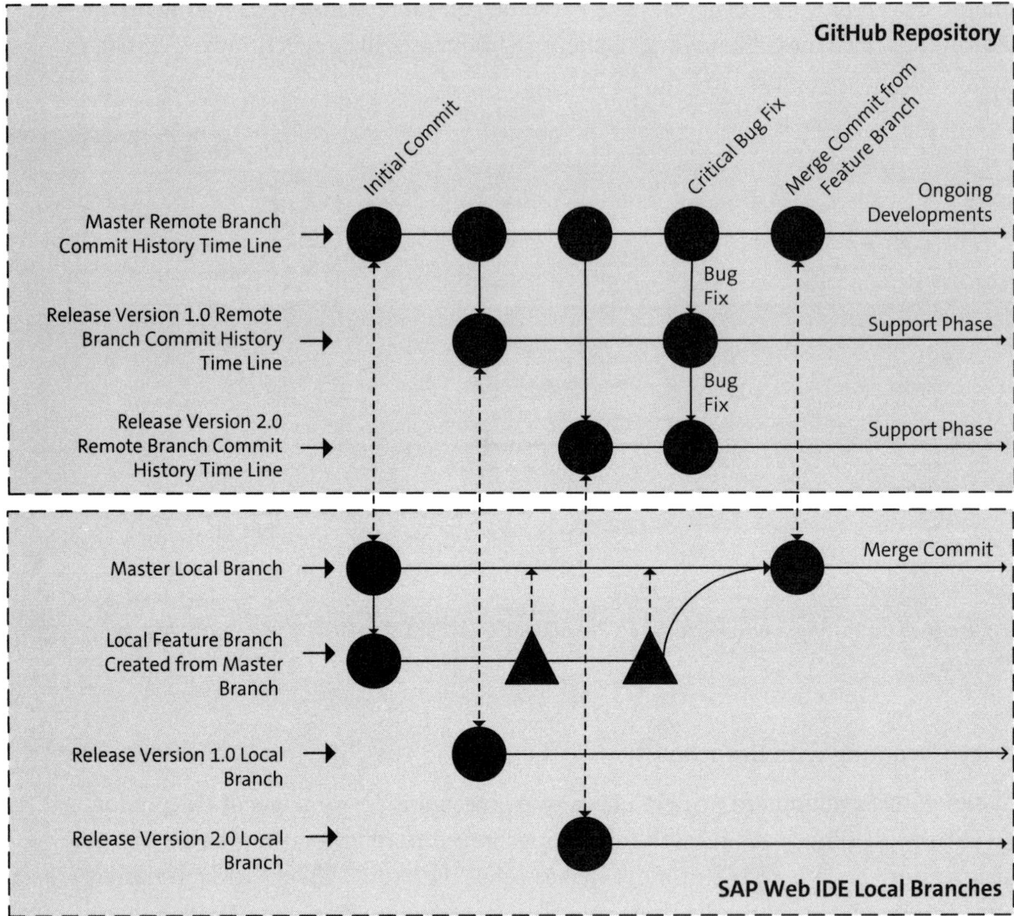

Figure 9.36 Working with Multiple Remote and Local Branches

First, let's create a new remote branch called `ReleaseVersion1.0` in the GitHub. Open the repository for the project, click on the **Branch:master** button shown in Figure 9.37 ❶, and type in the new branch name ❷. Then, click on the **Create branch: ReleaseVersion1.0** option ❸ in the bottom-left of the screen.

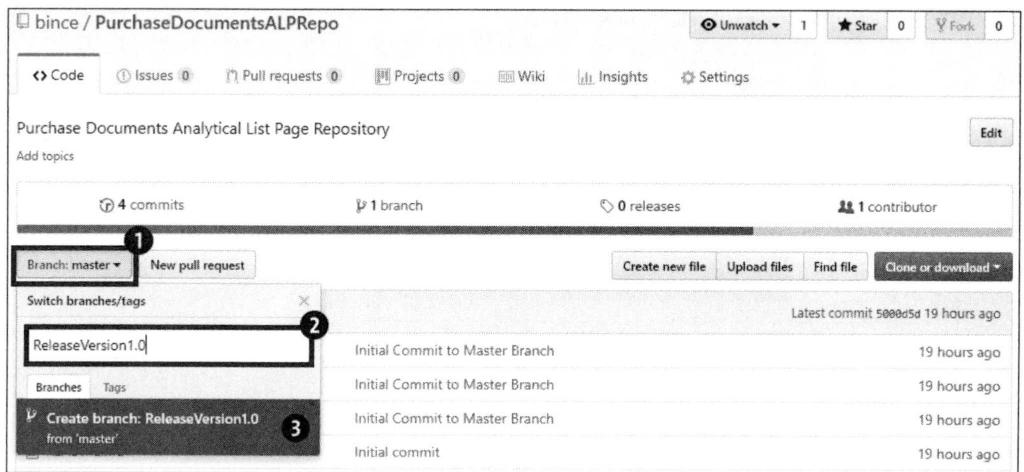

Figure 9.37 Creating a New Remote Branch in GitHub

Now, let's create a new remote branch named `ReleaseVersion2.0` using SAP Web IDE. Right-click on the project and go to **Git • Create Remote Branch**, as shown in Figure 9.38.

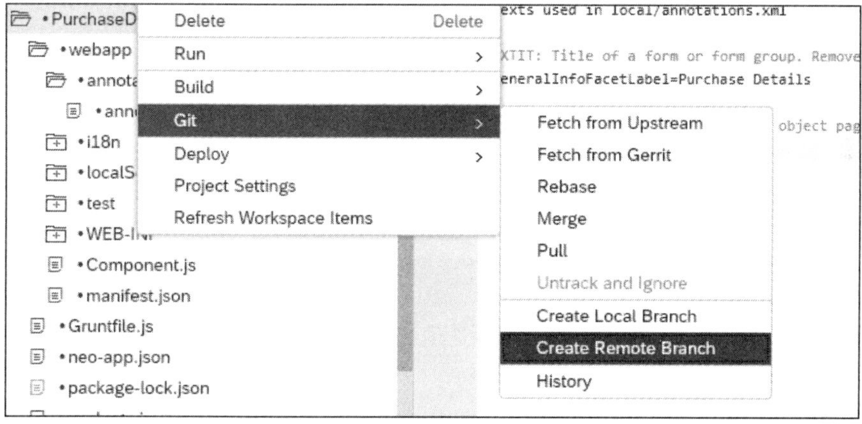

Figure 9.38 Creating a New Remote Branch from SAP Web IDE

In the new popup window, select the **Source Branch** as the remote branch **origin/master**, as shown in Figure 9.39. Enter the **Branch Name** as "ReleaseVersion2.0"; a copy will be made from the `Master` remote branch so that all the changes so far will be carried forward to the new remote branch).

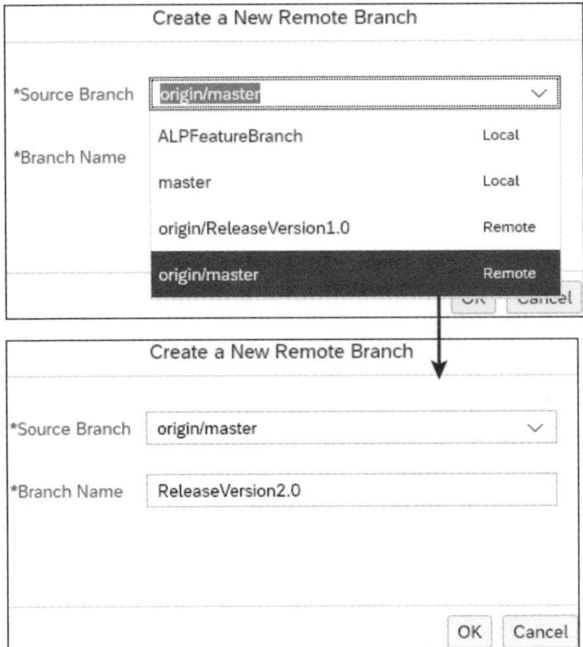

Figure 9.39 Creating a New Remote ReleaseVersion2.0 Branch

After the new remote branches have been created, you can start creating the local branches within the SAP Web IDE in the Git pane ❶. Click on the + icon ❷ next to the **Branch** dropdown list, as shown in Figure 9.40. In the popup window, select the **Source Branch** from which you want to create your local branch and click on the **OK** button ❸.

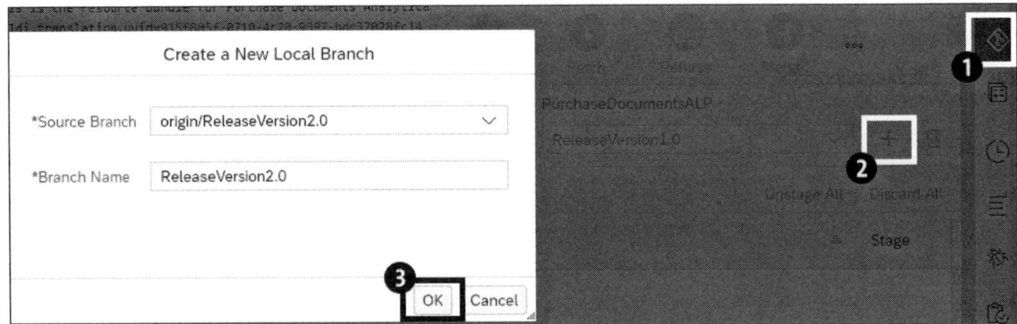

Figure 9.40 Creating a New Local Branch from Remote ReleaseVersion2.0

Create all the local branches based on your project requirements. After all the branches have been created, you'll see them in the **Branch** dropdown list in the Git pane in the SAP Web IDE, as shown in Figure 9.41.

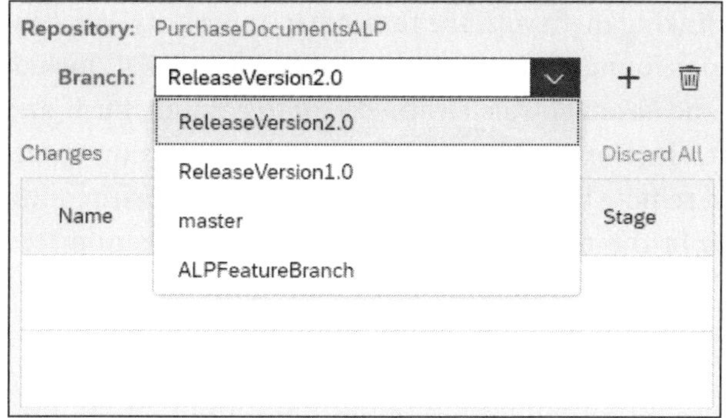

Figure 9.41 Overview of All Branches in SAP Web IDE Git Pane

You can also view all your remote branches directly in the GitHub page, as shown in Figure 9.42. With this approach, developers can easily work on different branches based on project release cycles or feature releases. Multiple developers on your team can work on the same project much more easily.

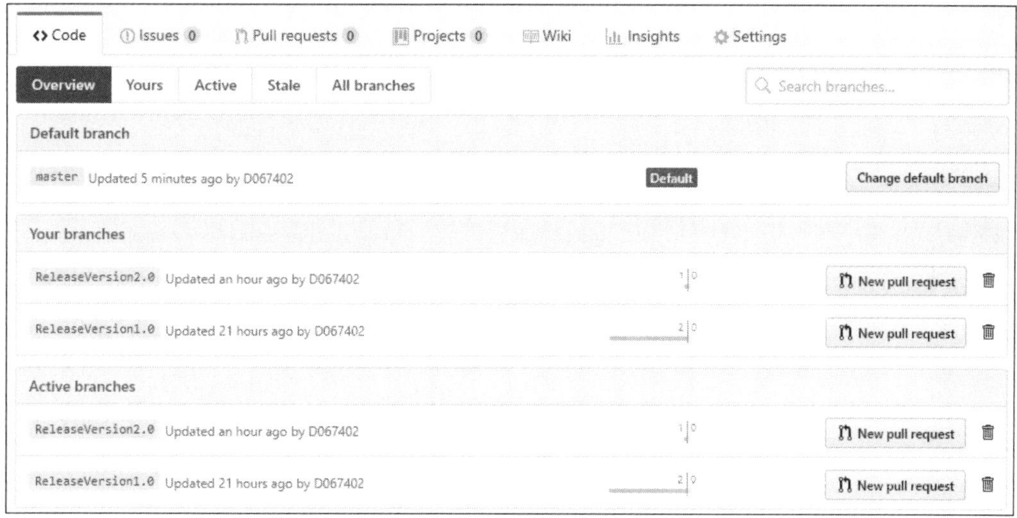

Figure 9.42 Overview of All Remote Branches in GitHub

9.3 Summary

In this chapter, you learned about the Git repository and how to use GitHub as an extension to create and manage repositories in Git. We covered creating local repositories in the SAP Web IDE and linking them with the remote Git repository. We went through the basic GitHub options found in the Git pane of the SAP Web IDE, including **Pull**, **Fetch**, **Rebase**, **Merge**, and **Reset**. You also learned how to commit, push, and stage codes into remote repositories from the SAP Web IDE. We discussed how to create multiple local branches and remote branches, as well as how to work with multiple branches for development. In the next chapter, you'll learn about automated testing on the SAP S/4HANA platform.

Chapter 10
Automated Testing

Automated testing is key for ensuring software quality across software releases and for catching bugs early and consistently. In this chapter, you'll learn how to create automated tests for all layers of your SAP S/4HANA applications, from the SAP HANA database over the ABAP business logic to the SAPUI5 frontend.

Traditionally, software was tested manually by testers following scripts ensuring consistent testing for each release. The software was deployed to a testing environment, and the testers did black-box style testing by clicking through the user interface (UI) of the application to check whether anything was broken, a time-consuming and tedious process that quickly becomes unfeasible. The only way to escape this negative spiral of manual repetitive testing is to automate the tests as much as possible. If your software is accompanied by a comprehensive automated test suite, determining whether your software works or not is a matter of seconds, not hours or days. Consequently, test automation is the foundation for shorter release cycles and faster customer feedback; automated tests are an integral part of any build pipeline that automatically tests and, if successful, deploys the software to a test or production environment. To achieve good coverage over all functional aspects and parts of the software, an extensive test suite usually consists of several layers, as depicted in the test automation pyramid shown in Figure 10.1.

Unit tests written using test-driven development (TDD) make up the foundation layer of the pyramid. These tests specify the software at the lowest possible level, usually on the public method or function level, and are written before the production code. These tests can play a decisive role in increasing code quality by enforcing testability, decoupling, and modularity. When developing applications for the SAP S/4HANA platform, you can write unit tests in the backend by using ABAP Unit, which is integrated into the ABAP runtime, and by using QUnit, which is included in the SAPUI5 Software Development Kit (SDK), in the frontend. A rule of thumb to follow is one unit test class/object per ABAP or JavaScript class/object and several test methods/

functions for one production method/function covering all code paths (*happy path* and *edge cases*). In testing, a happy path is a standard test case that does not check any exceptional or error conditions. In contrast, edge cases are exceptional cases where the program logic meets boundaries due to specific inputs. Edge cases are prone to bugs and should therefore be tested carefully.

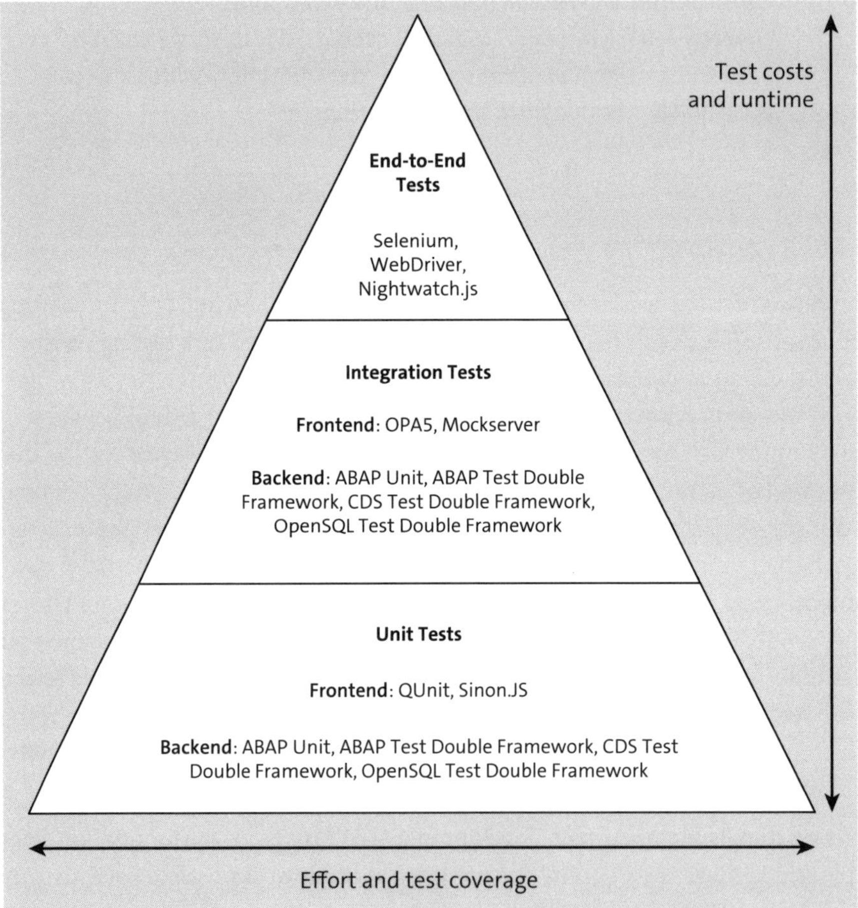

Figure 10.1 Test Pyramid Layers and Respective Testing Tools for SAP S/4HANA Applications

As indicated by the width of this layer of the pyramid, unit tests outnumber all other tests in the pyramid, and these tests should cover your code as close to 100% as reasonable. Because the SAP S/4HANA platform is database-centric and operations on data should be pushed down to SAP HANA, either via core data services (CDS) views or Open SQL, SAP provides CDS Test Double Framework to help you test their contained logic and calculations isolated from their underlying views and tables using ABAP Unit as a test runner. To isolate methods under test containing ABAP business logic from their dependencies or depended-on components (DOC), you can use the ABAP Test Double Framework. The counterpart in the frontend, included with the SAPUI5 SDK, is Sinon.JS.

In *integration tests*, several previously unit-tested software modules (e.g., several classes) are combined and tested together. In the SAP S/4HANA backend, you can use the same technologies as for unit tests to write integration tests. You can isolate these tests from additional unwanted dependencies using one or more of the provided test double frameworks and only test the integrations relevant for your particular test case. In the frontend, integration tests can be written using the One-Page Acceptance (OPA5) framework included with the SAPUI5 SDK. To isolate these tests from the backend, you can use a mock server with mock data to handle OData read requests locally by returning predefined mock data. A mock server is also capable of dealing with write accesses (POST, PUT, MERGE) to OData entities by persisting them in-memory for the runtime of the test.

In end-to-end (E2E) tests, you'll want to test the application how an end user would test the app via its UI but in an automated way. E2E tests give you the most confidence that the application is working correctly because they cover both the frontend and the backend of the application as well as their interaction and integration. At the same time, such tests are usually more fragile and slow compared to isolated unit or integration tests. In the SAP S/4HANA environment, executing such tests requires a dedicated test system with existing master data and stable Customizing; otherwise, these tests might fail often and lead to a lot of false positives. Maintaining a large set of E2E tests can quickly become a full-time job if there is no dedicated and stable test system. Therefore, E2E tests usually cover only the standard process of an application without testing all edge cases. Edge cases are supposed to be covered by lower-level tests. Since the UI part of SAP S/4HANA applications is in the end standard HTML5, you can use any E2E test framework used for testing web applications. A common option for E2E testing of web applications is Selenium and its WebDriver API. Thus, in Section 10.3, we'll create a small E2E test example using Nighwatch.js and Selenium under the hood.

In this chapter, you'll learn how to use various testing frameworks in the frontend and backend to cover all layers of the testing pyramid when developing applications on the SAP S/4HANA platform.

10.1 Backend Test Automation

Let's first look at how to write unit tests for the main technologies working in the backend of an SAP S/4HANA application: ABAP and CDS. We'll start by introducing ABAP Unit and subsequently develop an ABAP unit test for a CDS calculation. During the development of our unit tests, we'll also introduce dependency injection techniques to isolate the code under test (CUT) from its depended-on components (DOC), primarily the object factory class pattern, and use the ABAP Test Double Framework for creating test doubles. In the next section, we'll look at the CDS Test Double framework in depth. By the end of this section, you'll be able to write your own unit tests for the backend part of your SAP S/4HANA applications.

10.1.1 Unit Testing (ABAP Unit)

ABAP Unit is SAP's unit testing framework for ABAP. Unit tests for ABAP classes are typically implemented in a local test class of a global class to be tested with the addition of `FOR TESTING` of the `CLASS` statement. The test class will contain several test methods, which also have the addition `FOR TESTING` added to their method definitions. In addition to the test methods, the class can contain *test fixture* methods that are called at predefined times by the ABAP Unit Runner; for instance, the static `class_setup()` and `class_teardown()` methods will be called before and after the test methods are run.

These methods can be used for general setup and cleanup activities relevant for the whole test suite. The `setup()` and `teardown()` methods, if present, will be called before and after each test method execution. The sequence in which the actual test methods are executed is undefined. The test fixture methods can therefore be used to create, re-create, and clean up a defined state before and after a test method is executed. Additionally, a new instance of the test class is created for each test method, which prevents unwanted side effects due to states conserved between different test method runs. Figure 10.2 shows the sequence in which the ABAP Unit Runner invokes the methods of the local test class in an Unified Modeling Language (UML) sequence diagram. To check the result of a method under test, SAP provides the `CL_ABAP_UNIT_ASSERT` class, which contains different static methods for comparing expected and actual values.

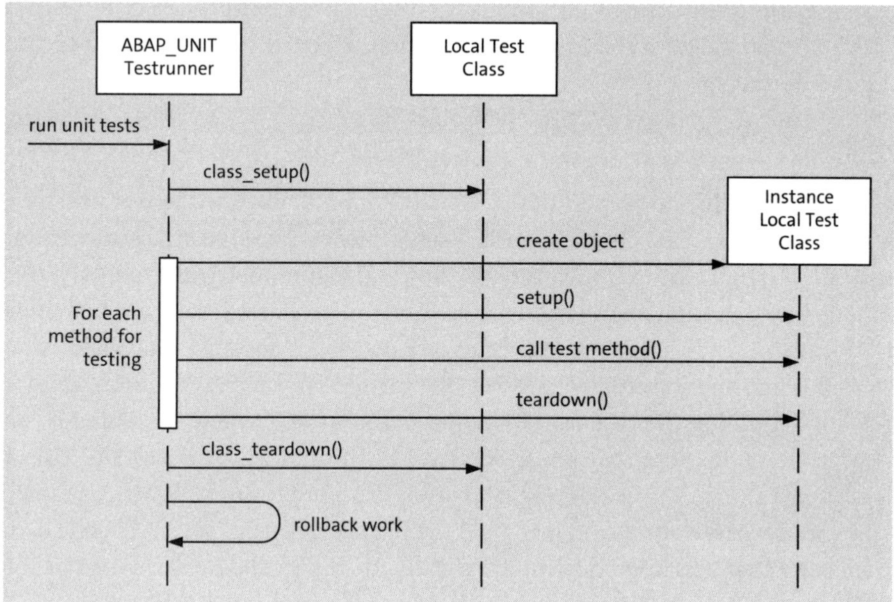

Figure 10.2 UML Sequence Diagram for an ABAP Unit Test Run

Create an ABAP Unit Test in ABAP Development Tools

You can create a local test class for a global ABAP class opened in the editor of the ABAP development tools in Eclipse by selecting the **Test Classes** tab, entering "test-Class" into the editor, and pressing Ctrl+Space and then Enter. The `testClass` code template, which consists of a local skeleton unit test class, will be inserted into the editor, as shown in Figure 10.3.

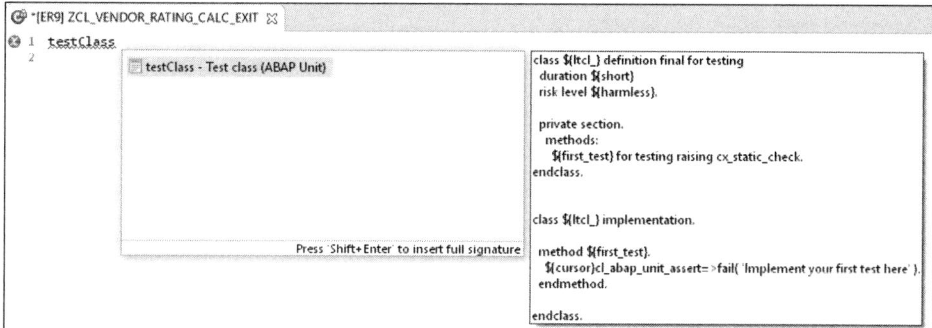

Figure 10.3 Creating a Unit Test Class Skeleton Using the Provided ABAP Development Tools testClass Code Template

You can run unit tests using the shortcut Ctrl+Shift+F10 or Ctrl+Shift+F11 (which also includes the info how much of the actual code is covered or run through by your tests).

Add a Virtual Element to a Core Data Services View

Let's say you need to add an additional **Vendor Rating** field added to our purchase order item OData and CDS entity (`Z_C_PurchaseDocumentItemLrp`) to indicate a vendor quality rating ranging from 0 to 5 stars, as shown in Figure 10.4. Unfortunately, this information isn't present on the database, at least not in a format easily consumable by a CDS view. Luckily, an ABAP service class (`zcl_vendor_service`) is available that provides this information conveniently via the `get_vendor_rating()` method. Vendor ratings are a common use case for a virtual element in a CDS view populated by an ABAP exit. However, note that you cannot yet push the logic down to SAP HANA using CDS views, and the business logic is simply too complex to rewrite in a reasonable time frame. The only option is to read the field values using an ABAP code exit. Keep in mind that this approach might negatively impact the performance of the application since not all data processing is being pushed down into SAP HANA.

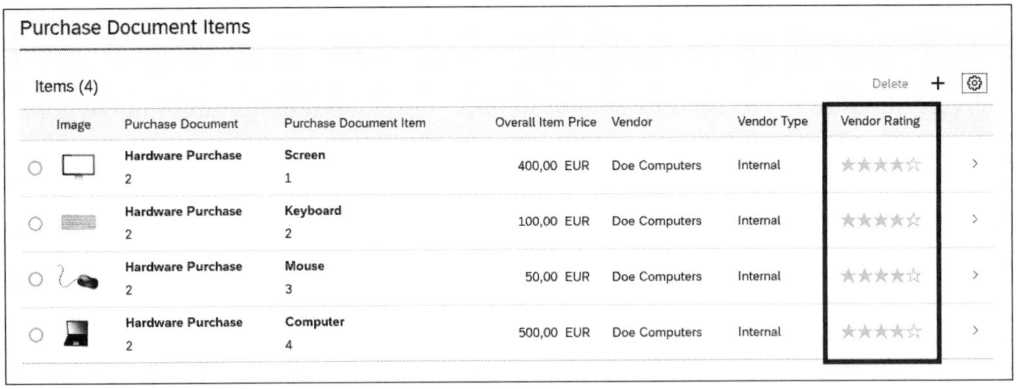

Purchase Document Items

Items (4) Delete +

Image	Purchase Document	Purchase Document Item	Overall Item Price	Vendor	Vendor Type	Vendor Rating
	Hardware Purchase 2	Screen 1	400,00 EUR	Doe Computers	Internal	
	Hardware Purchase 2	Keyboard 2	100,00 EUR	Doe Computers	Internal	
	Hardware Purchase 2	Mouse 3	50,00 EUR	Doe Computers	Internal	
	Hardware Purchase 2	Computer 4	500,00 EUR	Doe Computers	Internal	

Figure 10.4 New in ABAP: Calculated Vendor Rating Column

Listing 10.1 shows how you can add the virtual `VendorRating` field to the field list of the `Z_C_PurchaseDocumentItemLrp` CDS view. The field is virtual because it doesn't exist on the database. The values of the virtual field (or virtual element) are calculated by the `ZCL_VENDOR_RATING_CALC_EXIT` ABAP class.

```
...
@EndUserText.label: 'Vendor Rating'
@ObjectModel.virtualElementCalculatedBy: 'ABAP:ZCL_VENDOR_RATING_CALC_EXIT'
virtual VendorRating: abap.int1(0),
...
```

Listing 10.1 Add the Virtual VendorRating Field to the Z_C_PurchaseDocumentItemLrp CDS View

Create an ABAP Code Exit for a Virtual Core Data Services Element

The `zcl_vendor_rating_calc_exit` must implement the interface `if_sadl_exit_calc_element_read`, which has two methods (`get_calculation_info()` and `calculate()`), as shown in Figure 10.5.

The `get_calculation_info()` method is called before data is selected from the database via the generic Service Adaptation Definition Language (SADL) CDS entity `SELECT` (in our case, on `Z_C_PurchaseDocumentItemLrp`). The `calculate()` method is called after the original data is read from the database. Its purpose is to calculate the virtual elements based on the original data. Figure 10.6 shows an oversimplification of when the methods are invoked by the SADL engine using a UML sequence diagram.

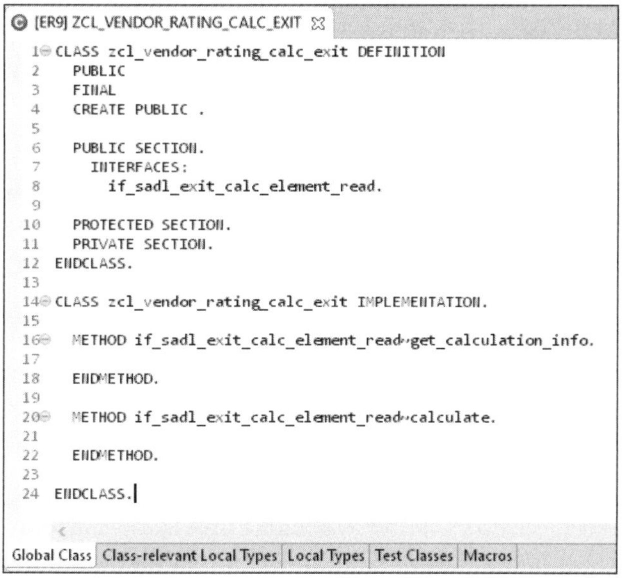

```
[ER9] ZCL_VENDOR_RATING_CALC_EXIT
CLASS zcl_vendor_rating_calc_exit DEFINITION
  PUBLIC
  FINAL
  CREATE PUBLIC .

  PUBLIC SECTION.
    INTERFACES:
      if_sadl_exit_calc_element_read.

  PROTECTED SECTION.
  PRIVATE SECTION.
ENDCLASS.

CLASS zcl_vendor_rating_calc_exit IMPLEMENTATION.

  METHOD if_sadl_exit_calc_element_read~get_calculation_info.

  ENDMETHOD.

  METHOD if_sadl_exit_calc_element_read~calculate.

  ENDMETHOD.

ENDCLASS.
```

Global Class | Class-relevant Local Types | Local Types | Test Classes | Macros

Figure 10.5 ABAP Calculation Exit for Vendor Ratings zcl_vendor_rating_calc_exit, Which Must Implement the Interface if_sadl_exit_calc_element_read

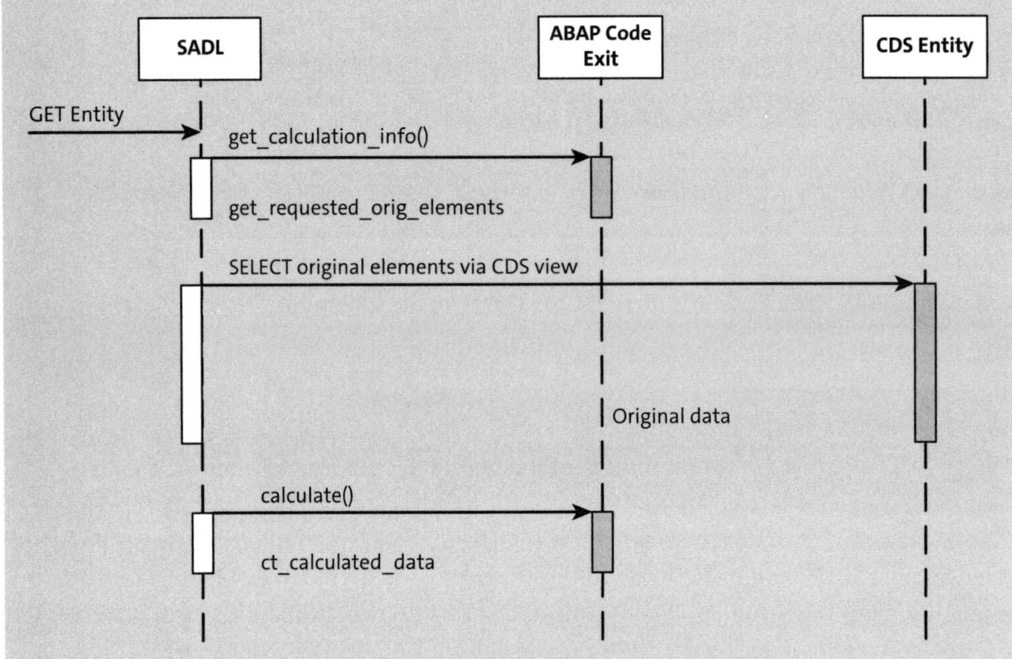

Figure 10.6 SADL Performs the Generic Database Select and Invokes the get_calculation_info() and calculate() Methods of the ABAP Exit in This Sequence

Implement the get_calculation_info() Method Using Test-Driven Development

In the `get_calculation_info()` method, you must provide all fields that will be required to later calculate the virtual element values in the `calculate()` method. In our case, the `VENDOR` field will need to be selected from the database if the `VendorRating` field is requested because the `VENDOR` will need to be passed as a parameter to the `get_vendor_rating()` method of the `zcl_vendor_service` class. With this specification, let's write our first `vendor_rating_selected` test, shown in Figure 10.7. We'll create an instance of the calculation exit and call its `get_calculation_info()` method, passing the `VENDORRATING` field (as a requested calculated field) and the entity name of our CDS views as parameters.

The test will fail because we haven't yet implemented anything in our CUT according to the TDD practice. Let's fix this problem by simply appending the `VENDOR` field to the `et_requested_orig_elements` table inside the `get_calculation_info()` method of the `zcl_vendor_rating_calc_exit` class. However, what happens if the `VENDORRATING` field isn't contained in the `it_requested_calc_elements` table? In this case, you shouldn't append the VENDOR field to the requested original elements table (et_requested_orig_elements) because, for performance reasons, we should always only read data that is requested. We can write a test for this scenario as shown in Figure 10.8.

```
[ER9] ZCL_VENDOR_RATING_CALC_EXIT

CLASS ltcl_vendor_rating_calc_exit DEFINITION FINAL FOR TESTING
  DURATION SHORT
  RISK LEVEL HARMLESS.

  PRIVATE SECTION.
    METHODS:
      vendor_rating_selected FOR TESTING RAISING cx_sadl_exit.
ENDCLASS.


CLASS ltcl_vendor_rating_calc_exit IMPLEMENTATION.

  METHOD vendor_rating_selected.
    " If VendorRating is requested we must also read the Vendor
    DATA(lo_vendor_rating_calc_exit) = NEW zcl_vendor_rating_calc_exit( ).

    lo_vendor_rating_calc_exit->if_sadl_exit_calc_element_read~get_calculation_info(
      EXPORTING
        it_requested_calc_elements = VALUE #( ( `VENDORRATING` ) )
        iv_entity                  = 'Z_C_PURCHASEDOCUMENTITEMLRP'
      IMPORTING
        et_requested_orig_elements = DATA(lt_requested_orig_elements)
    ).

    cl_abap_unit_assert=>assert_table_contains( line = `VENDOR` table = lt_requested_orig_elements ).
  ENDMETHOD.

ENDCLASS.

Global Class | Class-relevant Local Types | Local Types | Test Classes | Macros
```

Figure 10.7 Local Test Class with the First Test Method for Our Vendor Rating ABAP Calculation Exit

```
METHOD unknown_calc_field.
  NEW zcl_vendor_rating_calc_exit( )->if_sadl_exit_calc_element_read~get_calculation_info(
    EXPORTING
      it_requested_calc_elements = VALUE #( ( `UNKNOWN` ) )
      iv_entity                  = 'Z_C_PURCHASEDOCUMENTITEMLRP'
    IMPORTING
      et_requested_orig_elements = DATA(lt_requested_orig_elements)
  ).

  cl_abap_unit_assert=>assert_table_not_contains( line = `VENDOR` table = lt_requested_orig_elements ).
ENDMETHOD.
```

Figure 10.8 Making Sure the VENDOR Field Isn't Added to the Requested Original Elements Table If the VENDORRATING Field Isn't Requested

We can fix this test by checking whether the VENDORRATING field is requested or contained in the importing table it_requested_calc_elements. If not, simply don't append the VENDORRATING field to the et_requested_orig_elements exporting table, as shown in

Figure 10.10. Additionally, we need to make sure that our calculation exit can't be called for any entity other than Z_C_PurchaseDocumentItemLrp. The corresponding test is shown in Figure 10.9. If the entity doesn't equal Z_C_PurchaseDocumentItemLrp, a zcx_unkown_entity exception, inherited from cx_sadl_exit, should be thrown. The static cl_abap_unit_assert=>fail() method call can only be reached if the exception hasn't been thrown. The actual final implementation of the get_calculation_info() method is shown in Figure 10.10.

```
METHOD unkown_entity.
  TRY.
      NEW zcl_vendor_rating_calc_exit( )->if_sadl_exit_calc_element_read~get_calculation_info(
        EXPORTING
          it_requested_calc_elements = VALUE #( ( `VENDORRATING` ) )
          iv_entity                  = 'UnknownEntity'
        IMPORTING
          et_requested_orig_elements = DATA(lt_requested_orig_elements)
      ).
      cl_abap_unit_assert=>fail( msg = 'zcx_unknown_entity not raised'
                                 level = if_aunit_constants=>critical ).

    CATCH zcx_unknown_entity.
  ENDTRY.
ENDMETHOD.
```

Figure 10.9 If the Passed Entity Isn't Equal to Z_C_PurchaseDocumentItemLrp, Expect an zcx_unknown_entity Exception

```
METHOD if_sadl_exit_calc_element_read~get_calculation_info.
  IF iv_entity <> 'Z_C_PURCHASEDOCUMENTITEMLRP'.
    RAISE EXCEPTION TYPE zcx_unknown_entity.
  ENDIF.
  IF line_exists( it_requested_calc_elements[ table_line = 'VENDORRATING' ] ).
    APPEND 'VENDOR' TO et_requested_orig_elements.
  ENDIF.
ENDMETHOD.
```

Figure 10.10 Final Implementation of the get_calculation_info method() for the VENDORRATING Field

Implement the calculate() Method Using TDD and an Object Factory Class

In the next step, you'll implement the calculate() method of the exit in a TDD fashion. Figure 10.11 shows our test implementation. The calculate() method of the ABAP exit is being called with an original data table containing VendorA. Additionally, we'll request the VENDORRATING element to be calculated. As a result, we expect the original data to be extended with a vendor rating of 5 (stars).

```
METHOD get_rating_for_vendor.
  " Arrange
  DATA lt_original_data TYPE STANDARD TABLE OF z_c_purchasedocumentitemlrp.
  lt_original_data = VALUE #( ( purchasedocument = '1' purchasedocumentitem = '1' vendor = 'VendorA' ) ).

  DATA lt_calculated_data TYPE STANDARD TABLE OF z_c_purchasedocumentitemlrp.
  lt_calculated_data = VALUE #(   ).
  "Act
  NEW zcl_vendor_rating_calc_exit( )->if_sadl_exit_calc_element_read~calculate(
    EXPORTING
      it_original_data           = lt_original_data
      it_requested_calc_elements = VALUE #(  ( `VENDORRATING` )  )
    CHANGING
      ct_calculated_data         = lt_calculated_data
  ).
  " Assert
  DATA lt_expected_calulcated_data TYPE STANDARD TABLE OF z_c_purchasedocumentitemlrp.
  lt_expected_calulcated_data = VALUE #(
     ( purchasedocument = '1' purchasedocumentitem = '1' vendor = 'VendorA' vendorrating = 5 ) ).

  cl_abap_unit_assert=>assert_equals( act = lt_calculated_data exp = lt_expected_calulcated_data ).
ENDMETHOD.
```

Figure 10.11 Test for the calculate() Method of the ABAP Calculation Exit

Of course, the test will initially fail since we haven't implemented anything yet inside the `calculate()` method of our ABAP exit class `zcl_vendor_rating_calc_exit`. In contrast to the `get_calculation_info()` method, the `calculate()` method has a dependency to another ABAP class since the vendor rating must be read via an already existing `zcl_vendor_service` ABAP service class, as shown in Figure 10.12. The class has a public method `get_vendor_rating()`, which returns the rating for a certain vendor that must be passed as a parameter.

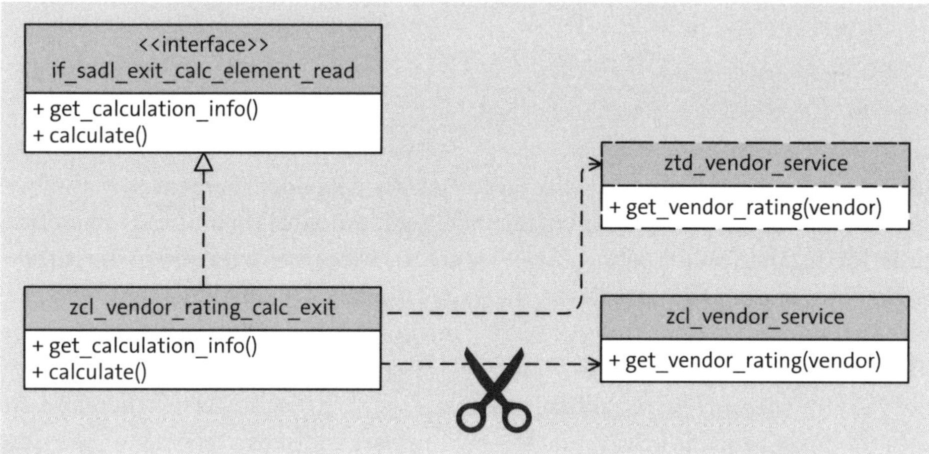

Figure 10.12 Ratings for a Vendor Must be Read via the zcl_vendor_service Class

Because we don't need to test the get_vendor_rating() dependency inside our unit test (we assume that this functionality already has its own unit test and is working properly), we must find and replace this dependency at test runtime with a test double (ztd_vendor_service), which is a test-specific equivalent returning fixed predefined ratings. Using a test double instead of the actual dependency allows you to focus on testing the code you're implementing and prevents your tests from failing when dependencies fail. Therefore, if your test fails, you'll know the problem lies in your code, and you can immediately localize the problem without having to analyze the code's dependencies. To be notified of bugs and regressions in the get_vendor_rating() method when interacting with the calculate() method, you might consider writing an integration test.

To make the dependency replaceable in a test, you can't simply instantiate the vendor service inside the calculate method. You must make this dependency injectable into the zcl_vendor_rating_calc_exit class using one of the dependency injection techniques listed in Table 10.1.

Technique	Description
Constructor injection	The dependencies are provided and set through the constructor of the class.
Setter injection	The class provides a setter method for each dependency.
Object factory class	The class uses an object factory to fetch its dependencies. At test runtime, the object factory can be configured to return test doubles instead of the actual dependencies.

Table 10.1 Dependency Injection Techniques

In our example, we'll use the object factory class dependency injection technique because it provides a single point of injection for test doubles in unit and integration tests, for instance, on the package level. Figure 10.13 shows an overview of the pattern in the form of a UML class diagram. Instead of directly instantiating the vendor service (zcl_vendor_service), the calculate() method fetches an instance of the service via the zcl_object_factory class's static get_vendor_service() method. The zcl_vendor_service will only be instantiable by the zcl_object_factory class. Therefore, its creation must be made private and the factory class added as a friend. Additionally, we'll introduce an interface for our vendor rating class (zif_vendor_service) to make its concrete implementation replaceable since the calculate() method no longer depends on a concrete implementation but on an abstraction (*dependency inversion principle*). At test runtime, you can then use an injector class (ztcl_object_injector), which is a friend of the object factory (zcl_object_factory), to inject a test double for the vendor service (ztd_vendor_service) by overwriting its private static go_vendor_service attribute with the test double.

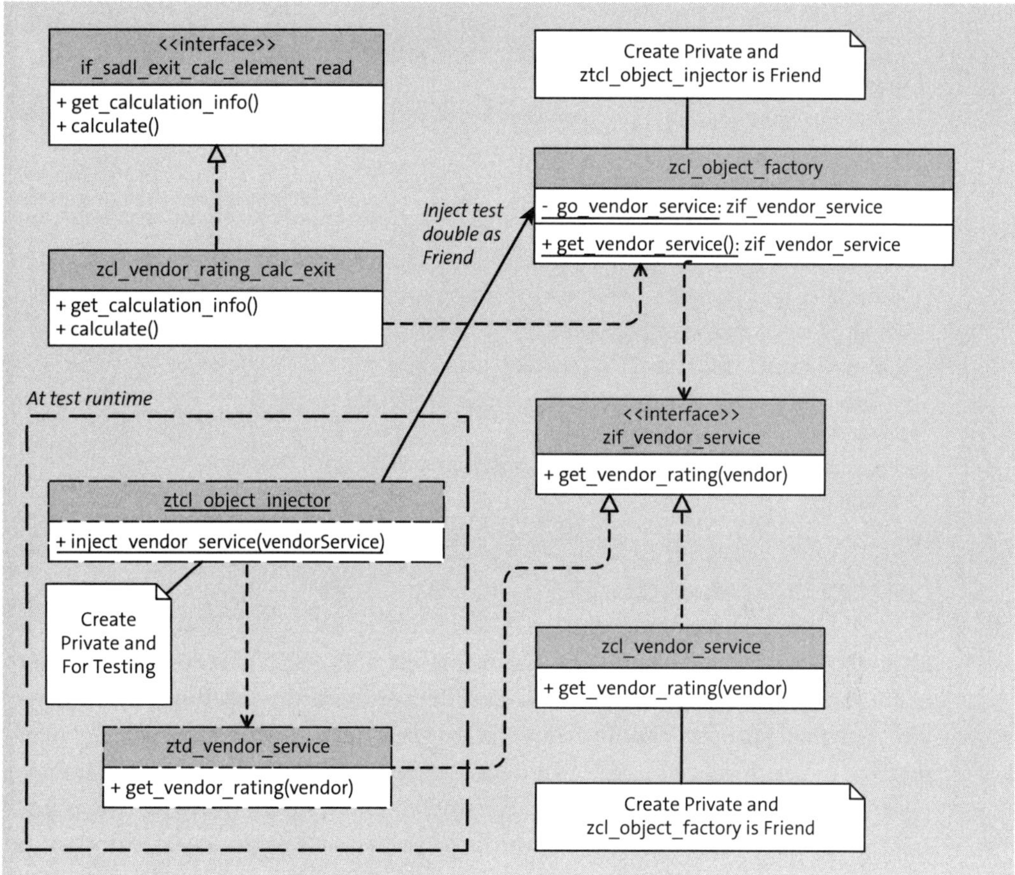

Figure 10.13 Object Factory Class Dependency Injection Technique for Our Vendor Rating Example

Listing 10.2 shows the full implementation of the factory class for our example. The get_vendor_service() creates a new instance, if not already created, and saves the instance in the static go_vendor_service class attribute. Note also that we won't return a reference to the concrete vendor service implementation but instead a reference to its interface.

```
CLASS zcl_object_factory DEFINITION
  PUBLIC
  FINAL
  CREATE PRIVATE
  GLOBAL FRIENDS ztcl_object_injector.
  PUBLIC SECTION.
    CLASS-METHODS get_vendor_service
RETURNING VALUE(ro_vendor_service) TYPE REF TO zif_vendor_service.
  PROTECTED SECTION.
  PRIVATE SECTION.
CLASS-DATA go_vendor_service TYPE REF TO zif_vendor_service.
ENDCLASS.

CLASS zcl_object_factory IMPLEMENTATION.
  METHOD get_vendor_service.
    IF go_vendor_service ISN'T BOUND.
      go_vendor_service = NEW zcl_vendor_service( ).
    ENDIF.
    ro_vendor_service = go_vendor_service.
  ENDMETHOD.
ENDCLASS.
```

Listing 10.2 Object Factory Class Implementation

Listing 10.3 shows the full implementation of the test double injector class we want to use at test runtime to replace the actual vendor service with a test double vendor service. For that purpose, the implementation provides the `inject_vendor_service()` method to which we can pass a test double object (`io_vendor_service_td`). Since the injector and factory class are friends, the implementation can overwrite the private static `go_vendor_service` attribute of the factory class. As a result, the factory class can return the test double on future requests instead of the actual implementation of the vendor service.

```
CLASS ztcl_object_injector DEFINITION
  PUBLIC
  FOR TESTING
  FINAL
  CREATE PRIVATE .
  PUBLIC SECTION.
```

```
    CLASS-METHODS inject_vendor_service
      IMPORTING
        io_vendor_service_td
          TYPE REF TO zif_vendor_service.
  PROTECTED SECTION.
  PRIVATE SECTION.
ENDCLASS.

CLASS ztcl_object_injector IMPLEMENTATION.
  METHOD inject_vendor_service.
    zcl_object_factory=>go_vendor_service =
        io_vendor_service_td.
  ENDMETHOD.
ENDCLASS.
```

Listing 10.3 Test Double Injector Class Implementation

To create a test double, you can either use the ABAP Test Double Framework or create your own local test double class that implements the `zif_vendor_service` interface. In general, test doubles can be classified as one of the test double types listed in Table 10.2.

Test Double Type	Description
Dummy	A dummy satisfies syntax requirements, for instance, implements the required interface, but does nothing else.
Fake	A fake is a simple lightweight implementation of a DOC.
Stub	A stub replaces a DOC and provides test-specific *indirect input* to the CUT, for instance, returns predefined values that affect the behavior of the CUT in a certain way.
Spy	A spy captures *indirect output* calls to other components for later verification, for instance, if you want to make sure that a certain method is called by the CUT.
Mock	A mock is an extension of fake, spy, and stub that can verify *indirect input* and/or *output* according to given expectations.

Table 10.2 Different Test Double Types

Listing 10.4 shows how you can create a stub for the vendor service using the ABAP Test Double Framework and inject it into the object factory. The code must be executed before we call the CUT, which in our case is the `calculate()` method of the test. If you look back to our initial test method in Figure 10.11, the code sequence must be inserted directly before the `Act` comment.

```
" (1) Create the test double of interface type
DATA tdo_vendor_service
    TYPE REF TO zif_vendor_service.
tdo_vendor_service ?= cl_abap_testdouble=>create(
    'zif_vendor_service' ).
" (2) Configure the test double behavior
cl_abap_testdouble=>configure_call(
    tdo_vendor_service )->returning( 5 ).
" (3) Configure the test double method
tdo_vendor_service->get_vendor_rating(
    iv_vendor = 'VendorA' ).
" (4) Inject the test double
ztcl_object_injector=>inject_vendor_service(
    tdo_vendor_service ).
```

Listing 10.4 Create a Stub for the Vendor Service DOC Using the ABAP Test Double Framework and Inject It into the Object Factory

As shown in Figure 10.14, the final implementation of the `calculate()` method passes our test and fetches an instance of the vendor service (`zif_vendor_service`) via the object factory (`zcl_object_factory`).

```
METHOD if_sadl_exit_calc_element_read~calculate.
  CHECK it_original_data IS NOT INITIAL.

  IF line_exists( it_requested_calc_elements[ table_line = 'VENDORRATING' ] ).
    DATA lt_calculated_data TYPE STANDARD TABLE OF z_c_purchasedocumentitemlrp.
    MOVE-CORRESPONDING it_original_data TO lt_calculated_data.

    LOOP AT lt_calculated_data ASSIGNING FIELD-SYMBOL(<fs_calculated_data>).
      <fs_calculated_data>-vendorrating =
          zcl_object_factory_purch=>get_vendor_service( )->get_vendor_rating(
               iv_vendor = <fs_calculated_data>-vendor  ).
    ENDLOOP.
    MOVE-CORRESPONDING lt_calculated_data TO ct_calculated_data.
  ENDIF.
ENDMETHOD.
```

Figure 10.14 Final Implementation of the calculate() Method

10.1.2 Unit Testing (Core Data Services Test Double Framework)

In Chapter 4, you saw some examples of the CDS unit test when we wrote tests for several calculated fields contained in our purchase document and item CDS views. In general, you should write unit tests for CDS views that contain any kind of calculation logic, for instance, calculations, conversions, or Boolean expressions. You shouldn't write tests for views that simply act as projections of database tables and that don't contain any logic. Unit tests for CDS views are also based on ABAP Unit and the ABAP Unit Runner. However, to find and replace first-level DOC CDS views or database tables of a CDS entity CUT, we can't use conventional ABAP dependency injection methods because the CDS view logic is executed in the underlying database. Therefore, the DOCs must be replaced inside the database, as shown in Figure 10.15. Moreover, you'll also need be able to insert test-specific data into the test doubles so that this data is returned when executing the CUT.

These challenges are addressed by the CDS Test Double Framework, which has been available since SAP S/4HANA 1610 Support Package Stack (SPS) 03. The CDS Test Double Framework enables unit testing of CDS views by performing the following tasks:

- Creating updatable doubles for each DOC of the CDS entity CUT
- Creating a copy of the CDS entity CUT and replacing its DOC with the previously created updatable doubles while preserving the CUT's actual logic

You can also turn on/off the corresponding data control language (DCL) of the CDS entity CUT using the CDS Test Double Framework. Unless you really want to implement authorization tests, we recommended switching the DCL off to truly isolate the CUT for unit testing.

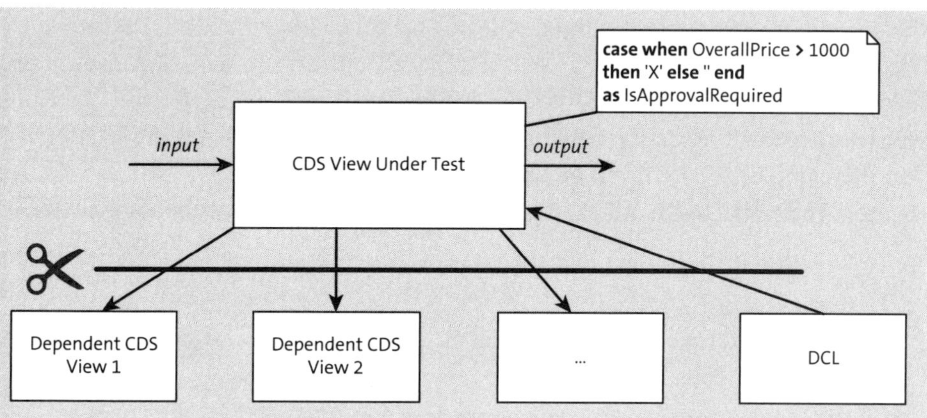

Figure 10.15 Cutting Dependencies to DOC CDS Views and Replacing Them with Test Doubles

In Chapter 4, Section 4.6.2, we showed you how to create a unit test for a CDS view using the wizard approach by right-clicking on a CDS view in the **Project Explorer** and choosing **New Test Class.** An alternative, more manual approach is to use the Eclipse quick assist. You first must create a global class, including a local test class, which is linked to the CDS view using a test reference (`! @testing`) by pressing Ctrl+1. You can then trigger the quick assist popup window and selectively generate the different parts of the CDS unit test, for instance, the CDS test fixtures, as shown in Figure 10.16.

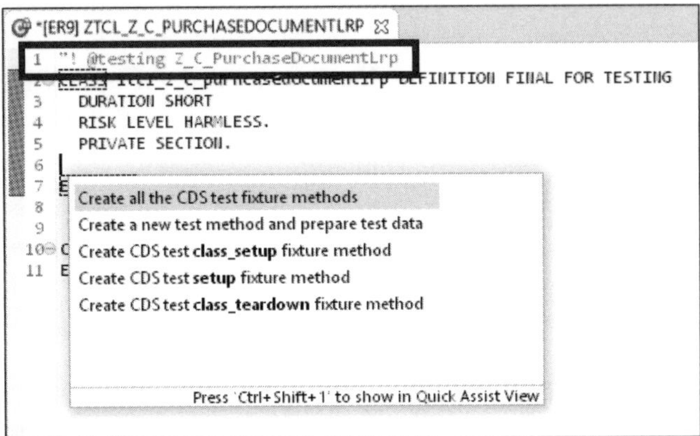

Figure 10.16 Linking the Test Class to the CDS Repository Object Using a Test Reference (! @testing) and Triggering the Quick Assist Using a Keyboard Shortcut

Listing 10.5 shows a minimal CDS unit test skeleton for a CDS entity or view CUT (`<CDS_ENTITY_UNDER_TEST>`). The `cl_cds_test_environment=>create( '<CDS_ENTITY_UNDER_TEST>' )` call inside the `class_setup` method will create the test environment by first creating the updatable test doubles for the first-level dependencies of the CUT. Then, the CUT itself will be cloned and its dependencies replaced with test doubles. Before each test method, the data contained in the test doubles is cleared in the `setup` test fixture, which is called before each test method. After all tests have completed, the test doubles and the clone of the CUT will be destroyed using the static `class_teardown` fixture method. The actual test methods (`some_test_method`) always follow the same pattern:

1. *Given/Arrange*: Insert data into the test doubles (only as much as required for the test).
2. *When/Act*: Perform an Open SQL select on the CDS entity and store the result in an internal ABAP table.
3. *Then/Assert*: Assert that the actual result (`act_results`) is as expected by using one of the methods provided by the `CL_ABAP_UNIT_ASSERT` class.

```
"! @testing <CDS_ENTITY_UNDER_TEST>
CLASS ltcl_<CDS_ENTITY_UNDER_TEST> DEFINITION FINAL FOR TESTING
  DURATION SHORT
  RISK LEVEL HARMLESS.
  PRIVATE SECTION.
CLASS-DATA: environment TYPE REF TO   if_cds_test_environment.
CLASS-METHODS: class_setup RAISING cx_static_check, class_teardown.
    METHODS setup.
METHODS some_test_method FOR TESTING RAISING cx_static_check.
ENDCLASS.

CLASS ltcl_<CDS_VIEW_UNDER_TEST> IMPLEMENTATION.
  METHOD class_setup.
    environment = cl_cds_test_environment=>create( '<CDS_ENTITY_UNDER_
TEST>' ).
  ENDMETHOD.

  METHOD setup.
    environment->clear_doubles( ).
  ENDMETHOD.

  METHOD class_teardown.
    environment->destroy( ).
  ENDMETHOD.

  METHOD some_test_method.
    " given
    lt_table_stub = VALUE #( ( ) ). " TODO: Specify test data
    environment->insert_test_data( i_data = lt_table_stub ).
    " when
    SELECT * FROM <CDS_ENTITY_UNDER_TEST> INTO TABLE
    @DATA(act_results).
    " then
    cl_abap_unit_assert=>fail(
      msg = 'Place your assertions here' ).
  ENDMETHOD.
ENDCLASS.
```

Listing 10.5 Minimal CDS Unit Test Skeleton for a CDS Entity CUT

You can also write hierarchy tests for CDS views where the first-level dependencies of the CDS entity CUT are no longer automatically identified and replaced with test doubles. Instead, developers can specify views or tables deeper in the CDS hierarchy to be replaced with test doubles. Figure 10.17 shows an example; instead of replacing the first-level DOC CDS views (DOC 1 and DOC 2) automatically, CDS hierarchy tests allow us to replace the DB Table 1 and DB Table 2 to also include the DOC views in our test. Although an integration test rather than a unit test, this kind of hierarchy test lets you test a defined part of the CDS view stack instead of a single CDS view.

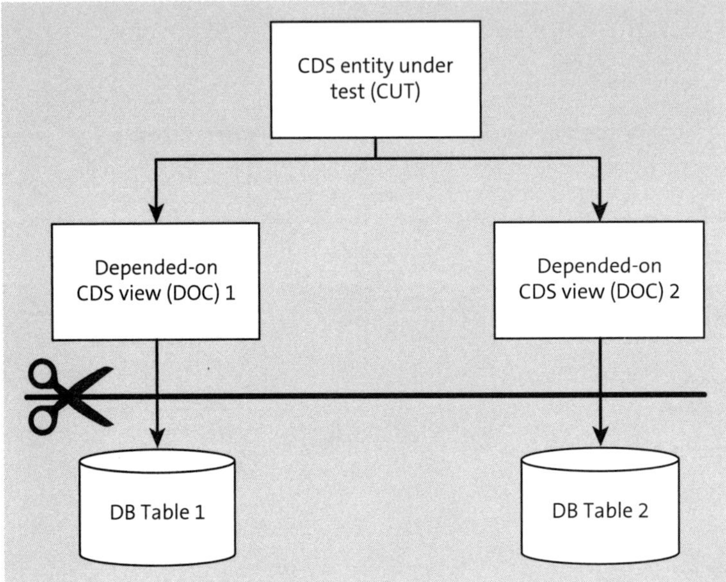

Figure 10.17 Replacing DB Tables 1 and 2 to Include DOC 1 and 2 in the CDS Hierarchy Test

In addition to the CUT, a hierarchy test requires the specification of a dependency list (`i_dependency_list`), which must contain a view or table for each hierarchy path, as shown in Listing 10.6; otherwise, an exception will be thrown. The idea is that the test should never interact with the actual database in order to isolate the tests from any real data. Updatable test doubles will be created for the selected dependencies, and entities above the selected dependencies are cloned to select from the test doubles while preserving their logic. The rest of the test structure is similar to a standard CDS unit test, so we're won't repeat this information in this context.

```
cl_cds_test_environment=>create( i_for_entity = '<CDS_ENTITY_UNDER_TEST>' i_
dependency_list =
VALUE #( ( name = '<DB Table 1>' type = 'TABLE' )( name =
 '<DB Table 2>'   type = 'TABLE' ) ) ).
```

Listing 10.6 Adding the Dependency List to Environment Creation

To test code pushdown to SAP HANA using Open SQL, you can use the Open SQL Test Double Framework, as shown in Listing 10.7. Like the hierarchy CDS Test Double Framework, you must specify a list of dependencies for which you want to create updatable test doubles.

```
cl_osql_test_environment=>create( i_dependency_list = VALUE #
( ( '<View1>' ) ( '<View2>' )  ) ).
```


Listing 10.7 Create Test Doubles Using the Open SQL Test Double Framework

10.2 Frontend Test Automation

The UI part of SAP S/4HANA applications is based on the SAPUI5 JavaScript framework and requires JavaScript-compatible unit and integration testing frameworks for writing automated tests. Consequently, the SAPUI5 SDK comes with QUnit and Sinon.JS for writing unit tests and OPA5 along with a mock server for writing UI integration tests. In this section, you'll learn how to write a UI unit test for a JavaScript method using QUnit and isolate the method from a dependency using Sinon.JS. Additionally, we'll look at using OPA5 for writing integration tests.

10.2.1 Unit Testing (QUnit)

Let's say you want to implement a new column in the SAP Fiori elements list report application we developed in Chapter 4 to displays the total delivery time for a purchase document in days, as shown in Figure 10.18. We'll define the total delivery time for a purchase document as the delivery time of its purchase document item with the longest delivery time; for instance, if a purchase document has two items with delivery dates 20 and 30 days from now, we'll consider 30 days as the total delivery time of the purchase document.

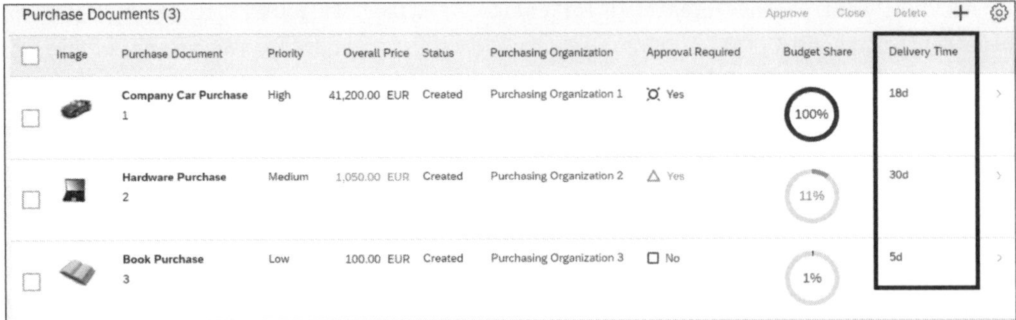

Figure 10.18 New Delivery Time Column Displaying the Total Delivery Time of All Purchase Document Items

You can implement the new **Delivery Time** column as a new UI column extension in the same way we implemented the **Budget Share** column in Chapter 4, Section 4.7. We'll add the new field to our already-existing column and cell fragment definitions and calculate its value using the formatter (`formatter.js`). This time, we won't perform any calculations directly in the formatter; instead, the formatter will delegate the calculation to the `getDeliveryTime()` method of a `DeliveryTimeHelper.js` class with a dependency to a `deliveryDateService.js` object (as shown later in Figure 10.20 for the final implementation).

The `deliveryDateService.js` dependency is injected using constructor injection. To treat the service like a black box, we'll only pass the purchase document ID to its `getDeliveryDatesOfItems()` method, which will return the delivery dates of all purchase document items as an array of date objects. The service itself might therefore call another RESTful service providing this data. In the `DeliveryTimeHelper.js`, we then must identify the max delivery date among the item delivery dates, calculate the days between today and the max delivery date, and format the result as a string; for instance, 18 days should be displayed as **18d**.

Figure 10.19 shows the unit test for the delivery time calculation. Like ABAP Unit, QUnit also provides test fixtures or hooks (`before,beforeEach,afterEach,after`), which are executed before and after the test suite or each unit test execution. In the `beforeEach` method, we're using Sinon.JS to create a stub for the `deliveryDateService.js` object's `getDeliveryDatesOfItems` method.

DeliveryTimeHelper.js ×

```
sap.ui.define(["fiori/manage/purchase/documents/purchasedocumentslrp/model/DeliveryTimeHelper",
        "fiori/manage/purchase/documents/purchasedocumentslrp/model/deliveryDateService",
        "sap/ui/thirdparty/sinon"
    ],
    function (DeliveryTimeHelper, oDeliveryDateService, sinon) {
        "use strict";

        var PURCHASE_DOCUMENT = "1";

        QUnit.module("Get Delivery Time in Days", {
            beforeEach: function () {
                var oDeliveryServiceStub = sinon.stub(oDeliveryDateService, "getDeliveryDatesOfItems");
                var oToday = new Date();
                var oDeliveryDate1 = new Date().setDate(oToday.getDate() + 6);
                var oDeliveryDate2 = new Date().setDate(oToday.getDate() + 5);
                oDeliveryServiceStub.returns([oDeliveryDate1, oDeliveryDate2]);
            },
            afterEach: function () {
                oDeliveryDateService.getDeliveryDatesOfItems.restore();
            }
        });

        QUnit.test("6 days until delivery of all Purchase Document Items", function (assert) {
            // Arrange
            var oDeliveryTimeHelper = new DeliveryTimeHelper(oDeliveryDateService);
            // Act
            var iDaysUntilDelivery = oDeliveryTimeHelper.getDeliveryTime(PURCHASE_DOCUMENT);
            // Assert
            assert.strictEqual(iDaysUntilDelivery, "6d", "OK - Returned: " + iDaysUntilDelivery);
        });
    });
```

Figure 10.19 Isolated Unit Test for the DeliveryTimeHelper.js Class's getDeliveryTime Method

Let's make the `getDeliveryTime` method return two dates (today + 5 days, today + 6 days) in an array. In the `afterEach` method, we'll restore the stubbed method after each test execution. In the actual test case, we'll create an instance of the `DeliveryTimeHelper.js` class and inject the `deliveryDateService.js` object (with the stubbed `getDeliveryDatesOfItems` method) using a constructor injection. Then, we'll call the `getDeliveryTime` method, which is the CUT to ensure that the returned string equals 6d as the total delivery time since the purchase document should be equal to the maximum delivery time among its items.

In the previous example, you saw how you can use Sinon.JS to isolate CUT from dependencies in JavaScript using its stub application programming interface (API). In addition to its stub API, Sinon.JS also provides an API for creating mocks and spies.

> **Note**
> For further information concerning Sinon.JS, refer to the official documentation at *https://sinonjs.org*.

DeliveryTimeHelper.js ×

```
sap.ui.define(["sap/ui/base/Object"], function (BaseObject) {
    var DeliveryTimeHelper = BaseObject.extend("fiori.manage.purchase.documents.purchasedocumentslrp." +
        "model.DeliveryTimeHelper", {

            constructor: function (oDeliveryDateService) {
                this.oDeliveryDateService = oDeliveryDateService;
            },

            _getMaxDeliveryDate: function (aDeliveryDates) {
                return new Date(Math.max.apply(null, aDeliveryDates));
            },

            _getDaysUntilDelivery: function (oMaxDeliveryDate) {
                var oToday = new Date();
                var deliveryTimeInMilliseconds = oMaxDeliveryDate - oToday;
                return Math.ceil(deliveryTimeInMilliseconds / (1000 * 60 * 60 * 24));
            },

            getDeliveryTime: function (sPurchaseDocument) {
                var aDeliveryDates = this.oDeliveryDateService.getDeliveryDatesOfItems(sPurchaseDocument);

                var oMaxDeliveryDate = this._getMaxDeliveryDate(aDeliveryDates);
                jQuery.sap.log.debug("Max Delivery Date Purchase Document Items: " + oMaxDeliveryDate.toString());

                var iDays = this._getDaysUntilDelivery(oMaxDeliveryDate);
                return "" + iDays + "d";
            }
        });

    return DeliveryTimeHelper;
});
```

Figure 10.20 Final Implementation of the DeliveryTimeHelper.js Class with the getDeliveryTime Method Called inside the Formatter (formatter.js) to Trigger the Delivery Time Calculation

10.2.2 Integration Testing (OPA5)

The OPA5 framework enables you to write integration tests for the UI part of your SAP S/4HANA applications, as shown in Figure 10.20. You've already seen an example of an OPA5 test in Chapter 7, Section 7.2.4, where we wrote a test for the creation of a purchase document. If the test needs to be isolated from the backend OData service, you can additionally use the `sap.ui.core.util.MockServer`, which will interfere with the standard OData requests sent from the frontend and return mock data instead.

Figure 10.21 shows the overall structure of an OPA5 test suite. OPA5 can use QUnit as a test runner, and the usual entry point for an OPA5 integration test suite is therefore an *opaTests.qunit.html* file that will load QUnit, run the tests, and display the result. The tests will be organized into journeys that will be collected in an *allJourneys.js* file, which is then the only file the *opaTests.qunit.html* file needs to load. Journeys describe tests in a behavior-driven development (BDD) style, which nondevelopers will be able to understand. The concrete implementations of these behavior specifications are delegated to the page objects.

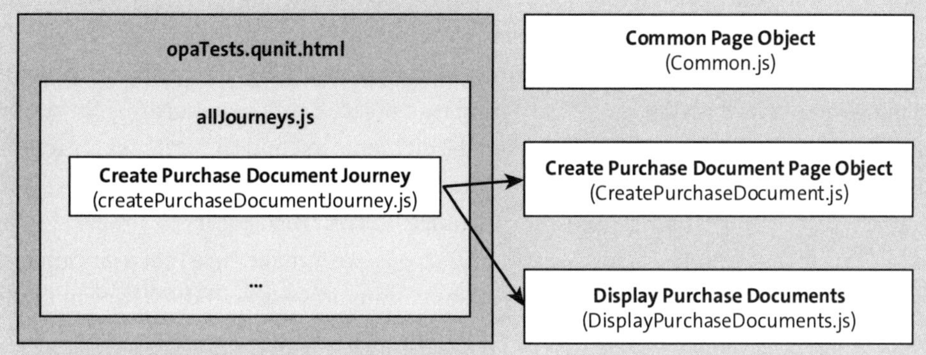

Figure 10.21 Structure of OPA5 Integration Tests

Journeys

A journey describes a test in an understandable high-level form and is always organized according to the *given-when-then* pattern, as shown in Listing 10.8. The `iStartTheApp()` *arrangement* is usually implemented in the common page object (`Common.js`) because it will be used in all journeys. The app can either be started in a UIComponent (recommended when using a mock server) or in an IFrame. The `When` object provides access to the *actions* of loaded page objects, and the `Then` object provides access to their *assertions*.

```
sap.ui.define([
 "sap/ui/test/opaQunit"
], function (opaTest) {
 "use strict";
 QUnit.module("<MODULE_DESCRIPTION>");

 opaTest("<TEST_DESCRIPTION>", function (Given, When, Then) {
```

```
  Given.iStartTheApp();
  When.onThe<PAGE_OBJECT>.<iDoSomething>;
  Then.onThe<PAGE_OBJECT>.<iCheckSomething>;
});
```

Listing 10.8 Basic Structure of an OPA5 Journey

Page Objects

Page objects contain the actual implementation of arrangements, actions, and assertions used in journeys. Listing 10.9 shows the basic structure of a page object. The baseClass property inherits the arrangements, actions, and assertions needed within more than one test case from a common base object. The actions object contains arrangements and actions, and the assertions object contains assertions. In action functions, we usually try to find a certain UI element first and then trigger an action. Predefined matchers and actions can be found below the sap.ui.test.matchers and sap.ui.test.actions namespaces, for instance, sap.ui.test.matchers.Properties or sap.ui.test.actions.Press. In assertion functions, we'll make sure that a certain element is present (or not) on the UI and/or has certain properties. If the UI doesn't look like as expected, the assertion will time out and fail.

```
sap.ui.define([
 "sap/ui/test/Opa5",
 "./Common",
 "sap/ui/test/actions/Press",
 "sap/ui/test/matchers/Properties",
], function (Opa5, Common, Press, Properties) {
 "use strict";
 Opa5.createPageObjects({
  onThe<PAGE_OBJECT>: {
   baseClass: Common,
   actions: {
    <iDoSomething>: function(){
     return this.waitFor({
      id:"<CONTROL_ID>",
      viewName:"<VIEW_NAME>",
      actions: new Press(),
      errorMessage: "<SOME_ERROR_MESSAGE>"
     });
```

```
      }
     },
     assertions: {
      <iCheckSomething>: function(){
       return this.waitFor({
        id:"<CONTROL_ID>",
        viewName:"<VIEW_NAME>",
        matchers : new Properties({
         isSelected: true
        }),
        success: function () {
         Opa5.assert.ok("true", "<SOME_SUCCESS_MESSAGE>");
        },
        errorMessage: "<SOME_ERROR_MESSAGE>"
       });
      }
     }
    }
  });
});
```

Listing 10.9 Structure of a Page Object Containing Actions and Assertions

10.3 End-to-End Test Automation Tools

To test the interaction and functioning of all components of software ranging from the UI to the database access, you'll need to create a small set of meaningful end-to-end (E2E) tests covering the core processes of your applications. Since the UI part of SAP S/4HANA applications runs in browsers, you can use standard browser testing tools to create E2E tests. The de facto standard toolset for automating browsers is *Selenium*. In this section, we'll create an E2E test for the same scenario, as in Chapter 7 where we developed an OPA5 integration test to create a purchase document and verify its successful creation in the subsequently displayed table showing all available purchase documents. However, in this case, we won't use a mock server because we're writing an E2E test and want to verify that everything is working, which also includes our OData backend service.

10.3.1 Setting Up Nightwatch.js

We'll create our E2E tests using Nightwatch.js, a wrapper containing Selenium/WebDriver that allows you to write the tests in JavaScript (Node.js). You can install Nightwatch.js via node package manager (npm) and save its dependency in our *package.json* file using the following command: `npm install -save nightwatch`. Additionally, you must download the Selenium server Java Archive (.jar) (*http://s-prs.co/498822*), which Nightwatch uses to connect to the various browsers. In our case, we also must download the *ChromeDriver* (*http://s-prs.co/498823*) since we want to run our tests in the Chrome browser.

The Nightwatch.js test runner by default expects a *nightwatch.json* configuration file from the current folder. Listing 10.10 shows our simple configuration file. The `src_folders` property specifies that your tests can be found in the *tests* folder. In the `selenium` object, you'll tell Nightwatch where to start the Selenium server process (`server_path`) and the browser driver Selenium will use (in our case, the ChromeDriver `webdriver.chrome.driver`), and where to find it.

```
{
  "src_folders" : ["tests"],
  "output_folder" : "reports",
  "selenium" : {
    "start_process" : true,
    "server_path" : "./bin/selenium-server-standalone-3.9.1.jar",
    "port" : 4444,
    "cli_args" : {
      "webdriver.chrome.driver" : "./bin/chromedriver.exe"
    }
  },
  "test_settings" : {
    "default" : {
      "launch_url" : "http://localhost",
      "selenium_port"  : 4444,
      "selenium_host"  : "localhost",
      "silent": true,
      "screenshots" : {
      "enabled" : false,
      "path" : ""
    },
    "desiredCapabilities": {
      "browserName": "chrome"
```

```
        }
      }
    }
}
```

Listing 10.10 Our nightwatch.json Configuration File

> **Note**
>
> For more detailed instructions on how to set up Nightwatch.js, refer to the official *Getting Started* guide at *http://s-prs.co/498824*.

10.3.2 Creating the Create Purchase Document End-to-End Nightwatch.js Test

Now, you can create a Nightwatch test, which we'll call `createPurchaseDocument.js` as shown in Figure 10.22. As in our OPA5 test developed in Chapter 7, Section 7.2.4, first navigate to the create screen of your freestyle application.

createPurchaseDocument.js

```
module.exports = {
  PURCHASE_DOCUMENT_ID: 0,

  before: function(browser) {
    console.log('Setting up...');
  },

  after: function(browser) {
    console.log('Closing down...');
  },

  'Create Purchase Document': function(browser) {
    browser
      .url("                    " +
        "/sap/bc/ui5_ui5/ui2/ushell/shells/abap/FioriLaunchpad.html?" +
        "sap-language=&sap-client=928#PurchasingDocument-create")
      .waitForElementPresent("input[id*=purchaseDocumentSmartField]", 6000)
      .setValue("input[id*=purchaseDocumentSmartField]", this.PURCHASE_DOCUMENT_ID)
      .setValue("input[id*=descriptionSmartField]", "Nightwatch.js test doc")
      .click("button[id*=savePurchaseDocumentButton]")
      .useXpath() // switch to xpath for selecting nodes
      .waitForElementPresent("//div[@class='sapMObjectIdentifierTitle']/" +
        "a[text()='Nightwatch.js test doc']", 6000)
      .pause(3000)
      .end();
  },
};
```

Figure 10.22 Creating a Purchase Document Using Nightwatch.js and Verifying Its Successful Creation by Checking That the Document Is Displayed in the Smart Table on the Next Page

Then, in about 6 seconds (6000 milliseconds), the **Purchase Document ID** input field should appear. If the field appears, enter data into the mandatory ID and description fields and click the **Save** button. So far, we've used Cascading Style Sheet (CSS) selectors to select HTML elements. By calling the `useXpath()` method, we'll switch to using XPath selectors and check whether the previously entered *Nightwatch.js test doc* description is present in a link (a) inside a `div` with the `sapMObjectIdentifierTitle` class attribute value.

As a reminder, when we save a purchase document in our freestyle application, we're immediately forwarded to a list report displaying all purchase documents in a table. By looking for the description inside an object identifier (`sap.m.ObjectIdentifier`) control, which should be present in the first column of the table, we can make sure that the creation was successful. If the *Nightwatch.js test doc* description doesn't become visible within 6 seconds, the test will time out and fail.

10.3.3 Running the Create Purchase Document End-to-End Nightwatch.js Test

Since we haven't installed Nightwatch.js globally, the easiest way to execute the test is to add an entry to the `scripts` object in our *package.json* file, as shown in Listing 10.11. The `npm test` command will trigger the `nightwatch` command without any arguments as Nightwatch knows, due to our *nightwatch.json* configuration file, from where to start the selenium server and where to find our tests (*tests* folder).

```
"scripts": {
 "test": "nightwatch"
}
```

Listing 10.11 Test Scripts Entry in the package.json File for Our Nightwatch Test

Now, you can execute the test by entering `npm test` on the command line from within the root folder of our E2E tests. Figure 10.23 shows the output of the test run on the console. The test will ensure that the elements using the `waitForElementPresent` method appear on the page within a certain time frame (6 seconds); otherwise, the test will fail. Be sure that the second argument specifying the timeout in milliseconds isn't too low or the tests might fail due to temporary system performance issues.

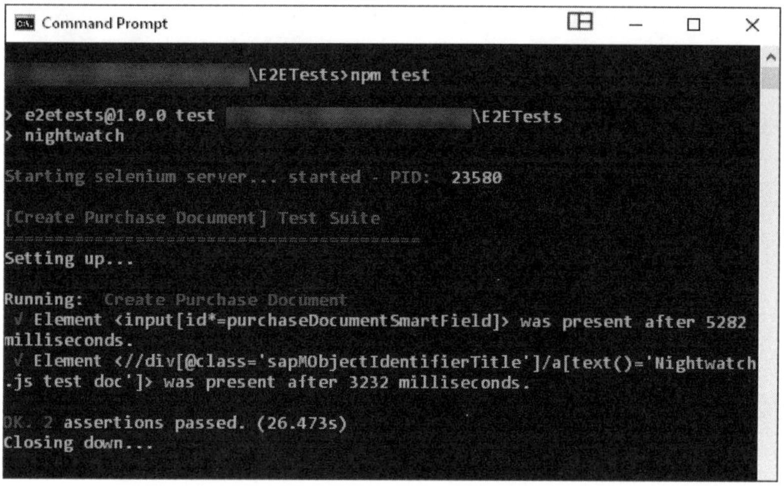

Figure 10.23 Execution of the Create Purchase Document E2E Test

10.4 Summary

In this chapter, we introduced you to the testing pyramid and its different layers from an SAP S/4HANA perspective. In general, good functional test coverage over software can only be achieved by implementing all layers of the testing pyramid. Consequently, frameworks and tools exist to cover all layers of the testing pyramid when developing applications for SAP S/4HANA. We also showed you in detail how to write unit tests for the backend (ABAP Unit) and frontend (QUnit) parts of your application that form the foundation of the testing pyramid and how to decouple your code to make it testable using dependency injection techniques. Unit tests greatly outnumber other test forms and when done right, early use of TDD positively influences the overall code quality by enforcing decoupling. Unit tests are therefore the most critical layer of the testing pyramid and deserve the most attention and effort.

Integration tests test several components together and can be developed in the backend using ABAP Unit and in the frontend using OPA5, including a mock server to isolate them from the backend OData service. E2E tests give you the most confidence that our software is working as a whole by automating tests for the most common processes or steps. However, their overall number should be kept relatively small since they are usually slow and require a stable test environment. A commonly used toolset for integration testing is Selenium, which we demonstrated using Nightwatch.js, which serves as a Node.js wrapper for Selenium. A high degree of test automation according to the testing pyramid is also a prerequisite for continuous integration and continuous delivery, which we'll explore in the next chapter.

Chapter 11
Continuous Integration

Continuously integrating code changes into a main code line, accompanied by automated tests provides immediate feedback to developers and prevents integration problems and regression bugs. In this chapter, we'll look at the tools and best practices enabling continuous integration (CI) for SAP S/4HANA applications.

Shipping software to customers fast and frequently is one of the core principles of agile software development and fosters faster customer feedback and greater customer satisfaction. Especially in cloud-based environments, release cycles have been getting shorter and shorter or have even been completely removed by the principle of continuous deployment where new features are immediately deployed to production in a completely automated way as soon as they are finished. Delivering software to customers in short cycles requires a high degree of automation where steps that had been manual in the past, for instance, uploading a software artifact to a certain system or repository, must be automated completely. Moreover, test automation can play a crucial role in automating deployments as usually a lot of time must be invested in testing software for bugs and regressions introduced with new features before it can be released to customers with manageable risk. Therefore, a high degree of test coverage is of utmost importance so you can deliver software frequently and safely to end users. The ability to ship or deploy bug-free and regression-free software fast is a competitive advantage for any company, organization, or development team.

In the following, we'll provide you with an overview of the practices and tools that support faster release cycles while still ensuring quality when developing applications for SAP S/4HANA. We'll start with a general introduction to continuous integration (CI), continuous delivery, and continuous deployment. The rest of the chapter is split into separate frontend and backend sections due to their usage of completely different technology stacks. In the frontend, which consists of our JavaScript-based SAPUI5 freestyle or SAP Fiori elements application developed in the SAP Web IDE full-stack, you can make use of widely adopted tools and technologies, such as GitHub, ESLint, Grunt, Jenkins, Docker, and Node.js, to build the stages and steps of our CI/CD pipelines. Therefore, you'll learn in this chapter how you can set up a simple CI pipeline for a frontend SAPUI5 project using the tools and technologies we'll explore in this chapter.

In contrast, in the backend, you'll still completely rely on the classic ABAP technology stack and the Change and Transport System (CTS) for transporting SAP S/4HANA-relevant backend development objects, such as core data services (CDS) views or ABAP classes, between the different SAP systems in the system landscape. Nevertheless, several tools, such as the ABAP Test Cockpit (ATC) or the ABAP Unit Runner, support faster release cycles by ensuring code quality through continuous checks and testing. Consequently, we'll show you how you can set up a kind of CI/CD pipeline in the ABAP backend as well by using the ATC and the ABAP Unit Runner.

11.1 Introduction

In this section, we'll provide you with a quick introduction to CI, continuous delivery, and continuous deployment and outline their differences. Continuous delivery and continuous deployment are often confused although they can be clearly distinguished. However, after reading this introductory section, you'll be able to clearly distinguish these three different software engineering approaches.

11.1.1 Continuous Integration

CI is one of the 12 original practices of the Extreme Programming (XP) software development methodology that originated in the late 1990s. The main aim of CI is to prevent integration problems by integrating changes to software frequently (even multiple times per day) into a central main code line hosted in a Source Code Management (SCM) system, for instance, Git. The SCM system represents the single source of truth for the software. Following the principle of CI reduces the overall risk and uncertainty in a software project since the individual parts of the software are constantly integrated into the main code line, so you'll always know where the project stands. Bug and integration problems are detected at earlier stages and not collected until the end of the project, which could result in *integration hell*. Additionally, CI is a foundation for customer feedback throughout the development project since this approach fosters runnable and presentable software.

Figure 11.1 shows a simple CI pipeline. As soon as a new feature is committed to the SCM system, the `Build` stage is triggered, which in turn might consist of several steps to ensure that the software can be compiled and that the different parts fit together. If this stage is successful, a set of tests is executed in the subsequent `Test` stage, for instance, static code checks and unit and integration tests. In this way, developers can get early feedback about their changes and can fix potential issues while still fresh in their minds.

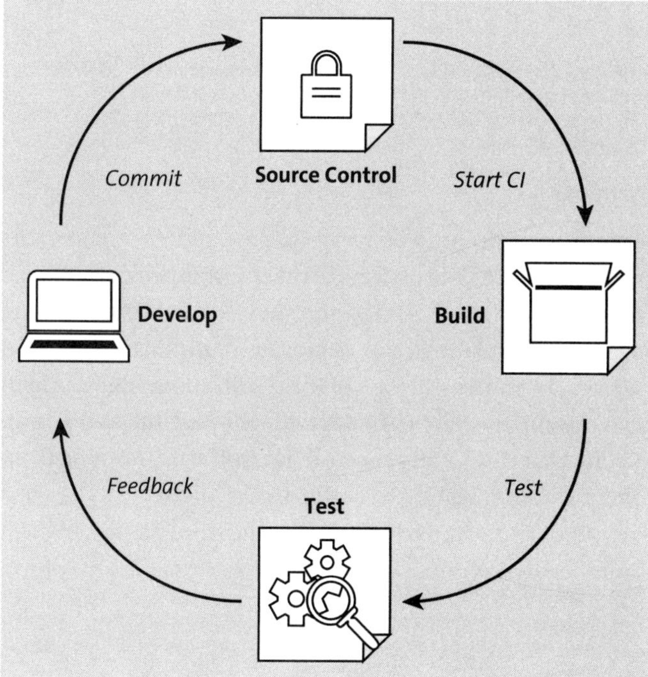

Figure 11.1 Simple CI Pipeline Consisting of Build and Test Stages

11.1.2 Continuous Delivery

Continuous delivery takes CI a step further. As soon as the CI process is finished successfully, you can reliably ship the software to your customers or deploy it to production at any time, as shown in Figure 11.2. Whether the software is shipped or deployed is decided by your development team or a delivery manager. Delivery requires that the software be built, tested, and available in an immediately shippable or deployable format as the output of the CI process. The actual delivery to end users must also be automated and should not require more effort than pressing a button.

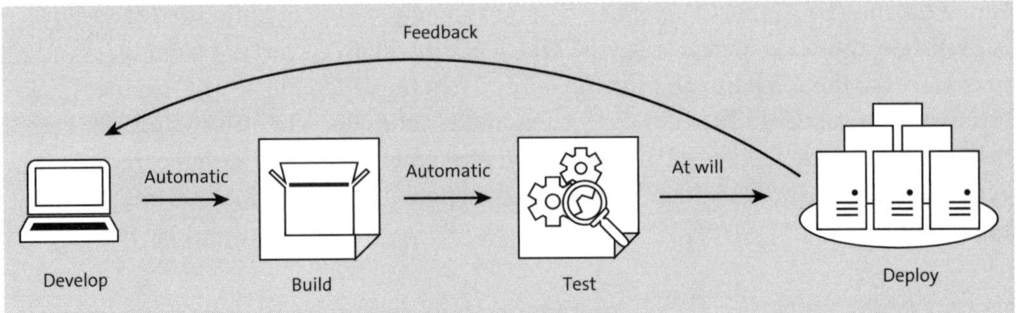

Figure 11.2 Simple Continuous Delivery Pipeline the Software Artifact We've Built and Tested Can Be Deployed at Will

11.1.3 Continuous Deployment

Continuous deployment extends continuous delivery further and eliminates any manual steps and decisions taken before the software artifact is shipped or deployed to production. As soon as the software is built and tested successfully, your software can be automatically shipped to your customers or deployed to production without any further human interaction, as shown in Figure 11.3. Continuous deployment requires the automation of every single step of the deployment pipeline and a comprehensive automated test suite that covers all aspects of the software, ranging from unit and integration tests over to system testing to performance and security testing. Out of CI, continuous delivery, and continuous deployment, the third has the highest velocity and shortest customer feedback loop.

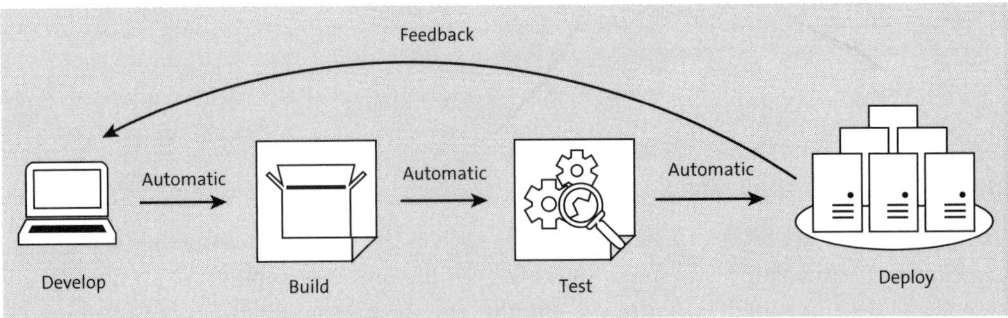

Figure 11.3 Simple Continuous Deployment Pipeline in Which the Build, Test, and Deploy Stages Are Completely Automated

11.2 Setting Up a Continuous Integration Pipeline for SAPUI5 on the ABAP Server

In this section, we'll set up a simple CI pipeline to make an SAPUI5 project, developed in the SAP Web IDE full-stack and stored in GitHub, ready for deployment on the SAP Gateway hub system, as shown in Figure 11.4. We'll use the Jenkins automation server to create a CI pipeline consisting of `build` ❶, `test` ❷, and `deploy` ❸ stages. The pipeline will be triggered on each push to the remote Git SCM system. In the `build` stage, we'll create a new, separate, deployment-ready version of our project, for instance, by minifying the project's files and doing other optimizations. We'll also perform some static code checks at this stage using ESLint, which will analyze our code for common mistakes or bad practices.

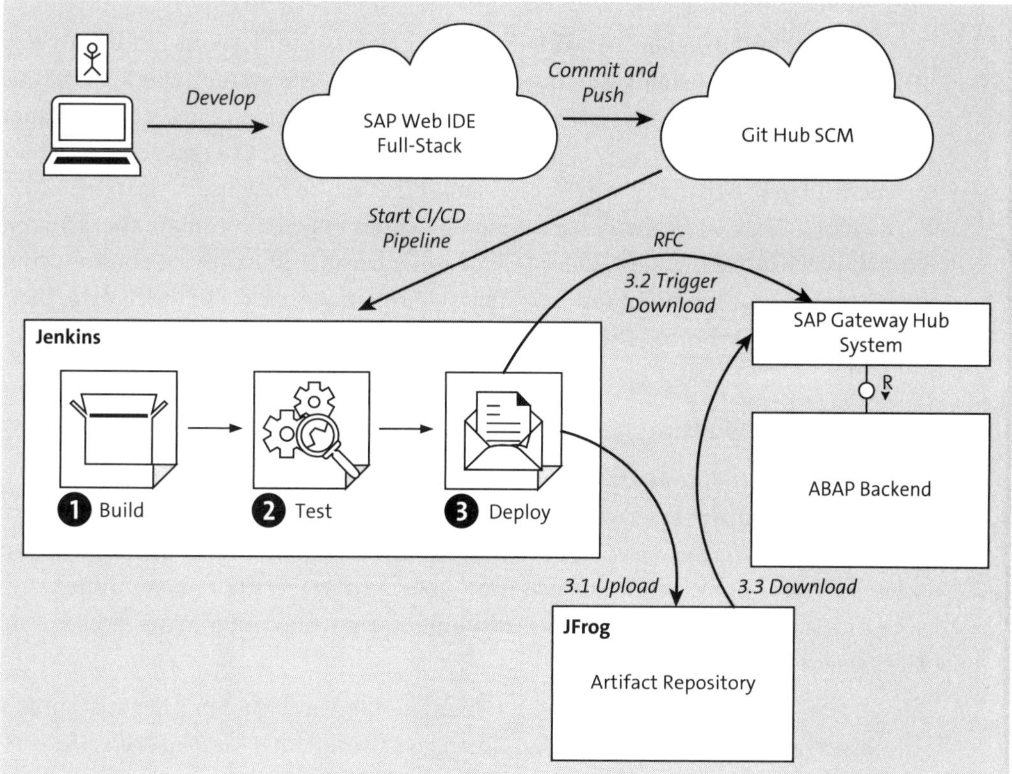

Figure 11.4 Simple CI/CD Pipeline Taking an SAPUI5 Application from the SAP Web IDE Full-Stack and GitHub over a Jenkins Automation Server to the SAP Gateway Hub System

In the `test` stage, we'll run the previously developed QUnit unit test and OPA5 integration test of the project to ensure that we didn't introduce any regressions with our new changes and to ensure that our software works as defined in our tests (as seen in Chapter 7, Section 7.2.4). In the `deploy` stage, we'll store the deployment-ready project as a ZIP file in the cloud version of the JFrog Artifactory software repository (*https://jfrog.com/artifactory/*). In this way, at any time, we'll have access to deployable versions of our project for each build, which are also centrally stored. Additionally, we'll outline the steps necessary to automatically deploy the SAPUI5 project to the SAP Gateway hub ABAP system after successful `build` and `test` stages, which would enable continuous deployment. To deploy SAPUI5 projects from within a CI/CD pipeline, the SAP Gateway hub system provides remote function call (RFC) function modules that can be used to trigger the download of the SAPUI5 project from a software repository and its deployment.

By now, you should be familiar with developing SAPUI5 applications in the SAP Web IDE full-stack and managing the source code with a Git SCM system. Our focus in this section will therefore be on setting up the Jenkins automation pipeline. Many other alternatives exist for setting up CI/CD pipelines, for instance, Concourse CI, Bamboo, or Travis CI, but Jenkins is widely used and offers a nice new user experience (UX) called Blue Ocean, which makes setting up pipelines easy. To automate the different stages, we'll use the Grunt JavaScript task runner because SAP provides best practice Grunt plug-ins for the `build` and `test` stages. Another alternative to the JFrog Artifactory repository for storing the built project, would, for instance, be Sonatype Nexus.

11.2.1 Setting Up a Local Jenkins Automation Server

Usually, a Jenkins automation server runs on a dedicated server or cloud environment; however, in our case, we'll set the Jenkins server up locally on our (Windows 10) machine for testing purposes. Additionally, we'll want to run our Jenkins automation sever as well as our pipeline stages inside Docker containers to ensure unified runtime environments. To install Docker on your local machine, refer to the Docker website (*www.docker.com*).

Blue Ocean, the latest UX for Jenkins, makes building automation pipelines simple. The fastest way to try out Jenkins Blue Ocean is to use the *jenkinsci/blueocean* (*https://hub.docker.com/r/jenkinsci/blueocean/*) Docker image, which already contains the Blue Ocean suite of plug-ins. You can run this Docker image as a container on Windows by entering the `docker run` command shown in Listing 11.1 into the Windows command prompt.

```
docker run ^
-u root ^
--rm ^
-d ^
-p 8080:8080 ^
-v jenkins-data:/var/jenkins_home ^
-v /var/run/Docker.sock:/var/run/Docker.sock ^
--name jenkins ^
jenkinsci/blueocean
```

Listing 11.1 Run the Jenkins Blue Ocean Docker Image as a Docker Container on Windows

The `docker run` command runs a Docker image as an isolated Docker container, which is essentially an isolated process with its own networking, file system, and process tree. In addition to the `jenkinsci/blueocean` argument, which is the image we want to fetch from Docker Hub and run locally on our machine, we're providing several flags and options: The `-u root` option and argument runs the container with the root user. The `--rm` flag makes Docker automatically clean up the container and remove the file system on exit. The `-d` flag runs the container in detach mode as a background process and outputs the container ID to the command prompt. The `-p 8080:8080` option and argument maps the 8080 port of the host system (your local machine) to the 8080 port of the Docker container. The `-v jenkins-data:/var/jenkins_home` option and argument maps the `/var/jenkins_home` container directory to the Docker volume with the name `jenkins-data` to persist the Jenkins settings between container restarts. The `-v /var/run/Docker.sock:/var/run/Docker.sock` option and argument maps the Docker daemon of the Docker container to the Docker daemon running on your local machine. This option is needed as we want to use additional Docker containers as unified runtime environments inside our pipeline. Finally, the `--name jenkins` option and argument defines the name `jenkins` for our container.

You can now access your locally running Jenkins server on *http://localhost:8080*. The Jenkins password needed to unlock Jenkins when running it for the first time is written to the Jenkins console log, which you can display with the `docker logs jenkins` command. After unlocking Jenkins, the installation wizard will guide you through the remaining installation steps. Simply accept the suggestions and create an admin user.

Note

For a more detailed description on how to install and run Jenkins in Docker, refer to the official Jenkins documentation at *https://jenkins.io/doc/book/installing/#docker*.

11.2.2 Creating an Initial Jenkinsfile

In Jenkins, pipelines, which takes code from an SCM system to end users, are defined using a declarative `Jenkinsfile`. The `Jenkinsfile` must be part of the GitHub-managed SAPUI5 project and reside in the root folder of the project. Figure 11.5 shows the initial `Jenkinsfile`, which we'll add to the freestyle application developed in Chapter 7 and push to our GitHub repository to put it under version control. The `Jenkinsfile` already contains the three stages we want to implement: `build`, `test`, and `deploy`. We'll implement the steps of the respective stages in the following subsections.

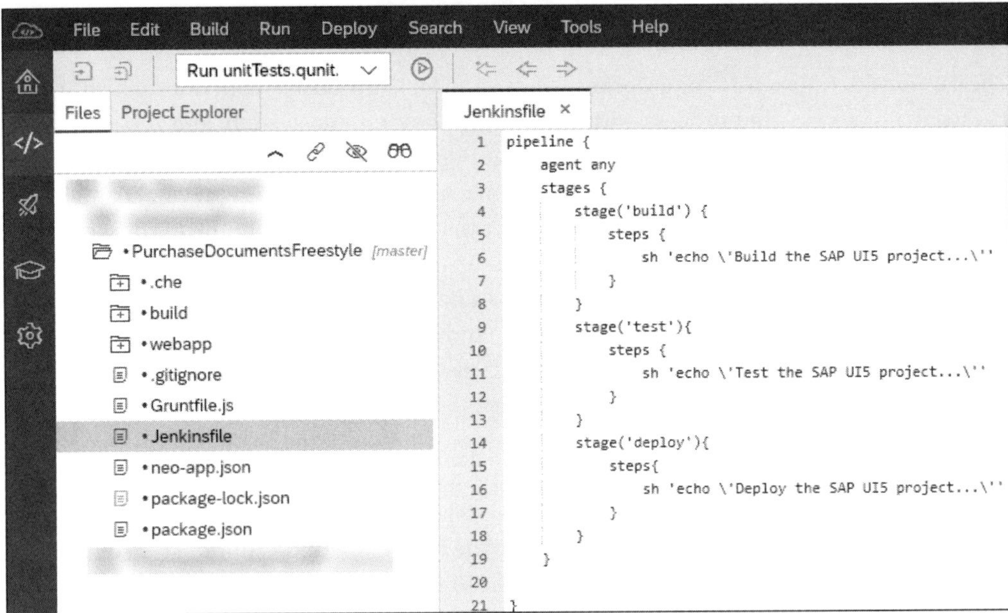

Figure 11.5 Initial Jenkinsfile for an SAPUI5 Project Containing Build, Test, and Deploy Stages

11.2.3 Creating the Continuous Deployment Pipeline

To create a pipeline in your running Jenkins Docker container, as shown in Figure 11.6, you must navigate to the *http://localhost:8080/blue/pipelines* URL ❶ and click on the **Create New Pipeline** button ❷.

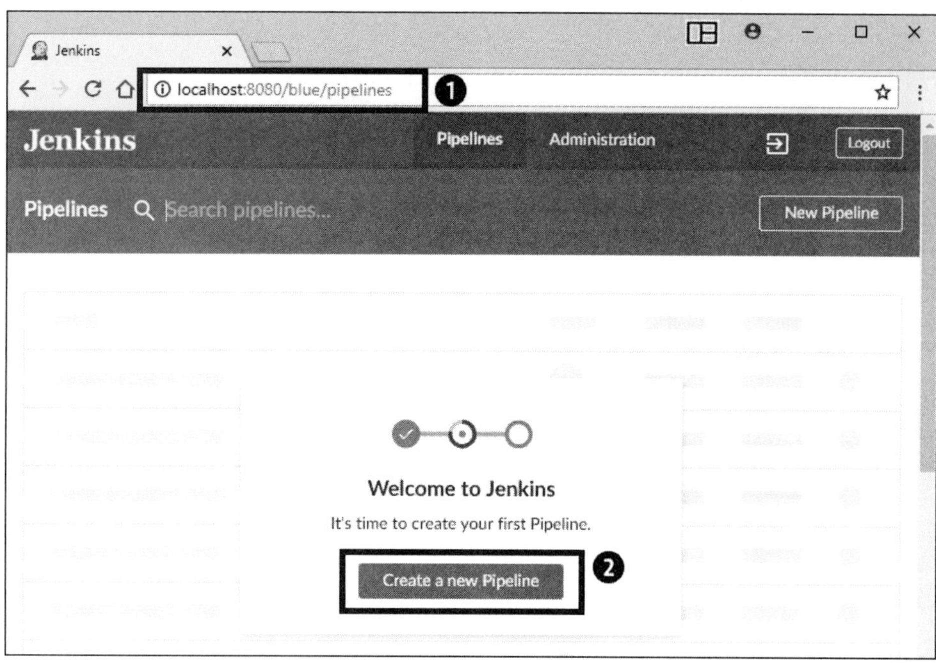

Figure 11.6 Starting the Pipeline Creation Process in Jenkins Blue Ocean

On the **Create Pipeline** page, as shown in Figure 11.7, you must first select where to store your SAPUI5 project code ❶, which in our case is a GitHub repository. When running the pipeline, Jenkins will first clone our project and must therefore authorize itself with GitHub. To create an access token for GitHub, simply click on the **Create an access token here** link ❷, which will forward you to your GitHub account's **Settings/Developer Settings/Personal Access Token** area. Leave the selected scopes as they are, provide a name for the token, generate the token, and paste this token into the input field. Next, you must select the GitHub account for which you've created the access token ❸. Finally, select the repository for which you want to create the pipeline ❹ and click on **Create Pipeline** ❺, as shown in Figure 11.7.

A multibranch Jenkins pipeline project will be created behind the scenes and immediately run the pipeline definition for each found branch containing a `Jenkinsfile`. When you click on the previously created pipeline, you'll see an overview of all currently active pipeline runs in the **Activity** view. As shown in Figure 11.8, our pipeline was immediately executed on our single `master` branch.

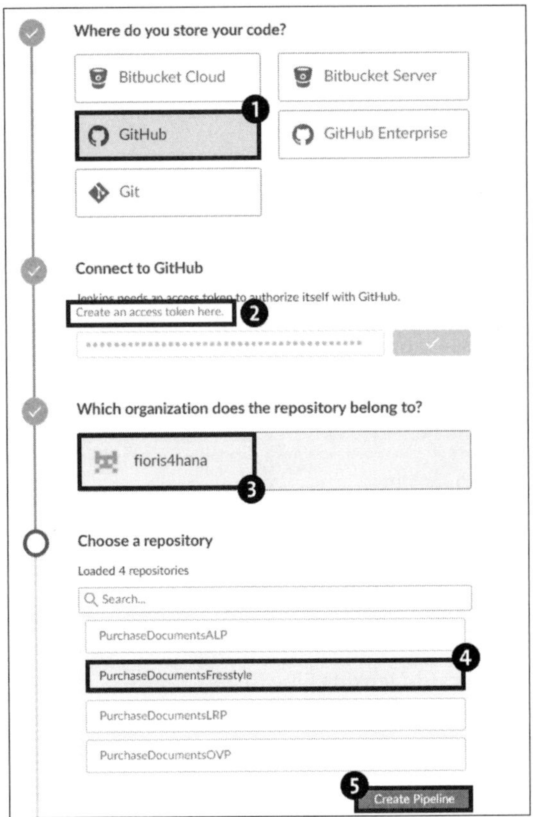

Figure 11.7 Creating a Pipeline for an SAPUI5 Project Stored in a GitHub Repository

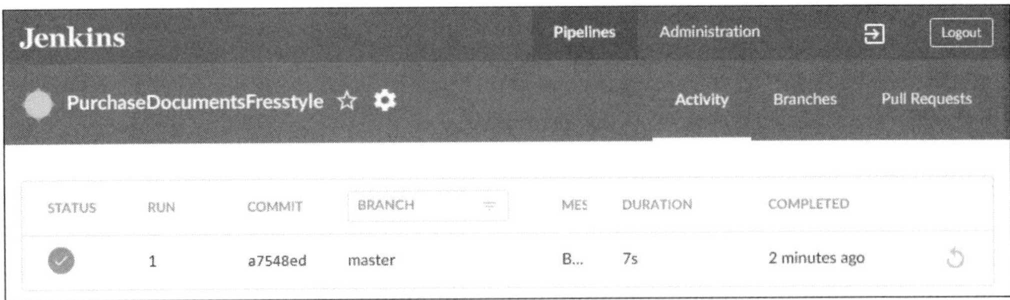

Figure 11.8 Initial Run of Our Pipeline

When you click on a pipeline run entry, you'll see a more detailed view of the pipeline run, including all the stages and steps, as shown in Figure 11.9.

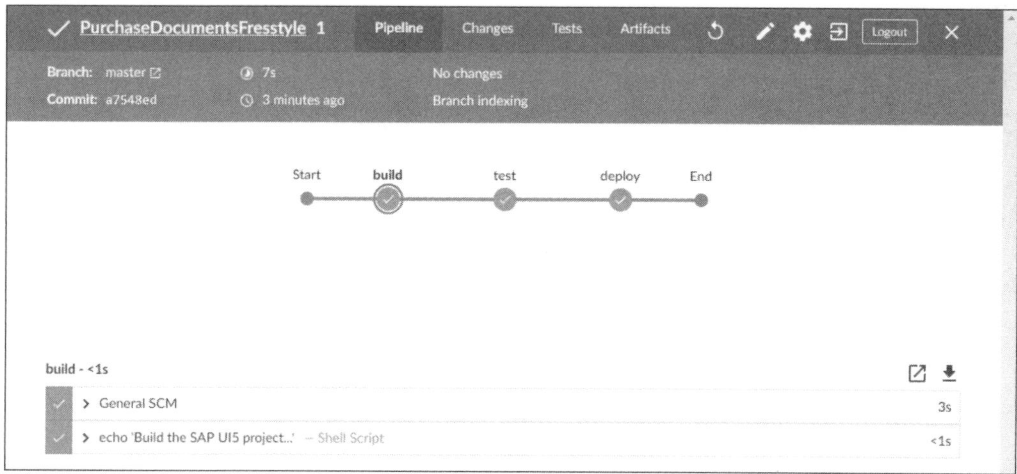

Figure 11.9 Our Executed Pipeline in the Jenkins Pipeline Run Details View

11.2.4 SAPUI5 Grunt Plug-ins

Whenever you create a new project in the SAP Web IDE full-stack, by default, the project will also generate a *Gruntfile.js* and a *package.json* file because the SAP Web IDE full-stack comes with a Node.js environment as part of the IDE, including the Grunt JavaScript task runner. Using the Grunt task runner, you can automate certain steps required for making a project ready for delivery or deployment, such as minifying JavaScript code or executing unit and integration tests. Thus, we'll use the Grunt task runner to execute different tasks inside the steps of our different pipeline stages. Additional Grunt plug-ins can be installed using the Node.js package manager (npm) and must be declared as development dependencies in the *package.json* file. Grunt tasks to be executed must be specified in the *Gruntfile.js* file.

SAP currently provides two best practice Grunt plug-ins for building and testing an SAPUI5 project:

- `@sap/grunt-sapui5-bestpractice-build`
- `@sap/grunt-sapui5-bestpractice-test`

Both plug-ins are published on the SAP npm registry *https://npm.sap.com*. To associate `@sap` scoped packages with the SAP registry, you must execute the `npm config set @sap:registry` *https://npm.sap.com* command. After the scope has been associated with the registry, every `npm install` command for a package with the scope (`@sap`) will request packages from the associated registry (*https://npm.sap.com*).

Note

If you're developing OpenUI5 applications, make sure you look at the UI5 tooling for automating the build of applications: *https://sap.github.io/ui5-tooling/*.

11.2.5 Implementing the Build Stage

To implement the `build` stage of our pipeline, we can use the `@sap/grunt-sapui5-bestpractice-build` Grunt plug-in. The plug-in contains several tasks for cleaning, linting, and building the project. Let's briefly look at each:

- The `clean` task deletes the *dist* folder where build results are stored and which contains previous build results.
- The *lint* task executes static code checks on the SAPUI5 project's code using ESLint rules defined in an *.eslintrc* configuration file that must be present in the root folder of the project. If no *.eslintrc* file is present, a default check configuration will be used. The result of the *lint* task will be written to the `di.code-validation.core_issues.json` file inside the *dist* folder.
- The `build` task creates a new version of the project, which is ready and optimized for deployment in a productive environment; for instance, this task will minify Cascading Style Sheets (CSS) and JavaScript files and create a *Component-preload.js* file bundling all project files (views, controllers) and reducing file sizes and the necessary number of requests to load them. The result of the build step will be stored in the *dist* folder.

Let's add the plug-in to the list of `devDependencies` inside the *package.json* file, as shown in Listing 11.2. The plug-in will then be installed as soon as the `npm install` command is executed inside the root folder of our project.

```
{
  "name": "PurchaseDocumentsFreestyle",
  "version": "0.0.1",
  "description": "Purchase Document Freestyle App",
  "private": true,
  "devDependencies": {
    "@sap/grunt-sapui5-bestpractice-build": "1.3.62"
  }
}
```

Listing 11.2 package.json File Containing a Dependency to the @sap/grunt-sapui5-best-practice-build Grunt Plug-In

To make the tasks contained in the build plug-in executable, first you must load the plug-in inside the *Gruntfile.js* file, as shown in Listing 11.3. Then, you'll register a new `buildProject` task and add a task list to it containing the `clean`, `lint`, and `build` tasks provided by the plug-in.

```
module.exports = function (grunt) {
 "use strict";
 grunt.loadNpmTasks("@sap/grunt-sapui5-bestpractice-build");
 grunt.registerTask("buildProject", [
  "clean",
  "lint",
  "build"
 ]);
};
```

Listing 11.3 Gruntfile.js file Loading the @sap/grunt-sapui5-bestpractice-Build Plug-In Containing the Clean, Lint, and Build Tasks and Declaring Them as the buildProject Tasks

As soon as the *package.json* and *Gruntfile.js* files are created, the SAP Web IDE full-stack will also enable a `Build` option for executing the Grunt `default` task locally in the IDE if defined in the *Gruntfile.js* file, as shown in Figure 11.10.

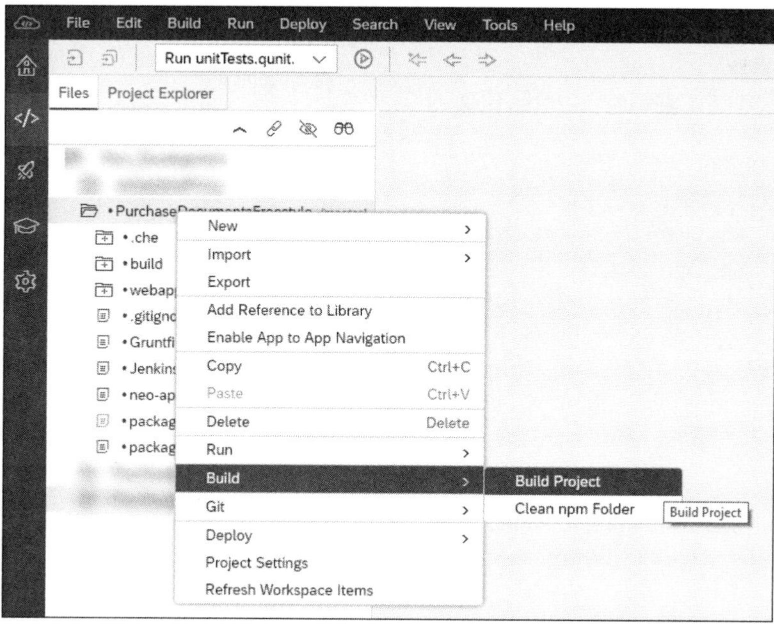

Figure 11.10 Building the SAPUI5 Project in the SAP Web IDE Full-Stack

To execute the buildProject task in the build stage of your Jenkins pipeline, you must adapt the *Jenkinsfile* and the *package.json* file. In the *package.json* file, add a new build script to its scripts property that will execute the buildProject Grunt task and output as much information as possible (Grunt -verbose option), as shown in Listing 11.4.

```
"scripts": {
 "build": "grunt buildProject --verbose"
}
```

Listing 11.4 Add a Build Script Executing the Grunt buildProject Task to the package.json File

In the *Jenkinsfile*, as shown in Listing 11.5, first you must specify the node Docker image (*https://hub.Docker.com/_/node/*) as the unified runtime environment inside the agent section. The build process requires a Node.js environment because we're using the Grunt JavaScript task runner and npm to manage our development dependencies. At the runtime of the pipeline, the Docker image will be pulled from the Docker Hub and run as a container containing our application. In the build stage of the pipeline, we'll add three steps: The npm config set @sap:registry ***https://npm.sap.com*** command will enable the installation of @sap scoped packages from the SAP npm registry; the npm install command will install our dev dependency to the build Grunt plug-in; and the npm run-script build command will execute the Grunt buildProject task(s) clean, lint, and build specified in the *Gruntfile.js* file of the SAPUI5 project.

```
pipeline {
    agent {  docker { image 'node:8.11.3' } }
    stages {
        stage('build') {
            steps {
                sh 'npm config set @sap:registry        https://npm.sap.com'
                sh 'npm install'
                sh 'npm run-script build'
            }
        }
...
    }
}
```

Listing 11.5 Jenkinsfile Containing the Build Stage, Which Is Using the node:8.11.3 Docker Image as the Unified Runtime Environment

To run the newly added build pipeline steps inside your Jenkins container, you must commit and push the changes to your Git repository.

11.2.6 Automatically Triggering Builds on Git Push

In general, Jenkins can be made to automatically execute the pipeline on a change being pushed to the Git repository in two ways:

- Have Jenkins periodically poll the Git repository for changes
- Have the Git repository notify Jenkins on each change pushed to Git

To enable the first (less efficient) approach, simply go to the classic configure Jenkins job view (*http://localhost:8080/job/PurchaseDocumentsFresstyle/configure*) and enable a periodic scan of your SCM system under the **Scan Repository Triggers** tab, specifying a certain time interval, as shown in Figure 11.11. As soon as Jenkins detects a change in a Git branch during one of the periodic checks, the pipeline for the branch will be triggered. This configuration will also work with our local Jenkins Docker container since the Git repository doesn't require access to the Jenkins server in this case. The Jenkins server just periodically checks the publicly accessible GitHub repository for changes.

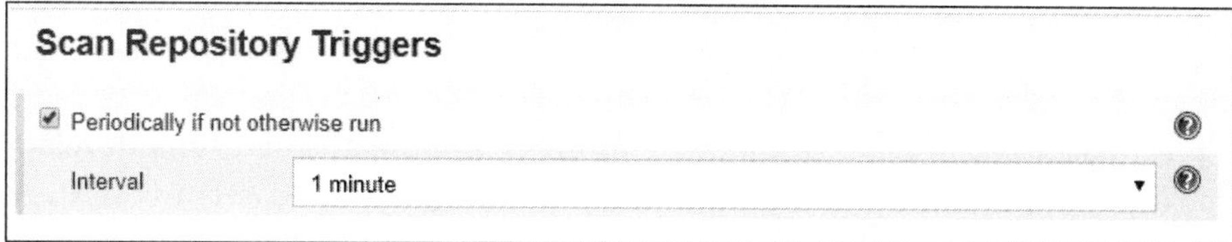

Figure 11.11 Polling the SCM for Changes Using a 1-Minute Interval

The second approach can be implemented using Git hooks. Git hooks are scripts that are executed each time a certain event occurs, for instance, when a change is pushed to the repository. Usually the *post-receive* server-side hook is used for notifying CI servers of a new change and to trigger the build. In this case, the Git repository notifies the Jenkins server of a change. The Jenkins server must therefore be reachable by the Git repository.

Note

For more information on the Git hook approach, consult the Git and GitHub Jenkins plug-in documentation:

- *http://s-prs.co/498825*
- *http://s-prs.co/498826*

11.2.7 Implementing the Test Stage

In the `test` stage of our pipeline, we'll run the unit (QUnit) and integration (OPA5) tests contained in the *test* folder of our SAPUI5 project in one of two ways. We can either user the `@sap/grunt-sapui5-bestpractice-test` Grunt plug-in just as we used the best practice build Grunt plug-in and load its `test` task, or we can create our own custom test configuration instead.

> **Note**
>
> When you create the `test structure` for an SAPUI5 project inside SAP Web IDE, the IDE will automatically add and configure the `@sap/grunt-sapui5-bestpractice-test` Grunt plug-in and its tasks.

Internally, the `@sap/grunt-sapui5-bestpractice-test` Grunt plug-in uses Karma (*http://karma-runner.github.io/2.0/index.html*), the karma-grunt plug-in (*https://github.com/karma-runner/grunt-karma*), and the karma-openui5 adapter (*https://github.com/SAP/karma-openui5*) for configuring and running SAPUI5 tests as a Grunt task. If your `test` stage requires more flexibility, for instance, different browsers and test reporters, you can also create a custom test configuration based on these tools instead of using the prebundled best practice test plug-in. Figure 11.12 shows the necessary development dependencies in the *package.json* file for setting up our custom `test` stage implementation.

package.json ×

```
{
    "name": "PurchaseDocumentsFreestyle",
    "version": "0.0.1",
    "description": "Purchase Document Freestyle App",
    "private": true,
    "devDependencies": {
        "@sap/grunt-sapui5-bestpractice-build": "1.3.62",
        "karma": "2.0.4",
        "grunt-karma": "2.0.0",
        "karma-openui5": "0.2.3",
        "karma-chrome-launcher": "2.2.0",
        "karma-qunit": "2.1.0",
        "qunit": "2.6.1",
        "karma-junit-reporter": "1.2.0",
        "karma-coverage": "1.1.2"
    },
    "scripts": {
        "build": "grunt buildProject --verbose",
        "test": "grunt testProject  --verbose"
    }
}
```

Figure 11.12 Development Dependencies Required in the package.json File for Creating a Custom Test Stage

Figure 11.13 shows our custom test configuration for the `karma` Grunt task. First, we must load the `grunt-karma` plug-in. Next, we'll add a configuration for the `karma` task with an `options` property holding the common configuration for all targets. The *dist* folder will be defined as the `basePath` of our configuration since we want to run the tests inside the previously built version of our project stored in the *dist* folder.

```
Gruntfile.js ×

    grunt.loadNpmTasks("grunt-karma");
    grunt.config.merge({
        karma: {
            options: {
                basePath: "./dist/",
                frameworks: ["qunit", "openui5"],
                openui5: {
                    path: "https://sapui5.hana.ondemand.com/1.54.4/resources/sap-ui-core.js" // eslint-disable-line
                },
                client: {
                    openui5: {
                        config: {
                            theme: "sap_belize",
                            language: "EN",
                            resourceroots: {
                                "fiori.create.pruchase.documents.PurchaseDocumentsFreestyle": "/base",
                                "test": "/base/test"
                            }
                        },
                        tests: [
                            "test/unit/allTests",
                            "test/integration/AllJourneys"
                        ]
                    }
                },

                files: [{
                    pattern: "**",
                    included: false,
                    served: true,
                    watched: true
                }],
                browsers: ["Chrome"],

                reporters: ["progress", "junit", "coverage"],
                junitReporter: {
                    outputDir: "../testResult",
                    outputFile: "result.xml",
                    useBrowserName: false
                },
                preprocessors: {
                    "/!(test|localService|coverage)/!(*dbg*).js": ["coverage"]
                },
                coverageReporter: {
                    type: "html",
                    dir: "../coverage/",
                    subdir: ".",
                    includeAllSources: true
                },
```

Figure 11.13 Custom Karma Configuration inside the Gruntfile.js File

The karma-openui5 adapter loads the SAPUI5/OpenUI5 framework from a specified location in the openui5 property, for instance, a content delivery network (CDN). Additionally, you must specify where your unit and integration tests are located (tests) and map the SAPUI5 namespaces to the right paths relative to the basePath (base). We'll run these tests inside the Chrome browser, which we can make available using a custom Docker image or by installing it in the Node.js container before running the pipeline. To report our test results, we'll add additional coverage (coverageReporter) and junit (jUnitReporter) reporters.

In addition to the common options configuration, we'll add a special ci target for our CI build, which will use Chrome in headless mode and run our tests in CI mode (singleRun). Headless mode will run chrome without displaying its actual UI which is great for automated testing as a UI is not required in this case. Furthermore, we'll register the karma:ci target as the testProject task inside the *Gruntfile.js* file, as shown in Figure 11.14.

```
        // Continuous Integration (CI) settings
        ci: {
            browsers: ["ChromeHeadlessNoSandbox"],
            customLaunchers: {
                ChromeHeadlessNoSandbox: {
                    base: "ChromeHeadless",
                    flags: ["--no-sandbox"]
                }
            },
            singleRun: true
        }
    }
});
grunt.registerTask("testProject", [
    "karma:ci"
]);
```

Figure 11.14 CI Target inside the Karma Configuration and the Registration of the karma:ci Target as the testProject Task inside the Grunfile.js File

To run the testProject task using npm, we'll add a test entry to the scripts property of the *package.json* file as we did for the buildProject task: "test": "grunt testProject --verbose".

The test stage inside the Jenkinsfile should resemble the code shown in Listing 11.6.

```
stage('test'){
    steps {
        sh 'npm run-script test'
```

```
    }
}
```

Listing 11.6 Test Stage of Our Pipeline inside the Jenkinsfile

Note

For further information on how to set up Karma as a test runner for SAPUI5 unit and integration tests, refer to the SAPUI5 Software Development Kit (SDK) test automation documentation at *http://s-prs.co/498827*.

11.2.8 Implementing the Deploy Stage

In the `deploy` stage of the pipeline, first we'll want to upload the project to our JFrog Artifactory cloud account. Therefore, we'll need to install the JFrog Artifactory plug-in for Jenkins via **localhost:8080 • Manage Jenkins • Manage Plugins**. In the pipeline definition, we'll then package our project as a ZIP file and upload it to our generic SAPUI5 artifact repository inside our JFrog Artifactory cloud account using a scripted pipeline step written in the Groovy language, as shown in Figure 11.15.

```
stage('deploy'){
    steps{
        // Package the dist folder as a zip file
        sh "cd dist && zip -r  ../${BUILD_ZIP_FILE_NAME} * && cd .."
        // Upload the zip file to JFrog Artifactory
        script{
            def server = Artifactory.server 'ART'
            def uploadSpec = """{
              "files": [
                {
                  "pattern": "${BUILD_ZIP_FILE_NAME}",
                  "target": "UI5/"
                }
              ]
            }"""
            def uploadBuildInfo = server.upload(uploadSpec)
            server.publishBuildInfo uploadBuildInfo
        }
    }
}
```

Figure 11.15 Packaging the dist Folder as a ZIP File and Uploading it to Our JFrog Artifactory Repository

To add a unique ID to each successfully built SAPUI5 artifact, we'll use the Jenkins `BUILD_NUMBER` environment variable inside the `environment` directive of the pipeline:

BUILD_ZIP_FILE_NAME = "PurchaseDocumentFreestyleUI5App-0.${env.BUILD_NUMBER}.zip".

Keep in mind that the deploy stage will only be reached if the preceding stages have executed successfully; for instance, if failures in unit tests arise due to regressions, the current state of the project won't be deployed. Figure 11.16 shows the result of successful pipeline executions. Production-ready and tested SAPUI5 projects are uploaded to the SAPUI5 repository in JFrog Artifactory from which applications can be downloaded and deployed to the SAP Gateway hub system.

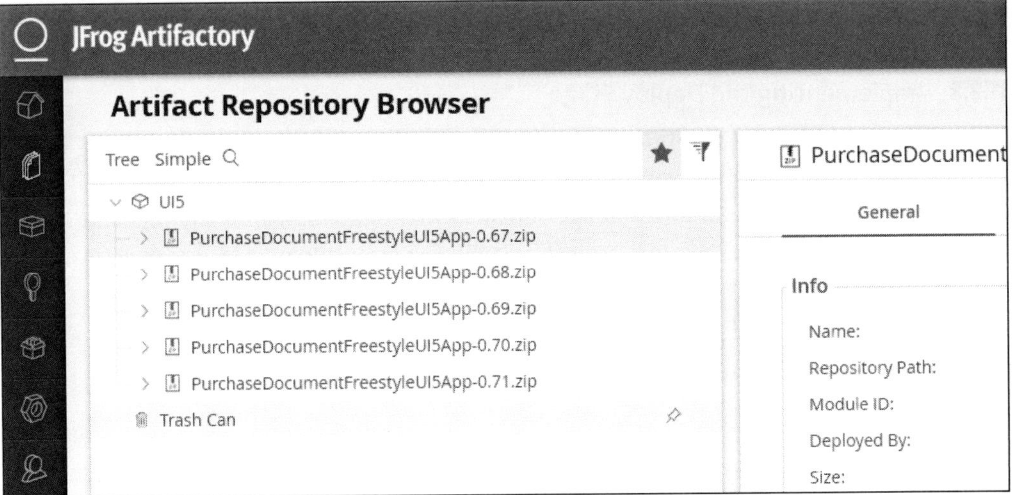

Figure 11.16 Uploaded Production-Ready SAPUI5 Projects inside the SAPUI5 Artifactory Repository

Note

For further information concerning Jenkins and JFrog Artifactory, refer to the official documentation:

- *www.jfrog.com/confluence/display/RTF/Jenkins+Artifactory+Plug-in*
- *www.jfrog.com/confluence/display/RTF/Working+With+Pipeline+Jobs+in+Jenkins*

Up to this point, our pipeline has implemented a CI process that included build and test stages as well as a deploy stage for uploading the pipeline's packaged result to a software repository. However, this process can't yet be considered continuous deployment because deploying the frontend project to our SAP Gateway hub system has not been fully automated. For both automated and manual deployments of SAPUI5 projects stored in a software repository to the SAP Gateway hub system, SAP provides the ABAP function module `/UI5/UI5_REPOSITORY_LOAD_HTTP` and, since SAP S/4HANA 1809, its simplified successor `/UI5/REPO_LOAD_FROM_ZIP_URL`. Both function modules are RFC enabled and can therefore be called remotely, for instance, by CI/CD scripts. In particular, these modules expect a URL to a ZIP file where the project can be downloaded and deployed, for instance, the URL to an SAPUI5 project artifact stored in a software repository such as JFrog Artifactory. To call SAP RFC-enabled function modules from within Grunt tasks, you can use the SAP RFC connector for Node.js (*https://github.com/SAP/node-rfc*). As a prerequisite, you must install the SAP NetWeaver RFC SDK and make it available in the runtime environment of your CI/CD pipeline, in our case, the Docker container (*http://s-prs.co/498828*).

To deploy the project to the SAP Gateway hub system, you can add a custom Grunt task `deployProjectToGateway` to our *Gruntfile.js*, as shown in Listing 11.7. Inside the task, you could then call the `/UI5/UI5_REPOSITORY_LOAD_HTTP` function module passing a URL pointing to the latest version of our project stored in JFrog Artifactory or some other software repository. This Grunt task might use the SAP RFC Connector Node.js library to upload the SAPUI5 project to the ABAP frontend server.

```
grunt.registerTask("deployProjectToGateway", function () {
...
});
```

Listing 11.7 Custom deployProjectToGateway Grunt Task

Like the previous `build` and `test` stages, you could add a `script` entry for the Grunt deploy task (`"deploy": "grunt deployProject --verbose"`) to the *package.json* file and call the script from the `deploy` stage inside the `Jenkinsfile`.

Note

If you need to transport the SAPUI5 project in your development landscape, for instance, from the development system (DEV) to the quality assurance system (QAS), you can additionally use the RFC-enabled `BAPI_CTREQUEST_CREATE` and `BAPI_CTREQUEST_RELEASE` function modules.

For further information concerning CI and continuous deployment, check out the comprehensive *Continuous Integration (CI) Best Practices with SAP* guide at *www.sap.com/developer/tutorials/ci-best-practices-intro.html*.

11.3 Continuous Integration on the ABAP Server

Classic ABAP development relies on the Change and Transport System (CTS) for transporting development objects between systems in the SAP landscape. This requirement hasn't changed for the backend part of SAP S/4HANA applications. The CDS, Business Object Processing Framework (BOPF), ABAP, and OData backend artifacts required for your OData service solely make use of the standard ABAP development lifecycle management. A classic SAP landscape usually consists of a development system (DEV) ❶, quality assurance system (QAS) ❷, and production system (PROD) ❸, as shown in Figure 11.17.

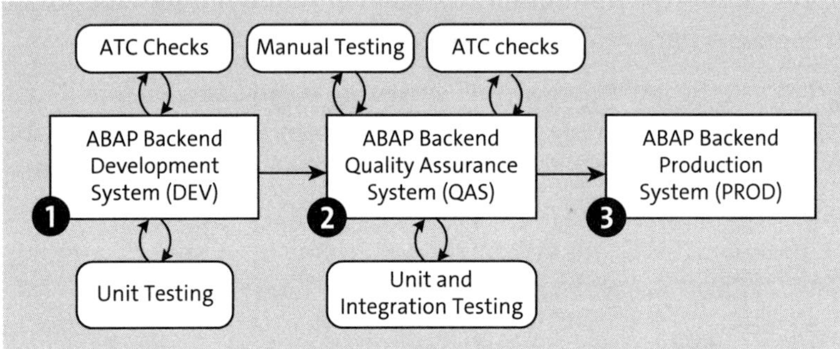

Figure 11.17 Classic ABAP Change and Transport System (CTS) Deployment Pipeline

The QAS serves as the main code line of our ABAP backend where new features developed in the DEV system(s) are integrated. From a CI standpoint, you can integrate changes frequently by releasing transport requests in the DEV system on a regular basis (usually daily) can be beneficial. As with SAPUI5 frontend projects, this approach fosters runnable software, encourages customer feedback, and prevents integration hell. Therefore, the classic ABAP system landscape can also be considered as a kind of a CI/CD pipeline where code from developers is integrated in a QAS system before being deployed into production. Before developers release their transport requests in the DEV system, they should get feedback about the quality of their development via static code checks and ABAP unit tests to catch bugs as early as possible in the pipeline. Subsequently, in the QAS system, automated tests and checks should be periodically run, for instance, every night to detect integration problems and regressions because solely integrating the transports into a main code line is not enough to verify that the software is actually working. Manual testing could be supplemental but should not be required. If the test and checks executed in the QAS system are all clear, we can transport the new features to the PROD system. To prevent the transport of erroneous objects to the next stage of the pipeline, we might want to establish quality gates (Q gates) at transport releases in the DEV and QAS systems. By automating the testing required in the DEV and QAS systems, you could significantly reduce the time needed for getting features into production and could increase quality by reducing (regression) bugs reaching the PROD system. The main tool that supports the just outlined scenario in the ABAP backend is the ABAP Test Cockpit (ATC).

11.3.1 Quality Checking Using the ABAP Test Cockpit

Based on the Code Inspector, the ATC is SAP's standard quality assurance infrastructure for all kind of checks and tests. In this section, you'll get a high-level overview of the best practice setup for an ATC test infrastructure, usually established by a quality manager. Additionally, you'll learn how to work with ATC checks locally as a developer in a development system to catch bugs at the earliest possible stage of the CI/CD pipeline.

ABAP Test Cockpit Best Practice Infrastructure Setup

The best practice recommendation for ATC quality checking introduces ATC checks at four different levels on the DEV and QAS systems, as shown in Figure 11.18:

❶ Developers continuously run ATC checks from the ABAP development tools in Eclipse when developing in the DEV system.

❷ The development team checks their development objects continuously using automatic ATC checks in the DEV system.

❸ As soon as a developer or development team releases a transport, the contained objects are checked using ATC checks, which implements a Q gate between the DEV and QAS systems.

❹ In the *ATC master system* (QAS system), the quality manager periodically runs mass quality checks and publishes the results to the *ATC satellite* DEV system(s) as the active ATC result, which also serves as a Q gate between the QAS and PROD system.

Usually, this test infrastructure is set up by a quality manager who will define the central code line or, in ABAP terms, the consolidation or quality system, where mass regression tests should happen. The QAS can be supplied from several different DEV systems, so continuously checking for integration problems and regressions—for instance, method signature changes where callers weren't yet updated, missing dependencies present in other not-yet-released transports, or side effects introduced with new features that break older functionality—is important.

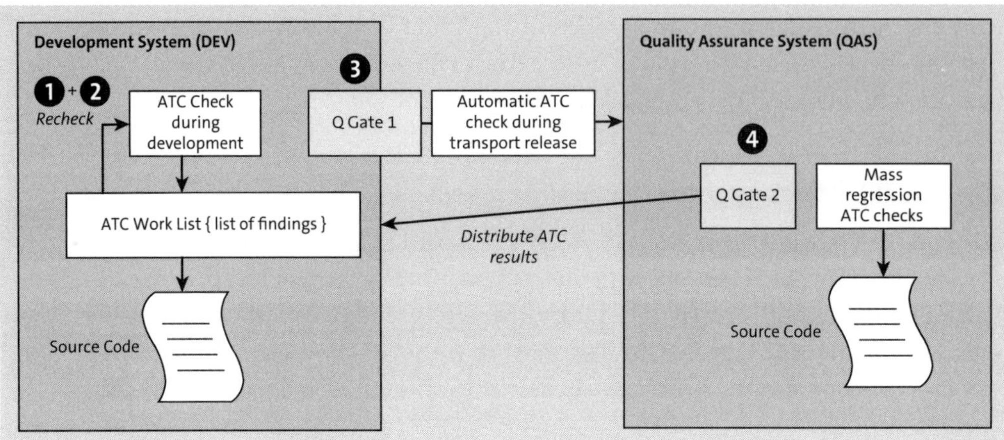

Figure 11.18 Illustration of the ATC Checks Executed in the Different Systems

When setting up the test infrastructure for an SAP landscape, the quality manager will first define the ATC master system where central ATC quality checking will take place on a regular basis, for instance, daily, as mentioned earlier, usually the QAS system of the landscape. The development or correction systems (DEV) that transport new ABAP development objects, such as CDS views, ABAP classes, or SAP Gateway artifacts, to the QAS systems are the ATC satellite systems. In the second step, the ATC master system and the ATC satellite systems must be connected via trusted RFC connections so that the ATC master system can distribute the central ATC results to the ATC satellite systems. In the third step, the quality manager will set up and schedule the ATC check locally on the ATC master system using Transaction ATC, including whether the ATC checks will also be executed on transport release in the satellite systems. What checks are concretely executed must be previously defined in the form of a global SCI variant using Transaction SCI. static code checks can be included as can dynamic tests in the form of ABAP unit tests. Finally, each development ATC satellite system can download the ATC configuration settings defined in the ATC master system, for instance, the SCI check variant using Transaction ATC. As a result, developers can run the same ATC checks locally as the quality manager does in the central consolidation system.

Dealing with ABAP Test Cockpit Checks Locally in a Development System

As a developer in the DEV system, you can execute a local (default) ATC check variant for a currently opened development object in the ABAP development tools in Eclipse using the shortcut [Ctrl]+[Shift]+[F2] or by right-clicking on the development object in the **Project Explorer** view and selecting **Run As • ABAP Test Cockpit**. The ATC work list will then be displayed in the **ATC Problems** view, as shown in Figure 11.19. If the view isn't visible, navigate to **Window • Show View • Other • ATC Problems** and select the view.

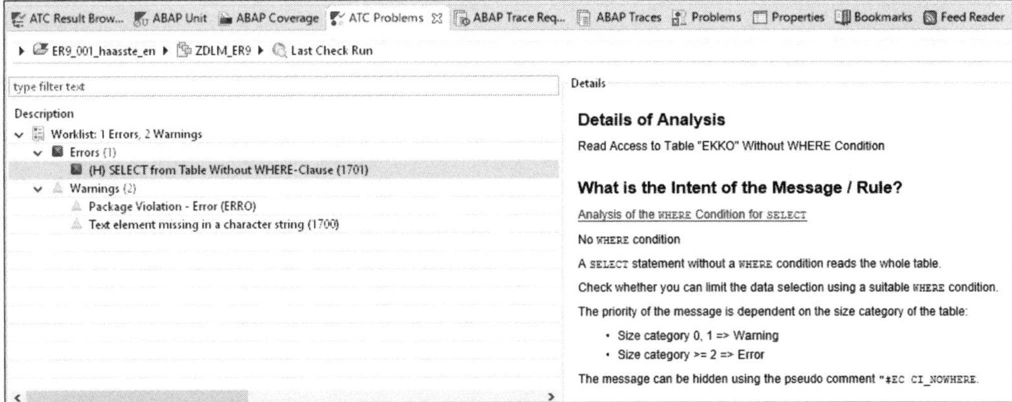

Figure 11.19 The Result of a Local ATC Check in the ATC Problems View

To run a different check variant, for instance, a locally defined stricter check variant than the default check variant from the ATC master system, you can open the context menu of a development object in the **Project Explorer** and choose **Run As • ABAP Test Cockpit With.**

To display the ATC check result distributed by a central ATC master system, you must open the **ATC Result Browser** view, as shown in Figure 11.20. You can do this by choosing **Window • Show View • Other • ATC Result Browser.**

You can also create a feed for the currently active ATC result and receive notification messages for findings by first displaying the **Feed Reader** view (**Window • Show View • Other • Feed Reader**) and then choosing **Add Feed Query • ATC Findings** from the context menu of the system. The **New Feed Query** dialog box will open, where you'll then configure the exact ATC results you want to receive notifications for, for instance, ATC errors for your objects with priority 1 or 2, as shown in Figure 11.21.

ATC Result Browser | ABAP Unit | ABAP Coverage | ATC Problems | Properties | Feed Reader | Search | History | (x)= Variables

type filter text

Description	Errors	Warnings	Infos	Check Variant
ER9_001_haasste_en				
Active Result: ZO9: Thursday, CW30 2018 (findings assigned to me)	1	353	239	ZDLM_ZO9
Results of my Check Runs				
Today (1)				
TESTZFIORIPURCHDEMO	75	53	4	ZDLM_ER9
Yesterday (5)				
Z_C_PURCHASEDOCUMENTLRP	3	1	0	ZDLM_ER9
Z_I_PURCHASEDOCUMENT	4	0	0	ZDLM_ER9
ZCL_A_SET_STATUS	0	0	0	ZDLM_ER9
ZCL_A_SET_STATUS	0	0	0	ZDLM_ER9
ZCL_A_SET_STATUS	0	0	0	ZDLM_ER9
Older (4)				

Figure 11.20 Active ATC Result Distributed by the ATC Master System

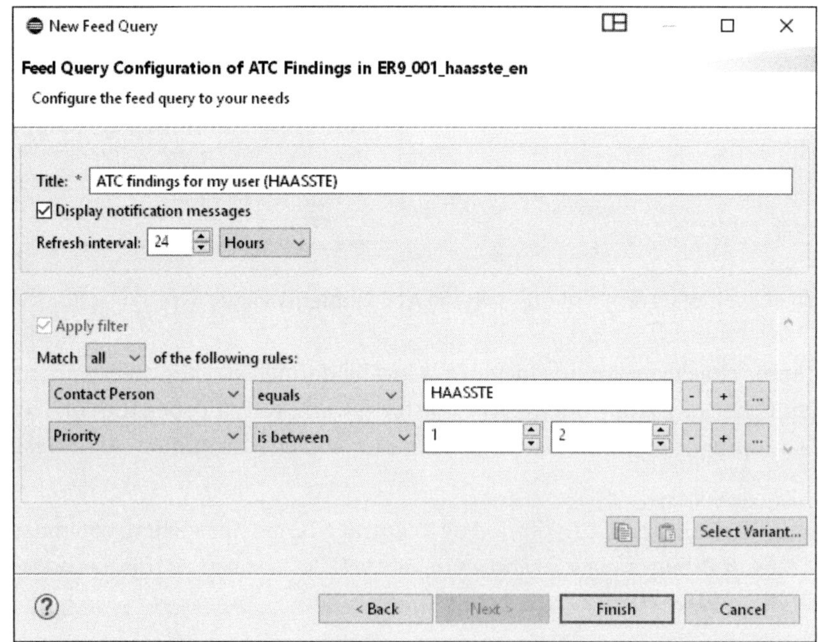

Figure 11.21 Creating a Feed That Includes Notifications for the Currently Active ATC Result Filtered by Your SAP User ID

11.3.2 Scheduling ABAP Unit Tests Using the ABAP Unit Runner

Lightweight regression testing in a development or quality system can also be done using the ABAP Unit Runner (program RS_AUCV_RUNNER). Compared to setting up an ATC infrastructure, setting up a periodically running ABAP Unit Runner job is simple and can be achieved without involving the SAP Basis team. Therefore, using the ABAP Unit Runner could be a first step to continuous regression and integration testing. With the ABAP Unit Runner, you can run unit tests by packages ❶ and notify certain people (usually the quality manager or developer) of test results always or only when errors arise ❷, as shown in Figure 11.22.

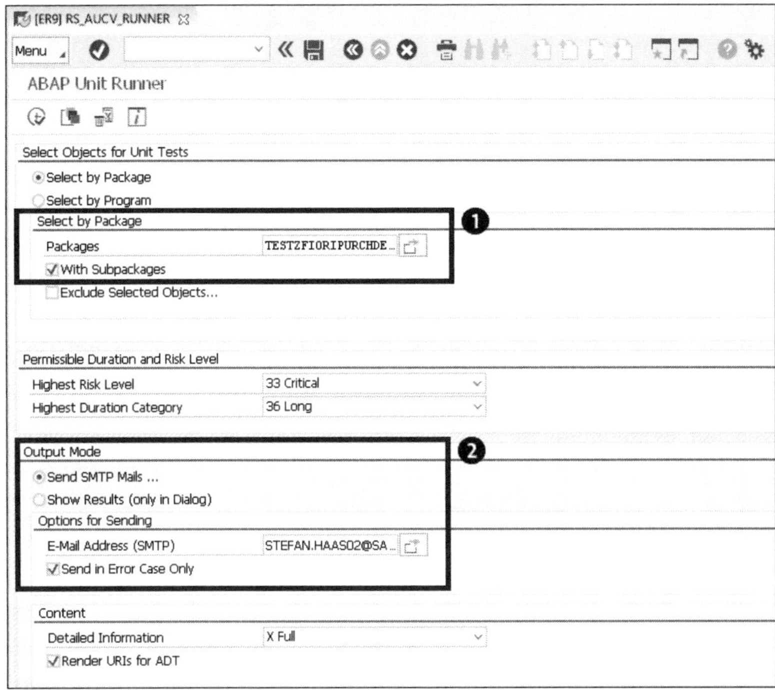

Figure 11.22 Running ABAP Unit Tests by Packages and Notifying Responsible Developers by Email in Case of Errors

To periodically schedule unit tests as a background job, first you must save the previously selected packages and entered email recipients as a variant of the report by clicking the **Save** button or by choosing **Menu • Go To • Variants • Save as Variant**. For our example, we'll call our variant `Z_UNIT_TESTS`.

To define a background job for our unit test variant, we must use Transaction SM36, as shown in Figure 11.23. First, we'll provide a name for our job ❶, then specify what our job will run by clicking the **Step** button ❷, and finally specify when our job should run via the **Start condition** button ❸.

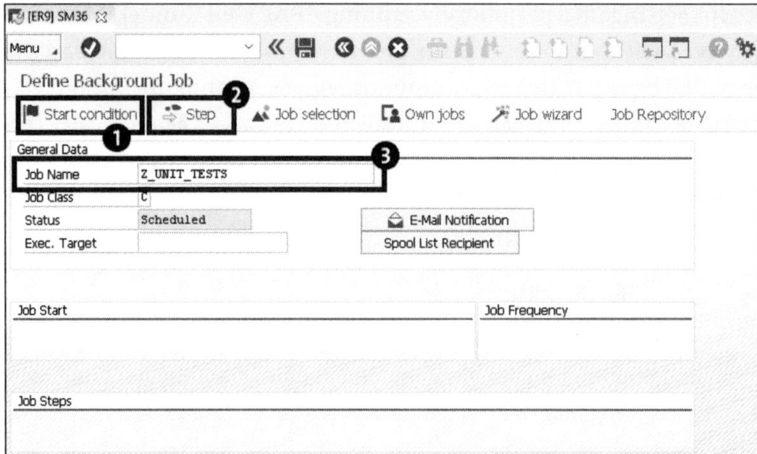

Figure 11.23 Define a Background Job in Transaction SM36 for Running the ABAP Unit Tests periodically

Figure 11.24 shows the configuration we entered inside the **Create Step 1** dialog: the ABAP Unit Runner report **RS_AUCV_RUNNER** and our **Z_UNIT_TESTS** variant containing our packages and email recipients.

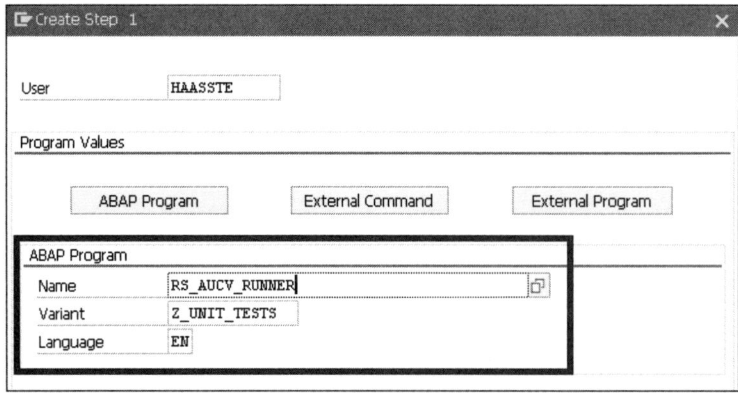

Figure 11.24 Adding the ABAP Unit Runner and Our Previously Saved Variant to the Job Definition

In the **Start Time** dialog, shown in Figure 11.25, opened by the **Start Condition** button, you must enter the start date and time for your job ❶ and the **Period Values** ❸, for instance, **Daily** if we want the job to run every day at the time specified in the **Scheduled**

Start Time field. The **Period Values** dialog box can be opened by clicking the **Period Values** button ❷. Don't forget to save everything.

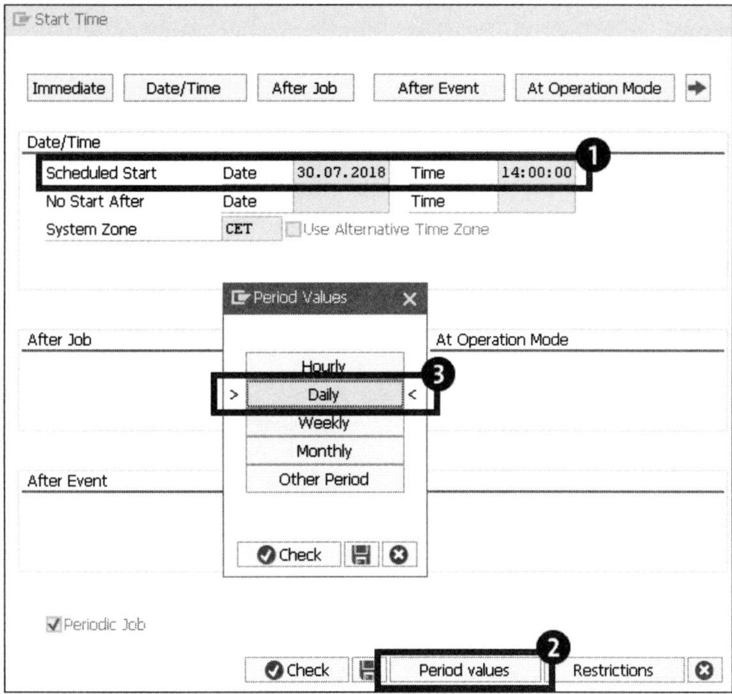

Figure 11.25 Scheduling the Background Job Daily Starting from a Certain Date

To display and check the service, use Transaction SM37.

11.4 Summary

This chapter provided you with an overview of CI practices you might want to establish when developing applications for SAP S/4HANA in the SAPUI5 frontend as well as in the ABAP backend. The tools and approaches we presented in this chapter will support you in reducing release cycles, (regression) bugs, and risks, which in turn foster faster customer feedback and satisfaction. We could only scratch the surface in this chapter because CI itself could take up a whole book, but we hope that we've at least introduced you the idea of using an SAPUI5 Jenkins pipeline for integration, test, and deployment automation. You might want to extend the pipeline further, for instance, with a code review process based on a protected master branch and the

GitHub workflow (pull requests) or an additional end-to-end (E2E) stage. Additionally, we introduced you to the ATC infrastructure as a best practice setup for the ABAP backend, discussed how to carry out ATC checks locally as a developer in the development system, and examined using the ABAP Unit Runner as a lightweight alternative for running unit tests. With this chapter, we've now covered the whole development process for SAP S/4HANA applications, starting from the design over the actual implementation to continuous integration and testing.

In the next chapter you'll learn how you can also manage your ABAP source code with Git and how you can import the source code discussed in this book into your local SAP S/4HANA system.

Chapter 12
ABAP on Git

In Chapter 9, you learned about version control using the SAP Web IDE for SAPUI5 applications. In this chapter, you'll get familiar with a new feature that SAP has introduced to link ABAP development objects to Git: ABAP on Git (abapGit). We'll use ABAP on Git to export and import development objects between systems.

ABAP on Git is an open source project (more details can be found at *https://docs.abapgit.org/*) used as a ABAP client for Git. Supported from ABAP 7.02 and above, like any other Git project, abapGit allows version control of the code committed to the repository. We walked you through some basic concepts behind Git in Chapter 9. In this chapter, first we'll link abapGit with an online repository and then we'll upload a code directly into the Git, then we'll import this code into another system. We'll also export the source codes of our applications using abapGit as ZIP files, which we created in Chapters 4 to 7, and then we'll import this file directly into another system using abapGit. (This process will be helpful for importing the source codes of this book directly into your development system to out try the applications we created.) So, let's start by walking through the steps for setting up abapGit for the rest of this chapter.

12.1 Creating a Git Repository

You learned how to create repositories in Chapter 9, but for this example, we'll create a new repository that we'll use throughout this chapter. Log in to your GitHub account and click **New**, as shown in Figure 12.1.

Provide a name and description for the new repository of your abapGit project, as shown in Figure 12.2. Make sure you select the **Initialize this repository with a README** checkbox so that the repository is initialized.

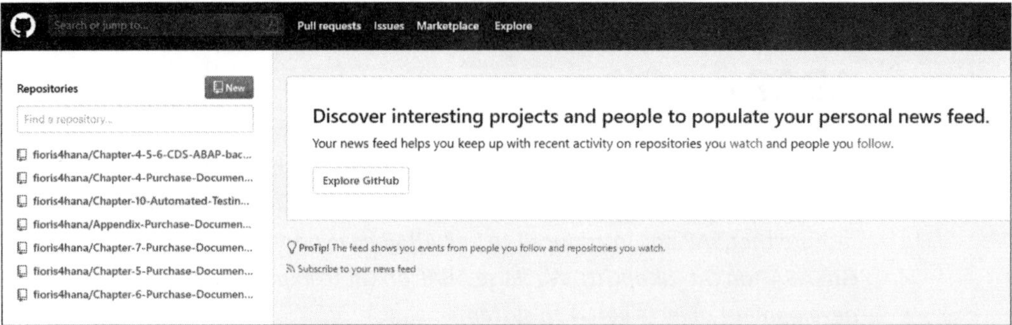

Figure 12.1 Creating a New Repository for abapGit

Create a new repository

A repository contains all project files, including the revision history. Already have a project repository elsewhere? Import a repository.

Owner: fioris4hana / Repository name *: ABAPGitRepo

Great repository names are short and memorable. Need inspiration? How about scaling-fiesta?

Description (optional): Repository for ABAP on Git

Public — Anyone can see this repository. You choose who can commit.

Private — You choose who can see and commit to this repository.

Skip this step if you're importing an existing repository.

Initialize this repository with a README — This will let you immediately clone the repository to your computer.

Add .gitignore: None | Add a license: None

Create repository

Figure 12.2 Creating a New Repository for abapGit

Once the repository is been created and initialized, click on the **Clone or download button**, and you'll be able to see the URL for this repository, as shown in Figure 12.3. Make a note of this URL because you'll need this information later when you clone this GitHub repository into the Eclipse IDE.

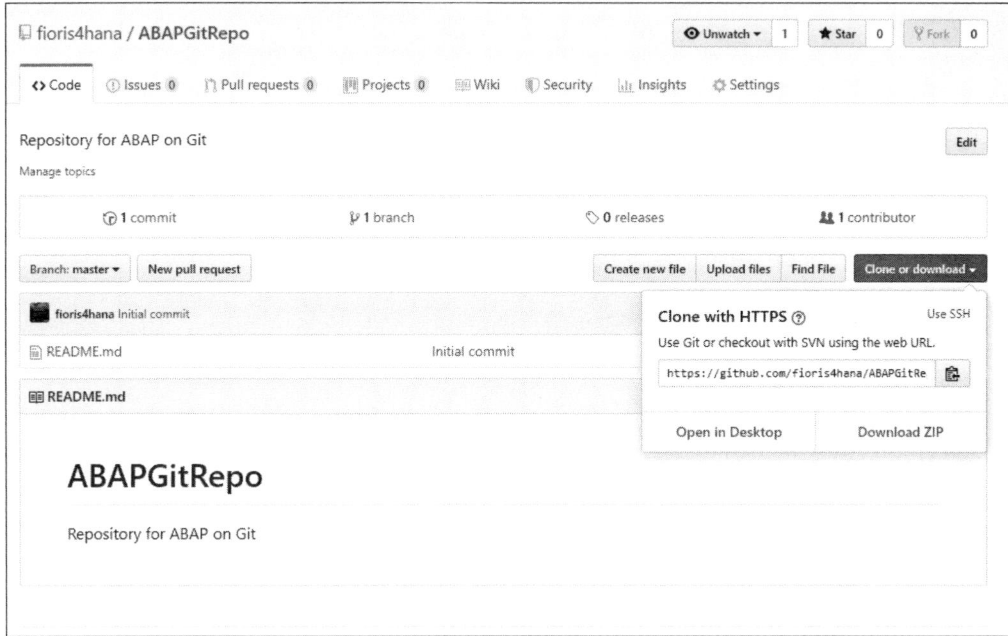

Figure 12.3 URL Link for Cloning the Created Repository

12.2 Installation and Setup

Now, let's begin the abapGit installation and setup process. To start the abapGit program, you'll need to download the report program's source code from *https://docs.abapgit.org/* under the **Latest build** section. You'll need to create a local report program in your system with this source code, as shown in Figure 12.4, and then execute it. This program will let you connect your ABAP system with the GitHub repositories.

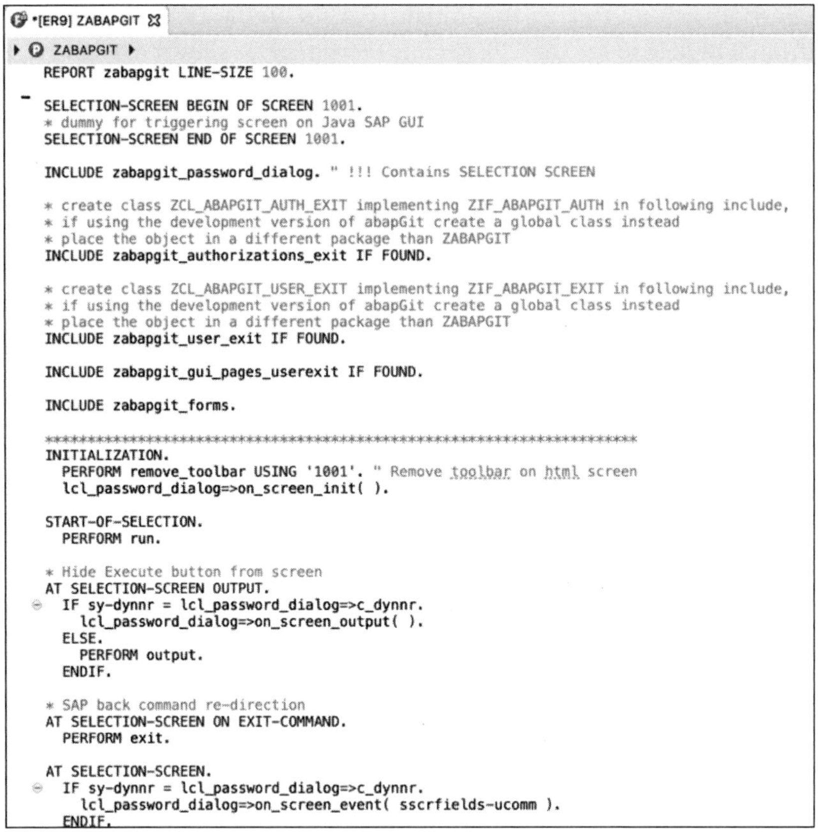

```
*[ER9] ZABAPGIT
ZABAPGIT
REPORT zabapgit LINE-SIZE 100.

SELECTION-SCREEN BEGIN OF SCREEN 1001.
* dummy for triggering screen on Java SAP GUI
SELECTION-SCREEN END OF SCREEN 1001.

INCLUDE zabapgit_password_dialog. " !!! Contains SELECTION SCREEN

* create class ZCL_ABAPGIT_AUTH_EXIT implementing ZIF_ABAPGIT_AUTH in following include,
* if using the development version of abapGit create a global class instead
* place the object in a different package than ZABAPGIT
INCLUDE zabapgit_authorizations_exit IF FOUND.

* create class ZCL_ABAPGIT_USER_EXIT implementing ZIF_ABAPGIT_EXIT in following include,
* if using the development version of abapGit create a global class instead
* place the object in a different package than ZABAPGIT
INCLUDE zabapgit_user_exit IF FOUND.

INCLUDE zabapgit_gui_pages_userexit IF FOUND.

INCLUDE zabapgit_forms.

**********************************************************************
INITIALIZATION.
  PERFORM remove_toolbar USING '1001'. " Remove toolbar on html screen
  lcl_password_dialog=>on_screen_init( ).

START-OF-SELECTION.
  PERFORM run.

* Hide Execute button from screen
AT SELECTION-SCREEN OUTPUT.
  IF sy-dynnr = lcl_password_dialog=>c_dynnr.
    lcl_password_dialog=>on_screen_output( ).
  ELSE.
    PERFORM output.
  ENDIF.

* SAP back command re-direction
AT SELECTION-SCREEN ON EXIT-COMMAND.
  PERFORM exit.

AT SELECTION-SCREEN.
  IF sy-dynnr = lcl_password_dialog=>c_dynnr.
    lcl_password_dialog=>on_screen_event( sscrfields-ucomm ).
  ENDIF.
```

Figure 12.4 abapGit Report Program

Figure 12.5 shows the abapGit home screen. Different options are available when setting up the project: **Online** will let you connect to an online GitHub repository, and **Offline** will let you import or export development objects as ZIP files. For our example, we'll use the online option to connect a local package with the GitHub repository we created earlier.

Click on the **Online** link and provide the URL of the online GitHub repository, as shown in Figure 12.6, which we created earlier. Also, you must provide a package name (you'll use your local package on your ABAP system) so that the ABAP package will be linked to the repository, thereby enabling all future development objects created in this package to be uploaded to this repository. The upload has be done manually, it will not be uploaded or synced automatically every time you make a change in your linked development package.

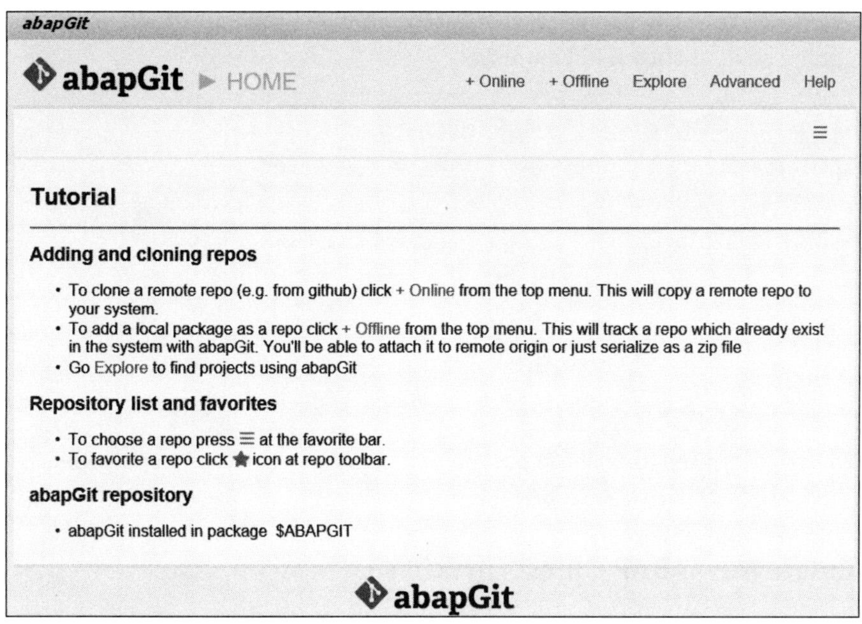

Figure 12.5 abapGit Home

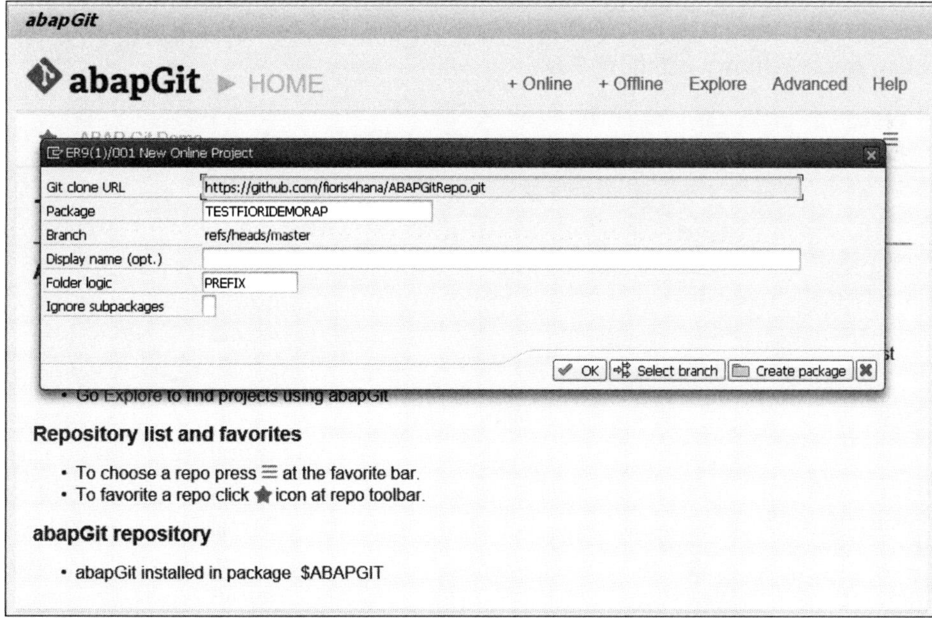

Figure 12.6 Linking ABAP Local Package with abapGit with Online Repository

Once the repository is synchronized, you'll see the GitHub repository details in your abapGit home page, as shown in Figure 12.7.

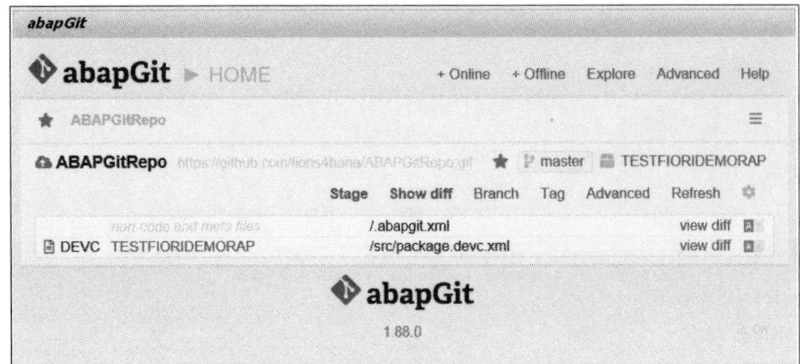

Figure 12.7 abapGit Linked to Online Repository

12.3 Create New ABAP Objects in Eclipse

Once you've linked your ABAP package with the online repository, now you'll need to create some development objects to test whether we can push changes from the package to the repository. For our example, we'll create an ABAP class. Right-click on the package name in the Eclipse Project Browser and select **New • ABAP Class** to create a new class, as shown in Figure 12.8.

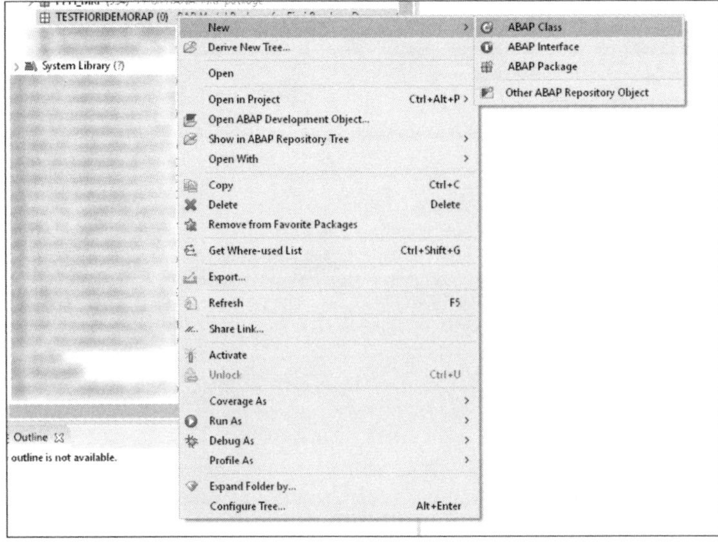

Figure 12.8 Creating abap Objects in Eclipse

Provide a name and description for the class and then click on the **Next** button to create the class, as shown in Figure 12.9.

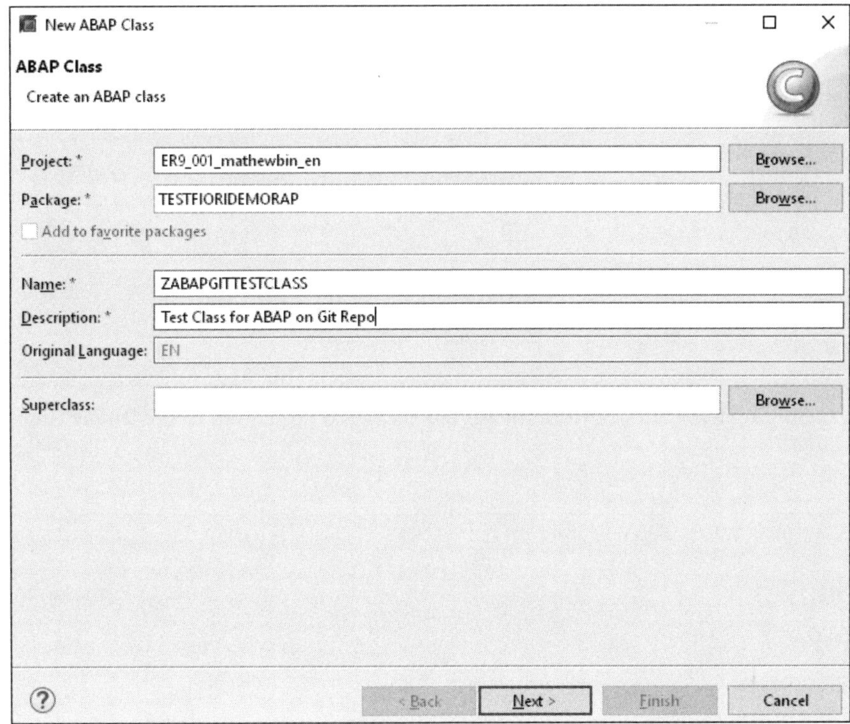

Figure 12.9 Creating an ABAP Class in Eclipse

12.4 Staging and Committing ABAP Code to Git

Now that you've created some development objects in your package, let's submit our changes to the repository. Execute the abapGit report program like we did earlier in Section 12.2 to bring up the abapGit home page. Open your GitHub project using the **Explore** button, or if you already have the abapGit report running with the project open, click on the **Refresh** button to see the new changes. As shown in Figure 12.10, details about the new **CLASS** object are displayed on the home page. Click on the **Stage** button to make the changes ready for commit to the online GitHub repository.

Now, click on the **Add all and Commit** button, which will commit all four of our unsaved changes back to the online repository, as shown in Figure 12.11.

Figure 12.10 Staging the Changes from the ABAP Package to Be Pushed to the Online Git Repository

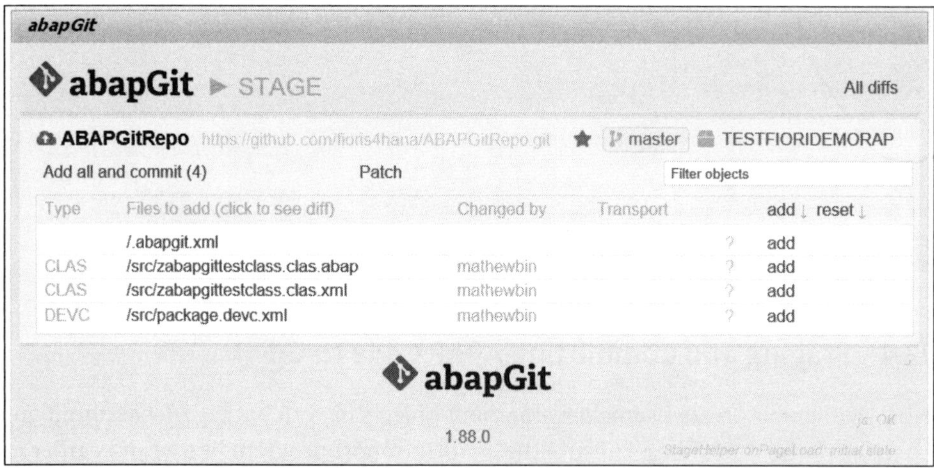

Figure 12.11 Commit Local Changes to the Online GitHub Repository Using abapGit

Before the commit, you'll be presented with a window to enter details about the committer. A *committer* the person who is submitting the code, so that the repository can keep track of the changes. Enter these details and press **Commit**, as shown in Figure 12.12.

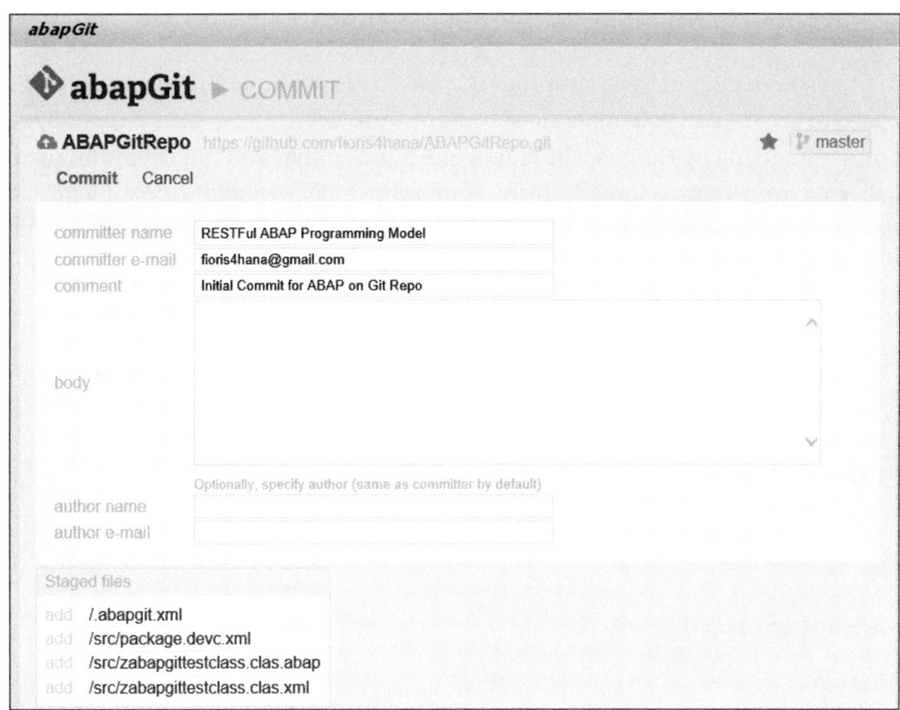

Figure 12.12 Submitting the Changes Using abapGit

Now, if you open your GitHub repository from the GitHub website, you'll see the new commits applied to the repository, as shown in Figure 12.13.

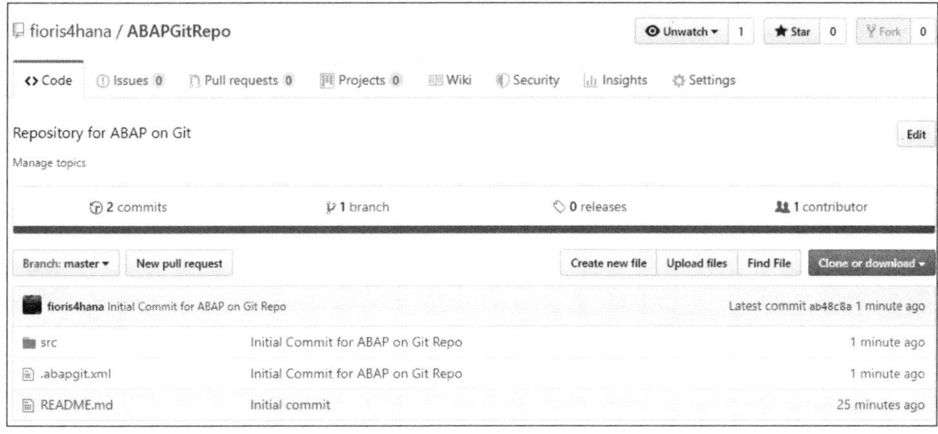

Figure 12.13 Online GitHub Repository Updated with Changes from the ABAP System

12.5 Setting Up the abapGit Plugin in Eclipse

Now, in most development environments, you'll have multiple GitHub repositories you need to access, and you might need to clone a project to a new SAP system. So, we recommend setting up the abapGit plugin in Eclipse so that you can clone and manage all your repositories directly from your Eclipse IDE. To add a new plugin, in Eclipse, go to **Help • Install New Software**. Enter the URL *http://s-prs.co/498829* and click **Next** to finish the installation, as shown in Figure 12.14.

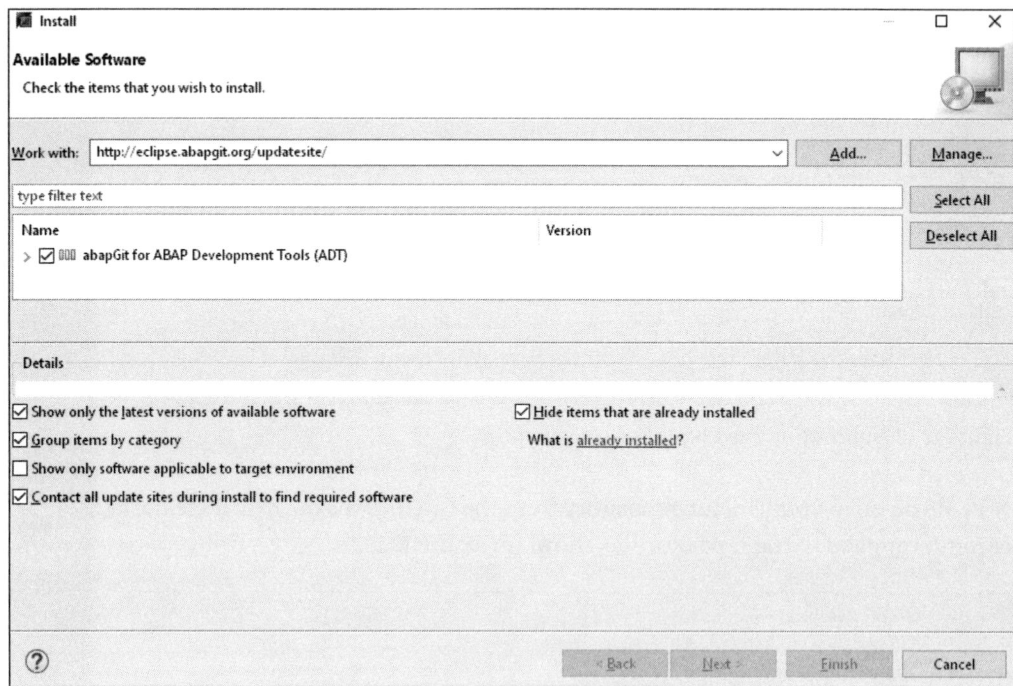

Figure 12.14 Installing the abapGit for ABAP Development Tools in Eclipse

12.6 Connecting to abapGit Repositories

Now, let's open the view for our abapGit repositories. Go to **Window • Show View Other** or press [ALT]+[SHIFT]+[Q] and then press [Q] again. The view list will appear, as shown in Figure 12.15, where you'll select **abapGit Repositories** from the list and then click **Open**.

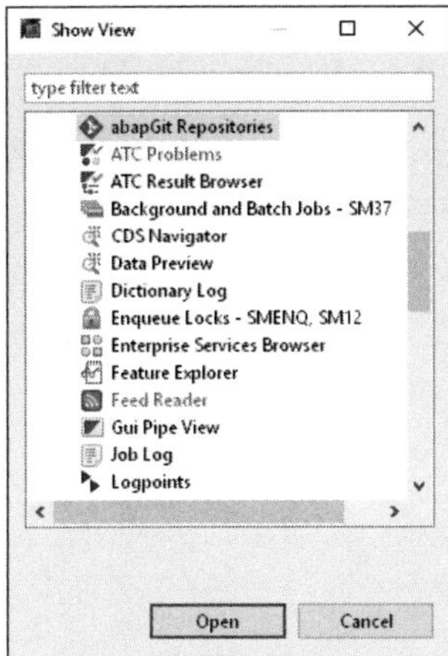

Figure 12.15 abapGit Repositories View

12.7 Cloning Git Repository into Eclipse

In the abapGit repositories view, click on the **+** icon on the top right of the view. Enter the URL of the GitHub repository and click **Next** to open the project, as shown in Figure 12.16.

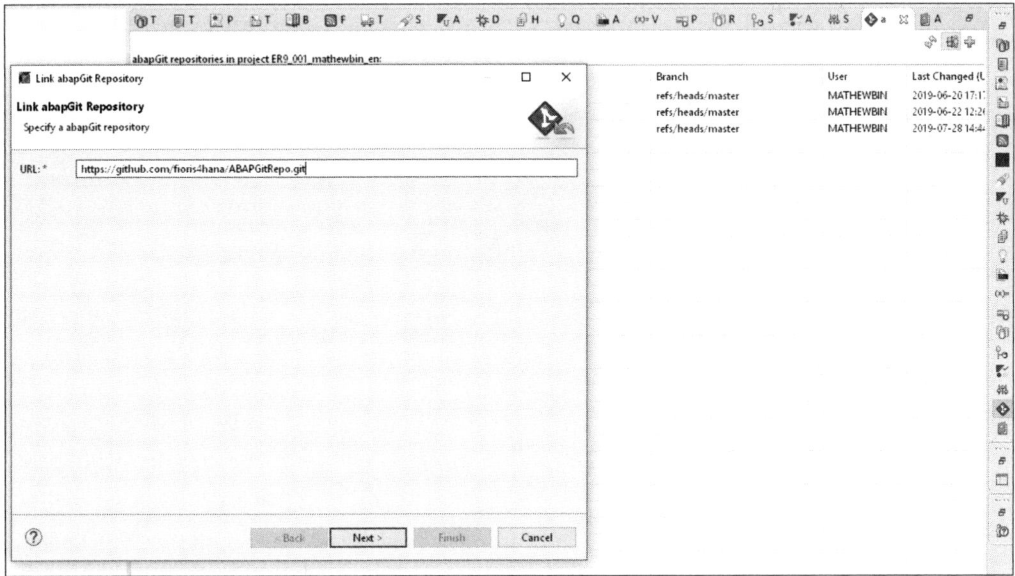

Figure 12.16 Cloning the GitHub Repository to Eclipse

On the next screen, enter the name of the package to which the development objects from the GitHub repository need to be cloned. Select the **Pull after link** checkbox so that the latest changes will be created into your local package, as shown in Figure 12.17.

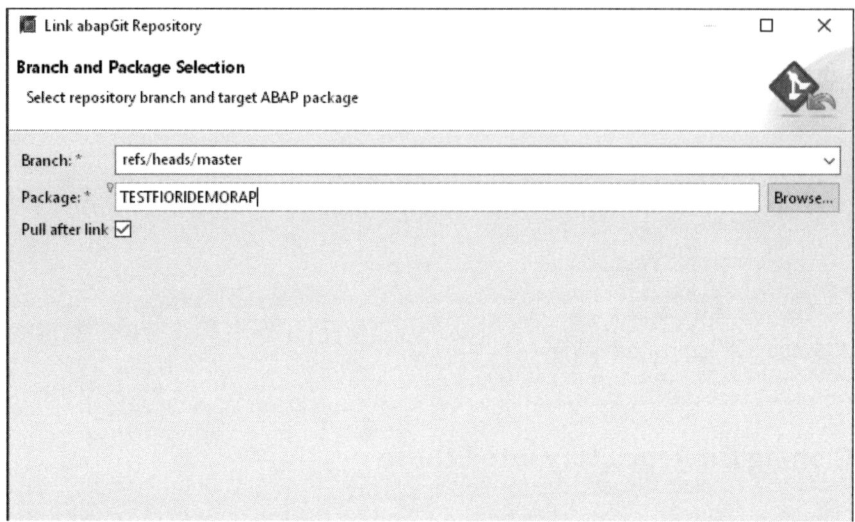

Figure 12.17 Select the Package to which the Project Needs to Be Cloned

Now, you'll see the development objects in your new package. In our case, we cloned the repository with the sample ABAP class we created earlier in Section 12.3, as shown in Figure 12.18.

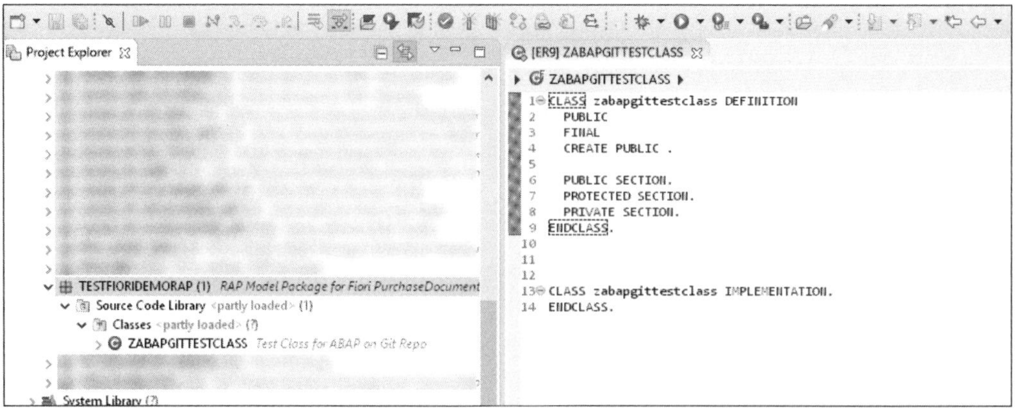

Figure 12.18 ABAP Object Created and Committed to the GitHub Repository Using abapGit and Now Cloned to Eclipse

12.8 Exporting Existing Packages as ZIP Files from a System Using abapGit

Some scenarios may require you to import the source codes of this book into your system. A common issue with the source code for the first edition of this book was that readers were confused about how to import the source codes directly into their systems. Thus, we've decided to include this chapter in this edition of the book, so that the readers won't have to refer elsewhere to figure out how to import the source code for this book using abapGit.

But first, we need to export our development objects. (The exported ZIP file of these development objects will be available in the GitHub repositories we created for this book, and you can find more details about these resources in the download section for this book on the SAP PRESS website.) Click on the **Advanced** button and select **Package to Zip** link, as shown in Figure 12.19.

Figure 12.19 Exporting ABAP Packages as ZIP Files

In the wizard that opens, enter the name of the package to be exported, and on the next screen, you'll see the option to save the ZIP file to your local file system, as shown in Figure 12.20.

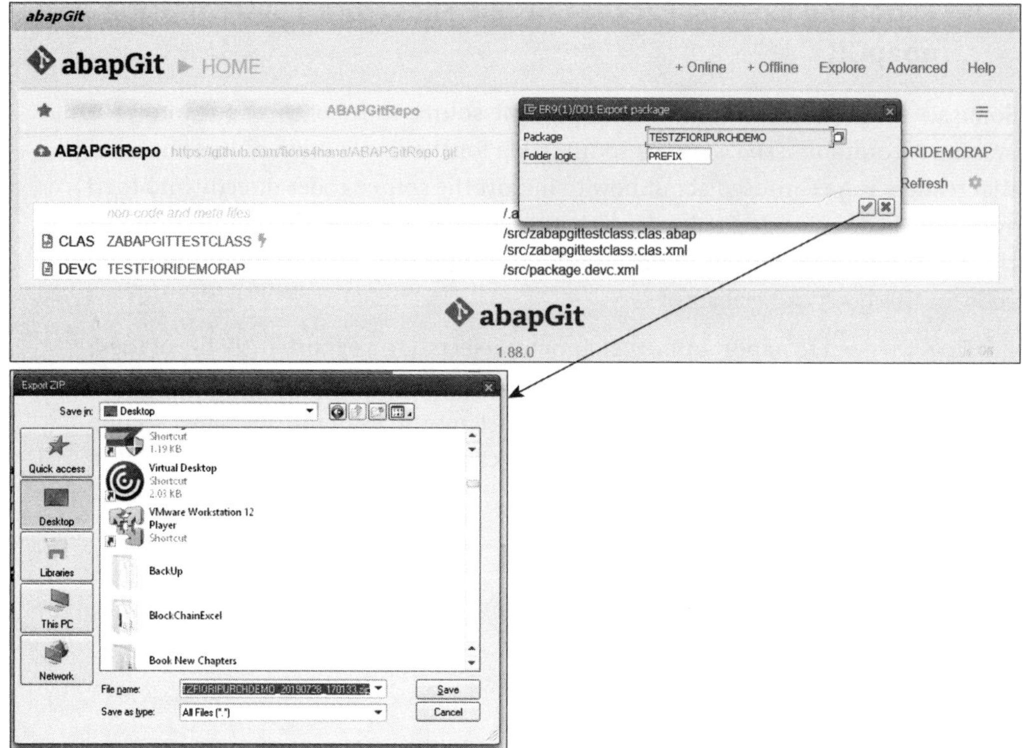

Figure 12.20 Specify the Package to Export as a ZIP File

12.9 Importing Package ZIP Files into Another ABAP System Using abapGit

Now, we need to import these ZIP files into another ABAP system. First, execute the abapGit report in the target system and click the **Offline** button on the abapGit home page. In the next window, enter the name for your Git project and for the target package into which the development objects should be imported, as shown in Figure 12.21.

Now, in this new Git project, click on the **Import** button to import our ZIP files into the ABAP system, as shown in Figure 12.22.

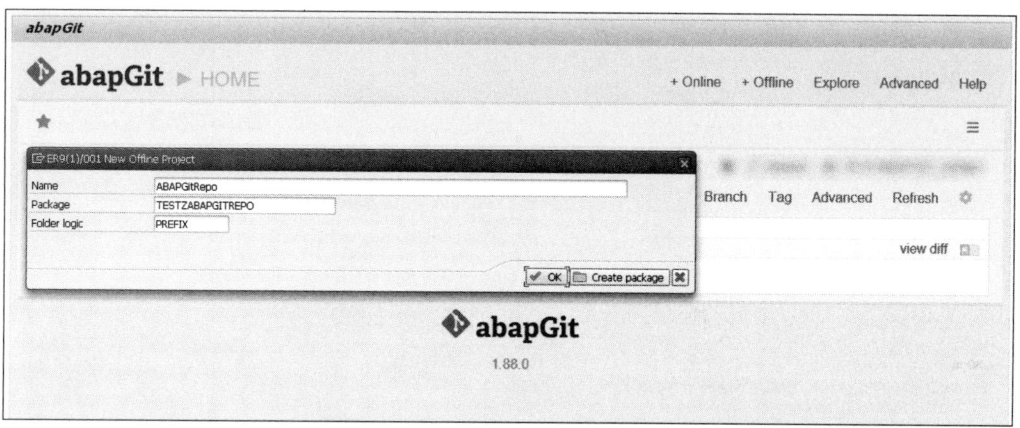

Figure 12.21 Creating an Offline Project in Another ABAP System Using abapGit

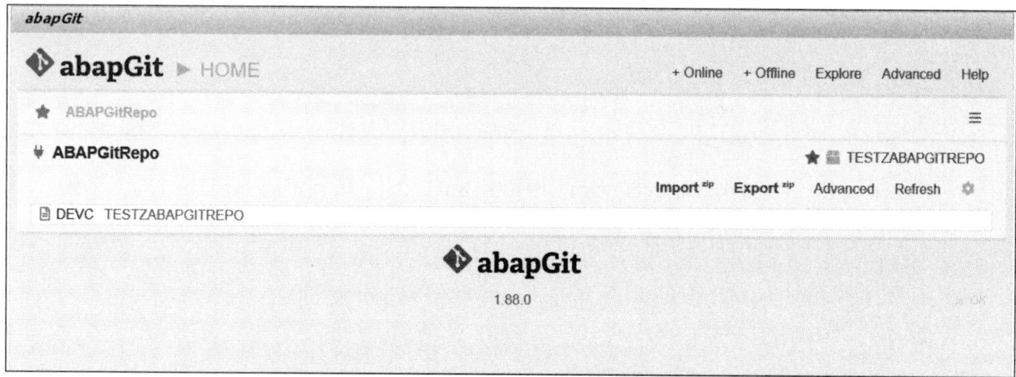

Figure 12.22 Importing the ABAP Package ZIP File into the System Using abapGit

On the next screen (Figure 12.23), you'll see a list of all development objects ready for import. Click on the **Pull** button to complete the import of the objects to your local package. When using the actual ZIP file of source code for this book, even though you can import the source code from the provided ZIP files, the related behavior definitions and business services (service definitions and service bindings) will not be imported via abapGit. You'll need to create these files on your own in your system.

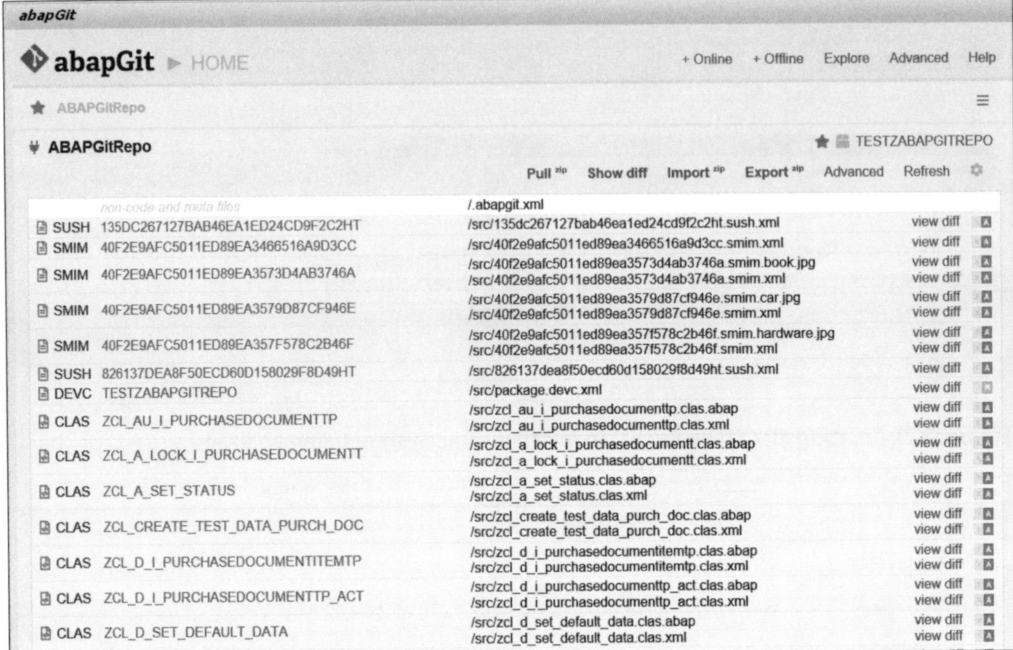

Figure 12.23 List of All Objects from GitHub That Can Be Imported into the ABAP System Using abapGit

12.10 Summary

In this chapter, you learned how to use ABAP on Git, a new open source feature to create ABAP objects and push them into a GitHub repository. You also learned how to set up and install the Git repository tool in Eclipse. We used the Git repository tool to clone an online GitHub project directly into the Eclipse. You also learned how to export ABAP packages as ZIP files and how to import them into another ABAP system using abapGit. In the next appendix, we'll learn how to develop application on the SAP Cloud Platform development.

Appendix A
Developing Applications on the SAP Cloud Platform

This appendix provides information on another option for developing cloud applications for SAP S/4HANA: side-by-side extensibility with the SAP Cloud Platform. This overview of developing and deploying a sample application uses the SAP Cloud Platform programming model.

A.1 Introduction to SAP Cloud Platform

SAP Cloud Platform is an enterprise Platform-as-a-service (PaaS) that gives end users the ability to build, extend, and integrate their own business applications. The SAP Cloud Platform acts as a development platform by providing various cloud-based services and technologies such as the Internet of Things (IoT), machine learning, artificial intelligence (AI), easy-to-use application programming interfaces (APIs), and more.

Unlike SAP S/4HANA, SAP S/4HANA Cloud relies on ready-to-use services and key-user tools for customizing the standard delivered apps. SAP S/4HANA Cloud prevents access to the SAP NetWeaver backend to ensure seamless system upgrades without the incompatible changes that sometimes occur with SAP S/4HANA when customers can add custom changes to the backend system. Access to the SAP S/4HANA Cloud is based on the SAP Fiori launchpad and via the applications in the launchpad that are provided as tiles. The standard delivered apps can be customized and extended via key-user tools (known as in-app extensibility), and fully custom applications can be deployed into SAP Cloud Platform (known as side-by-side extensibility).

Let's consider a simple example of developing and deploying a custom application following the concept of side-by-side extensibility. To accomplish this task, SAP provides the SAP Cloud Platform application programming model.

A.2 SAP Cloud Platform Application Programming Model

The SAP Cloud Platform application programming model gives developers the ability to create enterprise applications with ease. The programming model contains development tools, libraries, and ready-to-use APIs to help with delivering applications. Although the new SAP Cloud Platform application programming model is compatible with multiple development environments, for this example, we'll be using the SAP Web IDE full-stack. Figure A.1 shows an overview of the SAP Cloud Platform application programming model.

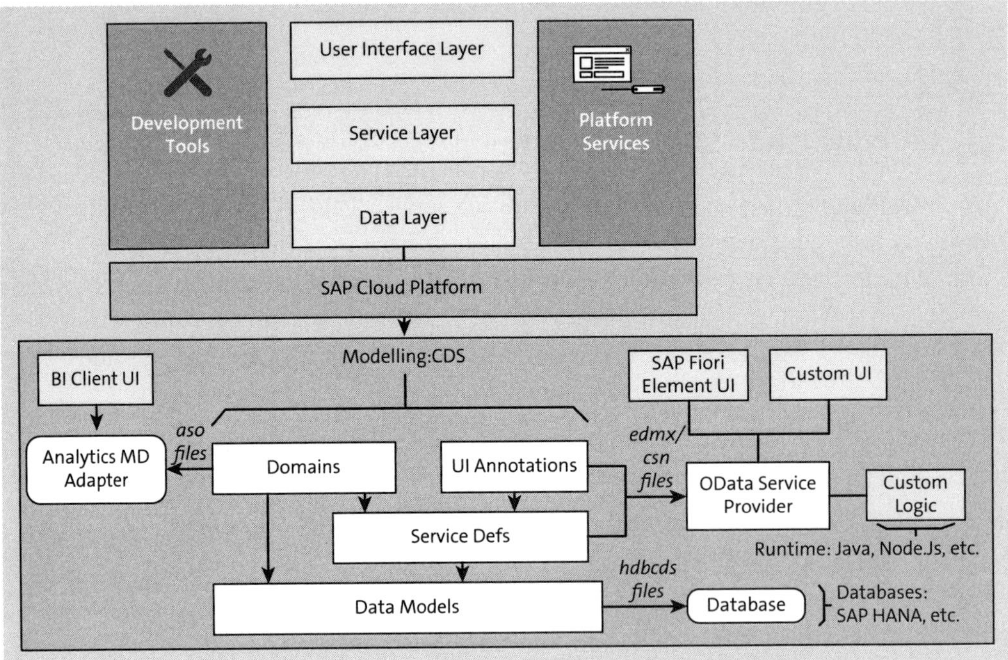

Figure A.1 Overview of the SAP Cloud Platform Application Programming Model

The new SAP Cloud Platform application programming model offers multiple features:

- **Data and service models**
  Supports various data models and services, such as JavaScript Object Notation (JSON), YAML, and core data services (CDS).

- **Database support**
  Supports different databases, including SAP HANA; standard SQL databases (MySQL, Oracle, etc.); and Java Persistence API (JPA) model generation to take advantage of JPA support from other databases. SAP Cloud Platform also supports custom mappings to certain databases.
- **SAP Fiori markup**
  Native SAPUI5 support and use of SAP Fiori elements for generating the user interface (UI) and OData for the data services. The SAP Fiori elements UI is generated directly from CDS-based UI annotations via the OData service, which provides the metadata definitions for generating the SAP Fiori elements-based app.
- **Generic service providers**
  Supports a set of libraries to handle a wide variety of service providers automatically, such as the following:
  - Connection management
  - Locale and principle management
  - Protocol conversion from various channels, including OData, to ensure compatibility with other sources
  - Incoming requests and rerouting them to the respective request handlers
- **Generic handlers**
  Supports generic handlers for metadata; create, read, update, and delete (CRUD) operations; batch requests; `DRAFT` feature support; and so on.
- **Custom handler APIs**
  In addition to a list of ready-to-use APIs, developers can add custom handlers on the OData service level for the CDS views such as the following:
  - `this`: Gives the current instance of a service.
  - `phase`: Gives access to the different phases of a request such as `before`, `after`, and `on`.
  - `event`: Gives access to the events such as `CRUD`, `COMMIT`, and custom definitions based on an action or function on an entity.
  - `entity`: Gives access to entities exposed by the service to place custom handlers.
  - `handler`: Gives the actual function that is being implemented, represented by the syntax "`(cds)=>{}`". For example:

```
cds.serve('name-service').with (function(){
this.before('READ',()=> {}))
})
```

- **Data access**
  To read data from custom sources, a set of libraries and language bindings are provided that make use of CDS models and query languages.
- **Service integration**
  To leverage SAP S/4HANA services, other applications or services, and SAP S/4HANA Cloud SDK.
- **Data replication**
  Via CDS models available from SAP S/4HANA, SAP Cloud Platform applications can replicate models and annotations and consume them.

> **Note**
> For more details about the features provided by the SAP Cloud Platform application programming model, visit *http://s-prs.co/498830*.

A.3 Developing an App on SAP Cloud Platform Using the SAP Web IDE Full-Stack

With the introduction of the SAP Web IDE full-stack, you no longer need to switch back and forth between the Eclipse IDE and the old SAP Web IDE to develop apps. The SAP Web IDE full-stack now gives you all the necessary tools to generate CDS views, services, data models, and UI developments. This comprehensiveness makes developing, building, deploying, testing, and extending apps on SAP Cloud Platform a lot easier.

> **Note**
> To learn more about the SAP Web IDE full-stack, visit *http://s-prs.co/498831*.

A.3.1 Setting Up the SAP Web IDE Full-Stack in SAP Cloud Platform

To set up the SAP Web IDE full-stack, you must register for a free trial in the SAP Cloud Platform and enable the SAP Web IDE full-stack service from the Neo trial within SAP Cloud Platform. You'll also need to set up Cloud Foundry within the SAP Cloud Platform for our example. To register for a trial account in SAP Cloud Platform, visit *https://account.hanatrial.ondemand.com*. After you've set up an account, click the **Neo Trial** account, as shown in Figure A.2.

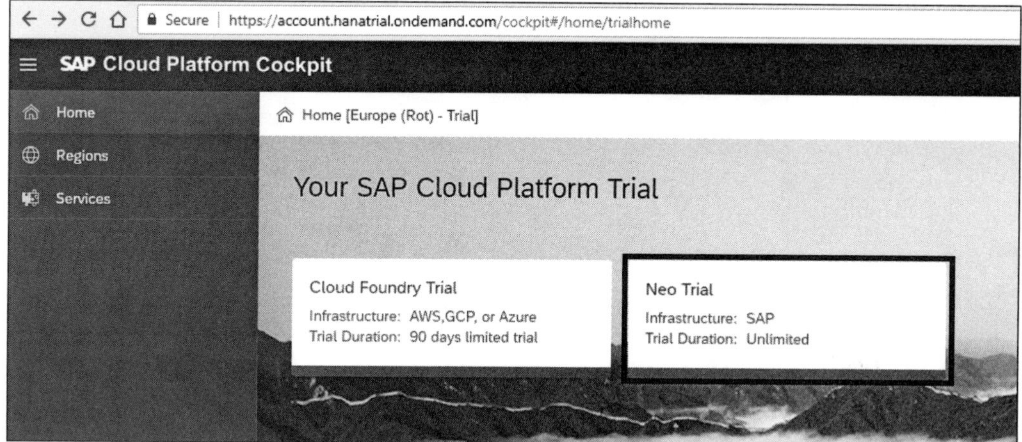

Figure A.2 Setting Up a Neo Trial Account

Then, in **Services** on the left, click the **SAP Web IDE Full-Stack** tile, as shown in Figure A.3, and enable the solution if not yet enabled. Next, click the **Go to Service** link on the next page. You'll be redirected to the SAP Web IDE full-stack home page. Bookmark this link because we'll come back to the SAP Web IDE later.

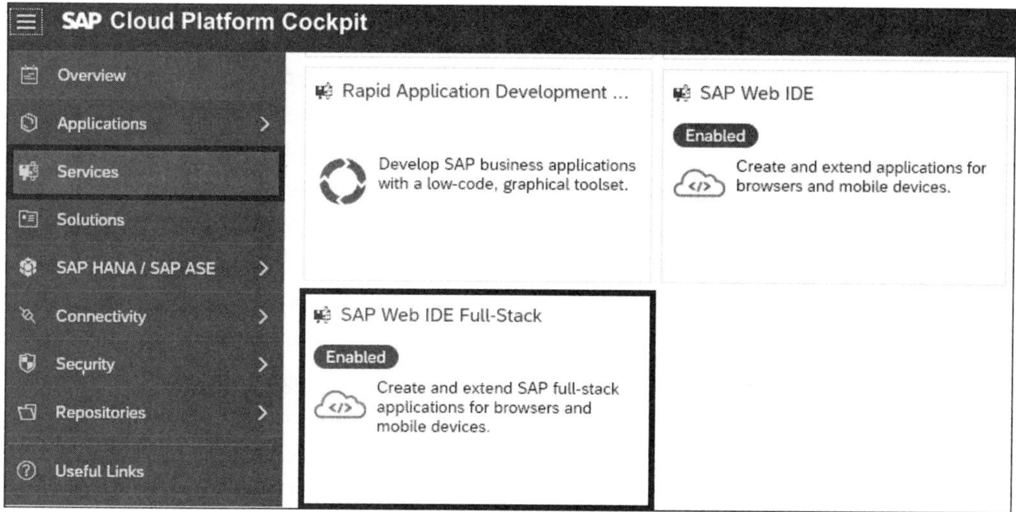

Figure A.3 Enabling the SAP Web IDE Full-Stack Service in SAP Cloud Platform

Now, you'll need to enable the Cloud Foundry trial on SAP Cloud Platform. Navigate to the SAP Cloud Platform cockpit home page, click **Cloud Foundry Trial** ❶ as shown in Figure A.4, and then select the region ❷ closest to you.

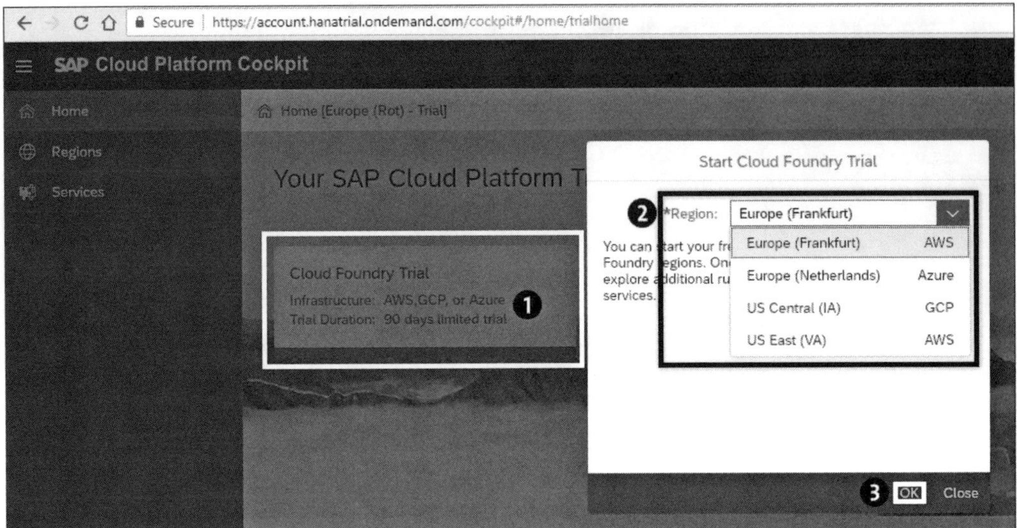

Figure A.4 Enabling the Cloud Foundry Trial

After Cloud Foundry is set up, open the SAP Web IDE full-stack and, as shown in Figure A.5, navigate to **Tools • Preferences** ❶ and select **Cloud Foundry** from the left side of the tab ❷. Select the API endpoint, which you'll get from the Cloud Foundry home page. After you've selected an API endpoint, the **Organization** tab ❸ and the space will be automatically generated from your endpoint (assuming that you haven't created additional subaccounts or spaces in the Cloud Foundry account). After the Cloud Foundry settings are listed, click the **Install Builder** ❹ button at the bottom. A builder application will be installed for your SAP Web IDE into the Cloud Foundry. Finally, click the **Save** ❺ button.

> **Note**
>
> A *space* in Cloud Foundry is like a development area or package that you reserve for your application developments; you can register OData services, deploy applications, and more in this space. The memory allocated to the space is limited with a trial account, so you won't be able to deploy too many apps into this space. To learn more about the relation between spaces, orgs, and subaccounts in Cloud Foundry, go to *http://s-prs.co/498832*.

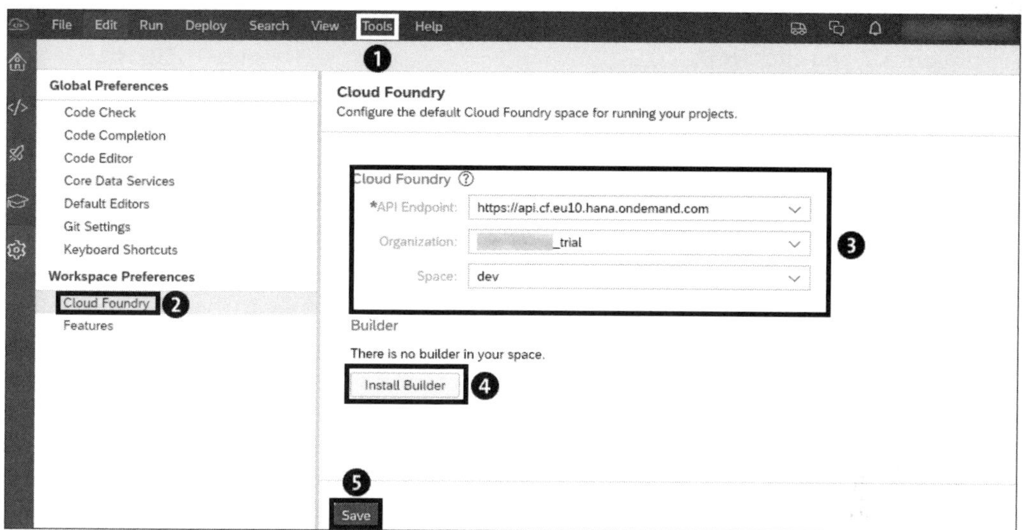

Figure A.5 Linking the Cloud Foundry Space with the SAP Web IDE

A.3.2 Creating a Full-Stack Business Application in SAP Web IDE

Now let's create an SAP full-stack business application. Navigate to **File • New • Project from Template** or press `Ctrl`+`Alt`+`Shift`+`O`. From the list of templates, select **SAP Cloud Platform Business Application** template, as shown in Figure A.6, and click **Next**.

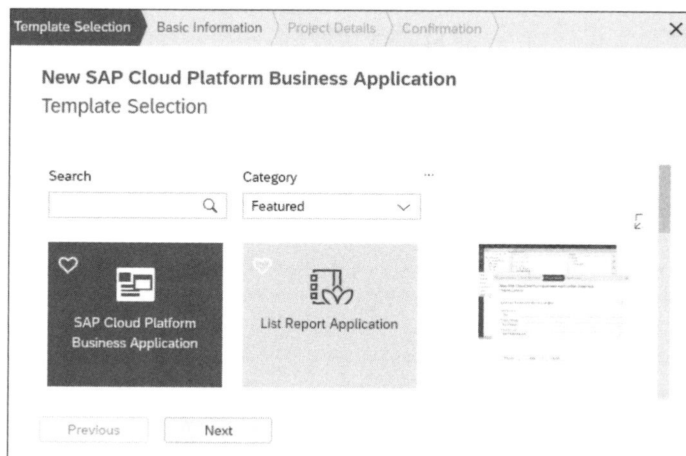

Figure A.6 Selecting the SAP Cloud Platform Business Application Template

Give the project a name (for our example, "PurchaseDocumentSCP"), as shown in Figure A.7, and click **Next**.

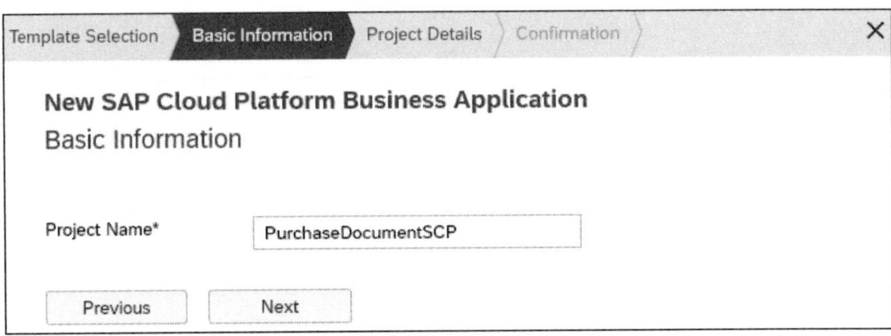

Figure A.7 SAP Cloud Platform Business Application Basic Information

Next, enter the **Template Customization** details for the app (for example, using the values shown in Table A.1). Select the **Use HTML5 Application Repository** checkbox, as shown in Figure A.8, since we'll need this feature later to add a UI. Click the **Finish** button to generate the template app.

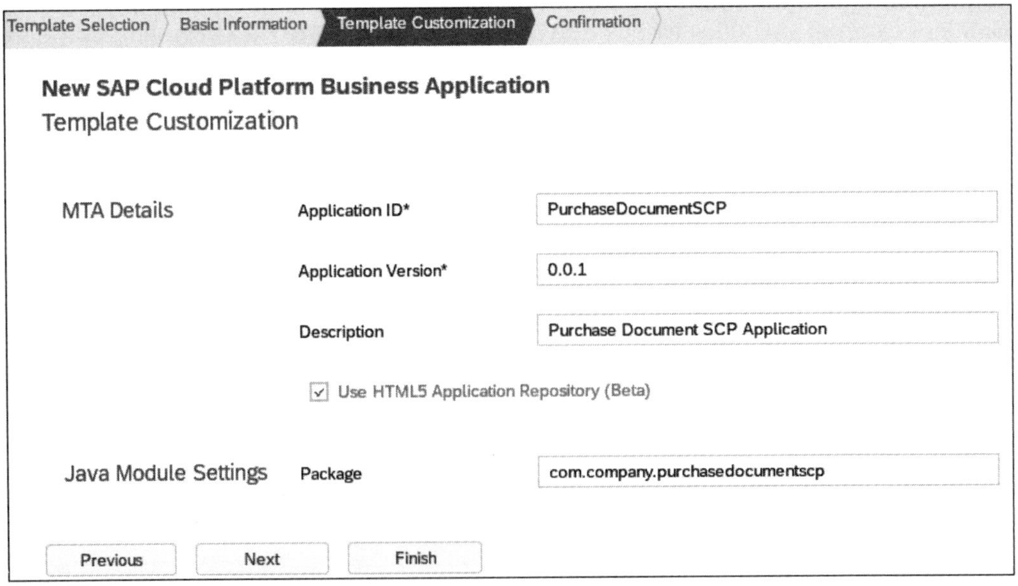

Figure A.8 Template Customization for an SAP Cloud Platform Business Application

Field	Parameter
Application ID	"PurchaseDocumentSCP"
Application Version	0.0.1 (Default value)"
Description	"Purchase Document SCP Application"
Package	"com.company.purchasedocumentscp"

Table A.1 Values for SAP Cloud Platform Business Application Template Customization

A.3.3 Creating a New Data Model for the Application

Our plan is to make a simplified version of the Purchase Document list report page (LRP) app we created in Chapter 4. Before adding the SAP Fiori elements app into our project, you'll need to create the relevant CDS views and data models and deploy them into Cloud Foundry using the SAP Web IDE full-stack.

But first, let's get familiar with some components in this template project. Figure A.9 shows the folder structure of the template project that we just created. These include:

❶ Database module

❷ Java module

❸ Multi-target application config file

❹ Referenced by SAP Web IDE builder tool

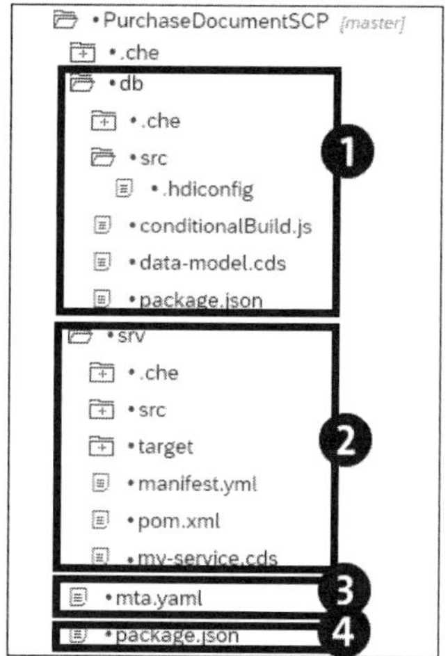

Figure A.9 Template App Structure Overview

In this structure, the following files are needed for the application we're going to create in this chapter:

- `data-model.cds`
  This file is under the folder named *db* (this folder is the database module of our app) and is used to create a data model for the application. The framework will compile this data model into the relevant database view in SAP HANA by converting the contents of this file into a compatible type ending with *.hdbcds* (which we'll discuss later in this chapter). Then, the framework will create the schemas/views in the Cloud Foundry database via the SAP HANA Deployment Infrastructure.
- `my-service.cds`
  The content of this file helps generate the required OData service for our application (this file is inside the Java module of the project, as shown in Figure A.10). This file generates a service definition from our previously created *data-model.cds* file and generates two additional files under the folder path **srv • main • resources • edmx**, as shown in Figure A.10. The *csn.json* (Core Schema Notation) file in the folder is a JavaScript Object Notation (JSON) file, which contains the structure of the CDS models. The *.xml* file is the Entity Data Model XML (EDMX) file used for the OData service.

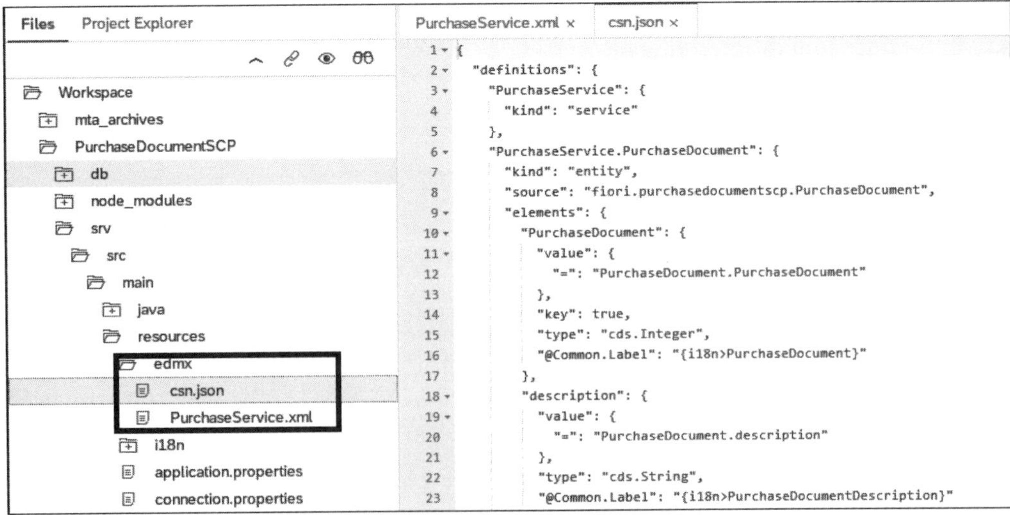

Figure A.10 Java Module for Generating and Extending OData Services

The *srv* folder itself is a Java module containing a Java application that can be used to implement custom logic on the generated OData services. This custom logic acts like the extension classes in the OData project.

- `mta.yaml`
  The Multi-Target Application (MTA) file is used to specify the prerequisites for and dependencies with Cloud Foundry. When deployed into Cloud Foundry by the SAP Web IDE, the application refers the *mta.yaml* file and deploys all the modules and services specified within it.
- `package.json`
  The SAP Web IDE builder tool executes the Node.js package manager (npm) commands defined in this file, shown in Figure A.11, for compiling the *.cds* files for the application deployment.

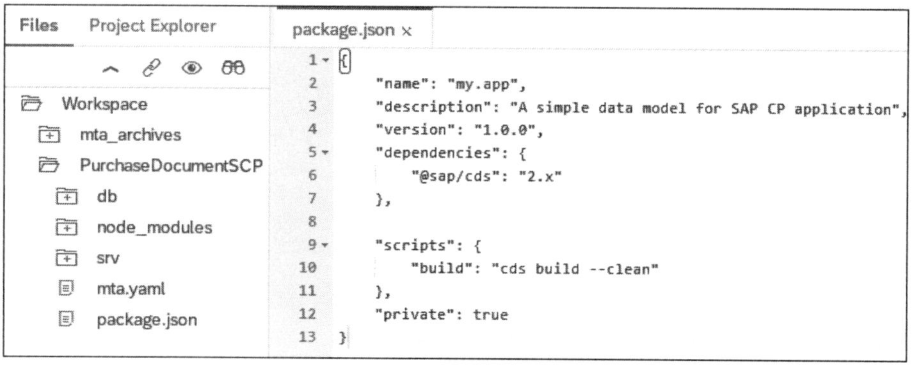

Files Project Explorer

Workspace
- mta_archives
- PurchaseDocumentSCP
  - db
  - node_modules
  - srv
  - mta.yaml
  - package.json

package.json ×

```
{
    "name": "my.app",
    "description": "A simple data model for SAP CP application",
    "version": "1.0.0",
    "dependencies": {
        "@sap/cds": "2.x"
    },

    "scripts": {
        "build": "cds build --clean"
    },
    "private": true
}
```

Figure A.11 Package.json File Used by the SAP Web IDE Builder Tool

At this point, we need to set up a data model to form the structure of our CDS views. The template project already includes a dummy data model. We'll edit this data model to adjust it for our requirements. Navigate to the *db* folder and replace the contents of the *data-model.cds*. We'll split the codes that will go into the *data-model.cds* into three parts for easy understanding (the source code for all the applications described in this chapter will be available for download at the SAP PRESS website, *www.sap-press.com/4988*):

- `PurchaseDocument`
  As shown in Figure A.12, the entity `PurchaseDocument` is defined in a similar way to the original CDS view for the Purchase Document LRP app in Chapter 4. The `PurchaseDocPriority` has an association to a custom entity type `Priorities` (which acts as the value help for the **Priority** field). Similarly, the `PurchaseDocumentItem` is

defined as an association of (0...*) cardinality to the `PurchaseDocmentItems` entity. As a result, the necessary navigation properties between the entities will be generated when the service is generated and deployed to the Cloud Foundry.

data-model.cds ×

```
namespace fiori.purchasedocumentscp;
// Declare Main Entities for the App
entity PurchaseDocument{
    key PurchaseDocument      : Integer @(title: '{i18n>PurchaseDocument}');
    description               : String @(title: '{i18n>PurchaseDocumentDescription}');
    status                    : String @(title: '{i18n>Status}');
    purchasingOrganization    :String @(title: '{i18n>OrgUnit}');
    PurchaseDocPriority       : Association to Priorities     @( title: '{i18n>Priority}',
                                                                 Common: {
                                                                     Text: {$value: PurchaseDocPriority.name, "@UI.TextArrangement": #TextOnly},
                                                                     ValueList: {entity: 'Priorities', type: #fixed},
                                                                     ValueListWithFixedValues});
    PurchaseDocumentItem      :Association to many PurchaseDocumentItems on PurchaseDocumentItem.PurchaseDocument = $self;
}
```

Figure A.12 Defining the PurchaseDocument Entity Type in the Data Model

- **`PurchaseDocumentItems`**
  The `PurchaseDocumentItems` entity, shown in Figure A.13, has a `Price` field and a `Currency` field that require value helps from custom entity types such as `Currency` and `QuantityUnit`. In addition, the `PurchaseDocument` field needs an association back to the `PurchaseDocument` entity.

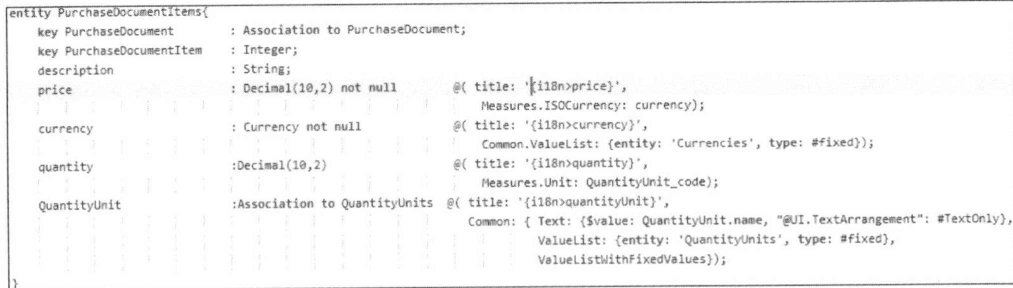

```
entity PurchaseDocumentItems{
    key PurchaseDocument        : Association to PurchaseDocument;
    key PurchaseDocumentItem    : Integer;
    description                 : String;
    price                       : Decimal(10,2) not null        @( title: '{i18n>price}',
                                                                    Measures.ISOCurrency: currency);
    currency                    : Currency not null             @( title: '{i18n>currency}',
                                                                    Common.ValueList: {entity: 'Currencies', type: #fixed});
    quantity                    :Decimal(10,2)                  @( title: '{i18n>quantity}',
                                                                    Measures.Unit: QuantityUnit_code);
    QuantityUnit                :Association to QuantityUnits  @( title: '{i18n>quantityUnit}',
                                                                  Common: { Text: {$value: QuantityUnit.name, "@UI.TextArrangement": #TextOnly},
                                                                            ValueList: {entity: 'QuantityUnits', type: #fixed},
                                                                            ValueListWithFixedValues});
}
```

Figure A.13 Defining the PurchaseDocument Items Entity Type in the Data Model

- **`CustomEntityTypes`**
  Because we need a value help for the **Priority** field, we must declare a custom type named **PRIORITIES**, as shown in Figure A.14. In addition, the `Currency` and `QuantityUnit` are required for `Price` and `Quantity` fields, so we'll declare them as custom types.

```
// Declare Custom Types
type Currency            : String(3) @title: '{i18n>currencyCode}' @ValueList.entity: Currencies;
type QuantityUnit        : String(3) @title: '{i18n>quantityUnitCode}' @ValueList.entity: QuantityUnits;
type PurchaseDocPriority : String(1) @title: '{i18n>priority}' @ValueList.entity: Priorities;
// Declare Custom Type Entities
entity Currencies {
  key code : Currency;
      name : String;
}
entity QuantityUnits {
  key code : QuantityUnit;
      name : String;
}
entity Priorities {
  key code : PurchaseDocPriority;
      name : String;
}
```

Figure A.14 Defining Custom Entity Types in the Data Model

A.3.4 Defining an OData Service for the Application

Now let's define/register our CDS views as an OData service. Navigate to the folder *srv*, rename the *my-service.cds* file to *purch-service.cds*, and add the code shown in Figure A.15. When deployed into Cloud Foundry, this file will register our CDS view as an OData service. The entities defined in this file will be exposed by the OData service, which we'll use later for our HTML5-based UI app.

```
*purch-service.cds ×
using fiori.purchasedocumentscp from '../db/data-model';

service PurchaseService {
  entity PurchaseDocument        @readonly as projection on purchasedocumentscp.PurchaseDocument;
  entity PurchaseDocumentItems   @readonly as projection on purchasedocumentscp.PurchaseDocumentItems;
  entity Priorities              @readonly as projection on purchasedocumentscp.Priorities;
  entity Currencies              @readonly as projection on purchasedocumentscp.Currencies;
  entity QuantityUnits           @readonly as projection on purchasedocumentscp.QuantityUnits;
}
```

Figure A.15 Defining the OData Service

A.3.5 Defining User Interface Annotations for Core Data Services Views

At this point, we have our basic CDS views and our OData service defined, but we still need to create a UI to consume our OData service later using SAP Fiori elements app. To generate the SAP Fiori elements UI, we'll need to add UI annotations to our CDS view. Because our app is a list report page application, we must annotate our `PurchaseDocument` and `PurchaseDocumentItems` CDS views. Create a new file named

purch-annotations under the **PurchaseDocumentSAP Cloud Platform • srv** folder. We'll split the entity annotations into three parts for easy understanding (all three parts go into the same *purch-annotations* file):

- **PurchaseDocument**
  In the LRP app, we want to display all the fields by default in the table. Thus, as shown in Figure A.16, we've added the `UI{LineItem:[ ]}` syntax to specify the required fields. Much like the CDS view UI annotations we created in previous chapters, the syntax is only slightly different. Similarly, we added the `SelectionFields` property for the default filter fields to come up in the filter bar. Then, we added the `HeaderInfo`, `HeaderFacets`, and `FieldGroups` for the purchase document object page. Now, to link our `PurchaseDocumentItem` CDS view's UI annotations for `LineItem` to appear in the object page area of our `PurchaseDocument`, we added the `UI.Facets:[{$Type:'UI.ReferenceFacet'}]` annotation.

```
annotate PurchaseService.PurchaseDocument with @(
//List Report Page Filter field level annotations
    UI: {
        SelectionFields: [ PurchaseDocument, status, purchasingOrganization, PurchaseDocPriority_code ],
//List Report Page Table level annotations
        LineItem: [ {$Type: 'UI.DataField',Value: PurchaseDocument},
                    {$Type: 'UI.DataField',Value: description},
                    {$Type: 'UI.DataField',Value: status},
                    {$Type: 'UI.DataField',Value: purchasingOrganization},
                    {$Type: 'UI.DataField',Value: PurchaseDocPriority_code }]},
//Object Page header level annotations
    UI: {
        HeaderInfo: {
            TypeName: '{i18n>PurchaseDocument}',
            TypeNamePlural: '{i18n>PurchaseDocuments}',
            Title: { Value: PurchaseDocument },
            Description: { Value: description}},
        HeaderFacets: [
        {$Type: 'UI.ReferenceFacet', Label: '{i18n>generalInformation}', Target: '@UI.FieldGroup#GeneralInformation', "@UI.Importance": #High }],
//Object Page Field Group level annotations
        FieldGroup#GeneralInformation: {
            Data: [
                {$Type: 'UI.DataField',Label: '{i18n>PurchaseDocumentDescription}', Value: description},
                {$Type: 'UI.DataField',Label: '{i18n>Priority}', Value: PurchaseDocPriority.name},
                {$Type: 'UI.DataField',Label: '{i18n>Status}', Value: status }]} },
//Linking to PurchaseDocumentItem entity
    UI.Facets: [
        {$Type:'UI.ReferenceFacet',Label:'{i18n>PurchaseDocumentItems}',Target:'PurchaseDocumentItem/@UI.LineItem' }]);
```

Figure A.16 UI Annotations for the PurchaseDocument CDS View

- **PurchaseDocumentItems**
  Similarly, we must specify which fields should be the default columns for the `PurchaseDocumentItems` entity, so we'll use the `LineItem` annotation, as shown in Figure A.17. In this case, we don't want any fields in the filter bar, so we won't annotate the `SelectionFields`. For the object page of this CDS view, we'll annotate the fields for `HeaderInfo`, `HeaderFacets`, and `FieldGroup`,

```
annotate PurchaseService.PurchaseDocumentItems with @(
//List Report Page Table level annotations
    UI: { LineItem: [   {$Type: 'UI.DataField',Value: PurchaseDocumentItem},
                        {$Type: 'UI.DataField',Value: description},
                        {$Type: 'UI.DataField',Value: price},
                        {$Type: 'UI.DataField',Value: currency},
                        {$Type: 'UI.DataField',Value: quantity }]},
//Object Page header level annotations
    UI: {
        HeaderInfo: {
            TypeName: '{i18n>PurchaseDocumentItem}',
            TypeNamePlural: '{i18n>PurchaseDocumentItems}',
            Title: { Value: PurchaseDocumentItem },
            Description: { Value: description}},
        HeaderFacets: [
            {$Type: 'UI.ReferenceFacet', Label: '{i18n>generalInformationItem}', Target: '@UI.FieldGroup#GeneralInformation', "@UI.Importance": #High }],
//Object Page Field Group level annotations
        FieldGroup#GeneralInformation: {
            Data: [ {$Type: 'UI.DataField',Label: '{i18n>PurchaseDocumentItemDescription}', Value: description},
                    {$Type: 'UI.DataField',Label: '{i18n>quantity}', Value: quantity},
                    {$Type: 'UI.DataField',Label: '{i18n>price}', Value: price},
                    {$Type: 'UI.DataField',Label: '{i18n>currency}', Value: currency }]}
        });
```

Figure A.17 UI Annotations for the PurchaseDocumentItems CDS View

- **`ValueHelp`**
  The `ValueHelp` entities also must be annotated to prevent unwanted fields like the `code` and `name` coming up in the filter bar settings. Therefore, we'll annotate those fields with the `@UI.HiddenFilter` property, as shown in Figure A.18.

```
//Hide ValueHelp Entities from Filter bar
annotate PurchaseService.Priorities {
    code @UI.HiddenFilter;
    name @UI.HiddenFilter;
}
annotate PurchaseService.Currencies {
    code @UI.HiddenFilter;
    name @UI.HiddenFilter;
}
annotate PurchaseService.QuantityUnits {
    code @UI.HiddenFilter;
    name @UI.HiddenFilter;
}
```

Figure A.18 UI Annotations for the ValueHelp CDS Views

A.3.6 Adding a Database for the Application

At this stage, we have our CDS views with the required UI annotations, data model for the database, and our OData service definition. However, if you generate our OData service now and test it, no data will be return because we haven't added any records into our database. So, let's add some records via a set of *.csv* files to import records to our database tables. Navigate to **PurchaseDocumentSCP • db • src** and create a new folder named **csv**.

Now, let's create our CSV files. Right-click on the **csv** folder and navigate to **New • File**. Create one *.csv* file each for all the entities we've defined in the *data-model.csv* file, as shown in Figure A.19. You must create records in the *.csv* files that are separated by a comma (,). In addition to these files, create another file in the same folder named *Data.hdbtabledata*.

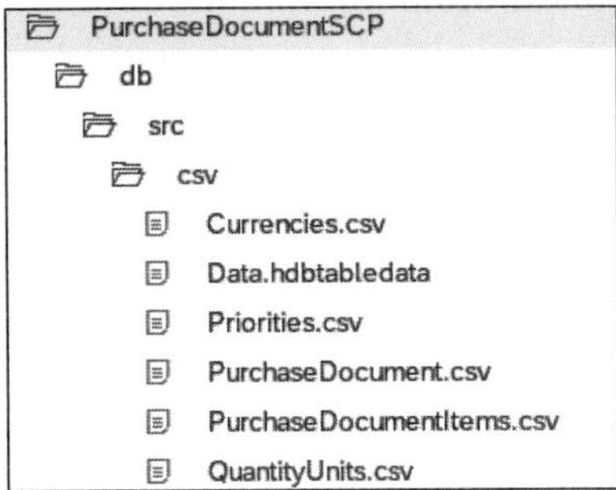

Figure A.19 Creating a csv File for All the Entities Defined in the Data Model

Figure A.20 shows the sample syntax for the *Data.hdbtabledata* file to make it read from the *.csv* files and import them into our tables defined in the data model.

Data.hdbtabledata ×

```
{
    "format_version": 1,
    "imports": [
        {
            "target_table": "FIORI_PURCHASEDOCUMENTSCP_PURCHASEDOCUMENT",
            "source_data": {
            "data_type": "CSV",
                "file_name": "PurchaseDocument.csv",
                "has_header": true
            },
            "import_settings": {
            "import_columns": [
                    "PURCHASEDOCUMENT",
                    "DESCRIPTION",
                    "STATUS",
                    "PURCHASINGORGANIZATION",
                    "PURCHASEDOCPRIORITY_CODE"
                ]
            }
        },
```

Figure A.20 Syntax for Reading from csv Files into the OData Model Tables

Note

Alternatively, you can import data files from existing OData APIs by right-clicking on the **srv** folder and navigating to **New • Data Model from External Service**. Then, you must select **SAP API Business Hub** and then select the required OData service from the list of available APIs. But, for our example, since we're relying on a custom table, we had to create our own records.

A.3.7 Deploying the Application on Cloud Foundry

Finally, let's generate our OData service, defined in the *purch-services.cds* file, by deploying the Java application in the *srv* folder to the Cloud Foundry. Right-click on the **srv** folder and go to **Run • Run as Java Application,** as shown in Figure A.21.

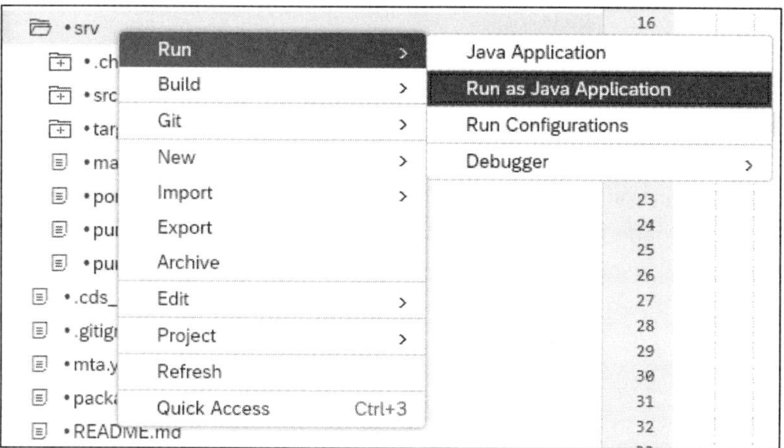

Figure A.21 Registering the OData Service by Deploying the Java Application

After the deployment is successful, you'll get the OData endpoint link highlighted in blue on top of the console window, as shown in Figure A.22.

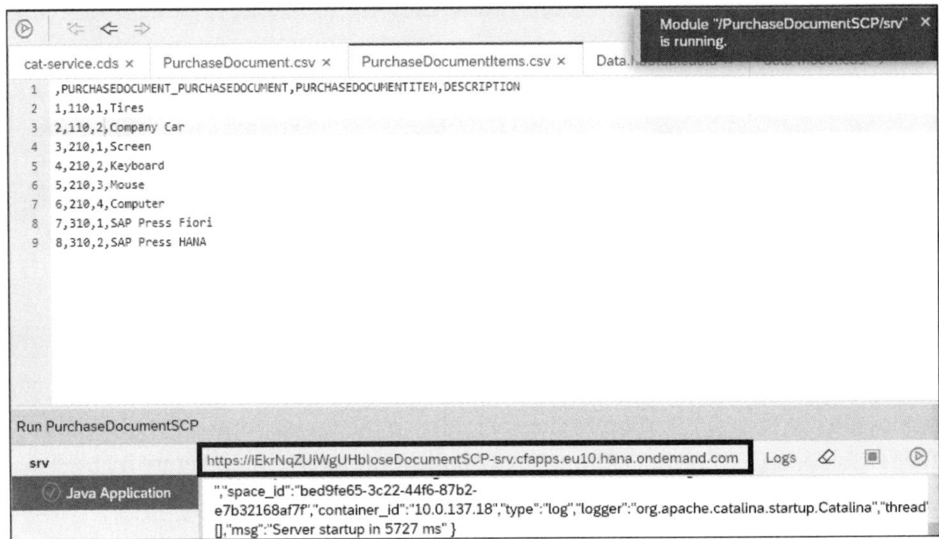

Figure A.22 OData Endpoint Generated Successfully

A.3.8 Consuming the OData Service

Now, we have our OData service. Let's check whether all our entities are returning the correct data that we uploaded from those *.csv* files into our database. Run the OData endpoint URL in your browser, and you should see the response of our OData service listing all the entities defined in our *purch-service.cds* file in the *srv* folder, as shown in Figure A.23.

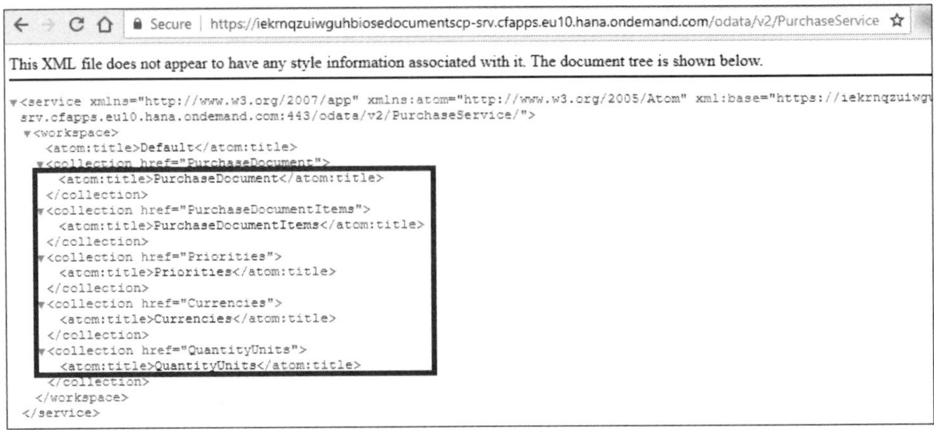

Figure A.23 Testing the OData Service

Let's test our PurchaseDocument entity set now. Execute the URL ending with */PurchaseService/PurchaseDocument*, and you should get the result shown in Figure A.24.


```
Secure | https://iekrnqzuiwguhbiosedocumentscp-srv.cfapps.eu10.hana.ondemand.com/odata/v2/PurchaseService/PurchaseDocument
This XML file does not appear to have any style information associated with it. The document tree is shown below.
<feed xmlns="http://www.w3.org/2005/Atom" xmlns:m="http://schemas.microsoft.com/ado/2007/08/dataservices/metadata"
xmlns:d="http://schemas.microsoft.com/ado/2007/08/dataservices" xml:base="https://iekrnqzuiwguhbiosedocumentscp-
srv.cfapps.eu10.hana.ondemand.com:443/odata/v2/PurchaseService/">
 <id>...</id>
 <title type="text">PurchaseDocument</title>
 <updated>2018-08-19T17:31:12.894Z</updated>
 <author>...</author>
 <link href="PurchaseDocument" rel="self" title="PurchaseDocument"/>
 <entry>
  <id>
  https://iekrnqzuiwguhbiosedocumentscp-srv.cfapps.eu10.hana.ondemand.com:443/odata/v2/PurchaseService/PurchaseDocument(110)
  </id>
  <title type="text">PurchaseDocument</title>
  <updated>2018-08-19T17:31:12.895Z</updated>
  <category term="PurchaseService.PurchaseDocument" scheme="http://schemas.microsoft.com/ado/2007/08/dataservices/scheme"/>
  <link href="PurchaseDocument(110)" rel="edit" title="PurchaseDocument"/>
  <link href="PurchaseDocument(110)/PurchaseDocPriority" rel="http://schemas.microsoft.com/ado/2007/08/dataservices/related/PurchaseDoc
  type="application/atom+xml;type=entry"/>
  <link href="PurchaseDocument(110)/PurchaseDocumentItem" rel="http://schemas.microsoft.com/ado/2007/08/dataservices/related/PurchaseDoc
  title="PurchaseDocumentItem" type="application/atom+xml;type=feed"/>
  <content type="application/xml">
   <m:properties>
    <d:PurchaseDocument>110</d:PurchaseDocument>
    <d:description>Company Car Purchase</d:description>
    <d:status>Created</d:status>
    <d:purchasingOrganization>PurchasingOrg1</d:purchasingOrganization>
    <d:PurchaseDocPriority_code>1</d:PurchaseDocPriority_code>
```


Figure A.24 Testing the PurchaseDocument Entity Set

Next, let's test whether our `PurchaseDocument` to `PurchaseDocumentItem` association is working properly. In this test, you'll need to test the URL with one of our purchase document numbers in it, so let's test for purchase document `110` and check whether the association to `PurchaseDocumentItem` is returning all the relevant items for the purchase document. Test the URL ending with */PurchaseService(110)/PurchaseDocumentItem*, and you should get the result shown in Figure A.25. The query result is showing the correct result, which means our association is working.

Figure A.25 Testing Associations between PurchaseDocument and Item

As a final step, our application needs to update its EDMX files, which will be used when we add a UI to the app. (The wizard will use the *.xml* file to identify the entities and associations for generating the template app.) Right-click on the root folder and navigate to **Build • Build CDS**, as shown in Figure A.26, which will compile the OData service and generate the EDMX files.

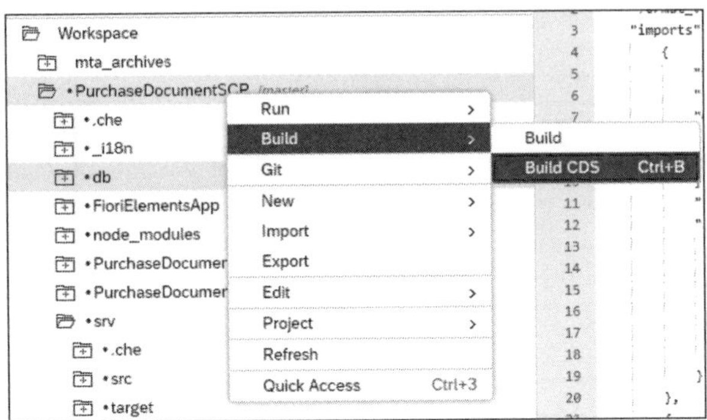

Figure A.26 Compiling the OData Services to Generate EDMX Metadata Files

A.3.9 Building a User Interface to Display the Data

We're done with building our base application for setting up the CDS views and OData service for consumption. However, we still need a UI to display the data we tested earlier in the browser via the OData endpoints. To add a UI, right-click on the root folder and navigate to **New • HTML5 Module**, as shown in Figure A.27.

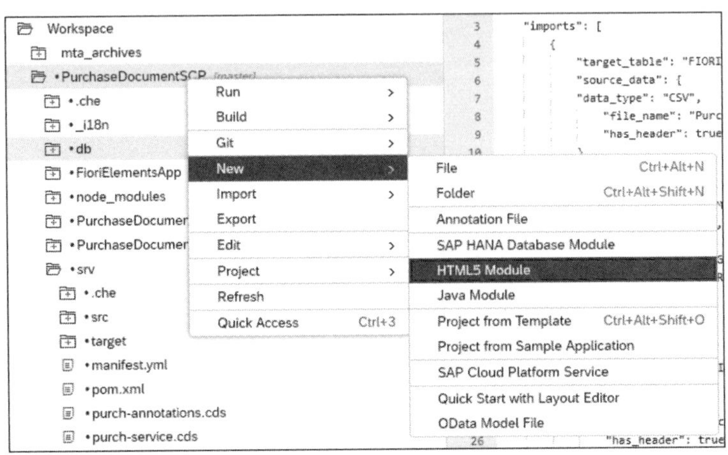

Figure A.27 Adding an HTML5-Based UI to the App

Select the **List Report Application** from the **Template Selection** wizard, as shown in Figure A.28.

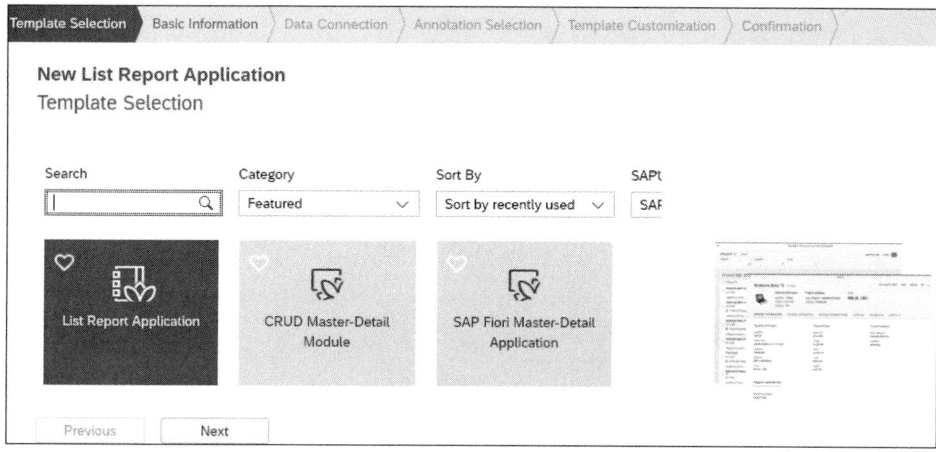

Figure A.28 HTML5 Template Selection

Fill in the **Basic Information** for our app. Enter the **Module Name** as "FioriElementsApp" as well as the remaining information shown in Figure A.29 and click the **Next** button. We followed similar steps in Chapter 4 when we created a list report application.

Template Selection | Basic Information | Data Connection | Annotation Selection | Template Customization | Confirmation

New List Report Application

Basic Information

Module Name* FioriElementsApp

App Descriptor Data

Title* PurchaseDocumentLRP

Namespace fiori.manage.purchase.documents.purchasedocumentslrp

Description Purchase Document List Report App

Previous Next

Figure A.29 Purchase Document LRP Basic Information

In the **Data Connection** window, select **Sources** as **Current Project**, and the framework will detect the services from the EDMX files we generated earlier. Our **PurchaseService** should appear in the list, as shown in Figure A.30. Click the **Next** button.

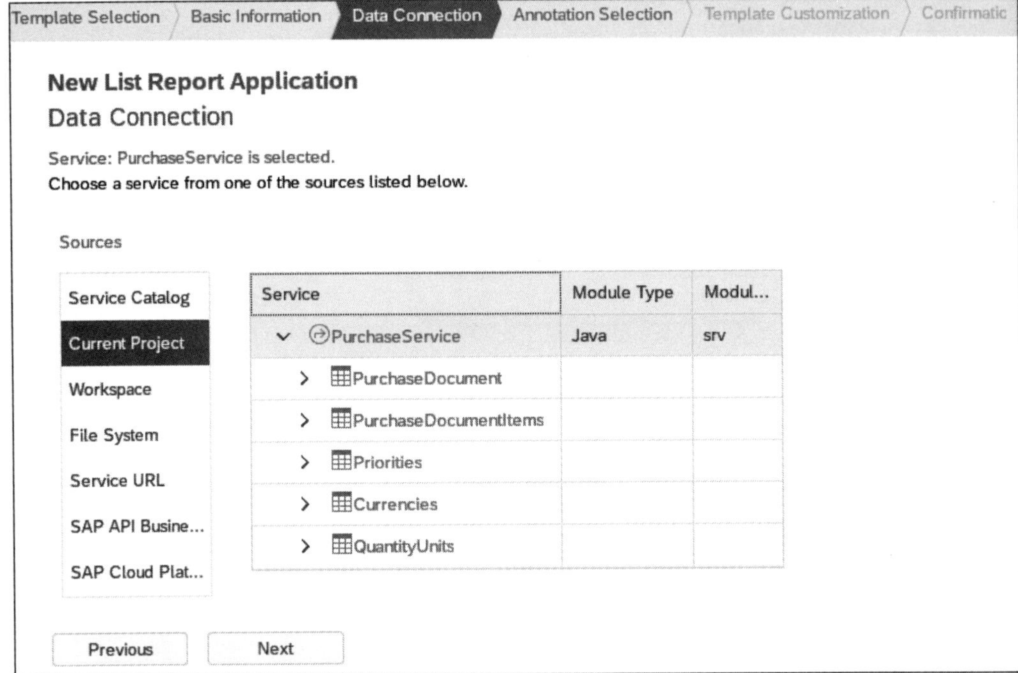

Figure A.30 PurchaseDocument LRP: Selecting the Data Connection

In the next window, select the **PurchaseDocument** as the main **OData Collection**, and the **PurchaseDocumentItem** should be automatically selected by the framework and will be added to the **OData Navigation** field, as shown in Figure A.31. Click **Finish** to generate the list report template app.

Now, let's run our application. Right-click on the HTML5 module we just added and go to **Run • Run flpSandBox.html**, as shown in Figure A.32.

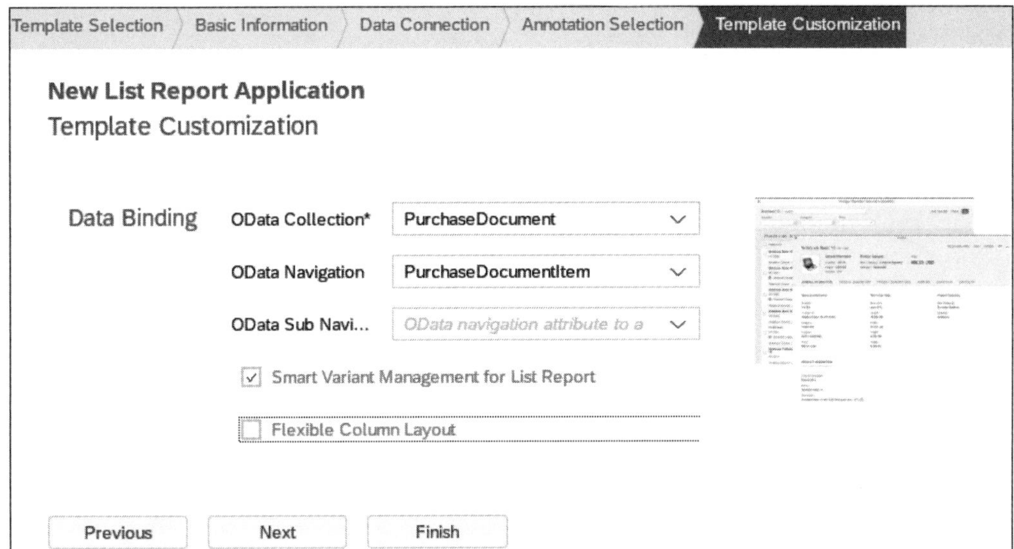

Figure A.31 PurchaseDocument LRP Template Customization

•FioriElemen
•node_mod
•PurchaseD
•PurchaseD
•srv
•.che
•src
•target
•manifest.
•pom.xml
•purch-an
•purch-se
•.cds_gen.lc
•.gitignore

Run
Build
Git
New
Import
Export
Archive
Edit
Project
Refresh
Quick Access Ctrl+3
UI Adaptation Editor
Migrate to ALP

Run flpSandbox.html
MockData
Run as Web Application
Run as Unit Test
Run as SAP Fiori Launchpad Sandbox
Run Configurations

```
},
{
    "target_table": "FIORI_PURCHASEDOCUMENT
    "source_data": {
    "data_type": "CSV",
        "file_name": "PurchaseDocumentItems
        "has_header": true
    },
    "import_settings": {
    "import_columns": [
```

Figure A.32 Run Configurations for the PurchaseDocument LRP App

You should see the app displaying the data from our OData service and all the UI annotations, which we specified in our *purch-annotations.cds* file, should also be reflected accordingly in the UI, as shown in Figure A.33. Now, let's check the object page and the navigation. Click on one of the table rows to go to the object page.

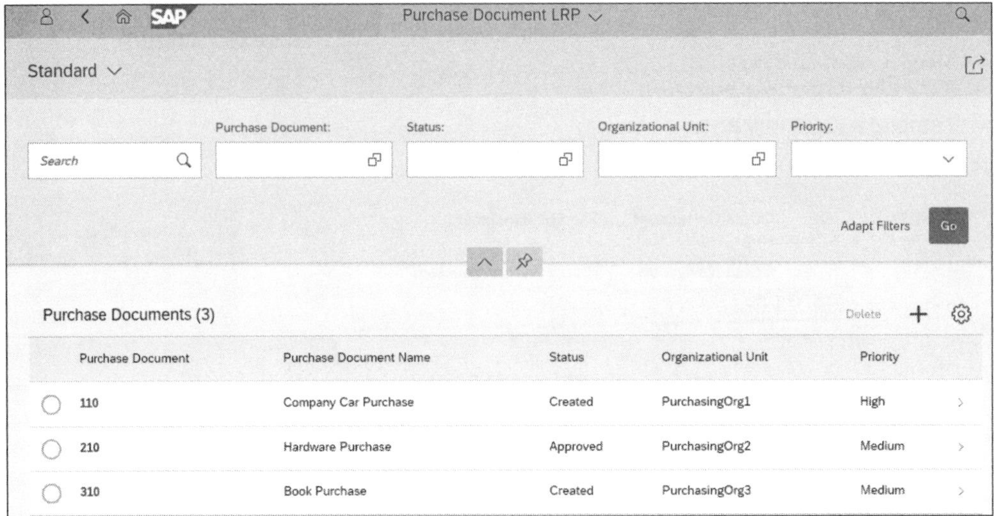

Figure A.33 Purchase Document LRP Object Page Output

In the object page of the app, shown in Figure A.34, you should see that all the UI annotations are working. But notice in the table level fields heading, the **PurchaseDocumentItem** and **Description** seem to be missing i18n translations. We can resolve this issue by updating our *purch-annotations.cds* file or directly in the *data-model.cds* file using the annotation modeler tool of the SAP Fiori elements app.

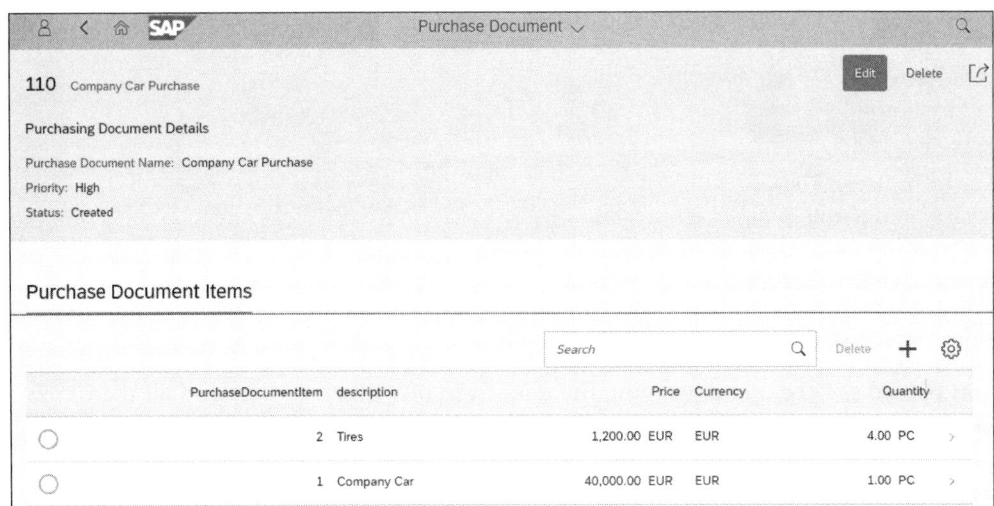

Figure A.34 Purchase Document Object Page Output

A.3.10 Modifying the User Interface Using the Annotation Modeler

To modify the UI of our SAP Fiori elements LRP app, first, you'll need to generate the annotation file. Navigate to **FioriElementsApp • webapp • localService** folder, right-click on the **localService**, and navigate to **New • Annotation File**, as shown in Figure A.35.

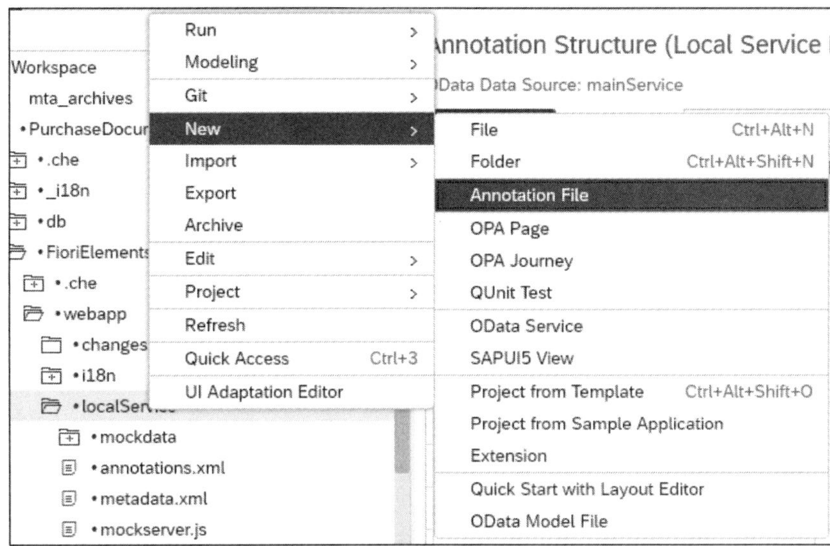

Figure A.35 Adding a New Annotation File to the Project

In the popup window, provide a name for the annotation files and click **Next**, as shown in Figure A.36.

New Annotation File Settings | Confirmation

Annotation File

New Annotation File Settings

Create empty annotation file based on metadata

File name: annotations

OData Service: mainService

Previous | Next

Figure A.36 New Annotation File Details

Open the annotations file, and you'll see that the annotation modeler tool has already detected all the existing UI annotations within the entity sets of the CDS view. In our case, we need to override the `purchaseDocumentItem` and `description` columns in the `LineItem` to add a label for the fields. Therefore, select the relevant `LineItem` and click on the **Clone for overriding** icon ❶ on the far right of the table, as shown in Figure A.37. This process will make a copy of that row so that we can add or modify its properties.

Figure A.37 Annotation Modeler Displaying the UI Annotations from Service

Add the **Label** properties for both the columns and link the labels to the *i18n* files named as `Purchase Document Item` and `Purchase Document Item Name`, as shown in Figure A.38.

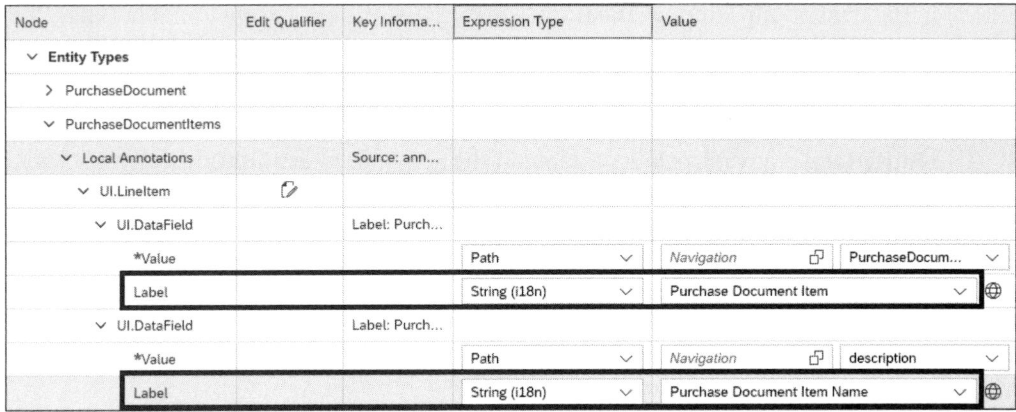

Figure A.38 Adding Custom UI Annotations to the PurchaseDocumentItems Entity

A.3.11 Adding Custom Logic to the OData Service

At this point, we finally have an SAP Fiori elements LRP app that consumes the OData service we generated via the Java application. But the Java application in the *srv* folder doesn't just generate services based on our data model; it also gives us the flexibility of registering custom handlers to different hook operations for the service. These hooks will allow us to add custom logic before and after the main logic as well as to override generic CRUD operations. For this example, we'll add a custom hook to add an additional property to the `PurchaseDocument` entity result set. Adding hooks to our existing Java app in the *srv* folder is relatively easy. Right-click on the **srv** folder and navigate to **New • Entity Operation Hooks**, as shown in Figure A.39.

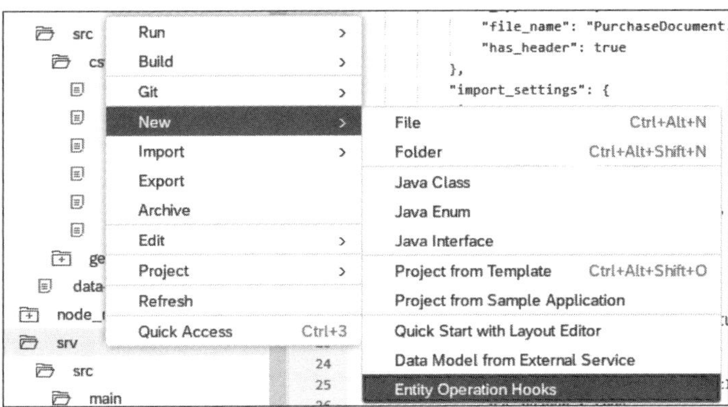

Figure A.39 Creating a New Entity Operation Hook

In the next popup window, the framework will list the entity sets that it has detected from the service, as shown in Figure A.40. Select the **PurchaseDocument** entity, click **Next**, and then click **Confirm** to generate the Java handler class for implementing the hook operations. As shown in Figure A.41, the Java handler class (**PurchaseDocumentEntityHandler.java**) has been created in the app under **PurchaseDocumentSCP • srv • main • java • com • company • purchasedocumentscp • handlers • purchaseservice**.

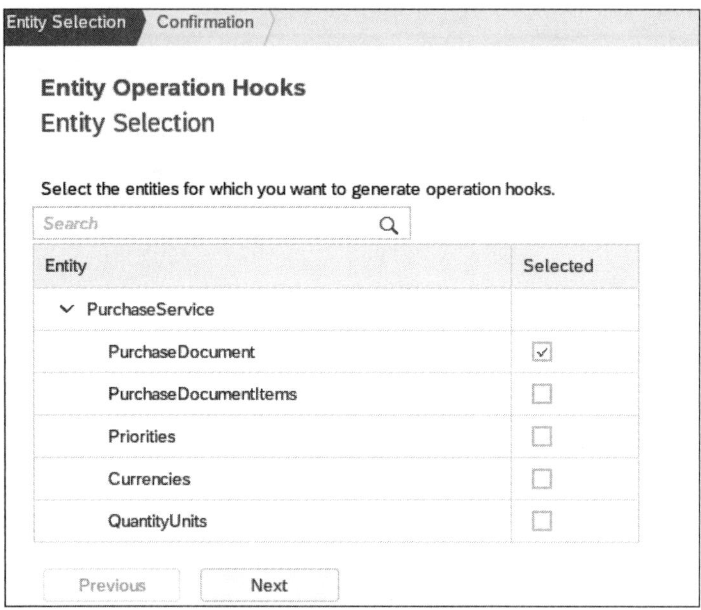

Figure A.40 Selecting the Entity for the Hooks

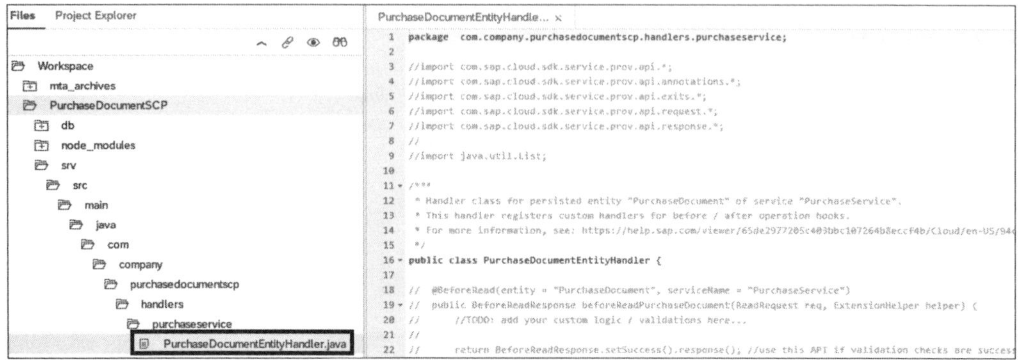

Figure A.41 Java Class Handler Created for PurchaseDocument Entity Hook Operations

The framework already has inserted sample code (commented out by default) for all the supported hook methods for after, before, and CRUD events. You can go through all this code and uncomment the methods that are relevant. For our scenario, we only need two hook events:

- `@AfterRead`
  This even is triggered immediately after the read operation on an entity in a service is carried out, so you should uncomment the codes for that. As shown in Figure A.42, we've opted to include an additional property named `comments` with the value "`Cloud Foundry Says Hello`" to the `PurchaseDocument` entity set.
- `@AfterQuery`
  This event is triggered after a query operation on an entity in a service is complete. We've also added our `Comments` property along with its value to this event.

After this step, you'll need to redeploy your Java application to the Cloud Foundry by right-clicking on the **srv** folder and going to **Run • Run as Java Application**. Now, your OData result for the `PurchaseDocument` entity set will have this additional custom property. By using these operation hooks, you can implement various logic such as validations for requests coming from the app, custom authorization checks, modifications of the incoming results, and so on.

```
package  com.company.purchasedocumentscp.handlers.purchaseservice;

import com.sap.cloud.sdk.service.prov.api.*;
import com.sap.cloud.sdk.service.prov.api.annotations.*;
import com.sap.cloud.sdk.service.prov.api.exits.*;
import com.sap.cloud.sdk.service.prov.api.request.*;
import com.sap.cloud.sdk.service.prov.api.response.*;
import java.util.List;
import java.util.ArrayList;

public class PurchaseDocumentEntityHandler {

    @AfterRead(entity = "PurchaseDocument", serviceName = "PurchaseService")
    public ReadResponse afterReadPurchaseDocument(ReadRequest req, ReadResponseAccessor res, ExtensionHelper helper) {
        EntityData data = res.getEntityData();
        EntityData modifiedData = EntityData.getBuilder(data).addElement("comments", "Cloud Foundry Says Hello").buildEntityData("PurchaseDocument");
        return ReadResponse.setSuccess().setData(modifiedData).response();}

    @AfterQuery(entity = "PurchaseDocument", serviceName = "PurchaseService")
    public QueryResponse afterQueryPurchaseDocument(QueryRequest req, QueryResponseAccessor res, ExtensionHelper helper) {
        List<EntityData> dataList = res.getEntityDataList(); //original list
        List<EntityData> modifiedList = new ArrayList<EntityData>(dataList.size()); //modified list
        for(EntityData data : dataList){
          EntityData modifiedData = EntityData.getBuilder(data).addElement("comments", "Cloud Foundry Says Hello").buildEntityData("PurchaseDocument");
          modifiedList.add(modifiedData);}
        return QueryResponse.setSuccess().setData(modifiedList).response();}
}
```

Figure A.42 Added Custom Logic for AfterRead and AfterQuery Hook Operations

Note

To learn more about adding custom logic to your service, visit *http://s-prs.co/498833*.

A.4 Summary

In this appendix, you learned about SAP Cloud Platform and the application programming model used for developing apps for SAP Cloud Platform. We walked through the steps for creating a simple Java-based application and deployed it in SAP Cloud Platform. We also discussed how to create data models, CDS annotations, and databases, as well as register OData services using the SAP Web IDE full-stack tool. Then, we added a UI using SAP Fiori elements as an HTML5 module into this app and consumed the OData service we created earlier. We also covered modifying the UI using the annotation modeler tool in the SAP Web IDE and added custom logic via hook operations to the OData service we registered.

Appendix B
The Authors

Stefan Haas is currently working as an IT Specialist at BMW Group's IT center in Munich, Germany. Before that, he was a senior developer at SAP working on enterprise asset management applications for SAP S/4HANA within the digital supply chain and manufacturing lines of business. He is an experienced full stack developer on all layers of SAP S/4HANA, ranging from SAP HANA, core data services, and ABAP to OData, SAP Gateway, SAP Fiori, SAPUI5, and JavaScript. Additionally, he was a fellow at the machine learning engine team at SAP's predictive maintenance and service cloud solution. He holds a master's degree in computer science, with a minor in business, from Ludwig Maximilian University of Munich and is a certified Cloud Foundry developer.

Bince Mathew is a senior developer at SAP with more than ten years of experience in providing solutions on various SAP mobility platforms. He is an expert in areas such as SAP Fiori, SAP S/4HANA, SAP Syclo, SAP Mobile Platform (formerly Sybase Unwired Platform), SAP Afaria, and the Internet of Things. He has worked with industry verticals such as manufacturing and retail. He is an SAP Certified Technology Associate for SAP Fiori and a published author with a focus on SAP Fiori developments. He was also given the best speaker award for SAP Fiori at the SAP Inside Track event held by SAP. He is active in the SAP Community on topics related to SAP mobility.

Index

B

C

D

E

F

G

H

I

J

K

L

Q

R

S

T

U